Microsoft SQL Server 7.0 Programming

John Papa, MCP, MCT and MCSD,
Matthew Shepker, MCSE, MCT, et al.

SAMS

Unleashed

Microsoft SQL Server 7.0 Programming Unleashed

Copyright ©1999 by Sams Publishing

International Standard Book Number: 0-672-31293-X

Library of Congress Catalog Card Number: 98-85912

Printed in the United States of America

First Printing: *June 1999*

01 00 99   4 3 2 1

Trademarks

All terms mentioned in this book that are known to be trademarks or service marks have been appropriately capitalized. Sams Publishing cannot attest to the accuracy of this information. Use of a term in this book should not be regarded as affecting the validity of any trademark or service mark.

Warning and Disclaimer

Every effort has been made to make this book as complete and as accurate as possible, but no warranty or fitness is implied. The information provided is on an "as is" basis. The authors and the publisher shall have neither liability or responsibility to any person or entity with respect to any loss or damages arising from the information contained in this.

EXECUTIVE EDITOR
Rosemarie Graham

ACQUISITIONS EDITOR
Neil Rowe

DEVELOPMENT EDITOR
Sakhr Youness

MANAGING EDITOR
Jodi Jensen

PROJECT EDITOR
Dawn Pearson

COPY EDITOR
Lisa Lord

INDEXER
Johnna Vanhoose

PROOFREADER
Mike Henry

TECHNICAL EDITOR
Sakhr Youness

INTERIOR DESIGN
Gary Adair

COVER DESIGN
Aren Howell

COPY WRITER
Eric Bogert

LAYOUT TECHNICIANS
Ayanna Lacey
Heather Miller
Amy Parker

Contents at a Glance

APPENDIXES

Table of Contents

APPENDIXES   855

About the Authors

Johnny Papa (a MCP, MCT and MCSD) is a trainer and a developer with Blue Sand Software, Inc in Raleigh, NC. He wears many hats at Blue Sand, along with his partner Peter DeBetta, as they have created an environment that fosters creativity and stresses quality. Johnny has co-authored several books including Sams *SQL Server 6.5 Programming Unleashed* and the upcoming release of Wrox's *Professional ADO/RDS 2.0 with ASP*. In addition, he contributes articles to *Visual Basic Programmer's Journal* and *Microsoft Interactive Developer* (MIND). Johnny prides himself on his close knit Sicilian family and attributes all that he has become and all that he will achieve to God, his parents John and Peggy, and his loving wife, Colleen. You can contact him at Johnny@BlueSand.com or through http://www.BlueSand.com on the Internet.

Matthew Shepker is a SQL Server consultant and network integrator in Overland Park, KS. Matthew has been working with SQL Server for over 4 years in a variety of business applications including online transaction processing, decision support systems and other custom software. He has co-authored two other books and has written one book. Matthew is an MCSE, MCT and is currently one test from his MCSD. Matthew currently lives in Overland Park, KS, with his wife, Misty.

Irfan Chaudhry has been working as a consultant for the past several years working with various sized clients from Fortune 500 to legal firms mainly on NT-based projects. He has his MCSE and is currently working on his MCSD. Irfan has written and been published previously on the topics of Windows NT Server and Microsoft Internet Information Server. Currently, he is working as a Senior Network Engineer at Affiliated Distributors based out of King of Prussia, PA.

Ted Daley brings more than 10 years of experience in the computer industry and the business world. Ted is currently the lead consultant and teacher for MB Consulting, a firm specializing in providing database expertise to a variety of federal, state, educational, and commercial clients throughout the US. His consulting and training efforts focus on Microsoft SQL Server on the Windows NT platform. His expertise spans enterprise-wide reporting, decision support and data warehousing systems. He can be reached at teddaley@cizer.com.

Tim Hatton is a software developer with over seven years experience writing mission critical, client-server applications using PowerBuilder and PowerJ. He is currently serving as Software Development Manager at Demos Consulting Group in Norwell, MA.

Michael Lambrellis has been working in the computer industry as a developer, consultant, team leader and now IT coordinator. Recently he has been developing with SQL Server. Michael lives in Australia with his wife Georgia and his daugher Areti. Personal interestes include computers, his family, and spicy food.

Randy Charles Morin has degrees in both computer science and commerce from the University of Windsor. He is currently employed as a software developer at 724 Solutions Inc. in Toronto, Ontario, Canada. He is co-author of both *COM/DCOM Primer Plus* and *COM/DCOM Unleashed*. He is also webmaster of the KBCafe website (www.kbcafe.com). Randy was born in Cobalt, Ontario. He is married to Bernadette and they have one daughter, Adelaine. They live together in Brampton, Ontario. His wife dreams of moving to Redmond and vacationing in Hawaii, but then all wives do. His one-year old daughter dreams of cats, dogs, bubbles, and balls. Randy spends most of his free time playing with his daughter while watching NHL hockey games. His only remaining dream in life is to finally see the Toronto Maple Leafs win the Stanley Cup. And maybe upgrading his 486 laptop. LEAFS RULE!

William Robison, a Microsoft Certified Systems Engineer and Technical Lead with TRW, Inc. in Fairfax, VA, has more than ten years' experience in application, server, and complete system design and development. His professional experience includes a range of architectural, design and programming tasks on platforms from desktop PCs, Windows NT, and UNIX servers, up to and including IBM mainframe applications. To this work he brings over five years' experience with RDBMS applications, including ODBC programming to SQL Server from version 4.3 through version 7. Mr. Robison's professional interests include physical modeling, simulation and visualization.

Dan Ryan is a software developer with eight years experience. He is a Microsoft Certified Professional with extensive experience in SQL Server, Oracle, and Visual Basic. He is a consultant with Andersen Consulting and lives in Washington, D.C. He has a Web site at http://www.ryansoftware.com and can be reached at dan@ryansoftware.com.

Michael Searer is president of Searer Solutions, Inc. a Wilmington, Delaware-based software and consulting services company. He has worked with SQL Server since the initial release of Microsoft SQL Server for Windows NT. In addition to his Microsoft SQL Server database services, he provides development and consulting services for SQL Server based implementations of the SBT Executive Series client/server accounting system. Michael can be reached at msearer@searer.com.

Rick Tempestini lives in Chalfont, Pennsylvania with his wife and two sons. Rick earned his master's degree in Information Science from Penn State University. He is a Microsoft Certified Solution Developer as well as a Certified Sybase DBA and Certified Sybase Performance and Tuning Specialist. Rick is an independent consultant working for GreyMatter, Inc. with clients in Pennsylvania, New Jersey and Delaware.

Paul Thurrott, author of more than a dozen books, is a Web developer and the publisher of WinInfo, the Windows news and information mailing list. Paul was awarded the Microsoft MVP status for his authoritative answers to questions from Visual InterDev users around the world. In addition to his Web development, Paul has been affiliated with online groups including WUGNET, the SiteBuilder Network, and ClubWin.

Sakhr Youness is a software architect and senior computer consultant the Detroit area, Michigan. He is a Microsoft Certified Solution Developer with long experience using Microsoft tools to develop client/server and multitier applications with Oracle or MS SQL Server as the back end. He has a long experience in Microsoft SQL Server and Oracle database design and development. He provided technical editing for a number of SQL Server 7.0, Oracle, Visual Basic, and Visual Studio books. Recently he has been working on developing multitier, client/server, and Web-based applications.

Dedication

Johnny Papa

This book is dedicated to my grandma Kay, who taught me how to play cards and always made me smile. May you rest in the hands of God; we all miss you.

Matt Shepker:

*To my wife, Misty. I sometimes have a hard time being a computer nerd...
I can't imagine being married to one. Thank you.*

Acknowledgments

Johnny Papa:

Foremost, I would like to thank my family. To my wife, Colleen, thank you for supporting me through long nights and endless weekends of preparing this book. You are my rock, which without, I would certainly fall. To my mother, Peggy, thanks for everything you've inspired me to become and especially for the support and the enduring love you've freely given. Although it may seem otherwise at times, I'll always love you. To my father, John, I can only hope to become half of the man you are. You are my best friend and I am very proud to be your son. To my sisters Julie, Sandy, Laurie and Debbie, thank you for staying so close. Our family is the source from which I have always drawn my strength. And to my Kadi girl, for keeping me company on long nights of writing. Without you all, I could never have come so far.

I'd like to thank Carole Bohn for supporting my dreams and visions. You've been a good friend to me. I'd also like to thank Erik Johnson, Brian Sokolowski, Saju Joshua, and Bruce Suitt; good friends who inspired ideas for contributions to this book through our conversations. To Chris Putnam, thanks for giving me the freedom to spread my wings in this area—it paid off. To Charlotte Taber, Jim Matthews and Timoth Lederman at Siena, thanks for preparing me for my future—you are not forgotten. And to all of the students who sparked my mind in new avenues, thank you all.

When Peter and I started this venture, we didn't realize how many people it takes to make a book get on the shelves and into your hands. And we'd like to thank Corrine Wire, Rosemarie Graham, and Marla Reece-Hall at Macmillan for putting the personal touch into this hectic business. We'd also like to thank the authors who helped make our vision a reality. Without them, we couldn't have made this book the successful tool that it has become.

To Peter DeBetta, a wonderful friend, partner, colleague and fellow Robert Frost fanatic; a special thank you for getting me involved in my first book. I have often said that Peter is the only one I could go into business with as I had to find someone shorter than me.

And to those who I have not mentioned here but have made a lasting impression on this book, thank you for your contributions. The fact that you're reading this book is a testament to the people who inspired us, the authors, to reach out and write this book. Without the publishers, editors, reviewers and all of the family, friends and colleagues who inspired us, this book simply wouldn't have existed. Thank you all.

Finally, a special thank you to my sister Julie. (Go Yankees!) We've always been close and I cherish the times we spend together. You've inspired me more than you know to achieve more than I ever thought I could. You're not only my sister, but also a very close friend.

Johnny Papa

"Two roads diverged in a wood, and I,

I took the one less traveled by,

And that has made all of the difference."

–Robert Frost

Matt Shepker:

Most authors will tell you that writing a book is a labor of love. Most of these same authors will only tell you this after they have completed their book. There are a lot of people that deserve credit for helping us all get from the "What in the world did I just get myself into" stage and the "It was a labor of love" stage. First of all, this book would have never gotten off the ground without the hard work of Neil and Rosemarie. Dawn and Sakhr, thank you for keeping us honest. And, of course, thanks to all of out friends and loved ones who were ignored while we were diligently creating this labor of love.

Tell Us What You Think!

As the reader of this book, *you* are our most important critic and commentator. We value your opinion and want to know what we're doing right, what we could do better, what areas you'd like to see us publish in, and any other words of wisdom you're willing to pass our way.

As a publisher for Sams Publishing, I welcome your comments. You can fax, email, or write me directly to let me know what you did or didn't like about this book—as well as what we can do to make our books stronger.

Please note that I cannot help you with technical problems related to the topic of this book, and that due to the high volume of mail I receive, I might not be able to reply to every message.

When you write, please be sure to include this book's title and author as well as your name and phone or fax number. I will carefully review your comments and share them with the author and editors who worked on the book.

Fax: 317-581-4770

Email: mstephens@mcp.com

Mail: Michael Stephens
             Sams Publishing
             201 West 103rd Street
             Indianapolis, IN 46290 USA

Introduction

Why Read This Book?

That's a good question. Well, let me give you a brief background on where the idea of the book came from. In the summer of '96, Peter DeBetta and I were working together on similar projects involving SQL Server. More often than we liked, we were posing questions to each other that we could not find the answer to in any references, whether it was on the Internet, in magazines, or in books. It got to the point where the reference materials we had on SQL Server were virtually useless when it came to solving complex T-SQL or other programming issues with SQL Server. As we became the prominent experts in the area, "How do you call ActiveX Servers from a scheduled task?" and "How do we create a cross-tab query?" were common questions posed to us from our colleagues. Finally, one of Peter's students sparked an idea in him: "Why not write all the practical experiences we've learned from our programming experiences in a book?" After some initial research, Peter approached me on the topic and together we spawned *SQL Server 6.5 Programming Unleashed*.

Since then, Peter and I have joined forces and stretched out to create a development environment that fosters the creative mind that asks (and usually solves) the questions often answered in this book. As the technologies changed over the past year, we realized that there were new ideas and technologies that we should include in the 7.0 version of this book. Besides, with the major overhaul of SQL Server, how could we resist putting together a new comprehensive programming bible?

So the book evolved into what you're reading now. This book is not meant to be a DBA's handbook or an administrative guide, nor is this book meant to teach you SQL or the basics of SQL Server. Rather, this book is intended as a reference with practical examples to jumpstart you in the areas you need. You don't have to read Chapter 1, "Taking Advantage of the Tools," through to the end. You can jump right to a specific chapter and reap its benefits.

You can see that this book came from a real-world database programming environment combined with the ideas from training numerous developers in these topics. You know the topics in this book are useful because they all came from real problems in real applications that we've all hit. So why should you read this book? Because you've probably asked some of the tough questions that have been answered in this book.

What Will I Learn from This Book?

We've catapulted past the basics in *Microsoft SQL Server 7.0 Programming Unleashed* right to the intermediate and advanced database programming topics. This book is designed to be a hard-core concentrated programming book for anyone who programs against a SQL Server database.

In this book you will find real insight into the problems facing programmers today. As an instructor, I find that the majority of my students don't want to hear about the syntax of T-SQL or how to create a stored procedure. Rather, they want to know how they can program some T-SQL within a stored procedure to run their business rules on a nightly basis. Programmers simply want to know how it pertains to what they need to accomplish in their real-world scenario. Most books give you the definition of what a tool or technology is. This book takes that idea one step further by offering you insight on why you should care about these technologies and how you can use them to implement your solutions.

Because of the advanced nature of some of the topics, we do assume you have a basic knowledge of SQL and relational database exposure. To get an idea of what we've compiled in this book for you, take a look at the following list:

- Advanced T-SQL programming topics, including query optimization, stored procedures, cursors, dynamic execution, triggers, and the ever-popular date and string manipulation functions.

- The newest features of SQL Server 7.0 that can be used to further your applications' power.

- Multiple-tiered application programming is extensively defined with several examples because this topic just will not go away in the foreseeable future.

- Database migration from other databases, such as Oracle, Access, and the original SQL Server: Sybase SQL Server.

- Connecting through programming APIs such as DAO, RDO, and the latest technology to hit the stage: ADO. ADO connects through OLE DB—what Microsoft dubs the successor of ODBC. We'll jump into all these topics and explain how we can manage SQL Server databases programmatically through SQL-DMO.

- Scheduling tasks to run periodically throughout the day, week, or month can be achieved more easily than ever in SQL Server 7.0. We'll hit this topic because it has a multitude of enhancements since the previous versions.

Conventions Used in This Book

The following conventions are used in this book:

- Code lines, commands, statements, variables, and any text you type or see on the screen appears in a `computer` typeface.

- Placeholders in syntax descriptions appear in an *`italic computer`* typeface. Replace the placeholder with the actual filename, parameter, or whatever element it represents.

- *Italics* highlight technical terms when they first appear in the text and are being defined.

- A special icon ➡ is used before a line of code that is really a continuation of the preceding line. Sometimes a line of code is too long to fit as a single line in the book, given the book's limited width. If you see ➡ before a line of code, remember that you should interpret that "line" as part of the line immediately before it.

- As a part of the *Unleashed* series, this book also contains notes, tips, and warnings to help you spot important or useful information more quickly. Some of these are helpful shortcuts to help you work more efficiently.

Advanced Programming Techniques

PART

I

IN THIS PART

Taking Advantage of the Tools

CHAPTER 1

With the release of SQL Server 7 Microsoft has enhanced existing tools and added new tools. This chapter will review some of the features that are particularly useful when developing database applications.

Microsoft Management Console

Enterprise Manager is Microsoft's tool for managing and administering SQL Server. In previous versions of SQL Server, Enterprise Manager was a standalone application. In SQL Server 7.0, Microsoft has restructured Enterprise Manager as a Microsoft Management Console (MMC) snap-in.

The Microsoft Management Console is a framework application that offers a common console environment for administrative and management tools. In addition to providing a hosting environment, the MMC also integrates snap-ins from other applications, including those from other manufacturers. The MMC doesn't perform any application management; it's the MMC snap-in that supplies the actual management capabilities.

A MMC *snap-in* is a single set of management behavior. A tool such as Enterprise Manager is a set of one or more MMC snap-ins that has been saved as an MMC file. MMC allows administrators to integrate one or more snap-ins into their own MMC file so they can create their own customized task-oriented administrative tools. To create these tools, administrators enter the author mode in MMC.

The MMC window is contained within a Multiple Document Interface (MDI) frame window. The MMC MDI window allows you to open multiple copies of the same console to display different contexts at the same time. The management tools may also open one or more windows within the MMC MDI for their work. MDI frame windows allow you to open and arrange contained windows in any way that you like.

The MMC console window is a split-screen window that has a scope pane (lefthand pane), results pane (righthand pane), status bar, description bar, and a command bar.

The *scope pane* on the lefthand side contains the console tree, which is a display of the hierarchy of manageable objects, tasks, or views. This tree view can be configured to display the nodes as large icons, small icons, a list, or a detailed list. When a node of the tree is selected in the scope pane, the righthand *results pane* is updated to display the scope pane's context results.

MMC offers users several views of their administrative tools. Two sets of views are usually available—one for the advanced or power user and one for the less experienced or occasional user. For the power users, a tree view of the manageable objects that can be acted on is displayed.

For the less experienced user, a taskpad is often used, which is a graphical display of available tasks for the given context. Each task could be a wizard, a task tool, or another taskpad. By grouping tasks into a taskpad for a given context, good administration practices can be suggested for the less experienced user.

Managing SQL Server with Enterprise Manager

Enterprise Manager is a MMC administrative application that provides a split-screen representation of SQL Server's management capabilities. The lefthand screen, or scope pane, displays the *console tree*, which is a hierarchy of manageable database objects. The righthand screen, or results pane, displays the context-sensitive list of management capabilities. The results pane can be configured to display views of the management capabilities, including a listing of the hierarchy of objects or the task associated with the current context. Figure 1.1 shows Enterprise Manager in the database server context with the Getting Started taskpad.

FIGURE 1.1

The MMC SQL Server Enterprise Manager.

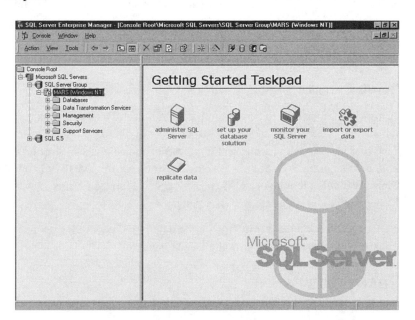

The top level of the hierarchy is Microsoft SQL Servers. At this level, you can create new SQL Server groups, which are listed at the next hierarchy level. Below the SQL Server Group hierarchy level is the list of registered SQL servers. Below the SQL servers are the hierarchies of the database objects available. Under databases is the list of data-bases created, and under the specific database is the list of database objects, such as tables, stored procedures, and roles. At each hierarchy level, you have access to tasks, tools, and views for the given context. By selecting an object, you can see the available context options in the results pane; you can also right-click on the object for a pop-up menu of available actions.

Tools

Tools are grouped on the Tools menu bar. Tools used on a specific object can be accessed with a right-click on the object in either the scope pane or results pane depending.

Tools include Wizards, Database Scripting, Database Backup and Restore, as well as external applications, such as SQL Server Query Analyzer and SQL Server Profiler. You can also add in other third-party tools.

Wizards

SQL Server 7 includes many wizards for administration and development. A *wizard* is an interactive set of questions that help users perform a specific operation, such as backup, maintenance plan development, index tuning, HTML generation, full-text indexing, data transformation, and replication.

Tasks

A *task* is an operation to be performed on an object. Database objects, such as databases, tables, and procedures, have tasks associated with them. Available tasks depend on the type of database object selected. For example, some database-level tasks that are avail-able are Generate SQL Scripts, Backup, Restore, Shrink Database, and Maintenance Plan. Available table tasks are Manage Triggers, Manage Permissions, Display Dependencies, and Generate SQL Scripts.

You select a task by right-clicking on the database object in the scope pane or by right-clicking on a database object in the results pane.

Taskpads

Two sets of taskpads are included in Enterprise Manager. One taskpad is at the database server level. By selecting the database server, you have a taskpad available that gives you easy-to-use access to administrative and development tools and wizards. The context for these tools is the database server level.

At the database level context is another taskpad that gives you detailed information on the selected database. Several tabs on the taskpad allow you to select what information you want to view, such as database size, backup details, file space, log space, and table space (see Figure 1.2).

FIGURE 1.2

The database taskpad.

Database Diagram

A database diagram tool has been added to SQL Server 7 that allows you to visually represent your database with the tables and the relationships between them. With this tool, you can completely develop your database design and maintain it. It can reverse engineer an existing database by determining the database structure and creating the diagram from this.

To create a new database diagram from an existing database, you must first select the database in the scope pane. Then right-click the database, and choose New, Select Database Diagram. This option is available under the Action menu, too. It brings up the Create Database Diagram Wizard shown in Figure 1.3 that steps you through the process. You are prompted to select which tables to add to your diagram. If you have the Add Related Tables Automatically check box checked then related tables are added automatically for you. You can then select how many levels of related tables to add. For example, in the Pubs database, if you select only the Authors table and have one level of related tables, then the Titleauthor table is also selected for you.

FIGURE 1.3

*The Diagram
Wizard.*

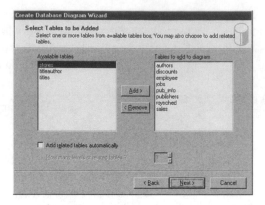

After the tables have been selected, the wizard asks if you want to have the tables arranged automatically or if you would rather do it manually. After they're arranged, the tables and their relationships are displayed onscreen.

After the diagram has been created and is displayed, you can make changes to a table by selecting the table and either right-clicking to bring up a pop-up menu or by choosing the View menu option. You have more options available when you use the pop-up menu for a table, such as changing the view of the table (see Figure 1.4).

FIGURE 1.4

*Available options
in the database
diagram.*

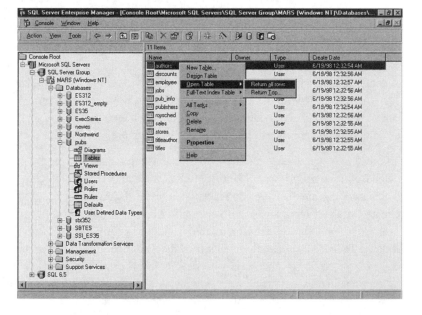

When you make a change to the table definition, such as adding a column, the table has an asterisk after the name.

Creating or modifying the database diagram changes the database, too, when you save the database diagram. If you don't want the change to be made in the database, you can't save the diagram.

You can, however, save the changes that were made by generating a change script; to do that, right-click in the results pane and choose Save Change Script from the pop-up menu. You can also set an option on this screen that generates a change script every time you save the database diagram. This is ideal for a typical business environment that has ongoing changes. You can make your database changes in the development database with this tool and have the changes saved in a script file, which can be used to update your test and production databases.

Although this is a helpful tool, you should still investigate tools such as Erwin and PowerDesigner. They give you the same functionality as the database diagram tool, plus additional features. For instance, you can model your entire database without actually creating it.

Data Maintenance with Open Table

A handy new feature in SQL Server 7 is the Data in Table window that gives a resultset update capability. This update window is similar to the Table Datasheet view in MS Access. You can easily add new rows and update existing rows by simply adding or changing data.

To access the Data in Table window, select the table to open and either right-click for the pop-up menu (see Figure 1.5) or choose Action, Open Table from the menu and select either Return All or Return Top. Selecting Return Top pops up a response window to ask how many rows to return. After the rows are displayed, you can change your SQL statement, add tables, and show different panes for your query.

The Open Table tool automatically creates and sends the appropriate insert or update query to the database when the focus moves off the row. To insert null data into a cell, press Ctrl+0. When data has been modified but not saved, the row indicator to the left of the row changes from a triangle to a pencil. When the data has been saved to the database, the row indicator changes back to a triangle.

FIGURE 1.5

*Retrieving data
from a table.*

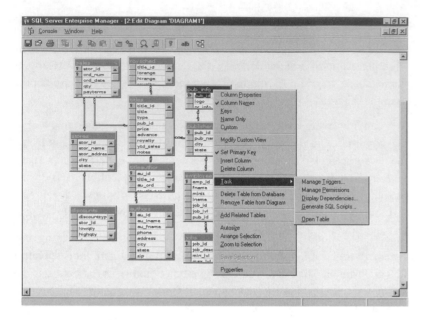

You can also delete rows by changing the query type. You have to explicitly execute the query after you change the query type. Be aware that all rows displayed will be deleted.

SQL Server Profiler

The SQL Server Profiler tool gives an administrator the ability to monitor and log the activities that occur on the database server. The activities include events such as SQL statements and SQL statements within stored procedures. These activities are monitored at the user level.

Deadlocks can also be monitored using Profiler. A deadlock occurs when two transactions are running and both are waiting to lock a resource that the other transaction already has locked. For example, user Bob has table A locked and is trying to lock table B within his transaction. At the same time, user Sally has table B locked and is trying to lock table A within her transaction. When this occurs, the database will automatically terminate one of the two transactions and roll it back to its original state. The transaction that was not terminated will continue on without anyone knowing that the transaction was involved in a deadlock. It is difficult to tell which transactions and tables are involved in deadlocks without capturing events in SQL Server Profiler.

These capabilities allow you to performance-tune your application, debug stored procedures, and find deadlocks in your SQL scripts. You can also replay your logged events in the server, so you can reproduce those events you're debugging.

The Create Trace Wizard helps you create a SQL Server Profiler trace. This and other wizards are available by selecting the Wizards option under the Tools menu. Located in the Management group of wizards is the Create Trace wizard. After you select this wizard, it steps you through creating a trace to find a particular type of problem, such as identifying the cause of a deadlock.h

Querying SQL Server with Query Analyzer

The Query Analyzer tool provides a workspace to perform select, update, delete queries and database definition queries using SQL scripts. It replaces the WISQL application of previous versions. Query Analyzer provides functionality in writing and executing queries that's similar to WISQL, and it adds some important new features.

If you need to check the structure of a table or the data it contains, you can use Query Analyzer to quickly get the information you need. When selecting data, you can save the results as a tab-delimited file or as a comma-separated file. This can be a quick way to export data to another application or computer system.

When writing scripts, you can test your scripts for syntax and for performance without actually executing the statement. This option is the Show Query Plan setting on the General tab of the Current Connection Options window available under the Query menu. This is useful when writing larger SQL scripts, so you can check your script while writing it.

Configuration

Under the File menu is the Configure window, where you can change the default file extensions for queries and results. This option can be handy for saving scripts for different purposes with different extensions. For example, you could save table creation scripts with a .ddl extension instead of the default .sql extension to help differentiate these types of scripts from data manipulation scripts.

Context-Sensitive Help

Context-sensitive help for Transact-SQL is available in the query pane. Press Shift+F1 after selecting all or part of your SQL script to display the context-specific help on Transact-SQL syntax in the Help window (see Figure 1.6).

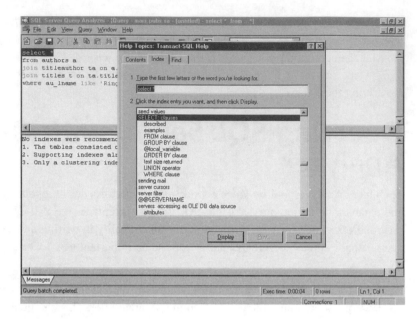

FIGURE 1.6

Context sensitive help.

Color Coding and Fonts

One of the first things you will notice in Query Analyzer is the color coding. For example, the default color coding is blue for keywords, green for comments, and red for strings. You can change the default color coding by accessing the Font window under the View menu item or by right-clicking the mouse on either pane of the Query Analyzer window. In the Font window, you can also change the fonts used in Query Analyzer. Notice that the color coding and font settings are specific to the pane currently selected. This means you can select different fonts for the query and the resultsets. The font settings are also used when printing.

Results Pane

When running your query, you have the option of displaying the resultset in the standard results pane or a grid results pane. One of the advantages of using the grid results pane, shown in Figure 1.7, is that you can resize a column by dragging one of its edges.

FIGURE 1.7

Query results in a grid.

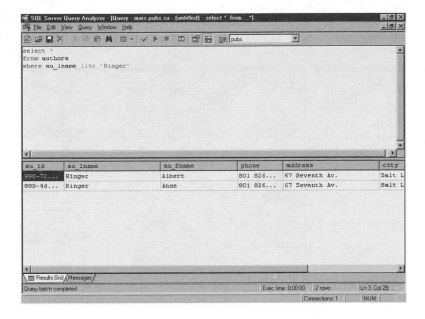

Graphical SQL Execution Plan

Query Analyzer provides a graphical execution plan with details on each execution step that supply the optimizer's reasons and explanations for the query plan. Details include estimated row counts and estimated costs for the step. The explanation for the step describes how the particular operation works. Figure 1.8 shows that a bookmark lookup is being used and displays relevant statistics for the step. The execution plan even gives warnings when statistics on tables are missing and should be updated. The Show Query Plan option provides similar, but less detailed, information in a text-only format. This option is available by using the SET SHOWPLAN_TEXT ON statement.

Clicking Display Estimated Execution Plan on the Query menu accesses the graphical execution plan.

Index Analysis

An analysis of your query for possible index performance improvements is available by choosing Query, Index Analysis from the menu or by pressing Ctrl+I. Query Analyzer displays the results of the index analysis. The analysis might be a suggested index scheme. If the analysis can't find an index scheme, then no indexes are recommended, as shown in Figure 1.9. Notice the list of reasons for not recommending many indexes.

FIGURE 1.8

*Estimated SQL
execution plan.*

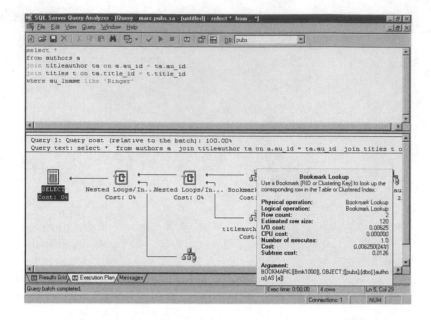

FIGURE 1.9

An index analysis.

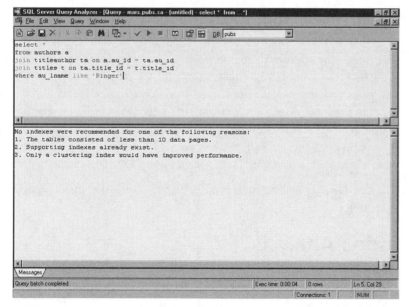

If Query Analyzer can determine that a new index will enhance your query's performance, a dialog box prompts you to accept the recommended index. After accepting the index, the query is created. This is an easy-to-use tool to get indexing recommendations for queries when you need them to run with the best performance possible.

When generating indexes, you should be aware of their performance downside, however. Indexes can lower performance of database inserts, deletes, and updates because both the index and the underlying data must be updated and maintained. You have to balance the expected performance increases against the potential impact of additional database work in maintaining the index.

Summary

Compared with other database vendors, Microsoft has always provided one of the richest database tool sets with the SQL Server product. They have continued this tradition by enhancing the SQL Server tool set in both functionality and ease of use. By utilizing these tools, programmers can effectively develop great database applications.

CHAPTER 2

Beyond the Basics of Data Manipulation Language

When you first begin working with Structured Query Language (SQL), you will probably think that it is rather simple in comparison to other programming languages. How far can you take a statement, such as SELECT, that has approximately only a dozen clauses to specify everything you need? As you delve deeper, you will find that the syntax is very complicated. Nesting statements, dynamic execution, and advanced functions and expressions all gave SQL the extra power and capability to do even the most difficult tasks.

As you investigate further, you will find that with all SQL's complexity, it has no standard naming conventions. You will even notice a lack of consistency in many procedures. Without such standards or consistency, debugging someone else's code can be a nightmare.

Therefore, the purpose of this chapter is two-fold: to help establish a standard convention for objects and to explore some of the more advanced features of Transact-SQL (T-SQL).

Naming Conventions

As a programmer, it seems that everywhere you look, someone has established naming conventions for one thing or another. When it comes to database servers and various flavors of Structured Query Language, no one has taken the plunge and stated, "This is the way you should name your variables, and so on." To date, no one has yet established a set of naming conventions for Microsoft SQL Server's Transact-SQL language.

What's Good for the Goose: Microsoft's Own Discrepancies

Even Microsoft does not use a standard naming syntax in its system stored procedures. Examine the code snippets in Listings 2.1 and 2.2 from the sp_help and sp_rename system stored procedures.

LISTING 2.1   SAMPLE CODE FROM THE sp_help SYSTEM STORED PROCEDURE

```
create proc sp_help
    @objname nvarchar(776) = NULL          -- object name we're after
as
    -- PRELIMINARY
    set nocount on
    declare @dbname sysname

    -- OBTAIN DISPLAY STRINGS FROM spt_values UP FRONT --
    declare @no varchar(35), @yes varchar(35), @none varchar(35)
```

LISTING 2.2 SAMPLE CODE FROM THE sp_rename SYSTEM STORED PROCEDURE

```
CREATE PROCEDURE sp_rename
    @objname     nvarchar(776),     -- up to 3-part "old" name
    @newname     sysname,           -- one-part new name
    @objtype     varchar(13) = null  -- identifying the name
as
Set nocount    on
Set ansi_padding on

Declare @objtypeIN        varchar(13),
        @ExecRC           integer,
        @CurrentDb        sysname,
        @CountNumNodes    integer,
        @UnqualOldName    sysname,
        @QualName1        sysname,
        @QualName2        sysname,
        @QualName3        sysname,
        @OwnAndObjName    nvarchar(517),   -- "[owner].[object]"
        @objid            integer,
        @xtype            char(2),
        @indid            smallint,
        @colid            smallint,
        @cnstid           integer,
        @parent_obj       integer,
        @xusertype        smallint,
        @ownerid          smallint,
        @objid_tmp        integer,
        @xtype_tmp        char(2),
        @retcode          int,
        @replinfo         int,
        @replbits         int
```

In the sp_help procedure, both the @objname parameter and @objid variable start with obj, yet they are of different data types. In the sp_rename procedure, @objname, @newname, and @objtype are all of the varchar data type. Some of the variables use a title case type of naming as well: @CurrentDb and @CountNumNodes. Some even use a data type indication: @Int1 and @Int2.

Perhaps it would be wiser to name all these items so that their names reflect the type of data they can hold, as shown in the Listing 2.3.

LISTING 2.3   MODIFIED SAMPLE OF THE sp_help STORED PROCEDURE

```
create proc sp_help
    @ncvobjname nvarchar(776) = NULL        -- object name we're after
as
    -- PRELIMINARY
    set nocount on
    declare @dbname sysname
    declare @chvNo varchar(35)
    declare @chvYes varchar(35)
    declare @chvNone varchar(35)
```

For the same reasons that intCounter and strName are easier to read when programming in Microsoft Visual Basic, coding @chvObjName and @intObjId can assist you when programming in T-SQL. The original question still begs an answer, however: What are the naming conventions in SQL Server T-SQL? Microsoft has mentioned certain elements when naming indexes and the like: Use the table name and field names, for example. You can take the rules one step further.

The Name of the Game

Naming conventions for both data types and objects need to be established. Primarily, there needs to be syntax for the names. Title case has always been a popular feature used in naming objects, and so the tradition will be carried on. A set of standard prefixes is necessary so that items can be easily identified in code. Keep in mind that some restrictions apply when you name variables and objects in SQL Server:

- First, identifier names cannot exceed 128 characters. Although this seems like a lot, it can be restricting at times, especially when you are accurately trying to describe the role an object plays in the database. Because the prefixes use two or three characters, you are left with that many fewer characters to name your objects and variables.

- Second, an item's name might begin only with a letter or the following characters: _ (underscore), # (pound or hash), or @ (at symbol). Furthermore, the @ and # symbols have special meanings. The @ symbol represents a local variable in T-SQL, so you might not use it when naming a database object. The # symbol represents a temporary object. A local variable cannot use an initial # in its name.

- Next, an identifier might contain alphanumeric characters or any of the following symbols: # (pound or hash), $ (dollar), or _ (underscore). You have no restrictions on placement within the name, as long as the initial character follows the rule previously mentioned.

- Next, you cannot use a SQL Server reserved work as an identifier.
- Finally, spaces and other characters are not allowed in identifier names. Also, you cannot use keywords, such as `table`, as an object name.

> **NOTE**
>
> It wouldn't be programming unless there was some exception to the rule—and of course, there is: quoted identifiers. By using quoted identifiers in T-SQL, you can create table names such as `"This Is My Table"`, `"This&That"`, or even `"table"`. Quoted identifiers allow for nonstandard names in an environment that prefers standard names. Although SQL Server supports quoted identifiers, it is strongly recommended that you do not use this technique.

The Conventions

When determining naming conventions for T-SQL, you must still adhere to the rules for identifiers as described by Microsoft. The conventions listed here describe conventions that are in accordance with those rules.

Local variables use a lowercase, three-letter prefix with all remaining words in title case. Table 2.1 gives you a listing of conventions for data types and some examples.

TABLE 2.1   THE DATA TYPE NAMING CONVENTIONS FOR T-SQL

Data Type	*Prefix*	*Example*
int	int	@intObjectId
smallint	ins	@insCounter
tinyint	iny	@inyQuantity
float	flt	@fltValue
real	rel	@relInterest
numeric	num	@numMass
decimal	dec	@decVolume
money	mny	@mnyTotal
smallmoney	mns	@mnsSalary
bit	bit	@bitTerminated
datetime	dtm	@dtmBirth
smalldatetime	dts	@dtsBeginAccount

continues

TABLE 2.1   CONTINUED

Data Type	Prefix	Example
char	chr	@chrLastName
varchar	chv	@chvAddress1
nvarchar	ncv	@ncvFirstName
binary	bny	@bnyFlags
varbinary	bnv	@bnvData
text	txt	@txtMemo
ntext	ntx	@ntxNotes
image	img	@imgPicture
cursor	cur	@curTableNames
uniqueidentifier	uig	@uidIdentifier

Although `ntext`, `text`, and `image` are valid data types, they might not be declared as local variables. Keep in mind that local variables must begin with a single @ (at) symbol.

Objects use a lowercase, two-letter prefix with all remaining words in title case. The exceptions are tables and columns, neither of which use a prefix, although the title case rule still applies. Table 2.2 lists the object naming conventions.

TABLE 2.2   DATABASE OBJECT NAMING CONVENTIONS FOR T-SQL

Object	Prefix	Example
Table	None	SalesReps
Column	None	AuthorId
View	vw	vwContractAuthors
Stored procedure	pr	prDeleteTerminatedReps
Rules	rl	rlZipCheck
Defaults	df	dfStandardQuantity
User-defined data types	dt	dtAddressLine
Index (clustered)	ic	icAuthorFullName
Index (nonclustered)	in	inClientStateCity
Primary key (clustered)	pc	pcCustomerId
Primary key (nonclustered)	pn	pnStateLookupId
Foreign key	fk	fkRepCompanyId
Trigger	tr	trStoreDelete
Cursor	cr	crTables

Some Additional Notes

Microsoft does use some standard naming conventions for its objects in SQL Server. System and extended stored procedures use sp_ and xp_ prefixes, respectively, with a few exceptions. Systems tables start with a sys prefix. Try to stay away from naming your objects in a like manner. If you create a system stored procedure, however, sp_ is the most appropriate way to name it.

Keep in mind that, like the Reddick naming conventions used in Visual Basic for Applications, the objective here is to provide an industry standard for naming identifiers in SQL Server. So when you do change someone else's code, or even your own code, six months down the road, your task will be much easier if you can quickly identify the type of each object and variable.

Using Subqueries and Inline Views

Now that naming conventions are under control, it's time to do a little programming. You will be learning to do some more advanced queries in T-SQL using both subqueries and inline views, also known as *derived tables*. Both techniques offer a means of embedding SELECT statements within other T-SQL statements. You will examine examples of both to better understand how they work and when they are appropriate to use.

> **NOTE**
>
> Throughout this chapter, you will use the pubs database in SQL Server for the sample code.

Subqueries in T-SQL

Subqueries come in two varieties: simple and correlated. Subqueries are SELECT statements nested within another T-SQL statement. Generally, subqueries are used within the WHERE or HAVING clause of another SELECT, INSERT, UPDATE, or DELETE statement, another subquery, or even as an expression.

Simple Subqueries

Start off by examining a SELECT statement with a simple subquery, as shown in Listing 2.4.

LISTING 2.4   A SIMPLE SUBQUERY

```
SELECT     title, price
FROM       titles
WHERE      title_id IN
           (SELECT   title_id
           FROM      sales
           WHERE     qty > 30)
```

This statement returns a list of books that have had more than 30 copies sold. Using the pubs database, you get a total of four rows affected (returned). Only those titles whose title_id exist in the sales table and had more than 30 copies sold are returned by the subquery. This list is used as the criteria for the list of titles that will be returned. You have another way to get the same results, and although the next statement in Listing 2.5 is indeed different, it is semantically the same.

LISTING 2.5   A SIMPLE SUBQUERY USING THE EXISTS CLAUSE

```
SELECT     title, price
FROM       titles
WHERE      EXISTS
           (SELECT   *
           FROM      sales
           WHERE     sales.title_id = titles.title_id
           AND       qty > 30)
```

Again, if a title_id *exists* in the sales table with more than 30 copies sold, only then is it listed by the main SELECT statement. To better understand the semantics, look at the results with one of the query options turned on. Figure 2.1 shows the Current Connection Options box and an option that has been set: Show Query Plan.

FIGURE 2.1

The Current Connection Options dialog box.

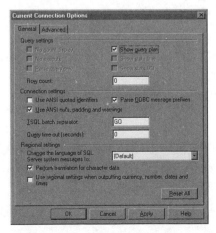

After turning these options on, you can execute the two SELECT statements to get the results shown in Figures 2.2 and 2.3 for Listings 2.4 and 2.5, respectively.

FIGURE 2.2

The query plan for Listing 2.4.

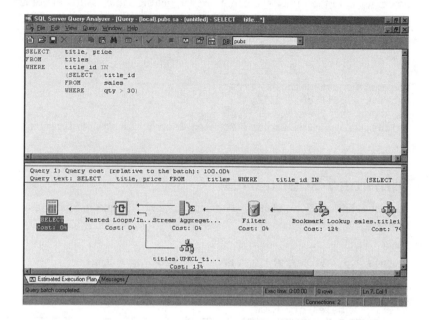

FIGURE 2.3

The query plan for Listing 2.5.

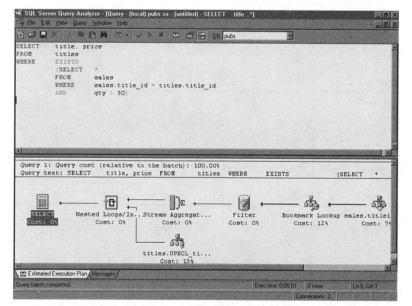

As you examine the results of these two statements, as shown in the following code, you will see that both queries produce the same results. Behind the scenes, SQL Server processes both the same. You can, however, get the same results in yet another manner. By using table joins instead of subqueries, you get the same set of data returned and, most likely, keep processing down on your server.

```
title                                                          price
-------------------------------------------------------------  -----
You Can Combat Computer Stress!                                  2.99
Secrets of Silicon Valley                                      20.00
Is Anger the Enemy?                                            10.95
Onions, Leeks, and Garlic: Cooking Secrets of the Mediterranean 20.95

(4 row(s) affected)
```

Joins and Subqueries

Examine the following SELECT statement (Listing 2.6) and its query plan as shown in Figure 2.4.

LISTING 2.6   SELECTING TITLES BASED ON SALES VIA A JOIN

```
SELECT     titles.title, titles.price
FROM       titles JOIN sales ON sales.title_id = titles.title_id
WHERE      sales.qty > 30
```

Sure, SQL Server returns the rows in a different order, but the results are the same. The semantics are quite different, however, so they need further discussion.

LISTING 2.7   THE RESULTS FROM LISTING 2.6

```
title                                                          price
-------------------------------------------------------------  -------
Secrets of Silicon Valley                                      20.0000
Is Anger the Enemy?                                            10.9500
Onions, Leeks, and Garlic: Cooking Secrets of the Mediterranean 20.9500
You Can Combat Computer Stress!                                 2.9900

(4 row(s) affected)
```

FIGURE 2.4

The query plan for Listing 2.6.

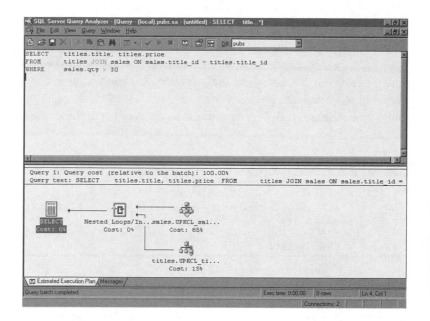

2

Notice in the Query Plan section that an EXISTS is not being performed. Rather, the SELECT statement finds the data from the sales table and then uses the clustered index from the titles table to find the matching titles.

In most cases, a join in the SELECT statement is easier and more efficient than an equivalent subquery. My recommendation is to use joins whenever possible instead of subqueries for better performance.

> **NOTE**
>
> Using indexes can greatly affect the Stats I/O of a T-SQL statement. Be sure that key fields (the columns being joined) in both tables are indexed for better lookup performance.

Further Subquery Considerations

Based on what you have read so far, there doesn't seem to be a good time to use subqueries. So why use them at all? Well, situations do exist where (no pun intended) a subquery can do the job that a join just cannot do. Say that you want to get a list of titles that sold more than the average sales quantity. A SELECT statement with a join alone cannot accomplish this task. You need to use a subquery to get the job done, as shown in Listing 2.8.

LISTING 2.8 SELECTING TITLES THAT SELL MORE THAN THE AVERAGE

```
SELECT    titles.title, titles.price
FROM      titles JOIN sales ON sales.title_id = titles.title_id
WHERE     sales.qty >
          (SELECT AVG(qty)
          FROM sales)
```

Why must you use the subquery? Simply put, you cannot compare aggregate values—in this case, AVG(qty)—with non-aggregate values—qty, in this example. When performing a SELECT statement, if you select the average quantity and the quantity, you must use GROUP BY on the second quantity (because it is not being aggregated), which in turn prevents you from finding the average quantity. Look at the following statement in Listing 2.9 and its results.

LISTING 2.9 SELECTING qty AND AVG(qty) FROM THE sales TABLE

```
SELECT    qty, AVG(qty) AS avgqty
FROM      sales
GROUP BY  qty

qty     avgqty
------  -----------
3       3
5       5
10      10
15      15
20      20
25      25
30      30
35      35
40      40
50      50
75      75

(11 row(s) affected)
```

Notice how the avgqty column and the qty column are always equal. Because you need to group by the qty column, you see only the average quantity for each unique quantity. The average of 3 is 3, the average of 3 and 3 is 3, and so on.

Correlated Subqueries

A correlated subquery relies on the main query for its processing. In essence, a correlated subquery cannot exist on its own. If you were to compare simple and correlated subqueries to English syntax, a simple subquery would be an independent clause, and a correlated subquery would be a dependent clause. A correlated subquery relies on a value from the main query to retrieve its rows, so you will always see a column from the main query being referenced by the subquery. Listing 2.10 is an example of a correlated subquery.

LISTING 2.10 A CORRELATED SUBQUERY

```
SELECT    DISTINCT au_lname, au_fname
FROM      authors
WHERE     100 IN
          (SELECT royaltyper
          FROM titleauthor
           WHERE titleauthor.au_id = authors.au_id)
```

Observe how the subquery references a column from the main query. The subquery could not exist on its own because the main query supplies the value for au_id during the execution of the query. As usual, most cases of correlated subqueries can be replaced with a join. In many cases, the join is easier to read and more efficient behind the scenes. So why use a correlated subquery? Just like the example shown in Listing 2.9, sometimes the job can be done only with a subquery. The best advice, however, is to use a join when possible. You usually gain speed, and joins tend to be easier to decipher when you look back on your code.

Inline Views (Derived Tables)

Originally introduced in SQL Server 6.5, ANSI inline views (*derived tables* in SQL Server) enable you to create a temporary view on demand without the physical storage for the view. Derived tables are just another form of an embedded SELECT statement. Instead of performing complicated joins, a derived table gives you an alternative to the SELECT statement with no change to the query's performance. Examine Listings 2.11 and 2.12 to see the difference.

LISTING 2.11 SELECTING AUTHORS AND TITLES USING ONLY JOINS

```
SELECT    au_lname, title
FROM      authors a JOIN titleauthor ta ON a.au_id = ta.au_id
          JOIN titles t ON t.title_id = ta.title_id
```

LISTING 2.12 SELECTING AUTHORS AND TITLES USING DERIVED TABLES

```
SELECT    a.au_lname, tt.title
FROM      authors a JOIN
          (SELECT title, au_id FROM titleauthor ta
          JOIN titles t ON t.title_id = ta.title_id) tt
          ON a.au_id = tt.au_id
```

These two examples work the same but look very different. The SELECT statement in Listing 2.11 joins authors to titleauthor to titles. Behind the scenes, two are initially joined, and then the third is joined to those results. The SELECT statement in Listing 2.12 shows the work happening behind the scenes in the query itself. First, titleauthor is joined to titles, and then authors is joined to those results.

> **NOTE**
>
> The parentheses and the table alias following the derived table are both required when performing a query with derived tables.

In most cases, there is no net benefit to using derived tables in your T-SQL code. However, you will sometimes encounter queries that have too many joins to be readable. In these cases, using several inline views can help make reading the query easier on the eyes and the mind without sacrificing performance. If you look at the execution plans of the two queries, as shown in Figures 2.5 and 2.6, you will see that these queries are executed in the exact same way.

FIGURE 2.5

The query plan for Listing 2.11.

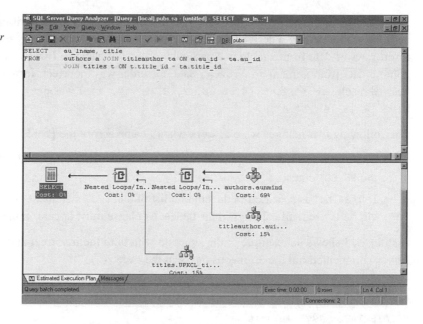

FIGURE 2.6

The query plan for Listing 2.12.

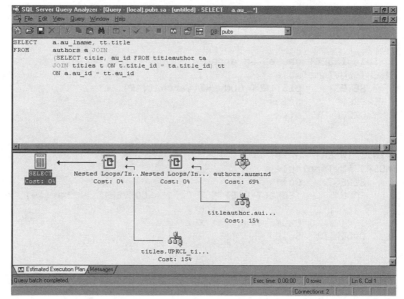

2

BEYOND THE
BASICS

Just recently, however, I came across a situation where a query I was writing could not be done without either a derived table in the syntax or the creation of a view. I wanted to insert rows of data from a table in a particular order, but because I was converting the column data from numeric to character data, the order was incorrect. Instead of the desired results of 1, 2, 3, 4, 5, 6, 7, 8, 9, 10, 11, I was getting 1, 10, 11, 2, 3, 4 ,5 ,6 ,7 ,8 ,9.

The following two features were at work when I came across the problem:

- The INSERT statement requires that only the fields being inserted can be present in the SELECT clause.

- If DISTINCT is specified in the column list of a SELECT statement and an ORDER BY clause is used, all columns in the ORDER BY clause must appear in the column list.

Listing 2.13 shows an example of the situation with both the incorrect and correct query. I have commented out the erroneous query in the code.

LISTING 2.13 A QUERY THAT REQUIRES A DERIVED TABLE

```
CREATE TABLE #MyTempTable
(
    ThisCol varchar(10)
)

/* This INSERT causes an error
INSERT #MyTempTable
    SELECT    DISTINCT CONVERT(varchar(10), qty)
    FROM      sales
    ORDER BY  qty
*/

--This INSERT works
INSERT #MyTempTable
    SELECT    Col1
    FROM      (SELECT DISTINCT Col1 = CONVERT(varchar(10), qty),
                      Col2 = qty
              FROM    sales) xyz
    ORDER BY  Col2


SELECT * FROM #MyTempTable

DROP TABLE #MyTempTable
```

The first `INSERT` causes an error because the `qty` column in the `ORDER BY` clause is not in the column list. The `INSERT` statement would fail if I added the additional column to the list because it requires its input to be exact (just one column). So I retrieved the distinct set of data in the derived table, allowing me to use the `ORDER BY` clause on the numeric column. The main `SELECT` is a simple query, with no `DISTINCT` clause, so this action is perfectly valid.

The derived table could have been made into a view, but it would have been no more efficient. If this inline view is unique to this operation in the database, you have no need to add the storage overhead. A derived table in this situation is exactly what is needed.

Outer Joins, Cross Joins, and Self-Joins

For most queries that are performed, the standard inner join suffices when trying to retrieve data from more than one table. Situations do arise, however, when you need to retrieve information that is not common to both tables. This is where outer and cross joins come in handy. Perhaps you need to select information from more than one instance of the same table. Self-joins do the job nicely.

Outer Joins

Outer joins come in three varieties: left, right, and full. Left and right outer joins vary only in the order of the tables listed in the `FROM` clause. A full outer join is the combination of both a left and right outer join being performed at the same time, which, by the way, is not possible—hence the need for the full outer join. Keep reading to find out more.

Left and Right Outer Joins

You can start with an example of a left outer join. In Listing 2.14, you want to retrieve all titles and their associated quantity of sales. If the title has no sales, you still want to see it listed.

LISTING 2.14   SELECTING ALL TITLES AND ASSOCIATED SALES USING A LEFT OUTER JOIN

```
SELECT     sales.qty, titles.title
FROM       titles LEFT OUTER JOIN sales
           ON titles.title_id = sales.title_id
```

> **NOTE**
>
> You'll notice in Listing 2.14 that the older syntax for joins—that is, =, *=, =*, and so on—is not used. That is because this syntax is not ANSI SQL compliant, and using these symbols occasionally produces undesired results when trying to exclude data. Although you might have to do a little more typing, you don't have to worry about having problems like this arise.

Unlike an inner join, all rows from the outer table will be included in the results plus any matching rows in the other table. So all titles will be listed, regardless of whether they have been sold. By inspecting the results of Listing 2.14 in the following output, you see that two titles in particular have a (null) value in the qty column. Because neither of these books have their title_id as an entry in the sales table, there is no qty value to display—so a (null) is displayed instead. If an inner join had been used instead, neither of these titles would appear in the result list, as seen in Listing 2.15.

LISTING 2.15 THE RESULTS FROM LISTING 2.14

```
qty     title
------  ----------------------------------------------------------------
5       The Busy Executive's Database Guide
10      The Busy Executive's Database Guide
25      Cooking with Computers: Surreptitious Balance Sheets
35      You Can Combat Computer Stress!
15      Straight Talk About Computers
10      Silicon Valley Gastronomic Treats
25      The Gourmet Microwave
15      The Gourmet Microwave
(null)  The Psychology of Computer Cooking
30      But Is It User Friendly?
50      Secrets of Silicon Valley
(null)  Net Etiquette
20      Computer Phobic AND Non-Phobic Individuals: Behavior Variations
3       Is Anger the Enemy?
75      Is Anger the Enemy?
10      Is Anger the Enemy?
20      Is Anger the Enemy?
25      Life Without Fear
15      Prolonged Data Deprivation: Four Case Studies
25      Emotional Security: A New Algorithm
40      Onions, Leeks, and Garlic: Cooking Secrets of the Mediterranean
20      Fifty Years in Buckingham Palace Kitchens
20      Sushi, Anyone?

(23 row(s) affected)
```

NOTE

Other rows are listed multiple times; these titles have more than one entry in the sales table and will be displayed for each sale of that particular title.

NOTE

You can use the `ISNULL` function to change the null values to a zero numeric value.

By the way, you can get the same results by using a right outer join. The only difference is the order of the tables in the FROM clause. The relative position of the table to the outer join clause determines whether you choose left or right. In the previous example, you wanted all results from the table to the left of the clause, so a left outer join was used. Left and right outer joins are processed in the same fashion by SQL Server. Listing 2.16 shows the same query using a right outer join, and Figures 2.7 and 2.8 show the query plan results from each. Notice how they are indeed parsed exactly the same.

LISTING 2.16 SELECTING ALL TITLES AND ASSOCIATED SALES USING A RIGHT OUTER JOIN

```
SELECT     sales.qty, titles.title
FROM       sales RIGHT OUTER JOIN titles
           ON titles.title_id = sales.title_id
```

FIGURE 2.7

The query plan for Listing 2.14.

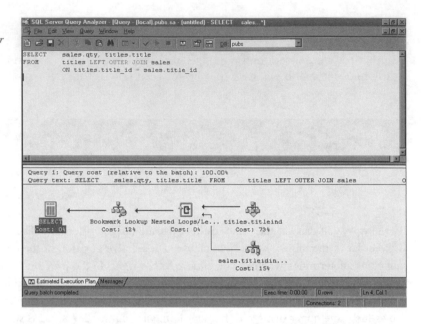

FIGURE 2.8

The query plan for Listing 2.16

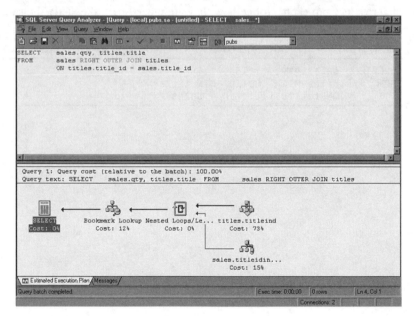

Now take this one step further by listing only those books that have not been sold (see Listing 2.20). The query needs only a minor adjustment to return the desired results.

LISTING 2.17 SELECTING TITLES THAT HAVE NOT BEEN SOLD

```
SELECT     sales.qty, titles.title
FROM       titles LEFT OUTER JOIN sales
           ON titles.title_id = sales.title_id
WHERE      sales.title_id IS NULL
```

The addition of the WHERE clause makes all the difference. But why check if the title_id is null in the sales table? Well, if the title_id in the titles table has no entry in the sales table, there will be no matching title_id in the sales table. This query will return only the two titles that have no sales, as shown in Listing 2.18.

LISTING 2.18 THE RESULTS OF THE QUERY IN LISTING 2.20

```
qty     title
------  ------------------------------------------------------------------
(null)  The Psychology of Computer Cooking
(null)  Net Etiquette

(2 row(s) affected)
```

> **NOTE**
>
> Actually, all column values for that title in the sales table will be null, so any column in the sales table can be used to check for the existence—or lack there-of. It is best to compare related columns, however, for the sake of consistency.

Full Outer Joins

Full outer joins combine the technology of left and right outer joins into one statement. The example in Listing 2.19 shows a full outer join with a derived table that uses a right outer join. Although it is more complicated, it gives the desired results: Show authors with no matching titles and titles with no matching authors. Keep in mind that you can always create a view to replace the inline view of this query.

2

BEYOND THE
BASICS

LISTING 2.19   SELECTING ORPHANED AUTHORS AND TITLES

```
SELECT    a.au_lname, tt.title
FROM      authors a FULL OUTER JOIN
          (SELECT au_id, title FROM titleauthor ta
          RIGHT OUTER JOIN titles t ON t.title_id = ta.title_id) tt
          ON a.au_id = tt.au_id
WHERE     a.au_lname is null or tt.title is null
```

The results, as shown in Listing 2.20, are a list of author's last names (au_lname) with a null value in the title column and titles with a null value in the au_lname column.

LISTING 2.20   THE RESULTS FROM THE QUERY IN LISTING 2.19

```
au_lname                          title
--------------------------------- ---------------------------------
NULL                              The Psychology of Computer Cooking
Greene                            NULL
Smith                             NULL
Stringer                          NULL
McBadden                          NULL

(5 row(s) affected)
```

Cross Joins

The least common type of join, a cross join, is not a join at all; it is the Cartesian product of all the rows from all tables participating in the SELECT statement. For example, if you want to generate a list of the combination all authors with all titles, you can create a SELECT statement, as in Listing 2.21.

LISTING 2.21   A CROSS JOIN OF AUTHORS AND TITLES

```
SELECT    au_lname, title
FROM      authors CROSS JOIN titles
```

The result of this query, too long to show here—414 rows to be exact—is the combination of each author with each title. This is an impractical means of selecting data. Normally, you would not want all items from both tables as a set of results. Sometimes, however, a cross join can be advantageous.

A colleague of mine, for example, wrote a client/server application using a cross join in this scenario: An inventory table needs to be cleared each month and populated with each warehouse. For each warehouse, each product must be listed. So, my colleague uses a stored procedure that truncates the inventory table and then performs a cross join between the products and warehouses tables to repopulate the inventory table with all products from all warehouses.

Another practical example occurs when you need to create sample data for, say, an authors table. You can create a table with a list of first and last names and then do a cross join on itself to create a larger list of names to perform tests on your database. Listing 2.22 demonstrates this by using the authors table to create a `testauthors` table.

LISTING 2.22　CREATING A `testauthors` TABLE USING A CROSS JOIN

```
SELECT    a1.au_fname, a2.au_lname
INTO      testauthors
FROM      authors a1 CROSS JOIN authors a2
```

Self-Joins

Self-joins are not a special kind of join. In fact, a self-join is really an inner or outer join on the same table. For example, imagine you want to get a list of titles that have the same price. You can write a SELECT statement, as follows in Listing 2.23.

LISTING 2.23　SELECTING BOOKS THAT HAVE THE SAME PRICE

```
SELECT    DISTINCT t1.price, t1.title
FROM      titles t1
          JOIN titles t2 ON t1.price = t2.price
          AND t1.title_id <> t2.title_id
```

The process involves using the `titles` table twice in the join. Notice how the table aliasing is used to create the join of titles with itself. This query also uses two expressions in the ON clause of the join. The first matches the prices in the first instance of the `titles` table with the second instance. The second part makes sure that a title in the first instance does not match with a title in the second instance, thus preventing a title from being displayed if it finds itself as a match (which will happen because the price of the same title is the same). The results of this query are shown in Listing 2.24.

LISTING 2.24 THE RESULTS OF THE QUERY IN LISTING 2.23

```
price                   title
--------------------    -----------------------------------------------
2.99                    The Gourmet Microwave
2.99                    You Can Combat Computer Stress!
11.95                   Cooking with Computers: Surreptitious Balance Sheets
11.95                   Fifty Years in Buckingham Palace Kitchens
19.99                   Prolonged Data Deprivation: Four Case Studies
19.99                   Silicon Valley Gastronomic Treats
19.99                   Straight Talk About Computers
19.99                   The Busy Executive's Database Guide

(8 row(s) affected)
```

The systypes system table gives you another example of a self-join. User-defined data types might, on occasion, need to be resolved to their base data type. You will see this method used in several other chapters of this book. To do this, you must perform a self-join on systypes, as shown in Listing 2.25.

LISTING 2.25 RESOLVING BASE DATA TYPES FROM USER-DEFINED DATA TYPES

```
SELECT      t1.name, t2.name
FROM        systypes t1 JOIN systypes t2
            ON t1.type = t2.type
WHERE       t1.usertype >= 100
AND         t2.usertype < 100
AND         t2.usertype NOT IN (18,80)
```

This query joins systypes to itself based on the type column of each table. The first line of the WHERE clause makes sure that only user-defined data types are listed from the first instance of systypes (t1). The next two lines exclude user-defined data types and the timestamp and sysname data types from the second instance of systypes (t2), preventing a data type from t1 from matching to itself or a system user-defined data type in t2. The 100 value is the lowest value that a user-defined data type will be in the usertype column. The values of 18 and 80 represent the sysname and timestamp data types, respectively.

If you join the results of this query with syscolumns, you can generate a list of column names and base data types. This list can then be used to generate the same table in another database that does not have the same user-defined data types of the original database, as shown in Listing 2.26.

LISTING 2.26 SELECTING BOOKS THAT HAVE THE SAME PRICE

```
name                                name
--------------------------------    ---------------------------
id                                  varchar
tid                                 varchar
empid                               char

(3 row(s) affected)
```

The nature of any relational database requires performing joins between the tables. Most joins you create are relatively simple, but some situations do require more complex joins of data on more than just two or three tables. You can sleep soundly knowing that SQL Server can do the job—and do it well.

More Advanced DELETE and UPDATE Statements

The DELETE and UPDATE statements tend to be used in their simple forms: Delete or update a row based on a particular column's value. Just like a SELECT statement, however, DELETE and UPDATE can use joins and subqueries when evaluating what data should be deleted or updated. This less-often-used feature allows for some powerful capabilities when modifying or deleting data.

> **TIP**
>
> When you practice using DELETE and UPDATE, be sure to place your DELETE and UPDATE statements between a BEGIN TRAN and ROLLBACK TRAN so that the changes aren't permanent.

The DELETE Statement: A Second Look

Let's examine a simple DELETE statement that removes rows from the sales table based on the supplied title_id (see Listing 2.27).

LISTING 2.27 DELETING ROWS FROM THE sales TABLE

```
DELETE    sales
WHERE     title_id = 'BU1032'
```

This statement removes two rows from the sales table based on the title_id of 'BU1032'. But what if you want to remove all sales for a particular publisher? You need to find the titles associated with that particular publisher and then remove those from the sales table. Here is where a join helps. Why not perform a join to the titles and publishers table (as shown in Listing 2.28) to find those sales associated with that publisher?

LISTING 2.28 DELETING SALES FOR A PARTICULAR PUBLISHER BY id

```
DELETE    sales
FROM      sales
          JOIN titles t ON sales.title_id = t.title_id
WHERE     t.pub_id = '1389'
```

Or use Listing 2.29 if you want to delete based on the name of the publisher.

LISTING 2.29 DELETING SALES FOR A PUBLISHER BY NAME

```
DELETE    sales
FROM      sales
          JOIN titles t ON sales.title_id = t.title_id
          JOIN publishers p ON t.pub_id = p.pub_id
WHERE     p.pub_name = 'Algodata Infosystems'
```

As you can see, a join can be performed in the DELETE statement to find and delete only those rows that match with data in other tables. The join does its comparison and limits the number of rows in the sales table that will be deleted. In other words, delete sales records only when you find a matching title (by some publisher).

Subqueries Revisited

You can also use subqueries to restrict what rows in a table are deleted. The example in Listing 2.29 has the same results as Listing 2.30, but uses a subquery in place of a join.

LISTING 2.30   DELETING SALES FOR A PUBLISHER USING A SUBQUERY

```
DELETE    sales
WHERE     title_id IN
          (SELECT    title_id from titles
           WHERE     pub_id = '1389')
```

> **NOTE**
>
> Although this query is less efficient, it's easier to read. As usual, you should stick to joins whenever possible, but there are exceptions to this rule, as shown in Listing 2.31.

LISTING 2.31   DELETING SALES BASED ON THE AVERAGE QUANTITY OF SALES

```
DELETE    sales
WHERE     qty <
          (SELECT AVG(qty) from sales)
```

This query deletes all sales whose quantity is less than the average quantity in the sales table. There's no equivalent DELETE statement that uses a join to perform the same task. A subquery is not only useful in this situation, but necessary.

The New and Improved UPDATE Statement

Actually, the UPDATE statement is nothing new to T-SQL. But just like a DELETE statement, it can use joins and subqueries to limit the data needing to be updated. UPDATE statements can use joins or subqueries to limit the rows that are updated, and they can also use a subquery as an expression for the update value.

Limiting Rows to Be Updated

As with the other queries that you have been looking at, you can use subqueries to limit the rows that you are trying to update. The code in Listing 2.32 shows you how to do this.

2

BEYOND THE
BASICS

LISTING 2.32   UPDATING ROYALTIES FOR BOOKS THAT SELL WELL

```
UPDATE    titleauthor
SET       royaltyper = royaltyper * 1.1
WHERE     title_id IN
          (SELECT   title_id
           FROM     sales
           GROUP BY title_id
           HAVING   sum(qty) >=30)
```

As you can see, the `royaltyper` is being increased by 10% for all titles that have a total sales quantity of 30 or more. Again, the subquery is the only solution because the comparison involves using an aggregate to determine what titles have sold well.

Assigning Update Values Using Subqueries

What about using the results of a subquery as the update value for a column? The UPDATE statement in Listing 2.33 does just that. Using a correlated subquery, it updates the `royaltyper` column of `titleauthor` to be the sum of all sales for the particular book. Although it's perhaps not practical in the real world, it does demonstrate the ability to use subqueries with a new twist.

LISTING 2.33   UPDATING `royaltyper` BASED ON TOTAL SALES

```
UPDATE    titleauthor
SET       royaltyper = (SELECT   SUM(qty)
                        FROM     sales
                        WHERE    sales.title_id = titleauthor.title_id)
```

How about one step further: updating the `royaltyper` to be 10% greater than the total sales quantity for those titles that have sold a total of 30 or more copies. Take a look at Listing 2.34 for the answer. It is simply a compilation of the two UPDATE statements used in Listings 2.32 and 2.33.

LISTING 2.34   UPDATING `royaltyper` USING TWO SUBQUERIES

```
UPDATE    titleauthor
SET       royaltyper = 1.1 * (SELECT   SUM(qty)
                              FROM     sales
                              WHERE    sales.title_id = titleauthor.title_id)
WHERE     title_id IN
          (SELECT   title_id
           FROM     sales
           GROUP BY title_id
           HAVING   sum(qty) >=30)
```

> **TIP**
>
> If you do decide to run these data modification statements without a BEGIN TRAN and ROLLBACK TRAN, you always have the option of running the instpubs.sql script located in the \mssql7\install\ directory of SQL Server. This script file re-creates the original pubs database. Just be sure to log in as sa, or you might get unwanted results.

Aggregate Functions

SQL Server provides several functions, known as *aggregate functions*, that perform calculations on a set of values and return a single value to the user. These can be used to count all the rows in a table, determine the minimum or maximum values in a table, or determine the average of all the values in a table. Aggregate functions can be used only in the SELECT clause, in a COMPUTE or COMPUTE BY clause, or in a HAVING clause. The aggregate functions are outlined in Table 2.3.

TABLE 2.3 AGGREGATE FUNCTIONS

Function	Action
AVG	Returns the average of all non-NULL values in a group.
COUNT	Returns the number of all items in a group.
MAX	Returns the largest of all the values in a group.
MIN	Returns the smallest of all the values in a group.
SUM	Returns the sum of all non-NULL values in a list. SUM can be used only with numeric expressions.
STDEV	Returns the standard deviation of all values in an expression.
STDEVP	Returns the standard deviation for the population of all values in an expression.
VAR	Returns the variance of all values in an expression.
VARP	Returns the variance for the population of all values in an expression.

AVG

The AVG function returns the average of all values in a specified group. NULL values are ignored when using the AVG function. The syntax of the function is as follows:

```
AVG([ALL ¦ DISTINCT] expression)
```

Argument	Description
ALL	The ALL argument forces SQL Server to apply the function to all values in the group. This is the default.
DISTINCT	The DISTINCT argument forces SQL Server to apply the function only to each unique instance of a value, ignoring any repeated instances of the value.
expression	The expression is the list of values that are going to be considered. These must be a numeric data type.

COUNT

The COUNT function returns the number of all values in a specified group. The syntax of the function is as follows:

```
COUNT({[ALL ¦ DISTINCT] expression] ¦ *})
```

Argument	Description
ALL	The ALL argument forces SQL Server to apply the function to all values in the group. This is the default.
DISTINCT	The DISTINCT argument forces SQL Server to apply the function only to each unique instance of a value, ignoring any repeated instances of the value.
expression	The expression is the list of values that are going to be considered. The values can be any data type except uniqueidentifier, text, image, or ntext.
*	This specifies that all rows in the table should be counted.

MAX

The MAX function returns the maximum of all values in a specified group. The syntax of the function is as follows:

```
MAX([ALL ¦ DISTINCT] expression)
```

Argument	Description
ALL	The ALL argument forces SQL Server to apply the function to all values in the group. This is the default.
DISTINCT	The DISTINCT argument forces SQL Server to apply the function only to each unique instance of a value, ignoring any repeated instances of the value.
expression	The expression is the list of values that are going to be considered. These values can be any data type except for the bit data type.

MIN

The MIN function returns the minimum of all values in a specified group. The syntax of the function is as follows:

```
MIN([ALL ¦ DISTINCT] expression)
```

Argument	Description
ALL	The ALL argument forces SQL Server to apply the function to all values in the group. This is the default.
DISTINCT	The DISTINCT argument forces SQL Server to apply the function only to each unique instance of a value, ignoring any repeated instances of the value.
expression	The expression is the list of values that are going to be considered. These values can be any data type except for the bit data type.

SUM

The SUM function returns the total of all values in a specified group. The syntax of the function is as follows:

```
SUM([ALL ¦ DISTINCT] expression)
```

Argument	Description
ALL	The ALL argument forces SQL Server to apply the function to all values in the group. This is the default.
DISTINCT	The DISTINCT argument forces SQL Server to apply the function only to each unique instance of a value, ignoring any repeated instances of the value.
expression	The expression is the list of values that are going to be considered. These values can be any numeric data type except for the bit data type.

STDEV

The STDEV function returns the standard deviation of all values in a specified group. The syntax of the function is as follows:

STDEV(*expression*)

Argument	Description
expression	The *expression* is the list of values that are going to be considered. These values can be any numeric data type except for the bit data type.

STDEVP

The STDEVP function returns the standard deviation for the population of all values in a specified group. The syntax of the function is as follows:

STDEVP(*expression*)

Argument	Description
expression	The *expression* is the list of values that are going to be considered. These values can be any numeric data type except for the bit data type.

VAR

The VAR function returns the variance of all values in a specified group. The syntax of the function is as follows:

VAR(*expression*)

Argument	Description
expression	The *expression* is the list of values that are going to be considered. These values can be any numeric data type except for the bit data type.

VARP

The VARP function returns the variance for the population of all values in a specified group. The syntax of the function is as follows:

VARP(*expression*)

Argument	Description
expression	The *expression* is the list of values that are going to be considered. These values can be any numeric data type except for the bit data type.

The GROUP BY and HAVING Clauses

The GROUP BY and HAVING clauses are used in a SELECT statement to provide extra groups of data, especially when using aggregate functions.

GROUP BY

The GROUP BY clause is used in a SELECT statement to specify groups that the output data is supposed to be put in and, when an aggregate function is present, will calculate a summary value for each group. The syntax for the GROUP BY clause is as follows:

```
[ GROUP BY [ALL] group_by_expression [,...n] [ WITH { CUBE ¦ ROLLUP } ]]
```

Argument	Description
ALL	When the ALL option is specified, all rows and groups are returned, even those that do not meet the requirements that are set forth in the WHERE clause of the SELECT statement. The ALL option cannot be specified when you use the CUBE or ROLLUP operators.
group_by_expression	The group_by_expression is the name of the expression on which you want the results to be grouped by.
WITH CUBE	When the CUBE operator is specified, summary data is added to the resultset. This summary data is used to represent every possible combination of every group and subgroup.
WITH ROLLUP	The ROLLUP operator is used to provide summary data in the resultset. The groups are summarized in hierarchical order, from the lowest level to the highest level.

HAVING

The HAVING clause is used to specify a search condition for a group or an aggregate function. The HAVING clause is similar to a WHERE statement, and, in fact, when it is used without a GROUP BY or an aggregate function, it works just like a WHERE clause. The syntax for the HAVING clause is as follows:

```
[ HAVING <search_condition> ]
```

Argument	Description
<search_condition>	The <search_condition> is any condition that must be met by the group or aggregate function.

Unions

A UNION is a way of combining two or more queries into a resultset that consists of all queries in the union. This can be used to combine data that resides in different tables—for example, an order processing system that contains a table for each region that the company has stores in. In this case, you will deal with stores east and west of the Mississippi River, thus producing two tables: stores_east and stores_west. To get a list of all stores, you would run the following query:

```
SELECT * FROM stores_east
UNION
SEECT * from stores_west
```

There are a few rules for using the UNION clause:

- The number of columns must be identical in all queries. If they are not identical, you must provide an explicit NULL for the missing columns.
- All data types must be compatible. This does not mean that the data types must be the same, rather that they must be compatible through implicit conversion.

Summary

You have come to the end of this chapter on programming with T-SQL. As you have seen, T-SQL has some more advanced capabilities that give you better flexibility when retrieving, modifying, and deleting data. Using these features allows SQL Server to do work that might otherwise have been done by a business server or client application. Try to take advantage of SQL Server's capability to manipulate and modify data—that's what it was designed for.

Furthermore, if these advanced statements can be encapsulated in stored procedures, you have gained even better performance. By placing these more complicated T-SQL statements in stored procedures, you parse and compile them ahead of time, cutting down on the time it takes to do the job.

Finally, no rule says you can't go further than what's shown here or in any other references on T-SQL. Experiment with new combinations of T-SQL statements to create procedures that do what you never expected. You will see plenty of examples of experimentation throughout the book. Just close your eyes and take the plunge.

CAUTION

About the final statement in this chapter: Under no circumstances should you ever try out new code on a production server. Always use a test server to try out new code. Be sure to perform backups on a regular basis, too, so you don't have to rebuild test databases.

2

Optimizing Queries

CHAPTER 3

Indexes can make or break the performance of SQL Server if implemented without much thought. Most database developers know to put an index on the primary key fields of a table and even the foreign key fields of related tables. There are questions that need to be taken into consideration, though. What type of index should you use? Do you need to put indexes on other fields within a particular table? When should you use a composite index?

Locks and transaction isolation levels are another necessary part of optimizing performance and selecting the types of queries to use. For example, you might eventually need to know whether using read uncommitted isolation levels is better than using read committed isolation levels. A better understanding of locks and isolation levels helps you, the programmer, make better choices about indexes and table structure.

These and other questions are answered in the following section, but to understand when to use indexes, you must understand their actual structure.

A Closer Look at Index Structures

SQL Server provides for two types of indexes: clustered and nonclustered. Although the role of any index is to speed data retrieval and updates, each type of index is tuned to perform certain jobs more effectively. In some cases, either type of index provides similar data retrieval speeds, but the performance from those same indexes can differ greatly when there's a minor change to the query.

Nonclustered Indexes

Most people are familiar with the concept of nonclustered indexes, although they might not be aware of it. This type of index is similar to an index of a book or labels on filing cabinet drawers. You use the index to find out where an item is located, and then you use the information in the index to go to that item (be it on a page or in a drawer—or a row of data).

Examine Figure 3.1 to see a better picture of a nonclustered index.

This figure is abridged for readability. It shows the index root with its first two entries: Alvin and Marti. The index root is a page of data that contains evenly dispersed entries from the entire set of data from the indexed column. The number of entries that fit in this initial page depends on the size of the column being indexed.

Figure 3.1

The structure of a nonclustered index.

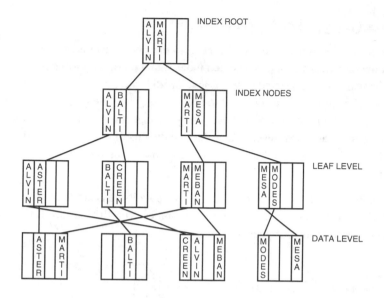

Next, each entry points to another page in the index node level. The first page of data contains evenly dispersed entries from the first item in the index root to the second item in the index root. Depending on how many rows are in the table being indexed, the number of levels in the index nodes vary. This figure shows just one level, but larger tables with larger indexed columns could increase the number of levels of index nodes.

Imagine you were trying to find an order number that ranged from 1 to 1048576. If each index page could hold only four entries, the index root would contain 1, 262144, 524288, and 786432. The first page in the first index node level would contain 1, 65536, 131072, and 196608. The first page in the next index node level would contain 1, 16384, 32768, and 49152. The first page in the next index node level would contain 1, 4096, 8192, and 12288. This would continue until the eighth level, known as the *leaf level*, where the first page would contain 1, 2, 3, and 4; the second page would contain 5, 6, 7, and 8; and so on.

This leaf level points to the actual data (in the data level) being sought and is not necessarily in any particular order—hence the crossing of the lines in Figure 3.1. The name "Marti" was entered before the name "Alvin," so it comes before that entry in the table's data pages. Information in a book (such as this one) is not presented in alphabetical order, but by topic instead. The last names in a customer table are not necessarily in alphabetical order; rather, they're ordered based on when they were entered into the table.

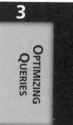

Clustered Indexes

Clustered indexes are a little different from their nonclustered counterparts. A textbook uses the equivalent of a nonclustered index, but a dictionary or encyclopedia uses a mechanism like a clustered index. Encyclopedias are often separated into volumes based on the letter of the topic you want to investigate. Then the topics are listed alphabetically, and the pages are marked to indicate the topic that starts on that page and the one that ends on that page (leaf level). However, the data itself is already in order. There's no need to find the topic in the index and then look it up based on some page number reference.

This is how a clustered index functions. The data itself is actually reorganized to match with the index nodes and, therefore, is combined with the leaf level. Examine Figure 3.2 for a better view of this phenomenon.

FIGURE 3.2

The structure of a clustered index.

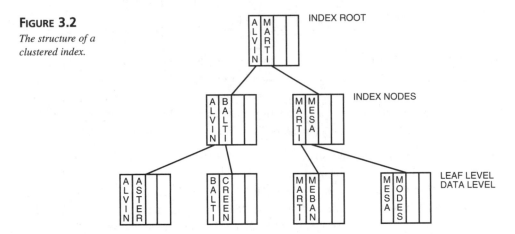

This structure has the potential to both increase and decrease performance when manipulating data. You will read more about this in the coming sections.

Because the data and leaf levels are now one, clustered indexes require less space than an equivalent nonclustered index. Also, because the data is reorganized with the clustered index, you can create only one clustered index per table, as opposed to nonclustered indexes; you can have up to 249 of them.

Clustered Versus Nonclustered Indexes

So when should you use a clustered index and when should you use a nonclustered index? Let's look at some examples and determine which index would be a better choice.

ORDER BY and GROUP BY Clauses

If you are often selecting data and using the ORDER BY and the GROUP BY clauses, either type of index helps with SELECT performance. If you typically select customers and sort by last and first name, either index gives you a quick means of retrieving that data. Some of the following factors might sway you to use one type or the other, however.

Returning a Range of Values

For example, if you're returning all names between 'Smith' and 'Talbert', or orders for dates between '11/1/98' and '11/30/98', and you do this sort of thing often, you're better off using a clustered index on the particular column on which the range is based. Because clustered indexes already contain the data in a sorted order, it's more efficient for retrieving data in a particular range. A clustered index needs to find only the start and end of the data to retrieve all of it, unlike a nonclustered index, which needs to look up each entry from the leaf level in the data level.

One or Few Unique Values in Columns

Some columns in your table will contain few, if any, unique values, such as a status column that contains only the values Inactive, Active, or Terminated. In such a case, it's not wise to use any type of index on that column. The justification is simple: If you have a table with 15,000 rows, approximately one-third, or 5,000, of the rows will contain Active in the status column. It's just as efficient, if not more so, to scan the entire table than to look up each entry in the index pages and then find the actual data page on which each row with an Active status resides. Listing 3.1 is an sample script that creates a simple table with few unique values and an index on the column containing those highly duplicated values. Don't be alarmed when this script takes a few minutes to run (you will be inserting 15,000 rows).

LISTING 3.1 CREATING A TABLE WITH FEW UNIQUE VALUES

```
CREATE TABLE FewUniques
(
    Id    int    IDENTITY(1,1) NOT NULL,
    Status  char(10) NULL
)
GO

SET IDENTITY_INSERT FewUniques ON
DECLARE  @intCounter int
BEGIN TRAN
SELECT  @intCounter = 1
```

continues

continues

LISTING 3.1 CONTINUED

```
WHILE    @intCounter <= 15000
BEGIN
    INSERT FewUniques (Id, Status) VALUES (@intCOunter, 'Active')
    SELECT @intCounter = @intCounter + 3
END

SELECT  @intCounter = 2
WHILE    @intCounter <= 15000
BEGIN
    INSERT FewUniques (Id, Status) VALUES (@intCOunter, 'Inactive')
    SELECT @intCounter = @intCounter + 3
END

SELECT  @intCounter = 3
WHILE    @intCounter <= 15000
BEGIN
    INSERT FewUniques (Id, Status) VALUES (@intCOunter, 'Terminated')
    SELECT @intCounter = @intCounter + 3
END
COMMIT TRAN

SET IDENTITY_INSERT FewUniques OFF
GO

DUMP TRANSACTION pubs WITH NO_LOG
GO

CREATE INDEX inFewUniquesStatus
ON FewUniques (Status)
GO
```

Next, you can run the two SELECT statements shown in Listing 3.2. Be sure to turn on the Query options Show Stats I/O from the Current Connection Options screen. The results will amaze you.

LISTING 3.2 SELECTING TABLE DATA WITH AND WITHOUT AN INDEX

```
--Force the Query Optimizer to use a table scan
SELECT  *
FROM    FewUniques WITH(index(0))
WHERE   Status = 'Inactive'

--Force a particular index to be used by the Query Optimizer
SELECT  *
FROM    FewUniques WITH(index(inFewUniquesStatus))
WHERE   Status = 'Inactive'
```

Notice the extra code in parentheses after the table name in each query. This feature, known as an *optimizer hint*, is discussed in the "Using Index Optimizer Hints" section later in this chapter. The Stats I/O information, as seen in Listing 3.3, shows two very different results. The first SELECT statement forced a table scan and needed to perform only 45 reads from memory (all the data was in memory because it was just inserted, so no disk or physical reads needed to be done). The second SELECT statement required 5,018 reads.

LISTING 3.3   THE STATS I/O RESULTS FROM LISTING 3.2

```
--Stats I/O from table scan access (comment was added)
Table 'FewUniques'. Scan count 1, logical reads 45, physical reads 0,
➥ read-ahead reads 0.
--Stats I/O from indexed access (comment was added)
Table 'FewUniques'. Scan count 1, logical reads 5018, physical reads 0,
➥ read-ahead reads 0.
```

The statistics page, the index root, the index nodes, and the data pages all must be read when selecting data with an index. This normally decreases the number of reads required, but when the number of records being returned is high, more reads are required.

Low Number of Unique Values

What if the number of unique values increases? And what if the table is larger? As the number of rows in the table and the number of unique values in a column grow, the index becomes more beneficial. Examine and run the code in Listing 3.4.

LISTING 3.4   CREATING A TABLE WITH A LOW NUMBER OF UNIQUE VALUES

```
DROP TABLE FewUniques
GO

CREATE TABLE FewUniques
(
    Id     int     IDENTITY(1,1) NOT NULL,
    Status char(10) NULL,
    Col3   char(20) NOT NULL,
    Col4   char(50) NOT NULL
)
GO

DECLARE  @intNum int
SELECT   @intNum = 0
```

continues

LISTING 3.4   CONTINUED

```
BEGIN TRAN

WHILE    @intNum <= 1300
BEGIN
  INSERT FewUniques VALUES (CHAR(@intNum % 26 + 65), 'test3', 'test4')
  SELECT @intNum = @intNum + 1
END

COMMIT TRAN
GO

--Force the Query Optimizer to use a table scan
SELECT  *
FROM   FewUniques WITH(index(0))
WHERE    Status = 'B'

--Create and Force a particular index to be used by the Query Optimizer
CREATE CLUSTERED INDEX icFewUniquesStatus
ON FewUniques (Status)
GO
SELECT  *
FROM   FewUniques WITH(index(icFewUniquesStatus))
WHERE    Status = 'B'
```

Listing 3.5 shows the results of querying this table. Note that the clustered index was much more efficient at retrieving the data. Because the data resides on the leaf level of the index, no additional jump to the data pages was necessary to read the data. Therefore, fewer page reads needed to be performed.

LISTING 3.5   STATS I/O FROM LISTING 3.4

```
--Stats I/O from table scan access (comment was added)
Table 'FewUniques'. Scan count 1, logical reads 16, physical reads 0,
➥ read-ahead reads 0.
--Stats I/O from clustered indexed access (comment was added)

Table 'FewUniques'. Scan count 1, logical reads 3, physical reads 1,
➥ read-ahead reads 2.
```

High Number of Unique Values and Updating Indexed Column Data

As you have seen, clustered indexes help when there are some unique values on the column being examined, but a nonclustered index is the preferred method of data access when the number of unique values increases to the number of rows in the table. Although the number of pages read will not vary much from nonclustered to clustered index access, the write performance of the table is now in question.

Whenever you make a change to the column that is indexed, SQL Server has to make modifications to the index using that column. When using a clustered index, this requires possible changes to the index root, changes to the index nodes, and the insertion of the entire row in the data/leaf level, potentially requiring a shift of rows.

When you modify a column that has a nonclustered index, the index root could change, index nodes will change, and the leaf level will change. But the data level, which is separate from the leaf level, does not need to be shifted around because rows are appended if needed. Because the data pages are handled separately from the index pages, less movement of entire rows of data is required. This allows for quicker modifications to the data.

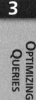

> **TIP**
>
> Remember to update the statistics (UPDATE STATISTICS) and rebuild your indexes (DBCC DBREINDEX) on a regular basis. Over time, indexes become fragmented, just as a hard drive does. Rebuilding an index is really a kind of index defragmentation. Updating statistical information helps the Query Optimizer make better decisions about how it should process the query. Statistics are always updated when you rebuild an index.

Frequently Updated Columns

If you're using the indexed column instead to find the row that needs to be updated, a clustered index gets to the data faster. If you never update the columns on which the clustered index is built, you will not hurt performance when updating data because the index's data isn't involved. You will see more about this topic in the "Using Indexes for Retrieving and Updating Data" section later in this chapter.

Returning a Range of Values

The winner—most of the time—is the clustered index. The exception to the rule is explained in a later section, but for most cases, the clustered index does a much better job of retrieving a range of data. Listings 3.6 through 3.8 show the table and index creation, the two SELECT statements (using nonclustered and clustered indexes), and the Stats I/O results from both.

LISTING 3.6   CREATING A TABLE WITH MANY UNIQUE VALUES

```
DROP TABLE FewUniques
GO

CREATE TABLE FewUniques
(
    Id     int    IDENTITY(1,1) NOT NULL,
    status char(20) not null
)
GO

DECLARE  @intNum int
SELECT   @intNum = 0

BEGIN TRAN

WHILE   @intNum <= 5000
BEGIN
  INSERT FewUniques VALUES ('test' + convert(char(6),@intNum))
  SELECT @intNum = @intNum + 1
END

COMMIT TRAN
GO
```

LISTING 3.7   RETRIEVING A RANGE OF ROWS

```
SELECT  Status
FROM    FewUniques WITH(index(0))
WHERE   Id BETWEEN 1000 and 1500
GO

CREATE CLUSTERED INDEX icFewUniquesId
ON FewUniques (Id)
GO

CREATE INDEX inFewUniquesId
ON FewUniques (Id)
GO
```

```
SELECT  Status
FROM    FewUniques WITH(index=(nFewUniquesId))
WHERE   Id BETWEEN 1000 and 1500

SELECT  Status
FROM    FewUniques WITH(index=(cFewUniquesId))
WHERE   Id BETWEEN 1000 and 1500
```

LISTING 3.8   STATS I/O RESULTS FROM LISTING 3.7

```
--Stats I/O from table scan access (comment was added)
Table 'FewUniques'. Scan count 1, logical reads 22, physical reads 0,
➡ read-ahead reads 8.
--Stats I/O from nonclustered indexed access (comment was added)
Table 'FewUniques'. Scan count 1, logical reads 1060, physical reads 2,
➡ read-ahead reads 0.
--Stats I/O from clustered indexed access (comment was added)
Table 'FewUniques'. Scan count 1, logical reads 4, physical reads 0,
➡ read-ahead reads 0.
```

Even the table scan was more efficient than the nonclustered index. As I stated earlier, if more than a few rows are being returned, using a nonclustered index is generally a poor choice. The clustered index requires the least number of reads to get the job done. SQL Server searches for only the first and last values in the index node pages and finds the first and last page on which the data resides. Then the data/leaf pages are read sequentially to get the requested information.

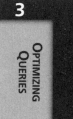

Primary and Foreign Keys

The decision to create a clustered index on a primary key really depends on whether another index would benefit more by being clustered. It isn't necessary to make the primary key a clustered index. Another index, one that has frequent range retrievals, for example, might be a better candidate for the clustered index. If this situation exists, use your good judgment and make the primary key a nonclustered index.

As for foreign keys, the same rule applies. Keep in mind, however, that foreign keys often contain repeated values, being the "many" side of a one-to-many relationship, and thus often fit the criteria for becoming a clustered index. Again, you're not obliged to make a foreign key a clustered index, but if it's the best candidate, there should be no question in your mind. If the table contains both a primary and foreign key, the decision becomes a little more involved.

> **NOTE**
>
> For example, the titles table in the pubs database could have been designed to have a clustered index on the pub_id field and a nonclustered index on the title_id (primary key) field. The pub_id of titles will not have a unique set of data because most publishers produce more than one book. A clustered index on the pub_id column would be wiser than one on the title_id column because the latter has no duplicates. Therefore, you would see better overall performance when retrieving data from titles and publishers. If the publishers table is rarely joined to the titles table, or only a few titles are ever selected when joining to the publishers table, the present scenario of a clustered index on the title_id field and no index on the pub_id field is better.

The key is to know what types of queries are performed. The more you know about what the users are retrieving from the database, the easier the decisions are about what types of indexes to use.

Table 3.1 contains a summary of when to use clustered and nonclustered indexes.

TABLE 3.1   COMPARING THE USAGE OF CLUSTERED AND NONCLUSTERED INDEXES

Action/Description	Use Clustered	Use Nonclustered
Columns often grouped/ordered by	Yes	Yes
Return a range of values	Yes	No
Low number of unique values	Yes	No
High number of unique values	No	Yes
One or a few unique values	No	No
Low number of returned rows	No	Yes
Frequently updated columns	No	Yes
Foreign key columns	Yes	Yes
Primary key columns	Yes	Yes
Frequent indexed column modifications	No	Yes

Of course, you regularly encounter situations that really are a combination of these conditions. Test out each type of index and see which one best does the job for you.

The Dos and Don'ts of Composite Indexes

When creating *composite*, or multi-column, indexes, it's important to keep a few rules in mind. The order of the columns plays an important role in the efficiency of the index and even the Query Optimizer's decision to use the index. Too many columns can also dramatically increase the size of the index, taking up more space and requiring more time to find the information being sought.

The following are the rules for dealing with composite indexes:

- Don't include columns that no longer result in a unique set of data.

    For example, if the index on the `lastname` and `firstname` columns contains very few duplicates, don't add the `middlename` column. You're only increasing the number of pages that need to be searched to find the same information.

> **TIP**
>
> The following SELECT statement finds duplicate items within Col1 and Col2 in Table1:
> ```
> SELECT  Col1, Col2, COUNT(*) as Total
> FROM    Table1
> GROUP BY Col1, Col2
> HAVING  COUNT(*) > 1.
> ```

- Columns that will not be individually searched should never be listed first in the index.

    For example, if you often search by `lastname` and `firstname` or just `lastname`, then `firstname` should not appear as the initial column of the composite index of `lastname` and `firstname`. If it does come before `lastname`, the search for just the `lastname` will never use the index, and if you force the use of that index, it will be very inefficient.

- If you often retrieve data from only one or just a few fields of the table, a nonclustered index can cut down on the number of reads required if it contains all the fields being retrieved.

This is known as a *covered query*. If the index contains all the data that needs to be retrieved, there's no need to go to the data pages to get the data because the index already can supply all the requested information. Covered queries should only be used if the same few columns are very frequently requested. In addition, do not forget about performance when modifying data. If some of these fields are updated frequently, the index needs more maintenance from you and SQL Server. If speeding up the SELECT statement doesn't make up for slowing down these updates, a covered query is not recommended.

For example, say you create an index on the authors table that contains the following columns: au_lname, city, state, and phone. You're requesting the information (for a directory listing) from these four columns on a regular basis. However, you find that the authors tend to move a lot, requiring changes to the city, state, and phone columns as frequently as you look up the information. The index is causing the updates to move much more slowly because three of the four columns get updated often, and the retrieval increase does not make up for that lost time. Therefore, it's time to lose the index.

Listing 3.9 creates some more sample data to test the covered query scenario. Listing 3.10 selects data using both a clustered and nonclustered index. Listing 3.11 shows that the nonclustered index requires fewer reads to get the same data, even though a range of values is being retrieved.

LISTING 3.9 CREATING A TABLE WITH MANY UNIQUE VALUES

```
DROP TABLE FewUniques
GO

CREATE TABLE FewUniques
(
    Id   int   IDENTITY(1,1) NOT NULL,
    status char(20) not null
)
GO

DECLARE  @intNum int
SELECT  @intNum = 0

BEGIN TRAN

WHILE   @intNum <= 5000
BEGIN
  INSERT FewUniques VALUES ('test' + convert(char(6),@intNum))
  SELECT @intNum = @intNum + 1
END

COMMIT TRAN
GO

CREATE CLUSTERED INDEX icFewUniquesId
ON FewUniques (Id)
GO

CREATE INDEX inFewUniquesId
ON FewUniques (Id)
GO
```

LISTING 3.10 SELECTING DATA VIA A COVERED QUERY

```
SELECT  Id
FROM    FewUniques WITH(index(nFewUniquesId))
WHERE   Id BETWEEN 1000 and 1500

SELECT  Id
FROM    FewUniques WITH(index(cFewUniquesId))
WHERE   Id BETWEEN 1000 and 1500
```

LISTING 3.11 STATS I/O RESULTS FROM LISTING 3.10

```
--Stats I/O from nonclustered indexed access (comment was added)
Table 'FewUniques'. Scan count 1, logical reads 2, physical reads 0,
➡ read-ahead reads 0.
--Stats I/O from clustered indexed access (comment was added)
Table 'FewUniques'. Scan count 1, logical reads 4, physical reads 0,
➡ read-ahead reads 0.
```

The results show that fewer data pages were required to be read by the nonclustered index because it contained most of the data being retrieved. It even beat the clustered index on range retrieval (because the data/leaf level pages take up more room). If the table had a larger row size, the nonclustered index would be that much more efficient than its clustered counterpart.

Can I Have Too Many Indexes?

Indexes can certainly help with data retrieval performance, but too many indexes can lead to inefficiency. With each index that you add to a table, that much more work must be done to maintain the set of indexes. Standard maintenance tasks, like updating table statistics and rebuilding indexes, take longer with each new index you create. If an index is based on a column that gets updated, that is also additional work for SQL Server to perform every time you update that column.

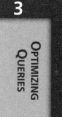

> **NOTE**
>
> If you're creating a data warehouse and few updates will be performed on the data, have at it. Create all the indexes you need to help speed up data retrieval. If, on the other hand, you're creating an *online transaction processing* (*OLTP*) database, you probably should keep the number of indexes to a minimum so that the data modifications will be faster.

Part of the standard database testing should include trying various combinations of clustered and nonclustered indexes. Some scenarios would reveal that several indexes fit in both the clustered and nonclustered index categories. The only way to find out which is best is to try each. Test out queries with each type and see which is more beneficial. Then let each test run for a few days or so and check with the users to see if they notice any difference in performance.

> **TIP**
>
> Try varying the order of clustered and nonclustered indexes when you're asking the users about performance. You might find that they always see an increase on the second go-around, for example. If you vary the order of your index type when testing with users and see a pattern like this, you know they are being primed to see better, or worse, performance the second time around. You must then rely on your own tests to see what works best.

Using Indexes for Retrieving and Updating Data

When is an index good for both data retrieval and modification? When the field of the index is used to locate data for retrieval and modification but is not modified itself, and when data is more frequently updated than inserted or deleted from the table. For example, the authors table in the pubs database has a key column au_id, which is used to find the author for retrieval and updates but is never modified itself.

All indexes cause a decrease in performance when inserting data. Because there's new information being introduced to the table, the index must react accordingly. If a new author is inserted into the authors table, a new entry in all indexes must also be added, adding time to the process.

The performance can increase when deleting data from a table if the field of the index is used to locate the rows to be deleted. Although some maintenance by SQL Server is required when removing a row from a table, the increased speed in finding the record to be deleted normally outweighs the decreased speed of that maintenance. If you delete an author with an au_id of '123-45-6789' by using an index that has a key of only au_id, this index speeds the search for said author. Although an entry must be removed from the index (because the row is no longer in the table), the amount of time it takes to do this is much less than the amount of time saved by using the index to find the author in the first place.

Updating data always results in a performance increase if the field in the index is used to locate the row and if that field is not changed by any of the updates. If you update the field within an index, you cause the same maintenance by SQL Server that results in a performance decrease. If you were to update the author whose au_id was '111-22-3333' and an index using just au_id was present, using it would decrease the amount of time needed to find the record and make the change. Without it, SQL Server would have to search the entire table to make sure it found all records that needed updating.

Retrieving data usually results in a speed boost if the indexes' field is used to locate the data. Keep in mind the information already presented to you in this chapter. If you select all rows of a table, it's best to use no index because the additional page reads of the index are just added onto the number of data pages in the table, resulting in more work for SQL Server.

Indexes, Transactions, and Data Manipulation

This section aims to fill in a few gaps before going on to the discussion of locking and query optimization. The topic of transaction isolation levels introduces the four basic locking schemes in SQL Server.

Transaction Isolation Levels

SQL Server syntactically provides for the four transaction isolation levels as prescribed in the ANSI-SQL standard. These are the four transaction isolation levels:

- Read uncommitted
- Read committed
- Repeatable read
- Serializable

Two of these, repeatable read and serializable, are functionally the same in SQL Server and are provided for compatibility with ANSI-SQL (so it's actually only three isolation levels). Read committed is the default isolation level for SQL Server connections. Transaction isolation levels can be set as follows:

```
SET TRANSACTION ISOLATION LEVEL READ COMMITTED
```

This setting is on a per-connection basis and lasts until the connection is dropped or the transaction isolation level is changed. You can temporarily override the setting by influencing the Query Optimizer (see "Using Locking Optimizer Hints" later in this chapter).

Read Uncommitted

Potentially, read uncommitted gives you the greatest increase in performance because it reads data regardless of its current locking state. Locking concurrency does not exist as far as this level is concerned. However, it also provides for the least data integrity, allowing you to read data that has not yet been committed (mid-transaction). Imagine if a user was running a long update on some book prices, and at the same time another user was retrieving title prices with read uncommitted in effect. If the first update was rolled back, the second user's data would be incorrect, reflecting whatever values were in the table at the time it was read. Therefore, in any application that requires the data that is displayed on the user's screen be 100% correct should avoid using this isolation level.

Read Committed

Read committed is the default setting for SQL Server. When data is being modified, a request to read that data waits until the modifier's transaction has finished. This prevents data from being read until it has been committed, which gives you better data integrity but slows down performance. This isolation level still allows for nonrepeatable reads to occur.

Repeatable Read and Serializable

When SQL Server reads data, normally the lock is released as soon as SQL Server is done. However, repeatable read and serializable cause locks to be held on data being read until the transaction in which the read exists has finished. Serializable isolation prevents what is known as the *phantom phenomenon*—reading different values from the same data within a single transaction. Repeatable read isolation still allows for phantom reads, but prevents nonrepeatable reads. Although these two transaction isolation levels provide for the best data integrity, they also have the biggest potential for performance decrease because they hold locks on data being read. Unless it's vital to have consistent reads within the same transaction, these two should be avoided.

> **NOTE**
>
> SQL Server treats both repeatable read and serializable the same, even though standard ANSI-SQL differentiates between the two (although it's a subtle differentiation). Because they work the same in SQL Server, you can use either one when coding.

How Transactions and Indexes Affect Locking

Now to the heart of the matter. I have mentioned locking only in passing until this point, but now you'll examine SQL Server's locking mechanism and how indexes and transaction isolation levels affect it. First, you'll see what types of locks are available in SQL Server. Next, you'll investigate how you can use indexes to decrease locking concurrency. Finally, you'll take a look at transaction scopes and the locking mechanism.

The Spectrum of Locks

SQL Server 7.0 has greatly increased the functionality of its locking mechanism over that of SQL Server 6.5. SQL Server 7.0 enables a multigranular locking scheme. To allow for the least cost of locking, resources are locked at the lowest level appropriate to perform the task at hand. For example, low granularity locking, such as a single row, increases concurrency but requires more overhead as more and more rows are locked. On the other hand, locking at a higher granularity, such as an entire table, decreases the amount of overhead required but greatly decreases the concurrency. Table 3.2 shows the different resources that SQL Server can lock. They are listed in order of least to greatest granularity.

TABLE 3.2 LOCKABLE RESOURCES AND THEIR DESCRIPTIONS

Resource Type	Description
RID	A RID, or Row Identifier, is used to lock individual rows within a table. It allows rows to be updated, inserted, and deleted without locking entire pages.
Key	A key lock is a row lock in an index.
Page	A page lock locks an entire 8KB page in a table or index, including all rows on that page.
Extent	An extent lock locks a contiguous group of eight pages. As with a page lock, it locks all rows contained on all pages within the extent.
Table	A table lock locks an entire table, including all the data and indexes in the table.
DB	A DB, or database lock, locks an entire database and all tables in the database.

SQL Server locks these resources using different lock modes based on the type of activity being performed. Table 3.3 outlines the lock modes that SQL Server can use.

TABLE 3.3   LOCK MODES AND DESCRIPTIONS

Lock Mode	*Description*
Shared	Shared locks are used for operations that do not modify data, such as SELECT statements. Shared locks are released as soon as the data has been read. Multiple users can acquire shared locks on the same objects, but no user can acquire an update or exclusive lock on an object that has a share lock on it.
Update	Update locks are used when an UPDATE operation takes place. They are needed to stop a specific type of deadlock that can occur during an update. During an UPDATE operation, SQL Server reads a record, which acquires a shared lock on the affected records and then actually modifies the records, which uses an exclusive lock. If two users attempt this, both will acquire shared lock on the same record, and both users will attempt to update their locks to exclusive locks. A lock wait will occur because each are waiting for the other to release the lock, and a lock wait occurs. SQL Server will detect the lock wait and kill on of the transactions, causing a dead lock. Only one user can acquire an update lock on an object. If the data modification actually occurs, the lock is upgraded to an exclusive lock.
Exclusive	Exclusive locks are used during data modification operations, such as INSERTs, UPDATEs, and DELETEs. This type lock ensures that no other users can access the object that is locked.
Intent shared	Intent shared locks indicate that the transaction intends to place shared locks on some but not all of the resources lower down the hierarchy. For example, a transaction can place an intent shared lock on a table if it appears that most of the rows in a table are going to be read.
Intent exclusive	Intent exclusive locks are used to indicate a transaction to modify some but not all of the resources lower down the hierarchy.
Shares with intent exclusive	This type of lock indicates that a transaction will read all the resources further down the hierarchy and modify some of them by placing intent exclusive locks on them.
Schema	There are two types of schema locks that can be used. A schema modification lock is taken when any type of data definition language, such as adding a column or dropping a table, is performed. A schema stability lock is taken when SQL Server is compiling a query and keeps any scheme modifications from taking place.

Lock Mode	Description
Bulk Update	A bulk update lock is taken when SQL Server is bulk copying data into a table. When these locks are held, multiple processes can bulk copy data into a table while stopping users who are not copying data in from accessing the data.

Using Indexes to Decrease Locking Concurrency

So why all the talk about locking? Well, it just so happens that if you can lock as few rows as possible when manipulating data, you can potentially increase SQL Server's performance by not making processes wait for locked data to be freed. If 200 users are modifying different customers' data, it's more beneficial to lock only the single row on which the individual customer's information resides than to lock the entire table.

So how do you request row locks instead of table locks? By using indexes, of course. As mentioned earlier, an index on a field that locates the data to be modified increases performance by going right to the page where the data resides, instead of wading through all the data pages to find the particular row. If you go directly to the row in the table, you need to lock only that row, rather than many pages or the entire table, when updating the data.

This helps increase performance yet again. Not only are fewer pages read when making the change to the row, but fewer pages are locked, potentially preventing others from having to wait until your modification has finished.

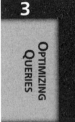

Transaction Scope, Transaction Isolation Levels, and Locking

Certain locking rules apply within a transaction, depending on what type of transaction isolation level is currently in effect. Table 3.4 describes those differences.

TABLE 3.4 TRANSACTION ISOLATION LEVELS AND LOCKING EFFECTS

Isolation Level	Lock Type and Length	
	Shared	Exclusive
Read uncommitted	As Needed	Length of Transaction
Read committed	As Needed	Length of Transaction
Repeatable read	Length of Transaction	Length of Transaction

As you can see, Shared locks are normally held only while data is actually being retrieved. The Shared lock is released once that process is done, even if the transaction has not yet finished. This is why the phantom phenomenon can happen. If the transaction isolation level is set to repeatable read (or serializable), the Shared lock is held for the length of the transaction. Exclusive locks are always held for the length of the transaction, regardless of the isolation level.

What does this mean? It means your transactions should be only as long as needed to maintain data integrity. Lengthy transactions that modify data (that is, that use Exclusive locks) can slow down SQL Server by making other processes wait for those transactions to finish. The longer a transaction containing data modification statements takes to execute, the greater the potential for locking concurrency.

Listing 3.12 shows a sample script that holds onto a Shared lock in the authors table. It also has a delay that lasts two minutes to give you time to check the current server activity.

LISTING 3.12 TESTING TRANSACTION ISOLATION LEVELS

```
SET TRANSACTION ISOLATION LEVEL REPEATABLE READ
GO

BEGIN TRAN

SELECT  *
FROM    authors
WHERE   au_lname = 'Green'

WAITFOR DELAY '00:02:00'

ROLLBACK TRAN
GO
```

The Activity Legend reveals that page table intent locks are being taken out by SQL Server when retrieving the data. The Current Activity window (see Figure 3.3) shows that the shared locks are held until the transaction is finished (in other words, until the WAIT-FOR and ROLLBACK TRAN statements are done).

FIGURE 3.3

The Current Activity window while shared page locks are in effect.

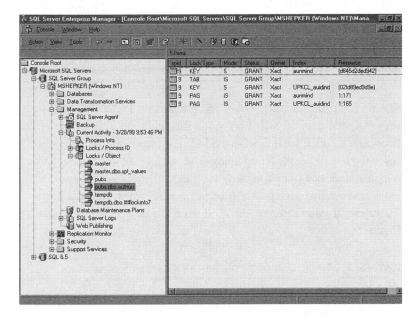

Optimizing the Query Optimizer

Now you get to the good stuff: telling SQL Server how to perform its queries. SQL Server has excellent decision-making capabilities when it comes to figuring out which index, if any at all, would get the job done most efficiently. Sometimes, however, complicated queries with many joins and elaborate WHERE clauses can be interpreted incorrectly. SQL Server has a mechanism to override the Query Optimizer's decision and specify exactly what indexes, locking, and table order should be used to get or change the data.

Using Index Optimizer Hints

You have already seen this feature in action in previous sections of this chapter. Listing 3.13 demonstrates two examples of data retrieval with index optimizer hints from the authors table.

LISTING 3.13 INDEX OPTIMIZER HINTS

```
SELECT  au_lname, au_fname
FROM    authors WITH (INDEX(0))

SELECT  au_lname, au_fname
FROM    authors WITH(INDEX(1))
```

continues

```
WHERE   au_id = '213-46-8915'

SELECT  au_lname, au_fname
FROM    authors WITH(INDEX(aunmind))
WHERE   au_lname = 'Green'
```

The first SELECT statement shows the hint WITH (INDEX(0)) to force a table scan when retrieving the data. In SQL Server 7.0, this option works only when there is not a clustered index on the table. The second SELECT statement uses the hint WITH(index(1)) to force the use of the clustered index. The third SELECT statement forces the use of the nonclustered index aunmind with the hint WITH(index(aunmind)). The index number and name are interchangeable (except for table scans, where a 0 needs to be used). Therefore, if you preferred, the third SELECT statement could have been as shown in Listing 3.14.

LISTING 3.14 A VARIATION ON INDEX OPTIMIZER HINTS

```
SELECT  au_lname, au_fname
FROM    authors WITH (index(2))
WHERE   au_lname = 'Green'
```

Because the aunmind index in the authors table has an ID of 2, either value can be used by the Query Optimizer.

> **TIP**
>
> The index ID can be found in the sysindexes table of the database in which the index resides. An ID of 0 means no index, and an ID of 1 always represents the clustered index. IDs 2 through 255 represent nonclustered indexes.

Using Locking Optimizer Hints

Let's take the example in Listing 3.14 one step further. By changing the optimizer hint, you can make SQL Server do an exclusive table lock on the authors table (as shown in Listing 3.15 and Figure 3.4).

LISTING 3.15 FORCING AN EXCLUSIVE TABLE LOCK

```
BEGIN TRAN

SELECT  *
FROM    authors (tablockx)
```

```
WHERE    au_lname = 'Green'

WAITFOR DELAY '00:02:00'

ROLLBACK TRAN
GO
```

FIGURE 3.4

*The Current
Activity window
while an exclusive
table lock is in
effect.*

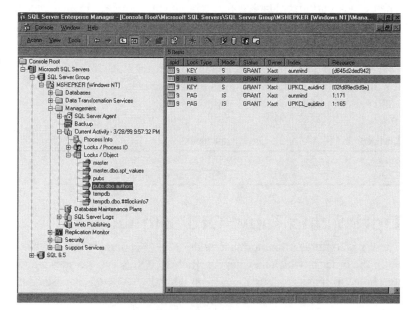

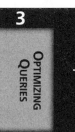

This script gives activity results like those shown in Figure 3.4. The SELECT statement
uses the optimizer hint of `tablockx` to keep exclusive table locks in place until the transaction has finished.

The available locking optimizer hints are shown in Table 3.5.

TABLE 3.5   LOCKING OPTIMIZER HINTS AND DESCRIPTIONS

Optimizer Hint	*Description*
holdlock	Hold the lock until the end of the transaction.
nolock	Do not use locks when retrieving data.
paglock	Use page locks.
tablock	Use a table lock.
tablockx	Use an exclusive table lock.
updlock	Use an update lock.

The `holdlock` optimizer hint can be used to hold shared locks for the duration of the transaction. This should already sound familiar to you in the form of serializable and repeatable read transaction isolation levels. If you would prefer to occasionally hold shared locks, you would be better off keeping the default transaction isolation level of read committed and using the `holdlock` optimizer hint as needed.

The `nolock` optimizer hint has the same functionality as the read uncommitted transaction isolation level. It forces the reading of uncommitted data by not requiring any locks while reading the data (thus bypassing the blocking by any exclusive locks).

One final note about index and locking optimizer hints: You can combine both types, but it's important to list the index hint last. The code in Listing 3.16 shows an example of a valid set of optimizer hints.

LISTING 3.16 MIXING OPTIMIZER HINTS

```
SELECT  *
FROM    authors (paglock holdlock index=aunmind)
```

Optimizing Table Order in Queries

There's no optimizer hint to place in the SELECT statement that forces tables to be selected in the order in which they appear. Rather, SQL Server decides which table is the better choice to select from first, based on what data is being requested and what's in the WHERE clause. So when tables are joined, SQL Server decides which one it uses first.

Well, not exactly. You see, there's a way to force the Optimizer to use the tables in the order they are presented. It's just not part of the SELECT statement itself. Rather, you use the SET FORCEPLAN statement to tell SQL Server to use the table order as it appears or to decide on its own. Examine Listing 3.17 and its query plan (see Figure 3.5).

LISTING 3.17 JOINING THREE TABLES

```
SELECT  au_lname, title
FROM    titles t
    JOIN titleauthor ta ON ta.title_id = t.title_id
    JOIN authors a ON a.au_id = ta.au_id
WHERE   au_lname = 'Green'
```

Although the `titles` table is listed first, then `titleauthor`, and finally `authors` in the FROM clause, `authors` is used first by the Query Optimizer because its data is being preselected. You can force SQL Server to use the tables as they appear, as shown in Listings 3.18 and Figure 3.6.

FIGURE 3.5

The Graphical Showplan of the query in Listing 3.17.

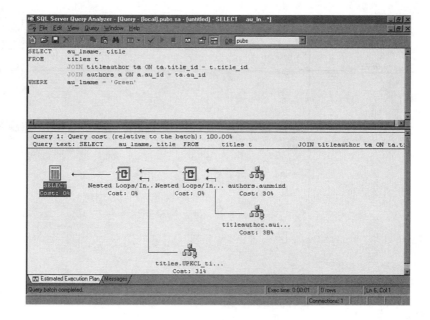

LISTING 3.18 USING THE SET FORCEPLAN STATEMENT

```
SET FORCEPLAN ON

SELECT  au_lname, title
FROM    titles t
    JOIN titleauthor ta ON ta.title_id = t.title_id
    JOIN authors a ON a.au_id = ta.au_id
WHERE   au_lname = 'Green'

SET FORCEPLAN OFF
```

Now SQL Server is using titles first, then titleauthor, and finally authors, just as they are listed in the FROM clause. In this case, however, examination of the Stats I/O would reveal that the latter is much more inefficient than the former. SQL Server decided to use authors first because it would cut down on the number of lookups in the other tables by limiting the authors table to a single or few rows. In most cases, SQL Server makes the best decision, but if you find a complex join query that's running more slowly than you think it should, you might want to play around with table order and the SET FORCEPLAN statement.

FIGURE 3.6

The Graphical Showplan of the query in Listing 3.19.

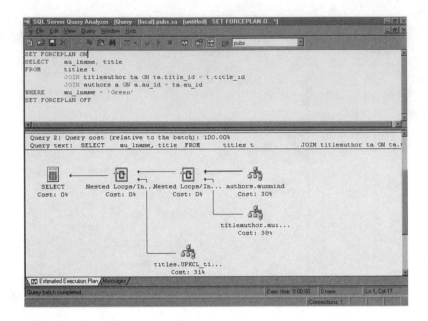

Using the SQL Server Profiler

SQL Server 7.0 has provided a new and powerful utility that enables a DBA to collect data and monitor system performance and user activity. The types of events that SQL Server Profiler can track are login attempts, connects and disconnects, Transact-SQL INSERTs, UPDATEs and DELETEs, and Remote Procedure Call batch status. After collecting information in the form of traces, you can then use the traces to analyze and fix server resource issues, monitor login attempts, and correct locking and blocking issues. A trace is simply a file where you capture server activity and events for later use. The main uses for the SQL Server Profiler are as follows:

- Monitoring performance
- Identifying problem queries and users

What to Trace

SQL Server Profiler can collect specific data about server activity. When creating a trace that will be used in monitoring performance, you should select events that are relevant to resource issues. The following trace events should be selected to assist you in tracking performance issues:

- Locks
- Stored procedures
- Transactions

Along with selecting the entire event categories, you will want to select the application name and process ID, object ID, and database ID. After collecting data from the capture, you can analyze it using one of the techniques described later in this chapter.

To start SQL Server Profiler, create a trace, and monitor it, follow these steps.

1. Start SQL Enterprise Manager and connect to the server that you will be running a trace on. From the Tools menu, choose SQL Server Profiler. The SQL Server Profiler application, shown in Figure 3.7, will open.

FIGURE 3.7

The SQL Server Profiler application enables a DBA to collect data and monitor system performance and user activity.

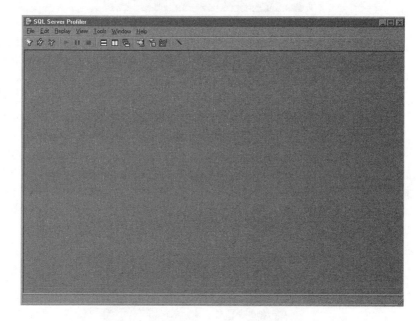

2. If you want to start a predefined trace, select File, Open, and select Trace Definition.
3. To create a new trace, click the New Trace button on the toolbar, or click on the File menu and then choose New, Trace. The Trace Properties dialog box, shown in Figure 3.8, opens.
4. In the Name box, type the name that you will use to identify the trace.

FIGURE 3.8

In the General dialog box, you define what the trace will capture.

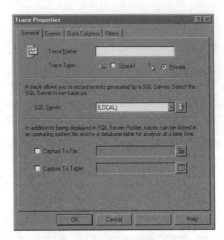

5. In the Type area, choose either a Private trace or a Shared trace. If the trace is going to be used by people other than the user that created it, choose Shared. The default is a Private trace.

6. The General tab also enables you to choose where you want the captured data to go. If you want to record the data for later analysis, choose to capture the file either to a table or to a file. The default option is to simply record events to the screen.

7. On the Events tab, shown in Figure 3.9, you can specify which SQL Server events you want to trace. In this dialog, you can choose specific options that you want to record. For the sake of this exercise, choose SQL Operators and click the Add>> button. This will track all SQL Statements such as INSERTs, UPDATEs, SELECTs, and DELETEs that are made against your database.

FIGURE 3.9

On the Events tab, you can choose events to monitor.

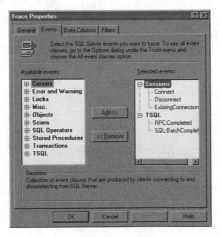

8. On the Data Columns tab, shown in Figure 3.10, you can select the data you want to capture for each traced event. This includes information about the user and any server objects that are accessed. In most cases, you will not need to change anything in this tab.

FIGURE 3.10

On the Data Columns tab, you can select which you can collect.

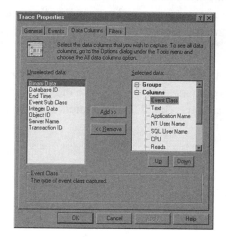

9. On the Filters tab, shown in Figure 3.11, you can choose specific criteria to include or exclude. For example, by default, any events that are generated by SQL Server Profiler are ignored. For these purposes, you will leave this with its default settings.

FIGURE 3.11

On the Filters tab, you can choose criteria for determining which events to capture.

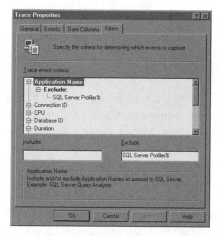

10. After you have set the options, click the OK button and the trace will automatically start. If you are tracing to the screen, you will begin to see information.

Identifying Problem Queries and Users Using SQL Server Profiler

As you probably already know, users are the first people to place the blame of poor performance on you. Most users don't understand that sudden and unexpected poor performance is most often the result of either an untrained user or a badly written query. Users don't always understand that running a query that returns 100,000 rows during the busiest time of the day can cause problems.

SQL Server Profiler can be used to help outline problem queries that can either be rewritten or scheduled for off-peak hours and users who are in need of retraining. When setting up a trace that will be used in tracking this information, you should set it up with the following events:

- SQL operators
- Transact-SQL statements
- Indexes used
- Databases used
- Duration of execution

Using the Index Tuning Wizard

The Index Tuning Wizard is a tool that is new to SQL Server 7.0 that enables administrators to create and modify indexes without knowledge of the structure of the database, hardware platforms and components, or how end-user applications interact with the database. The wizard analyzes data that is collected with the SQL Server Profiler and then makes recommendations about the effectiveness of the indexes that are on the system and any new ones that may need to be created. These recommendations are in the form of a script that can be run to drop and re-create indexes on the system.

1. From SQL Enterprise Manager, click the Tools drop-down box and select Wizards. This will open the Select Wizard dialog box. Click the plus sign next to Management and select Index Tuning Wizard; then click the OK button.

2. Click the Next button.

3. In the Select SQL Server and Database dialog, choose the name of the SQL Server and the name of the database that you will be analyzing and click the Next button.

4. From the Identify Your Workload dialog, choose I Have a Saved Workload File if you have already created one using SQL Profiler. If you have not, choose the I Will Create a Workload File on My Own option. This will open SQL Profiler for you to create a workload file. For these purposes, I will assume you already have a workload file.

5. From the Specify the Workload screen, select either the file or the SQL Server table that contains the trace information and click the Next button.

6. In the Select Which Tables to Tune dialog, SQL Server will automatically choose all the tables in the database for tuning. If you want to exclude any tables, you do so here.

7. When you click the Next button, the Index Tuning Wizard begins to analyze the data you collected and specify indexes based on that. When it has completed analyzing, it will open the Index Recommendations dialog box, specifying which indexed need changed or added. Examine this information and click Next.

8. The next dialog enables you to choose either to save the changes as a script file that enables you to apply the changes when you want, or allow SQL Server to make the changes for you.

Summary

In all honesty, the information in this chapter describes only some of the SQL Server optimization techniques. Network performance, NT Server performance, application design, and so on, all have an effect on how well your SQL Server does its job.

Great queries and indexes mean nothing if there's not enough memory on the NT server where SQL Server resides. What might appear to the users to be poor performance could be alleviated not by playing with indexes, but by installing faster network cards or using switches on the network. Applications that issue client-based transaction statements and hold them open can slow down a server to a crawl.

Be sure to check all possibilities when you need to increase performance. Work with the network administrators and application programmers. Make sure everyone is doing his or her part to make SQL Server perform to the best of its ability.

3

OPTIMIZING
QUERIES

Advanced Transact-SQL Statements

IN THIS CHAPTER

When developing databases using SQL Server, there are many times you will run into problems that cannot be solved using standard SQL Statements. There are many advanced functions that can help you during these times. Many of these statements will be covered in the preceding chapters, although there are several that you will use frequently that deserve special attention.

Using CAST and CONVERT

The CAST and CONVERT statements can be used to change an expression from one data type into another. Both the CAST and CONVERT statements can be used when concatenating data to form strings for output. The syntax for the CAST statement is

```
CAST(expression AS data_type)
```

The *expression* is any valid SQL Server expression. The *data_type* is the data type that you want to change the expression into. The following code snippet will outline a simple use of the CAST statement.

```
DECLARE @intValue     INTEGER
SELECT @intValue = 50
PRINT 'The value of @intValue is ' + CAST(@intValue AS VARCHAR(10))
```

The CONVERT statement provides very similar functionality to the CAST statement, with an extra twist when converting string data to DATETIME or DATETIME data into strings. The syntax of the CONVERT statement is

```
CONVERT (data_type[(length)], expression `[, style])
```

The *data_type* is the data type that you will be converting the *expression* into. The *length* is used when you are converting into a data type that requires a length, such as VARCHAR or CHAR. The style is used primarily when you are converting DATETIME data into string data. You must specify the style number, as outlined in Table 4.1, that you want the output string to look like. For example, to format the current date into the ANSI standard, you would execute the following code:

```
CONVERY (VARCHAR(16), GETDATE(), 102)
```

TABLE 4.1 CONVERSION STYLES WHEN CONVERTING TO AND FROM DATETIME

Without century (yy)	With century (yyyy)	Standard	Input/Output
- hh:miAM±	0 or 100 (*)	Default	mon dd yyyy
1	101	USA	mm/dd/yy
2	102	ANSI	yy.mm.dd
3	103	British/French	dd/mm/yy
4	104	German	dd.mm.yy
5	105	Italian	dd-mm-yy
6	106	-	dd mon yy
7	107	-	mon dd, yy
8	108	-	hh:mi:ss
-	9 or 109 (*)	Default + milliseconds	mon dd yyyy hh:mi:ss:mmmAM±
10	110	USA	mm-dd-yy
11	111	JAPAN	yy/mm/dd
12	112	ISO	yymmdd
-	13 or 113 (*)	Europe + milliseconds	dd mon yyyy hh:mi:ss:mmm (24h)
14	114	-	hh:mi:ss:mmm (24h)
- (24h)	20 or 120 (*)	ODBC canonical	yyyy-mm-dd hh:mi:ss
-	21 or 121 (*)	ODBC canonical + milliseconds	yyyy-mm-dd hh:mi:ss.mmm (24h)

Printing Information

The PRINT statement allows you to display a custom message to the user. The message can have up to 8,000 ASCII characters and include variables. The variables can be local or global, but if they are not of the CHAR or VARCHAR data type, their type must be changed by using the CONVERT function.

Listing 4.1 is an example of a PRINT statement that shows how variables are used to concatenate data and then print it. Notice the way CONVERT functions are used to change the data types from INT to VARCHAR.

LISTING 4.1   PRINTING WITH VARIABLES

```
DECLARE @intMinQty INT, @intNumOrders INT, @chrOutputText CHAR(60)

/* define the variables                                      */
SELECT @intMinQty = 15
SELECT @intNumOrders = COUNT(*) FROM sales WHERE qty > @intMinQty

/* Concatenate the string using CONVERT to format the variables */
SELECT @chrOutputText = 'There are '
                  + CONVERT(VARCHAR,@intNumOrders)
                  + ' orders with a quantity greater than '
                  + CONVERT(VARCHAR, @intMinQty)

PRINT @chrOutputText

/*  CODE RESULTS   -   DO NOT RUN CODE AFTER THIS LINE        */

(1 row(s) affected)
(1 row(s) affected)
(1 row(s) affected)

There are 13 orders with a quantity greater than 15
```

Each SELECT statement in Listing 4.1 returns a count message. These messages can be suppressed by preceding the first SELECT statement with the SET NOCOUNT ON statement and placing a SET NOCOUNT OFF statement after the last statement. Listing 4.2 shows Listing 4.1 after it's been modified to suppress the additional messages. Always remember to include SET NOCOUNT OFF or the counts will continue to be suppressed.

WARNING

Aside from the obvious benefit of not having to see all the row count information, there is another benefit to turning the row count off. This is that you can speed up stored procedure performance by reducing the amount of network traffic that is required to send the results back to the front end.

LISTING 4.2 USING THE SET NOCOUNT OPTION TO SUPPRESS COUNT MESSAGES

```
SET NOCOUNT ON
DECLARE @intMinQty INT, @intNumOrders INT, @chrOutputText CHAR(60)

/* define the variables                                         */
SELECT @intMinQty = 15
SELECT @intNumOrders = COUNT(*) FROM sales WHERE qty > @intMinQty

/* Concatenate the string using CONVERT to format the variables */
SELECT @chrOutputText = 'There are '
                    + CONVERT(VARCHAR,@intNumOrders)
                    + ' orders with a quantity greater than '
                    + convert(VARCHAR, @intMinQty)

PRINT @chrOutputText
SET NOCOUNT OFF

/*  CODE RESULTS  -   DO NOT RUN CODE AFTER THIS LINE         */

There are 13 orders with a quantity greater than 15
```

When returning messages from procedures, you should always use a PRINT statement rather than a SELECT statement. SELECT statements should be reserved for data processing or output. The PRINT statement is useful for communicating the status or outcome of a procedure to the user (not the programmer), but it should not be used to send critical messages. For that purpose, you should use the RAISERROR statement, which is covered in the section "Purposely Causing Errors" later in this chapter.

The sysmessages System Table

All the messages that can be returned by SQL Server are stored in the sysmessages table in the master database. There are around 3,000 predefined messages, to which you can add your own messages. The structure of the sysmessages table is shown in Table 4.2.

4

ADVANCED TRANSACT-SQL STATEMENTS

TABLE 4.2   THE STRUCTURE OF THE sysmessages TABLE

Column	Data Type	Description
Error	INT	Unique message identifier.
Severity	SMALLINT	Severity level of the error.
Dlevel	SMALLINT	Gives descriptive level of message.
Description	VARCHAR(510)	Error description with place-holders for parameters.
MsgLangid	SMALLINT	Language (default is NULL).

TIP

You can list all the defined messages in sysmessages by running the following statements.

```
SELECT error, severity, description
FROM master..sysmessages
ORDER BY error
```

Explaining Severity Levels in sysmessages

Each of the messages in the sysmessages table has a severity value, which is used to control how the message is treated. Table 4.3 is a summary of the severity levels, giving some idea of how they affect you as a programmer and your users.

TABLE 4.3   ERROR MESSAGE SEVERITY LEVELS

Error Range	Notes
0–10	These are informational messages (not errors), a way of reporting additional information after a command has executed. Sample error: 15343 New message added.
11–16	These are basic errors. Sample error: 504 Stored procedure '%.*s' not found.
17	Caused by reaching the limit of a configurable system

Error Range	Notes
	parameter. These cannot always be solved by a user and require either the DBO or SA to change a setting for the database. Sample error: `7111 Can't log text value because log is out of space.`
18	A software-based error. The batch can finish and the SQL Server connection is maintained. Sample error: `516 - Attempt to get system date/time failed.`
19	Some physical resource limit has been reached. The SA could help resolve these errors, or the transaction might have to be performed differently. Sample error: `701 There is insufficient system memory to run this query.`
20	Fatal error in the current process. The current process will be terminated, but the database integrity will be unaffected. Sample error: `2806 Stored procedure '%.*s' is corrupted. Must re-create procedure.`
21	Fatal error in database process. Any active process in the current database is terminated to protect the database integrity.
22–23	Fatal error. Database or table integrity suspect. Database or table integrity has been affected by a system failure.
24	Hardware error.
25	Internal system error.

WARNING

For errors 0 through 18, the user's session normally isn't interrupted. All errors in the range of 19–25 are fatal errors that cause at least the current process to be terminated. For errors over 20, the current process is terminated—other processes in the database are terminated and the connection to SQL Server is lost.

4

ADVANCED
TRANSACT-SQL
STATEMENTS

Defining Your Own Messages

You can add, change, and delete user-defined messages in the sysmessages table by using the system stored procedures sp_addmessage(), sp_altermessage(), and sp_dropmessage().

Adding Entries to sysmessages

By using the system stored procedure sp_addmessage(), you can add your own user-defined messages to the sysmessages table. You can choose a message identification number between 50,001 and 2,147,483,647, which leaves just a little room for growth! The description can be up to 255 characters in length. If you decide to include variables in the error, remember to leave space for them. Listing 4.3 shows the code for adding a message and the successful return from the server.

LISTING 4.3   ADDING A MESSAGE TO THE SYSMESSAGES TABLE

```
sp_addmessage 50001, 12, 'A number greater than 0 was
                                    expected. Please retry'

/*  CODE RESULTS   -    DO NOT RUN CODE AFTER THIS LINE         */

New message added.
```

If you try to add a message with an existing message_id, the code will fail, as shown in Listing 4.4.

LISTING 4.4   ADDING A MESSAGE TO THE SYSMESSAGES TABLE WITH AN EXISTING MESSAGE_ID

```
sp_addmessage 50001, 12, 'The specified value for %s was invalid.'

/*  CODE RESULTS   -    DO NOT RUN CODE AFTER THIS LINE         */

Msg 15043, Level 16, State 1
You must specify 'REPLACE' to overwrite an existing message.
```

If you really want to overwrite the error, add the REPLACE option to the end of the line. Notice that there are two more options added to the line in Listing 4.5. The first sets the language for the message (it defaults to U.S. English), and the second determines whether the message will be recorded in the Windows NT Application Log.

LISTING 4.5   ADDING A MESSAGE TO THE sysmessages TABLE USING THE REPLACE OPTION

```
sp_addmessage 50001, 12, 'The specified value for %s was invalid.'
                              , US_English, TRUE, REPLACE

/*  CODE RESULTS   -   DO NOT RUN CODE AFTER THIS LINE        */

Replacing message.
New message added.
```

> **TIP**
>
> Before adding error messages to the sysmessages table, you should contact the system administrator to make sure you use an acceptable message_id and to determine what the severity of the error should be.

Changing the State of Entries in sysmessages

If you need to alter the state of a message you have placed in sysmessages, you can use the sp_altermessage() system stored procedure, which allows you to change whether a particular message is written to the Windows NT Event Log by default.

LISTING 4.5   ALTERING THE STATE OF A MESSAGE IN THE sysmessages TABLE

```
sp_altermessage 50001, WITH_LOG, FALSE

/*  CODE RESULTS   -   DO NOT RUN CODE AFTER THIS LINE        */

Message altered.
```

Deleting Entries in sysmessages

Any of the user-defined messages in the sysmessages table can be deleted by using the sp_dropmessage() stored procedure. Listing 4.6 shows an example of the stored procedure call and the results returned.

LISTING 4.6   DELETING A MESSAGE IN THE sysmessages TABLE

```
sp_dropmessage 50001

/*   CODE RESULTS   -   DO NOT RUN CODE AFTER THIS LINE          */

Message dropped.
```

Purposely Causing Errors

You saw in the "Printing Information" section how to notify the user of progress and status. Now you'll learn how to notify the user or the programmer when things are not going according to plan.

You can use the RAISERROR statement to return an error that's handled by the system in the same way as the standard errors. The RAISERROR statement can also set a system flag using the WITH LOG option so that the error is recorded into the Windows NT Event Log. Any error written to the Windows NT Application Log is also written to the SQL Server Error Log.

The syntax of the function is

```
RAISERROR ({msg_id ¦ msg_str}{, severity, state}[, argument[,...n]] )[WITH
option[,...n]]
```

The msg_id is the number of an error that can be retrieved out of the sysmessages table. For user defined errors, you must use numbers over 50,000. msg_ids under 50,000 are reserved for SQL Server, although you can raise any of these errors with a msg_ids over 13,000. Alternatively, you can create an ad hoc message and use it in place of the msg_id. The severity option is a number that determines the severity level of the error. Severity levels between 0 and 18 are considered non-fatal errors and can be raised by any user. Severity numbers from 19 to 25 are fatal errors and can only be raised by the systems administrator. When a fatal error occurs, the client application will receive the error and then the connection to the SQL Server will be terminated. The state option is a number from 1 to 127 that represents the information about the state of a process when the error is invoked. This state information is determined by the developer and normally it is only meaningful to the developer. The argument can be used when creating ad hoc messages to fill in placeholders within the message string. The option value is a custom option that can be used this error message. The valid options are

Value	Description
LOG	The LOG option specifies that the error is to be written to the SQL Server and Windows NT error log. The errors written to the error log are currently limited to 440 bytes in length.
NOWAIT	This option causes the error to be sent to the client. immediately.
SETERROR	This option causes the @@ERROR variable to be the msg_id of the error that has just been generated, no matter what the severity level.

WARNING

To issue a RAISERROR with a severity level of 19 or higher requires system administrator privileges.

Listing 4.7 demonstrates how to return a message that is already in the sysmessages table.

LISTING 4.7   RETURNING A sysmessages ENTRY THAT REQUIRES A PARAMETER

```
RAISERROR(14056, 16, 1)

/*  Build a string to display the current value of the global   */
/*  variable @@error. You do not normally have to do this; this  */
/*  step is for the purposes of this example.                    */
SELECT @chrPrintMsg = 'The value of @@error is ' +
                                           CONVERT(char,@@error)

PRINT   @chrPrintMsg

/*  CODE RESULTS    -    DO NOT RUN CODE AFTER THIS LINE          */

Server: Msg 14056, Level 16, State 1, Line 1
The subscription could not be dropped at this time.

The value of @@error is 14056
```

4

ADVANCED
TRANSACT-SQL
STATEMENTS

> **TIP**
>
> If you look in the sysmessages table, you will see that many entries have para-
> meters. For example, in Listing 4.7 the error contains '%.*s'. This example
> requires two parameters—the first is the length of the string, and the second is
> the string value.

Listing 4.8 returns an error that is not already defined in the sysmessages table. For
errors that do not exist in the sysmessages table, but that are generated using RAISERROR,
set @@error to the message_id number 50,000 unless the severity is less than 10. If the
severity is less than 10 and you want to set @@error to an actual value, you need to use
the WITH SETERROR option.

LISTING 4.8   RAISING A MESSAGE NOT DEFINED IN sysmessages

```
DECLARE @chrPrintMsg CHAR(255)

/*  Raise the error, giving the error text, severity, and state. */
RAISERROR('Undefined error raised using the WITH SETERROR option'
                                        ,1,2) WITH SETERROR

/*  Build a string to display the current value of the global   */
/*  variable @@error. You do not normally have to do this; this */
/*  step is for the purposes of this example.                   */
SELECT @chrPrintMsg = 'Using WITH SETERROR sets the error number ' +
                      generated to ' + CONVERT(char,@@error)
PRINT @chrPrintMsg

/*  CODE RESULTS   -   DO NOT RUN CODE AFTER THIS LINE          */

Undefined error raised using the WITH SETERROR option

(1 row(s) affected)

Using WITH SETERROR sets the error number generated to 50000
```

The CASE Expression

The CASE expression is an extremely powerful tool. In its simplest form, it allows only
equality comparisons to be made. By using the more advanced CASE expression syntax,
multiple Boolean comparisons can be made to determine the action to be taken.

The Simple CASE Expression

One of the uses of the simple CASE statement is to expand values to give the user more meaningful output. For the purposes of this example, assume that the `titles` table does not have a type field and that this information can be found in the first two characters of the `title_id`. Each line in the CASE statement looks for equality between the substring function that isolates the first two characters of the `title_id`. When it finds equality, it assigns the text string to the output field `BookType`.

LISTING 4.9   USING THE CASE EXPRESSION TO EXPAND A LIST

```
SELECT  title_id,
        CASE SUBSTRING(title_id,1,2)
                WHEN 'BU' THEN 'Business'
                WHEN 'MC' THEN 'Modern Cooking'
                WHEN 'PC' THEN 'Popular Computing'
                WHEN 'PS' THEN 'Psychology'
                WHEN 'TC' THEN 'Traditional Cooking'
        END AS BookType
FROM titles
```

The following shows the output from the query:

```
title_id BookType
-------- ------------------
PC1035   Popular Computing
PS1372   Psychology
BU1111   Business
PS7777   Psychology
TC4203   Traditional Cooking
PS2091   Psychology
PS2106   Psychology
PC9999   Popular Computing
TC3218   Traditional Cooking
PS3333   Psychology
PC8888   Popular Computing
MC2222   Modern Cooking
BU7832   Business
TC7777   Traditional Cooking
BU1032   Business
MC3021   Modern Cooking
MC3026   Modern Cooking
BU2075   Business

(18 row(s) affected)
```

4

ADVANCED
TRANSACT-SQL
STATEMENTS

AUTOMATIC CODE GENERATION FOR CASE EXPRESSIONS

When you're creating these types of queries, you can save a lot of typing and the associated mistakes by using a query to build the main parts of the code. For example, the main section of Listing 4.9 could be generated by the code in Listing 4.10. After running the query, just cut and paste the code back into the query window and complete the statements. This method becomes a great help if the list is much longer than the one used in the example.

LISTING 4.10   AUTO-GENERATING THE CODE FOR LISTING 4.9

```
select distinct 'WHEN '''
                + SUBSTRING(title_id,1,2)
                + ''' THEN' from titles

/*  CODE RESULTS   -    DO NOT RUN CODE AFTER THIS LINE             */

--------------
WHEN 'BU' THEN
WHEN 'MC' THEN
WHEN 'PC' THEN
WHEN 'PS' THEN
WHEN 'TC' THEN

(5 row(s) affected)
```

Advanced CASE Expressions

The simple CASE expressions used in the previous section are only a fraction of the power that CASE can bring to your code. In this section, the full power of the CASE expression is unleashed.

Summarizing Data Using the CASE Expression

The CASE expression can be a great way to get more control when summarizing data. In this example, a report is required to return the total sales for each day of the week. At first it seems simple, but a CASE-based solution produces a more elegant result.

In Listings 4.11 and 4.12, both queries return the correct totals for the sales on that day. At first glance, the code in Listing 4.11 appears to be superior because it performs the task in fewer statements.

LISTING 4.11 SELECTING THE TOTAL SALES BY WEEKDAY: SIMPLE QUERY

```
SELECT   sum(qty) AS Total,
         datename(weekday, ord_date) AS Weekday
FROM     sales
GROUP BY datename(weekday, ord_date)
```

LISTING 4.12 USING A CASE EXPRESSION TO SUM SALES BY WEEKDAY

```
SELECT   sum(qty) AS Total,
         CASE datepart(weekday, ord_date)
                 WHEN 1 THEN 'Sunday'
                 WHEN 2 THEN 'Monday'
                 WHEN 3 THEN 'Tuesday'
                 WHEN 4 THEN 'Wednesday'
                 WHEN 5 THEN 'Thursday'
                 WHEN 6 THEN 'Friday'
                 WHEN 7 THEN 'Saturday'
         END AS Weekday
FROM sales
GROUP BY datepart(weekday, ord_date)
```

But look at the output from Listing 4.11:

```
Total         Weekday
-----------   -------------------------------
130           Monday
115           Saturday
45            Sunday
40            Thursday
78            Tuesday
85            Wednesday

(6 row(s) affected)
```

You notice that the days are out of order, making it difficult read as a report. The following is the output from Listing 4.12:

```
Total         Weekday
-----------   ---------
45            Sunday
130           Monday
78            Tuesday
85            Wednesday
40            Thursday
115           Saturday

(6 row(s) affected)
```

You will notice that the results have all of the same days, but they are in the correct order, therefore making it easier to read.

Using the CASE Expression with Complex Conditions

In the previous section you were using simple equalities to establish which part of the CASE statement would be executed. This section shows how the CASE expression allows Boolean expressions to be used. In Listing 4.13, you can compare the value in ytd_sales and then discount the book based on that value. In addition to the Boolean logic at the end of the WHEN expressions, there is an ELSE expression. If none of the Boolean logic is true, the code in the ELSE expression is executed.

LISTING 4.13 A CASE EXPRESSION WITH COMPLEX CONDITIONAL TERMS

```
SELECT
title_id, price, ytd_sales,
"DiscountPrice" =
            CASE
                WHEN ytd_sales < 1000 THEN
                                CONVERT (SMALLMONEY, price * .50)
                WHEN ytd_sales < 3000 THEN
                                CONVERT (SMALLMONEY, price * .85)
                ELSE price
            END

FROM titles
```

The following is the output from Listing 4.13:

```
title_id price                          ytd_sales  DiscountPrice
-------- ----------------------------   ---------- ----------------------------
BU1032   19.99                          4095       19.99
BU1111   11.95                          3876       11.95
BU2075   2.99                           18722      2.99
BU7832   19.99                          4095       19.99
MC2222   19.99                          2032       16.99
MC3021   2.99                           22246      2.99
MC3026   (null)                         (null)     (null)
PC1035   22.95                          8780       22.95
PC8888   20.00                          4095       20.00
PC9999   (null)                         (null)     (null)
PS1372   21.59                          375        10.80
PS2091   10.95                          2045       9.31
PS2106   7.00                           111        3.50
PS3333   19.99                          4072       19.99
PS7777   7.99                           3336       7.99
```

TC3218	20.95	375	10.48
TC4203	11.95	15096	11.95
TC7777	14.99	4095	14.99

(18 row(s) affected)

Look at this output and use the ytd_sales column to compare the values in the price column to those in the DiscountPrice column. See how the values were affected depending on which part of the CASE statement was executed.

Summarizing Data Using the Searched CASE Expression

You can further extend the power of the CASE expression by basing the expression on the results of a SELECT statement. The SELECT statement is placed in parentheses and replaces the field name in the Boolean expression of the standard CASE expression.

Listing 4.14 shows a query where an output field is created based on the value of the SELECT statement, summing the sales quantity of each store in the stores table. If the output field does not meet any of the conditions of the WHEN expression, it's placed in the last category of the ELSE expression. The output demonstrates how useful the CASE expression can be when there's data to be summarized or sorted.

LISTING 4.14 USING A SELECT-BASED CASE EXPRESSION

```
SELECT DISTINCT st.stor_name,

'Sales Rating' =
    CASE
      WHEN (SELECT SUM(sa.qty) FROM sales sa
                                WHERE st.stor_id = sa.stor_id) < 10
          THEN 'Poor'
      WHEN (SELECT SUM(sa.qty) FROM sales sa
                                WHERE st.stor_id = sa.stor_id) < 80
          THEN 'Average'
      WHEN (SELECT SUM(sa.qty) FROM sales sa
                                WHERE st.stor_id = sa.stor_id) < 100
          THEN 'Good'
      ELSE 'Excellent'
    END,

'Sales Total' = (SELECT SUM(sa.qty) FROM sales sa
```

continues

4

ADVANCED
TRANSACT-SQL
STATEMENTS

LISTING 4.14 CONTINUED

```
                                    WHERE st.stor_id = sa.stor_id)

FROM stores st, sales sa

ORDER BY 'Sales Total'

stor_name                              Sales Rating Sales Total
-------------------------------------- ------------ -----------
Eric the Read Books                    Poor         8
Fricative Bookshop                     Average      60
Bookbeat                               Good         80
News & Brews                           Good         90
Barnum's                               Excellent    125
Doc-U-Mat: Quality Laundry and Books   Excellent    130
 (6 row(s) affected)
```

Updating Data Using the CASE Expression

The CASE expression is not limited to selecting and summarizing data. It can also be used to update tables. Listing 4.15 shows how to use a CASE expression with the UPDATE statement to update the payterms field in the sales table, based on that store's sales performance. In this case you need to use a correlated subquery (see Chapter 2, "Beyond the Basics of Data Manipulation Language") to enable making a summation of the qty field. Based on the outcome of the selection, the value of payterms is updated to a new value. When you use a CASE expression with an update statement, large amounts of data can quickly be updated to new values based on a series of conditional expressions.

LISTING 4.15 USING CASE TO UPDATE DATA

```
UPDATE sales

SET payterms =
    CASE
        WHEN (SELECT SUM(qty) FROM sales s1
            WHERE sales.stor_id = s1.stor_id) < 10
            THEN 'On Invoice'
        WHEN (SELECT SUM(qty) FROM sales s1
            WHERE sales.stor_id = s1.stor_id) < 100
            THEN 'Net 30'
        ELSE 'Net 60'
    END
GO
SELECT stor_id, SUBSTRING(ord_num,1,5) ord_num,
       ord_date, qty, payterms, title_id FROM sales
GO
```

The resultset from this query is as follows:

```
(21 row(s) affected)

stor_id ord_num ord_date                        qty     payterms      title_id
------- ------- ----------------------------    ------  -----------   --------
6380    6871    Sep 14 1994 12:00AM             5       On Invoice    BU1032
6380    722a    Sep 13 1994 12:00AM             3       On Invoice    PS2091
7066    A2976   May 24 1993 12:00AM             50      Net 60        PC8888
7066    QA744   Sep 13 1994 12:00AM             75      Net 60        PS2091
7067    D4482   Sep 14 1994 12:00AM             10      Net 30        PS2091
7067    P2121   Jun 15 1992 12:00AM             40      Net 30        TC3218
7067    P2121   Jun 15 1992 12:00AM             20      Net 30        TC4203
7067    P2121   Jun 15 1992 12:00AM             20      Net 30        TC7777
7131    N9140   Sep 14 1994 12:00AM             20      Net 60        PS2091
7131    N9140   Sep 14 1994 12:00AM             25      Net 60        MC3021
7131    P3087   May 29 1993 12:00AM             20      Net 60        PS1372
7131    P3087   May 29 1993 12:00AM             25      Net 60        PS2106
7131    P3087   May 29 1993 12:00AM             15      Net 60        PS3333
7131    P3087   May 29 1993 12:00AM             25      Net 60        PS7777
7896    QQ229   Oct 28 1993 12:00AM             15      Net 30        BU7832
7896    TQ456   Dec 12 1993 12:00AM             10      Net 30        MC2222
7896    X999    Feb 21 1993 12:00AM             35      Net 30        BU2075
8042    423LL   Sep 14 1994 12:00AM             15      Net 30        MC3021
8042    423LL   Sep 14 1994 12:00AM             10      Net 30        BU1032
8042    P723    Mar 11 1993 12:00AM             25      Net 30        BU1111
8042    QA879   May 22 1993 12:00AM             30      Net 30        PC1035

(21 row(s) affected)
```

Distributed Transactions

When you're dealing with data found on two servers, data that's modified on one server needs to be updated on the other. This requires a *distributed transaction*. For example, say you're selling books. Before you can sell a book, you have to verify that you have copies in stock. When the sale is agreed on, you must remove the correct quantity from the stocklist. If all the tables were based in one database, or even in several databases on one server, you could use a series of the transactions discussed in Chapter 3, "Optimizing Queries." In this example, the store of books is kept on a remote database. To ensure consistency, a distributed transaction is used.

4

ADVANCED
TRANSACT-SQL
STATEMENTS

Why Use the Distributed Transaction Coordinator (DTC)?

The DTC gives you a way to ensure data consistency when data is manipulated across more than one server. In Chapter 3, you saw how to handle data consistency with transactions when the data was based on a single server. When you need to update data in several locations, a more complex system is required to prevent the data inconsistency that occurs if one of the other servers cannot complete its transactions. The DTC provides a simple method of controlling the transactions across several servers, managing the process.

Behind the Scenes in the DTC

Each computer involved in a distributed transaction has a local transaction manager. All application and resource managers work through their local transaction managers, which work together to manage transactions that span more than one system. Each distributed transaction consists of a two-phase commit protocol.

When the application first generates the distributed transaction, in this case using the `BEGIN DISTRIBUTED TRANSACTION` statement, the DTC on the local machine (known as the *commit coordinator*) sends a message to the remote computer and sets up a relationship (see Figure 4.1, step 1). Each system informs its transaction manager that this transaction is connected to the local transaction manager on the other system. The remote system sends an agree message to the local system (see Figure 4.1, step 2). These incoming and outgoing relationships between the systems and their local transaction managers form a tree called a *commit tree*. Any member of the commit tree has the right to abort its local transaction at any time, which in turn aborts the transaction on all the systems involved.

After the relationship is set up, the local DTC sends a prepare request to each of the remote systems involved in the transaction (see Figure 4.1, step 3). Each remote server prepares the transaction and reports back to the commit coordinator that it's prepared (see Figure 4.1, step 4). Until it receives a commit or abort from the commit coordinator, the transaction remains in doubt on that system. The commit coordinator maintains an entry in its distributed transaction log until all remote systems have confirmed that they have finished the transaction. The transaction can be completed by any of the steps 5A, 6, 5B, or 5C in Figure 4.1.

FIGURE 4.1

Sequence of operations for distributed transactions.

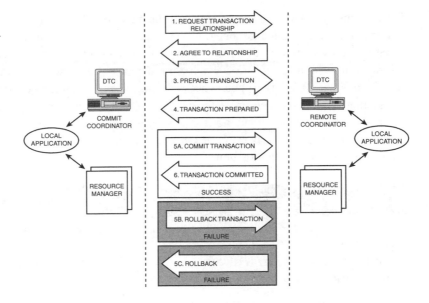

In steps 5A and 6, the transaction succeeds at the local computer and the remote is told to commit. The cycle is done when the remote computer responds to the commit coordinator that its commit was successful.

In steps 5B and 5C, the transaction fails and is rolled back. The difference between the two is that in step 5B, the remote system initiates the rollback, and in step 5C, the local system calls for the rollback.

If one of the systems fails at any time while the query is still in doubt, the local transaction manager on that computer determines the fate of the transaction when the computer restarts. It uses the information stored in its log file to decide whether it had been informed of the outcome of any incoming transactions. If any incoming transactions remain in doubt after the computer checks the log file, the commit coordinator for that transaction is queried to determine the outcome. The local transaction manager also determines the outcomes of any transactions for which it was the commit coordinator. It also responds to the requests from the other servers involved in the transaction, who are waiting to complete the transaction.

WARNING

One of the biggest problems with distributed transactions is that whenever the transaction is in doubt, any resources modified by the transaction remain locked until a commit or abort is received. To minimize this problem, it is especially important to use small, fast-executing transactions.

Transactions that remain in doubt for a long period can be a real problem, but the DTC gives you a graphical tool for resolving these stalled transactions. This tool can be used on either the commit coordinator or on the remote system to force the outcome of transactions in doubt. To show the current transactions, right-click on the DTC in the Server Manager window of SQL Enterprise Manager and select the Transactions option. Right-click again on entries in the log to commit, abort, or forget the transactions. The Forget option is sometimes required to remove transactions that have been manually completed from the event logs of other servers that have already committed the transaction.

NOTE

Only transactions that are in doubt can be forced by using the DTC Transactions Manager in SQL Enterprise Manager.

Using the DTC to Maintain Consistency Across Systems

One reason to use the DTC is that you might need to update several tables across two or more servers. If you need to update a large amount of complex data on many servers, you should also consider using *replication* (see Chapter 16, "Replication").

There are several key elements to consider when you're setting up the transactions. First, you initialize the DTC with the `BEGIN DISTRIBUTED TRAN (DISTRIBUTED TRANSACTION)` statement. There will be at least two stored procedures. One is based locally at the server initiating the transaction to update the local data. The other is on the remote server and handles the update of the remote data. After all the data manipulation is finished and successful, the `COMMIT TRAN` is issued by the local procedure. If the remote procedure tries to abort the procedure by using a `ROLLBACK` statement, an error is generated because the transaction has scope only on the commit coordinator. If the remote procedure doesn't finish and an error is generated, the distributed transaction is rolled back.

> **NOTE**
>
> If you want two servers to use distributed transactions, they must be connected by running the system stored procedures `sp_addserver()` and `sp_addremotelogin()`, or connected to each other by using the Manage Remote Servers dialog, accessed by choosing Server, Remote Servers from the menu in Enterprise Manager.

Listing 4.16 shows the stored procedure that's used to update the remote server. It takes the `job_id` passed from the local `jobs` table and updates the remote `jobs` table with the new job description.

LISTING 4.16 STORED PROCEDURE TO UPDATE THE REMOTE DATABASE USING THE DTC

```
CREATE PROCEDURE prUpdateJobs(@insJob_Id smallint,
                             @chvJob_Desc varchar(50)) AS
UPDATE jobs SET job_desc = @chvJob_Desc WHERE job_id = @insJob_Id
```

Listing 4.17 is the stored procedure on the local machine that updates the local table and then calls the remote stored procedure passing the same information. After calling the remote procedure, the two updates are committed to the databases. If either of the queries fails, the changes made within the scope of the transaction are rolled back.

LISTING 4.17 LOCAL STORED PROCEDURE TO UPDATE THE LOCAL TABLE

```
CREATE PROCEDURE prUpdateJobs(@insJob_Id      smallint,
                             @chvJob_Desc    varchar(50),
                             @chvServerName  varchar(30)) AS

declare @chvExecStr varchar(255)

/* Start a Transaction */
```

4

ADVANCED TRANSACT-SQL STATEMENTS

```
BEGIN DISTRIBUTED TRANSACTION UpdateJobs

/* Change Local Jobs Table */
UPDATE jobs SET job_desc = @chvJob_Desc where job_id = @insJob_Id

/* Make a string with the remote server name and            */
/* stored procedure to execute                              */
/* Syntax for remote procedure call is NTSQL2.pubs..prUpdateJobs*/
select @chvExecStr = @chvServerName + '.pubs..prUpdateJobs '

/* Update remote server.                                    */
exec @chvExecStr @insJob_id, @chvJob_Desc

/* Commit the MS DTC transaction */
COMMIT TRANSACTION
```

The EXECUTE statement for the stored procedure is shown in Listing 4.18. Note that the only return is that no rows were returned. In this case, no news is good news. If you examine the jobs table on each server, both should have changed the job_desc field to 'CEO' for the job_id 5.

LISTING 4.18 EXECUTING THE PROCEDURES WITH SUCCESSFUL RESULTS

```
exec prUpdateJobs 5,'CEO', NTSQL2

This command did not return data, and it did not return any rows
```

To simulate a failure, you can prevent the remote code from running by stopping the DTC on NTSQL2. Now when you execute the query as shown in Listing 4.19, the update fails on the remote server because the DTC cannot establish a link. The DTC returns an error and rolls back the query. If you now requery the jobs on the two servers, the job_desc for job_id will remain at 'CEO', unaffected by the query.

LISTING 4.19 EXECUTING THE PROCEDURES WITH FAILED RESULTS

```
EXEC prUpdateJobs 5,'Chief Executive Officer', NTSQL2

Msg 8501, Level 16, State 1
DTC on server 'NTSQL' is unavailable
Msg 8524, Level 16, State 1
The current transaction couldn't be exported to remote site.
                                        It has been rolled back.
```

Using the DTC for Paired Transactions

Another use of the DTC is to update two different tables that must remain synchronized across two different servers. In your example, whenever a sale is entered, the same quantity of books must be deducted from the remote database table bookinv. The bookinv table contains an inventory list. Listing 4.20 shows the code for creating a table of book inventory and populating it with some sample data. The table should be created in the pubs database of the remote machine.

LISTING 4.20 CREATING A BOOK INVENTORY TABLE WITH SAMPLE DATA

```
CREATE TABLE bookinv
(
        title_id        tid
                CONSTRAINT p1_constraint PRIMARY KEY NONCLUSTERED,
        quantity        integer,
        location        char(2),
        lastaudit       datetime
)

INSERT INTO bookinv
SELECT DISTINCT title_id,
                COALESCE(CONVERT(int,RAND(ytd_sales)*100),10),
                SUBSTRING(type,1,2),
                pubdate
FROM titles
```

Listing 4.21 shows .the remote server's stored procedure for checking and updating the remote table. It is called by sending the title_id and the quantity requested. At line 7, the available quantity for the book_id is found from the bookinv table. At line 10, a check is made to ensure that enough books are available to be removed from stock.

If there are not enough books, lines 11 through 17 are executed. These lines build an error message and then raise an error stating that the transaction cannot be completed.

If there are enough books, lines 19 through 28 are executed. Line 22 updates the table with the correct amount of books removed from the stock number. Lines 24 through 27 build and print a message that states the successful transfer of the books from inventory.

4

ADVANCED
TRANSACT-SQL
STATEMENTS

LISTING 4.21   CREATING A REMOTE STORED PROCEDURE FOR CHECKING AND UPDATING
THE BOOK INVENTORY TABLE

```
 1: CREATE PROCEDURE prUpdatebookinv(@tidTitles tid,
 2:                                  @intQty int) AS
 3:
 4: Declare @intAvailQty int, @chvOutputMsg varchar(255)
 5:
 6: /* Get quantity of available books in inventory   */
 7: SELECT @intAvailQty = (SELECT quantity FROM bookinv
 8:                                  WHERE title_id = @tidTitles)
 9:
10: IF @intAvailQty - @intQty < 0
11:     BEGIN
12: /* If available quantity is less than zero, then raise error */
13:          SELECT @chvOutputMsg = 'There are only '
14:                  + CONVERT(varchar(10),@intAvailQty)
15:                  + ' available, remote transaction denied'
16:          RAISERROR (@chvOutputMsg, 16, -1)
17:     END
18: ELSE
19:     BEGIN
20: /* If available quantity is greater than zero,          */
21: /* update the inventory table                           */
22:          UPDATE bookinv SET quantity = quantity - @intQty
23:                                  WHERE title_id = @tidTitles
24:          SELECT @chvOutputMsg = 'There were '
25:                  + CONVERT(varchar(10),@intAvailQty)
26:                  + ' available, remote transaction succeeds'
27:          PRINT @chvOutputMsg
28:     END
```

Listing 4.22 is the local stored procedure. It requires a title_id, quantity of books, the
StorID, and the remote server name. At line 11, the remote procedure call is built, and at
line 15, an order number is generated. At line 18, the distributed transaction UpdateJobs
is started. The first action in the distributed transaction, in lines 21 and 22, is to update
the local titles table, increasing the sales quantity in the ytd_sales field. Then an entry
is added to the sales table in lines 25 through 28, recording the sale. After the local
changes are made, the remote stored procedure is called in line 31. The final statement
block in lines 33 through 42 decides whether an error has been generated in either of the
procedures. If so, the distributed transaction is rolled back, restoring the tables. If there is
no error, the database changes are committed. This strategy is possible because if the
value of @@error is set in the remote stored procedure, the value of @@error is still visible to the calling procedure.

LISTING 4.22 CREATES THE LOCAL STORED PROCEDURE THAT CONTROLS THE DISTRIBUTED
TRANSACTION

```
 1: CREATE PROCEDURE prCreateSale (@tidTitleid tid,
 2:                                @intQty int,
 3:                                @chrStorId char(4),
 4:                                @chvServerName varchar(30)) AS
 5:
 6: DECLARE @chvExecStr varchar(255),
 7:         @chvOrdNum varchar(20)
 8:
 9: /* Make a string with the remote server name and      */
10: /* stored procedure to execute.                       */
11: SELECT @chvExecStr = @chvServerName
12:                     + '.pubs..prUpdatebookinv '
13:
14: /* Generate an order number. */
15: SELECT @chvOrdNum = @chrStorId + SUBSTRING(@tidTitleId,1,2)
16:
17: /* Start a transaction. */
18: BEGIN DISTRIBUTED TRANSACTION UpdateJobs
19:
20: /* Update local titles table. */
21: UPDATE titles SET ytd_sales = ytd_sales + @intQty
22:               WHERE title_id = @tidtitleid
23:
24: /* Add entry to local sales table. */
25: INSERT sales(stor_id, ord_num, ord_date, qty
26:                                 , payterms, title_id)
27:    VALUES (@chrStorId, @chvOrdNum, GETDATE(), @intQty
28:                                 , 'Net 60', @tidtitleid)
29:
30: /* Update remote server.                          */
31: EXEC @chvExecStr @tidtitleid, @intQty
32:
33: IF @@error > 0
34:     BEGIN
35:         ROLLBACK TRAN
36:         PRINT 'TRANSACTION WAS ROLLED BACK'
37:     END
38: ELSE
39:     BEGIN
40:         COMMIT TRAN
41:         PRINT 'TRANSACTION WAS COMMITTED'
42:     END
```

4

ADVANCED
TRANSACT-SQL
STATEMENTS

When the EXECUTE command shown in Listing 4.23 is issued, the procedure tries to remove 100 books of the book type 'BU1032' from the remote bookinv table, update the year-to-date sales in the titles table, and enter a sales record in the sales table. In this case, the procedure fails because there are only 40 books available. The distributed transaction is rolled back, leaving the database in its original state. You can check the states of the tables involved and confirm that this happens by running a query against each of the tables.

LISTING 4.23 EXECUTING THE STORED PROCEDURE, WITH AN UNSUCCESSFUL OUTCOME

```
EXEC prCreateSale 'BU1032',100,'6380','NTSQL2'

/*  Enter only the EXEC statement - sample output follows. */

Msg 50000, Level 16, State 1
There are only 40 available; remote transaction denied.
TRANSACTION WAS ROLLED BACK
```

In Listing 4.24, the sales demand is only 20 books, an amount that the available inventory can support. In this case, the remote query is successful, the distributed transaction is successful, and the updates are written to the tables in both the remote and local databases. Listings 4.25 and 4.26 show sample data, with the queries used to create them. Run them before and after the queries are executed to help show what is happening in the database tables.

LISTING 4.24 EXECUTING THE STORED PROCEDURE, WITH A SUCCESSFUL OUTCOME

```
EXEC prCreateSale 'BU1032',20,'6380','NTSQL2'

/*  Enter only the EXEC statement - sample output follows. */

There were 40 available; remote transaction succeeds.
TRANSACTION WAS COMMITTED
```

LISTING 4.25 CHECKING QUERIES AND SAMPLE DATA FOR THE LOCAL DATABASE

```
/* Run these two queries against the local database. */

SELECT stor_id, convert(char(10),ord_num), ord_date, qty, title_id
                                              FROM SALES
GO

SELECT title_id, ytd_sales FROM titles
GO
```

```
/* Sample data for local database after a fresh install of pubs */

stor_id          ord_date                         qty     title_id
-------          ----------                       ------  --------
6380    6871     Sep 14 1994 12:00AM              5       BU1032
6380    722a     Sep 13 1994 12:00AM              3       PS2091
7066    A2976    May 24 1993 12:00AM              50      PC8888
7066    QA7442.3 Sep 13 1994 12:00AM              75      PS2091
7067    D4482    Sep 14 1994 12:00AM              10      PS2091
7067    P2121    Jun 15 1992 12:00AM              40      TC3218
7067    P2121    Jun 15 1992 12:00AM              20      TC4203
7067    P2121    Jun 15 1992 12:00AM              20      TC7777
7131    N914008  Sep 14 1994 12:00AM              20      PS2091
7131    N914014  Sep 14 1994 12:00AM              25      MC3021
7131    P3087a   May 29 1993 12:00AM              20      PS1372
7131    P3087a   May 29 1993 12:00AM              25      PS2106
7131    P3087a   May 29 1993 12:00AM              15      PS3333
7131    P3087a   May 29 1993 12:00AM              25      PS7777
7896    QQ2299   Oct 28 1993 12:00AM              15      BU7832
7896    TQ456    Dec 12 1993 12:00AM              10      MC2222
7896    X999     Feb 21 1993 12:00AM              35      BU2075
8042    423LL922 Sep 14 1994 12:00AM              15      MC3021
8042    423LL930 Sep 14 1994 12:00AM              10      BU1032
8042    P723     Mar 11 1993 12:00AM              25      BU1111
8042    QA879.1  May 22 1993 12:00AM              30      PC1035

(21 row(s) affected)

title_id ytd_sales
-------- -----------
BU1032   4095
BU1111   3876
BU2075   18722
BU7832   4095
MC2222   2032
MC3021   22246
MC3026   (null)
PC1035   8780
PC8888   4095
PC9999   (null)
PS1372   375
PS2091   2045
PS2106   111
PS3333   4072
PS7777   3336
TC3218   375
TC4203   15096
TC7777   4095

(18 row(s) affected)
```

Listing 4.26 Checking Queries and Sample Data for the Remote Database

```
/* Run this query against the remote database. */

SELECT * FROM bookinv

/* Results for a bookinv created against a fresh install of pubs*/

title_id quantity    location lastaudit
-------- ----------- -------- --------------------------
BU1032   40          bu       Jun 12 1991 12:00AM
BU1111   38          bu       Jun 9 1991 12:00AM
BU2075   86          bu       Jun 30 1991 12:00AM
BU7832   40          bu       Jun 22 1991 12:00AM
MC2222   20          mo       Jun 9 1991 12:00AM
MC3021   21          mo       Jun 18 1991 12:00AM
MC3026   10          UN       Dec 11 1997  1:35AM
PC1035   87          po       Jun 30 1991 12:00AM
PC8888   40          po       Jun 12 1994 12:00AM
PC9999   10          po       Dec 11 1997  1:35AM
PS1372   3           ps       Oct 21 1991 12:00AM
PS2091   20          ps       Jun 15 1991 12:00AM
PS2106   1           ps       Oct 5 1991 12:00AM
PS3333   40          ps       Jun 12 1991 12:00AM
PS7777   33          ps       Jun 12 1991 12:00AM
TC3218   3           tr       Oct 21 1991 12:00AM
TC4203   50          tr       Jun 12 1991 12:00AM
TC7777   40          tr       Jun 12 1991 12:00AM

(18 row(s) affected)
```

> **Warning**
>
> MS DTC doesn't support the SAVE TRAN statement that can be used in standard transactions. If a SAVE TRAN is used within a distributed transaction, it is ignored with no error. If the transaction is subsequently rolled back or aborted, the entire transaction is rolled back to the BEGIN DISTRIBUTED TRANSACTION.

Troubleshooting DTC Procedures

One issue with using the DTC is that transactions spread across more than one node can be difficult to troubleshoot. There are several things you can do to minimize problems, however. First, keep your transactions short and simple. A large transaction is difficult to debug and maintains many page locks for a significant period during its processing. You can refer to Chapter 14, "Writing Effective Code," for some useful techniques for writing simple code.

Debugging DTC Procedures

If you encounter a problem with a distributed transaction, first try to run the code piece by piece using the Query Manager. If no problems are found when the code is run locally, place a number of extra commands in the transaction that either return the values being used or use a temporary table to store the variables as they change in the procedures. When you use a table, remember that any changes made within the transaction are rolled back if the transaction fails. If this is the case, record all the values just before the BEGIN DISTRIBUTED TRANSACTION statement. If you still can't find the bug, try separating the transaction into several smaller ones. This method will probably produce a better-written procedure with many shorter transactions.

Summary

This chapter has shown you a number of ways to use T-SQL statements to improve your applications and manage distributed transactions. As you have seen, CASE expressions are a helpful way to label, organize, and summarize your output and sift through complex conditions. You've also seen reusable code that uses the PRINT statement, messages you define in the sysmessages system table, and the RAISERROR function to give your application's user easy-to-understand, informative error messages.

Of course, you might be working on a system that requires multiple servers and distributed transactions. This chapter has also shown you how to create a remote stored procedure for checking and updating data on a remote server as well as code for checking queries and sample data for the local database. These examples should help you keep data on multiple servers concurrent by monitoring these distributed transactions.

4

ADVANCED
TRANSACT-SQL
STATEMENTS

Effective Use of Built-in Functions

CHAPTER 5

Functions are an important, powerful feature that allow you to accomplish tasks without having to write a lot of code. Just imagine trying to use SQL to compute the tangent of a line to a circle without using built-in functions. This chapter not only reviews all of SQL Server's functions, but also explains some effective methods for implementing these functions.

Making Computations Work with Mathematical Functions

Mathematical functions give you a means to perform operations on numeric data. Although this book assumes you're familiar with the order of operations, it's imperative that you know the order of mathematical computations. Many decisions have been made based on erroneous reports in which the order of operations was misunderstood. Table 5.1 shows a complete list of mathematical functions available in SQL Server.

TABLE 5.1 MATHEMATICAL FUNCTIONS

Function	Description
ABS	Returns the absolute value of numeric data.
ACOS	Returns the arc cosine in radians of any number passed to the function. The input range is from –1 to 1, and the output range is 0 to pi.
ASIN	Returns the arc sine in radians of any number passed to the function. The input range is from –1 to 1, and the output range is –pi/2 to pi/2.
ATAN	Returns the arc tangent in radians of any number passed to the function. The input range is infinity, meaning unbounded at both ends, and the output range is –pi/2 to pi/2.
ATN2	Returns the arc tangent in radians of the two numbers (y/x) passed to the function. The input range is infinity, meaning unbounded at both ends, and the output range is –pi to pi.
CEILING	Returns the value representing the smallest integer that is greater than or equal to the *input_number*.
COS	Returns the cosine of any number passed as an angle in radians to the function.
COT	Returns the cotangent of any number passed as an angle in radians to the function.
DEGREES	Converts radians to degrees.
EXP	Returns e raised to the nth power, where e = 2.71828183.
FLOOR	Returns the value representing the largest integer that is less than or equal to the *input_number*.

Function	Description
LOG	Returns the natural logarithm of some *input_number*, which is greater than zero.
LOG10	Returns the logarithm of some *input_number* calculated on the *input_base*. The base must be a positive value greater than 1, and the *input_number* must be a positive number greater than 0.
PI	Constant value of pi = 3.141592653589793.
POWER	Returns a number (*input_x*) raised to the power of a number (*input_y*). *Input_x* and *input_y* can be any number, but if *input_x* is negative, *input_y* must be an integer.
RADIANS	Converts from degrees to radians.
RAND	Returns random number from 0 to 1.
ROUND	Rounds the *input_x* number to the number of places specified. If the number of places specified is positive, it rounds to the right of the decimal. If the number of places specified is negative, it rounds to the left of the decimal. If no places are specified, the default is 0, which rounds to the nearest integer.
SIGN	Returns a value of 1 if the number is greater than zero, 0 if the number is zero, or −1 if the number is less than zero.
SIN	Returns the sine of any number, which is passed as an angle in radians, to the function.
SQRT	Returns the square root of an *input_number*. The value of the *input_number* must not be negative.
SQUARE	Returns the square of the *input_number*.
TAN	Returns the tangent of any number, which is passed as an angle in radians, to the function.

Out of all the mathematical functions, the most useful are ABS, CEILING, FLOOR, POWER, RAND, ROUND, and SQRT. If you are an engineer, implementing the trigonometric functions should be second nature. In business applications, these seven functions prove their worth. Their practical business uses are discussed in the following sections.

ABS

The ABS function returns the absolute value of any number passed to it. Regardless of whether the number passed is negative or positive, the ABS function always returns the number as positive. The syntax for the ABS function is as follows:

```
ABS(input_number)
```

The next several examples discussed should theoretically never happen if there's strong control over the quality of data input, whether from a file, keyboard, or EDI processing. However, in reality, data inputs cannot be fully trusted, so the ABS function provides some security at the processing end. While integrating and mechanizing many business environments, very few database packages provide financial functions. The first sample calculates the economic ordering quantity.

Implementing ABS to Reduce Input Errors

The ABS function can come in handy in management's never-ending efforts to reduce costs. For example, when analyzing trends, management attempts to reduce purchase and inventory costs by using the economic ordering quantity (EOQ) formula. This formula is as follows:

```
EOQ = SQRT(2 * Abs(S) * Abs(O) / Abs(C))
```

S is the total sales in units, O is the ordering cost for each order, and C is the carrying cost for each order. Although the formula could be calculated using the square root function only, negative input can occur, resulting in trying to take the square root of a negative (imaginary) number. To avoid this condition, you can implement the ABS function as it's shown in the following line. For this example, assume that S = 2,000 units, O = $8.00, and C = $0.20.

```
SELECT SQRT(2.0*ABS(2000.0)*ABS(-8.0)/ABS(0.20))
```

Your output should look similar to the following:

```
-----------------------
400.0
(1 row(s) affected)
```

> **TIP**
>
> When using the SQRT function, all data types must be the same. If you alter the data to be a mix of integers and real values, you get an arithmetic overflow error.

One of the most exciting features of functions and formulas is that you can now store this value. As your input parameters change, you can store the updated value and use EDI to automatically figure your purchasing requirements. The next example is also taken from real code used for tracking claim payments for an insurance company.

Using ABS as an Audit Tool

When a claim is made, a claims adjuster sets up a loss reserve and an expense reserve before any payments are made on the claim. Eventually, if the claim is valid, the insurer makes loss and expense payments to process the claim. The total of these four fields is called the *total incurred*. Logically, the reserve dollars, which are used to set aside anticipated funds for settling claims, should be reduced to $0.00 after the claim is paid.

When you're auditing a firm's data, instead of checking to see if loss reserve plus expense reserve equals zero, use absolutes—ABS(loss reserve) and ABS(expense reserve)—to see if the sum is zero. Running both queries should have resulted in the same returned count of selected records, but did not. Ultimately, a bug was discovered in the system, which reports loss reserve as negative and expense reserve as positive for the same amount only under specific conditions, resulting in these discrepancies. As you can see, a simple function can have many uses!

CEILING

The CEILING function returns the value representing the smallest integer that is greater than or equal to the *input_number*. The syntax for the CEILING function is as follows:

```
CEILING(input_number)
```

Have you ever wondered how the average family has 2.35 kids? How you can order 1.3 cars for your sales lot? By replacing the ABS function (shown previously as the EOQ calculation) with the CEILING function, you no longer need to worry about placing an order with a noninteger quantity. The CEILING function always rounds up to the next integer. The next example demonstrates the use of the CEILING function with the EOQ calculation.

```
SELECT CEILING(SQRT(2.0*ABS(1985.0)*ABS(-8.0)/ABS(0.20)))
```

Your output should look similar to the following:

```
- - - - - - - - - - - - - - - - - - - - - -
399.0
(1 row(s) affected)
```

This function could also be used to round up dollars to the next integer without using the ROUND function.

5

EFFECTIVE USE
OF BUILT-IN
FUNCTIONS

FLOOR

This function returns the value that represents the largest integer that is less than or equal to the *input_number*. The syntax for the FLOOR function is as follows:

```
FLOOR(input_number)
```

The FLOOR function can be used to compute the modulus, as shown in the following section. It can also be used to retrieve the decimal portion of a number relatively quickly.

Using FLOOR to Calculate the Modulus

Surprisingly, SQL Server does not build the MOD function into its function library. However, using the FLOOR function as your basis, you can create a modulus function. The modulus returns the remainder of one number divided into another number. The following line shows the SQL Server code for returning the modulus using sample data. The formula to return the modulus is x-y*FLOOR(x/y), so in this example, 5 divided by 2 returns a remainder of 1.

```
SELECT 5-2*FLOOR(5/2)
```

Your output should look similar to the following:

```
- - - - - - - - - - - - - - - - - - - - -
1
(1 row(s) affected)
```

The T-SQL in the preceding example is equivalent to the mathematical equation 5 Mod 2. You can even use this function with floating numbers. Another use for FLOOR is to produce the decimal portion of a float value.

Using FLOOR to Make Some Cents

Again, Microsoft does not provide a TRUNC function. To mimic part of this function, you can use FLOOR to determine the decimal portion of any number. You could use string functions to accomplish this task, but FLOOR gives you a faster and more elegant solution. The formula to compute the decimal value of any number is x - FLOOR(x), as shown here:

```
SELECT 1.22-FLOOR(1.22)
```

Your output should look similar to the following:

```
- - - - - - - - - - - - - - - - - - - - -
0.22
(1 row(s) affected)
```

SQL Server also lets you integrate two functions in this manner. For example, you could find the decimal portion of the value of pi by integrating the PI function with the FLOOR function like the following:

```
SELECT PI() - FLOOR(PI())
```

POWER

The POWER function returns a number (*input_x*) raised to the power of a number (*input_y*). Although *input_x* and *input_y* can be any number, if *input_x* is negative, *input_y* must be an integer. Almost every business implements the POWER function to some extent.

Calculating the Present Value with the POWER Function

The formula to compute the present value is $FV*(1/(1+i)^n)$; FV is the future value, i is the interest rate, and n is the number of periods. The next example calculates the present value using SQL Server functions. For this example, you assume that the future value is 1,464, the interest rate is 10%, and the number of periods is 4.

```
SELECT 1464*(1/POWER((1+.10),4))
```

Your output should look similar to the following:

```
---------------------------------
1002.7397260273972602739726027397 26
(1 row(s) affected)
```

The length of this result's decimal part can be fixed under the ROUND section, discussed later in this chapter.

RAND

RAND is another specialty function. One of the most common complaints in the information technology field is the lack of testing potential candidates. SQL Server, Oracle, Dataease, Informix, and the like have been used to generate tests used by businesses as well as schools. One database holds the actual questions (in text format) with a unique key on a QuestionNumber column from 1 to *n* (the highest number of your questions). This database cannot be accessed by the user. When the user takes an exam, the system automatically copies all 100 exam questions into the true test database randomly with the RAND function. Everyone should have the same questions, but in a different sequence. After the user has finished the exam, it's then graded automatically. This process disables the login ID used to take the exam, so the user can't change his or her answers.

The basic code for implementing this can be seen in Listing 5.1. The code for actually implementing the testing portion, which would be written in Visual Basic or Visual C++, of this is beyond the scope of this book.

LISTING 5.1   USING THE RAND SPECIALTY FUNCTION

```
CREATE TABLE Questions
(
    intQuestionID       INT,
    vchQuestionText     VARCHAR(512)
)
GO

CREATE TABLE TestQuestions
(
    intQuestionID       INT,
    vchQuestionText     VARCHAR(512)
)
GO

/*  This section populates the questions table */

DECLARE @intCounter       INT
DECLARE @vchQuestion      VARCHAR(64)

SET NOCOUNT ON

SELECT @intCounter = 1

WHILE (@intCounter <= 100)
BEGIN
     SELECT @vchQuestion = 'Test Question #' +
            CONVERT(VARCHAR(8), @intCounter)
     INSERT INTO Questions VALUES (@intCounter, @vchQuestion)
     SELECT @intCounter = @intCounter + 1
END
GO

/* This section generates the random questions */

DECLARE @intQuestionID      INT

SET NOCOUNT ON

DELETE FROM TestQuestions
SELECT @intQuestionID = CEILING(RAND()*100)

WHILE (SELECT COUNT(*) FROM TestQuestions) < 100
BEGIN
     WHILE (SELECT COUNT(*) FROM TestQuestions
```

```
            WHERE intQuestionID = @intQuestionID) = 1
    BEGIN
            SELECT @intQuestionID = CEILING(RAND()*100)
    END
    INSERT INTO TestQuestions
            SELECT * FROM Questions
            WHERE intQuestionID = @intQuestionID
END
```

ROUND

The ROUND function rounds the *input_x* number to the number of places specified. If the number of places specified is positive, the function rounds to the right of the decimal. If the number of places specified is negative, it rounds to the left of the decimal. If no places are specified, the default is 0, which rounds to the nearest integer. The syntax for the ROUND function is as follows:

```
ROUND(input_x,<places_to_round>)
```

In the previous section on the POWER function, the code snippet calculated the present value by using the POWER function. The result was calculated to 32 decimal places. Because the output should be in monetary format, there are two options. First, convert the data type to money by using the CONVERT function. The SQL coding required to do that follows:

```
SELECT CONVERT(money,1002.7397260273972602739726)
```

This option is adequate for most situations. However, if you have just run this T-SQL, you notice that it results in an error. There are too many decimal places for the code to translate the number into a MONEY data type. What's the other solution?

The second means is to use the ROUND function, which computes faster than the first option. The following line applies the ROUND function to the present value calculation:

```
SELECT ROUND(1464*(1/POWER((1+.10),4)),2)
```

Your output should look similar to the following:

```
-----------------------------------
1002.7400000000000000000000000000000000
 (1 row(s) affected)
```

The only disadvantage with ROUND is that the function uses zeros for placeholders to retain the data type.

> **TIP**
>
> Most of you have seen reports that display money values and a total dollar amount at the end of the report. Sometimes the dollar amounts do not sum to the exact dollar amount shown in the total. Most often, this occurs because the aggregates carry the computations out to 32 decimal places. The output, however, displays only two decimal places, rounding when conditions are met. This usually occurs when complex calculations are performed on columns.
>
> One way to address this problem is to avoid printing the report first and enter the data into a table. You can then track the fraction remaining from the third decimal place to the thirty-second decimal place. Every time the fraction adds to a penny, add (or subtract, if necessary) the penny to the amount for the next record.

SQUARE

The SQUARE function squares the *input_number* that is passed into it. Here's the syntax of the command:

```
SQUARE(input_number)
```

SQRT

The SQRT function returns the square root of a value 0 or greater. The syntax of SQRT is as follows:

```
SQRT(input_number)
```

Again, the *input_number* can't be negative or an error will result. Refer to the ABS or EOQ examples in the "Implementing ABS to Reduce Input Errors" section for the syntax using the SQRT function.

Calculating Dates with Date Functions

Date calculations are frequently used in most business applications, such as due dates, interest computations, aging reports, loan calculations, birthdays, and the number of days left in a pregnancy. SQL Server date functions perform CHAR (or VARCHAR) to DATETIME (or SMALLDATETIME) conversions automatically. Before you can even work with the date functions, you need to understand the components of the date, listed in Table 5.2.

TABLE 5.2   PARTS OF THE DATE

Date Part	Description	Value Range
YY	Year	1753 to 9999
QQ	Quarter	1 to 4
MM	Month	1 to 12
DY	Day of year	1 to 366
DD	Day of month	1 to 31
WK	Week of year	1 to 53
DW	Weekday	1 to 7 or Sun to Sat
HH	Hour	0 to 23 (military time)
MI	Minute	0 to 59
SS	Second	0 to 59
MS	Millisecond	0 to 999

NOTE

SQL Server treats any dates with the last two digits of the year less than 50 as the next century and any dates with the last two digits greater than or equal to 50 as the current century. Therefore, 01/01/70 is treated as 1970, but 01/01/36 is treated as 2036. As a general rule, try to use a four-digit year whenever possible.

For example, assume you are trying to calculate a 30-year mortgage that started in 1940 and ended in 1970. You enter 40 to 70 as the year range. SQL Server translates that year range into 2040 to 1970, which would yield a starting date 70 years following the ending date of the loan! In addition, consider that some countries have 100-year loans. This obviously causes problems if the year is not expressed as all four digits.

SQL Server allows you to configure the four-year cutoff date in either SQL Enterprise Manager of through the use of the `sp_configure` command.

Table 5.3 lists all of SQL Server's available date functions.

5

EFFECTIVE USE
OF BUILT-IN
FUNCTIONS

TABLE 5.3   DATE FUNCTIONS

Function	Description
DATEADD	Returns the result of adding a time interval to a date.
DATEDIFF	Returns the time interval between two dates in the format specified for the *datepart* parameter.
DATENAME	Returns the text representation of the date as specified by *datepart*.
DATEPART	Returns an integer of the *datepart* specified from a date.
GETDATE	Returns the current system date and time.
DAY	Returns an integer representing the day *datepart* of the specified date.
MONTH	Returns an integer representing the month *datepart* of the specified date.
YEAR	Returns an integer representing the year *datepart* of the specified date.

The DATEADD Function

This function allows you to add a time interval to a date to arrive at the new date. It's used all the time in business for calculating due dates, aged dates, and shipping and delivery dates. The syntax for the DATEADD function is as follows:

DATEADD(*datepart*,*number*,*date*)

The *datepart* could be any of the values listed in Table 5.2, but it is unlikely that you will add seconds or milliseconds to a date. The following SELECT statement calculates the due date of an invoice with a net term of 30.

SELECT DATEADD(DY,30,'10/01/98')

Your output should look similar to the following:

```
------------------
Oct 31 1998 12:00AM
 (1 row(s) affected)
```

Notice that the date function completes all string conversions and returns the output in the SQL Server standard date format. All these date functions perform this conversion automatically.

The DATEDIFF Function

DATEDIFF returns the difference between two dates as specified by *datepart*. The syntax for the DATEDIFF function is as follows:

DATEDIFF(*datepart*,*date1*,*date2*)

The next SELECT statement calculates the number of days past due for an invoice.

```
SELECT DATEDIFF(DY,'08/30/98','10/01/98')
```

Your output should look similar to the following:

```
- - - - - - - - - - - - - - - - - -
32
 (1 row(s) affected)
```

In reality, the first date would be a field called DueDate, and the second date would be a field called CurrentDate (or a specified period-ending date). The system automatically calculates the number of days past due and ages the invoices accordingly. From here, you can automatically send out different types of notices based on the number of days past due. This system could also be used to determine whether a customer gets a discount with terms 2%/10 net 30. If the customer pays within ten days, the invoice is discounted 2%. As you can see, date functions play an important role in all businesses.

> **NOTE**
>
> Keep in mind that the function returns an INTEGER value. Although you probably won't exceed the maximum value for an INTEGER when computing the difference for days, weeks, and months, you could potentially exceed an INTEGER's value range when taking the difference on times, especially with milliseconds. For example, the difference in milliseconds between September 1, 1973 and September 1, 1975 is approximately 63 billion milliseconds (1000ms×60sec×60min×24hr×365dy×2yr). If you calculate this and try setting the result to an INTEGER value, you get an arithmetic overflow error.

The DATENAME Function

This function returns a date's character string representation. The syntax for the DATENAME function is as follows:

```
DATENAME(datepart,date)
```

To find the day of the week, use this line:

```
SELECT DATENAME(DW,'10/01/98')
```

Your output should look similar to the following:

```
- - - - - - - - - - - - - - - - - -
WEDNESDAY
 (1 row(s) affected)
```

You can use this function in a letter saying, for example, you will call the customer on Monday, August 12. Keep in mind that the only *datepart* values that return a character string are the day of the week (DW) and the month (MM).

The DATEPART Function

This function returns the integer value of the *datepart* specified. (Note that the DATEPART function is different from the *datepart* parameter.) For example, the DATEPART function can be used to return the numerical representation of the current month of the year. The syntax for the DATEPART function is as follows:

```
DATEPART(datepart,date)
```

This SELECT statement extracts the month from a date:

```
SELECT DATEPART(MM,'Oct 31 1998')
```

Your output should look similar to the following:

```
- - - - - - - - - - - - - - - - - -
10
 (1 row(s) affected)
```

One practical use of this function is searching for all sales within the month of October, for example. Maybe you stored the month in an INTEGER column separated from the rest of the date. If so, the T-SQL in this DATEPART example could be embedded in a WHERE clause to retrieve all sales for October.

The GETDATE Function

The GETDATE function returns the current system date and time of the server. GETDATE accepts no parameters, yet it is one of the most useful functions. You can use this value to update an audit field in triggers. The syntax for GETDATE looks like this:

```
SELECT GETDATE()
```

Your output should look similar to the following:

```
- - - - - - - - - - - - - - - - - -
Aug 12 1998 5:30PM
(1 row(s) affected)
```

A good use of GETDATE is stamping the name of the user who ran the report and the date the report was generated. This information makes an excellent audit trail because the user can't change the server date and time. My report endings always show these two lines with the actual values filled in:

Report Generated By: ...

Report Generated On: ...

The first line displays the system username, and the second uses `GetDate` to display current date and time. Your auditors will thank you for adding these two items.

The DAY Function

The DAY function returns an integer that represents the day datepart of a specified date. This function is the equivalent to using DATEPART(*dd, date*).

The MONTH Function

The MONTH function returns an integer that represents the month datepart of a specified date. This function is the equivalent to using DATEPART(*mm, date*).

The YEAR Function

The YEAR function returns an integer that represents the year datepart of a specified date. This function is the equivalent to using DATEPART(*yy, date*).

Using String Functions to Manipulate Strings

A good portion of data stored in a database is composed of string data. SQL Server has several powerful functions that can be used to manipulate strings. Table 5.4 is a summary of all available string functions.

TABLE 5.4 STRING FUNCTIONS

Function	*Description*
+	Concatenates two or more strings.
ASCII	Returns the decimal equivalent of a single ASCII character. If a string is passed, only the first character is translated.
CHAR	Returns the corresponding ASCII character represented by the decimal number passed in this function. The decimal equivalent must be passed in an INTEGER format. This function has the opposite effect of ASCII. If a value other than 0–255 is used, NULL is returned.
CHARINDEX	Returns the starting position of a string pattern found within a string.
DIFFERENCE	Used to compare two strings. A value from 0–4 is returned, with 4 being the best match, which means the two strings are identical.

continues

TABLE 5.4   CONTINUED

Function	Description
LEFT	Returns the part of a string starting from the left and moving right the specified number of spaces.
LEN	Returns the number of characters in the string passed into it.
LOWER	Converts all characters to lowercase.
LTRIM	Removes leading blank spaces from a string.
NCHAR	Returns the Unicode character with the given integer code, as defined by the Unicode standard.
PATINDEX	Returns the starting position of the first occurrence of a pattern found in a string. The difference between this and CHARINDEX is that if the string can be found anywhere, you need to use wildcards with PATINDEX.
REPLACE	Replaces all instances of a string with a different string.
QUOTENAME	Returns a Unicode string with delimiters added to make the string a valid SQL Server delimited identifier. The delimiter can be a single quote mark ('), a double quote mark ("), or a left and right bracket ([ ]). If nothing is entered, the brackets are used.
REPLICATE	Repeats one or more characters a specified number of times in a string.
REVERSE	Returns a character string in reverse order.
RIGHT	Returns part of a character string starting from the right to as many characters specified.
RTRIM	Removes trailing blank spaces.
SOUNDEX	Returns a four-character SOUNDEX code to compare the similarity between two strings.
SPACE	Returns a string of spaces repeated the number of times specified.
STR	Converts numeric data to string data.
STUFF	Deletes a specified number of characters at a starting position in the first string and inserts all the characters from the second string at the deletion point from the first string.
SUBSTRING	Returns all or part of a string as specified.
UNICODE	Returns the integer value for the first character of the input string, as defined by the Unicode standard.
UPPER	Converts all letters to uppercase.

The most commonly used string functions listed in Table 5.4 are CHARINDEX, DIFFERENCE, LOWER, LTRIM, RTRIM, REVERSE, STR, SUBSTRING, and UPPER. The following sections give you a description and syntax of each of them. Several examples using a combination of these functions follow.

The CHARINDEX Function

This function returns the starting position of a pattern specified in a string value. The syntax for the CHARINDEX function is as follows:

CHARINDEX(*pattern,string_value*)

The pattern can be one or more characters. One possible use is eliminating commas within string values. This function finds only the first occurrence—if a string has more than one comma, you have to locate the comma, write out the new string without the comma, and repeat the search for the comma until no more values are found (when the function returns a value of 0).

The DIFFERENCE Function

This function returns a value between 0–4 to compare the similarities between strings using SOUNDEX. The higher the value, the closer the match. A value of 0 means no match, and a value of 4 reflects an exact string match. The syntax for the DIFFERENCE function is as follows:

DIFFERENCE(*string1,string2*)

You can use this function when searching for names or addresses. For instance, if you need the name Kathy Ward and are not sure if it is spelled Cathy, Kathy, Kathie, or some other way, selecting all values of 3 or greater should locate the record. Because this feature is not case sensitive, you don't need to worry about having to convert to all uppercase or all lowercase and doing a match based on case.

Soundex values are useful when an operator is taking an order from a customer over the phone. For example, a customer named Colleen Hogan calls to place an order for 100 widgets. The operator searches for Colene Hogan and finds the match almost instantly. The customer does not have to worry about spelling her name because the DIFFERENCE function found all logical matches.

The LOWER Function

This function converts all alphabetic characters to lowercase. All nonalphabetic characters remain unchanged. The syntax for the LOWER function is as follows:

LOWER(*input_string*)

This function can be used with other functions to correct data-entry mistakes. Some people input all characters in uppercase, some all in lowercase, and some in proper case.

The LTRIM Function

This function removes all leading spaces in a string. The syntax for the LTRIM function is as follows:

```
LTRIM(input_string)
```

It's commonly used to correct data-entry mistakes or to correct data during data migration, data conversion, EDI, or some other data importing. You can combine this function with RTRIM to remove all leading and trailing spaces from a string.

The REVERSE Function

This function reverses all characters in a string. The syntax for the REVERSE function is as follows:

```
REVERSE(input_string)
```

The REVERSE function also accepts a column as input. You can use it embedded within a SQL query, possibly to set default passwords. For example, you can place a trigger on a table that holds a list of users. When a new user is inserted into the table, the trigger updates the Password field to be the reverse of the username.

The RTRIM Function

This function removes trailing blank spaces at the end of the string. The syntax for the RTRIM function is as follows:

```
RTRIM(input_string)
```

It's commonly used to correct data-entry mistakes or to correct data during data migration, data conversion, EDI, or some other data importing. Another use for this function is applying it on a CHAR column in a SELECT statement. Sometimes the data in a CHAR column does not completely fill the column, so it's padded with spaces.

The STR Function

This function converts numeric-type data to string data. The syntax for the STR function is as follows:

```
STR(input_number,total_length,decimal)
```

The `input_number` is the numeric data to be converted to string data. Optionally, the `total_length` can be used to specify the total length of the string, including sign, spaces, digits, and the decimal point. The `decimal` parameter is also optional and specifies the number of places to the right of the decimal (the default length is 10). The results from this function are often used to concatenate string data for output.

The SUBSTRING Function

The SUBSTRING function returns all or part of a character string. The syntax for the SUBSTRING function is as follows:

```
SUBSTRING(input_string,starting_position,length)
```

The `input_string` is the string or column name that you want to retrieve a subset of. The `starting_position` is the location in the `input_string` where your subset begins. The `length` is the number of characters to extract from the `input_string` beginning at the `starting_position`. Some practical uses of the SUBSTR function are parsing a phone number column for the area code, retrieving the last name from a name column, or getting the final six digits from a UPC code.

Examples Using String Functions

SQL Server gives you a limited set of string manipulation functions. However, by using these built-in functions, you can manufacture your own custom string functions. Several examples are offered here so that you can see many different cases in which advanced string manipulation was required. Keep in mind that although the following examples use a SELECT statement with fixed data, they could be altered to use columns from a table. You might even want to consider creating your own custom stored procedures with output parameters returning the outcome of complex string manipulations.

Using Strings to Reverse the Order of a Name

In database conversion projects, names are often stored in a single field. This sample takes a name stored in one field in the format First Name, Last Name, and converts it to Last Name, First Name. In reality, you can use this method in a stored procedure to actually split the data into two separate fields. When a middle initial or suffix is involved, the concept is the same, but a slightly more complex method is used. See to Listing 5.2 for sample T-SQL that changes the order of the first and last name.

LISTING 5.2 CHANGING THE ORDER OF A NAME

```
DECLARE @chvFullName VARCHAR(30),
        @chvReorderedName VARCHAR(30)
SELECT @chvFullName = 'Julie Ely'
SELECT @chvReorderedName =
  SUBSTRING(@chvFullName, -- create Last Name
        (CHARINDEX(" ",@chvFullName) + 1 ) ,
        30) +
        ', ' + -- Comma and Space Separator
        SUBSTRING(@chvFullName, -- Create First Name
        1 ,
        (CHARINDEX(" ",@chvFullName) - 1 ))
PRINT @chvReorderedName
```

Your output should look similar to the following:

```
----------------------------------------
Ely, Julie
(1 row(s) affected)
```

The first three lines use the SUBSTRING function to extract the last name. Although the string data is a name, it could easily be a column from a table. To arrive at the starting position, CHARINDEX is used to locate the space between the first name and the last name, and adds 1 to the value of the space's position to calculate the starting position of the last name. There is no need to determine the length; you get the remainder of the string only if you supply a length longer than the string. The concatenation function adds the comma and space separator to the last name. Finally, the first name is concatenated again by using the SUBSTRING function. The first string parameter is the fixed name. The starting position should always be 1, as specified in the listing, and the ending position uses the CHARINDEX function to locate the space separator and subtract 1 to arrive at the length.

Again, this assumes a few items:

- The name is always first name, space, last name.
- The field length and type is set to char(30).
- No spaces precede the first name.
- No middle initial or suffix has been entered.

NOTE

If you plan on using either name part independently, it's better database design to create two separate columns, one for the first name and another for the last name. This method also allows you to perform faster searches by first or last name using indexes.

Any of these limitations could be worked out with SQL Server, such as using LTRIM in the computation to eliminate spaces before the name even begins. The REVERSE function can be used, by looking at the location of the first space, to see if there is a suffix or middle initial. The field length can be assigned by using the DATALENGTH function, which is discussed later in this chapter.

Changing Strings to Sentence Case

As robust as SQL Server's functions are, being able to convert a line of data to sentence case is one feature that's not offered. *Sentence case* means capitalizing the first character of a string and lowercasing the remaining characters. The following code converts a sentence to sentence case.

```
SELECT UPPER(SUBSTRING("this Is a tEst.",1,1)) +
    LOWER(SUBSTRING("this Is a tEst.",2,20))
```

Your output should look similar to the following:

```
--------------------
This is a test.
(1 row(s) affected)
```

This process extracts the first character with the SUBSTRING function in the first line and converts it to uppercase with the UPPER function, regardless of its original case when selected. The rest of the line is selected again by the SUBSTRING function and converted to lowercase with the LOWER function in the second line. To improve this code, you could look for instances of the period and automatically capitalize the first character after the period. You have to factor out abbreviations, too, such as Mr. and Dr., as well as numbers with decimals, such as "You've just won $9,999.99". This method could be applied similarly to capitalize the first letter in every word.

Using Strings to Extract the Decimal Portion of a Real Number

Because SQL Server does not provide any type of TRUNCATE function, a second method to extract the decimal portion of a real number is demonstrated in the following example. The first method is described in this chapter's section "Using FLOOR to Make Some Cents."

```
SELECT SUBSTRING(STR(4.1313,20,6),
        CHARINDEX(".",STR(4.1313,20,6)),7)
```

Your output should look similar to the following:

```
---------
0.131300
(1 row(s) affected)
```

You could now apply the CONVERT function to change the data back to a real number. The SUBSTRING function is used in the first line to extract the decimal portion of the real number. The first parameter uses the STR function to convert from the number to the string data type. The starting position is determined by locating the decimal place with the CHARINDEX function in the second line. Because you want a length of six decimal places, SUBSTRING's last parameter in the second line is set to a value of 7 to include the decimal point and six significant digits. As you can see, you can make use of SQL Server functions to accomplish the same task in many different ways.

Using String Functions to Search for Phonetically Similar Data

One continuing problem with customer service is trying to look up a customer name and not finding it. This problem could be caused by a data-entry error or the service agent could be entering the name incorrectly. The DIFFERENCE function allows you to extract close or exact matches from a string. The following lines show you how to locate the name Kathy Ward.

```
SELECT DIFFERENCE("Kathy Ward","kathy WARD"),
        DIFFERENCE("KATHY Ward","Cathy Ward"),
    DIFFERENCE("KATHY Ward","Cathie Ward")
```

Your output should look similar to the following:

```
----------- ----------- -----------
4           3           3
(1 row(s) affected)
```

This example reflects two points. As you can see in lines 1 and 2, case does not matter with the DIFFERENCE function. The second item you should notice is the output results. An exact match is always a value of 4, and a very close match is a value of 3. You could do a SELECT statement from a table that selects only records with a difference value of 3 or greater. This method should locate the information you're looking for.

Using Text and Image Functions in SQL

In SQL Server, you can store text and image data with the TEXT and IMAGE data types. Functions are provided so that you can work with these data types in a table. Table 5.5 lists the available TEXT and IMAGE functions.

TABLE 5.5   TEXT AND IMAGE FUNCTIONS

Function	*Description*
TEXTPTR	Points to the starting location of the text stored in the column.
TEXTVALID	Checks to make sure the TEXTPTR is valid.

These functions can be combined with several other functions, such as PATINDEX to find a matching pattern in the text or DATALENGTH to get the size of the text or image stored.

Using SQL Functions to Retrieve System Information

SQL Server has functions that return information about the database and server. These functions can retrieve system data, such as usernames, database names, and column names. Other functions, such as NULLIF and COALESCE, can be used to embed logic into SQL queries. The system functions are listed in Table 5.6.

TABLE 5.6   SYSTEM FUNCTIONS

Function	*Description*
APP_NAME	Returns the name of the application for the current connection, if one has been set for the connection by the application.
COALESCE	Returns the first non-NULL expression. Very similar to the CASE statement, but looks for non-NULL versus the Boolean values TRUE or FALSE.
COL_LENGTH	Returns the column length for a specified column in a table.
CURRENT_TIMESTAMP	Returns the current date and time. This function is equivalent to using GETDATE().
CURRENT_USER	Returns the name of the current user. This function is equivalent to using USER_NAME.
DATALENGTH	Returns the actual length of the data. Useful only for CHARACTER, BINARY, TEXT, and IMAGE data types. All other data types are fixed.
DB_ID	Returns the database identification number.
DB_NAME	Returns the name of the database.
GETANSINULL	Returns a value of 1 if the database supports the rules of ANSI NULL.
HOST_ID	Returns the workstation ID number.
HOST_NAME	Returns the name of the workstation.

continues

5

EFFECTIVE USE
OF BUILT-IN
FUNCTIONS

TABLE 5.6 CONTINUED

Function	Description
IDENT_INCR	Returns the increment value as specified when creating an identity column.
IDENT_SEED	Returned the SEED value, or starting value, used for an identity column. (It does not, however, tell you what the current or next incremental value is; this information can be retrieved from system tables.)
INDEX_COL	Returns the name of the column indexed.
ISDATE	Determines whether an input expression is a valid date.
ISNULL	Replaces NULL entries with a specified expression.
ISNUMERIC	Determines whether an input expression is a valid numeric expression.
NEWID	Creates a new unique value of type *uniqueidentifier*.
NULLIF	If *expression1* is equivalent to *expression2*, the expression is NULL. It's similar to the way a CASE statement works.
OBJECT_ID	Returns the database object ID number.
OBJECT_NAME	Database object name.
PARSE_NAME	Returns the specified part of an object name, which can be the server name, database name, owner name, or object name.
PERMISSIONS	Returns a value that indicates the permissions for the statement, object, or column for the current user.
SESSION_USER	This function returns the username and can be used as a default in a table.
STATS_DATE	Returns the date when the specified index was last updated.
SYSTEM_USER	Returns the value for the current system username.
SUSER_ID	Returns the login user ID number.
SUSER_NAME	Returns the login user's name.
SUSER_SID	Returns the security identification number (SID) for the user's login name.
USER_ID	Returns the user's database ID number.
USER	Returns the user's database ID name.

The most commonly used system functions are DATALENGTH, ISNULL, HOST_NAME, SUSER_NAME, and USER, which are explained in more detail in the following sections.

The DATALENGTH Function

This function returns the actual length of data specified in an expression or column. If the data passed to the DATALENGTH function is NULL, NULL is returned. Keep in mind that when used with a CHAR data type, this function always returns the defined length of the variable or column.

> **TIP**
>
> If you do get a NULL value when one is not desired, you could use the ISNULL function to replace the NULL value with one or more spaces (or some other default value). The ISNULL function is discussed in the next section.

The syntax for the DATALENGTH function is as follows:

```
DATALENGTH(input_data)
```

The *input_data* can be a column, an expression, or data. This function is useful only for CHARACTER, BINARY, TEXT, and IMAGE data types. All other data types are returned as fixed values whether data exists or not. This function counts all values, including spaces.

> **TIP**
>
> Microsoft states that because trailing spaces are stored at the end of the column, this function is useless for fixed-width character columns, but all you have to do is use the RTRIM function before the DATALENGTH function to return the actual length of meaningful data.

This function might be classified as a string function because it's used so often with string functions. Most of the time this function is used to determine the length of a string variable or column.

Using the DATALENGTH Function with String Functions

You saw an example of using string functions to convert a line of text to sentence case earlier in this chapter. However, the length of the data was hard-coded. The next segment of code adds the function DATALENGTH to work with any scenario.

```
SELECT UPPER(SUBSTRING("this Is a tEst.",1,1)) +
    LOWER(SUBSTRING("this Is a tEst.",2,
        (DATALENGTH("this Is a tEst.")-1)))
```

5

EFFECTIVE USE
OF BUILT-IN
FUNCTIONS

Your output should look similar to the following:

```
- - - - - - - - - - - - - -
This is a test.
(1 row(s) affected)
```

One noticeable difference is that the number of characters produced is no longer 20, but the actual string you want. By adding line 3, you now subtract 1 from the actual length of the data because the first letter of the sentence has already been counted.

Using DATALENGTH and COL_LENGTH Functions on a Table

What's the difference between the DATALENGTH and COL_LENGTH functions? The following code answers that question by applying those functions to the table titles.

```
SELECT title,DATALENGTH(title) "Actual",
       COL_LENGTH('titles','title')"Defined"
   FROM titles
       ORDER BY DATALENGTH(title)
```

Your output should look like the following:

```
title                                             Actual Defined
-------------------------------------------------- ------ -------
Net Etiquette                                         13     80
Sushi, Anyone?                                        14     80
Life Without Fear                                     17     80
Is Anger the Enemy?                                   19     80
The Gourmet Microwave                                 21     80
But Is It User Friendly?                              24     80
Secrets of Silicon Valley                             25     80
Straight Talk About Computers                         29     80
You Can Combat Computer Stress!                       31     80
Silicon Valley Gastronomic Treats                     33     80
The Psychology of Computer Cooking                    34     80
Emotional Security: A New Algorithm                   35     80
The Busy Executive's Database Guide                   35     80
Fifty Years in Buckingham Palace Kitchens             41     80
Prolonged Data Deprivation: Four Case Studies         45     80
Cooking with Computers: Surreptitious Balance Sheets  52     80
```

The Actual_Width column used the DATALENGTH function in line 1 to compute the actual length stored in the column. The COL_LENGTH function returns the defined length of the column, which was defined as a maximum length of 40. In addition, you can see from line 4 that you can use ORDER BY with an expression using the DATALENGTH function.

The ISNULL Function

This function allows you to replace NULL values with a specified value. The syntax for the ISNULL function is as follows:

```
ISNULL(expression,replacement_value)
```

The *expression* can be any column, data, or calculated data. The *replacement_value* is substituted whenever a NULL value is selected. This function is useful when changing NULL values in a column to default values. This function can also be used with aggregate functions to count values including NULL values.

The ISNULL function is commonly used when selecting data for a sales report, for example. Imagine that the Standard Cost column in a query could contain NULL values. When a query is run containing this field in the select list, you might want to see 0 in lieu of NULL values.

The HOST_NAME Function

This function returns the name of the workstation on which you are working. The syntax for the HOST_NAME function is as follows:

```
HOST_NAME()
```

No parameters are required. This function is most often used when implementing database security.

> **WARNING**
>
> This function's return value is determined by the front-end application on the connected workstation. If the front-end application supplied SQL Server with this value, then that is what's returned from HOST_NAME. The SQL Query Analyzer is an example of an application that fits this description. However, if a front-end application does not supply the information to SQL Server, HOST_NAME returns blank. In short, it is the front-end application connected to SQL Server that determines whether the HOST_NAME function will return the name of the host application.

The SUSER_NAME Function

This function returns the name of the user logged into the server. The syntax for the SUSER_NAME function is as follows:

```
SUSER_NAME()
```

5

EFFECTIVE USE OF BUILT-IN FUNCTIONS

No parameters are required. This function is most often used when implementing database security. For example, you can refer to this function in a trigger when you want only certain users to be able to increase the price of a title. You can use this function in update and delete triggers when you want to store the name of the user who made the change.

The USER Function

This function returns the name of the user logged into the database. The syntax for the USER function is as follows:

```
USER()
```

No parameters are required. This function is most often used when implementing database security. As opposed to the SUSER_NAME function, this function returns the name of the user logged into the database. Keep in mind that if you alias yourself as DBO, USER returns DBO as the user logged into the database. In contrast, SUSER_NAME returns the name of the user logged into the server. Logged in as SA, USER returns DBO and SUSER_NAME returns SA.

Summary

SQL Server has many powerful functions. This chapter teaches you different methods for manipulating data with math functions, string functions, system functions, text functions, date functions, and the CONVERT function. Although the examples showed some varied and complex uses of functions, they demonstrate only a small portion of what you can really do with these built-in functions, including making your own functions by using stored procedures.

Using Cursors

CHAPTER 6

A *cursor* is a mechanism that allows you to access individual rows of data instead of working with the entire set of rows (as is done with a SELECT, UPDATE, or DELETE statement). By dealing with each row separately, you can gather information piece by piece and perform actions against the data on a row-by-row basis, thus decreasing overhead and potential blocking situations. You can also use the data to generate T-SQL code and immediately execute or print it. Another way you can look at cursors is that they are the closest things you can get to an array using T-SQL code.

Cursor Declaration

You are probably familiar with the basics of cursor usage, including declarations, so this section is short. A cursor's definitions, as well as all the rules that apply to cursor usage, are covered in this chapter.

Defining a Cursor

The DECLARE statement is used not only to define variables used in code, but also to create a cursor's definition. There are actually two supported ways to declare a cursor in SQL Server 7.0. SQL Server supports both the SQL-92 syntax and the T-SQL syntax. The syntax for the SQL-92 cursor appears in the following snippet.

```
DECLARE cursor_name [INSENSITIVE] [SCROLL] CURSOR
FOR select_statement
[FOR {READ ONLY ¦ UPDATE [OF column_name [,...n]]}]
```

The required portions consist of the essential items: DECLARE, the cursor variable, CURSOR, FOR, and the SELECT statement. The *cursor_name* variable is the name that you later use to refer to the cursor and must adhere to the standard naming conventions of SQL Server. The keyword CURSOR states that this variable is of type cursor. The FOR keyword and the SELECT statement define the cursor contents.

- INSENSITIVE - This option causes a copy of the cursor data to be put in tempdb. Because of that, the cursor sees no changes to the data. This option is sometimes known as a *snapshot* or *static* cursor. It does not allow direct updates to the data contained in the cursor.
- SCROLL - This option allows you to move backward and forward through the cursor. Without this option, you can move forward only one row at a time. Although this seems limiting, you do not usually need to do anything but go through and collect or update the data.

- FOR READ ONLY - This option specifies that the cursor is just that—read-only. By default, data contained in the cursors are updateable, and this option overrides that. FOR UPDATE states that the cursor is updateable, which as you now know is the default—so why use it? The optional column list allows you to specify individual columns that can be updated. Without it, all columns are updateable. Another reason to use this option is that scrollable cursors and cursors that use an ORDER BY clause in the SELECT statement are read-only and not sensitive by default; now you need to use the FOR UPDATE option to update underlying data.

The T-SQL version of a cursor allows for quite a few more keywords that allows for some different functionality. Microsoft's official statement is that it is going to move away from the T-SQL standard, but it has enhanced the T-SQL cursor declaration in SQL Server 7.0. The following is the T-SQL cursor syntax:

```
DECLARE cursor_name CURSOR
[LOCAL ¦ GLOBAL]
[FORWARD_ONLY ¦ SCROLL]
[STATIC ¦ KEYSET ¦ DYNAMIC ¦ FAST_FORWARD]
[READ_ONLY ¦ SCROLL_LOCKS ¦ OPTIMISTIC]
[TYPE_WARNING]
FOR select_statement
[FOR UPDATE [OF column_name [,...n]]]
```

The required portions of this type of cursor are the same as the SQL-92 ones. In fact, if you leave out any of the other options listed here, you have a SQL-97 cursor. These differences actually make the T-SQL cursor a more powerful implementation. The following is a list of the different keywords and their use.

- LOCAL The LOCAL keyword is used to define the scope of the cursor. LOCAL means that only the calling batch, stored procedure, or trigger can utilize the cursor. The cursor is implicitly deallocated when the batch, stored procedure, or trigger has completed processing.

- GLOBAL The GLOBAL keyword is also used to define the scope of the cursor. When a cursor is declared as GLOBAL, the cursor has a life of the connection. When the user that created the cursor logs off, the cursor will be implicitly deallocated.

- FORWARD_ONLY FORWARD_ONLY is used to declare a cursor that can only be scrolled from the first row to the last row. With a FORWARD_ONLY cursor, FETCH NEXT is the only way you can get data from the cursor.

- SCROLL As with the a SQL-92 cursor, the SCROLL keyword indicates that you can move in any direction through the data in the cursor.

- STATIC The STATIC keyword is used to indicate that SQL Server should make a copy of the data and place it into tempdb. If data in the base table is modified, the changes will not be reflected in the cursor.

KEYSET A KEYSET cursor is one in which the order of the rows within the cursor is fixed when the cursor is first opened. A set of identifying keys is copied into a table in tempdb called keyset. Any changes made to the nonidentifying keys are displayed when the cursor is scrolled through. Inserts into the table are not shown in the cursor. If a row in the cursor is deleted, when the user attempts to fetch it, SQL Server will return an @@FETCH_STATUS of -2.

- DYNAMIC A DYNAMIC cursor is one in which any changes made to the base data is available during the fetch. The data, number of rows, and order of rows can change from fetch to fetch.

- FAST_FORWARD The FAST_FORWARD option specifies a FORWARD_ONLY, READ_ONLY cursor with certain performance enhancements turned on. If FAST_FORWARD is specified, you cannot also specify SCROLL, FOR_UPDATE, or FORWARD_ONLY.

- READ_ONLY The READ_ONLY option is used to specify a cursor through which no data can be changed. The type of cursor cannot be referenced in a WHERE CURRENT OF statement.

- SCROLL_LOCKS The SCROLL_LOCKS option causes SQL Server to lock each row as it is read into the cursor. This is done to ensure that locks and updates that are made through the cursor will succeed.

- OPTIMISTIC The use of the OPTIMISTIC keyword specifies that SQL Server will not lock each row as it reads it. In this scenario, if row that is being updated or deleted has changed since the cursor has been opened, the modification will fail.

- TYPE_WARNING The TYPE_WARNING option is used to instruct SQL Server to return an error to the client if the specified cursor type is implicitly changed from one type to another.

You see several examples of cursor declarations throughout this chapter, but one simple declaration is shown in Listing 6.1. This cursor lets you manipulate titles and quantities in which the qty is currently greater than 10.

LISTING 6.1 EXAMPLE OF A CURSOR DECLARATION

```
DECLARE crTitleSales CURSOR FOR
    SELECT  title, qty
    FROM    titles t
        JOIN sales s ON t.title_id = s.title_id
    WHERE   qty > 10
```

Rules of Cursor Use

There are two aspects of cursors discussed here: the scope of a cursor and how its declaration affects its final form. The latter topic is discussed first, showing how various types of SELECT statements can have different effects on the actual cursor created. You also see how various types of cursors affect performance and some other rules for use. The scope of a cursor shows how cursors maintain their existence even after a procedure has finished and returned to the client.

Cursor Facts

Here are some facts about cursors:

- Forward-only (non-scrollable) cursors are better for performance if used on large tables.

- Forward-only cursors are dynamic by default, which makes the cursor quicker to open and allows it to update row data.

- You may not declare a cursor on a table that is created within the same batch or stored procedure.

- You can create a cursor on a temporary table that was created in the same batch or stored procedure.

- You can create a cursor on a table that is created in the same batch or stored procedure if you create the cursor dynamically. This type of cursor reflects any changes that have been made to the table since the cursor has been created.

- The keywords COMPUTE, FOR BROWSE, and INTO are not allowed in the SELECT statement of a cursor declaration.

- If UNION, DISTINCT, GROUP BY, or HAVING are used, if an outer join is used, or if a constant expression is included in the SELECT list of the SELECT statement, the cursor will be insensitive.

- Cursors declared as insensitive are always read-only, too.

Listing 6.2 demonstrates what happens if you try to update a cursor declared as insensitive.

LISTING 6.2   ATTEMPT TO DECLARE AN INSENSITIVE, UPDATABLE CURSOR

```
DECLARE crAuthors INSENSITIVE CURSOR FOR
    SELECT * FROM authors
    FOR UPDATE
```

This statement fails and returns the following error:

```
Msg 16929, Level 16, State 1
Cursor is read only
```

The cursor never gets created because of conflicting credentials. You can't update the data if you are no longer browsing the original data. Even though this is a forward-only cursor, it is read-only by default and cannot be made updateable.

There you have it—the rules are straightforward, and all exceptions have been listed. The other aspect of cursors—scope—is discussed next.

Cursor Scope

Cursors exist throughout the life of a connection. A cursor declared earlier during a connection's existence is available until either the connection is closed or the cursor is destroyed. How do you destroy a cursor? Simply deallocate it, as shown in Listing 6.3.

LISTING 6.3 DECLARING AND DEALLOCATING A CURSOR

```
DECLARE crAuthors INSENSITIVE CURSOR FOR
    SELECT * FROM authors

/*Other code that uses the cursor*/

DEALLOCATE crAuthors
```

Unless you deallocate a cursor, it not only remains available for use, but it can even be left open and fetched from as needed while the connection is maintained. For example, you can declare a cursor in one batch. You can open the cursor later. Still later you can fetch data from the cursor and continue to do so periodically. The cursor remains open until you close it and remains available until the cursor is destroyed.

Opening, Closing, and Moving Through Cursors

Now that you are familiar with the concepts of opening and closing a cursor, we will look into how to actually access the data that is contained in the cursor. There are several steps that you need to take to get at and cycle through the data. The statements required to do this will be outlined in the following few sections.

The OPEN and CLOSE Statements

The OPEN and CLOSE statements allow you to open the cursor for use and close it when you're finished. Although you must always explicitly open a cursor, there are a couple of ways to close it without explicitly stating so.

The first is the SET statement option, which causes a cursor to close when a transaction (implicit or explicit) finishes. By using the statement in the following snippet, you can ensure that a cursor closes at the end of a stored procedure or batch.

```
SET CURSOR_CLOSE_ON_COMMIT ON
```

If you want to make sure a cursor is closed each time you make a call to the server, you can turn on this option and sleep soundly.

> **NOTE**
>
> Keep in mind that the cursor is still allocated, even if you explicitly close it with the CLOSE statement or force its closure with SET CURSOR_CLOSE_ON_COMMIT ON. Be sure to deallocate it if you do not plan on using it again, but want to keep the connection open.

Another method is to simply close the current connection. This action not only closes the cursor, but it also deallocates it. If you want to maintain the current connection, this method obviously is not the preferred one.

Recycling a Cursor

You all know that recycling helps save the environment and is a good thing to do. Just because you can keep a cursor open for the lifetime of a connection, however, does not mean you should—particularly if you hold the lock by using optimizer hints or with the Repeatable Read or Serializable transaction isolation level. The end result is that you can tie up data pages and prevent modifications from occurring, thus creating more concurrency issues and dropping performance. In essence, this sort of recycling potentially has only bad effects on the SQL Server environment. Listing 6.4 shows an example of how to declare a cursor that blocks modifications.

LISTING 6.4 DECLARING A CURSOR THAT BLOCKS MODIFICATIONS

```
/*Either use the holdlock optimizer hint...*/
DECLARE crAuthors CURSOR FOR
    SELECT * FROM authors (holdlock)

/*...or set the transaction isolation level*/

SET TRANSACTION ISOLATION LEVEL REPEATABLE READ

DECLARE crAuthors CURSOR FOR
    SELECT * FROM authors (holdlock)
```

If either section in Listing 6.6 is used to declare the cursor, opening without closing the cursor leaves a page and table intent lock on the authors table. The only real advantage might be that you alone can make changes to the data by using the UPDATE statement for the particular row that the cursor is located.

> **WARNING**
>
> This method of holding locks holds a lock on remaining rows of the data page where the cursor is located. If you are going to hold the lock, keep the time frame as short as possible; otherwise, you might start negatively affecting performance by increasing locking concurrency.

In general, a cursor is declared, opened, closed, and deallocated all within the same procedure or batch. You usually do everything that you want to do and have no need to keep the cursor hanging around.

> **WARNING**
>
> If your batch or procedure fails part of the way through or if you execute a RETURN statement before deallocating or closing the cursor, you might accidentally leave the cursor open or allocated.

The FETCH Statement

You can declare, open, close, and deallocate a cursor. The last bit is fetching data. This is where the fun begins. For starters, the name itself begs for some sort of dog joke.

The FETCH statement is the key to using cursors. You're going to take a look at its standard use and then dig a little deeper to find some interesting methods and uses of cursors in general.

Standard Use of FETCH

The FETCH statement has the most complicated syntax of all the cursor statements, as shown in Listing 6.5.

LISTING 6.5   FETCH SYNTAX

```
FETCH
[[NEXT ¦ PRIOR ¦ FIRST ¦ LAST ¦ ABSOLUTE {n ¦ @n} ¦ RELATIVE {n ¦ @n}]
FROM]
name_of_cursor
[INTO @variable1, @variable2, ...]
```

The only required elements are the actual word FETCH and the name of the cursor from which you are fetching data. The power of using cursors does not come from this simple use. Before exploring further, however, examine the rest of the syntax. First, there are several options, listed in Table 6.1, that allow control of what you fetch.

TABLE 6.1   FETCH DIRECTIVES

Directive	*Description*
NEXT	Retrieves the next row in the cursor.
PRIOR	Retrieves the previous row in the cursor.
FIRST	Retrieves the first row in the cursor.
LAST	Retrieves the last row in the cursor.
ABSOLUTE	Using a literal int, smallint, tinyint, or a variable of these data types, retrieves the nth physical row in the cursor. For negative values of n or @n, the cursor counts backward from the last row of the cursor.
RELATIVE	Using a literal int, smallint, tinyint, or a variable of these data types, retrieves the nth relative row from the current row position of the cursor. For negative values of n or @n, the cursor counts backward from the current row of the cursor.

If you do use any of the FETCH directives, you must also use the FROM clause—no exceptions. The last part of the syntax deals with storing retrieved row data into variables. The number of variables must match the number of columns, and each variable must fit in size and match in type the data type of the corresponding column from the selected column list.

Cursor Thresholds

How do you know if you've finished moving through a cursor? SQL Server supplies a global variable—@@FETCH_STATUS—to help you find the answer. If @@FETCH_STATUS contains a value of 0, then everything is all right. If it contains another value, you have a situation on your hands. The next two sections explain this variable in more detail.

Moving Past the End of the Cursor Set

Moving past the beginning or end of the cursor row set results in @@FETCH_STATUS containing a value of -1. You can use a WHILE statement and check the value of @@FETCH_STATUS so that fetching stops when there are no longer any rows to retrieve. Examine the code snippet in Listing 6.6.

LISTING 6.6   CHECKING @@FETCH_STATUS WITH A WHILE STATEMENT

```
FETCH NEXT FROM crColumnTypes INTO @chvName, @chvNameType
WHILE (@@FETCH_STATUS <> -1)
BEGIN
      SELECT @chvPrint = '     @' + @chvName + ' ' + @chvNameType
      PRINT @chvPrint
      FETCH NEXT FROM crColumnTypes INTO @chvName, @chvNameType
END
```

As long as the cursor has not moved past the end of the row set, @@FETCH_STATUS will not contain a value of -1. You keep fetching the rows until that point. Notice how a FETCH is performed before entering the WHILE construct. This method prevents you from entering the loop if there are no rows at all in the cursor. Another FETCH (at the end) is performed within the loop after processing the data, so that the loop isn't executed any further if you have again moved past the end of the cursor.

Dealing with Deleted Rows

What if the row itself has been deleted since opening the cursor? The cursor looks for it and can position itself on it—even if it has been deleted. Again, your friend @@FETCH_STATUS provides a way to take care of the situation. A value of -2 indicates that you have moved onto what once was a row in the underlying data.

> **TIP**
>
> If the cursor is declared INSENSITIVE, there's no need to check for missing rows in the cursor (@@FETCH_STATUS = -2). Because the cursor is actually a copy of the underlying data, rows cannot be deleted from the cursor's row set.

You don't want the WHILE construct to check for a missing row; this causes an exit from the loop as soon as a deleted row is encountered. Rather, you need to check within the looping structure as shown in Listing 6.7, which is an enhancement of Listing 6.6.

LISTING 6.7 CHECKING FOR ROW EXISTENCE IN A CURSOR

```
FETCH NEXT FROM crColumnTypes INTO @chvName, @chvNameType
WHILE (@@FETCH_STATUS <> -1)
BEGIN
    IF (@@FETCH_STATUS <> -2)
    BEGIN
        SELECT @chvPrint = '  @' + @chvName + ' ' + @chvNameType
        PRINT @chvPrint
    END
    FETCH NEXT FROM crColumnTypes INTO @chvName, @chvNameType
END
```

As you can see, the check for the row's existence occurs within the loop. If the row is present, the data is used to print information. If not, the loop carries on and fetches the next row of data. What if the row has been deleted? All the variables contain NULL values, so they aren't of much use to you.

WARNING

If @@FETCH_STATUS returns -2, the variables into which the data was retrieved all contain NULL values. If the selected columns of a present row all support and actually contain NULL values, however, the variables all contain NULL values, too. Existence of NULL values in these variables does not ensure that the row has been deleted. You must use @@FETCH_STATUS to verify whether a row has been deleted.

Some Advanced Cursor Uses

You're going to take a big leap in this section by learning how cursors can be used to help perform many productive tasks. This section wraps up by discussing a stored procedure currently used to help generate a stored procedure that updates a table. There's a lot of code, as well as some fairly complicated cursors and SELECT statements. Take your time while all the details are explained.

Generating Stored Procedure Code from a Stored Procedure

The lines of this code have been numbered for easier reference and ease of explanation.

Look through the code in Listing 6.8 and see if you understand what's being done. The more difficult items involve some complex CASE expressions, including nested ones, within SELECT statements that are part of cursor declarations. In this procedure, you enter the name of the table you are going to update and the key for that table.

LISTING 6.8   GENERATING NEW PROCEDURE CODE FROM A STORED PROCEDURE

```
0001: CREATE PROC prGenerateUpdateProc
0002: @chvTable varchar(30),
0003: @chvKey varchar(30)
0004: AS
0005: SET NOCOUNT ON
0006: DECLARE
0007:    @chvName varchar(30),
0008:    @intType int,
0009:    @chvNameType varchar(255),
0010:    @chvPrint varchar(255),
0011:    @chvName2 varchar(30),
0012:    @chvNameType2 varchar(255),
0013:    @chvMessage varchar(255),
0014:    @intReturnVal int,
0015:    @chvDBName varchar(30)
0016:
0017:  IF NOT EXISTS
0018:    (SELECT  *
0019:     FROM   sysobjects so
0020:     JOIN   syscolumns sc
0021:        ON so.id = sc.id
0022:     WHERE   so.name = @chvTable
0023:     AND    sc.name = @chvKey)
0024:  BEGIN
0025:    SELECT @intReturnVal = 1
0026:    SELECT @chvMessage = 'Either table ''%s'' or column ''%s''' +
➥ ' does not exist in the database ''%s''.'
0027:    SELECT @chvDBName = DB_NAME()
0028:    RAISERROR (@chvMessage, 10, -1, @chvTable, @chvKey, @chvDBName)
0029:    RETURN @intReturnVal
0030:  END
0031:
0032:  DECLARE crColumnTypes SCROLL CURSOR FOR
0033:    SELECT sc.name AS name,
0034:       st2.name +
0035:       CASE
0036:       WHEN st2.type IN (37,45,39,47)
```

```
0037:            THEN '(' + RTRIM(CONVERT(varchar(10),sc.length)) + ') '
0038:          WHEN st2.type IN (55, 63)
0039:            THEN '(' + RTRIM(CONVERT(varchar(10),sc.prec)) + ', '
0040:             + RTRIM(CONVERT(varchar(10),sc.scale)) + ') '
0041:          ELSE ' '
0042:          END +
0043:          CASE sc.status & 8
0044:          WHEN 0 THEN 'NOT NULL'
0045:          WHEN 8 THEN 'NULL'
0046:          END AS type
0047:      FROM  syscolumns sc
0048:          JOIN systypes st ON sc.usertype = st.usertype
0049:          JOIN systypes st2 ON st.type = st2.type
0050:      WHERE id = OBJECT_ID(@chvTable)
0051:      AND   st2.usertype < 100
0052:      AND   st2.name NOT IN ('sysname','timestamp')
0053:      ORDER BY sc.colid
0054:
0055:  DECLARE crColumns SCROLL CURSOR FOR
0056:      SELECT sc.name AS name,
0057:          CASE
0058:          WHEN st2.type IN (37,45) THEN
0059:             CASE
0060:             WHEN sc.status & 8 = 8 THEN 1
0061:             WHEN sc.status & 8 = 0 THEN 8
0062:             END
0063:          WHEN st2.type IN (39,47) THEN
0064:             CASE
0065:             WHEN sc.status & 8 = 8 THEN 2
0066:             WHEN sc.status & 8 = 0 THEN 9
0067:             END
0068:          WHEN st2.type IN (38, 106, 108, 109, 110) THEN 3
0069:          WHEN st2.type = 111 THEN 4
0070:          WHEN st2.type IN (48, 52, 55, 56, 59, 60, 62, 63, 122) THEN 5
0071:          WHEN st2.type = 50 THEN 6
0072:          WHEN st2.type IN (58, 61) THEN 7
0073:          END AS type
0074:      FROM  syscolumns sc
0075:          JOIN systypes st2 ON sc.type=st2.type
0076:      WHERE  id = OBJECT_ID(@chvTable)
0077:      AND    st2.usertype < 100
0078:      AND    st2.name NOT IN ('sysname','timestamp')
0079:      ORDER BY sc.colid
0080:
0081:  SELECT @chvPrint='CREATE PROC prUpdate' + @chvTable
0082:
0083:  PRINT @chvPrint
0084:
0085:  OPEN crColumnTypes
```

continues

LISTING 6.8   CONTINUED

```
0086:
0087:  FETCH NEXT FROM crColumnTypes INTO @chvName, @chvNameType
0088:  IF (@@fetch_status <> -1)
0089:  BEGIN
0090:    WHILE 1 = 1
0091:    BEGIN
0092:      FETCH RELATIVE 0 FROM crColumnTypes INTO @chvName, @chvNameType
0093:      FETCH RELATIVE 1 FROM crColumnTypes INTO @chvName2,
@chvNameType2
0094:      SELECT  @chvName2 = @chvName,
0095:              @chvNameType2 = @chvNameType
0096:      SELECT @chvPrint = '    @' + @chvName2 +
➡ SPACE(34-DATALENGTH(@chvName2)) + @chvNameType2
0097:      IF (@@fetch_status <> -1)
0098:      BEGIN
0099:        SELECT @chvPrint = @chvPrint + ', '
0100:        PRINT @chvPrint
0101:      END
0102:      ELSE
0103:      BEGIN
0104:        PRINT @chvPrint
0105:        BREAK
0106:      END
0107:    END
0108:  END
0109:
0110:  CLOSE crColumnTypes
0111:
0112:  PRINT 'AS'
0113:  PRINT ''
0114:  PRINT 'DECLARE '
0115:
0116:  OPEN crColumnTypes
0117:  FETCH NEXT FROM crColumnTypes INTO @chvName, @chvNameType
0118:
0119:  WHILE (@@fetch_status <> -1)
0120:  BEGIN
0121:    IF (@@fetch_status <> -2)
0122:    BEGIN
0123:      SELECT @chvPrint = '    @' + @chvName + '2' +
0124:          SPACE(33-DATALENGTH(@chvName)) + @chvNameType + ','
0125:      PRINT @chvPrint
0126:    END
0127:    FETCH NEXT FROM crColumnTypes INTO @chvName, @chvNameType
0128:  END
0129:
0130:  CLOSE    crColumnTypes
0131:
0132:  PRINT '    @intReturnVal              int,'
```

```
0133:   PRINT '      @chvMessage                varchar(255),'
0134:   PRINT '      @inyCount                  tinyint'
0135:   PRINT ''
0136:   PRINT 'SELECT @intReturnVal = 0'
0137:   PRINT 'SELECT '
0138:
0139:   OPEN crColumnTypes
0140:
0141:   FETCH NEXT FROM crColumnTypes INTO @chvName, @chvNameType
0142:   IF (@@fetch_status <> -1)
0143:   BEGIN
0144:     WHILE 1 = 1
0145:     BEGIN
0146:       FETCH RELATIVE 0 FROM crColumnTypes INTO @chvName, @chvNameType
0147:       FETCH RELATIVE 1 FROM crColumnTypes INTO @chvName2,
➥@chvNameType2
0148:       SELECT   @chvName2 = @chvName,
0149:               @chvNameType2 = @chvNameType
0150:       SELECT @chvPrint = '     @' + @chvName2 + '2 = ' + @chvName2
0151:       IF (@@fetch_status <> -1)
0152:       BEGIN
0153:         SELECT @chvPrint = @chvPrint + ','
0154:         PRINT @chvPrint
0155:       END
0156:       ELSE
0157:       BEGIN
0158:         PRINT @chvPrint
0159:         BREAK
0160:       END
0161:     END
0162:   END
0163:
0164:   CLOSE crColumnTypes
0165:
0166:   SELECT @chvPrint = 'FROM    ' + @chvTable
0167:   PRINT @chvPrint
0168:   SELECT @chvPrint = 'WHERE    ' + @chvKey + ' = @' + @chvKey
0169:   PRINT @chvPrint
0170:   PRINT ''
0171:   PRINT 'IF @@ROWCOUNT = 0'
0172:   PRINT 'BEGIN'
0173:   PRINT '   SELECT @intReturnVal = -1'
0174:   SELECT @chvPrint= '   SELECT @cvrMessage = ''' + @chvTable + ' with
➥Id of '' + '
0175:   PRINT @chvPrint
0176:   SELECT @chvPrint= '   RTRIM(CONVERT(varchar(10), @' + @chvKey + '))
➥+ '
0177:   PRINT @chvPrint
0178:   PRINT '   '' was not found.'''
0179:   PRINT '   PRINT @cvrMessage'
```

continues

LISTING 6.8   CONTINUED

```
0180:  PRINT '    RETURN @intReturnVal'
0181:  PRINT 'END'
0182:  PRINT ''
0183:  PRINT 'SELECT  @inyCount = 0'
0184:  PRINT ''
0185:  PRINT 'BEGIN TRAN'
0186:
0187:  OPEN crColumns
0188:
0189:  FETCH NEXT FROM crColumns INTO @chvName, @intType
0190:
0191:  WHILE (@@fetch_status <> -1)
0192:  BEGIN
0193:    IF (@@fetch_status <> -2)
0194:    BEGIN
0195:      IF @chvName <> @chvKey
0196:      BEGIN
0197:        IF @intType = 1
0198:          SELECT @chvPrint = 'IF COALESCE(@' + @chvName +
0199:            '2, 0x0) <> COALESCE(@' + @chvName + ', 0x0)'
0200:        ELSE IF @intType = 2
0201:          SELECT @chvPrint = 'IF COALESCE(@' + @chvName +
0202:            '2, '''') <> COALESCE(@' + @chvName + ', '''')'
0203:        ELSE IF @intType = 3
0204:          SELECT @chvPrint = 'IF COALESCE(@' + @chvName +
0205:            '2, 0) <> COALESCE(@' + @chvName + ', 0)'
0206:        ELSE IF @intType = 4
0207:          SELECT @chvPrint = 'IF COALESCE(@' + @chvName +
0208:            '2, ''1/1/1900'') <> COALESCE(@' +
0209:            @chvName + ', ''1/1/1900'')'
0210:        ELSE
0211:          SELECT @chvPrint = 'IF @' + @chvName + '2 <> @' + @chvName
0212:          PRINT @chvPrint
0213:          PRINT 'BEGIN'
0214:          PRINT '    SELECT @inyCount = @inyCount + 1'
0215:          SELECT @chvPrint = '    UPDATE ' + @chvTable +
0216:            ' SET ' + @chvName + ' = @' + @chvName
0217:          PRINT @chvPrint
0218:          SELECT @chvPrint = '    WHERE ' + @chvKey +
0219:            ' = @' + @chvKey
0220:          PRINT @chvPrint
0221:          PRINT 'END'
0222:          PRINT ''
0223:      END
0224:    END
0225:    FETCH NEXT FROM crColumns INTO @chvName, @intType
0226:  END
0227:
0228:  CLOSE crColumns
```

```
0229:   DEALLOCATE crColumns
0230:   DEALLOCATE crColumnTypes
0231:
0232:   PRINT 'IF @inyCount = 0'
0233:   PRINT 'BEGIN'
0234:   PRINT '    ROLLBACK TRAN'
0235:   PRINT '    SELECT @intReturnVal = 1'
0236:   PRINT '    SELECT @chvMessage =  ''No changes were detected. '' + '
0237:   PRINT '                 ''No changes were made.'''
0238:   PRINT '    PRINT @chvMessage'
0239:   PRINT '    RETURN @intReturnVal'
0240:   PRINT 'END'
0241:   PRINT 'ELSE'
0242:   PRINT 'BEGIN'
0243:   PRINT '    COMMIT TRAN'
0244:   PRINT '    RETURN @intReturnVal'
0245:   PRINT 'END'
0246:
0247:   SET NOCOUNT OFF
0248:
0250:   GO
0251:
```

Declaring the Procedure and Some Variables

Lines 1 through 16 are simply the CREATE statement for the stored procedure and some variable declarations used in the code. The procedure takes two arguments: the table name and the key field. Lines 17 through 31 check to make sure that the table and column passed into the procedure do exist and, if not, return an error.

NOTE

The prGenerateUpdateProc stored procedure can only be used on tables that have a single field that acts as the identifying column for the row.

The Cursors

Lines 32 through 52 declare one of two cursors used in this procedure. This cursor is used three times in the procedure. It selects two columns: the name column from the syscolumns table (which holds all the column names for every table), and a second value, which evaluates out to the actual data type (and size or precision and scale, if necessary).

Lines 36 and 37 handle `char` and `binary` data types and add the column length in a pair of parentheses after the data type name. Lines 38 through 40 handle decimal and numeric data types and add the precision and scale values in a set of parentheses. Instead of just getting `varchar` or `numeric` as the data type, you get `varchar(10)` or `numeric(5, 3)` instead. Line 41 adds nothing and is for all other data types (because they don't require any size information). Lines 43 through 46 add the phrase `= NULL` or nothing to the end of the string to reflect the column's nullability.

The join in lines 47 through 49, from `syscolumns` to `systypes` to `systypes`, is required to get the base data type of each column. The `ORDER BY` clause provides the original column order.

Lines 53 through 77 define a second cursor. Again, two columns are selected: the column name and an `int` value, which evaluates out to reflect the category of the data type, including its nullability. The return values from the nested `CASE` expression are shown in Table 6.2.

TABLE 6.2   DATA TYPE CATEGORIES FROM LISTING 6.8

Value	Description
1	Nullable `binary` and `varbinary`
2	Nullable `char` and `varchar`
3	Nullable numerics (`money`, `int`, `real`, `decimal`, and so on)
4	Nullable `datetime` and `smalldatetime`
5	Not nullable numerics (`money`, `int`, `real`, `decimal`, and so on)
6	Bit (not nullable by definition)
7	Not nullable `datetime` and `smalldatetime`
8	Not nullable `binary` and `varbinary`
9	Not nullable `char` and `varchar`

You see these values crop up in a later portion of the code, when the cursor is actually created and data is fetched. Although the values 5 through 9 are distinguished from one another later in the code, this always supplies a base category of data types and can be used for other procedures.

Printing Information

This procedure prints all the information to the results pane of the SQL Query Tool window. The `SET NOCOUNT ON` statement on line 6 prevents the dreaded `"Rows Affected"` message from appearing among the printed information. The variable `@chvPrint` is used to print all pertinent information. You see it used in a SELECT statement, often immediately followed by a PRINT statement. In addition, many lines contain static information being printed (32 lines, to be exact). Look at the results to see how the static lines being printed fit into the scheme.

Using the Cursors

The heart of the procedure is most definitely the use of the two defined cursors. The first cursor, crColumnTypes, is used to generate the parameters for the stored procedure. One little problem, however, is that you do not want a comma on the last item in the list. See the following snippet to better understand (this example was generated from the authors table).

```
CREATE PROC prUpdateauthors
    @au_id              id ,
    @au_lname            varchar(40),
    @au_fname            varchar(20),
    @phone              char(12),
    @address             varchar(40)= NULL,
    @city           varchar(20)= NULL,
    @state            char(2)= NULL,
    @zip            char(5)= NULL,
    @contract            bit
AS
```

Notice how the last item, @contract, does not have a comma at the end. This presents a problem from a code-generation standpoint: how to avoid putting the comma on the last item. A little trick that indicates the last row of the cursor is used, so the comma could not be appended on the last item.

Generating the Parameters

Line 87 performs the initial row data FETCH. The IF statement in line 88 checks to see whether you have gone past the end of the cursor, as does line 97. Then you execute a WHILE statement with an expression that is always true. You use a BREAK statement to get out of the loop.

The two FETCH statements on lines 92 and 93 are the key to finding out if you are on the last row. The first selects the cursor row data from the current row (no row movement) into @chvName and @chvNameType by using the Relative 0 clause. The second fetches the next row of data into @chvName2 and @chvNameType2. These values are immediately replaced in lines 94 and 95 with those in @chvName and @chvNameType.

Why bother doing this? You now have the current row data in @chvName2 and @chvNameType2 and have also moved forward a row. If you were on the last row of the cursor, the first FETCH would get the data and the second FETCH would move you past the end of the cursor. You now store the initial value to print in line 94 and then check to see if you have moved too far. Again, if you were not on the last row before the loop began, the comma would be appended to the variable @chvPrint and printed (lines 99 and 100). If you were on the last row, the second FETCH would put you past the end, and lines 104 and 105 would execute, simply printing the last item with no comma and breaking from the loop.

Generating the Variable Declarations

This first cursor is closed on line 110 and opened for a second run in lines 116 through 130 to generate most of the declared variables (shown in Listing 6.9). Why isn't the second loop through the data concerned with the final comma? You are appending additional DECLARE statements to the end, so the comma has to be on all the generated rows, and the PRINT statement can take care of the final comma not appearing (line 132).

LISTING 6.9   THE DECLARE STATEMENT SECTION RESULTS

```
DECLARE
    @au_id2             id,
    @au_lname2          varchar(40),
    @au_fname2          varchar(20),
    @phone2             char(12),
    @address2           varchar(40),
    @city2              varchar(20),
    @state2             char(2),
    @zip2               char(5),
    @contract2          bit,
    @intReturnVal       int,
    @chvMessage         varchar(255),
    @inyCount           tinyint
```

Creating the SELECT Statement

The cursor is used for a third time in lines 139 through 164. Using the same mechanism as the first instance of this cursor, it creates the column list portion of the SELECT statement that retrieves the current values based on the key field in @chvKey. Once again, the comma is left off the last item printed. Listing 6.10 shows the final results of lines 139 through 164. Lines 166 through 170 add the FROM and WHERE clause portions.

LISTING 6.10   THE SELECT STATEMENT SECTION RESULTS

```
SELECT
    @au_id2 = au_id,
    @au_lname2 = au_lname,
    @au_fname2 = au_fname,
```

```
         @phone2 = phone,
         @address2 = address,
         @city2 = city,
         @state2 = state,
         @zip2 = zip,
         @contract2 = contract
FROM     authors
WHERE    au_id = @au_id
```

Second Cursor, Only Use

After lines 176 through 191 add some error-trapping code in the results, lines 192 through 231 add the bulk of the code in the results. Using the data type category from the second cursor, it generates the appropriate check to see if the existing data has changed. If the field is not nullable, it prints a simple check (the second part of Listing 6.11). If the field is nullable, it creates a check using the COALESCE function and the appropriate default data for the column's data type. Because the notes column is of the varchar data type, it uses a default of an empty string (''). However, because orig_price is of the money data type, it uses a default of 0.

LISTING 6.11 A PORTION OF THE RESULTS FROM THE SECOND CURSOR

```
IF @phone2 <> @phone
BEGIN
    SELECT @inyCount = @inyCount + 1
    UPDATE authors SET phone = @phone
    WHERE au_id = @au_id
END

IF COALESCE(@address2, '') <> COALESCE(@address, '')
BEGIN
    SELECT @inyCount = @inyCount + 1
    UPDATE authors SET address = @address
    WHERE au_id = @au_id
END

IF COALESCE(@address2, '') <> COALESCE(@address, '')
BEGIN
    SELECT @inyCount = @inyCount + 1
    UPDATE authors SET address = @address
    WHERE au_id = @au_id
END
```

Cleaning Up

The remaining lines of code destroy the cursors, print some final code in the results pane, and turn the NOCOUNT setting back to its start value of off.

There you have it. All in all, this procedure should be digestible. There are some complicated constructs in the procedure, but nothing you can't figure out or learn by examining in detail. Use this procedure as an example or even as part of other procedures that you need or want to create. Take a good look at the system stored procedures in the master database. You can find plenty of great code from which you can learn quite a lot.

Using Cursors to Modify Data

Now take a deep breath. You have just absorbed a lot of information. This last section covers the concept of modifying data based on the cursor position. First, you see how to update and delete rows with a cursor. You then examine a procedure that randomly selects a title and reduces its price by 50%—something your standard UPDATE statement cannot do.

A Cursor Cannot UPDATE or DELETE (By Itself)

A cursor does not actually update or delete row data on its own. Rather, it is used with an UPDATE or DELETE statement to get the job done. The WHERE clause of either statement can contain the phrase Where Current Of and the name of the cursor. Look at the following example in Listing 6.12.

LISTING 6.12   DELETING AN AUTHOR WITH A CURSOR

```
DECLARE crAuthors SCROLL CURSOR FOR
    SELECT  *
    FROM    authors
    FOR UPDATE

OPEN crAuthors

FETCH NEXT FROM crAuthors
FETCH NEXT FROM crAuthors
FETCH NEXT FROM crAuthors
FETCH NEXT FROM crAuthors
FETCH NEXT FROM crAuthors
FETCH NEXT FROM crAuthors

BEGIN TRAN —Start transaction

DELETE authors WHERE CURRENT OF crAuthors

ROLLBACK TRAN —Undo the delete so you don't have to re-add the row

CLOSE crAuthors

DEALLOCATE crAuthors
```

After opening the cursor, you fetch six consecutive rows (this particular row won't break any referential integrity rules) and then delete the row by using the DELETE statement and the Where Current Of clause. The cursor provides the position, and the DELETE provides the action.

Advanced Updating Using a Cursor

This last code example alters the titles table and creates a stored procedure to randomly change one title's price to be 50% of its original value. The additional column is used to store the original price, and the procedure resets all entries before choosing a new title to reduce in price. Seems like a simple task, and with this procedure it is. It could not be done, however, with a conventional T-SQL UPDATE statement. Once again, look through the code in Listing 6.13.

LISTING 6.13 RANDOMLY SELECTING A TITLE TO UPDATE

```
 1: ALTER TABLE titles
 2: ADD orig_price money NULL
 3:
 4: GO
 5:
 6: CREATE PROC prHalfPriceTitle
 7: AS
 8:
 9: DECLARE  @intCount int,
10:      @intRow int,
11:      @chvDiscard varchar(6),
12:      @chvPrint varchar(255)
13:
14: BEGIN TRAN
15:
16: SELECT @intCount = COUNT(*) FROM titles (holdlock)
17: WHERE orig_price IS NULL AND price IS NOT NULL
18: SELECT @intRow = CONVERT(int, RAND() * @intCount) + 1
19:
20: DECLARE crTitles SCROLL CURSOR FOR
21: SELECT title_id FROM TITLES
22: WHERE orig_price IS NULL and price IS NOT NULL
23:
24: OPEN crTitles
25:
26: FETCH ABSOLUTE @intRow FROM crTitles INTO @chvDiscard
27:
28: IF @@FETCH_STATUS >=0
29: BEGIN
30:      UPDATE titles SET price = orig_price WHERE orig_price IS NOT NULL
```

continues

LISTING 6.13 CONTINUED

```
31:        UPDATE titles SET orig_price = NULL WHERE orig_price IS NOT NULL
32:        UPDATE titles SET orig_price = price WHERE CURRENT OF crTitles
33:        UPDATE titles SET price = price * .5 WHERE CURRENT OF crTitles
34: END
35: ELSE
36:        PRINT 'No titles to update.'
37:
38: CLOSE crTitles
39: DEALLOCATE crTitles
40:
41: SELECT  title_id,
42:        price,
43:        orig_price,
44:        title
45: FROM    titles
46: WHERE    orig_price IS NOT NULL
47:
48: COMMIT TRAN
49:
50: GO
```

Lines 1 through 5 perform the alter to the `titles` table and add the `orig_price` column for storing the original price of the discounted book. Lines 6 through 13 take care of the procedure creation and variable declarations. Line 14 starts a transaction that's completed on line 48. Why have a transaction at all? You are going to find the current number of titles and use that value to pick one at random. If titles are added or deleted after the count is taken, but before the discount is applied, you might get an error (choosing a book that doesn't exist) or not give a new title a chance for discount.

The key to making a shared table lock stick around while you make your discount changes is in lines 16 and 17, which also return the count. The holdlock optimizer hint directs SQL Server to hold the lock for the duration of the transaction. Everyone will be able to read the `titles` table data, but only you can update it now.

Line 18 generates a random number from 1 to the number of titles. Lines 20 through 22 define the scrollable cursor, which you use to choose the row to be updated. Lines 16, 17, and 22 use a condition in which `orig_price` contains a NULL value and price does not contain a NULL value. This condition prevents books with a NULL price from being updated—50% of NULL is NULL, so there's no need to try changing a NULL price.

Lines 24 through 38 use the cursor to pick the row to be updated. The random value is used with the `FETCH ABSOLUTE` statement to move to the randomly selected row. As long as your @@FETCH_STATUS is not -1 or -2, you perform four updates.

6

The first update resets all prices to their original value. The second sets every row's orig_price value to NULL. The third stores the value in the price column of the current cursor row into the orig_price column. The fourth sets the price of the current cursor row to 50% of its value.

Line 39 destroys the cursor—you have no further need for it. Lines 41 through 46 select the changed row back to the client. Finally, lines 48 through 50 commit the cursors and>transaction and end the procedure.

Summary

You have seen some simple and some very complicated uses of cursors. Cursors can definitely make life easier for tasks that are repetitive or normally impossible with T-SQL. Try to experiment with them because it's the only way to know what really can be done. In addition, get familiar with the system tables. They hold a lot of useful information. Listing 6.8 relies entirely on them.

Stored Procedures

CHAPTER 7

Why Use Procedures?

Stored procedures offer many advanced features not available in the standard SQL language. The ability to pass parameters and perform logic allows the application designer to automate complex tasks. In addition, these procedures being stored at the local server reduces the amount of bandwidth and time required to execute the procedure. Besides the ability to create your own procedures, Microsoft supplies you with several stored procedures that are ideal for manipulating data at the system and administrative levels. The only way you can change data in a system table is by using system stored procedures or by changing a parameter to allow any query to update a systems table, which is never recommended. By providing these stored procedures, SQL Server prevents you from needing to write thousands of lines of code or from accidentally modifying data in a system table.

> **NOTE**
>
> This chapter assumes you are a member of the db_ddladmin role or have similar permissions. You should either sign on as the systems administrator or contact the system administrator for the appropriate user access.

System Stored Procedures

The most commonly used system stored procedures can be grouped into administrative, assistance, configuration, and monitoring categories.

Administrative Stored Procedures

An actual sample of user-based administration can be found in the section "Advanced Uses of Stored Procedures" later in this chapter. The administrative stored procedures for users include sp_addrole, sp_addlogin, sp_grantdbaccess, sp_addrolemember, sp_droprole, sp_droplogin, sp_revokedbaccess, sp_password, and sp_who. Database administrative stored procedures use sp_certify_removable, sp_create_removable, sp_attach_db, and sp_dboption.

Some smaller companies may distribute their databases for use by customers, suppliers, and so forth, using removable media. In planning for this requirement, you should create the database using sp_create_removable. You can then verify that all objects in the database can be removed with sp_certify_removable. After copying the data to a backup device, you can install at any location on the database by using sp_dbinstall. Before you can use the database, you need to use sp_dboption to place the database back online. I have used this for many small applications at branch offices to track sales. A procedure can then be used to export the data on a daily basis and send it to the main office so the data can be merged with the primary database. This keeps all the branch offices' numbers and information confidential.

The syntax of these four procedures is discussed in the following sections.

sp_create_removable

```
sp_create_removable databasename, syslogical, sysstorage, sysdsize,
loglogical, logphysical, logsize, datalogical, dataphysical, datasize
```

The *databasename* is the name of the database to create. The *syslogical* parameter is a logical name associated with where the system tables will be stored at the *sysstorage* location, requiring *sysdsize* megabytes of storage. The *loglogical* parameter is a logical name associated with where the system logs will be stored at the *logphysical* location, requiring *logsize* megabytes of storage. Finally, the *datalogical* parameter is a logical name associated with where the data will be stored at the *dataphysical* location, requiring *datasize* megabytes of storage. You can have up to 16 different logical and physical parameters.

Here's an example of creating a removable database:

```
sp_create_removable sales, salessys, 'c:\sales\data\salessys.dat',3,
  saleslog,'c:\sales\data\saleslog.dat',6,
  salesdata,'c:\sales\data\salesdata.dat',20
```

You can try the preceding sample code only after you have created the c:\sales and c:\sales\data subdirectories on the SQL Server. This is usually a hard concept to grasp without an illustration, so try following these steps and creating the database to see this in action. In this case, you could install this database even over a network with sp_attach_db.

sp_certify_removable

```
sp_certify_removable databasename,[AUTO]
```

The *databasename* is the name of the database to certify. The optional *AUTO* parameter attempts to give all ownership of the objects in the database to the systems administrator. Otherwise, you have to perform this with a variety of SQL scripts. You could now certify the database created earlier by entering

```
sp_certify_removable sales
```

This code takes the database offline. You can now copy the database files and then use the sp_attach_db stored procedure to reconnect the files on another server.

sp_attach_db

```
sp_attach_db dbname, filename1, [filename 2-16]
```

This stored procedure is used to attach database files to a server to re-create a database. To install a database, enter the following code:

```
sp_attach_db 'testpubs', testpubs_file1, testpubs_file2
```

This attaches the database testpubs to the server using the files *testpubs_file1* and *testpubs_file2*.

> **NOTE**
>
> If are attempting to attach a database that has more than 16 files, you must use the CREATE DATABASE statement with the FOR ATTACH clause.

```
sp_dboption
sp_dboption [databasename,option,{TRUE|FALSE}]
```

To get a list of options, type sp_dboption at the SQL prompt. Each of these options can be turned on or off by using the values TRUE or FALSE. To set the database online, enter the following sample code:

```
sp_dboption sales,'offline',FALSE
```

This sets the database offline value to FALSE, which brings the database back online. This is a great way to segregate and back up databases for quick and easy distribution. Ideally, you would write SQL scripts to load these databases at other locations automatically.

Using Stored Procedures for Gathering Information

The following procedures help you when dealing with SQL Server: sp_help, sp_help-constraint, sp_helpdb, sp_helprole, sp_helpprotect, sp_helpserver, sp_helpsort, sp_helptext, and sp_helpuser. These are all features that are built into the SQL Server, putting data at your fingertips that would normally require that you write large queries.

Using Stored Procedures for Configuration and Fine-Tuning

The following stored procedures are the most commonly used for configuring information on SQL Server: sp_addtype, sp_configure, sp_droptype, sp_recompile, and sp_serveroption. While you could configure SQL Server to change system values with your own stored procedures, this is not recommended.

The syntax and use of these stored procedures are discussed in the next few sections.

sp_addtype

This stored procedure allows you to create your own specific data types, including how SQL Server handles NULL values. You could define such fields as Hire Date, Pay Rate, SS#, or other common fields. This is the syntax for sp_addtype:

```
sp_addtype typename, SQLtype[,NULLhandler]
```

The *typename* parameter is the name you use to identify the new data type. The *SQLtype* parameter is a valid SQL Server data type. The optional *NULLhandler* allows you to specify how to handle NULL values—you can either accept them or reject them. However, you can override how NULLs are handled when creating tables. Here's an example of creating your own data type:

```
sp_addtype HireDate,datetime,"NOT NULL"
```

After you create the data type, you can run a query against systypes table to validate the existence of the new data type.

sp_droptype

If you no longer need a user-defined data type, this stored procedure removes it from the database permanently. The syntax for sp_droptype is as follows:

```
sp_droptype typename
```

The user-defined data type cannot be dropped if existing tables reference the data type. Make sure all references have been removed before dropping this data type.

sp_configure

This is the most dangerous system stored procedure available. Using it improperly could cause problems in SQL Server. This is the syntax for sp_configure:

```
sp_configure [configname[,configvalue]]
```

Running this procedure with no parameters gives you the current configuration. If you have altered some of the configuration values, you might need to shut down and restart the server before the update takes effect. You can get configuration information for a certain item by specifying the configuration name, and you can change the configured value by specifying the new value. A common use for this procedure is to increase the number of connections that can be made to the server. The default is 0, which allows unlimited connections. The following example will increase, and limit, it to 300:

```
sp_configure "user connections",300
```

To make this change work, you need to shutdown and restart the SQL Server.

> **NOTE**
>
> Be cautious when changing values. One configuration value of `"allow updates"`, which lets a user change values within all system tables, should ideally never be allowed. That means you could write your own stored procedures and `ad_hoc` queries to directly modify system variables if you set the value to TRUE.

sp_recompile

This stored procedure forces all triggers and stored procedures to recompile the next time the table is accessed. The syntax for this stored procedure is as follows:

```
sp_recompile tablename
```

Stored procedures and triggers are compiled only when they are created. Any changes you make to the table, such as adding indexes, could cause sluggish performance from the trigger or stored procedure because the procedure will not use the index. You should always run this procedure after altering a table to keep your system optimized.

sp_serveroption

This stored procedure allows you to configure the type of SQL Server. Here's the syntax for this stored procedure:

```
sp_serveroption [servername.option,{true¦false}]
```

Using no parameters returns the available server options that can be set for any server. If you want to change a server to a distribution server, you would code the following:

```
sp_serveroption DIST,TRUE
```

sp_procoption

```
sp_procoption, procname, option, value
```

This stored procedure replaced the `sp_makestartup` stored procedure. The `procname` option is the name of the stored procedure that you want to change. The `option` value is the option you're going to turn on or off. Currently, the only valid value for it is `startup`. The `value` option is used to turn the option on (or true) or off (or false). For example, to turn a procedure called `pr_updatestatistics_pubs` into a startup procedure, you would use the following code:

```
sp_procoption pr_updatestatistics_pubs, startup, true
```

Using Stored Procedures to Monitor the System

The more common stored procedures used for monitoring SQL Server are `sp_monitor` and `sp_spaceused`.

sp_monitor

You can use this stored procedure to monitor the performance of your SQL Server. This is the syntax:

```
sp_monitor
```

If you start seeing many dropped packets, you need to look for network congestion and try to solve the problem. If there are many read/write errors, there could be an I/O bottleneck at the server or problems with the storage device. If the CPU usage is more than 80 percent, you might want to add more CPUs. This process should be run every day. If you bring down the server once per week, you might want to make it an auto-executing procedure.

sp_spaceused

Another method for monitoring your system is to review the space used by a table in a database. You can also displace the disk space reserved and used by an entire database. Here's the syntax:

```
sp_spaceused [tablename[,@updateusage={TRUE¦FALSE}]]
```

The `tablename` is the name of the table you want to review. If no parameters are specified, information is displayed on the current database. If an index is removed or added, this stored procedure could produce invalid information. If you suspect the output is wrong, add `@updateusage=TRUE` to correct this problem. This process should be done during off-peak hours because it could take a long time to run.

Extended Stored Procedures

Extended stored procedures allow you to access SQL Server as though the procedure were local by using DLLs (dynamic link libraries). If the DLL causes an error, SQL Server removes the problem thread but doesn't stop running. If you want to create your own external procedures, you can use a language such as C or C++. This topic in itself would require several chapters.

Using Extended Procedures for Messaging

Messaging should be an integral part of your SQL Server. Here are some benefits of using messaging with SQL Server and a mail client:

- If a procedure fails, you can email or page the user responsible for maintaining the server.
- You can attach output from a query to an email message and then forward it to the appropriate parties.
- You can send email if performance hits a critical point.
- Messaging can be integrated with Alerts.

Setting up mail can be a daunting task. I have found that even though MAPI (Messaging Application Programming Interface) is supported, Microsoft Exchange seems to integrate better with the SQL Server than with Windows NT mail or any other mail system. The steps to set up messaging are as follows:

1. Make sure the post office is installed.
2. Make sure the clients attached to the post office are installed.
3. Set up a user named something like SQLSERVER to send and receive mail to and from SQL Server.
4. Run SQL Setup and set up services to make sure the Mail Client automatically starts when SQL Server starts. The login name should be the same name that was set up in step 3.
5. You can now send and receive mail, using sp_processmail to process all incoming mail.

After the mail client is installed and running, you can then use the external procedures xp_deletemail, xp_readmail, xp_sendmail, xp_findnextmessage, and sp_processmail to send and receive mail.

Here are some samples of sending mail:

```
xp_sendmail 'jpeterson', @query = 'sp_monitor'
```

This code sends the output from this stored procedure to the user tatwood. Here's another example:

```
xp_sendmail @recipients = 'mshepker,mrdavis',
@message = 'Server rebooted on 2/21/1999 4:26PM',
@copy_recipients = 'jpeterson',
@subject = 'Server Status'
```

This example uses actual variables to specify how the message is formatted. Using email can automate many mundane tasks, especially if you use a stored procedure to automatically email several users with meaningful output.

7

STORED
PROCEDURES

TIP

Each line can store a maximum of 7,990 characters. If your output exceeds this limit, there's an elegant solution to the problem. Simply create a table with two or more columns that can store each line of text, but make sure the length of each variable is under 7,990 characters and the total of all the columns equals the line length. You can now run a SELECT statement extracting all columns and send this information through email with no problems. If the line length is 12,000 characters, you could create one column of 7,990 characters and another of 4010 characters. Each row is now broken into two columns, but the combined total matches the output of 12,000 characters.

Accessing the Operating System with External Procedures

One nice feature is the ability to access operating system commands on SQL Server by using xp_cmdshell. You should grant this access *only* to system administrators. Granting PUBLIC permissions is a large security loophole. Here's the syntax of this stored procedure:

```
xp_cmdshell "command"[,no_output]
```

The *command* parameter is any operating system command, surrounded by quotes. You can optionally add *no_output* if you don't want to display output. Here's an example of using this stored procedure:

```
xp_cmdshell "dir c:\"
```

This code sends the contents of the server's root directory to the console. A better use is in the next example:

```
DECLARE @myresult int
EXEC @myresult = xp_cmdshell "dir c:\status.txt"
IF (@myresult = 0)
  PRINT "Success"
ELSE
  PRINT "Failure"
```

Instead of looking at output, why not use a procedure to test for the existence of a file? Other uses include running programs on the server or even shutting the server down. Again, be very careful about who has access to this external procedure.

Creating Your Own Stored Procedures

Now that we have looked at a lot of the system stored procedures, it is time to look at creating you own. There are several advantages to writing your own procedures. First of all, you are able to take extremely complex SQL statements and create the stored procedure. Then, to use those SQL statements, all the user has to do is to run the stored procedure. There is also a security advantage to using stored procedures. After the stored procedure has been created, all access to the underlying tables can be revoked to the users. As long as the user has the ability to run the stored procedure, access to the tables is implied.

The syntax used to create a stored procedure is:

```
CREATE PROC[EDURE] procedure_name [;number]
[{@parameter data_type} [VARYING] [= default] [OUTPUT]]
[,...n]
[WITH {RECOMPILE | ENCRYPTION | RECOMPILE, ENCRYPTION}]
[FOR REPLICATION]
AS
sql_statement [...n]
```

As you can see, there are only two required arguments that must be passed into the CRE-ATE PROCEDURE statement: *procedure_name* and the *sql_statements* required to make the stored procedure. The *procedure_name* must conform to the standard SQL Server naming conventions and must be unique within the database. The *sql_statements* are any number of valid SQL statements to be included in the stored procedure. All of the other arguments are optional. The *@parameter* portion of the CREATE PROCEDURE statement is explained in detail in the next section. The [WITH {RECOMPILE | ENCRYPTION | RECOM-PILE, ENCRYPTION}] allows you to choose how the procedure is going to be stored and executed. If you specify the RECOMPILE option, SQL Server will not cache the execution plan of the stored procedure and will recompile it every time the procedure is executed. The ENCRYPTION option allows you to encrypt the text of the stored procedure when it is stored in the syscomments table. In previous versions of SQL Server, these procedures would have to be dropped and recreated if you need to transfer the database or upgrade to a new version of SQL Server. SQL Server 7.0 has the ability to read the encrypted comments and recreate the stored procedure without having to recreate the stored procedure without encryption. The FOR REPLICATION option allows you to create a stored procedure that cannot be executed on a subscribing server and is used when creating filtering stored procedures that are executed only by replication. This option cannot be used with the RECOMPILE option.

Now that you have seen the syntax for creating a stored procedure, it is time to look at the creation of some simple stored procedures. The simplest stored procedure is one that selects from a table and returns it to the user. The following example creates a stored procedure called procTitleAuthorPublisher that involves a complex SQL statement that returns authors, the books that they wrote and the name of the publisher:

```
CREATE PROCEDURE procTitleAuthorPublisher
AS
SELECT au_lname, au_fname, title, pub_name
FROM authors a INNER JOIN titleauthor ta
   ON a.au_id = ta.au_id INNER JOIN titles t
   ON t.title_id = ta.title_id INNER JOIN publishers p
   ON t.pub_id = p.pub_id
GO
```

While creating simple stored procedures with hardcoded where clauses can be very useful, there is much more that you can do using parameters.

All About Parameters in Stored Procedures

You will find that stored procedures are extremely powerful features within SQL Server. So far, we have primarily looked at creating stored procedures that merely select data and return it to the client. With the use of parameters, you can make your stored procedures much more useful as well as powerful.

To add a parameter to your stored procedure, you must declare it. You do this by giving the parameter a name, a data type and determining if you will allow a default value to be used if the user does not supply one. The following example shows the creation of a stored procedure that selects only the author, title, and publisher information for the specified author:

```
CREATE PROCEDURE procTitleAuthorPublisher
@lastname varchar(40),
```

```
@firstname varchar(20)
AS
SELECT au_lname, au_fname, title, pub_name
FROM authors a INNER JOIN titleauthor ta
    ON a.au_id = ta.au_id INNER JOIN titles t
    ON t.title_id = ta.title_id INNER JOIN publishers p
    ON t.pub_id = p.pub_id
WHERE au_fname = @firstname AND
    au_lname = @lastname
GO
```

After you create this stored procedure, you will execute it by running the following statement:

```
procTitleAuthorPublisher 'Locksley', 'Charlene'
```

This will return the titles that were written by Charlene Locksley. One of the problems with this type of stored procedure is that if you to not pass it one of the parameters that it is expecting, you will get an error. One way to get around this is to set up the parameters to use a default value. To do this, put an equal sign followed by the default value after the definition of the parameter, as shown in the following example:

```
CREATE PROCEDURE procTitleAuthorPublisher
@lastname varchar(40) = '%',
@firstname varchar(20) = '%'
AS
SELECT au_lname, au_fname, title, pub_name
FROM authors a INNER JOIN titleauthor ta
    ON a.au_id = ta.au_id INNER JOIN titles t
    ON t.title_id = ta.title_id INNER JOIN publishers p
    ON t.pub_id = p.pub_id
WHERE au_fname LIKE @firstname AND
    au_lname LIKE @lastname
GO
```

When you execute this stored procedure, you do not have to pass any of the parameters in. If you do not pass anything in, you will retrieve a listing of all of the authors, titles, and publishers.

The OUTPUT Parameter

The OUTPUT parameter is a very special type of parameter. It allows you to return data directly into a variable that can be used in other processing. The value that is returned is the current value of that parameter when processing of the stored procedure completes.

In order to save this value, the calling SQL script must also use the OUTPUT keyword when calling the procedure. The following example shows how to create a simple stored procedure that utilizes the OUTPUT keyword:

```
CREATE PROCEDURE procAddValues
    @intVal1   INT,
    @intVal2   INT,
    @intTotal  INT OUTPUT
AS
SET NOCOUNT ON
SELECT @intTotal = @intVal1 + @intVal2
GO
```

To execute this stored procedure, and return the value into a variable, you must call is using the OUTPUT keyword, as seen in the following example:

```
DECLARE @intVal1   INT
DECLARE @intVal2   INT
DECLARE @intTotal  INT
SELECT @intVal1 = 15
SELECT @intVal2 = 9
EXEC procAddValues @intVal1, @intVal2, @intTotal OUTPUT
PRINT 'The total of ' + CONVERT(VARCHAR(5), @intVal1) + ' and ' +
    CONVERT(VARCHAR(5), @intVal2) + ' is ' +
    CONVERT(VARCHAR(5), @intTotal) + '.'
GO
```

Returning Cursors as Parameters

SQL Server 7.0 provides you with the ability to return a cursor containing data to the calling stored procedure, trigger or batch statement through the use of the cursor data type. In order to use the cursor data type, you must also specify the VARYING and OUTPUT parameters. The following example demonstrates how to return a cursor from a stored procedure:

```
CREATE PROCEDURE procAuthorNames
    @curAuthorNames   CURSOR VARYING OUTPUT
AS
SET @curAuthorNames = CURSOR FOR
SELECT au_fname + ' ' + au_lname
FROM authors
OPEN @curAuthorNames
GO
```

To utilize the returned cursor, you must declare a variable of cursor type and pass it in to the stored procedure using the OUTPUT keyword, as seen in the following example:

```
DECLARE @curAuthors       CURSOR
DECLARE @vcharAuthorNames VARCHAR(64)
```

```
EXEC procAuthorNames @curAuthors OUTPUT
FETCH NEXT FROM @curAuthors INTO @vcharAuthorNames
WHILE (@@FETCH_STATUS = 0)
BEGIN
  PRINT @vcharAuthorNames
  FETCH NEXT FROM @curAuthors INTO @vcharAuthorNames
END
CLOSE @curAuthors
DEALLOCATE @curAuthors
GO
```

Modifying Data with Stored Procedures

So far, we have looked at stored procedures that select and display data. Stored procedures can also be used to modify data. The same advantages that you get in stored procedures that select data apply. Any valid insert, update or delete can be made into a stored procedure and can be run by executing a single line of code instead of running many lines of code. In the following example, a stored procedure, called procUpdateRoyalty is created that will update the royalty percentage of all the authors by a specified percentage rate:

```
CREATE PROCEDURE procUpdateRoyalty
    @fltPercentage   FLOAT
AS
UPDATE roysched SET royalty = royalty + royalty * (@fltPercentage / 100)
GO
```

ALTERing a Procedure

In previous versions of SQL Server, when one wanted to change the functionality of a stored procedure, you had to drop it, recreate, reassign permissions and then recompile any other stored procedures that referenced the stored procedure (to keep the dependencies in order). A new feature to SQL Server 7.0 allows you to ALTER a stored procedure without having to perform all of the other tasks. Through the use of the ALTER PROCEDURE statement, you can change a stored procedure without having to do all of this. The arguments for the ALTER PROCEDURE statement is the same as the CREATE PROCEDURE statement, as outlined above. The following is the syntax for the ALTER PROCEDURE statement:

```
ALTER PROC[EDURE] procedure_name [;number]
[{@parameter data_type } [VARYING] [= default] [OUTPUT]]
[,...n]
[WITH {RECOMPILE ¦ ENCRYPTION ¦ RECOMPILE , ENCRYPTION}]
[FOR REPLICATION]
AS
sql_statement [...n]
```

Integrating Messages into Stored Procedures

When developing and utilizing stored procedures, you will frequently need to return data to the user. SQL Server provides two ways to send text messages back to the user: the PRINT statement and the RAISERROR function. SQL Server also provides the ability to exit a stored procedure and return a numerical value to the calling procedure using the RETURN statement.

The PRINT Statement

The PRINT statement is used to return any user defined string of text to the client. You can also return complex strings that are built by combining SQL Server constants, such as @@ROWCOUNT; system functions, such as GETDATE(); and local variables. Along with simply returning information to the front end, you will find that the PRINT statement is extremely useful when troubleshooting stored procedures and checking the values of data. The following code snippet shows the combination of a user defined variable, a SQL Server constant and string data:

```
DECLARE @vcServerName VARCHAR(64)
SELECT @vcServerName = @@SERVERNAME
PRINT 'The computer ' + RTRIM(@vcServerName) + ' is running '
  + RTRIM(@@VERSION)
GO
```

The RAISERROR Function

Like the PRINT statement, the RAISERROR function is used to return informational messages to the user. Unlike the PRINT statement, the RAISERROR function also sets a system flag to record that an error has occurred. Using this function, you can return a message retrieved from the sysmessages table or create a message dynamically using user specified severity and state information. Once the message has either been retrieved or defined, it is sent back to the client as a server error message. There are three required and several optional parameters that can be passed into the RAISEROR function. The syntax of the function is:

```
RAISERROR ({msg_id ¦ msg_str}{, severity, state}[, argument[,...n]] )
[WITH option[,...n]]
```

7

STORED
PROCEDURES

The msg_id is the number of an error that can be retrieved out of the sysmessages table. For user defined errors, you must use numbers over 50,000. Msg_ids under 50,000 are reserved for SQL Server. Alternatively, you can create an ad hoc message an use it in place of the msg_id. The severity option is a number that determines the severity level of the error. Severity levels between 0 and 18 are considered non-fatal errors and can be raised by any user. Severity numbers from 19 to 25 are fatal errors and can only be raised by the systems administrator. When a fatal error occurs, the client application will receive the error and then the connection to the SQL Server will be terminated. The state option is a number from 1 to 127 that represents the information about the state of a process when the error is invoked. This state information is determined by the developer and normally it is only meaningful to the developer. The argument can be used when creating ad hoc messages to fill in placeholders within the message string. The option value is a custom option that can be used this error message. The valid options are:

Value	Description
LOG	The LOG option specifies that the error is to be written to the SQL Server and Windows NT error log. The errors written to the error log are currently limited to 440 bytes in length.
NOWAIT	This option causes the error to be sent to the client immediately.
SETERROR	This option causes the @@ERROR variable to be the msg_id of the error that has just been generated, no matter what the severity level.

The RETURN Statement

The RETURN statement can be used to return a numerical value after exiting a stored procedure. However, if you add a number after the RETURN statement, the number is returned. This number can be any non-zero number except for the reserved range of -1 to -99. If you intend to create your own message errors with RETURN, you should be consistent about the meaning and range of the integer values used. For instance, you could reserve return codes 100–199 for problems with the sales database.

Advanced Uses of Stored Procedures

This section explains advanced DML (Data Manipulation Language), cursors, stored procedures, system stored procedures and using advanced parameters. For example, your firm specializes in developing software for the finance sector. To maintain your competitive edge using technology, you hire consultants. The consultants, who compose over 70 percent of your staff, bring critical knowledge and expertise on current and existing technology. In a recent audit, it was discovered that login IDs still existed for consultants and regular employees who had been terminated by the company. Your job is to devise a method to handle this problem.

The solution, one of the many methods possible, involves concepts discussed throughout this book. You create two tables and several stored procedures to handle the administrative tasks. The two tables, identical copies of one another, store information about each user.

Creating the First Administrative Table

The first table stores information on all current users of the system. Run the code in Listing 7.1 to create the first table.

LISTING 7.1   CREATING THE USER-TRACKING TABLE

```
-- This sets up a table called myusers to store data on employees
CREATE TABLE myusers(
  UserID     varchar(30)NOT NULL PRIMARY KEY,
    FirstName  varchar(30),
  LastName   varchar(30),
  EmployeeType  char(1) NOT NULL, -- C-Contractor, P-Permanent
  DBAccess    varchar(30), -- Default database to access
  StartDate    datetime, -- Employee Start Date
  ExpDate    datetime -- Employee Expiration Date
  )
```

The UserID and DBAccess fields are identical to the syslogins table, which stores the entire set of login IDs for SQL Server. To get the field attributes, I used sp_help syslogins to display this information onscreen. The FirstName and LastName fields are 60 characters combined, which should be adequate for virtually 99 percent of the users. To track the employee type, the EmployeeType field stores a value of "C" for a contract programmer and a value of "P" for a permanent employee. The hire date and expiration date information is stored in this database for the automatic removal process. Your output, if successful, will be as follows:

```
This command did not return data, and it did not return any rows
```

Creating the Archive Administrative Table

Before an employee is removed from the myuser table and the syslogins table, it's a good idea to archive the information to a backup table. This process not only protects you from complaints by an accidentally deleted user, but it also helps track administrative costs and management abuse of the system. Run the code in Listing 7.2 to create the second archive table.

LISTING 7.2   CREATING THE SECOND ARCHIVE TABLE

```
-- This sets up a table called oldusers
-- to store data on terminated employees
CREATE TABLE oldusers(
  UserID     varchar(30),
    FirstName  varchar(30),
  LastName  varchar(30),
  EmployeeType  char(1) NOT NULL, -- C-Contractor, P-Permanent
  DBAccess     varchar(30), -- Default database to access
  StartDate     datetime, -- Employee Start Date
  ExpDate      datetime -- Employee Expiration Date
  )
```

Your output should appear as the following:

```
This command did not return data, and it did not return any rows
```

Now that the tables have been set up, you can start creating the procedures for adding a user, updating the user's expiration date, and deleting the user. One more notable difference—the UserID is no longer a primary key. This UserID field keeps track of how often managers forget to remind administrators to update the expiration date by extracting the count of records in the oldusers table greater than one.

Adding a User Login ID

The challenge in adding a login ID is to first add it to the myusers table and then add some of the same information to the syslogins table. However, as in any good system, input parameters should be checked for validity before any users are added. Because the overall procedure references an additional stored procedure that checks for the existence of the default database assigned to the user, you need to create this stored procedure first. Run the code in Listing 7.3 to create the pr_verifydb stored procedure.

LISTING 7.3   VERIFYING THE EXISTENCE OF THE DEFAULT DATABASE

```
/* This procedure verifies that the database exists before adding
   the new user to any of the tables  */
CREATE PROC pr_verifydb (@dbname varchar(30))
AS
DECLARE @dbid int
SELECT @dbid = dbid from sysdatabases -- Suppresses output
   where name = @dbname
IF @@ROWCOUNT = 0 -- No records match, create our own error codes!
   RETURN 50
RETURN 0 -- Everything is perfect!!!
```

Your output should appear as follows:

```
This command did not return data, and it did not return any rows
```

This stored procedure accepts the parameter @dbname, which holds the value passed by the pr_adduser stored procedure to test for the existence of the default database. The local variable @dbid stores the database ID associated with the default database in the sysdatabases table, if found. Not only does it suppress output to the screen, but it can be used to expand the procedure for other possibilities. The system variable @@ROWCOUNT tracks the number of rows selected. If any matches are found by using the SELECT statement, @@ROWCOUNT should be greater than 0. In fact, there should be only one database name stored, so the value should be either a 0 if the database name is not found or 1 if the database name is found.

Instead of a simple RETURN statement, it was decided to assign return codes to create distinct meanings. A value of 0 is assigned if the database is found. A value of 50 is assigned if the database is not found. Creating your own RETURN codes was discussed in detail in the sections "Using RETURN for More Meaningful Error Messages" and "Advanced Uses of Stored Procedures." You are now ready to create the stored procedure to add the user with the code in Listing 7.4.

7

STORED PROCEDURES

LISTING 7.4 GIVING A USER ACCESS TO SQL SERVER

```
/* This procedure adds users to the mytable database, and then
   adds the user to the login table. */
DROP PROC pr_adduser
GO

CREATE PROC pr_adduser (@UID varchar(30),@FN varchar(30),
   @LN varchar(30),@PW varchar(30),@EmpT char(1),
   @DB varchar(30),@SD datetime, @ED datetime)
AS
DECLARE @returnstat int -- Used to verify existence assigned database
BEGIN
/* The next several blocks of code test the parameters to make sure
the parameters are as close to accurate as possible. Every effort to
  error-check data should be made. */

   SELECT @UID = LTRIM(RTRIM(@UID))
   SELECT @FN = LTRIM(RTRIM(@FN))
   SELECT @LN = LTRIM(RTRIM(@LN))
   SELECT @PW = LTRIM(RTRIM(@PW))
   SELECT @DB = LTRIM(RTRIM(@DB))


--Check UserID for valid first character
   IF DATALENGTH(@UID) < 3 or DATALENGTH(@UID)>=30 or @UID = ""
     BEGIN
        RAISERROR ("User ID Must be from 3 to 30 characters"
          ,16,1)
        RETURN
     END

--Check UserID Length
   IF UPPER(SUBSTRING(@UID,1,1)) < "A" or
    UPPER(SUBSTRING(@UID,1,1)) > "Z"
     BEGIN
        RAISERROR ("User ID Must begin with a letter"
          ,16,1)
        RETURN
     END

-- Check First Name Length
   IF DATALENGTH(@FN) <= 1 or DATALENGTH(@FN) >= 31 or @FN = ""
     BEGIN
        RAISERROR ("The first name must be 2 to 30 characters"
          ,16,1)
        RETURN
     END
-- Check Last Name Length
   IF DATALENGTH(@LN) <= 1 or DATALENGTH(@LN) > =31 or @LN = ""
     BEGIN
```

7

```
        RAISERROR ("The last name must be 2 to 30 characters"
            ,16,1)
        RETURN
    END

-- Check Password Length
    IF DATALENGTH(@PW) < 8 or DATALENGTH(@PW) > 31 or @PW = ""
        BEGIN
        RAISERROR ("The password must be 8 to 30 characters"
            ,16,1)
        RETURN
    END

-- Check for valid Employee Type
    IF UPPER(@EmpT)<>"C" and UPPER(@EmpT)<>"P"
        BEGIN
        RAISERROR ("Employee type must be a 'C' or 'P'",16,1)
        RETURN
    END

-- Check to make sure the end date is not prior to the start date
    IF @SD >= @ED
        BEGIN
        RAISERROR ("The start date must be before ending
                [ie:ccc]date",16,1)
        RETURN
    END

-- Verify existence of assigned database
    EXEC @returnstat = pr_verifydb @DB
    IF @returnstat =50 -- Compare custom-made return value
        BEGIN
        RAISERROR("Assigned Database Does Not Exist!",16,1)
        RETURN
    END

/* Used to make sure no extra spaces are entered. Better to do this
   at one spot than to repeat this for entering the same data in two
   separate tables */


-- Add user to myusers table
    INSERT myusers(UserID,FirstName,LastName,EmployeeType,
        DBAccess,StartDate,ExpDate)
    VALUES (@UID,@FN,@LN,@EMPT,@DB,@SD,@ED)
-- Use system stored procedure to add users to system stored table
    EXECUTE sp_addlogin @UID,@PW,@DB
END
```

Your output should appear as follows:

```
This command did not return data, and it did not return any rows
```

As you can see, a lot of code was used to add eight parameters in some combination to two tables. The input parameters to the stored procedure are @UID to hold the user ID, @FN to store the first name, @LN to store the last name, @PW to store the password, @EmpT to store the employee type, @DB to store the default database name, @SD to store the start date, and @ED to store the expiration date. From examining the code, you will see that all but the @UID, @PW and @DB parameters are used to update the myusers table. These parameters are used to add the login using the *sp_addlogin* system stored procedure.

The extra code checks for potential input errors, reducing possible input error by the administrator. However, before the data is checked for errors, all leading and trailing spaces are removed with RTRIM and LTRIM. The most obvious item to check is the length of the character input parameters. The user ID is tested for a length between 3 to 30 characters by using the DATALENGTH function. The additional test—@UID = " "—tests for NULL or blank values that are not evaluated as integers. You will notice a consistent use of the functions LTRIM and RTRIM, which remove all leading and ending blank spaces to correct for input errors.

The second check on the user ID is to make sure that the first letter is a valid character, which should be an alphabetic character—the type allowed for creating the user ID in the syslogins table. Notice that SUBSTRING extracts the first character and UPPER converts the result to uppercase for comparison. This way, if the sort order does not treat uppercase and lowercase the same, this procedure won't require alteration. The first name and last name are tested for a length between 2 and 30 characters. The additional test—@FN = " "—is used to check for NULL values that aren't evaluated as integers.

The password length is similarly checked for a length between 8 and 30 characters. Next, the employee type is checked for valid values of "C" or "P". The expiration date is checked to make sure it's not before, or equal to, the hire date.

The last check verifies the existence of the default database, which uses the stored procedure pr_verifydb that you created in Listing 7.3. If the value of 0 is returned, there is a match. If 50 is returned, the database does not exist. If any of these parameters are invalid, you don't add the user to either table. This check is done by using the BEGIN and END statements, which encapsulate the entire procedure. If any error is found, the RAIS-ERROR statement displays the error message, and the RETURN statement that directly follows causes you to exit the stored procedure completely.

If all input is valid, the user is added to the `myusers` table with the `INSERT` statement. The system stored procedure `sp_addlogin` is called to add the user to the system database.

> **NOTE**
>
> Although you could have stored the password in the `myusers` table, the password would not be encrypted, so it would be a potential security risk.

To verify these processes, enter the next several users. If you do this all in one batch, make sure you have the keyword `EXEC` in front of each call to the stored procedure:

```
pr_adduser "jsule","john","sule","test1233","C","master",
    "12/10/97","12/10/98"
pr_adduser "matwood","michelle","atwood","test1233","C","master",
    "12/10/96","12/10/98"
pr_adduser "tatwood","tim","atwood","test1233","C","master",
    "12/10/97","12/10/98"
pr_adduser "ghodgson","greg","hodgson","test1233","C","master"
    ,"12/10/96","12/10/99"
pr_adduser "grerick","glen","rerick","test1233","C","master",
    "12/10/96","12/10/99"
pr_adduser "ahudson","ann","hudson","test1233","C","master",
    "12/10/96","12/10/97"
```

Modifying the End Date of the User

Instead of continually writing a script to update a user's expiration date, enter the code in Listing 7.5 to automate this process.

LISTING 7.5 UPDATING A USER'S EXPIRATION DATE

```
/* This procedure updates employee Expiration Date in case the
   employee will continue employment after the original
   Expiration Date */

CREATE PROC pr_updateuser(@UserID varchar(30), @NewExpDate datetime)
AS
UPDATE myusers -- Changes Expiration Date in the myusers table
   SET ExpDate = @NewExpDate
   Where UserID = @UserID
IF @@ROWCOUNT = 1 -- Checks to make sure process completed properly
   PRINT "User Updated"
ELSE
   PRINT "Invalid UserID entered"
```

7

STORED
PROCEDURES

Your output should appear as follows:

```
This command did not return data, and it did not return any rows
```

This stored procedure demonstrates updating data effectively with input parameters. The parameters passed are the user ID and the new expiration date. The procedure searches the data until a match is made and sets the original expiration date to the new expiration date. To improve on possible errors, whether an update occurred or not, the output was always the same. By adding the last IF statement to make sure that one row was displayed (User Updated), you could tell the administrator if they were successful.

Why is this stored procedure necessary? Most contract workers' dates are usually extended because corporate policy often dictates that renewals last three months. To test this process, run the following code:

```
pr_updateuser tatwood,"01/10/99"
```

Your output should be the following:

```
User Updated
```

Removing a User

You can now see two different methods for deleting a user. Run the code in Listing 7.6 for the first method.

LISTING 7.6 FIRST METHOD FOR DELETING A USER

```
CREATE PROC pr_deluser (@TD datetime )
AS
DELETE syslogins WHERE name IN(
   SELECT UserID FROM myusers
     WHERE EmployeeType = "C" and ExpDate <= @TD)
```

When you run the code, this is the output:

```
sg 259, Level 16, State 2
Ad-hoc updates to system catalogs not enabled.
System Administrator must reconfigure system to allow this.
```

Although your first thought might be to use sp_configure to allow for direct updates to system tables, followed by RECONFIGURE to save the changes, this is never a good idea. Any query could update a system table, easily causing database corruption. There has to be a better way. Before you can create the stored procedure to delete a user, you need to create one more stored procedure to copy the user into the archive oldusers database by running the code in Listing 7.7.

LISTING 7.7   ARCHIVING USER DATA

```
/* The purpose of this procedure is to copy a user's information
   into a permanent archive database before wiping the user from
   the system completely */
CREATE PROC pr_copyuser (@UID varchar(30) )
AS
INSERT INTO oldusers -- Database archiving the data
   SELECT *
     FROM myusers
     WHERE UserID = @UID
DELETE myusers -- Remove user from myusers table
   WHERE UserID = @UID
```

Your output should be the following:

```
This command did not return data, and it did not return any rows
```

This procedure accepts the UserId provided by the cursor, selects the data from the myusers table, copies all data into the oldusers table, and then deletes the row from the myusers table. You can now create the proper procedure to delete a user by running the code in Listing 7.8.

LISTING 7.8   PROPER METHOD FOR DELETING A USER

```
/* This procedure deletes a login ID in the system tables and
   deletes the employee from myusers table after the employee
   data has been copied to the oldusers table */
CREATE PROC pr_deluser (@TD datetime )
AS
SET NOCOUNT OFF
-- Cursor used to fetch employees who have expired
DECLARE getuser_curs CURSOR
   FOR
     SELECT UserID
     FROM myusers
     WHERE ExpDate <= @TD
-- Stores UserIDs that matched into temp variable
DECLARE @HoldID varchar(30)
-- Tracks number of users deleted instead of @@ROWCOUNT
DECLARE @MyCount int
-- Assigns initial count value to 0
SELECT @MyCount = 0
OPEN getuser_curs
FETCH NEXT FROM getuser_curs into @HoldID
-- Test myusers database for expired employees
WHILE @@FETCH_STATUS = 0 BEGIN
```

continues

7

STORED
PROCEDURES

LISTING 7.8 CONTINUED

```
    EXEC sp_droplogin @HoldID
    EXEC pr_copyuser @HoldID
-- If match, increments count of users deleted
    SELECT @MyCount = @MyCount + 1
    FETCH NEXT FROM getuser_curs into @HoldID
END
DECLARE @MyDisp varchar(50)
-- Displays text total of number of users deleted
SELECT @MyDisp = "Number of Users Deleted is " + ltrim(str(@MyCount))
PRINT @MyDisp
-- Cleanup of cursor work
CLOSE getuser_curs
DEALLOCATE getuser_curs
```

This process uses cursors within a stored procedure. The only parameter passed is the date you want to test against the expiration date. Two variables are declared: @HoldID stores the match of each user ID, and @MyCount stores the total number of matches. In this case, @@ROWCOUNT does not return a valid value. If a match occurs, a call is made to the system stored procedure sp_droplogin to remove the login from the system tables. The pr_copyuser procedure is called to archive the data and delete the user from the myusers table. A PRINT statement reflects the number of people deleted. For good memory management, all space used by the cursor is deallocated. To try this stored procedure, use the following example:

```
pr_deluser "04/10/99"
```

Your output should be the following:

```
Login dropped.
Login dropped.
Number of Users Deleted is 2
```

However, this process should be automated to run daily, getting the system date from SQL Server. You can use the code in Listing 7.9 to create a stored procedure to further automate this process.

LISTING 7.9 USING THE SYSTEM DATE AS A DEFAULT PARAMETER

```
DECLARE @myvalue varchar(12)
SELECT @myvalue=CONVERT(varchar(12), GETDATE())
EXEC pr_deluser @myvalue
```

If you run the stored procedure with GETDATE() as the parameter, you immediately receive an error message 170. You can't place functions on the same line as an EXEC statement. To work around this problem, you can create a temporary string value that holds the converted date by using the CONVERT function. This string is used as the parameter, which contains the current date.

Suggestions for Improving This Process

With these few procedures, the benefits for the administration of users are great. These procedures met the goals of the business situation. In addition, if managers forget to notify the administrators to change the expiration date and the user is deleted, this is tracked in the oldusers database. You could conceivably charge the department for the added administrative costs! However, there's room for improvement:

- You could add the fields in the myusers table to the Employee table and add a field to store the group, username, department, and manager name. This method wastes less space and allows you to use external stored procedures to email to the managers a list of employees about to be deleted within two weeks.

- Because users can have a group name and username in the system, and you can't remove the login ID if these items exist, you could use the added fields discussed previously to automate the removal from a group and the removal of the username to the database.

- You could add the ability to change a user from "C" (Contract) to "P" (Permanent).

- You could create a stored procedure to verify that a process creates the intended object successfully. You can do this by calling a system stored procedure (after a process runs) to test for the validity of the object created and return a more meaningful message.

- You could create a procedure to test for birthdays, names, and words in the password and disallow them.

- You could create a stored procedure to remove any non-alphabetic characters (except 0–9) from the user ID, first name, and last name.

Summary

This chapter has focused on stored procedures. These offer many advanced features not available using the standard SQL language. The ability to pass parameters and perform logic allows you to create powerful applications. With the use of stored procedures, your ability to program SQL Server is nearly unlimited.

Advanced String Manipulation and Bitwise Operators

Introduction

Along with stored procedures, character string functions offer unlimited possibilities for manipulating alphanumeric data. Chapter 5, "Effective Use of Built-In Functions," has several examples of combining character string functions as well as a function summary. SQL Server 7.0 also allows the use of bitwise operators instead of regular operators to improve the database's performance.

Advanced String Manipulation to Spell Currency

When you write a check or draft, you normally spell out the currency in the amount space. Most databases do not come with a built-in function to do this. However, most databases support the ability to create a series of functions or stored procedures to do that. To create this process using SQL Server 7.0, the values are broken down into components.

Spelling Single Digits

The first main component is spelling single digits, and the next component is spelling the tens column. Listing 8.1 is the stored procedure that creates the single digits.

LISTING 8.1 SPELLING SINGLE DIGITS

```
DROP PROC pr_single
GO
CREATE PROC pr_single @chrDigit CHAR(1), @chrSd VARCHAR(6) OUTPUT
AS
IF @chrDigit = '1'
  BEGIN
     SELECT @chrSd = "One"
   RETURN
   END
ELSE
IF @chrDigit = '2'
  BEGIN
     SELECT @chrSd = "Two"
   RETURN
   END
ELSE
IF @chrDigit = '3'
  BEGIN
     SELECT @chrSd = "Three"
```

```
      RETURN
   END
ELSE
IF @chrDigit = '4'
   BEGIN
      SELECT @chrSd = "Four"
   RETURN
   END
ELSE
IF @chrDigit = '5'
   BEGIN
      SELECT @chrSd = "Five"
   RETURN
   END
ELSE
IF @chrDigit = '6'
   BEGIN
      SELECT @chrSd = "Six"
   RETURN
   END
ELSE
IF @chrDigit = '7'
   BEGIN
      SELECT @chrSd = "Seven"
   RETURN
   END
ELSE
IF @chrDigit = '8'
   BEGIN
      SELECT @chrSd = "Eight"
   RETURN
   END
ELSE
IF @chrDigit = '9'
   BEGIN
      SELECT @chrSd = "Nine"
   RETURN
   END
ELSE
   SELECT @chrSd = ""
```

This stored procedure receives one character, which was converted to a character string before passing, and then returns a converted string number. This stored procedure works for the ones place and the hundreds place of any number. However, the pr_SpellCur (spell currency) stored procedure is limited to numbers of up to 999,000,000,000 dollars, which can easily be altered to an even higher number. This stored procedure simply tests for the values 0 through 9. When a match is made, @chrSd is assigned the appropriate string value, which is returned to the calling stored procedure.

> **TIP**
>
> When using nested IF statements, you should consider adding a RETURN statement when the appropriate match has been made. This avoids SQL Server having to execute all the IF statements.

Spelling the tens Column

The next stored procedure, in Listing 8.2, handles the tens column.

LISTING 8.2 SPELLING THE tens COLUMN

```
DROP PROC pr_twonum
GO
CREATE PROC pr_twonum @chrDigit CHAR(2), @chvDD VARCHAR(10) OUTPUT
AS
IF SUBSTRING(@chrDigit,1,1) = '1'
  BEGIN
   IF @chrDigit = '10'
     BEGIN
       SELECT @chvDD = "Ten"
       RETURN
     END
  ELSE
   IF @chrDigit = '11'
     BEGIN
       SELECT @chvDD = "Eleven"
     RETURN
   END
  ELSE
   IF @chrDigit = '12'
     BEGIN
       SELECT @chvDD = "Twelve"
     RETURN
   END
  ELSE
   IF @chrDigit = '13'
     BEGIN
       SELECT @chvDD = "Thirteen"
     RETURN
   END
  ELSE
   IF @chrDigit = '14'
     BEGIN
       SELECT @chvDD = "Fourteen"
     RETURN
   END
```

```
          ELSE
          IF @chrDigit = '15'
             BEGIN
                SELECT @chvDD = "Fifteen"
             RETURN
           END
          ELSE
          IF @chrDigit = '16'
             BEGIN
                SELECT @chvDD = "Sixteen"
             RETURN
           END
          ELSE
          IF @chrDigit = '17'
             BEGIN
                SELECT @chvDD = "Seventeen"
             RETURN
           END
          ELSE
          IF @chrDigit = '18'
             BEGIN
                SELECT @chvDD = "Eighteen"
             RETURN
           END
          ELSE
          IF @chrDigit = '19'
             BEGIN
                SELECT @chvDD = "Nineteen"
             RETURN
           END
      END

      IF SUBSTRING(@chrDigit,1,1) = '2'
         BEGIN
            SELECT @chvDD = "Twenty"
            RETURN
         END
      ELSE
      IF SUBSTRING(@chrDigit,1,1) = '3'
         BEGIN
            SELECT @chvDD = "Thirty"
         RETURN
         END
      ELSE
      IF SUBSTRING(@chrDigit,1,1) = '4'
         BEGIN
            SELECT @chvDD = "Forty"
            RETURN
         END
```

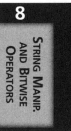

continues

LISTING 8.2   CONTINUED

```
ELSE
IF SUBSTRING(@chrDigit,1,1) = '5'
   BEGIN
     SELECT @chvDD = "Fifty"
     RETURN
   END
ELSE
IF SUBSTRING(@chrDigit,1,1) = '6'
   BEGIN
     SELECT @chvDD = "Sixty"
     RETURN
   END
ELSE
IF SUBSTRING(@chrDigit,1,1) = '7'
   BEGIN
     SELECT @chvDD = "Seventy"
     RETURN
   END
ELSE
IF SUBSTRING(@chrDigit,1,1) = '8'
   BEGIN
     SELECT @chvDD = "Eighty"
     RETURN
   END
ELSE
IF SUBSTRING(@chrDigit,1,1) = '9'
   BEGIN
     SELECT @chvDD = "Ninety"
     RETURN
   END
ELSE
   SELECT @chvDD = ""
```

This stored procedure accepts two values and sends the converted character string to the calling stored procedure. Because the teen values require different handling, you need two characters if the tens place has a value of 1. The first check uses the SUBSTRING function to determine whether the first character is a value of 1. If it is, the teen value is returned. If the value is not 1, the procedure returns the appropriate tens place value.

Putting It All Together

The pr_SpellCur procedure, shown in Listing 8.3, puts the conversion together.

LISTING 8.3   THE SPELL CURRENCY STORED PROCEDURE

```
DROP PROC pr_SpellCur
GO
CREATE PROC pr_SpellCur @mnyMonCon MONEY
    AS
DECLARE @intHoldlen INTEGER
DECLARE @chvDollout VARCHAR(255)
DECLARE @intCountdown INTEGER
DECLARE @@intRemLen INTEGER
DECLARE @intPosition INTEGER
DECLARE @chvHoldCHAR VARCHAR(100)
DECLARE @chvCompare VARCHAR(2)
DECLARE @chrWordChk CHAR(1)
DECLARE @chrCents CHAR(2)
SELECT @intHoldlen =
    CONVERT(INTEGER,DATALENGTH(LTRIM(STR(FLOOR(@mnyMonCon)))))
SELECT @chvHoldChar = LTRIM(STR(FLOOR(@mnyMonCon)))
SELECT @@intRemLen = @chvHoldlen
SELECT @chrCents = LTRIM(STR((@mnyMonCon-floor(@mnyMonCon))* 100))


WHILE @@intRemLen != 0
BEGIN

IF @chvHoldlen = 1 AND @chvHoldChar = '0'
   SELECT @chvDollout = @chvDollout + "Zero"

IF @@intRemLen % 3 = 0
   SELECT @intCountdown = 3
   IF SUBSTRING(@chvHoldCHAR,@chvHoldlen-@intRemLen+1,3) != "000"
     SELECT @chrWordChk = "Y"
   ELSE
     SELECT @chrWordChk = "N"
IF @@intRemLen % 3 = 1
  BEGIN
    SELECT @intCountdown = 1
    SELECT @chrWordChk = "Y"
  END
IF @@intRemLen % 3 = 2
  BEGIN
    SELECT @intCountdown = 2
    SELECT @chrWordChk = "Y"
  END
```

8

STRING MANIP.
AND BITWISE
OPERATORS

continues

LISTING 8.3   CONTINUED

```
WHILE @intCountdown != 0
BEGIN
   DECLARE @chvSpellIt VARCHAR(10)
   SELECT @@intRemLen = @@intRemLen - 1
   SELECT @intPosition = @chvHoldlen - @intRemLen

   IF @intCountdown = 3
     BEGIN
        SELECT @chvCompare =
           SUBSTRING(@chvHoldCHAR,@intPosition,1)
        EXEC pr_single @chvCompare,@chvSpellIt OUTPUT
        IF SUBSTRING(@chvHoldChar,@intPosition,1) != '0'
        SELECT @chvDollout = @chvDollout + @chvSpellIt +
                   " Hundred"
        SELECT @chvDollout = RTRIM(@chvDollout) + " "
     END
   IF @intCountdown = 2
     BEGIN
        SELECT @chvCompare =
           SUBSTRING(@chvHoldChar,@intPosition,2)
        EXEC pr_twonum @chvCompare,@chvSpellIt OUTPUT
        SELECT @chvDollout = @chvDollout + @chvSpellIt
        SELECT @chvDollout = RTRIM(@chvDollout) + " "
     END

   IF @intCountdown = 1 AND ((@intPosition != 1 AND
           SUBSTRING(@chvHoldChar,
     (@intPosition-1),1) != '1') OR @intPosition = 1)
     BEGIN
        SELECT @chvCompare =
           SUBSTRING(@chvHoldChar,@intPosition,1)
        EXEC pr_single @chvCompare,@chvSpellIt OUTPUT
        SELECT @chvDollout = @chvDollout + @chvSpellIt
        SELECT @chvDollout = RTRIM(@chvDollout) + " "
     END
   IF @@intRemLen = 9 AND @chrWordChk = "Y"
     SELECT @chvDollout = @chvDollout + "Billion "

   IF @@intRemLen = 6 AND @chrWordChk = "Y"
     SELECT @chvDollout = @chvDollout + "Million "

   IF @@intRemLen = 3 AND @chrWordChk = "Y"
     SELECT @chvDollout = @chvDollout + "Thousand "

   IF @@intRemLen = 0
     SELECT @chvDollout = @chvDollout + "Dollars "
     SELECT @intCountdown = @intCountdown - 1
   END
END
```

```
SELECT @chvDollout = RTRIM(@chvDollout) + " And " + RTRIM(@chrCents)
            + " Cents"
PRINT @chvDollout
```

The hardest part of this stored procedure is accounting for spaces between the spelling of numbers. If you have a value of 100, you cannot add an automatic space for tens and ones because you have two extra spaces in the spelling of the currency. To account for this, as well as the other placeholders, several variables are declared; those variables are summarized in Table 8.1.

TABLE 8.1 VARIABLES USED IN THE SPELL CURRENCY STORED PROCEDURE

Operator	Description
@mnyMonCon	Input parameter passed when calling the stored procedure. It holds the monetary value you convert to a spelled character string.
@chvHoldlen	Holds the total length of the number being converted, excluding the decimal portion. A number such as 1234.56 would store a value of 4.
@intRemLen	Holds the remaining length to be converted. As the numbers are converted from left to right, this variable retains the remaining length to convert.
@chvDollout	Holds the character string of the converted monetary amount.
@intCountdown	The process breaks the integer portion of the monetary number into groups of three digits, if available. @intCountdown is assigned the value if the length MOD 3 has a remainder other than 0; otherwise, @intCountdown is assigned a value of 3. This value then tracks the location of the hundreds, tens, and ones place when converting numbers into words.
@intPosition	Stores the position for the location in the integer portion of the monetary value. Calculated by taking @chvHoldlen - @intRemLen; used as a parameter with the SUBSTRING function to extract one or more characters.
@chvHoldChar	Stores integer portion of the monetary value to convert.
@chvCompare	Stores one or two characters, which are passed to the stored procedures to calculate hundreds, tens, and ones places.
@chrWordChk	Variable used to let the procedure know when to add the suffix, such as billion, million, and so on.
@chrCents	Stores the decimal part of the monetary value.

After the variables are declared, the procedure assigns values to several of these variables. The @chvHoldlen variable is assigned the total length by taking the FLOOR value, converting it to a character value with the STR function, and then using the LTRIM function to remove leading spaces. It then uses the DATALENGTH function to return the total length and uses the CONVERT function to convert the length of the string to an integer value. All of these functions are discussed in detail in Chapter 5.

As you can see, this code makes use of several functions to manipulate one character string. You need to use FLOOR because STR rounds up if the cents portion is over 50 cents. LTRIM is necessary to remove leading spaces because they aren't valid parts of the monetary value. Finally, the CONVERT function converts the returned value of DATALENGTH, which is not an integer value, into an integer value. The @chvHoldChar variable stores the integer portion of the monetary value using the same process of extraction, with the exception of using CONVERT and DATALENGTH. @@intRemLen is set equal to the value of @chvHoldlen. Both values are needed to locate the position in the conversion process to extract the required characters. The @chrCents variable stores the cents by taking the monetary value minus the FLOOR of the monetary value (which is now an integer) and calculates the cents. This value is multiplied by 100 to change the decimal value to a whole number, and the STR function then converts the integer values to characters. Finally, LTRIM finishes cleaning up the data by removing leading spaces.

At this point, you know that the total length of the integer portion, the character value of the integer value, and the decimal portion are all stored. You're now ready to begin the conversion process. A WHILE loop controls converting the integer portion by checking that the value of @@intRemLen is not equal to zero. That means you haven't yet converted all the numbers into words. Because a monetary value of 0.56 cents will catch the zero portion, the procedure checks for this occurrence and stores the word Zero (for zero dollars) to the output string @chvDollout.

To determine the remainder, the procedure takes the MOD of the remaining length and divides it by three. For modularity purposes, this procedure breaks the monetary value up into groups of threes to hold the hundreds, tens, and ones places. Any remainder other than zero is always the first one or two digits when the number does not have a hundreds or even a tens place. This remainder value is assigned to the @intCountdown variable to extract this block of character(s) and to track the location within this block. One extra check (to see whether the value is 000) with this remainder process occurs if there are characters in all three positions. If so, the @chrWordChk value is assigned a value of N, and the suffix does not print. If this check is not done, a value of 1000000 would yield an error string of "one million thousand dollars".

The second WHILE loop tracks the value of @intCountdown and continues until this value reaches 0. The remaining length is decremented by 1. The @intPosition variable is then calculated by taking the total length minus the remaining length. A local variable, @chvSpellIt, is declared to store the results when calling the stored procedures pr_single or pr_twonum. The result (@chvSpellIt) is concatenated to the @chvDollout variable. Three comparisons are made in this loop to check for a value of 1, 2, or 3 with the @intCountdown variable. If the value is 3, that indicates a value in the hundreds place and calls the stored procedure pr_single. To pass the single-character parameter required, SUBSTRING is used to extract the single character within the @chvHoldChar variable. The output, as long as this value is not 0, is concatenated to the @chvDollout variable including the suffix hundred. The @chvDollout value removes any undesirable trailing spaces by using RTRIM on the @chvDollout variable.

When @intCountdown has a value of 2, two characters are extracted. This is necessary to return the spelling of any teen values. Therefore, if 17 is passed, the procedure returns 17 instead of the word Ten. All values greater than 1 return the corresponding tens value, such as twenty, thirty, and so on. When @intCountdown is 1, the procedure makes sure the tens place did not have a value of 1. If it did, there's no need to call the stored procedure pr_single because the ones place has already been accounted. If the value can be converted, it follows the same procedure as the hundreds and tens place and concatenates the spelled words to the @chvDollout variable.

After the inner WHILE loop has finished, the procedure checks whether a suffix such as billion, million, or the like is required. If the @chrWordChk value is set to Y and the remaining length is 9, 6, or 3, the appropriate suffix of Billion, Million, or Thousand is added. It is at this point that you could add a check for 12 or 15 and add the appropriate suffix for numbers larger than 999,000,000,000 dollars. If the remaining length is zero, the word Dollars is appended to the @chvDollout variable and the outer WHILE loop exits. The decimal part, along with the word Cents, is now appended to the @chvDollout variable and this value is sent to the screen. You could also return this value if you need to store it in a table (or for any other purpose). Although this currency-spelling project could be done many different ways, it does demonstrate that you can combine functions seamlessly. It also demonstrates how you can put the functions to use right away to solve a business problem.

Using the Procedure to Spell Currency

Before you can test this process, run the code in Listing 8.4 to create a table and insert some data.

LISTING 8.4   CREATING TEST DATA FOR THE SPELL CURRENCY PROCEDURE

```
DROP TABLE test_spell
  GO
CREATE TABLE test_spell (
  SPELL money)
  GO

INSERT INTO test_spell (Spell) VALUES (123.22)
INSERT INTO test_spell (Spell) VALUES (1234.22)
INSERT INTO test_spell (Spell) VALUES (12345.22)
INSERT INTO test_spell (Spell) VALUES (123456.22)
INSERT INTO test_spell (Spell) VALUES (1234567.22)
INSERT INTO test_spell (Spell) VALUES (12345678.22)
INSERT INTO test_spell (Spell) VALUES (123456789.22)
INSERT INTO test_spell (Spell) VALUES (1234567890.22)
INSERT INTO test_spell (Spell) VALUES (1000000000.22)
INSERT INTO test_spell (Spell) VALUES (0.22)
```

After you have created the table and data, run the code in Listing 8.5 to see if the process will spell the currency.

LISTING 8.5   TESTING THE SPELL CURRENCY PROCEDURE

```
DECLARE @mnyHoldID MONEY
— Holds the dollar amount for money

— Declare a cursor for the money values
DECLARE cuMoney CURSOR
FOR
SELECT SPELL FROM test_spell

OPEN cuMoney
FETCH NEXT FROM cuMoney into @mnyHoldID
— Retrieves first row
WHILE @@FETCH_STATUS = 0 BEGIN
    EXEC pr_SpellCur @mnyHoldID
— Calls procedure spell currency
    FETCH NEXT FROM cuMoney into @mnyHoldID
END
CLOSE cuMoney
DEALLOCATE cuMoney
```

This batch process uses cursors to fetch one row at a time, and then calls the pr_SpellCur procedure to display the data in words instead of numbers. Your output should look like the following:

```
One Hundred Twenty Three Dollars And 22 Cents
One Thousand Two Hundred Thirty Four Dollars And 22 Cents
```

```
Twelve Thousand Three Hundred Forty Five Dollars And 22 Cents
One Hundred Twenty Three Thousand Four Hundred Fifty Six Dollars
➥And 22 Cents
One Million Two Hundred Thirty Four Thousand Five Hundred Sixty
➥Seven Dollars
And 22 Cents
Twelve Million Three Hundred Forty Five Thousand Six Hundred Seventy
➥Eight
Dollars And 22 Cents
One Hundred Twenty Three Million Four Hundred Fifty Six Thousand
Seven Hundred Eighty Nine Dollars And 22 Cents
One Billion Two Hundred Thirty Four Million Five Hundred Sixty Seven
➥Thousand
Eight Hundred Ninety Dollars And 22 Cents
One Billion Dollars And 22 Cents
Zero Dollars And 22 Cents
```

You can continue to add data to the table to test the procedure or incorporate this process into your current business needs. The final code in Listing 8.6 adds the capability to output the spelled currency and pass it back to the calling process, instead of just displaying the words to the screen.

LISTING 8.6   PASSING SPELLED CURRENCY AS A PARAMETER

```
DROP PROC pr_SpellCur
GO
CREATE PROC pr_SpellCur
@mnyMonCon money,
@chvDollout VARCHAR(255) OUTPUT
    AS
DECLARE @chvHoldlen INTEGER
DECLARE @intCountdown INTEGER
DECLARE @@intRemLen INTEGER
DECLARE @intPosition INTEGER
DECLARE @chvHoldChar VARCHAR(100)
DECLARE @chvCompare VARCHAR(2)
DECLARE @chrWordChk CHAR(1)
DECLARE @chrCents CHAR(2)
SELECT @chvHoldlen =
    CONVERT(integer,DATALENGTH(LTRIM(STR(FLOOR(@mnyMonCon)))))
SELECT @chvHoldCHAR = LTRIM(STR(FLOOR(@mnyMonCon)))
SELECT @@intRemLen = @chvHoldlen
SELECT @chrCents = LTRIM(STR((@mnyMonCon-floor(@mnyMonCon))* 100))


WHILE @@intRemLen != 0
BEGIN
```

continues

8

STRING MANIP.
AND BITWISE
OPERATORS

LISTING 8.6   CONTINUED

```
IF @chvHoldlen = 1 AND @chvHoldChar = '0'
   SELECT @chvDollout = @chvDollout + "Zero"

IF @@intRemLen % 3 = 0
   SELECT @intCountdown = 3
   IF SUBSTRING(@chvHoldChar,@chvHoldlen-@intRemLen+1,3) != "000"
     SELECT @chrWordChk = "Y"
   ELSE
     SELECT @chrWordChk = "N"
IF @@intRemLen % 3 = 1
  BEGIN
     SELECT @intCountdown = 1
     SELECT @chrWordChk = "Y"
  END
IF @@intRemLen % 3 = 2
  BEGIN
     SELECT @intCountdown = 2
     SELECT @chrWordChk = "Y"
  END

WHILE @intCountdown != 0
BEGIN
   DECLARE @chvSpellIt VARCHAR(10)
   SELECT @@intRemLen = @@intRemLen - 1
   SELECT @intPosition = @chvHoldlen - @intRemLen

   IF @intCountdown = 3
     BEGIN
        SELECT @chvCompare =
           SUBSTRING(@chvHoldCHAR,@intPosition,1)
        EXEC pr_single @chvCompare,@chvSpellIt OUTPUT
        IF SUBSTRING(@chvHoldCHAR,@intPosition,1) != '0'
        SELECT @chvDollout = @chvDollout + @chvSpellIt +
           " Hundred"
        SELECT @chvDollout = RTRIM(@chvDollout) + " "
     END
   IF @intCountdown = 2
     BEGIN
        SELECT @chvCompare =
           SUBSTRING(@chvHoldCHAR,@intPosition,2)
        EXEC pr_twonum @chvCompare,@chvSpellIt OUTPUT
        SELECT @chvDollout = @chvDollout + @chvSpellIt
        SELECT @chvDollout = RTRIM(@chvDollout) + " "
     END

   IF @intCountdown = 1 AND ((@intPosition != 1 AND
      SUBSTRING(@chvHoldCHAR,
     (@intPosition-1),1) != '1') OR @intPosition = 1)
     BEGIN
```

```
    SELECT @chvCompare =
        SUBSTRING(@chvHoldCHAR,@intPosition,1)
    EXEC pr_single @chvCompare,@chvSpellIt OUTPUT
    SELECT @chvDollout = @chvDollout + @chvSpellIt
    SELECT @chvDollout = RTRIM(@chvDollout) + " "
  END
IF @@intRemLen = 9 AND @chrWordChk = "Y"
  SELECT @chvDollout = @chvDollout + "Billion "

IF @@intRemLen = 6 AND @chrWordChk = "Y"
  SELECT @chvDollout = @chvDollout + "Million "

IF @@intRemLen = 3 AND @chrWordChk = "Y"
  SELECT @chvDollout = @chvDollout + "Thousand "

IF @@intRemLen = 0
  SELECT @chvDollout = @chvDollout + "Dollars "
  SELECT @intCountdown = @intCountdown - 1
  END
END

SELECT @chvDollout = @chvDollout + "And " + @chrCents + " Cents"
```

The only difference here is the addition of `@chvDollout` as an `OUTPUT` parameter. When calling this procedure, you need to add a second parameter to store the output. The following code provides a demonstration on how to call the stored procedure with parameters:

```
DECLARE @chvSpellIt VARCHAR(255)
EXEC pr_SpellCur 1100111553.66,@chvSpellIt OUTPUT
PRINT @chvSpellIt
```

Binary Operators

Binary, or bitwise, operators are used to perform binary addition and subtraction (the addition of 1s and 0s). Bitwise operations can be performed on `int`, `smallint`, and `tinyint` data. The bitwise NOT (~) operator can also be used with the bit data type.

Binary Operators in SQL Server

The four binary operators are summarized in Table 8.2, which work on integer or binary data types only. Speed is the main advantage of using binary operators because you're now talking in the computer's native language. In addition, you can use bitwise operators to convert binary or compressed data.

> **NOTE**
>
> When using binary operators, it's important to remember the order of operations. In this case, the bitwise operators are below the arithmetic operators such as + and -. If you want to add a value after the binary operation takes place, you need to add the appropriate parenthesis, such as (8 & 1) + 100. Forgetting the order of operations could result in corrupt data or reports.

TABLE 8.2 BINARY OPERATORS

Operator	*Description*
&	Bitwise, logical AND
¦	Bitwise, logical OR
^	Bitwise, logical EXCLUSIVE OR
~	Bitwise NOT

These operators work on a bit-level basis. Each bit is compared against the next. Each return bit result depends upon the bitwise operator.

Bitwise AND

The results of bitwise AND (&) follow:

```
1 & 1 = 1
1 & 0 = 0
0 & 0 = 0
0 & 1 = 0
```

Bitwise OR

The results of bitwise OR ([¦]) follow:

```
1 [¦] 1 = 1
1 [¦] 0 = 1
0 [¦] 0 = 0
0 [¦] 1 = 1
```

Bitwise EXCLUSIVE OR

The results of bitwise EXCLUSIVE OR (^) follow:

```
1 ^ 1 = 0
1 ^ 0 = 1
```

```
0 ^ 0 = 0
0 ^ 1 = 1
```

Bitwise NOT

The results of bitwise NOT (~)returns the opposite bit stream. For example, ~00001111 returns 11110000.

Comparing Values with Bitwise Operators

In any database language, users are allowed to enter data, whether it's from a menu or a data-entry screen. The first example, in Listing 8.7, selects numeric values from a menu and how you can use bitwise operators to evaluate the data.

LISTING 8.7   TESTING NUMERIC VALUES WITH BITWISE OPERATORS

```
DROP PROC pr_bitwise
   GO
CREATE PROC pr_bitwise
   AS
DECLARE @chvHold INTEGER
SELECT @chvHold = 2
IF ( @chvHold & 1) = 1
   BEGIN
    PRINT 'One Selected'
    RETURN
   END
IF ( @chvHold & 2) = 2
   BEGIN
    PRINT 'Two Selected'
    RETURN
   END

IF ( @chvHold & 3) = 3
   BEGIN
    PRINT 'Three Selected'
    RETURN
   END

IF ( @chvHold & 4) = 4
   BEGIN
    PRINT 'Four Selected'
    RETURN
   END
```

Notice that the @chvHold variable has been hard-coded to a value of 2. You could simply change it to a parameter for your own use. The decimal values are converted implicitly to binary values and compared with the & operator. If a match occurs, it prints out the option selected. Run the following code to test this stored procedure:

```
EXEC pr_bitwise
```

Your output should look like the following:

```
Two Selected
```

This same process is tested for alphanumeric choices. Run the code in Listing 8.8.

LISTING 8.8   TESTING ALPHANUMERIC VALUES WITH BITWISE OPERATORS

```
DROP PROC pr_bitalpha
    GO
CREATE PROC pr_bitalpha
    AS
DECLARE @chvHold INTEGER
SELECT @chvHold = ASCII('A')
IF ( @chvHold & 65) = 65
    BEGIN
     PRINT 'A Selected'
     RETURN
    END
IF ( @chvHold & 66) = 66
    BEGIN
     PRINT 'B Selected'
     RETURN
    END

IF ( @chvHold & 67) = 67
    BEGIN
     PRINT 'C Selected'
     RETURN
    END

IF ( @chvHold & 68) = 68
    BEGIN
     PRINT 'D Selected'
     RETURN
    END
```

The only difference here is that the character value needs to be converted to decimal for the binary operation to take place. The CONVERT function converts only characters 0–9, and no implicit conversion takes place in this database package. The only means is to use the ASCII function to return the ASCII value and compare this decimal result to see if a match exists. Run the following code to test this process:

```
EXEC pr_bitalpha
```

Your output should look like the following:

```
A Selected
```

The value A is selected because it was hard-coded, but again, you could easily pass parameters to this stored procedure. This is meant to demonstrate some of the nuances of bitwise operators. Another practical example follows with EBCDIC conversion.

EBCDIC Conversion with Binary Operators

I have worked in several small and large shops and have found ways to manipulate software packages to perform tasks that were never originally intended, partly because of a lack of programming tools. One case involved receiving EBCDIC data, including binary and packed fields from an IBM shop for proprietary EDI, which wasn't converted to ASCII. The source would not translate the file to ASCII, and Visual Basic was not yet implemented. If none of the fields were binary or compressed, you could easily import the binary data with SQL Server's BCP (Bulk Copy Program) and convert the EBCDIC text characters to ASCII characters with a simple translation table. However, most shops store number fields with COMP-3. This means that two numbers are stored in each byte, and the very last byte stores one number and the sign.

Because two numbers are stored in one byte, the first four bits compose one number, and the last four bits compose the second number. As you can see, 2^4 provides 16 possible values of 0 through 15, more than adequate for values of 0 through 9 to be stored in this field. To extract the two numbers, you simply declare a variable of type integer to store the value of the first byte & 11110000, and to store the first byte & 00001111. By using masking, the first number stored contains a replica of the first four bits because 0 AND any number always produces 0. The same goes for the last four bits. To implement this, you need to know the beginning and ending locations. You can store the values in a string, concatenating each value as extracted. Then, when you extract the sign, you can convert this string to an integer value, divide by 100 to add the decimal point, and then multiply by -1 if the number is negative.

Again, this section gives you guidelines if you want to use SQL Server to convert from EBCDIC to ASCII. The ideal method is for the source file to be translated into an ASCII comma-separated value, or to use a tool such as Visual C++ or Visual Basic to complete this task.

Another practical use for the bitwise operators is to evaluate bit data that's stored in tables. For example, assume that a table has 4-bit columns that represent the stages of an order. Each column represents whether the order has been credit-checked, priced, shipped, and closed. You could then write a query requesting all orders that have been credit-checked or priced, but not both. Execute the T-SQL in Listing 8.9 to create a sample table that contains the columns previously listed. This listing also inserts sample data into the table.

LISTING 8.9 CREATING A TABLE THAT STORES BIT DATA

```
DROP TABLE tableX
GO

CREATE TABLE tableX
(
bitPriced BIT,
bitCredit_checked BIT,
bitAllocated BIT,
bitShipped BIT
)
GO

INSERT tableX (bitPriced, bitCredit_checked, bitAllocated,
➥bitShipped)
VALUES (1,1,0,0)
INSERT tableX (bitPriced, bitCredit_checked, bitAllocated,
➥bitShipped)
VALUES (1,0,1,0)
INSERT tableX (bitPriced, bitCredit_checked, bitAllocated,
➥bitShipped)
VALUES (0,0,0,0)
INSERT tableX (bitPriced, bitCredit_checked, bitAllocated,
➥bitShipped)
VALUES (1,1,1,0)
GO
```

You can test this example by selecting all orders that have been priced or allocated, but not both. Listing 8.10 uses the EXCLUSIVE OR bitwise operator to resolve the search condition.

LISTING 8.10   SELECTING DATA USING BITWISE OPERATORS

```
SELECT *
FROM tableX
WHERE bitAllocated ^ bitPriced = 1
```

Using BIT columns not only saves space in the database, but also makes logic much cleaner and quicker because only the bits need to be compared. This final example of selecting orders by their stage of completion is a common business use. For example, you can also use bitwise operators to compare all survey applicants that fit a specific category of yes/no answers. As you can see, there are many uses for bitwise operators in business applications.

Summary

This chapter demonstrates methods of combining string functions, as well as other functions, for creating a procedure to spell currency. Although this procedure could spell values up to 999,000,000,000, the procedure is flexible enough to handle larger numbers. Bitwise operators are discussed and demonstrated for menu options. The CONVERT function does not convert alphabetic characters to integer; therefore, CONVERT could not be used. Because bitwise operators require integer or binary values, the best method is to use the ASCII function to return the character's integer value and use this result with the bitwise operator. Finally, if you're importing binary data and want to convert packed fields, the only method is to use these bitwise operators.

8

STRING MANIP.
AND BITWISE
OPERATORS

Dynamic Execution

CHAPTER 9

Putting all of the radical changes in SQL Server 7.0 aside, one thing hasn't changed: T-SQL is still as powerful as ever. With T-SQL, you can architect highly scalable stored procedures to aid your application development. This chapter focuses on the process of developing dynamic T-SQL statements and implementing them within stored procedures.

If you are unfamiliar with dynamic execution, don't worry. This chapter explains what dynamic execution is and how it can help you. Then you'll see how to create and run a dynamically executable T-SQL string and how cursors can provide even more flexibility. The chapter wraps up by showing why you would and wouldn't want to use dynamic execution by outlining its pros and cons.

What Is Dynamic Execution?

On a recent project on which I was asked to perform some maintenance, I noticed that the original development team created more than 500 stored procedures. Most of these stored procedures weren't doing anything more than retrieving a single resultset. The first thing I thought of was that this team really overcomplicated the project for those who would maintain it (me, in this case). The stored procedures that retrieved a single resultset could all have used a single scalable stored procedure using dynamic execution. (See Chapter 7, "Stored Procedures," for more information on stored procedures.) This might sound out of reach, but *dynamic execution* of T-SQL brings you this capability.

Dynamic execution enables you to use the same T-SQL statement to execute different queries. How do you do this? By using variables and the T-SQL EXEC (EXECUTE) statement, you can create scalable and reusable T-SQL.

> **TIP**
>
> You can use the EXEC keyword instead of using the EXECUTE keyword to achieve the same results. I prefer to use EXEC because it is fewer characters to type.

Valid Syntax of Dynamic Execution

You might have used the EXEC statement only to invoke standard, remote, and extended stored procedures. However, much more power can be unleashed by the EXEC statement. The EXEC statement can run valid T-SQL statements contained within single quotation marks, a string variable, or a concatenation of both. Whether you want to run a SELECT statement or an action query, dynamic execution gives you the flexibility to use the same SQL statement for several queries. Listing 9.1 shows the syntax to execute a SQL string with the EXEC statement.

LISTING 9.1 SYNTAX OF THE DYNAMIC EXECUTION OF T-SQL

```
EXEC ({@chvTSQLString ¦ 'T-SQL String'}
[ + {@chvTSQLString ¦ 'T-SQL String'}...])
```

@chvTSQLString represents the name of a string variable. This variable can be of the VARCHAR or CHAR data types and can contain multiple strings that, when concatenated, represent a valid T-SQL statement.

T-SQL String represents a string containing valid T-SQL statements. The string passed to the EXEC statement must be enclosed with single quotation marks. If more than one string is passed, the strings must be separated by spaces and concatenated with the plus (+) operator.

Further, both types of parameters—strings enclosed within single quotation marks and string variables—can be concatenated together and passed to the EXEC statement. A sample statement can be found below.

```
EXEC 'SELECT * FROM authors'
```

> **NOTE**
>
> The argument(s) used in the EXEC string must contain character data. All numeric data must be converted before using the EXEC statement or in the EXEC statement itself using the CONVERT function. In addition, any functions can be passed within the T-SQL string, on the condition that the arguments used in the EXEC string can be resolved to character data.

So Where Would I Use This?

When used with a stored procedure, execution of dynamic SQL enables the stored procedure to perform a different SQL statement based on the parameters passed to the stored procedure. You could use dynamic execution to select all fields from any table in the pubs database, for example, simply by changing the value of the argument you pass into the stored procedure. In the same manner, you could also change which fields you want to select, which criteria you want to specify, the order in which you want the resultset to be returned, and many other variations of any T-SQL statement.

9

DYNAMIC
EXECUTION

Dynamic execution of T-SQL is a rarely documented feature of SQL Server that is used frequently by database administrators (DBAs) and advanced users. It does provide the flexibility to manipulate T-SQL statements, but it also comes with limitations. If you learn to work within its constraints, however, dynamic execution can prove to be a valuable tool in developing enterprise applications—especially when used to retrieve metadata from system tables.

Creating the Executable String

Whether you are retrieving data from a table or writing data to the database, dynamic execution can help you get more use (or reuse) out of your T-SQL. Because you can use dynamic execution with any T-SQL statement, it is a great tool for writing database maintenance T-SQL. There is no reason why you couldn't change a table's schema using dynamic execution, for example.

The next few sections explain how you can use dynamic execution with data retrieval queries. Then you'll look at creating dynamic action queries and dynamic database altering scripts. Most of the examples use stored procedures to demonstrate the usefulness of dynamic execution.

> **TIP**
>
> Using stored procedures to contain your dynamic T-SQL gives you the capability to accept parameters and encapsulate the T-SQL. This makes your stored procedure appear as a black box to outside calling programs.

Dynamic Selects

A simple query such as retrieving the names of the authors in the Authors table can be written in T-SQL with or without the EXEC statement. To rewrite this SQL statement in an EXEC string, precede it with the EXEC keyword and enclose the T-SQL within quotation marks and parentheses. Listing 9.2 shows both methods.

LISTING 9.2   SIMPLE SELECT QUERY WRITTEN IN TWO WAYS

```
SELECT au_fname, au_lname FROM authors


EXEC ('SELECT au_fname, au_lname FROM authors')
```

Listing 9.2 shows how easy it is to rewrite a T-SQL statement using the EXEC statement. Both these queries return the same set of data. Even though you wouldn't use the latter method for this example, you could modify this same query to include variables for the fields. This requires that you define two variables in the batch to be used in the query and that you set the names of the au_fname and au_lname fields to these two variables, respectively. Listing 9.3 shows how to code and execute this query.

LISTING 9.3   SIMPLE SELECT QUERY WRITTEN USING VARIABLES FOR FIELD NAMES

```
DECLARE @chvField1 VARCHAR(128),
        @chvField2 VARCHAR(128),
        @chvSQL VARCHAR(8000)
SELECT @chvField1 = 'au_fname'
SELECT @chvField2 = 'au_lname'
SELECT @chvSQL = 'SELECT ' + @chvField1 + ', ' +
➥@chvField2 + ' FROM authors'
EXEC (@chvSQL)
GO
```

Notice that the variable @chvSQL was set equal to a concatenation of several literal strings and variables. Dynamic execution does not limit you to using one or the other. This query retrieves the same results as the queries in Listing 9.2. Because of the variables, however, this query offers more flexibility than the other queries offer. By changing the values of the field name variables to "phone" and "address", for example, you can reuse the rest of the code to retrieve different data fields from the same table.

> **NOTE**
>
> The variables declared in Listing 9.3 were defined as VARCHAR(128) because SQL Server limits the length of field names and table names to 128 characters. This convention is used throughout this chapter. You might also notice that Listing 9.3 uses a VARCHAR(8000) variable. This is the longest length T-SQL allows for its variable.

You can use this same idea to retrieve data in different sequences. By putting a variable after the ORDER BY statement, you can specify the field that you want to order the data. The query in Listing 9.4 returns all fields in the Authors table ordered by the authors' last name.

LISTING 9.4   SIMPLE SELECT QUERY THAT USES A VARIABLE FOR THE FIELD TO SEQUENCE THE RESULTSET

```
DECLARE @chvOrderBy VARCHAR(128),
        @chvSQL VARCHAR(8000)
SELECT @chvOrderBy = 'au_lname'
SELECT @chvSQL = 'SELECT * FROM authors ORDER BY ' + @chvOrderBy
EXEC (@chvSQL)
GO
```

Using dynamic execution, you have the option of replacing any part of a T-SQL statement with a variable. In some situations, you might want to retrieve all data from one table on one condition or another table on another condition. As the previous listings show, you can simply replace the dynamic part of the query with a variable. For this scenario, you would replace the table name with a variable. Listing 9.5 shows a variation of this situation where the table name of a query is substituted with a variable.

LISTING 9.5   SELECT QUERY WITH A TABLE NAME PASSED AS A VARIABLE

```
DECLARE @chvTable VARCHAR(128),
        @chvSQL VARCHAR(8000)
IF getdate() > '7/1/1997'
SELECT @chvTable = 'sales'
ELSE
SELECT @chvTable = 'authors'

SELECT @chvSQL = 'SELECT * FROM ' + @chvTable
EXEC (@chvSQL)
GO
```

Using Stored Procedures

After you create your dynamic T-SQL, it may be to your advantage to encapsulate the functionality inside of a stored procedure. To truly reap the benefits of using dynamic execution, you might want to call the dynamic T-SQL from several different batches or programs. You cannot do this if the dynamic execution is contained within a standard batch; this is where stored procedures enter the picture.

Suppose that you want to retrieve sales data ordered by one field in some cases, and ordered by another field in other cases. Suppose further that you need to be able to specify whether the data is sorted in ascending order or in descending order. As shown previously in this chapter, it is a simple task to do this in a batch. Using a stored procedure for this task provides a tremendous amount of flexibility, as shown in Listing 9.6.

LISTING 9.6 STORED PROCEDURE THAT RETURNS SALES DATA ORDERED BY A DYNAMIC FIELD IN DESCENDING OR ASCENDING ORDER

```
CREATE PROCEDURE SalesQtys
    @chvOrderBy VARCHAR(128) = 'qty',
    @chvSortType VARCHAR(4) = 'ASC'
AS
DECLARE @chvSQL VARCHAR(8000)
SELECT @chvSQL = 'SELECT stor_id, ord_num, title_id, qty'
SELECT @chvSQL = @chvSQL + ' FROM Sales'
SELECT @chvSQL = @chvSQL + ' ORDER BY ' +
        @chvOrderBy + ' ' + @chvSortType
EXEC (@chvSQL)
GO
```

The SalesQtys stored procedure accomplishes this task. You can now call this stored procedure, passing to it the field name to sort by and a sort type, which returns the sales data in a dynamic order. Further, stored procedures enable you to specify default values for arguments. You can call this stored procedure without passing it any arguments, thus making it appear like static T-SQL.

> **TIP**
>
> Use default values for stored procedures containing dynamic T-SQL when you can identify the most likely values you will pass to the stored procedure. This way, you will not have to pass any values for the majority of your cases.

You now can call the SalesQtys stored procedure from any batch or stored procedure. To return the resultsets in different orders, just pass the stored procedure the appropriate values for its arguments. Listing 9.7 shows how you can call the SalesQtys stored procedure from Listing 9.6 from different batches.

LISTING 9.7 CALLING THE SalesQtys STORED PROCEDURE FROM THREE DIFFERENT BATCHES, WITH DIFFERENT ARGUMENTS

```
SalesQtys @chvOrderBy = 'stor_id', @chvSortType = 'DESC'
GO
SalesQtys
GO
SalesQtys @chvOrderBy = 'title_id'
GO
```

9

DYNAMIC
EXECUTION

The first batch in Listing 9.7 will return the sales data sorted by the store in descending order. This batch passes both values into the SalesQtys stored procedure, thus overriding the default values for the arguments. The second batch does not pass any arguments to the stored procedure. In this batch, the data will be returned according to the default values of the SalesQtys stored procedure, by ascending quantity order. The last batch uses the title for the sort column and the default sort type, ascending order.

Retrieving Metadata

Listing 9.8 shows the stored procedure prNeedsQuotes, which, using the table name and field name, queries the system tables sysobjects, syscolumns, and systypes to determine the data type of a field. If the data type requires that single quotation marks surround the field's value, prNeedsQuotes returns a value of y in its output argument; otherwise, it returns a value of n. This stored procedure resolves user-defined data types to their base data types as well. Suppose that the field being checked is au_id in the Authors table, for example. It has a data type of the user-defined data type ID. Therefore, prNeedsQuotes determines the base data type of the user-defined type ID to be VARCHAR.

LISTING 9.8   THE prNeedsQuotes STORED PROCEDURE USES SYSTEM TABLES TO DETERMINE THE DATA TYPE OF A FIELD

```
CREATE PROCEDURE prNeedsQuotes
    @chvTable VARCHAR(128),
    @chvField VARCHAR(128),
    @chvNeedsQuotes CHAR(1) OUTPUT
AS
    DECLARE @chvDataType VARCHAR(128),
        @intUserType INT

------------------------------------------------------------------------
--- Determine the data type of the WHERE clause field by looking in
--- the system tables.
------------------------------------------------------------------------
    SELECT @chvDataType = LOWER(st.name), @intUserType = st.usertype
    FROM (sysObjects so INNER JOIN sysColumns sc ON so.id = sc.id)
        INNER JOIN sysTypes st ON sc.usertype = st.usertype
    WHERE so.type = 'U'
        AND so.name = @chvTable
        AND sc.name = @chvField
------------------------------------------------------------------------
--- If the usertype for this data type is > 100, then it is a
--- user defined data type.
--- In this case we must resolve it to its base data type.
------------------------------------------------------------------------
```

```
    IF @intUserType > 100
        BEGIN
            SELECT @chvDataType = LOWER(st2.name)
            FROM sysTypes st1 INNER JOIN sysTypes st2 ON st1.Type =
            ➡st2.Type
            WHERE st2.userType < 100
              AND st2.userType NOT IN (18, 80)
              AND st1.usertype = @intUserType
        END
-------------------------------------------------------------------
--- Based on the data type, determine whether the WHERE clause field value
--- needs to be enclosed within single quotations marks.
-------------------------------------------------------------------
 SELECT @chvNeedsQuotes =
        CASE @chvDataType
            WHEN 'char' THEN 'y'
            WHEN 'datetime' THEN 'y'
            WHEN 'datetimn' THEN 'y'
            WHEN 'smalldatetime' THEN 'y'
            WHEN 'text' THEN 'y'
            WHEN 'timestamp' THEN 'y'
            WHEN 'varchar' THEN 'y'              WHEN 'nvarchar' THEN 'y'
            WHEN 'nchar' THEN 'y'
            ELSE 'n'
        END
GO
```

Dynamic Deletes

Deleting data from tables is a relatively simple and common task. There can be several business rules in an application that warrant deleting rows from a table. You could create separate distinct stored procedures for each DELETE query, or you could use dynamic execution, as shown in Listing 9.9, to create one stored procedure that can handle all these business rules.

LISTING 9.9   CREATING A STORED PROCEDURE THAT WILL REMOVE ALL ROWS FROM WHICHEVER TABLE IS PASSED TO IT

```
CREATE PROCEDURE prDeleteData
    @chvTable VARCHAR(128)
AS
DECLARE @chvSQL VARCHAR(8000)
SELECT @chvSQL = 'DELETE ' + @chvTable
EXEC (@chvSQL)
GO
```

9

DYNAMIC
EXECUTION

The prDeleteData stored procedure accepts the name of a table and creates a valid T-SQL query that will remove all rows from that table. Notice that there is no default value for the table in Listing 9.9. There are two reasons for this: There may not be any one table from which you most often delete, and even if there were, you would be better off to specifically ask for a table to be deleted than to blindly accept a default table.

WARNING

Most developers have been burned once by forgetting to include a WHERE clause in their DELETE statement, thus losing all the data in that table. It needs to happen only once before you vow never again to execute a DELETE without cautious consideration.

The prDeleteData stored procedure is certainly powerful and reusable. Most of the time you want to limit your deletions to a subset of the data in a table, however. The News & Brews store, for example, might have closed and needs to be removed from the database. Another scenario could require you to remove data from the Sales table for sales of less than 10 products. The prDeleteData stored procedure shown in Listing 9.10 can certainly be modified to handle both these cases and still be able to delete all rows, if necessary.

LISTING 9.10 THE prDeleteData STORED PROCEDURE MODIFIED TO REMOVE DATA BASED ON CRITERIA SPECIFIED THROUGH ARGUMENTS

```
CREATE PROCEDURE prDeleteData     @chvTable VARCHAR(128),
                                  @chvWhereField VARCHAR(128) = NULL,
                                  @chvWhereFieldDataType VARCHAR(128) =
'CHAR',
                                  @chvOperator VARCHAR(2) = '=',
                                  @chvValue VARCHAR(128) = NULL
AS
DECLARE @chvSQL VARCHAR(8000), @chvQuotes CHAR(1)
SELECT @chvSQL = 'DELETE ' + @chvTable
-------------------------------------------------------------------------
--If the WHERE clause field is specified, then create the WHERE clause.
--Otherwise, do not specify a WHERE clause.
-------------------------------------------------------------------------
IF NOT @chvWhereField IS NULL
        BEGIN
            SELECT @chvSQL = @chvSQL + ' WHERE ' + @chvWhereField + ' ' +
                  @chvOperator + ' '
            SELECT @chvWhereFieldDataType =
LOWER(RTRIM(@chvWhereFieldDataType))
-------------------------------------------------------------------------
```

```
            -- If the datatype requires quotation marks, then enclose it
within them.
-------------------------------------------------------------------

        SELECT @chvQuotes = CASE @chvWhereFieldDataType
                WHEN 'char' THEN 'y'
                WHEN 'datetime' THEN 'y'
                WHEN 'datetimn' THEN 'y'
                WHEN 'smalldatetime' THEN 'y'
                WHEN 'text' THEN 'y'
                WHEN 'varchar' THEN 'y'
                ELSE 'n'
        END
        IF @chvQuotes = 'y'
                SELECT @chvSQL = @chvSQL + '''' + @chvValue + ''''
        ELSE
                SELECT @chvSQL = @chvSQL + @chvValue
        END
EXEC (@chvSQL)
GO
```

> **NOTE**
>
> Keep in mind that you cannot delete data from a table if it is referenced by data from another table. If you execute the `prDeleteData` stored procedure, you might get an error message that says `DELETE statement conflicted with COLUMN REFERENCE constraint`. That means the data could not be removed because of foreign key violations. This chapter assumes that you design your deletes to avoid this scenario. If you want to remove data from a table and delete all rows from other tables that reference that data, cascading delete triggers will do the trick (see Chapter 11, "Specialized Triggers").

9

DYNAMIC EXECUTION

You have a few options when executing the `prDeleteData` stored procedure shown in Listing 9.10. If you want to delete all data from a table, only specify the table name. If you want to delete only a subset of the data, specify the following: the table name (`@chvTable`), the field name for the criteria (`@chvWhereField`), the value to compare the field to (`@chvValue`), the data type of the field (`@chvWhereFieldDataType`), and the operator to use for the comparison (`@chvOperator`). However, even the operator can be omitted. If you leave the operator out, the procedure assumes that you want to check to see whether the field and value are equivalent. Otherwise, you can pass it whatever operator you need. Let's take a look at three ways we can implement this stored procedure in Listing 9.11.

LISTING 9.11   THREE WAYS TO CALL THE prDeleteData STORED PROCEDURE

```
--Deletes all data from the stores table
prDeleteData     @chvTable = 'stores'
GO

--Deletes all 'News & Brews" stores from the stores table
prDeleteData     @chvTable = 'stores',
      @chvWhereField = 'stor_name',
      @chvWhereFieldDataType = 'CHAR',
      @chvOperator = '=',
      @chvValue = 'News & Brews'
GO

--Deletes all 'News & Brews" stores from the stores table
prDeleteData     @chvTable = 'stores',
      @chvWhereField = 'stor_name',
      @chvValue = 'News & Brews'
GO
```

The first call to prDeleteData in Listing 9.11 deletes all data in the Stores table. The second and third calls to the prDeleteData stored procedure have exactly the same effect. Both calls delete any rows from the Stores table where the store's name is News & Brews. The second batch explicitly specifies all the arguments to prDeleteData. Because some of these arguments have default values, however, it is not necessary to pass values for them. The prDeleteData stored procedure has a default value of "=" for the @chvOperator argument and a default value of "CHAR" for the @chvWhereFieldDataType argument. Thus, the second batch yields the same results as the third batch.

The code in Listing 9.12 shows how you can delete all sales where the quantity is less than 10 units. Notice how the value for the operator is passed in as "<". Table 9.1 lists other possible operator values.

LISTING 9.12   USING THE prDeleteData STORED PROCEDURE TO REMOVE ALL SALES OF LESS THAN 10 TOTAL ITEMS

```
prDeleteData     @chvTable = 'sales',
      @chvWhereField = 'qty',
      @chvWhereFieldDataType = 'NUMERIC',
      @chvOperator = '<',
      @chvValue = '10'
GO
```

TABLE 9.1   VALID VALUES FOR THE @chvOperator ARGUMENT OF THE prDeleteData STORED PROCEDURE

Operator	Description
<	Less than
>	Greater than
=	Equal to
<=	Less than or equal to
>=	Greater than or equal to
!= or <>	Not equal to

If you take a close look at the prDeleteData stored procedure in Listing 9.10, you might notice that it requires you to pass the data type of the WHERE clause field. Otherwise, the stored procedure assumes that the data type is a character field. prDeleteData uses this information to determine whether the WHERE clause value needs to be enclosed in single quotation marks. However, you are probably thinking that this stored procedure should be able to determine what the data type of the field is without you explicitly telling it. Well, it certainly can determine the data type by using the prNeedsQuotes stored procedure from Listing 9.8.

The prNeedsQuotes stored procedure is quite practical. In fact, the final revised prDeleteData, shown in Listing 9.13, uses prNeedsQuotes, as do other stored procedures later in this chapter (such as Listing 9.14 and 9.17).

LISTING 9.13   THE FINAL REVISION OF prDeleteData USES prNeedsQuotes TO DETERMINE WHETHER THE WHERE CLAUSE VALUE NEEDS TO BE ENCLOSED IN QUOTES

```
CREATE PROCEDURE prDeleteData
    @chvTable VARCHAR(128),
    @chvWhereField VARCHAR(128) = NULL,
    @chvOperator VARCHAR(2) = '=',
    @chvWhereValue VARCHAR(128) = NULL
As

DECLARE @chvSQL VARCHAR(8000),
    @chvNeedsQuotes CHAR(1)

SELECT @chvSQL = 'DELETE ' + @chvTable

-------------------------------------------------------------------
--- If the WHERE clause field is specified, then create the WHERE clause.
--- Otherwise, do not specify a WHERE clause.
-------------------------------------------------------------------
```

continues

9

**DYNAMIC
EXECUTION**

LISTING 9.13 CONTINUED

```
IF NOT @chvWhereField IS NULL
    BEGIN
        SELECT @chvSQL = @chvSQL + ' WHERE ' +
@chvWhereField + ' ' + @chvOperator + ' '
```

```
--- The stored procedure prNeedsQuotes determines
--- the data type of the field by looking in the system
--- tables. It returns a value of  'y' or 'n' in the
--- Output argument @chvNeedsQuotes. 'y' means
--- that the field is a data type that requires quotation
--- marks around its value.
```

```
EXEC prNeedsQuotes      @chvTable = @chvTable,
                    @chvField = @chvWhereField,
                    @chvNeedsQuotes = @chvNeedsQuotes OUTPUT
```

```
--- If the data type requires quotation marks, then use them.
```

```
IF @chvNeedsQuotes = 'y'
            SELECT @chvSQL = @chvSQL + '''' + @chvWhereValue + ''''
        ELSE
            SELECT @chvSQL = @chvSQL + @chvWhereValue
    END
EXEC (@chvSQL)
GO
```

Dynamic Updates

What is probably more practical than using dynamic execution to perform deletes is using dynamic execution to perform updates. Listing 9.14 shows the stored procedure prUpdateData, which updates an unspecified field with an unspecified value in an unspecified table where another unspecified field is compared against a value. That sure was a mouthful and certainly confusing, so let's dissect this stored procedure.

The power in prUpdateData is the flexibility it has in allowing dynamic updates, and what gives it that power are the stored procedure's arguments. So how do you use this stored procedure? First, determine which table's data you want to update and pass that table's name to the @chvTable argument. Then pass the name of the field you want to update and the value for this field to the @chvSetField and @chvSetValue arguments, respectively. Finally, if you want to update all rows in the table, you are done. However, if you want to limit your update to a subset of rows, you need to specify your criteria. To do this, pass the name of the criteria's field, the operator for the comparison, and the value to be compared to the arguments @chvWhereField, @chvOperator, and @chvWhereValue, respectively.

LISTING 9.14 THE prUpdateData STORED PROCEDURE USING prNeedsQuotes TO DETERMINE WHETHER THE WHERE CLAUSE VALUE NEEDS TO BE ENCLOSED IN QUOTATION MARKS

```
CREATE PROCEDURE prUpdateData
    @chvTable VARCHAR(128),
    @chvSetField VARCHAR(128),
    @chvSetValue VARCHAR(128),
    @chvWhereField VARCHAR(128) = NULL,
    @chvOperator VARCHAR(2) = '=',
    @chvWhereValue VARCHAR(128) = NULL
AS

DECLARE @chvSQL VARCHAR(8000),
    @chvSetFieldQuotes CHAR(1),
    @chvWhereFieldQuotes CHAR(1)

SELECT @chvSQL = 'UPDATE ' + @chvTable + ' SET '

SELECT @chvSQL = @chvSQL + @chvSetField + ' = '
-----------------------------------------------------------------
--- The stored procedure prNeedsQuotes determines
--- the data type of the field by looking in the system
--- tables. It returns a value of 'y' or 'n' in the Output
--- argument @chvNeedsQuotes. 'y' means that
--- the field is a data type that requires quotation
--- marks around its value.
-----------------------------------------------------------------
EXEC prNeedsQuotes
    @chvTable = @chvTable,
            @chvField = @chvSetField,
            @chvNeedsQuotes = @chvSetFieldQuotes OUTPUT
-----------------------------------------------------------------
--- If the data type requires quotation marks, then
--- enclose it within them.
-----------------------------------------------------------------
 IF @chvSetFieldQuotes = 'y'
    SELECT @chvSQL = @chvSQL + '''' + @chvSetValue + ''''
 ELSE
    SELECT @chvSQL = @chvSQL + @chvSetValue


-----------------------------------------------------------------
--- If the WHERE clause field is specified, then
--- create the WHERE clause. Otherwise, do not
--- specify a WHERE clause.
-----------------------------------------------------------------
 IF NOT @chvWhereField IS NULL
    BEGIN
        SELECT @chvSQL = @chvSQL + ' WHERE ' +
@chvWhereField + ' ' + @chvOperator + ' '
```

9

DYNAMIC
EXECUTION

continues

LISTING 9.14   CONTINUED

```
-------------------------------------------------------------------
--- The stored procedure prNeedsQuotes determines
--- the data type of the field by looking in the system
--- tables. It returns a value of 'y' or 'n' in the Output
--- argument @chvNeedsQuotes. 'y' means
--- that the field is a data type that requires quotation
--- marks around its value.
-------------------------------------------------------------------
EXEC prNeedsQuotes
    @chvTable = @chvTable,
    @chvField = @chvWhereField,
    @chvNeedsQuotes = @chvWhereFieldQuotes OUTPUT
-------------------------------------------------------------------
--- If the data type requires quotation marks,
--- then use them.
-------------------------------------------------------------------
 IF @chvWhereFieldQuotes = 'y'
            SELECT @chvSQL = @chvSQL + '''' + @chvWhereValue + ''''
        ELSE
            SELECT @chvSQL = @chvSQL + @chvWhereValue
    END
 EXEC (@chvSQL)
 GO
```

Just as `prDeleteData` uses the `prNeedsQuotes` stored procedure to determine whether field values need to be enclosed within quotation marks, so does `prUpdateData`. However, `prUpdateData` calls the `prNeedsQuotes` stored procedure twice: once for the `@chvSetField` argument and once for the `@chvWhereField` argument.

Using Cursors with Dynamic Execution

These stored procedures that use dynamic execution use it to an extreme and are probably not the answer to all your problems. They are practical templates that you can use to model your dynamic execution stored procedures, however. Your situations might call for a simpler version of one of these stored procedures, but then again, you might require a more complex use of dynamic execution.

Have you ever wanted to drop all foreign keys so you could perform structural changes on a table without having to drop all the tables that reference it? Or maybe you need to drop all the triggers in the database because they are no longer used. Normally you would have to type the T-SQL to drop all these objects individually. Using cursors with dynamic execution makes these tasks relatively simple, however.

Let's examine the problem of dropping all triggers in the database. You may have dozens of triggers in your database, so I won't even suggest that you type the T-SQL to drop them all individually. So the task at hand becomes how to acquire a list of all the triggers. The names of all the objects in the database and what type of object they are, including triggers, are stored in the system table sysobjects. This is the logical place to start, so you'll query this table for the list of trigger names. The T-SQL in Listing 9.15 retrieves all triggers in the current database.

LISTING 9.15 RETRIEVING ALL THE TRIGGERS IN THE DATABASE FROM THE sysobjects TABLE

```
SELECT name FROM sysobjects WHERE type = 'TR'
```

NOTE

The sysobjects table contains a row for every object in the database. To get a list of these objects by type, you can use the same query as shown in Listing 9.15, substituting the value of 'TR' with one of the values shown in Table 9.2.

TABLE 9.2 VALID VALUES FOR THE TYPE FIELD IN THE sysobjects TABLE

Type	Description
C	Check constraint
D	Default
F	Foreign key
K	Primary key
P	Stored procedure
R	Rule
RF	Stored procedure for replication
S	System table
TR	Trigger
U	User-defined table
V	View
X	Extended stored procedure

9

DYNAMIC EXECUTION

The next step is to loop through the list of triggers using a cursor. Inside the loop, you will use dynamic execution to drop the triggers. Let's go over Listing 9.16, which begins by declaring a cursor called cuTriggers. You open this cursor on the list of triggers stored in the sysobjects table using the T-SQL from Listing 9.15. Then you loop through the cursor until there are no more triggers in the list. Each time through the loop, you execute a T-SQL statement to drop the current trigger using dynamic execution. Next, you get the subsequent trigger name from the cursor using the FETCH command. The loop needs an out condition, so you check the value of the @@fetch_status global variable. If it equals -1, you stop looping because there are no more rows in the cursor. Finally, you wrap up by releasing the memory reserved by the cursor using the DEALLOCATE command.

> **NOTE**
>
> Cursors are slow because they keep a connection open longer and require overhead so that we can traverse them. You should avoid using cursors when possible. Cursors are vital to some batch routines, however, such as when you want to create dynamic T-SQL using the system tables (see Listing 9.16).

LISTING 9.16 DROPPING ALL THE TRIGGERS IN THE DATABASE USING A CURSOR AND DYNAMIC EXECUTION

```
DECLARE cuTriggers CURSOR
    FOR
    SELECT name FROM sysobjects WHERE type = 'TR'

OPEN cuTriggers

DECLARE @chvTrigger VARCHAR(128)

FETCH NEXT FROM cuTriggers INTO @chvTrigger
WHILE (@@fetch_status <> -1)
BEGIN
    --------------------------------------------------------------------
    -- A @@fetch_status of -1 means that there are no more rows in the
      ➥cursor.
    -- Since we want to loop through all triggers, this will be our exit
      ➥clause.
    --------------------------------------------------------------------
    EXEC ("DROP TRIGGER "  + @chvTrigger)
    FETCH NEXT FROM cutriggers INTO @chvTrigger
END
DEALLOCATE cuTriggers
GO
```

The Pros and Cons of Dynamic Execution

Dynamic execution comes at the cost of creating code for which SQL Server creates a plan each time it is executed, however. Issues such as these are outlined in this section, along with other pros and cons you should consider before employing dynamic execution.

Clear Advantages of Dynamic Execution

Dynamic execution enables you to create scalable, reusable T-SQL code by combining the functionality of several batches of T-SQL into one flexible solution. You can also perform database schema T-SQL using dynamic execution, as shown in Listing 9.16. You can drop, create, and alter objects just as you can through static T-SQL.

All on-the-fly, you can specify the names of tables, SELECT list fields, WHERE clause fields, ORDER BY fields, GROUP BY fields, HAVING clause fields, database names, and any other previously untouchable aspects of T-SQL. As Listing 9.17 shows, you can also create an extremely generic SELECT statement. The stored procedure in this listing, prSelectData, uses the same basic code structure that the prDeleteData and prUpdateData stored procedures use. You can further modify prSelectData by adding more fields to the SELECT list or the ORDER BY list or even add a new clause to the query. Your choices are limited only by T-SQL; whatever it can do, so can you through dynamic execution.

LISTING 9.17 USING DYNAMIC EXECUTION, YOU CAN CREATE A GENERIC DATA RETRIEVAL STORED PROCEDURE

```
CREATE PROCEDURE prSelectData
    @chvTable VARCHAR(128),
    @chvSelectField VARCHAR(128),
    @chvWhereField VARCHAR(128) = NULL,
    @chvOperator VARCHAR(2) = '=',
    @chvWhereValue VARCHAR(128) = NULL,
    @chvOrderByField VARCHAR(128) = NULL,
    @chvOrderByType VARCHAR(4) = 'ASC'
AS

DECLARE @chvSQL VARCHAR(8000),
    @chvWhereFieldQuotes CHAR(1)

SELECT @chvSQL = 'SELECT ' + @chvSelectField + ' FROM ' + @chvTable
```

continues

9

DYNAMIC EXECUTION

LISTING 9.17 CONTINUED

```
--------------------------------------------------------------------
--- If the WHERE clause field is specified, then
--- create the WHERE clause. Otherwise, do
--- not specify a WHERE clause.
--------------------------------------------------------------------
 IF NOT @chvWhereField IS NULL
     BEGIN
         SELECT @chvSQL = @chvSQL +
     ' WHERE ' + @chvWhereField +
     ' ' + @chvOperator + ' '


     --------------------------------------------------------------------
     --- The stored procedure prNeedsQuotes determines
     --- the data type of the field by looking in the system
     --- tables. It returns a value of 'y' or 'n' in the Output
     --- argument @chvNeedsQuotes. 'y' means that
     --- the field is a data type that requires quotation marks
     --- around its value.
     --------------------------------------------------------------------
     EXEC prNeedsQuotes
         @chvTable = @chvTable,
         @chvField = @chvWhereField,
         @chvNeedsQuotes = @chvWhereFieldQuotes OUTPUT


     --------------------------------------------------------------------
     --- If the data type requires quotation marks, then
     --- use them.
     --------------------------------------------------------------------
     IF @chvWhereFieldQuotes = 'y'
             SELECT @chvSQL = @chvSQL + '''' + @chvWhereValue + ''''
         ELSE
             SELECT @chvSQL = @chvSQL + @chvWhereValue
     END

--------------------------------------------------------------------
--- If the ORDER BY field is specified, then create
--- the ORDER BY clause. Otherwise, do not
--- specify an ORDER BY clause.
--------------------------------------------------------------------
IF NOT @chvOrderByField IS NULL
    SELECT @chvSQL = @chvSQL +
    ' ORDER BY ' + @chvOrderByField +
    ' ' + @chvOrderByType
EXEC (@chvSQL)
GO
```

Despite the power and flexibility that dynamic execution yields, it seems to be the least-documented feature of SQL Server. Every time I need to find a definition or example of a SQL Server feature, all I have to do is open one of several SQL Server books or the online help utilities, and I am flooded with pages of information. For whatever reason, however, dynamic execution documentation is a scarce commodity. It is bizarre that such a useful tool appears to have been overlooked by so many references.

One of the most useful stored procedures I have put together is also one of the simplest. (Shown in Listing 9.18.) It is the prSysObjectsCount stored procedure and it uses dynamic execution of T-SQL to retrieve the count of all objects in a given database. I'll bet that on several projects you have worked on, you have had to establish a production and a test database. The structures start out identical and the struggle becomes keeping them in synch. And it probably seems that no matter what you do, the databases always manage to get out of synch. This is where the prSysobjectsCount stored procedure makes your life a little bit easier. This stored procedure returns the count of all objects in a given database. You can run this stored procedure twice: once for the test database and once for the production database. You then can compare the number of objects in both databases to see whether they are still in synch. This stored procedure could definitely be made more robust. You could make it tell you which objects are not in the other database or even have it schedule this to run every night and kick off an email to you with its results. I'll leave these features to later chapters.

LISTING 9.18   prSysobjectsCount RETURNS THE COUNT OF ALL OBJECTS IN A GIVEN DATABASE

```
CREATE PROCEDURE prSysobjectsCount
    @chvDatabase VARCHAR(128),
    @chvOwner VARCHAR (128) ='DBO'
AS
    EXECUTE ("
    SELECT      CASE Type
        WHEN 'U'  THEN 'User table'
        WHEN 'S'  THEN 'System table'
        WHEN 'P'  THEN 'Stored procedure'
        WHEN 'V'  THEN 'View'
        WHEN 'TR' THEN 'Trigger'
        WHEN 'F'  THEN 'Foreign key'
        WHEN 'D'  THEN 'Default'
        WHEN 'K'  THEN 'Primary key or Unique'
        WHEN 'C'  THEN 'Check constraint'
        WHEN 'L'  THEN 'Log'
        WHEN 'R'  THEN 'Rule'
        WHEN 'X'  THEN 'Extended stored procedure'
        WHEN 'RF' THEN 'Stored procedure for replication'
        END
```

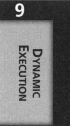

9

**DYNAMIC
EXECUTION**

continues

LISTING 9.18   CONTINUED

```
      AS 'Type',
      COUNT(*) AS Total
    FROM " + @chvDatabase + "." + @chvOwner + ".sysobjects
    GROUP BY Type")
GO
```

Common Pitfalls of Dynamic Execution

The prSysobjectsCount stored procedure does point out an interesting annoyance of dynamic execution: You must pass it a VARCHAR variable and/or character data. Because VARCHAR limits you to 255 characters, you have to concatenate multiple variables together to use long strings with the EXEC statement. You do have the option of using TEXT variables, but remember that they are limited because they cannot be local variables. This limitation does not stop you from coding useful dynamic execution T-SQL—it just frustrates you. Unlike most deterrents, however, the results often are worth the frustration.

Another pitfall of dynamic execution arises when you mix EXEC statements with non-EXEC statements. Now before you try this and see that prSysObjectsCount returns counts of all the objects, be aware that if you mix EXEC and non-EXEC statements, you risk getting unreliable results. What really would happen is that the counts would reflect the total number of objects in the current database before the stored procedure was executed.

It is important to note that the statements inside the EXEC statement are not compiled until the statement is executed. Combining statements that change the current database could result in errors or, worse, incorrect results. Shown in Listing 9.19 are some of the ways to misuse and correctly use the EXEC statement. For example, if you ran the third script from the context of the master database (or any database other than the pubs database) it would not work properly. This is because before the script can be executed, SQL Server first makes sure that all SQL is pointing to accurate objects for the current context unless a USE {database_name} syntax is used. Using the EXEC keyword basically tells SQL Server not to check its SQL.

LISTING 9.19   THE INCORRECT AND CORRECT WAYS TO USE THE EXEC STATEMENT

```
Correct:
USE pubs
SELECT stor_name FROM stores

OR

EXEC("USE pubs")
EXEC("SELECT stor_name FROM stores")
```

```
Incorrect:
EXEC ("USE pubs")
SELECT stor_name FROM stores
```

Another problem with dynamic execution is the lack of a dynamic array structure. Imagine how flexible your dynamic execution T-SQL could be if you could pass in an array of field names to the prSelectData stored procedure. Suddenly, the limitation of hard coding the number of fields in the SELECT list, the WHERE clause, or the ORDER BY clause would no longer hinder you. But nonetheless, this is a limitation and you must find alternative ways to work around it. One way to do this is to pass character-delimited strings that could be parsed to reveal the fields. There are other creative ways to get around this T-SQL limitation, however. Another way could be to create a table that holds all the data you need for your dynamic execution. You could just loop through the rows of the table, which would represent a different SELECT field. Whatever way you choose, the trick is to find the method that satisfies the situation.

Summary

Using dynamic execution with stored procedures provides a great deal of flexibility; however, it does come at a slight cost. The first time a stored procedure is executed, it is compiled and its query plan is stored in memory. The query plan is used each time the stored procedure is executed, thus making it faster. You can compare this to the first time you drove your car to work for your job interview, because you probably did not know where you were going (even if you did, just play along). But the next time you drove there, you remembered the way much more clearly. Stored procedures that use dynamic execution are compiled the first time they are executed, but the T-SQL could be different for each execution. Therefore, the query plan used the last time the stored procedure was executed cannot be reused and must be re-created. Imagine if your office moved every day—you would have to plan a new route to work every morning!

The time it takes to re-create the query plan is negligible in most cases, so you probably will not be concerned with this delay unless you are using dynamic execution in time-critical, business-critical situations. In these cases, it would be wise to perform some benchmarks on the dynamic execution stored procedure before implementing it in production applications.

Security Issues

CHAPTER 10

Information technology, specifically databases, is now an integral component of an organization's infrastructure. It ensures an organization's competitive edge in today's high-tech world. Industry, government, and individuals have become dependent on their data and have spent billions of dollars trying to maintain a secure environment for processing, exchanging, and storing information. Security is an essential part of managing databases. In this context, security refers to protecting the database against damage, theft, and unauthorized use. A well-developed security plan makes authorized use of the database easy, and unauthorized use or accidental damage difficult or impossible; it ensures users are allowed to do the tasks they are trying to do.

This chapter gives you an overview of the security features and the SQL Server 7.0 security model. It describes the components that make up the model and explains how SQL Server tracks each user and each securable object. It also shows how SQL Server validates access requests. SQL Server 7.0's security model includes built-in tools to control who accesses which objects (such as tables and stored procedures) and which action an individual user can take on an object (such as execute a stored procedure).

In this chapter, you will learn the following:

- How to set an authentication mode: Two choices are available to you—Windows NT Authentication Mode and Mixed Authentication Mode.
- Assign logins to users and roles: You can create login accounts from Windows NT users and groups, or you can create new SQL Server login accounts.
- Assign permissions to users and roles: After you have created accounts, you must assign permissions to enforce database security.
- How to plan a security system: There are five main issues to consider when you develop your plan.
- How to enforce security using views and stored procedures: Provides an additional level of security by allowing the administrator to set and manage permissions on the view or stored procedure, rather than on the objects to which they refer.
- How to manage application security: Application roles allow you to create a security environment for an application.

Implementing an Authentication Mode

The authentication stage identifies the user using a login account and verifies only the ability to connect with SQL Server. If authentication is successful, the user connects to SQL Server.

SQL Server supports two modes:

- Windows NT Authentication Mode (Windows NT Authentication)
- Mixed Mode (Windows NT Authentication and SQL Server Authentication)

Security Model

Before you begin selecting an authentication mode, let's discuss the elements of SQL Server's security architecture. Users and groups of users are the basic components of the security system. These entities are assigned an ID for security purposes and are referred to as *security principals*. It gives resource owners the ability to specify who can access their resources and to what extent they can be accessed.

The following are new additions to the SQL Server 7.0 security model:

- Allowing the use of Windows NT user and group accounts as SQL Server login identifiers.
- The introduction of SQL Server application and user roles, which replace SQL Server 6.5 aliases and groups.

SQL Server is fully integrated with the security system in Windows NT, allowing Microsoft clients to have a single username and password to access both SQL Server and Windows NT. SQL Server also uses Windows NT encryption features for network security. SQL Server provides its own security for non-Microsoft clients.

Groups and roles enable you to assemble users into a single unit that you can apply permissions to. Permissions can now be assigned directly to Windows NT users and groups. *Groups* are collections of users, local groups, and global groups within Windows NT. For more information about Windows NT users and groups, see your Windows NT documentation.

Roles are collections of SQL Server logins, Windows NT logins, Windows NT groups, or other roles, similar to Windows NT groups. Roles are convenient when equivalent Windows NT groups do not exist. A SQL Server user can be a member of multiple SQL Server roles. Now the administrator can manage database access and permissions using Windows NT groups or SQL Server roles.

Giving a user account membership in a group or role gives that user all the rights and permissions granted to the group or role. Group or role memberships offer an easy way to grant common capabilities to sets of users.

A two-stage process forms the foundation of the SQL Server Security model:

1. First, before users can gain access to any of the databases on a SQL Server, they must log on and be validated by SQL Server.

   Authentication accepts logon requests from a user and ensures that the user has a valid login account to access the server only. If authentication is successful, the user connects to SQL Server.

2. Second, users must have accounts in each database they want to access.

   Permissions validation checks to see if the user has permission to access databases on the server and perform whatever action the user is attempting. SQL Server maps SQL Server login authentication to user accounts in a database. This component enforces the access validation and policy defined by the administrator.

SQL Server supports two login authentication systems: SQL Server authentication and Windows NT authentication. Each system uses a different type of login account.

When using SQL Server authentication, a login account and password are created and stored on the SQL Server by a system administrator. Users must supply both the SQL Server login account and password when they connect to SQL Server.

When using Windows NT authentication, a Windows NT account or group is used instead; the user does not supply a SQL Server login account when connecting. A SQL Server system administrator must map either the Windows NT account or group to a valid SQL Server login account.

In Windows NT authentication, the user's access to SQL Server is controlled by his or her Windows NT account or group. That person does not have to provide a SQL Server login account when connecting. The SQL administrator must map either the Windows NT user or group account to a valid SQL Server login account.

Authentication Processing

SQL Server can use Windows NT to authenticate logins, or it can authenticate logins itself.

SQL Server Authentication

The following actions are taken when SQL Server authenticates logins:

- When a user requests a connection, SQL Server verifies that a login exists in the `syslogins` system table and that the specified password matches the previously recorded password.

- If there is no login account set up for the user, authentication fails and a connection is denied.

Windows NT Authentication

The following steps are taken when SQL Server processes logins that Windows NT authenticates:

- The user requests a trusted connection, which can be granted only if the user has been validated by Windows NT. This action passes only the user's Windows NT group and user account to SQL Server; no passwords are transmitted to the SQL Server.

  SQL Server does not have to validate the user separately; it knows that Windows NT has already accomplished this task.

- The connection request is approved if SQL Server finds the Windows NT user or group account in the `syslogins` system table.

> **NOTE**
>
> If you delete and re-create a user or group in Windows NT, you must do the same in SQL Server. SQL Server uses the Windows NT security identification number (SID) to identify user and group accounts.

- Depending on the account setup, the user's SQL Server login account is either the Windows NT user or group account.

- The Windows NT Authentication process also supports trusted domains. Therefore, all that's needed is to log on successfully to a single domain and be able to access multiple SQL Servers that are participating in the trusted domain model.

Choosing an Authentication Mode

Using SQL Server Enterprise Manager, you can configure the SQL Server security system to run in two modes: Windows NT Authentication Mode and Mixed Mode. A description of each mode and its advantages follows:

- In Windows NT Authentication Mode, only Windows NT Authentication is supported. It offers the following advantages:

- Provides more account policy features—secure validation, encryption of passwords, auditing, password expiration, minimum password length, and account lockout after an invalid password.

- Windows NT groups allow multiple Windows NT users to be granted access to SQL Server in one step.

10

SECURITY ISSUES

- User needs only one username and password for both Windows NT and SQL Server.

- In Mixed Mode, users can connect to SQL Server with Windows NT authentication or SQL Server authentication. This mode has the following advantages:

  - Supports a broader range of users—non–Windows NT clients, Internet clients, and mixed client groups.

  - Creates another layer of security over Windows NT.

  - An application can use a single SQL Server login and password.

Steps for Implementing an Authentication Mode

You must perform the following steps from a system administration account to implement authentication.

1. Configure the necessary network protocol. For trusted connections, you must use either Named Pipes, Multi-Protocol, or TCP/IP Sockets.

2. Set the security mode using Enterprise Manager:

   - Expand a server group.

   - Right-click on a server, and then choose Properties.

   - Click the Security tab.

   - Select the Windows NT Only option (for Windows NT Authentication Mode) or SQL Server and Windows NT (for Mixed Mode). See Figure 10.1.

3. You must stop and restart MSSQLServer service for the new settings to take effect.

FIGURE 10.1

Setting the authentication mode.

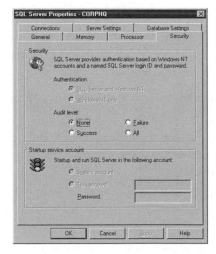

> **NOTE**
>
> To stop and start MSSQLServer service, use the Services icon in Control Panel, SQL Server Service Manager, or Enterpise Manger.

4. Create Windows NT users and groups.

5. Use Enterprise Manager to grant a Windows NT user or group login access to SQL Server.

6. For non-trusted connections only, create a new SQL Server login account.

Creating Login Accounts

As mentioned earlier, you can create login accounts from Windows NT users and groups or create new SQL Server login accounts. Login accounts are stored in the syslogins system table in the master database. During account creation, you can specify a default database that the user accesses at each connection to the SQL Server machine.

There are two approaches you can take to permit Microsoft Windows NT user or group accounts to connect to Microsoft SQL Server using Windows NT Authentication: Transact-SQL and SQL Enterprise Manager.

Transact-SQL

You can use the following system stored procedure to allow a Windows NT user or group to connect to SQL Server.

```
sp_grantlogin [@loginame =] 'login'
```

The *login* parameter is the name of the Windows NT user or group to be added. For a Windows NT global user, global group, local user, or local group, qualify the parameter by using the Windows NT domain name in the form *Domain\User*. If you decide to grant access to a built-in Windows NT local group, such as Adminstrators, specify BUILTIN\Administrators as the group name to add to SQL Server. The length of the combined domain name and user or group name string cannot exceed 128 characters.

Here are other system stored procedures you can use to manage Windows NT logins:

- sp_revokelogin—Removes the login entries from Microsoft SQL Server for the Microsoft Windows NT user or group created.

- sp_denylogin—Prevents a Microsoft Windows NT user or group from connecting to Microsoft SQL Server.

10

SECURITY ISSUES

SQL Enterprise Manager

To grant a Windows NT user or group login access to SQL Server using Enterprise Manager, perform the following steps:

1. Right-click on the Server to expand the folders.

2. Expand Security, right-click Logins, and then choose New Login.

3. Select Windows NT Authentication.

4. In the Name text box, enter the Microsoft Windows NT account (in the form DOMAIN\User) to grant access to Microsoft SQL Server. See Figure 10.2.

FIGURE 10.2

The New Login dialog.

> **NOTE**
>
> Changes to the Windows NT group membership don't affect the SQL Server login account.

Assigning Logins to Users and Roles

Before a user can access a database, you must set up a username as a login ID for that database. A database user is a security principal enabling object access permission control at the finest level of granularity. A user represents a single SQL Server login within the scope of the database in which the user is defined. You can map a SQL Server login account to a user account or roles in each database to which the user needs access.

Sysusers and sysprotects are two tables that store database-level system information for each database. The sysusers system table contains one row for each Microsoft Windows NT user, Windows NT group, Microsoft SQL Server user, or SQL Server role in the database. Sysprotects system contains information about permissions that have been applied to security accounts with the GRANT and DENY statements.

Assigning Logins to User Accounts

Use either SQL Server Enterprise Manager or the sp_grantdbaccess system stored procedure to grant a login account access to a database.

Transact-SQL

Use the following stored procedure to grant a user access to a database.

```
sp_grantdbaccess [@loginame =] 'login',[@name_in_db =] 'name_in_db'
```

The @loginame parameter is the name of the login for the new security account in the current database. It could be a Windows NT group, Windows NT user, or SQL Server user.

The @name_in_db parameter is the name for the account in the database. If not specified, login is used.

Here are some additional system stored procedures you can use to manage database access:

- sp_revokedbaccess—Removes a security account from the current database.
- sp_change_users_login—Changes the relationship between a SQL Server login and a SQL Server user in the current database.

SQL Enterprise Manager

Using SQL Enterprise Manager, you can grant a SQL Server login access to a database.

1. Double-click on the server to expand its folders.
2. Expand Databases; then expand the database the login will be granted access to.
3. Right-click Users, and then choose New Database User. This opens the General tab of the Properties window for New Users, shown in Figure 10.3.
4. In the Login Name drop-down list, select the Microsoft SQL Server login that database access will be granted to.

    Optionally, in the User Name text box, enter the username that the login is known by in the database. By default, it is set to the login name.

    Optionally, select database role memberships in addition to public (default).

FIGURE 10.3

Setting roles in the New User dialog.

Two default accounts are created in each database: dbo and guest. All members of the fixed server role System Administrators (sysadmin) are mapped to the dbo. All objects created by members of the sysadmin role belong to dbo. The dbo account cannot be deleted. The guest user account allows individuals with a SQL Server login account, but no database account, access to a database. To be mapped to the guest account, the following conditions must be met:

- The SQL Server login account is not currently mapped to a database user account.
- The database contains a guest user account.

By default, the guest user account is created only for the master and tempdb databases. This account also cannot be removed from these two databases. For all other newly created databases, the guest user account must be created and removed manually.

Assigning Logins to Roles

When several users share a common activity, it's easier to assemble them into a single unit called a "role" and assign permissions once to that specified role. Roles replace SQL 6.5 aliases and groups. Predefined roles relating to administrative functions have been included with SQL. In addition to predefined roles, you can also have user-defined roles.

Fixed Server Roles

The two types of predefined roles are fixed server and fixed database. *Fixed server roles* provide groupings with implied permissions necessary to perform administrative functions at the server level. These roles reside over the individual databases and are stored in the master syslogins system table. Table 10.1 lists all the fixed server roles.

TABLE 10.1 FIXED SERVER ROLES

Role	Description
sysadmin	Performs any activity in SQL Server
dbcreator	Creates and alters databases
diskadmin	Manages disk files
processadmin	Manages SQL Server processes
serveradmin	Configures server-wide settings
setupadmin	Installs replication
securityadmin	Manages and audits server logins

Use either SQL Server Enterprise Manager or the sp_addsrvrolemember system stored procedure to grant a login account access to a database.

Transact-SQL

To create a new user defined database role, use the following stored procedure.

```
sp_addsrvrolemember [@loginame =] 'login', [@rolename =] 'role'
```

The @loginame parameter is the name of the login being added to the fixed server role. It's a system-supplied, user-defined data type called sysname. The value can be a SQL Server login or a Windows NT user account. If the Windows NT login has not already been granted access to SQL Server, access is granted automatically.

The @rolename parameter is the name of the fixed server role in which the login is being added. Possible values are NULL or one of the values listed previously in Table 10.1.

For example, if you wanted to add the Windows NT user Research\JohnD to the sysadmin fixed server role, use the following code:

```
EXEC sp_addsrvrolemember 'Research\JohnD', 'sysadmin'
```

Additional system stored procedures you can use to manage fixed server role memberships are listed in Table 10.2.

TABLE 10.2 SYSTEM STORED PROCEDURES

System Stored Procedure	Description
sp_dropsrvrolemember	Removes a SQL Server login or Windows NT user or group from a fixed server role.
sp_helpsrvrole	Returns a list of the fixed server roles.
sp_srvrolepermission	Returns the permissions applied to a fixed server role.

10

SECURITY ISSUES

SQL Enterprise Manager

Using Enterprise Manager, you can create a new user-defined database role.

1. Double-click on the server to expand its folders.

2. Expand Security, and then click Server Roles (to view fixed server roles).

3. In the details pane, right-click the role, and then choose Properties (to view its members). See Figure 10.4.

FIGURE 10.4

*The Database
Role Properties
dialog for* public.

4. On the General tab, click Add, and then select the logins to add. Or select the login to remove, and then click the Remove button.

Fixed Database Roles

Fixed database roles are predefined groups created in each database. The data for these roles is stored in the sysusers system table of each database. You can add a user to more than one built-in database role. Being a member of one of these built-in roles gives a user rights and abilities to perform administrative tasks at the database level. They cannot be added, modified, or removed. The fixed database roles are described in Table 10.3.

TABLE 10.3   FIXED DATABASE ROLES

Role	Description
public	Maintains all default permissions.
db_owner	Performs the activities of all database roles.
db_accessadmin	Adds or removes database users, groups, and roles.
db_ddladmin	Adds, modifies, or drops database objects.

Role	Description
db_securityadmin	Manages roles and members of database roles and manages statement and object permissions.
db_backupoperator	Backs up and restores the database.
db_datareader	Reads data only from all tables.
db_datawriter	Adds, changes, or deletes data from all user tables.
db_denydatareader	Cannot see any data in the database.
db_denydatawriter	Cannot change data in any table.

> **NOTE**
>
> By default, every new database user is a member of the public database role. Created in every database including master, msdb, tempdb, model, and all user databases, its membership cannot be altered. This particular database role captures permissions for all the users in a database.

User-Defined Database Role

Your users' common needs might not always map easily to a fixed database role, or perhaps you don't have permissions to manage Windows NT users and groups. Therefore, you need to use a user-defined role. Keep in mind that a user can belong to more than one role in the same database, which means that more than one role can be active at any time. This gives you a flexible solution to set the correct level of security within a database. Assigning a user account membership in a role gives that user all the rights and permissions granted to the group.

For example, there might be a special activities committee composed of one member from each department. The members need access to a table created exclusively for them, and there is no group that consists of only these members. As mentioned earlier, you might not have permissions to create a Windows NT group. You could create a user-defined database role called SpecialEvents and add all the committee members. Then apply the necessary permissions to the role so that only these members have access to the table.

You can use SQL Enterprise Manager or the sp_addrole system stored procedure to create a new database role. This information is stored in the sysusers table of the current database—one for each role.

10

SECURITY ISSUES

Use the following stored procedure to create a new database role:

```
sp_addrole [@rolename =] 'role', [@ownername =] 'owner'
```

For example, to add a new role called SpecialEvents, owned by the dbo user, to the current database, use the following code:

```
EXEC sp_addrole SpecialEvents, dbo
```

After you have created your role, you can use SQL Enterprise Manager or the sp_addrolemember system stored procedure to add users or roles as members of the role.

The follwing stored procedure will allow you to add members to a database role:

```
sp_addrolemember [@rolename =] 'role', [@membername =] 'security_account'
```

To add a John to the SpecialEvents role, for example, use this code:

```
EXEC sp_addrolemember SpecialEvents, John
```

Table 10.4 lists additional system stored procedures available to manage database roles.

TABLE 10.4 SYSTEM STORED PROCEDURES

System Stored Procedure	Description
sp_droprole	Removes a role from the current database.
sp_droprolemember	Removes a security account from a role in the current database.

Assigning Permissions to Users and Roles

Security on SQL Server is further extended by the permissions granted to users to interact within each database. Permissions control how users access database objects. A user can be assigned permissions directly or as a member of a role. Also, a user can be a member of multiple roles with different permissions that give different levels of access to the same object. Each database has its own security system.

Types of Permissions

There are three types of permissions in SQL Server: object, statement, and implied.

Object Permissions

Object permissions regulate the use of certain statements on certain database objects. They are granted and revoked by the owner of the object. Object permissions apply to the statements and objects listed in Table 10.5.

TABLE 10.5   OBJECT PERMISSIONS

Statements	Objects
SELECT	Table/View
INSERT	Table/View
UPDATE	Table/View
DELETE	Table/View
REFERENCES	Table/Column
EXECUTE	Stored Procedure

Statement Permissions

A system administrator or database owner can assign *statement permissions* that allow individual users or groups to perform database tasks with the following self-explanatory statements:

```
CREATE DATABASE
CREATE TABLE
CREATE VIEW
CREATE PROCEDURE
CREATE INDEX
CREATE RULE
CREATE DEFAULT
BACKUP DATABASE
```

Implied Permissions

Implied permissions apply to activities that can be performed only by members of pre-defined system roles or owners of database objects. Fixed roles have implied permissions assigned to them, which can't be modified. Likewise, object owners have implied permissions allowing them to perform all activities with the object they own.

10

SECURITY ISSUES

Granting, Denying, and Revoking Permissions

Permissions for a user or role can exist in one of three states: granted, revoked, or denied. Information about permissions is stored in the sysprotects system table. Table 10.6 describes the possible states of each permission.

TABLE 10.6 PERMISSION STATES

Permission	State in sysprotects Table	Description
GRANT	Positive	Can perform action.
DENY	Negative	Cannot perform action.
REVOKE	None	Cannot perform action unless overridden by role membership.

Users can perform an action if they have been granted the permission directly or they belong to a role that has been granted the permission. You might be wondering how SQL Server resolves permission conflicts. For example, if a user has been assigned permissions explicitly or is a member of multiple roles, each with differently assigned permissions to the same resource, the user's effective permissions is always the cumulative or least restrictive of all permissions. There's one exception, however: If DENY is in the set of permissions, it overrides all other permissions and becomes the effective permission.

The right to GRANT, DENY, and REVOKE permissions belongs to members of the sysadmin, db_owner, and db_securityadmin fixed roles and to object owners. You can GRANT, DENY, and REVOKE permissions by using SQL Enterprise Manger or the GRANT statement.

The following example assigns SELECT permissions to the Sales role and assigns additional permissions to users John, Maria, and Lori for the Customers table. The graphic interface for the same permissions is shown in Figure 10.5.

```
GRANT SELECT
ON Customers
TO Sales
GO
GRANT INSERT, UPDATE, DELETE
ON Customers
TO John, Maria, Lori
GO
```

FIGURE 10.5

Setting permissions by role and individual user.

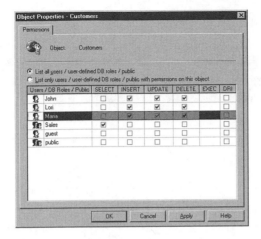

Denying permissions does the following:

- Removes the permission previously granted to the user or role.

- Overrides permissions that are inherited from another role.

- Prevents any permissions from being inherited in the future.

The following example shows SELECT, INSERT, and UPDATE permissions on the Customers table granted to the Sales role. Then specific permissions are denied from a few users who are members of the Sales role. Because DENY overrides all explicitly and inherited assigned permissions, these users (Lori, John, and Maria) have no access to the Customers table. See Figure 10.6 for the dialog in Enterprise Manager.

```
USE northwind
GO
GRANT SELECT, INSERT, UPDATE
ON customers
TO Sales
GO
DENY SELECT, INSERT, UPDATE
ON customers
TO John, Lori, Maria
```

Revoking a permission removes a granted permission, but it does not prevent the user or role from inheriting that permission in the future.

In this next example, the SELECT permission that had been granted to user Lori is deactivated. However, she can still query the table if the SELECT permission has been granted to any role of which she is a member.

```
REVOKE SELECT ON customers FROM Lori
```

10

SECURITY ISSUES

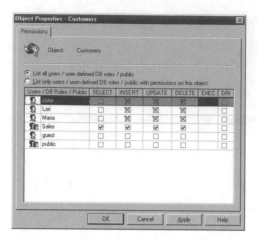

FIGURE 10.6

Denying table permissions to individual users in a group.

Planning Security

Developing a security policy involves four main issues:

- **Default login accounts**   Instead of using the sa built-in administrator login, assign all your administrator logins to the sysadmin fixed server role. This method allows them to login using their own login account. After installation, the sa login isn't assigned a password, so you should immediately assign a password to the sa login.

  The BUILTIN\Administrators default login is a member of the sysadmin role. You can disable this by removing the domain administrators from the local administrators group in Windows NT.

- **Guest user account**   When there is a guest user account, someone without a database user account can still access the database through the guest account. If you decide to use this account, assign the appropriate permissions to it.

- **Public role permissions**   Remember, the public role is a special role that includes all database user accounts and whose membership cannot be altered. You should pay close attention to which permissions to assign to this role.

- **Mapping logins to either user accounts or roles**   If a Windows NT group will perform similar activities, create a user account for the group and apply permission to it.

  If more than one login account will perform similar activities, create a role and assign the login accounts to that role.

  If a login account will perform administrative tasks, place the login in the appropriate fixed server or database role.

It is recommended that all objects be created by members of the sysadmin, db_owner, and db_ddladmin fixed roles only. This allows any user to refer to the object without specifying the owner name. Any object created by a member of the sysadmin role has the dbo as the owner.

When members from any other role create an object, they must specify dbo as the owner; otherwise, their username is used instead. You can change the object owner by using the sp_changeobjectowner system stored procedure as follows:

```
sp_changeobjectowner object, owner
```

Managing Application Security

You already looked at how to use login account verification and permissions to secure access to a database. You can also secure access at the application level by using views, stored procedures, and application roles.

Using Stored Procedures and Views to Manage Security

Stored procedures and views let you set up a security model specifically designed for applications. They allow you to manage security on the stored procedure and view, not on the underlying tables. Also, any changes to the objects referred to by the view or stored procedure are transparent to the user.

Using Application Roles to Manage Client Application Security

Application roles enable security for a particular application. They control indirect access to data through a specific application.

For example, you might allow all HR employees to use the hire processing program to enter new employee data into the personnel table. In this situation, you create an application role for the hire processing program.

Application roles have the following properties:

- These roles have no members; they are activated when the user runs the program.
- They require a password to be activated.
- After activating the application role, all other existing permissions in the current database, including those from role memberships, are lost.

You can use the `sp_addapprole` system stored procedure or the Enterprise Manager to create a new application role.

Transact-SQL

As with the other permissions, you can use both Transact-SQL and the SQL Enterprise Manager. The code looks like this:

```
sp_addapprole role, password
```

Here's how to add a new application role, HRApp, with the password HRDEPT6:

```
EXEC sp_addapprole 'HRApp', 'HRDEPT6'
```

SQL Enterprise Manager

Below are the steps to create a new application role using Enterprise Manager.

1. Double-click on the server to expand its folders.

2. Expand Databases; then expand the database in which to create a role.

3. Right-click Roles, and then choose New Database Role. See Figure 10.7.

FIGURE 10.7

Creating a new application role is comparable to setting permissions for other roles.

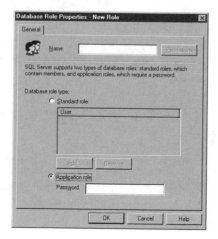

4. In the Name text box, enter the name of the new application role.

5. Select Application Role, and then enter a password.

To manage role permissions, use SQL Enterprise Manager or the GRANT, DENY, and REVOKE statements.

Here is an example of granting permissions to the HRApp application role to insert in the personnel table:

```
GRANT INSERT ON personnel TO HRApp
```

The client needs to execute the sp_setapprole system stored procedure to activate the application role. It must be executed by a direct Transact-SQL statement only. It cannot be executed within another stored procedure or from within a user-defined transaction.

The following needs to be considered when you're using application roles:

- The current application must provide the password, which can be encrypted.
- The scope of the application role is within the current database only. If the user accesses another database, the permissions in that database apply.
- Once activated, the application role can be deactivated only when the user disconnects from SQL Server.

Summary

This chapter has covered how to implement security, beginning with a description of how to set up an authentication mode for a server, and how to grant access to Windows NT users and groups and SQL Server users and roles. It has also shown you how to assign login accounts to users and roles and how to assign permissions to users and roles. Finally, it has described security planning, using views and stored procedures to manage security, and creating application roles to manage application security.

Specialized Triggers

CHAPTER 11

Quite often you want a business rule to execute immediately after a row has been inserted into a database. Other times, you want to reciprocate data updates throughout multiple tables. Through the use of triggers, you can accomplish these goals, as you'll see in this chapter. You'll also explore some of the new features of triggers introduced in SQL Server 7 and see how they can help you support an enterprise business solution.

For example, a trigger on the `sales` table is executed whether a T-SQL statement was run via `isql` or a new sale was entered by using an external application. Before tackling the practical business uses of triggers, I'll briefly discuss their technical aspects. This chapter, which assumes you have at least a minimal working knowledge of triggers, concentrates on their useful implementations. I'll begin the overview with a brief discussion of their components, such as the `inserted` and `deleted` tables and the `update()` function. Then I'll go over nesting and limitations of triggers. When triggers are created, information about them is stored in several system tables. I'll go through these system tables and the use of the information they store.

After finishing the overview, you'll jump straight into practical methods to enforce business rules, such as preventing a price increase of 25% or more on any title with sales of fewer than 100 units. SQL Server 7.0 introduces the `ALTER TRIGGER`, statement and I'll show how you can use this statement to edit your triggers. Then I'll review how triggers can be used to audit transactions and archive information. Triggers can be used to store system information about which SQL transactions are being executed most often. I'll discuss how this stored information can be used to improve database performance.

We all know foreign keys are faster than triggers at maintaining referential integrity (RI). However, triggers can maintain more complex relationships that foreign keys cannot handle. I'll go over these relationships and how triggers can enforce them. Afterward, I'll discuss some practical business uses of cascade deletes and cascade updates. Then, I'll wrap up by showing how you can keep two databases in sync using triggers to enforce real-time updates without using replication.

Nesting, Recursion, and Trigger Basics

A trigger is executed when SQL performs an action query on the table the trigger is linked to. For example, if an `update` statement occurs on the `titles` table, the `titles` table's update trigger (if one exists) is executed. Because triggers are performed when any of the three types of action queries are executed, there are three corresponding types of triggers:

- Update triggers
- Insert triggers
- Delete triggers

If the same action must be performed by more than one trigger on the same table, you can combine these triggers into one trigger. For example, if you want an email sent to you if someone inserts or deletes records from the discounts table, you can create one trigger that handles both types of action queries. Notice Listing 11.1, which contains a trigger that sends email to the user "Colleen" by using the xp_sendmail extended stored procedure (extended stored procedures are discussed in detail in Chapter 7, "Stored Procedures").

> **NOTE**
>
> The xp_sendmail extended stored procedure requires that SQL Mail be configured properly and started. SQL Mail, in turn, requires a valid Microsoft Exchange profile name for the startup user account of the MSSQLServer Service.

LISTING 11.1 THE TRIGGER trDiscounts_InsDel, WHICH SENDS AN EMAIL WHEN AN INSERT OR DELETE OCCURS ON THE discounts TABLE

```
CREATE TRIGGER trDiscounts_InsDel ON discounts
FOR INSERT, DELETE
AS
DECLARE @intRowCount INTEGER,
    @chvMsg VARCHAR(255)

SELECT @intRowCount = @@RowCount
SELECT @chvMsg = CONVERT(VARCHAR(10), @intRowCount ) + ' record(s) were '
SELECT COUNT(*) FROM inserted
IF @@error <> 0
    SELECT @chvMsg = @chvMsg + ' deleted from the discounts table.'
ELSE
    SELECT @chvMsg = @chvMsg + ' inserted into the discounts table.'
EXEC master..xp_sendmail 'Colleen', @chvMsg
RETURN
```

TIP

Keep in mind that a trigger is executed only once per action query, regardless of the amount of rows affected by the action query. For example, if you update 10 rows in the sales table, the update trigger on the sales table fires only once. When you design your triggers, be sure to account for multiple rows, one row, or even zero rows being affected. Even if you execute an update statement that does not affect any rows in a table, the table's trigger fires. In this case, you should leave a clause that exits the trigger immediately to minimize the length of time the lock is kept open.

NOTE

If you create a trigger (let's say an update trigger) with the same name as an existing trigger, the old update trigger is replaced. However, if you create an additional update trigger on a table, as long as the trigger names differ, both triggers will coexist. Both update triggers, in this case, fire when an update occurs on the given table.

The Inserted and Deleted Tables

Depending on which type of action query is performed, the trigger that is subsequently executed creates either one of the two temporary tables—the inserted table or the deleted table—or both. Refer to Table 11.1 to see which tables are created within a trigger for the corresponding action queries.

WARNING

You should be aware that the inserted and deleted tables can be referenced only by the trigger that created them. The scope of the inserted and deleted tables is limited to the trigger that caused their instantiation. If a trigger calls a stored procedure, that stored procedure cannot reference either the inserted or the deleted tables that were created when the trigger fired.

TABLE 11.1   THE TABLES CREATED BY THE VARIOUS TYPES OF TRIGGERS

Trigger Type	Inserted Table	Deleted Table
Insert	Yes	No
Update	Yes	Yes
Delete	No	Yes

> **NOTE**
>
> For the following discussion of `inserted` and `deleted` tables, please assume that the tables discussed have the appropriate triggers linked to them.

When a record is inserted into a table, the corresponding insert trigger creates an `inserted` table that mirrors the column structure of the table the trigger is linked to. For example, if you insert a row into the `titles` table, its trigger creates the `inserted` table using the same column structure of the `titles` table. For every row that was inserted into the `titles` table, a corresponding row is contained in the `inserted` table.

The `deleted` table also mirrors the column structure of the table it is linked to. When a `DELETE` statement is executed, every row that was removed from the table is contained in the `deleted` table within the delete trigger.

A trigger fired by an `UPDATE` statement creates both an `inserted` and a `deleted` table. Both of these tables have the same column structure as the table they are linked to. The `deleted` and `inserted` tables contain a "before and after" snapshot of the data in the linked table. For example, assume that you have executed the following T-SQL statement:

```
UPDATE titles SET advance = 5500 WHERE advance = 5000
```

The update trigger on the `titles` table is fired when this T-SQL statement is executed. The trigger's `inserted` and `deleted` tables contain a row for every data row that changed because of the T-SQL statement. The `deleted` table contains the data values of the row as they appeared before the `UPDATE` statement. The `inserted` table contains the data values of those same rows as they appear after the `UPDATE` statement.

The update() Function

Triggers can hamper the performance of T-SQL transactions and keep locks open while they execute. Therefore, if your trigger's logic needs to run only when certain columns' data is changed, you should check for those conditions. This is where the update() function steps in to make your life easier.

The update() function is available only in insert and update triggers. The update() function determines whether the column you pass to it has been affected by the insert or update statement that caused the trigger to be fired. Listing 11.2 shows an update trigger on the titles table that prevents the advance column from being altered.

LISTING 11.2 THE TRIGGER trTitles_Upd, WHICH ROLLS BACK ANY T-SQL THAT CHANGES THE advance COLUMN

```
CREATE TRIGGER trTitles_Upd ON titles
FOR UPDATE
AS

IF update(advance)
    ROLLBACK TRANSACTION

RETURN
```

The trTitles_Upd trigger checks whether any data in the advance column has been changed. If so, the trigger rolls back the transaction in its entirety. It is vital to use the update() function in a trigger to escape unnecessarily traversing the trigger's T-SQL logic. After all, why bother executing all the code in a trigger for a case that does not require it (especially because triggers keep the locks open on the affected tables while the triggers are executing)? The revised trigger trTitles_Upd in Listing 11.3 shows a practical example of a trigger that has an "escape clause" to avoid unnecessary work.

LISTING 11.3 THE TRIGGER trTitles_Upd, WHICH EXITS QUICKLY IF THE price COLUMN HAS NOT BEEN UPDATED

```
CREATE TRIGGER trTitles_Upd ON titles
FOR UPDATE
AS

DECLARE @chvMsg VARCHAR(255),
    @chvTitleID VARCHAR(6),
    @mnyOldPrice MONEY,
    @mnyNewPrice MONEY
DECLARE    cuPriceChange CURSOR
    FOR
```

```
    SELECT d.title_id, d.price, i.price
    FROM deleted d INNER JOIN inserted i ON d.title_id = i.title_id
IF update(price)
    BEGIN
        OPEN cuPriceChange
        FETCH NEXT FROM cuPriceChange INTO
            @chvTitleID, @mnyOldPrice, @mnyNewPrice
        WHILE (@@fetch_status <> -1)
        ------------------------------------------------------------
        -- @@fetch_status = -1 means no more rows in the cursor.
        ------------------------------------------------------------
            BEGIN
                SELECT @chvMsg = 'The price of title ' + @chvTitleID
                    + ' has changed from'
                    + ' ' + CONVERT(VARCHAR(10), @mnyOldPrice)
                    + ' to ' + CONVERT(VARCHAR(10), @mnyNewPrice)
                    + ' on ' + CONVERT(VARCHAR(30), getdate())
                    + '.'EXEC master..xp_sendmail 'Colleen', @chvMsg
                FETCH NEXT FROM cuPriceChange
                    INTO @chvTitleID, @mnyOldPrice, @mnyNewPrice
                SELECT @chvMsg = ''
            END
    DEALLOCATE cuPriceChange
    END
RETURN
```

The trTitles_Upd trigger in Listing 11.3 emails the user 'Colleen' for every price change. Because this trigger uses a cursor to loop through the affected rows, it degrades the performance of the original T-SQL statement that fired the trigger. That is why it is vital that the trigger checks whether the data in the price column has changed before it opens the cursor and loops through each affected row. The trTitles_Upd trigger in Listing 11.3 is smart enough to quit when there is no work to do, thus releasing the table locks that much earlier. You can test this trigger by executing any update on the titles table, such as the T-SQL in Listing 11.4.

LISTING 11.4 THE T-SQL THAT EXECUTES THE TRIGGER trTitles_Upd

```
BEGIN TRANSACTION
UPDATE titles SET price = price * .5 WHERE price < 10
ROLLBACK TRANSACTION
```

Notice that this listing changes the data in the titles table just long enough to execute the trigger (and the emails). Then the transaction is undone by the rollback command. If you execute an UPDATE statement against the titles table that does not affect the price column's data, the trigger trTitles_Upd exits when line 15 of Listing 11.3 returns false.

Keep in mind that the update() function does not really tell you whether a column's data has changed. Rather, it tells you if a change was attempted on the column. Specifically, here are the situations in which the update() function returns a value of true:

- The column is in the left side of the SET clause of an UPDATE statement.
- The column is in the columnlist of an INSERT statement.

Even if the data was not actually modified, the update() function returns true. For example, the following T-SQL causes the update() function to return true if it is passed the advance column:

```
UPDATE titles SET advance = advance
```

Notice that this T-SQL statement falls under the first bullet point in the previous list because the column is on the left side of the SET clause.

> **TIP**
>
> In addition to using the update() function to avoid traversing unneeded logic, you can count on the @@rowcount global variable. @@rowcount always contains the value of how many rows were affected by the most recent transaction on the current connection. Check the value of @@rowcount at the beginning of the trigger, and exit immediately if it equals 0 to circumvent any further processing.

Nesting Triggers

You might be wondering what happens when a trigger modifies another table that also has a trigger. In this case, the second trigger is executed, too. This situation is referred to as *nested triggers*. SQL Server allows you to prevent nested triggers from being executed by changing the value of the configuration option nested triggers from 1 to 0 (1, or ON, is the default value for this option). SQL Server 7 limits the levels of nested triggers to 32 deep (if this limit is exceeded, SQL Server raises an error). If you turn off trigger nesting, a trigger that modifies another table does not fire the second table's trigger. Keep in mind that if any of the triggers execute a ROLLBACK TRANSACTION, regardless of the nesting level, no further triggers are executed.

Recursive Triggers

In SQL Server 6.5 and earlier, if a trigger modifies the table it was defined on, it does not invoke itself recursively. Therefore, if an update trigger on the `sales` table updated the `sales` table, the trigger was not called on the second update. However, with the advent of SQL Server 7, you have the power to decide whether you want the triggers to be invoked recursively. Using the setting in `sp_dboption`, SQL Server 7 now allows recursive invocation of triggers by enabling the `Recursive Triggers` option. To enable recursive triggers, execute the following T-SQL, which sets the Recursive Triggers setting of `sp_dboption`:

```
EXEC sp_dboption 'pubs', 'Recursive Triggers', 'TRUE'
```

For example, assume that two update triggers, `trSales1` and `trSales2`, are defined on the `sales` table. The `trSales1` trigger recursively updates the `sales` table, and an `UPDATE` statement executes each `trSales1` and `trSales2` one time each. Further, the execution of `trSales1` triggers the execution of `trSales1` (recursively) and `trSales2`. In this example, the triggers are recursively executed for each update of the `sales` table, whether the update occurred in the trigger or external to the trigger.

> **NOTE**
>
> The `inserted` and `deleted` tables for a trigger contain rows corresponding only to the `UPDATE` statement that invoked the trigger.

T-SQL Limitations in Triggers

As powerful as triggers are, they do have limitations. Some T-SQL statements cannot be executed within the confines of a trigger. The following types of statements are restricted:

- All `CREATE` statements
- All `DROP` statements
- `ALTER` command (`DATABASE` nor `TABLE`)
- `TRUNCATE table`
- `SELECT INTO`
- Permission statements (`GRANT` nor `REVOKE`)
- `RECONFIGURE`
- `LOAD` statements (`TRANSACTION` nor `DATABASE`)
- All `disk` statements
- `UPDATE STATISTICS`

The Role of the System Tables with Triggers

Several system tables store varying information about triggers. Table 11.2 identifies and describes the role of the system tables that contain pertinent trigger information. (Chapter 7 discusses system stored procedures in length, and Appendix C, "Comparison of Development Tools," lists most of the system stored procedures. Refer to Appendix A, "The System Tables of the Master Database," for a listing of the system tables.)

TABLE 11.2   THE ROLE OF THE SYSTEM TABLES THAT STORE INFORMATION ABOUT TRIGGERS

System Table	Role
sysobjects	Stores a row per trigger. Each table row contains columns that reference the table's triggers.
sysdepends	Stores references between triggers and the tables they are linked to.
syscomments	Stores the T-SQL text of triggers.
sysprocedures	Stores a preparsed version of the trigger's query.

In addition, SQL Server provides the system stored procedures sp_helptext and sp_help to display information for SQL Server objects. Listing 11.5 shows the sp_helptext system stored procedure, which accepts a parameter of an object—in this case, a trigger name—and returns the T-SQL code that makes up that object.

LISTING 11.5   THE sp_helptext SYSTEM STORED PROCEDURE

```
CREATE PROCEDURE sp_helptext
@objname VARCHAR(92)
as
DECLARE @dbname VARCHAR(30)

SET NOCOUNT ON

/*
**   Make sure that the @objname is local to the current database.
*/
IF (@objname LIKE '%.%.%' AND
        SUBSTRING(@objname, 1, charindex('.', @objname) - 1) <> db_name()
)
        BEGIN
                RAISERROR(15250,-1,-1)
                RETURN (1)
        END
```

```
/*
**   See if @objname exists.
*/
IF (OBJECT_ID(@objname) IS NULL)
        BEGIN
        SELECT @dbname = db_name()
        RAISERROR(15009,-1,-1,@objname,@dbname)
                RETURN (1)
        END


/*
**   Find out how many lines of text are coming back,
**   and return if there are none.
*/
IF (SELECT COUNT(*) FROM syscomments WHERE id = OBJECT_ID(@objname)) = 0
        BEGIN
                RAISERROR(15197,-1,-1,@objname)
                RETURN (1)
        END

IF (SELECT COUNT(*) FROM syscomments WHERE id = OBJECT_ID(@objname)
    AND texttype & 4 = 0) = 0
        BEGIN
                PRINT 'The object''s comments have been encrypted.'
                RETURN(0)
        END

/*
**   Else get the text.
*/
SELECT text FROM syscomments WHERE id = OBJECT_ID(@objname)

RETURN (0)

GO
```

Let's take a closer look at this system stored procedure to see how it uses the system tables to retrieve information about the triggers (in this case). The first several lines of code verify that the object name passed to the stored procedure is valid. Then the object is checked to see whether its creation script was encrypted. If it was, the stored procedure is aborted. Finally, a simple SELECT statement retrieves the creation script for the object.

Listing 11.6 shows how a simple query can retrieve all user-defined tables and the names of the triggers that reference them. The `sysobjects` table has the `instrig`, `updtrig`, and `deltrig` columns, which contain the object IDs of the triggers that reference their respective tables. The `object_name()` and the `coalesce()` functions are system functions inherent to SQL Server. The `object_name()` function returns the name of the object, given the object's ID. The `coalesce()` function accepts a variant amount of arguments and returns the first non-null argument.

LISTING 11.6   RETRIEVING ALL THE TRIGGERS FOR EACH TABLE

```
SELECT name,
       COALESCE(OBJECT_NAME(instrig), 'N/A') AS InsertTrigger,
       COALESCE(OBJECT_NAME (updtrig), 'N/A') AS UpdateTrigger,
       COALESCE(OBJECT_NAME (deltrig), 'N/A') AS DeleteTrigger
FROM sysobjects
WHERE type = 'U'
ORDER BY name
```

How to Use Triggers to Enforce Business Rules

One of the best uses of a trigger is to enforce business-specific rules that cannot be enforced through any other SQL Server object. You could use an application development tool, such as Visual Basic, to enforce these more complex types of business rules. However, your users would have to go through this application for the business rules to be enforced. Otherwise, they could sidestep the rules completely. By placing these types of rules in triggers, you ensure that the rules will be enforced regardless of how the data is interfaced.

Let's assume you do not want to allow anyone to increase the price of any title by 25% or more of the title's current price. Let's also add the further restriction that this applies only to titles that have not yet sold 100 copies. A trigger is the perfect instrument to enforce this rule because any attempt to update this field will be caught by the trigger. Listing 11.7 shows a trigger that enforces this rule.

LISTING 11.7 PREVENTING PRICE INCREASES OF MORE THAN 25% USING A TRIGGER

```
CREATE TRIGGER trTitles_Upd ON titles
FOR UPDATE
AS

DECLARE @mnyOldPrice MONEY,
        @mnyNewPrice MONEY,
        @chvTitleID VARCHAR(6),
        @chvMsg VARCHAR(255),
        @intTotalQty INTEGER

IF UPDATE(price)
    ----------------------------------------------------------------
    -- There is no need to perform the following logic unless the
    -- price has been changed.
    ----------------------------------------------------------------
    BEGIN
        DECLARE cuPriceChange CURSOR
        FOR
        SELECT d.title_id, d.price, i.price
            FROM inserted i INNER JOIN deleted d
                ON i.title_id = d.title_id

        OPEN cuPriceChange

        FETCH NEXT FROM cuPriceChange INTO
            @chvTitleID, @mnyOldPrice, @mnyNewPrice

        WHILE (@@fetch_status <> -1)
        ----------------------------------------------------------------
        -- A @@fetch_status of -1 means there are no more rows in the
        ➥cursor.
        ----------------------------------------------------------------
        BEGIN
            ----------------------------------------------------------------
            -- Retrieve the total sales for this title.
            ----------------------------------------------------------------
            SELECT @intTotalQty = SUM(qty)
                FROM sales
                WHERE title_id = @chvTitleID


            ----------------------------------------------------------------
            -- If the total sales for this title is fewer than 100 units
            -- and the price has increased more than 25%, reverse the
            -- changes and notify an operator.
            ----------------------------------------------------------------
```

continues

LISTING **11.7** CONTINUED

```
          IF @mnyNewPrice > @mnyOldPrice * 1.25 AND @intTotalQty < 100
             BEGIN
                 SELECT @chvMsg = 'An attempt has been made to reduce'
                     + ' the price of title'
                     + ' ' + @chvTitleID + ' by more than 25% from'
                     + ' ' + CONVERT(VARCHAR(10), @mnyOldPrice) + ' to'
                     + ' ' + CONVERT(VARCHAR(10), @mnyNewPrice) + '.'
                     + ' This is transaction has been rolled back.'

                 PRINT @chvMsg
                 EXEC master..xp_sendmail 'Colleen', @chvMsg

                 ROLLBACK TRANSACTION

                 DEALLOCATE cuPriceChange

                 RETURN
             END

         FETCH NEXT FROM cuPriceChange
                 INTO @chvTitleID, @mnyOldPrice, @mnyNewPrice
   END

       DEALLOCATE cuPriceChange
     END
GO
```

Notice that the update() function is used immediately upon entering the trigger so that
you can circumvent any unneeded logic if the price has not changed. The cursor does not
even get declared if the price does not change. This is why you do not need to release the
memory the cursor reserves on every update. After the trigger's logic has determined that
an attempt was made to change the price of 0 or more titles, the affected rows are tra-
versed to examine the changes to the prices. If any price has increased by more than 25%,
the trigger formats an email message to send to user 'Colleen', rolls back all the
changes, releases the cursor's memory, and exits the trigger.

> **TIP**
>
> The trigger in Listing 11.7 rolls back all changes caused by the UPDATE statement
> if the price increase rule is violated. However, you can reverse specific changes
> based on business rules, too. Rather than roll back the entire transaction and
> exit, you can write an UPDATE statement inside the trigger to affect the same
> table that the trigger references. The UPDATE should simply change the price
> back to the original price (@mnyOldPrice). The updated trigger is shown in
> Listing 11.8.

LISTING 11.8   REVERSING PRICE INCREASES OF MORE THAN 25% BUT ALLOWING THE
CHANGES TO OTHER FIELDS IN THE TABLE

```
CREATE TRIGGER trTitles_Upd ON titles
FOR UPDATE
AS

DECLARE @mnyOldPrice MONEY,
        @mnyNewPrice MONEY,
        @chvTitleID VARCHAR(6),
        @chvMsg VARCHAR(255),
        @intTotalQty INTEGER

IF UPDATE(price)
    --------------------------------------------------------------------
    -- There is no need to perform the following logic unless the
    -- price has been changed.
    --------------------------------------------------------------------
    BEGIN
        DECLARE cuPriceChange CURSOR
        FOR
        SELECT d.title_id, d.price, i.price
            FROM inserted i INNER JOIN deleted d
                ON i.title_id = d.title_id

        OPEN cuPriceChange

        FETCH NEXT FROM cuPriceChange INTO
            @chvTitleID, @mnyOldPrice, @mnyNewPrice

        WHILE (@@fetch_status <> -1)
        ----------------------------------------------------------------
        -- A @@fetch_status of -1 means there are no more rows in the
        ➥cursor.
        ----------------------------------------------------------------
        BEGIN
            ------------------------------------------------------------
            -- Retrieve the total sales for this title.
            ------------------------------------------------------------
            SELECT @intTotalQty = SUM(qty)
                FROM sales
                WHERE title_id = @chvTitleID

            ------------------------------------------------------------
            -- If the total sales for this title is fewer than 100 units
            -- and the price has increased more than 25%, reverse the
            -- changes and notify an operator.
            ------------------------------------------------------------
```

continues

LISTING 11.8   CONTINUED

```
          IF @mnyNewPrice > @mnyOldPrice * 1.25 AND @intTotalQty < 100
            BEGIN
                SELECT @chvMsg = 'An attempt has been made to reduce'
                    + ' the price of title'
                    + ' ' + @chvTitleID + ' by more than 25% from'
                    + ' ' + CONVERT(VARCHAR(10), @mnyOldPrice) + '
to'
                    + ' ' + CONVERT(VARCHAR(10), @mnyNewPrice) + '.'
                    + ' This is transaction has been rolled back.'

                PRINT @chvMsg
                PRINT ''
                EXEC master..xp_sendmail 'Colleen', @chvMsg

                UPDATE titles
                    SET price = @mnyOldPrice
                    WHERE title_id = @chvTitleID
            END

        FETCH NEXT FROM cuPriceChange
                INTO @chvTitleID, @mnyOldPrice, @mnyNewPrice
END

    DEALLOCATE cuPriceChange
  END

GO
```

As shown in Listing 11.8, triggers can enforce rules that are more complex than can be defined using check constraints. The trigger trTitles_Upd references columns in an external table, sales. This cannot be done using a check constraint, but can be accomplished using a trigger.

> **NOTE**
>
> An update of a table in that table's trigger does not cause the trigger to fire recursively.

Real-Time Updates Between Databases

Sometimes you need data to be instantaneously copied from one database to another. For example, assume that you have a database holding inventory for your West Coast sales and another for your East Coast sales. The West Coast database is in Denver, and the East Coast database is in New York. Both databases contain a total view of the inventory and need to update each other when a sale has been made. You can accomplish this task through real-time updates using triggers.

A trigger on the inventory table of both databases that issues update statements on the opposite coast's database will do the trick in this case. On both databases' inventory tables, you can simply put a trigger for updates, deletes, and inserts that send the inventory changes across the country. This way, you can assure yourself of instantaneous updates and keeping the databases in sync.

However, be aware that you should not use recursive triggers in this case because that would send the inventory changes multiple times. Also, this creates quite a bit of network traffic. This method of real-time updates should be carefully thought out before implementing.

Auditing Triggers

You can also use triggers to audit transactions. For example, you might not want deleted sales data to be permanently lost. Rather, you would prefer to move the purged sales data to an archival `sales` table. The first step in this archival process is to create an `audit` table for the archived sales data. This table should mirror the column structure of the `sales` table while omitting the foreign keys that the `sales` table has. For this discussion, assume that you have created this table and have called it `SalesArchive`. You can use the T-SQL script in Listing 11.9 to create `SalesArchive`.

LISTING 11.9   THE TABLE CREATION SCRIPT FOR TABLE `SalesArchive`

```
CREATE TABLE SalesArchive
(
    stor_id       CHAR(4)          NOT NULL,
    ord_num       VARCHAR(20)      NOT NULL,
    ord_date      DATETIME         NOT NULL,
    qty           SMALLINT         NOT NULL,
    payterms      VARCHAR(12)      NOT NULL,
    title_id      tid,
)
GO
```

Transferring the purged sales data to the SalesArchive table allows you to query this data in the future. For example, you might want to run sales reports on historical data to forecast future sales by store. A delete trigger on the sales table can give you the ammunition to present these types of historical reports rather easily. Listing 11.10 shows the trigger trSales_Del, which transfers deleted sales data to the SalesArchive table.

LISTING 11.10   THE DELETE TRIGGER ON THE sales TABLE THAT ARCHIVES THE PURGED SALES DATA

```
CREATE TRIGGER trSales_Del ON sales
FOR DELETE
AS

INSERT SalesArchive
    SELECT stor_id, ord_num, ord_date, qty, payterms, title_id
        FROM deleted
GO
```

The beauty of this trigger is that it is so simple, yet powerful. After this trigger is in place, every sale that is deleted is subsequently transferred to the SalesArchive table. Regardless of how the sales data is purged (that is, from an iSQL window or a client application), the data is archived.

> **TIP**
>
> You could use a scheduled task with the trSales_Del trigger in Listing 11.10 to archive sales data. For example, you could schedule a task to run once a week that deletes all sales that occurred on or before the same day on the previous year. This task would kick off the sales table's delete trigger, which would then archive the sales, all done automatically.

Storing System Information

Triggers can be used to automatically store system information that defaults just can't handle. For example, assume that you want every table to contain two columns that represent who the last user to modify a row was and the day and time the modification occurred. Let's call these columns modify_date and modify_user. If you place an insert and update trigger on all tables that sets the values of these columns, you can use this information to query who performed each change on the system.

Listing 11.11 shows an update and insert trigger on the stores table that sets the values of the user who modified the table and the date and time the modification occurred. For this discussion, assume that you have altered the stores table to include these two new columns. Keep in mind that these columns must allow null values because they will not be included in an INSERT statement and because data already exists in this table. You can use the following T-SQL to add these two columns to the stores table:

```
ALTER TABLE stores
ADD modify_date DATETIME NULL
GO

ALTER TABLE stores
ADD modify_user VARCHAR(30) NULL
GO
```

LISTING 11.11   A SAMPLE TRIGGER ON THE stores TABLE THAT UPDATES THE
modify_date AND modify_user COLUMNS

```
CREATE TRIGGER trStores_InsUpd ON stores
FOR INSERT, UPDATE
AS

DECLARE @intRowCount int

SELECT @intRowCount = @@RowCount
IF @intRowCount > 0
    UPDATE stores
        SET modify_date = getdate(), modify_user = suser_name()
        WHERE stor_ID IN
        (
        SELECT stor_id FROM inserted
        )
GO
```

This trigger updates the `modify_date` and `modify_user` columns for all rows that have been affected by an `update` or an `insert` statement. Notice that this trigger handles all rows that are affected, as opposed to assuming that only one row was updated. This trigger also exits quietly if no rows were modified. You can execute the T-SQL from Listing 11.12 to test the newly created trigger's effects. This script will modify all California store names and roll back the changes. Then the script queries the before and after results to demonstrate the update trigger's effect.

LISTING 11.12 THIS SCRIPT TESTS THE TRIGGER CREATED FROM LISTING 11.11

```
BEGIN TRANSACTION

UPDATE stores
    SET stor_name = 'Test'
        WHERE state = 'CA'

SELECT * FROM stores

ROLLBACK TRANSACTION

SELECT * FROM stores
GO
```

> **NOTE**
>
> By selecting the data after the UPDATE statement and then again after the changes were rolled back, you can see how the `modify_date` and `modify_user` data changed. I could have queried the data before and after the update; however, I used a ROLLBACK here so that I wouldn't leave the data dirty.

Storing System Information in Custom Tables

Another way that triggers can store system information can help you determine what fields are most often modified. You can place an update trigger on a table that inserts a record into a storage table for every column that was affected by the original update. This information can then be used to analyze which users are most often changing which data. You can then adjust the permissions and/or the views accordingly.

For example, create a new table called `UpdateLog` as it appears in Listing 11.13. Then create an update trigger (also in Listing 11.13) on the `authors` table that inserts a record into the `UpdateLog` table for every column that was affected by the original UPDATE statement.

LISTING 11.13 THIS SCRIPT CREATES THE UpdateLog TABLE AND AN UPDATE TRIGGER ON
THE authors TABLE

```
CREATE TABLE UpdateLog
(
    table_name VARCHAR(30) NOT NULL,
    column_name VARCHAR(30) NOT NULL,
    updated_by VARCHAR(30) NOT NULL,
    updated_when DATETIME NOT NULL
)
GO

CREATE TRIGGER trAuthors_Upd ON Authors
FOR UPDATE
AS

DECLARE @intRowCount int

SELECT @intRowCount = @@RowCount
IF @intRowCount > 0
    BEGIN
        IF UPDATE(au_id)
            INSERT UpdateLog
                VALUES ('authors', 'au_id', suser_name(), getdate())

        IF UPDATE(au_lname)
            INSERT UpdateLog
                VALUES ('authors', 'au_lname', suser_name(), getdate())

        IF UPDATE(au_fname)
            INSERT UpdateLog
                VALUES ('authors', 'au_fname', suser_name(), getdate())

        IF UPDATE(phone)
            INSERT UpdateLog
                VALUES ('authors', 'phone', suser_name(), getdate())

        IF UPDATE(address)
            INSERT UpdateLog
                VALUES ('authors', 'address', suser_name(), getdate())

        IF UPDATE(city)
            INSERT UpdateLog
                VALUES ('authors', 'city', suser_name(), getdate())

        IF UPDATE(state)
            INSERT UpdateLog
                VALUES ('authors', 'state', suser_name(), getdate())
```

continues

LISTING 11.13 CONTINUED

```
    IF UPDATE(zip)
        INSERT UpdateLog
            VALUES ('authors', 'zip', suser_name(), getdate())

    IF UPDATE(contract)
        INSERT UpdateLog
            VALUES ('authors', 'contract', suser_name(), getdate())
    END

GO
```

This example uses the update() function to determine which columns were modified in the authors table. If the column's data was modified, the trigger inserts a record into the UpdateLog table. This information can then be used as a basis for designing views to data and permissions on data changes.

Referential Integrity with Triggers

A trigger can maintain referential integrity (RI) between two tables in much the same way a foreign key can. Foreign keys perform the same task more efficiently because they are tested before any data is changed, as opposed to triggers firing after the data changes. The primary benefit of triggers is that they can contain complex processing logic using T-SQL code. You can use the simple analogy of buying tickets to a movie to compare the relationship between foreign keys and triggers. If the movie is sold out, the ticket agent notifies you before you enter the theater. This scenario wastes no time, just like a foreign key. You are notified immediately if you will not be able to find a seat. However, imagine that the ticket agent sells you a ticket without checking whether the show is sold out. You buy your popcorn and search for a seat in the theater, but no seats are left. You then return to the ticket counter and get your refund. It's inefficient to make you buy snacks and your ticket without knowing whether you'll be able to find a seat.

After making such a strong argument for using foreign keys over triggers, I will justify why you would ever use triggers to enforce RI. Implementing triggers, in lieu of foreign keys, is vital to the success of cascading delete and update triggers. This will become evident later in this chapter when cascading triggers are discussed in detail.

Other types of RI can be enforced with triggers that foreign keys simply can't handle. A good example is a column that must contain a valid value from one of two other tables. Imagine that the authors table has a column that stores the account where the author electronically transfers his or her royalties. This account could be a bank account or a brokerage account; both accounts have different related information. Listing 11.14 helps you establish this new column in the authors table, create the new bank and brokerage tables, and fill them with some starter data.

LISTING 11.14   THIS SCRIPT ADDS THE account COLUMN TO THE authors TABLE AND CREATES THE NEW bank AND brokerage TABLES

```
ALTER TABLE authors
    ADD account VARCHAR(10) NULL
GO

CREATE TABLE bank
(
    account VARCHAR(10) NOT NULL PRIMARY KEY,
    name VARCHAR(50) NOT NULL
)
GO

CREATE TABLE brokerage
(
    account VARCHAR(10) NOT NULL PRIMARY KEY,
    name  VARCHAR(50) NOT NULL
)
GO

INSERT bank VALUES ('ABC', 'First Bank')
INSERT bank VALUES ('DEF', 'Second Bank')
INSERT bank VALUES ('XYZ', 'Third Bank')
GO

INSERT brokerage VALUES ('123', 'First Broker')
INSERT brokerage VALUES ('456', 'Second Broker')
INSERT brokerage VALUES ('987', 'Third Broker')
GO

sp_addmessage 56000, 10, 'Attempt to insert or update an invalid account.'
GO
```

You might have noticed that I threw in a custom message at the end of the script in Listing 11.14. (Messages are discussed in Chapter 7 under the section "The Basics of Messages"). You could have skipped this step and just printed a text message to the query window, but in an enterprise application, you want to raise an error in that case. You can raise an error by using this new custom message if the trigger finds that the RI has been violated.

Enforcing Complex RI with Triggers

Now that you have set up the basis of this discussion, you can see how a trigger enforces complex RI. Specifically, you will enforce the restriction that an account in the authors table must be a valid account from either the bank or brokerage table. To do this, place the trigger from Listing 11.15 on the authors table.

LISTING 11.15   THE trAuthors_InsUpd TRIGGER MAINTAINS A COMPLEX REFERENTIAL INTEGRITY RULE

```
CREATE TRIGGER trAuthors_InsUpd ON Authors
FOR UPDATE
AS

DECLARE @intRowCount int

SELECT @intRowCount = @@RowCount
IF @intRowCount > 0
    BEGIN
    IF (NOT EXISTS
            (
            SELECT account FROM bank WHERE account IN
                (SELECT account FROM inserted)
            UNION
            SELECT account FROM brokerage WHERE account IN
                (SELECT account FROM inserted)
            )
        )
            BEGIN
                RAISERROR(56000, 10, 1)
                ROLLBACK TRANSACTION
                RETURN
            END
    END
GO
```

Like the other triggers in this chapter, trAuthors_InsUpd exits immediately if no rows were affected. Then using a UNION query, the trigger checks whether all accounts in the inserted table are in the bank or brokerage tables (unions are discussed in Chapter 2, "Beyond the Basics of Data Manipulation Language"). If any account that was inserted or modified does not exist in the bank or the brokerage table, an error is raised and the transaction is undone. You can test this by executing the T-SQL script in Listing 11.16.

LISTING 11.16   TWO TEST SCRIPTS: THE FIRST SCRIPT VIOLATES THE RI AND THE SECOND
SCRIPT PASSES THE RI CHECK

```
-------------------------------------
--- This batch violates the RI.
-------------------------------------
BEGIN TRANSACTION

PRINT '---------------------'
PRINT 'BEGIN FIRST TRANSACTION'
PRINT ''
PRINT 'Updating the accounts to "xyz123"...'
PRINT ''
UPDATE authors SET account = 'xyz123'
PRINT 'Finished.'

COMMIT TRANSACTION
GO


-----------------------------------------
--- This batch passes the RI.
-----------------------------------------
BEGIN TRANSACTION

PRINT ''
PRINT ''
PRINT '-----------------------'
PRINT 'BEGIN SECOND TRANSACTION'
PRINT ''
PRINT 'Updating the accounts to "123"...'
PRINT ''
UPDATE authors SET account = '123'
PRINT 'Finished.'

COMMIT TRANSACTION
GO
```

Cascade Delete Triggers

As promised in the previous section, I'll now discuss the role triggers play in cascading
deletes and updates. Triggers can reciprocate deletions from one table through the related
tables' records in the database. You'll use the stores table for the example and concentrate on its relationships with the discounts and sales tables. For instance, a delete trigger on the stor_id column of the stores table causes a corresponding deletion of
matching rows in the tables discounts and sales. The trigger uses the stor_id column
as a unique key to locate and purge matching rows in the related tables.

Before you begin, you must drop the foreign keys on the discounts and sales tables that reference the stores table. You can either drop the foreign keys through the SQL Server Enterprise Manager's Manage Tables window or execute an alter table script. To drop foreign keys, you must first know the names of the constraints. If you did not name the foreign keys when you created them, SQL Server has given them unique names for you. To avoid figuring out which foreign keys to drop and what their names are, create and use the prDropForeignKeys stored procedure as shown in Listing 11.17. Simply pass the name of the table that you want all references dropped from, and the stored procedure does the dirty work.

LISTING 11.17 THE prDropForeignKeys STORED PROCEDURE DROPS THE FOREIGN KEYS THAT REFERENCE A GIVEN TABLE

```
CREATE PROCEDURE prDropForeignKeys
    @chvReferencedTable VARCHAR(30)
AS

DECLARE @chvTableWithForeignKey VARCHAR(30),
        @chvForeignKey VARCHAR(30),
        @chvSQL VARCHAR(255)

DECLARE cuFKs CURSOR
    FOR
    SELECT tb.name,
           fk.name
    FROM ((sysobjects tb INNER JOIN sysreferences r ON tb.id = r.fkeyid)
        INNER JOIN sysobjects fk ON r.constid = fk.id)
        INNER JOIN sysobjects refd_tb ON refd_tb.id = r.rkeyid
    WHERE refd_tb.name = @chvReferencedTable

OPEN cuFKs

FETCH NEXT FROM cuFKs INTO
    @chvTableWithForeignKey, @chvForeignKey

WHILE (@@fetch_status <> -1)
    BEGIN
        SELECT @chvSQL = 'ALTER TABLE ' + @chvTableWithForeignKey
                        + ' DROP CONSTRAINT ' + @chvForeignKey

        EXEC (@chvSQL)

        FETCH NEXT FROM cuFKs INTO
            @chvTableWithForeignKey, @chvForeignKey
    END

DEALLOCATE cuFKs
GO
```

Execute the stored procedure prDropForeignKeys, passing it the stores table as its argument. After you have dropped the DRI enforced by the foreign keys on the stores table, you can test a cascading delete trigger on the stores table. Listing 11.18 shows how the trigger trStores_Del cascades its deletions.

LISTING 11.18 AFTER ITS DATA HAS BEEN DELETED, THE TRIGGER trStores_Del DELETES CORRESPONDING ROWS FROM THE sales AND discounts TABLES

```
CREATE TRIGGER trStores_Del ON stores
FOR DELETE
AS

DECLARE @intRowCount int

SELECT @intRowCount = @@RowCount
IF @intRowCount > 0
    BEGIN
        DELETE sales
            WHERE stor_id IN
                (SELECT stor_id FROM deleted)

        DELETE discounts
            WHERE stor_id IN
                (SELECT stor_id FROM deleted)
END
GO
```

This trigger removes all sales and discounts for the stores that were deleted. You can test this trigger by executing the T-SQL script in Listing 11.19.

LISTING 11.19 THIS SCRIPT DEMONSTRATES THE CASCADING EFFECTS OF THE trStores_Del TRIGGER FROM LISTING 11.18

```
BEGIN TRANSACTION

DELETE stores WHERE stor_id = '8042'

SELECT COUNT(*) StoresAfterDelete FROM stores WHERE stor_id = '8042'
SELECT COUNT(*) SalesAfterDelete FROM sales WHERE stor_id = '8042'
SELECT COUNT(*) DiscountsAfterDelete FROM discounts WHERE stor_id = '8042'

ROLLBACK TRANSACTION

SELECT COUNT(*) StoresBeforeDelete FROM stores WHERE stor_id = '8042'
SELECT COUNT(*) SalesBeforeDelete FROM sales WHERE stor_id = '8042'
SELECT COUNT(*) DiscountsBeforeDelete FROM discounts WHERE stor_id =
'8042'
GO
```

Cascade Update Triggers

Cascading updates throughout related tables offer even more flexibility than cascading deletes do. You'll walk through two examples that unleash the power behind cascading updates. One example shows how you can update the value of the stor_id column in the stores table and have its related table references modified to reflect the change. The second example demonstrates how you can maintain derived data through a cascading update trigger. Both examples require that the foreign keys be removed from the stores table. (You can use the prDropForeignKeys stored procedure from Listing 11.17 to do this.)

> **WARNING**
>
> Because cascading deletes and updates require you to drop foreign key constraints on the respective tables, you must put logic in the triggers to enforce the referential integrity that was previously implemented by the foreign keys. For example, after dropping the foreign keys in the discounts and sales tables that reference the stores table, you must create triggers on all those tables to enforce the lost RI. Otherwise, you could change a stor_id in the sales table to an invalid value.

After dropping the foreign keys that referenced the stores table, create the trigger trStores_Upd as shown in Listing 11.20. This trigger updates the sales and discounts tables after its unique key (stor_id) has been updated.

LISTING 11.20 THE TRIGGER trStores_Upd UPDATES CORRESPONDING ROWS FROM THE sales AND discounts TABLES

```
CREATE TRIGGER trStores_Upd ON stores
FOR UPDATE
AS

DECLARE @intRowCount int

SELECT @intRowCount = @@RowCount
IF @intRowCount > 1
    BEGIN
        IF UPDATE(stor_id)
            ROLLBACK TRANSACTION
    END
ELSE
```

```
IF @intRowCount = 1
    BEGIN
        IF UPDATE(stor_id)
            BEGIN
                UPDATE sales
                    SET sales.stor_id = (SELECT stor_id FROM inserted)
                    FROM sales INNER JOIN deleted
                    ON sales.stor_id = deleted.stor_id
                UPDATE discounts
                    SET discounts.stor_id =
                        (SELECT stor_id FROM inserted)
                    FROM discounts INNER JOIN deleted
                    ON discounts.stor_id = deleted.stor_id
            END
    END
GO
```

WARNING

Notice that the trigger in Listing 11.20 handles only cases in which just one row
was updated. When you are cascading updates to primary keys, it is wise to
restrict the updates to affect one value at a time.

You can test this trigger by executing a T-SQL UPDATE statement that changes the value
of data in the stor_id column of the stores table.

Maintaining Derived Data

The second example of using cascading update triggers manages derived data. For example, assume that the title field exists in the sales table, denormalizing the data slightly.
This speeds up reporting for the sales department because it always requires the title to
be displayed on all its sales reports. This way, the sales reports do not have to hit both
the sales table and the titles table on each report. Add the column titles to the sales
table using the following script:

```
ALTER TABLE sales
ADD title VARCHAR(80) NULL
GO
```

Now create the trigger trTitles_Upd as shown in Listing 11.21. This trigger looks for
any changes to the name of any titles. If there are any changes, it copies them to the
sales table.

LISTING 11.21   THE trTitles_Upd TRIGGER COPIES ANY CHANGES IN THE titles.title COLUMN TO THE CORRESPONDING sales.title COLUMN

```
CREATE TRIGGER trTitles_Upd ON titles
FOR UPDATE
AS

DECLARE @intRowCount int

SELECT @intRowCount = @@RowCount
IF @intRowCount > 0
    BEGIN
        IF UPDATE(title)
            BEGIN
                UPDATE sales SET sales.title = inserted.title
                    FROM inserted INNER JOIN sales
                    ON inserted.title_id = sales.title_id
            END
    END
GO
```

Now your sales department can write a query selecting data from only the sales table. You can test this new trigger by using the following T-SQL script:

```
BEGIN TRANSACTION

SELECT title FROM titles  WHERE title_id = 'BU1111'
SELECT title FROM sales WHERE title_id = 'BU1111'

UPDATE titles
    SET title = 'My Title'
    WHERE title_id = 'BU1111'

SELECT title FROM titles  WHERE title_id = 'BU1111'
SELECT title FROM sales WHERE title_id = 'BU1111'

ROLLBACK TRANSACTION
GO
```

Summary

Triggers are powerful tools when used to support enterprise business solutions. I've shown how the `inserted` table, the `deleted` table, and the `update()` function can help enhance business applications. You've learned that triggers are an excellent means to enforce business rules and can audit transactions and archive system information with little effort. You've also seen that you can create multiple triggers on the same table to isolate code functionality. Also, using information gathered by triggers, you've seen how to improve database performance and determine which indexing schemes to implement. Triggers can even maintain complex RI where foreign keys just can't cut it. The introduction of recursion to triggers in SQL Server 7 gives you new power to control whether you want the triggers to call themselves. All these features, including real-time updates, are reasons that triggers are an integral part of any enterprise SQL Server application. Triggers can make your application soar.

CHAPTER 12

Updating Table Indexes and Statistics

Two often-overlooked aspects of database design are performance and tuning. Too often, developers—and sometimes database administrators (DBAs)—run out of time on tight schedules, and optimization of the database is the casualty. SQL Server has several built-in statements for optimizing and retrieving statistical information from a database. This chapter gives you guidelines on how to implement these statements, with useful utilities for improving performance on your server.

We begin by demonstrating two indexing techniques to improve database performance. These techniques show how planning index and table design, along with creating and indexing a manufactured column, improves the query time. Then we will move into a discussion of UPDATE STATISTICS, which optimizes indexes after data has been added. Finally, look at the DBCC statements that supply performance statistics on SQL Server.

Index Performance and Fine-Tuning

All too often, very little analysis is given to implementing useful indexes. If built correctly, indexes can give your application the "adrenaline boost" it needs. Let's begin by looking at the components of indexing. The first component is the actual design of the table and related indexes. Typically, for a data warehouse, you create many indexes for the stored data to ensure fast retrieval by your Decision Support Systems (DSS). In an Online Transaction Processing (OLTP) Database, having too many indexes is detrimental to performance because you're not only writing the data to the record, but also updating each of the clustered and nonclustered indexes. In the design phase, especially for real-time transaction processing, there are two methods for improving speed drastically.

Designing Indexes for Speed

The first method applies to tables in which multiple columns make the primary *unique* key, also known as the *composite* key. In lieu of creating a composite key on a table, you can create a new column that contains the data values for the columns that define the composite key. You can create a VARCHAR column with a length that's the sum of the lengths of the composite key. Then, store the composite key values in this new column, making it a single-column primary key. If you index this new column, it makes your table update much faster. For instance, if you have four fields that make up the primary key, you not only have to update four separate indexes, but as a record is added, all four indexes must be scanned for the combination you're attempting to write to a record. But because you've combined the four fields into a single column, only one index needs to be searched when you update or query a record. The extra hard drive space required to store the new column is somewhat, but not totally, offset by the space saved by creating a simpler indexing scheme. Remember, indexes are allocated hard drive space, too.

> **TIP**
>
> If you create a column to hold the concatenation of multiple fields, you run the risk of throwing your data out of synch. One way to prevent this from occurring is to place an update trigger on the table that updates the new column with the changes to the individual columns.

The second method allows for faster queries against data for real-time processing. Although creating multiple indexes decreases performance when you're adding records, having multiple indexes *increases* performance when you're running queries against the data. One solution to this difference in performance is to not create the additional indexes in the table, but instead create the indexes, run the query, and then drop the indexes. This technique will probably slow down queries against tables with few records, but tables with a high volume of records will show a significant improvement.

Distribution Pages and Storing Data with Stepping

Distribution pages are the second component in optimizing tables and indexes. SQL Server internally searches indexes for matches when running queries. It then creates a distribution page for each index it finds. So what does a distribution page store?

- Sample data values from the first indexed column in steps.
- The index density, which is the average number of duplicate rows in the index.

What is *stepping*? Imagine you have a statistical grouping of sequential data, and the information for every x number of records is bookmarked for reference. This concept is similar to how distribution pages work. The x number of records translates into the number of steps, and the grouping of data refers to the indexed data being queried.

So how does it work? A page can hold 8KB, with an overhead of a 32-byte header. This leaves 8,160 bytes available for the distribution page. Here's the formula to arrive at the number of steps for an index follows. For variable column indexes, the column width would be the maximum column widths.

```
(8160 - 2 - (number of key columns × 2 bytes))/(column width + 2)
```

Here's how to compute the number of steps for a CHAR(10) column:

```
(8160 · 2 · (1×2)/(10+2)
= 8156/12
= 676 steps.
```

If you have one million records with a step value of 676, a sample would be stored every 1,479 rows:

```
(1,000,000 rows / 676 steps = 1,479 rows/step)
```

> **NOTE**
>
> The more you increase the maximum column width, the lower the step number becomes. This creates more room for samples to be stored. So to reduce the indexing search time, you can increase the number of samples. This sounds strange, but it makes sense because when you index character columns, the first several characters will most likely be identical.

If you were searching for the product ID PSL123456, and SQL Server discovered PSL123444 at step 100 and PSL123466 at step 105, you would search five steps to locate the match in the index. As in the preceding example, if you had 1,479 rows/step × five steps, you would search a total of 7,395 rows—much faster than searching all one million records. In fact, a similar approach is commonly used in the C programming language for searching indexes of a table.

Using Index Densities Instead of Step Values

Although the step method can extract data for a simple search on a single column, other types of queries do not benefit from steps. Complex joins, advanced Data Manipulation Lanuguage (DML) with totals, composite indexes, and queries with calculations are among those queries that do not take full advantage of steps. In these cases, *index densities* are used in place of steps to narrow down the rows to search for matching criteria. Here is the formula for index densities:

```
Index density = 1/number unique values
```

Therefore, if you have one million records with 10,000 unique values, this would be the index density:

```
1/10,000 = .0001
```

The number of rows to search for a match would be as follows:

```
1,000,000 × .0001 = 100 rows
```

However, if the index consists of multiple columns, densities are stored for each of the combinations in column order. If you had columns called Product ID, Store ID, and Sales Associate ID, you would have a density for the following:

Product ID

Product ID and Store ID combined

Product ID, Store ID, and Sales Associate ID combined

The greater the number of columns, the lower the index density and the fewer rows that need to be searched. The fastest query generates searches on all three columns for the preceding case. Refer to the section "Using DBCC Statements to Monitor Your Database" for details on how to retrieve the steps and density for each index on a table.

Updating the Distribution Page

The distribution page is not updated every time a record is added. In a high-volume database, this would cause a huge performance loss. Therefore, when you initially create a table with no data, the distribution page remains empty. It's updated only when the following happens:

- You create an index on a table with existing data.
- You run the UPDATE STATISTICS statement.

From a systems administration point of view, you should create a utility to automatically update the distribution page at least once per week, or even daily if the data volume increases more than 10% per day. Fortunately, this utility is explained in the next section.

Creating a Utility to Optimize Table Indexes

Because it's unlikely that indexes will be added daily, you need to use the UPDATE STATISTICS statement to update the distribution page in order to optimize SQL Server. This is the syntax for the UPDATE STATISTICS statement:

```
UPDATE STATISTICS tablename [,index_name]
```

The *tablename* is the name of the table to optimize. If only the name of the table is specified, the distribution page for all indexes is updated. Optionally, if you specify the *index_name*, only the distribution page for that index is updated. Listing 12.1 is a utility for optimizing all indexes for all tables within the database.

LISTING 12.1   OPTIMIZING TABLES WITH UPDATE STATISTICS

```
DROP PROCEDURE pr_updateindex
GO
CREATE PROCEDURE pr_updateindex
     AS
SET NOCOUNT ON
DECLARE getindex_curs CURSOR
     FOR
          SELECT name   -- Table Name
          FROM sysobjects -- System Table
          WHERE type = 'U' -- User tables

-- hold name of table retrieved from sysobjects
DECLARE @holdtable varchar(30)
DECLARE @message varchar(40) -- Used to Display UPDATING message
-- Used to dynamically execute UPDATE STATISTICS statement
DECLARE @dynamic varchar(51)

OPEN getindex_curs
FETCH NEXT FROM getindex_curs into @holdtable
-- Test sysobjects database for user tables
WHILE @@FETCH_STATUS = 0 BEGIN
       SELECT @dynamic = "UPDATE STATISTICS " + @holdtable
       SELECT @message = "Updating " + @holdtable
       EXEC (@dynamic )
PRINT @message

       FETCH NEXT FROM getindex_curs into @holdtable
END
CLOSE getindex_curs
```

This stored procedure uses the UPDATE STATISTICS command to dynamically update the distribution page for all indexes on all user tables for the current database. The getindex_curs cursor retrieves each user table stored in the @holdtable variable, when type has a value of 'U'. A message is displayed with the word Updating concatenated with the name of the table. The UPDATE STATISTICS command, with the table name concatenated, is stored in the @dynamic variable. This variable is then executed to optimize all the indexes for the current table. The cursor is closed after all tables have been optimized. Type the following to execute this stored procedure:

```
EXEC pr_updateindex
```

Depending on the number of tables in the current database, your output will look similar to the following. These are the results from the pubs database:

```
Updating authors
Updating publishers
Updating titles
Updating titleauthor
Updating stores
Updating sales
Updating roysched
Updating discounts
Updating jobs
Updating pub_info
Updating employee
```

> **TIP**
>
> It's always a good idea to search for corrupted tables with the DBCC (Database Consistency Checker) statements CHECKDB or CHECKTABLE before attempting this operation, and it's best to do it when everyone is off the system.

Verifying When the Last Optimization Took Place

If you have never optimized the indexes of a table before, or want to see when the indexes of a table were last optimized, you can do that with the DBCC SHOW_STATISTICS statement. The sysindexes table stores the location of the distribution page. The format for the DBCC SHOW_STATISTICS statement is this:

```
DBCC SHOW STATISTICS (tablename, index_name)
```

The *tablename* parameter is the name of the table, and the *index_name* is the index you want. The following example uses tables and indexes created in Chapter 2, "Beyond the Basics of Data Manipulation Language":

```
DBCC SHOW_STATISTICS (salesne, sne)
```

Your output should be similar to this:

```
Updated               Rows        Steps        Density
------------------- ----------- ----------- -------------------
Dec 22 1997 11:26PM  13          12           0.0414201

(1 row(s) affected)
```

```
All density              Columns
-----------------------  -------------------------------
0.112426                 CDID
0.0887574                CDID, StoreID
0.0769231                CDID, StoreID, SalesDate

(3 row(s) affected)

Steps
-----------
       2005
       2006
       2007
       2007
       2008
       2008
       2009
       2009
       2010
       2018
       2020
       2022

(12 row(s) affected)

DBCC execution completed. If DBCC printed error messages,
see your System Administrator.
```

As you can see from the output, this distribution page holds a total of 12 steps, in which the data elements are also listed. Also notice that for each of the columns in the index, the index density changes as more columns are added.

Running Tasks Automatically

Now that you have the utility you can use to update the statistics in a database, you are probably trying to figure out how you are going to run these without having to think about it. In other words, how can you run these, and any other tasks, without having to remember to run them. There are two ways to execute tasks automatically, one when SQL Server first starts and one at scheduled times during the day.

Automatically Executing Stored Procedures

An automatically executing stored procedure is one that executes when SQL Server is started. These procedures are started after all of the databases on the server have been recovered, so you don't have to worry about attempting to run a procedure against a database that is inaccessible. These stored procedures, called autoprocs, can be used to alert the systems administrator that the server has been restarted, send out an email alerting the users that the server is accessible, and perform database maintenance tasks. To configure a stored procedure as an autoproc, you will use the sp_procoption system stored procedure. For example, if you wanted to configure the stored procedure that we created earlier in this chapter to run whenever the server is started, you would run the following in the SQL Server Query:

```
Analyzer:sp_procoption pr_UpdateIndex, startup, on
```

This will cause the pr_UpdateIndex stored procedure to run every time that the server is started.

12

UPDATING TABLE
INDEXES AND
STATISTICS

> **NOTE**
>
> You need to set the option: scan for startup procs to 1 (or on) using the system stored procedure sp_configure with the show advanced options option set to 1, if you want to automatically run stored procedures. Marking the first stored procedure as an autoproc with sp_procoption, sets this option to 1. On the other hand, when you use sp_procoption to un-mark the last stored procedure for autorun, this option is set to 0.

Scheduling Tasks

Through the SQL Server Agent, SQL Server provides the ability to schedule tasks to occur at any time. This is a very powerful feature of SQL Server that can be used to create very powerful lines of business applications. In this section, we will cover the creation of a T-SQL task that will update statistics on a database. For more information on the SQL Server Agent, see Chapter 29, "Scheduling Jobs and Using ActiveX Servers to Implement Business Solutions."

As we saw when we looked at updating statistics on a database, running the UPDATE STATISTICS command on large tables can be very processor and I/O intensive. In other words, this is something that you do not want to perform during production hours. This puts us in a real dilemma, because who wants to be onsite to run these commands at off hours? That is where the SQL Server Agent comes in handy. The following will walk you through setting up a task to perform this.

1. Open up SQL Server Enterprise Manager and connect to the server that you are going to set up the task on. Open the Management folder, then the SQL Server Agent folder and then click on the Tasks option. This will open up the screen shown in Figure 12.1.

Figure 12.1

The Tasks folder.

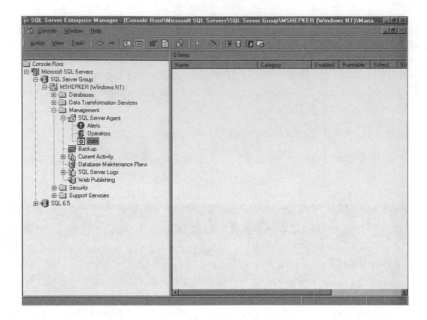

2. Right-click in the right hand pane and click on the New Job... option. This will bring up the New Job Properties window, as seen in Figure 12.2.

Figure 12.2

The New Job properties dialog General tab.

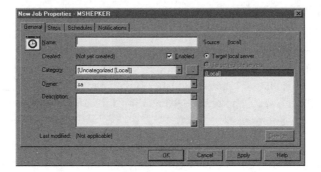

3. In the Name box, fill in the name that you want to call this task. In this case, use Update Statistics pubs. In the Category option, you can categorize this task by choosing one of the existing categories, or you can create your own. In this case, you can select the Database Maintenance option. Optionally, you can fill in a Description for this task. Once you have filled in these options, click on the Steps tab, as seen in Figure 12.3.

FIGURE 12.3

The New Job Properties dialog Steps tab.

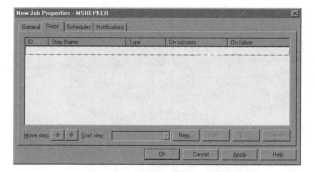

4. In the Steps tab, click on the New... button. This will open the New Job Step dialog, as seen in Figure 12.4.

FIGURE 12.4

The New Job Step *dialog General tab.*

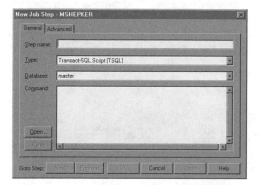

5. On the General tab, you will create the actual step that will update the statistics on the pubs database. In the Step name, fill in the name of this step. In this case, put Update Statistics. In the Type box, choose the type of step that this will be. Since you are running a stored procedure, choose Transact-SQL Script. In the database name section, you will choose the database, in this case pubs. In the command section, you will type the command that should be run. For this exercise, type in the following:

```
EXEC pr_updateindex
```

6. On the Advanced tab of the New Job Step dialog, as seen in Figure 12.5, you can specify options of how the SQL Server Agent will handle the successful execution or failure of this step. For this case, change the On success action to Quit the job reporting success. After you have completed this, press the OK button. If you have more that one step, simply create as many as you need.

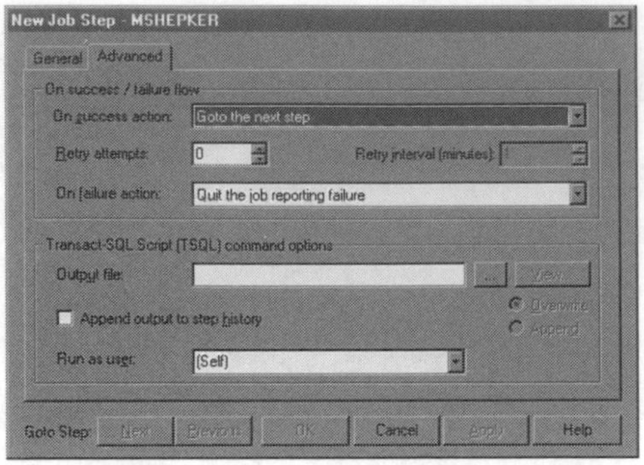

FIGURE 12.5

The New Job Step dialog Advanced tab.

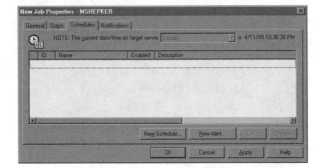

7. On the Schedules Tab, as seen in Figure 12.6, select the New Schedule... button.

FIGURE 12.6

The New Job Properties dialog Schedules tab.

8. The New Job Schedule Dialog will open, as seen in Figure 12.7, presenting you with several options for running this task. Most often, you will simply schedule the task to run at certain times during the day. Since you will want this task to run more than one time, you will select the Recurring option and then select the Change... button.

FIGURE 12.7

The New Job Schedule dialog.

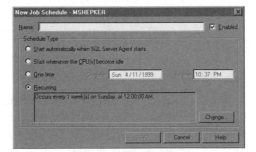

9. In the Edit Recurring Job Schedule dialog, as seen in Figure 12.8, you can choose how frequently the job will run. Since you will want to run this task during off-hours, you should choose a time late at night, when users are not logged in. After you have selected the time that you want to run this task and then press the OK button. At the New Job Schedule dialog, select the OK button again.

FIGURE 12.8
The Edit Recurring Job Schedule Dialog.

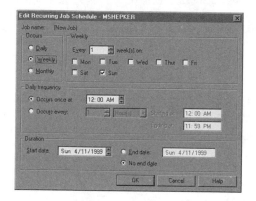

10. The last tab of the New Job Properties dialog, as seen in Figure 12.9, the Notifications tab, you can select how you want to be notified when the task has completed.

FIGURE 12.9
The New Job Properties Dialog Notifications Tab.

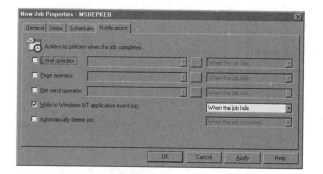

Using DBCC Statements to Monitor Your Database

The Database Consistency Checker, or DBCC, was originally intended to simply check the database's consistency. Over time, Microsoft has added many useful features to DBCC that can be used when troubleshooting SQL Server problems.

> **WARNING**
>
> DBCC is the most useful and powerful tool when trying to isolate and repair problems you're having with your databases. Aside from the supported DBCC commands, there are many others that are undocumented and unsupported by Microsoft. If you come across any of them, it's best to use them with caution and only after contacting your primary support provider. When repairing an error, some of the commands could cause more problems to your database because of other underlying problems.

With the release of SQL Server 7.0, Microsoft has added two new DBCC commands: CHECKFILEGROUP and SHRINKFILE. The SHRINKDB command has been revamped and renamed to SHRINKDATABASE. The following sections list the supported DBCC commands and their syntax.

CHECKALLOC

The CHECKALLOC command is used to check the allocation and usage of all pages in a specified database. CHECKALLOC acquires a schema lock on database objects before running to prevent changes to the schema of the database. There's no need to run CHECKALLOC if you're currently running CHECKDB. CHECKALLOC has replaced the NEWALLOC command. The syntax of the CHECKALLOC command is as follows:

```
DBCC CHECKALLOC ( 'database_name'
[, NOINDEX¦ { REPAIR_ALLOW_DATA_LOSS ¦ REPAIR_FAST ¦ REPAIR_REBUILD}]
) [WITH {ALL_ERRORMSGS ¦ NO_INFOMSGS}]
```

Where the options are:

Option	Description
NOINDEX	This option specifies that the nonclustered indexes on all nonsystem tables should not be checked. This option is provided for backward compatibility only.
REPAIR_ALLOW_DATA_LOSS	This option performs all of the same functions that the REPAIR_REBUILD option does except that it also will deallocate and reallocate all rows and pages that are causing errors and deletes any misallocated text objects. These actions can possibly cause some data loss. It is possible to perform these actions inside of a

	transaction which will allow the changes to be rolled back in the event that actual data loss occurs. The database must be in single user mode to run this command.
REPAIR_FAST	The REPAIR_FAST option causes SQL Server to perform simple repairs that can be performed quickly without risking data loss. The database must be insingle usermode to run this command.
REPAIR_REBUILD	This option performs all of the same checks that the REPAIR_FAST option but will also rebuild the indexes on the tables. The database must be in single user mode to run this command.
ALL_ERRORMSGS	This option specifies that SQL Server should return all error messages to the front end. SQL Server can return up to 200 errors per database object.
NO_INFOMSGS	This option specifies that SQL Server should suppress all informational messages and return only return true errors.

The most common error—2540—is returned by running CHECKALLOC in an active database. If you don't suspect problems in your database and you get this error from a CHECKALLOC command, it is most likely nothing to worry about.

CHECKCATALOG

The CHECKCATALOG function checks for consistency in the system tables. The system tables don't have foreign keys, so it's up to SQL Server to keep track of their consistency. It's rare to find problems with the system tables, but if it happens, the results can be catastrophic. The syntax of the CHECKCATALOG command is as follows:

```
DBCC CHECKCATALOG [(database_name)][ WITH NO_INFOMSGS]
```

> **NOTE**
>
> The DBCC CHECKCATALOG command should be run frequently to check the consistency of the system tables or system catalog.

12

UPDATING TABLE
INDEXES AND
STATISTICS

CHECKDB

If you have the time to run only one DBCC on your database, you should consider running CHECKDB, that performs a comprehensive check of all tables in the database for the following:

- Makes sure all data pages are properly linked. Data pages in SQL Server are in a double-linked list, meaning that page 1 in the list points to page 2 in the list, and page 2 points back to page 1.
- Makes sure all index pages are properly linked.
- Checks to make sure all indexes are in the correct sort order.
- Makes sure the row offsets are reasonable. The row offset specifies where on a data page the row resides.
- Makes sure that the data on each data page is readable and in logical form.

The syntax of the CHECKDB command is as follows:

```
DBCC CHECKDB ( 'database_name'
[, NOINDEX ¦ { REPAIR_ALLOW_DATA_LOSS ¦ REPAIR_FAST¦ REPAIR_REBUILD}])
[WITH {ALL_ERRORMSGS ¦ NO_INFOMSGS}]
```

Option	Description
NOINDEX	This option specifies that the nonclustered indexes on all nonsystem tables should not be checked. This option is will decrease the overall speed of execution of the command.
REPAIR_ALLOW_DATA_LOSS	This option performs all of the same functions that the REPAIR_REBUILD option does except that it also will deallocate and reallocate all rows and pages that are causing errors and deletes any misallocated text objects. These actions can possibly cause some data loss. It is possible to perform these actions inside of a transaction which will allow the changes to be rolled back in the event that actual data loss occurs. The database must be in single user mode to run this command.
REPAIR_FAST	The REPAIR_FAST option causes SQL Server to perform simple repairs that can be performed quickly without risking data loss. The database must be in single user mode to run this command.

REPAIR_REBUILD	This option performs all of the same checks that the REPAIR_FAST option but will also rebuild the indexes on the tables. The database must be in single user mode to run this command.
ALL_ERRORMSGS	This option specifies that SQL Server should return all error messages to the front end. SQL Server can return up to 200 errors per database object.
NO_INFOMSGS	This option specifies that SQL Server should suppress all informational messages and return only return true errors.

NOT ENOUGH TIME?

If you can run only one DBCC on your databases, you should run DBCC CHECKDB.

The normal output of a CHECKDB command run on the pubs database looks something like the following:

```
DBCC results for 'pubs'.
DBCC results for 'sysobjects'.
There are 93 rows in 1 pages for object 'sysobjects'.
DBCC results for 'sysindexes'.
There are 49 rows in 2 pages for object 'sysindexes'.
DBCC results for 'syscolumns'.
There are 477 rows in 7 pages for object 'syscolumns'.
    .
    .
    .
DBCC results for 'pub_info'.
There are 8 rows in 1 pages for object 'pub_info'.
DBCC results for 'employee'.
There are 43 rows in 1 pages for object 'employee'.
CHECKDB found 0 allocation errors and 0 consistency errors
➥in database 'pubs'.
DBCC execution completed. If DBCC printed error messages,
➥contact your system administrator.
```

12

UPDATING TABLE
INDEXES AND
STATISTICS

On large databases, the output of CHECKDB can be quite long if you don't specify the WITH NO_INFOMSGS option. In this case, the easiest way to look for errors is to choose Edit, Find and type **Msg** in the Find box after CHECKDB has finished running. If it comes back without finding anything, your database is clean. If not, you need to start investigating what the message is telling you.

CHECKFILEGROUP

The CHECKFILEGROUP command, new to SQL Server 7.0, enables you to check the structural integrity and allocation of all tables in a specified file group. CHECKFILEGROUP essentially performs all the checks that were performed by CHECKDB, CHECKALLOC, and TEXTALL on every table contained in a file group. The output of this command is very similar to that of the CHECKDB command. The syntax of the CHECKFILEGROUP command is as follows:

```
DBBC CHECKFILEGROUP [( [ {'filegroup_name'¦filegroup_id} ]
[, NOINDEX] ) ] [WITH NO_INFOMSGS]
```

> **NOTE**
>
> Running DBCC CHECKFILEGROUP on all of the file groups in a database attains similar results to running DBCC CHECKDB on the database.

CHECKIDENT

The CHECKIDENT command is used to check the current value of the identity column on a table and correct it, if needed. By specifying the NORESEED option, SQL Server compares the current value of the identity column and what that value should be. If you specify the RESEED option, SQL Server corrects the value of the identity column. The syntax of the CHECKIDENT command is as follows:

```
DBCC CHECKIDENT ('table_name'[, {NORESEED ¦ {RESEED
[, new_reseed_value]}}])
```

CHECKTABLE

The CHECKTABLE command performs the same functions as the CHECKDB command, but only to an individual specified table. This command is useful when you suspect problems with a single table and don't have the time needed to run a CHECKDB. The syntax of the CHECKTABLE command is as follows:

```
DBCC CHECKTABLE ( 'table_name' [, NOINDEX ¦ index_id ¦
{ REPAIR_ALLOW_DATA_LOSS ¦ REPAIR_FAST¦ REPAIR_REBUILD}]
) [WITH {ALL_ERRORMSGS ¦ NO_INFOMSGS}]
```

Option	Description
NOINDEX	This option specifies that the nonclustered indexes on all nonsystem tables should not be checked. This option is will decrease the overall speed of execution of the command.
REPAIR_ALLOW_DATA_LOSS	This option performs all of the same functions that the REPAIR_REBUILD option does except that it also will deallocate and reallocate all rows and pages that are causing errors and deletes any misallocated text objects. These actions can possibly cause some data loss. It is possible to perform these actions inside of a transaction which will allow the changes to be rolled back in the event that actual data loss occurs. The database must be in single user mode to run this command.
REPAIR_FAST	The REPAIR_FAST option causes SQL Server to perform simple repairs that can be performed quickly without risking data loss. The database must be in single user mode to run this command.
REPAIR_REBUILD	This option performs all of the same checks that the REPAIR_FAST option but will also rebuild the indexes on the tables. The database must be in single user mode to run this command.
ALL_ERRORMSGS	This option specifies that SQL Server should return all error messages to the front end. SQL Server can return up to 200 errors per database object.
NO_INFOMSGS	This option specifies that SQL Server should suppress all informational messages and return only return true errors.

If you want to check an index for corruption, you can supply the index ID of that index. To get the index ID, run the query in Listing 12.2. Replace dbname with the name of the database the table resides in and replace indname with the name of the index you want to investigate.

LISTING 12.2 THIS SQL QUERY ENABLES YOU TO GET THE INDEX ID FOR USE IN THE CHECKTABLE COMMAND

```
1 use dbname
2 go
3 select indid from sysindexes where name = 'indname'
4 go
```

DBREPAIR

The DBREPAIR command is used to drop a damaged or suspect database. It was used in earlier versions of SQL Server and has been provided for backward compatibility only. When running the DBREPAIR command, no one can be using the database that will be dropped. The syntax of the DBREPAIR command is as follows:

```
DBCC DBREPAIR ( database_name, DROPDB [, NOINIT] )
```

DBREINDEX

The DBREINDEX command rebuilds either one or all of the indexes in a specified table. There are two major advances with using the DBREINDEX command instead of manually dropping and re-creating the indexes. The first is that indexes that enforce PRIMARY KEY or UNIQUE constraints can be re-created without dropping and re-creating the constraints. The second is that the indexes can be re-created without having to know anything about the structure of the table. This is the syntax of the DBREINDEX command:

```
DBCC DBREINDEX ([table_name [, index_name [, fillfactor
➥   [, {SORTED_DATA ¦ SORTED_DATA_REORG}]]]]) [WITH NOINFOMSGS]
```

You must specify the table name for this command to work. If you only want to rebuild a single index in a table, you can specify it. To rebuild all indexes, you can specify ' '.

dllname (FREE)

The dllname (FREE) command is used to remove a dynamic linked library from SQL Server memory. Extended stored procedures use DLLs to provide functionality that would otherwise be unavailable. When an extended stored procedure is executed, the DLL is loaded into memory and remains in memory until SQL Server is shut down. With the dllname (FREE) command, you can remove a DLL from memory without shutting down SQL Server. The syntax of the command is as follows:

```
DBCC dllname (FREE)
```

INPUTBUFFER

The INPUTBUFFER command is used to display the first 255 characters of the last command that was sent to the server by a client. The command requires that you know the SPID (System Process ID) of the user you are investigating. The syntax of the command is as follows:

> ### GETTING A USER'S SPID
>
> You can get the SPID by running the sp_who stored procedure. The results of the command will return a list of users, their SPIDs, and other associated information.

```
DBCC INPUTBUFFER (spid)
```

NEWALLOC

The NEWALLOC command verifies all the extents in the database. This option has been retained for backwards compatibility only and has been replaced bt the CHECKALLOC command. The syntax of the NEWALLOC command is as follows:

```
DBCC NEWALLOC [(database_name [, NOINDEX])][ WITH NO_INFOMSGS]
```

The most common error—2540—is returned by running NEWALLOC in an active database. If you don't suspect problems in your database and you get this error from a NEWALLOC command, it is most likely nothing to worry about.

OPENTRAN

The OPENTRAN command is used to display information about the oldest active transaction in a specific database as well as the oldest replicated and nonreplicated transactions, if the database is published. This command is especially useful when troubleshooting problems with the transaction log filling up. When backing up the transaction log, only the inactive portion of the log is truncated. If a user's transaction is hung and the log isn't being truncated, OPENTRAN tells you and lets you kill the user's SPID. Here's the syntax of the OPENTRAN command:

```
DBCC OPENTRAN [('database_name'¦ database_id)][WITH TABLERESULTS
➥[,NO_INFOMSGS]]
```

The WITH_TABLERESULTS option returns the values in a table for retrieval at a later date.

12

UPDATING TABLE
INDEXES AND
STATISTICS

OUTPUTBUFFER

The OUTPUTBUFFER command enables you to view the last 255 characters SQL Server has sent back to the client, both in ASCII and hexadecimal format. You must pass the SPID of the user you are investigating. The syntax of the command is as follows:

```
DBCC OUTPUTBUFFER spid
```

PINTABLE

The PINTABLE command marks a table as "pinned." A pinned table forces SQL Server to leave the pages associated with the table in memory. This doesn't cause SQL Server to read all pages into memory; rather, it marks them as pinned as they are read by SQL statement. SQL Server logs updates and writes the changes to disk, if needed, but doesn't flush the pages from memory. This command is useful for very small, frequently accessed tables. This is the syntax of the PINTABLE command:

```
DBCC PINTABLE (database_id, table_id)
```

> **WARNING**
>
> If you pin a table that is larger that the size of the buffer cache, the SQL Server will have to be shut down and restarted, and the table will have to be unpinned before all of the pages are read into memory. This process requires a person who is a member of the sysadmin server role to run.

PROCACHE

The PROCACHE command is used by SQL Performance Monitor to investigate the procedure cache. The syntax of the command is as follows:

```
DBCC PROCCACHE
```

ROWLOCK

The ROWLOCK command is used to enable insert row locking on tables in SQL Server 6.5. SQL Server 7.0 automatically uses row locking and is supported only for backward compatibility. Here's the command's syntax:

```
DBCC ROWLOCK (db_id, table_id , set)
```

SHOWCONTIG

The SHOWCONTIG command scans the table that you specify for fragmentation. Fragmentation occurs when INSERTs, UPDATEs, and DELETEs are made against tables. After time, the order of the pages become so disorganized that read-ahead cache can do little to keep up with the physical reads required to get the information off the disk. The syntax of the SHOWCONTIG command is as follows:

```
DBCC SHOWCONTIG (table_id, [index_id])
```

To run the SHOWCONTIG command, you need to know the table ID of the table you are interested in. To do this, run the query in Listing 12.3. The index ID isn't required to run this command, and it will default to index ID 0 or 1. Replace *dbname* with the name of the database the table resides in and replace *tbl_name* with the name of the table you want to investigate.

LISTING 12.3 THIS SQL QUERY ENABLES YOU TO GET THE TABLE ID FOR USE IN THE SHOWCONTIG COMMAND

```
1 use dbname
2 go
3 select id from sysobjects where name = 'tbl_name'
4 go
```

The output of the SHOWCONTIG has several valuable pieces of information:

```
DBCC SHOWCONTIG scanning 'authors' table...
Table: 'authors' (117575457); index ID: 1, database ID: 5
TABLE level scan performed.
- Pages Scanned................................: 9
- Extents Scanned.............................: 5
- Extent Switches.............................: 6
- Avg. Pages per Extent.......................: 1.8
- Scan Density [Best Count:Actual Count].......: 28.57% [2:7]
- Logical Scan Fragmentation ..................: 88.89%
- Extent Scan Fragmentation ..................: 20.00%
- Avg. Bytes Free per Page....................: 2473.6
- Avg. Page Density (full)....................: 69.44%
```

The first number you need to pay attention to is the Scan Density. The optimal number for it is 100. The best count is the ideal number of extent changes if everything is contiguously linked. The actual count is the actual number of extents that the table extends across. The other returned values are as follows:

- Pages Scanned   This is the actual number of pages in the table or index that has been scanned.

- Extents Scanned   This is the actual number of extents in the table of index that has been scanned.

- Extend Switches   This is the number of times that the DBCC command had to switch from one extent to another.

- Avg. Pages per Extent   This is the number of pages per extent in the page chain.

- Logical Scan Fragmentation   This is the percentage of out of order pages returned from scanning the leaf pages of an index.

- Extent Scan Fragmentation   This is the percentage of out of order extents returned from scanning the leaf pages of an index.

- Avg. Bytes Free per Page   This is the average number of free bytes on all of the pages that have been scanned.

- Avg. Page Density (full)   This is the average page density as a percentage. The higher the number, the better.

Use DBCC DBREINDEX to rebuild the indexes on the table and correct the scan density information.

SHOW_STATISTICS

One of the most important jobs of a SQL administrator is to keep the database running quickly. Developers add indexes to their tables to help speed the performance of SELECTs made against their tables. SQL Server keeps statistics about the selectivity of those indexes and then uses those statistics to make decisions in query processing. Unfortunately, SQL Server doesn't always keep these statistics updated. After a great deal of information has been added, or the table had been truncated and reloaded, it's a good idea to run SHOW_STATISTICS to check the selectivity of the indexes in the table. The syntax of the SHOW_STATISTICS command is as follows:

```
DBCC SHOW_STATISTICS (table_name, target)
```

The *target* can be either an index or a collection of statistics. The most important bit of information to get out of the report returned from this is the density number, the number SQL Server uses to determine the selectivity of the index. You can multiply the number of rows by the density number to determine the selectivity. The lower the number, the more likely SQL Server is to use the index.

SHRINKDATABASE

The SHRINKDATABASE command is used to shrink the size of all the data files in a database. If you choose to specify a target percentage, SQL Server attempts to shrink all data files in a database to comply. SQL Server doesn't shrink the database files past the size needed to store the data. When running the SHRINKDATABASE command, you don't have to have the database in single-user mode. Users can continue to work while it is being shrunk. This is the command's syntax:

```
DBCC SHRINKDATABASE (database_name [, target_percent]
[,{NOTRUNCATE ¦ TRUNCATEONLY} ])
```

SHRINKFILE

The SHRINKFILE command is used to shrink the size of a single data file in a database. See the previous section, "SHRINKDATABASE," for more information. The syntax of the command is as follows:

```
DBCC SHRINKFILE ( {file_name ¦ file_id } [, target_size]
[,{NOTRUNCATE ¦ TRUNCATEONLY} ])
```

SQLPERF

The SQLPERF command is used to monitor the size of the transaction logs in all databases. This can be a good command to help you monitor your transaction logs to determine when to back them up or when to truncate them. This is the syntax of the SQLPERF command:

```
DBCC SQLPERF (LOGSPACE)
```

TEXTALL and TEXTALLOC

These commands are used to check databases that contain columns of text or image data types. These commands are retained in SQL Server 7.0 for backward compatibility.

TRACEOFF

The TRACEOFF command is used to turn off trace flags that have been set with the TRACEON command. Here's the command's syntax:

```
DBCC TRACEOFF (trace# [,…trace#])
```

TRACEON

The TRACEON command is used to turn on trace flags, which are used to change or control certain characteristics of SQL Server. The syntax of the command is as follows:

```
DBCC TRACEON (trace# [,...trace#])
```

TRACESTATUS

The TRACESTATUS command is used to display the current status of trace flags. This is the syntax of the command:

```
DBCC TRACESTATUS (trace# [, ...trace#])
```

UNPINTABLE

The UNPINTABLE command is used to mark a table as unpinned. This command, used with the PINTABLE command, doesn't automatically cause all pages to be flushed from memory; instead, it allows SQL Server to move them from memory as needed. The syntax of the command is as follows:

```
DBCC UNPINTABLE (database_id, table_id)
```

UPDATEUSAGE

The UPDATEUSAGE command corrects inaccuracies in the sysindexes table that can result in incorrect values when viewing database information in Enterprise Manager and running the sp_spaceused stored procedure. SQL Server doesn't automatically keep track of this information, so when you view the size of your database in Enterprise Manager, it might not be accurate. Here's the syntax of UPDATEUSAGE:

```
DBCC UPDATEUSAGE ({0 ¦ database_name} [, table_name [, index_id]])
```

If you pass UPDATEUSAGE a 0 in place of the database name, it checks the current database. The UPDATEUSAGE can take a long time to run and could result in a degradation of system performance. It should be run only if you suspect inaccuracies or during off-hours.

USEROPTIONS

The USEROPTIONS command is used to show the current working set of user options that were activated by using the SET command. The syntax of the command is as follows:

```
DBCC USEROPTIONS
```

Summary

This chapter demonstrated several techniques for improving performance by unleashing the power of indexes. Two methods of improving performance are planning the indexes in the design phase and using SQL's built-in optimizer to update table indexes. In the planning stage, different types of tables warrant different considerations. If the table is used for data warehousing, it is always a good idea to index as many fields as possible. Updates to the data warehouse are usually made in batch mode, so performance issues in adding records are meaningless. If the table is used for online transaction processing, the fewer indexes, the better.

If you create one field to store all the fields that would make the concatenated primary key, and make this single field the primary key, you will see a noticeable improvement in performance. Every time a record is added, all the indexes have to be searched to make sure the record is unique. When you narrow the search to one index, this improves the processing time greatly. If you must query these tables and there are many records, you might want to consider creating an index during processing time, running the query, and then dropping the index. The second method uses UPDATE STATISTICS, the statement that optimizes indexes after data has been added. This command updates the distribution page to account for any new or deleted records.

Finally, you witnessed the power of the remaining DBCC statements to supply performance statistics on SQL Server and learned about some powerful utilities.

Crosstabulation

Crosstabulation is one of those words that users of Microsoft Access, Seagate Crystal Reports, and the like are very familiar with. *Crosstabulation* is the process of taking data and transforming it into column names, so that data can be arranged in a cross-section–style format. For example, if you have a list of salespeople, clients, and sales amounts, instead of listing the first salesperson, the first client, and the sales, then the same salesperson, the next client, and the sales, and so on, what if you could have each salesperson listed alongside the left column, have the clients appear as columns, and have the total sales located where the two meet in the table?

This chapter will show you how to perform crosstabulation entirely within SQL Server Transact-SQL (T-SQL), and by doing so, it combines many of the topics discussed up to this point in the book. The real objective is to show you how to take the individual functions, statements, and expressions and make a complex, yet practical, stored procedure.

A Description of Crosstabulation

Not so long ago, I was teaching a SQL Server class when one of the students asked a question: "How do you crosstabulate data in SQL Server?"

My answers ranged from connecting to the SQL Server with Access and using a crosstab query to using a program like Seagate's Crystal Reports and creating a crosstab report. Not one of my responses mentioned SQL Server's capability to crosstabulate the data. I suppose I had always accepted this fact and never questioned it—until that day in class.

I did a little thinking over lunch, and that afternoon in class I spoke once again on the topic. I stated that there's no reason why SQL Server couldn't do it; I just have no idea how—and so I began my quest.

Essential Crosstabulation Considerations

As I began to delve deeper into the subject, I found many questions to consider: How do I return the data to the user? How do I create columns in this data structure that are actually row values? How do I validate a user's permissions on the requested data? Where do I start?

NOTE

I readily admit that I used my favorite resource during the initial and intermediate stages of developing these questions: friends, colleagues, and co-workers. The creative process played an important role in the entire development of this procedure; the human factor—not just reference books—helped solve the problem.

Before you get into the code, I would like to fill you in on the thought process that lead to it and a brief outline of its internals.

I decided to use a bottom-up approach, so I started by determining what I was going to return as the crosstabulated data results. A temporary table would be best, given the situation. However, it just couldn't be done. The temporary table required too much modification to structure and content, and T-SQL just couldn't do the job.

A permanent table is needed. What about all the users? Each user would need his or her own table. By using SQL Server's capability to have more than one table of the same name with different owners, this could be done. The only problem (to which I still haven't found a solution) occurs when a server login is aliased to an existing user in the database. That means multiple logins use the same database username. Therefore, they could potentially use the same table (which is named `Crosstable`) when crosstabulating data, a definite potential for conflict.

> **NOTE**
>
> More than one object can exist with the same name if the owner of those objects differ. Therefore, `dbo.Crosstable`, `joe.Crosstable`, and `mary.Crosstable` can coexist in a database. By having users own their crosstables, a simple `SELECT` statement (`SELECT * FROM Crosstable`) without the owner qualifier returns a given user his or her crosstabulated results. For example, if Mary ran that `SELECT` statement, she would get results from `mary.Crosstable` (as long as it existed) or `dbo.Crosstable` (if she didn't own an object named `Crosstable`).

Because of the nature of T-SQL, the crosstable could not be defined using dynamic execution. This ruled out using randomly generated names for the crosstable. I let this topic stew in my brain for a while, and even later found no better approach. I decided that I would not try to complicate matters further in this book by finding some contrived means of eliminating any chance of this conflict. If you happen to find an alternative solution, drop me a line and let me know. I will continue to update and place this procedure on my company's Web site and take all suggestions into account.

After the means of returning data was established, I went to work on the actual process. The parameters would consist of a column for the row header, a column for the column header, a column for the values to be aggregated, and the source itself (a table or a view).

13

Next, I check for the existence of the columns and source object. If all is well, two temporary tables are created to hold the row data and the column data. I create the crosstable, populate the rows from the row temporary table, and alter it using the data from the column temporary table. Altering the crosstable was also an issue. Data tends not to be usable as a column name because it often doesn't follow the rules for SQL Server identifiers. I considered using Quoted Identifiers, but this would be nonstandard; I resolved to parse through the data and remove illegal characters, as well as prefix the value with an underscore if the initial value is numeric.

Next, a cursor is created to hold all the data. As you iterate through the cursor rows, an EXECUTE statement is issued, updating the contents of the crosstable. When all is done, the crosstable results are returned and all tables and cursors are dropped and deallocated. This is the crosstab stored procedure's basic process, but a few other issues that needed addressing remained.

Security

Security didn't cross my mind at first; I figured it would be easy enough to handle when and if I needed to cross that bridge. When everything started falling into place, I came to a different realization.

Security knocked me for a loop, although it really was a very long SELECT statement within an IF statement that did the trick. The information was already stored in several system tables; I just needed to figure an efficient and graceful way to do the job. I'm not sure if my answer qualifies as either, but it gets the job done and is reliable. An entire section of this chapter is dedicated to explaining the security check process.

Aggregates

Another factor was the use of aggregates in the crosstabulated results. I was sure that a simple sum ability would not suffice, so an average, min, max, and count would also be needed. An additional parameter had to be added to handle this and some additional work, to determine which aggregate operation was good with which data types.

Date Grouping

True crosstab ability has to include date-range grouping such as year, quarter, month, week, and weekday. Matters became complicated very quickly when this factor was added to the process. Along with the additional parameter, which is needed to determine type, I had to create many additional checks using IF statements and CASE expressions. You should easily notice the majority of them in the procedure, and all are explained as they appear in the code.

The Procedure

The stored procedure is broken into sections, so that it's easier to work through and explain. The code, in actual order, is presented to you a portion at a time. Listing 13.1 shows the stored procedure declaration, as well as all the variable declarations used by the procedure.

LISTING 13.1 THE PROCEDURE AND VARIABLE DECLARATIONS

```
 1: CREATE PROCEDURE prCrosstab
 2:      @chrRowHead char(30),
 3:      @chrColHead char(30),
 4:      @chrValue char(30),
 5:      @chrSource char(30),
 6:      @inyType tinyint = 1,
 7:      @inyGrouping tinyint = 0
 8: AS
 9:
10: /*  Variables for the procedure  */
11: DECLARE
12:      @chvRow varchar(255),
13:      @chvCol varchar(255),
14:      @chvVal varchar(255),
15:      @chvType varchar(10),
16:      @chvRowType varchar(10),
17:      @chvColType varchar(255),
18:      @chvTemp varchar(255),
19:      @chvColTemp varchar(255),
20:      @chvRowTemp varchar(255),
21:      @intType int,
22:      @intRowType int,
23:      @intColType int,
24:      @chvExec varchar(255),
25:      @chvGroup varchar(255),
26:      @fltTemp float,
27:      @dtmTemp datetime,
28:      @insR smallint,
29:      @intColumn int,
30:      @intReturn int,
31:      @intTemp int,
32:      @intColNameLen int,
33:      @intMaxRowHead int
34:
35: SET NOCOUNT ON
```

This code is self-explanatory. The SET NOCOUNT ON statement isn't necessary, but makes debugging a lot simpler. You see a recurring PRINT statement throughout the code. I've added comments that I use to help me debug. The statement always occurs just before an EXECUTE statement, allowing you to print the actual string that is executed, so you know where to look if a problem occurs. In addition, Table 13.1 gives you information about the parameters and what values are expected to be passed into them.

TABLE 13.1 STORED PROCEDURE PARAMETER DESCRIPTIONS

Parameter	Description
@chrRowHead	Column that appears as the first column in the cross tabulated results
@chrColHead	Column whose data is transformed into new column names in the crosstabulated results
@chrValue	Column on which to perform aggregate function
@chrSource	Source table or view
@inyType	1-Sum, 2-Average, 3-Minimum, 4-Maximum, 5-Count
@inyGrouping	1-Weekday, 2-Week of Year, 3-Month, 4-Quarter, 5-Year

Verifying Object Existence

The next code portion has to verify that all the parameters were valid. The first step was to check for the existence of the three column names and the source table or view. After that, you need to make sure the aggregate is appropriate for the data type of the value column. Finally, the date grouping parameter needed to be verified against the column header column.

Verifying the Parameters

You should instantly recognize the statements used in Listing 13.2. You always see a similar statement when managing stored procedures and views in SQL Enterprise Manager. The source object's existence is verified by interrogating the sysobjects table. The three supplied columns are individually checked to see if they exist in the syscolumns table for the supplied source object.

LISTING 13.2 VERIFYING PARAMETER VALUES

```
1: /*  Check if source exists  */
2:
3: IF NOT EXISTS
4:      (SELECT *
```

```
5:      FROM sysobjects
6:      WHERE name = @chrSource
7:      AND type IN ('v','u'))
8: BEGIN
9:      RAISERROR 51001 'Source does not exist.'
10:     RETURN -1
11: END
12:
13: /*  Check for column existence  */
14:
15: IF NOT EXISTS
16:     (SELECT sc.name
17:     FROM syscolumns sc
18:         JOIN sysobjects so ON sc.id = so.id
19:     WHERE so.name = @chrSource
20:     AND sc.name = @chrColHead)
21: BEGIN
22:     RAISERROR 51002 'Invalid @chrColHead name.'
23:     RETURN -1
24: END
25:
26: IF NOT EXISTS
27:     (SELECT sc.name
28:     FROM syscolumns sc
29:         JOIN sysobjects so ON sc.id = so.id
30:     WHERE so.name = @chrSource
31:     AND sc.name = @chrRowHead)
32: BEGIN
33:     RAISERROR 51002 'Invalid @chrRowHead name.'
34:     RETURN -1
35: END
36:
37: IF NOT EXISTS
38:     (SELECT sc.name
39:     FROM syscolumns sc
40:         JOIN sysobjects so ON sc.id = so.id
41:     WHERE so.name = @chrSource
42:     AND sc.name = @chrValue)
43: BEGIN
44:     RAISERROR 51002 'Invalid @chrValue name.'
45:     RETURN -1
46: END
47:
48: /* Verify type is valid (1 (sum), 2 (avg), etc...) */
49:
50: IF @inyType <1 OR @inyType >5
51: BEGIN
52:     RAISERROR 51000 'Invalid crosstab type.'
53:     RETURN -1
54: END
```

The last portion of Listing 13.2 checks to see that the aggregate parameter value is not between 1 and 5. You could just as easily have coded it to read IF @inyType NOT BETWEEN 1 AND 5, or a variety of other ways. In any case, the first four parameters are simple to check. The fifth—the aggregate type—still needs additional verification, but this can only be done after you have found the base data types of the three columns.

Verifying the Data Types and Aggregates

Now you need to find the value column's data type and make sure it is valid for use with the requested aggregate type. Take a look at Listing 13.3.

LISTING 13.3   VERIFYING VALID DATA TYPES AND AGGREGATE CORRELATION

```
 1: /*  Create typestr to hold aggregate name  */
 2:
 3: SELECT @chvType =
 4:      CASE @inyType
 5:      WHEN 1 THEN 'SUM'
 6:      WHEN 2 THEN 'AVG'
 7:      WHEN 3 THEN 'MAX'
 8:      WHEN 4 THEN 'MIN'
 9:      WHEN 5 THEN 'COUNT'
10:      ELSE 'SUM'
11:      END
12:
13: /*  Get standard data type of @chrValue column  */
14:
15: SELECT @chvTemp = t2.name
16: FROM sysobjects o
17:      JOIN syscolumns c ON (o.id = c.id)
18:      JOIN systypes t1 ON (t1.usertype = c.usertype)
19:      JOIN systypes t2 ON (t1.type = t2.type)
20: WHERE t2.usertype < 100
21: AND t2.usertype <> 18
22: AND t2.usertype <> 80
23: AND o.type IN ('u','v')
24: AND o.name = @chrSource
25: AND c.name = @chrValue
26:
27: /*  Categorize types for aggregate check  */
28:
29: SELECT @intTemp =
30:      CASE
31:      WHEN @chvTemp IN ('int', 'smallint', 'tinyint', 'float', 'real',
32:            'decimal', 'numeric', 'money', 'smallmoney') THEN 1
33:      WHEN @chvTemp IN ('datetime', 'smalldatetime') THEN 3
34:      WHEN @chvTemp IN ('bit', 'char', 'varchar') THEN 5
35:      ELSE 100
```

```
36:        END
37:
38: /*  Validate existing data type is consistent with selected aggregate
*/
39:
40: IF @inyType < @intTemp
41: BEGIN
42:        RAISERROR 51020 'Crosstab type not valid with @chrValue
definition.'
43:        RETURN -1
44: END
45:
46: /*  Hold the data type for future use  */
47:
48: SELECT @chvColType = RTRIM(
49:        CASE @inyType
50:        WHEN 5 THEN 'int'
51:        ELSE CASE
52:            WHEN @chvTemp IN ('bit', 'char', 'varchar') THEN 'int'
53:            WHEN @chvTemp IN ('decimal', 'numeric') THEN 'float'
54:            ELSE @chvTemp
55:            END
56:        END)
57:
58: /*  Verify grouping is valid for colhead  */
59:
60: IF @inyGrouping <0 OR @inyGrouping > 5
61: BEGIN
62:        RAISERROR 51010 'Invalid crosstab grouping.'
63:        RETURN -1
64: END
```

Using a simple SELECT statement and a CASE expression, lines 3 through 11 create the string equivalent for the aggregate type to be used later in the code. Lines 15 through 25 find the value column's base data type.

> **NOTE**
>
> The base data types are defined as the initial data types (except sysname and timestamp) supplied by SQL Server. sysname and timestamp (both system-defined) and user-defined data types are resolved to their base data type by excluding them in the second instance of the systypes table. sysname has a usertype value of 18, timestamp is 80, and user-defined data types always have a usertype value greater than or equal to 100.

The data types are categorized into one of four values: 1, 3, 5, and 100. Lines 29 through 36 take care of this process. These values are not randomly chosen; lines 40 through 44 perform a check to see if the aggregate type is valid to use with the value column's data type. If the aggregate type is less than the data type category, the procedure raises an error and returns. Table 13.2 shows a list of data types, aggregates, and category values. Each data type supports any aggregate at an equal or greater level. Because the aggregates were already assigned a value when passed into the procedure, the data types are grouped, as shown in Table 13.2, and compared with the two values.

TABLE 13.2 DATA TYPES AND AGGREGATES

Category	Data Type	Aggregate
1	All numerics	Sum
2		Avg
3	datetime	Min
4		Max
5	All others	Count

In lines 48 through 56, you convert the value column's data type to int, if a count is requested. If not, bit, char, and varchar values are converted to int (because only a count can be performed on bit, char, and varchar), and numerics and decimals are converted into float. Finally, the last part of Listing 13.3 validates that the date grouping is indeed valid.

Column and Row Head Data Types

Listing 13.4 retrieves the base data type for both the column and row header columns.

LISTING 13.4 RETRIEVING THE COLUMN AND ROW HEAD DATA TYPES

```
1: /*  Get standard data type of @chrColHead column  */
2:
3: SELECT @chvTemp = t2.name
4: FROM sysobjects o
5:     JOIN syscolumns c ON (o.id = c.id)
6:     JOIN systypes t1 ON (t1.usertype = c.usertype)
7:     JOIN systypes t2 ON (t1.type = t2.type)
8: WHERE t2.usertype < 100
9: AND t2.usertype <> 18
10: AND t2.usertype <> 80
11: AND o.type IN ('u','v')
12: AND o.name = @chrSource
13: AND c.name = @chrColHead
```

```
14:
15: IF UPPER(@chvTemp) NOT IN ('CHAR', 'VARCHAR')
16:     SELECT @intColtype = 1
17: ELSE
18:     SELECT @intColtype = 0
19:
20: /*  Get standard data type of @chrRowHead */
21:
22: SELECT @chvRowType = t2.name
23: FROM sysobjects o
24:     JOIN syscolumns c ON (o.id = c.id)
25:     JOIN systypes t1 ON (t1.usertype = c.usertype)
26:     JOIN systypes t2 ON (t1.type = t2.type)
27: WHERE t2.usertype < 100
28: AND t2.usertype <> 18
29: AND t2.usertype <> 80
30: AND o.type IN ('u','v')
31: AND o.name = @chrSource
32: AND c.name = @chrRowHead
33:
34: IF UPPER(@chvRowType) NOT IN ('CHAR', 'VARCHAR')
35:     SELECT @intRowtype = 1
36: ELSE
37:     SELECT @intRowtype = 0
38:
39: /*  Categorize types for grouping check  */
40:
41: SELECT @intTemp =
42:     CASE
43:     WHEN @chvTemp IN ('int', 'smallint', 'tinyint', 'float', 'real',
44:          'decimal', 'numeric', 'money', 'smallmoney') THEN 1
45:     WHEN @chvTemp IN ('datetime', 'smalldatetime') THEN 3
46:     WHEN @chvTemp IN ('bit', 'char', 'varchar') THEN 5
47:     ELSE 100
48:     END
49:
50: /*  Validate existing data type is consistant with selected grouping
    ➥*/
51:
52: IF (@intTemp = 5 AND @inyGrouping > 0) OR (@intTemp = 1 AND
    ➥@inyGrouping >0)
53:     OR (@intTemp = 3 AND @inyGrouping = 0)
54: BEGIN
55:     RAISERROR 51030 'Crosstab grouping not valid with @chrColHead
        ➥definition.'
56:     RETURN -1
57: END
```

Lines 3 through 13 find the column head's data type. The next four lines categorize it as either a character or non-character data type. This information is later used to provide needed conversions. Lines 22 through 37 do the same for the row head data type.

The last portion (lines 41 through 57) validates that the column's data type is consistent with the date grouping parameter. If it is a date, the date grouping must be between 1 and 5; otherwise, the date grouping must be 0.

This procedure is designed so that future upgrades are as simple as possible. One thought was to add an alternative grouping for character data, so that results can be grouped on a certain number of initial characters. For example, group on the first character so that all items beginning with an *A* would be together, and so on. The date grouping parameter could then serve as two types of data grouping.

Checking Column Security

The next task was to check security. This was not part of the initial plan, but a later realization. I modeled the query after the one used in the sp_column_privileges system stored procedure. A rather complicated query, it checks to see if the number of columns with select permission equals 3. Each of the column parameters is checked in the query, and a value of 1 is returned to each that the current user has select rights for. If all three are accessible, the IF statement succeeds and the procedure continues. Otherwise, an error is raised and the procedure returns. Examine Listing 13.4.

LISTING 13.4   CHECKING PERMISSIONS

```
 1: /*  Check for permission on source  */
 2:
 3: IF user_id() <> 1
 4: BEGIN
 5:     IF (SELECT COUNT(DISTINCT c.name)
 6:         FROM syscolumns c, sysobjects o, sysprotects p,
 7:             sysusers u, master..spt_values v
 8:         WHERE c.name IN (@chrColHead, @chrRowHead, @chrValue)
 9:         AND c.id = o.id
10:         AND p.id = c.id
11:         AND c.colid = v.number
12:         AND v.type = 'p'
13:         AND o.id = object_id(@chrSource)
14:         AND (u.uid = user_id() OR u.uid IN
15:             (SELECT u1.uid
16:             FROM sysusers u1
17:             WHERE u1.gid = u1.uid
18:             AND u1.gid IN
19:                 (SELECT u2.gid
20:                 FROM sysusers u2
```

```
21:                           WHERE u2.uid = user_id()
22:                           OR u2.uid = user_id('public'))))
23:                   AND p.uid = u.uid
24:                   AND p.action = 193
25:                   AND p.protecttype = 205
26:                   AND columns IS NOT NULL
27:                   AND CASE SUBSTRING(p.columns, 1, 1) & 1
28:                           WHEN null THEN 255
29:                           WHEN 0 THEN CONVERT(tinyint,
30:                               SUBSTRING(p.columns, v.low, 1))
31:                           ELSE (~CONVERT(tinyint, ISNULL(
32:                               SUBSTRING(p.columns, v.low, 1), 0)))
33:                           END & v.high <> 0
34:                   AND NOT EXISTS
35:                       (SELECT *
36:                       FROM syscolumns c5, sysobjects o5,
37:                           sysprotects p5, sysusers u5,
38:                           master..spt_values v5
39:                       WHERE c.name IN (@chrColHead, @chrRowHead,
                          ➥@chrValue)
40:                       AND c5.colid = c.colid
41:                       AND c5.id = o5.id
42:                       AND p5.id = c5.id
43:                       AND c5.colid = v5.number
44:                       AND v5.type = 'p'
45:                       AND o5.id = object_id(@chrSource)
46:                       AND (u5.uid = user_id() OR u5.uid IN
47:                           (SELECT u6.uid
48:                           FROM sysusers u6
49:                           WHERE u6.gid = u6.uid
50:                           AND u6.gid IN
51:                               (SELECT u7.gid
52:                               FROM sysusers u7
53:                               WHERE u7.uid=user_id()
54:                               OR u7.uid=user_id('public'))))
55:                       AND p5.uid = u5.uid
56:                       AND p5.action = 193
57:                       AND p5.protecttype = 206
58:                       AND p5.columns IS NOT NULL
59:                       AND CASE SUBSTRING(p5.columns, 1, 1) & 1
60:                           WHEN NULL THEN 255
61:                           WHEN 0 THEN CONVERT(tinyint,
62:                               SUBSTRING(p5.columns, v5.low, 1))
63:                           ELSE (~CONVERT(tinyint,
64:                               ISNULL(SUBSTRING(p5.columns, v5.low, 1),
                              ➥0)))
65:                           END & v5.high <> 0)) <> 3
66:       BEGIN
67:           RAISERROR 51003 'Permission denied on column.'
68:           RETURN -1
69:       END
70: END
```

The first IF statement excludes the dbo from the search. There is no need to do extra processing for the owner of the database. The next IF statement spans lines 5 through 65. It contains a rather long SELECT statement.

In that statement, a count of the number of column names is the return value. The tables being queried are syscolumns, sysobjects, sysprotects (contains the security information), sysusers, and spt_values, from the master database.

Most of the query is straightforward. The name from syscolumns must be in the three supplied column names (line 8). Syscolumns and sysobjects are joined on their id columns. sysprotects and syscolumns are joined on their id columns as well (lines 9 through 10). The sysobjects id must match the supplied table or view for the procedure (line 13).

The current user's id must match the uid in sysusers, or any group to which the current user belongs (lines 14 through 22). The uid from sysprotects needs to match the uid from sysusers, and you look for an action of 193 (select permission) and a protecttype of 205 (permission is granted).

> **WARNING**
>
> If a user is a member of a group other than public, the user is not listed as a member of public in the sysusers table when it's queried—even though all users are always a member of public. When checking for a user's permissions, it's necessary to check the public group as well.

The subquery checks the same information, but with a NOT EXISTS clause. It finds those columns to which the user has been denied permission (sysprotects protecttype equals 206).

The spt_values table is used to find the bit positions for the columns column in the sysprotects table for which you are checking permissions. You primarily see it referenced in lines 27 through 33 and lines 59 through 65.

The first byte of data from the columns column (binary data type) is used in a CASE expression. The low value from spt_values is used to find another byte from the binary data. This value and the high value have a bit-wise AND performed against them. If the result is not 0, the user has permission to the specified column. Notice (for example, in lines 43 through 44) that the spt_values table's number column is matched with the colid from syscolumns and that the type is 'p' (permission). This ensures that the high and low column values pertain to that particular column in the table when checking permissions.

If all is well, the query returns a value of 3, meaning that the user has select permission on all three columns. If not, the main IF statement fails and the procedure raises an error and returns.

TIP

You can find information on the column definitions of the system tables and stored procedures in the appendixes of this book. The more you know about the system tables, the more ability you have to write robust stored procedures.

Generating the Column Header List

The next portion of the procedure creates the column and row header lists. It starts by simply defining two temporary tables, as shown in Listing 13.5.

LISTING 13.5   CREATING THE TEMPORARY TABLES

```
CREATE TABLE #colnames (colname varchar(255) NULL, colnumber int NULL)
CREATE TABLE #rownames (rowname varchar(255) NULL)
```

The next step is to generate the column names using data from the requested column head value.

Creating the `colnames` Table

Listing 13.6 creates an INSERT statement based on the data from the source table for the requested column. A few details needed to be handled in this code: date groupings, converting non-character data to char, and sorting according to original data type. The first item deals with creating the appropriate date grouping value for the requested parameter. The second item is required to make the data usable as a column name in the crosstable. The latter item is necessary when, for example, numeric data is converted into character data; the order is dictionary based when sorting numbers as characters (for example, 1, 10, 11, 2, 3, 4, 5, 6, 7, 8, 9), but you want the proper numerical order (1, 2, 3, 4, 5, 6, 7, 8, 9, 10, 11). Take a look at the code in Listing 13.6.

LISTING **13.6**   CREATING THE colnames TABLE

```
 1: /*  Insert distinct column data into #colnames   */
 2:
 3: SELECT @chvExec = 'insert #colnames select col1, col2 from '
 4:        + '(select distinct col1 = ' +
 5:        CASE @intTemp
 6:        WHEN 3 THEN
 7:             CASE
 8:             WHEN @inyGrouping IN (1,3) THEN 'datename(' +
 9:                  CASE @inyGrouping
10:                  WHEN 1 THEN 'weekday'
11:                  WHEN 3 THEN 'month'
12:                  END + ', ' + RTRIM(@chrColHead) + ')'
13:             ELSE CASE @inyGrouping
14:                  WHEN 2 THEN '''Week'
15:                  WHEN 4 THEN '''Quarter'
16:                  WHEN 5 THEN '''Year'
17:                  END + '_'' + ' + 'datename(' +
18:                  CASE @inyGrouping
19:                  WHEN 2 THEN 'week'
20:                  WHEN 4 THEN 'quarter'
21:                  WHEN 5 THEN 'year'
22:                  END + ', ' + RTRIM(@chrColHead) + ')'
23:             END
24:        ELSE CASE @intColType
25:             WHEN 1 THEN 'convert(varchar(255), ' + RTRIM(@chrColHead) +
                  ➥')'
26:             ELSE RTRIM(@chrColHead)
27:             END
28:        END + ', col2 = ' +
29:        CASE @intTemp
30:        WHEN 3 THEN 'datepart(' +
31:             CASE @inyGrouping
32:             WHEN 1 THEN 'weekday'
33:             WHEN 2 THEN 'week'
34:             WHEN 3 THEN 'month'
35:             WHEN 4 THEN 'quarter'
36:             WHEN 5 THEN 'year'
37:             END + ', ' + RTRIM(@chrColHead) + ')'
38:        ELSE '0'
39:        END + ', col3 = ' +
40:        CASE @intTemp
41:        WHEN 3 THEN 'datepart(' +
42:             CASE @inyGrouping
43:             WHEN 1 THEN 'weekday'
44:             WHEN 3 THEN 'month'
45:             WHEN 2 THEN 'week'
46:             WHEN 4 THEN 'quarter'
47:             WHEN 5 THEN 'year'
48:             END + ', ' + RTRIM(@chrColHead) + ')'
```

```
49:        ELSE RTRIM(@chrColHead)
50:        END + ' from ' + RTRIM(@chrSource) + ') xyz order by col3'
51:
52: --PRINT @chvExec
53: EXEC(@chvExec)
```

The SELECT statement created within the INSERT statement has three columns (of which only two are actually inserted). To achieve this, derived tables are used to create a result-set with three columns; only two of them are selected for the actual insert. The first column is generated in lines 4 through 28. If the column head's data type is a date (line 6), it is converted into the Datename for the particular date grouping type. If the Datename function were to return a numeric, the name of the date grouping and an underscore are prefixed to the number (for example, Quarter_4). The distinct clause used in line 4 causes a unique set of data to be returned (because one occurrence of each column header is desired). Listings 13.7 and 13.8 each show a sample execution of the prCrosstab procedure and what the generated insert would look like.

LISTING 13.7   A SAMPLE OF GENERATED CODE FROM prCrosstab

```
exec prcrosstab 'stor_id', 'ord_date', 'qty', 'sales', 1, 1 --weekday

insert #colnames
    select col1, col2
    from (select distinct col1 = datename(weekday, ord_date),
                 col2 = datepart(weekday, ord_date),
                 col3 = datepart(weekday, ord_date)
         from sales) xyz
    order by col3
```

LISTING 13.8   ANOTHER SAMPLE OF GENERATED CODE FROM prCrosstab

```
exec prcrosstab 'stor_id', 'ord_date', 'qty', 'sales', 1, 4 --quarter

insert #colnames
    select col1, col2
    from (select distinct col1 = 'Quarter_' + datename(quarter,
    ➥ord_date),
                 col2 = datepart(quarter, ord_date),
                 col3 = datepart(quarter, ord_date)
         from sales) xyz
    order by col3
```

13

CROSSTABULATION

> **NOTE**
>
> You might have noticed that all the generated code is lowercase. I chose to do this so it's easier to distinguish the generated code from the code of the actual stored procedure. You can call this formatting the exception to the rule of naming conventions.

The second column (Listing 13.6, lines 28 through 39) is a numeric used for dates only (0 otherwise), which is used for finding the column when the crosstable is updated later in the procedure. For non-dates, the value is simply converted to char and compared.

The third column (lines 39 through 50) is used to provide the proper sorting (as seen in the ORDER BY clause in line 50). By sorting on the appropriate data type, the columns are listed in proper order no matter what the original data type.

Finally, the generated INSERT statement is executed in line 53. Now that the #colnames table has the list of new columns for the crosstable, you need to verify that the number and length of the columns is valid.

Checking the Column Count and Length and Adding Row Data

In addition to verifying the column count and length of the column names, you also fill the #rownames table, if all is well, with the columns. Listing 13.9 shows the code to do the former.

LISTING 13.9 CHECKING COLUMN COUNT AND NAME LENGTH

```
 1: /*  Check column count  */
 2: IF (SELECT COUNT(*) FROM #colnames) > 1023
 3: BEGIN
 4:     DROP TABLE #colnames
 5:     RAISERROR 51004 'Distinct column count exceeded max of 1023.'
 6:     RETURN -1
 7: END
 8:
 9: /*  Verify colnames do not exceed max length  */
10: IF (SELECT MAX(DATALENGTH(RTRIM(colname)) - 1) FROM #colnames) > 29
11: BEGIN
12:     DROP TABLE #colnames
13:     RAISERROR 51050 'Column data length exceeded max of 30.'
14:     RETURN -1
15: END
```

Lines 2 through 7 check that there are fewer than 1023 columns. In addition to the row head column in the crosstable, there's room left for additional columns for summary data at a later upgrade. The check is a simple count of the number of rows in the #colnames table. Lines 10 through 15 check that the maximum length of data in colname is less than or equal to 29 characters (the limit for SQL Server column names is 30). One character is left for prefixing an underscore if a column begins with a number. This means that the title from the titles table could never work as the column head for the crosstable.

Next, you populate the #rownames table with character data (converted, if necessary) from the rowhead column of the source table or view. Again, dynamic execution performs the insert as shown in line 14 of Listing 13.10. Listing 13.11 shows a sample of the generated statement.

LISTING 13.10 POPULATING THE rowname TABLE

```
 1: /*  If all is OK, continue to add #rownames data  */
 2: SELECT @chvExec = 'insert #rownames select distinct ' +
 3:      CASE @intRowtype
 4:      WHEN 1 THEN 'convert(varchar(255), '
 5:      ELSE ''
 6:      END + RTRIM(@chrRowHead) +
 7:
 8:      CASE @intRowType
 9:      WHEN 1 THEN ') '
10:      ELSE ''
11:      END + 'from ' + @chrSource
12:
13: --PRINT @chvExec
14: EXEC(@chvExec)
```

LISTING 13.11 A SAMPLE INSERT GENERATED FROM prCrosstab

```
insert #rownames
     select distinct title_id
     from sales
```

Generating Cross-tabbed Reports

Now that the two temporary tables have been populated, move on to the crosstable itself.

Creating and Modifying the crosstable

Because of limitations in T-SQL, the crosstable must be defined statically in the stored procedure. A statement (with comments) was left in, which defines the actual length needed for the varchar data type of the rowhead column.

Listing 13.12 shows creating and altering the crosstable.

LISTING 13.12 CREATING AND ALTERING THE crosstable

```
 1: /*
 2:     Would be nice if you could use this value to define the
        ➥crosstable
 3:     but this table must be created in a non-dynamic fashion.
 4: */
 5: SELECT @intMaxRowHead =
        (SELECT MAX(DATALENGTH(RTRIM(rowname))) FROM #rownames)
 6:
 7: /*  Create crosstable  */
 8: /*  Define crosstable with rowhead field  */
 9: CREATE TABLE crosstable (rowhead varchar(255) NULL)
10:
11: /*  Alter crosstable by adding columns based on #colnames data  */
12:
13: DECLARE colname_cursor2 CURSOR FOR
14:     SELECT colname FROM #colnames
15:
16: OPEN colname_cursor2
17:
18: FETCH colname_cursor2 INTO @chvCol
19: WHILE @@fetch_status >= 0
20: BEGIN
21:     SELECT @chvColTemp=''
22:     IF @chvCol LIKE '%[^A-Z0-9]%'
23:     BEGIN
24:         SELECT @insR = 1
25:         WHILE @insR <= DATALENGTH(RTRIM(@chvCol))
26:         BEGIN
27:             SELECT @chvColTemp = RTRIM(@chvColTemp) +
28:                 CASE
29:                 WHEN SUBSTRING(@chvCol, @insR, 1) LIKE '[A-Z0-9_]'
30:                     THEN SUBSTRING(@chvCol, @insR, 1)
31:                 ELSE ''
32:                 END
```

```
33:                    SELECT @insR = @insR + 1
34:            END
35:            SELECT @chvCol = @chvColTemp
36:        END
37:        SELECT @chvExec = 'alter table ' + user_name() + '.crosstable add
    ➥' +
38:            CASE
39:            WHEN SUBSTRING(@chvCol,1,1) LIKE '[^1234567890]' THEN
                ➥@chvCol
40:            ELSE '_' + LTRIM(@chvCol)
41:            END
42:            + ' ' + @chvColType + ' null default (0)'
43:
44:        --PRINT @chvExec
45:        EXEC(@chvExec)
46:        FETCH colname_cursor2 INTO @chvCol
47: END
48:
49: CLOSE colname_cursor2
50: DEALLOCATE colname_cursor2
```

Line 9 defines the crosstable with a single nullable column named rowhead of varchar data type (length of 255). Next, a cursor is created based on the temporary table #colnames (lines 13 and 14). After opening the cursor, the column name is fetched into the variable @chvCol.

If all is well (data was fetched), then the column name is parsed. Line 22 checks to see if any illegal characters are in the name. If so, loop through the string and append only the valid characters onto the variable @chvColTemp. Lines 28 through 32 use a CASE expression and the SUBSTRING function to return the valid character and, if the character is invalid, to return an empty string.

After looping through the names of the columns, you alter the crosstable with the new column name. If the first character is a number (lines 38 through 41), an underscore is prefixed onto the name to make it valid. The data type that was determined earlier is used for the column data type. Line 42 defines the column as nullable with a default of 0.

Then execute the ALTER TABLE statement (see Listing 13.13 for an example) and move on to the next column, repeating the process until all columns have been added to the crosstable.

13

CROSSTABULATION

LISTING 13.13 A SAMPLE OF Alter Table STATEMENTS

```
alter table dbo.crosstable add Year_1992 smallint null default (0)
alter table dbo.crosstable add Year_1993 smallint null default (0)
alter table dbo.crosstable add Year_1994 smallint null default (0)
```

After all the columns have been appended to the table, the cursor is closed and deallocated (lines 49 and 50), finishing this portion of the procedure. You need to update all the values in the crosstable with the requested aggregate value column data from the source table or view.

Updating the crosstable Values

Updating the crosstable is a two-step process. First, you must append rows assigning only the first column (rowhead) with the row head data in the rownames temporary table. After placing this data in the crosstable, you can use it to perform updates on the table (you essentially have a chart to plot data against—see Listing 13.14 for an example).

Inserting the Initial Data into the crosstable

Listing 13.14 performs the insert that adds the initial data to the crosstable. It is a simple insert from the rownames table.

LISTING 13.14 ADDING THE INITIAL crosstable DATA

```
/*  Add #rowhead data to crosstable  */
SELECT @chvExec = 'insert ' + user_name() + '.crosstable (rowhead) select
    rowname from #rownames'

--PRINT @chvExec
EXEC(@chvExec)
```

LISTING 13.15 A SAMPLE OF THE crosstable TO THIS POINT IN TIME

```
/* If you were to complete the procedure (close cursors, drop temp
tables, and so forth */
/* you could then test to see what results were in the crosstable */
/* Because the procedure is not yet complete, this next statement will
not work correctly */
/* It is provided to demonstrate where the results listed below it
come from */
SELECT * FROM crosstable

/* These are only sample results */
rowhead   Year_1992 Year_1993 Year_1994
-------   --------- --------- ---------
```

6380	0	0	0
7066	0	0	0
7067	0	0	0
7131	0	0	0
7896	0	0	0
8042	0	0	0

Not much to look at, although it uses dynamic execution to do the job. You might not think it's a necessary step, but you find that the procedure won't work without it when you put the theory to practice. Listing 13.15 shows how the crosstable looks up to this point. It is primed and ready for updating.

> **NOTE**
>
> After dynamically altering the crosstable, I found that all future addressing of the table needed to be via dynamic execution as well. In theory, you cannot alter a table and add data to those columns in the same procedure or batch. The use of dynamic execution allows you to perform this act, however, by its very nature. Dynamically executed statements are considered part of their own batch— therefore, in a different scope from the batch or procedure that executed it.

Now you iterate through a cursor to fill the rest of the data in the table.

Populating the Remainder of crosstable with a Cursor

Listing 13.16 is actually only creating the cursor that's declared via dynamic execution. Listing 13.17 shows a sample cursor declaration and the prCrosstab call that created it. Take some time to examine both sets of code.

> **TIP**
>
> Because the scope of cursor declarations are connection-based and not batch- or procedure-based, declaring a cursor via dynamic execution allows it to be used by the calling procedure or batch.

13

CROSSTABULATION

LISTING 13.16 CREATING THE CURSOR TO POPULATE THE crosstable

```
 1: /*
 2:     Create cursor with @chrRowHead and @chrColHead groupings and
        ➥@chrValue
 3:     aggregate
 4: */
 5:
 6: SELECT @chvExec = 'declare colname_cursor3 cursor for select ' +
 7:     CASE @intRowType
 8:     WHEN 1 THEN 'convert(varchar(255), ' + RTRIM(@chrRowHead) + ')'
 9:     ELSE RTRIM(@chrRowHead)
10:     END + ', ' +
11:
12:     CASE
13:     WHEN @intTemp = 3 THEN
14:         CASE
15:         WHEN @inyGrouping IN (1,3) THEN 'datename(' +
16:             CASE @inyGrouping
17:             WHEN 1 THEN 'weekday'
18:             WHEN 3 THEN 'month'
19:             END + ', ' + RTRIM(@chrColHead) + ')'
20:         ELSE CASE @inyGrouping
21:             WHEN 2 THEN '''Week'
22:             WHEN 4 THEN '''Quarter'
23:             WHEN 5 THEN '''Year'
24:             END + '_'' + ' + 'datename(' +
25:
26:             CASE @inyGrouping
27:             WHEN 2 THEN 'week'
28:             WHEN 4 THEN 'quarter'
29:             WHEN 5 THEN 'year'
30:             END + ', ' + RTRIM(@chrColHead) + ')'
31:         END
32:     ELSE CASE @intColType
33:         WHEN 1 THEN 'convert(varchar(255), ' + RTRIM(@chrColHead) +
                ➥')'
34:         ELSE RTRIM(@chrColHead)
35:         END
36:     END + ', total = CONVERT(varchar(255),' + RTRIM(@chvType) + '(' +
37:
38:     RTRIM(@chrValue) + ')) from ' + RTRIM(@chrSource) + ' group by '
        ➥+
39:     RTRIM(@chrRowHead) + ', ' +
40:
41:     CASE @intTemp
42:     WHEN 3 THEN
43:         CASE
44:         WHEN @inyGrouping IN (1,3) THEN 'datename(' +
45:             CASE @inyGrouping
46:             WHEN 1 THEN 'weekday'
```

```
47:                    WHEN 3 THEN 'month'
48:                    END + ', ' + RTRIM(@chrColHead) + ')'
49:            ELSE CASE @inyGrouping
50:                    WHEN 2 THEN '''Week'
51:                    WHEN 4 THEN '''Quarter'
52:                    WHEN 5 THEN '''Year'
53:                    END + '_'' + ' + 'datename(' +
54:
55:                    CASE @inyGrouping
56:                    WHEN 2 THEN 'week'
57:                    WHEN 4 THEN 'quarter'
58:                    WHEN 5 THEN 'year'
59:                    END + ', ' + RTRIM(@chrColHead) + ')'
60:            END
61:        ELSE RTRIM(@chrColHead)
62:        END
63: --PRINT @chvExec
64: EXEC(@chvExec)
```

LISTING 13.17   A SAMPLE OF THE PRINTED RESULTS FROM LISTING 13.15

```
exec prcrosstab 'stor_id', 'ord_date', 'qty', 'sales', 1, 5

declare colname_cursor3 cursor for
    select stor_id,
           'Year_' + datename(year, ord_date),
           total = CONVERT(varchar(255),SUM(qty))
    from sales
    group by stor_id, 'Year_' + datename(year, ord_date)
```

Take a look at Listing 13.17. Notice that the results create a simple SELECT statement in the cursor with three columns: The row head values, the column names, and the requested aggregate for the value column. Now look at Listing 13.16. The first column (the row head) is defined in lines 7 through 10. An earlier test of the data type determines whether a conversion to varchar needs to be performed.

The second column (the column head) is a little more complex. It uses a functionality identical to that used to create the column names in the colnames table, so that the correct name is found for the update. Dates are converted to the appropriate grouping (lines 13 through 31). Other data types are converted if they are not of varchar type (lines 32 through 35). The total column is generated on lines 36 and 37. It's a simple conversion of the aggregate value to varchar.

Lines 38 through 62 create the GROUP BY statement again using the same methodology that created the initial column names. Once created, the cursor declaration is executed in line 64. The following results show a sample of the data that you iterate through to perform all the updates to the crosstable. Notice how the second column holds the column names for the crosstable and the last column (in this case) holds the summed values for each pair.

```
stor_id                                             total
-------  -----------------------------------------  ------
6380     Year_1994                                  8
7066     Year_1993                                  50
7066     Year_1994                                  75
7067     Year_1992                                  80
7067     Year_1994                                  10
7131     Year_1993                                  85
7131     Year_1994                                  45
7896     Year_1993                                  60
8042     Year_1993                                  55
8042     Year_1994                                  25
```

Now that the cursor exists, you are ready to update the crosstable.

Updating the crosstable

By iterating through the cursor just declared, you can update all the values in the crosstable. The next code segment, Listing 13.19, shows the portion of the procedure that performs those updates.

LISTING 13.19   UPDATING THE crosstable

```
 1: /*  Iterate through cursor and update crosstable  */
 2: BEGIN TRAN
 3: OPEN colname_cursor3
 4: FETCH colname_cursor3 INTO @chvRow, @chvCol, @chvVal
 5: WHILE @@fetch_status >= 0
 6: BEGIN
 7:     SELECT @chvColTemp=''
 8:     IF @chvCol LIKE '%[^A-Z0-9]%'
 9:     BEGIN
10:         SELECT @insR = 1
11:         WHILE @insR <= DATALENGTH(RTRIM(@chvCol))
12:         BEGIN
13:             SELECT @chvColTemp = RTRIM(@chvColTemp) +
14:                 CASE
15:                 WHEN SUBSTRING(@chvCol, @insR, 1) LIKE '[A-Z0-9_]'
16:                     THEN SUBSTRING(@chvCol, @insR, 1)
17:                 ELSE ''
18:                 END
```

```
19:                    SELECT @insR = @insR + 1
20:              END
21:              SELECT @chvCol = @chvColTemp
22:         END
23:         SELECT @chvExec = 'update ' + user_name() + '.crosstable set ' +
24:              CASE
25:              WHEN SUBSTRING(@chvCol,1,1) LIKE '[^1234567890]' THEN
                 ➥@chvCol
26:              ELSE '_' + LTRIM(@chvCol)
27:              END + ' = ' +
28:                   CASE
29:                   WHEN @chvVal IS NULL THEN '0'
30:                   ELSE RTRIM(@chvVal)
31:                   END + ' where  rowhead = '''
32:         SELECT @chvRow =
33:              CASE
34:              WHEN @chvRow IS NULL THEN 'NULL'
35:              ELSE RTRIM(@chvRow)
36:              END
37:         SELECT @chvRowTemp = ''
38:         IF @chvRow LIKE '%''%'
39:         BEGIN
40:              SELECT @insR = 1
41:              WHILE @insR <= DATALENGTH(RTRIM(@chvRow)) - 1
42:              BEGIN
43:                   SELECT @chvRowTemp = RTRIM(@chvRowTemp) +
44:                        CASE
45:                        WHEN SUBSTRING(@chvRow, @insR, 1) LIKE '[^'']'
                          ➥THEN
46:                             SUBSTRING(@chvRow, @insR, 1)
47:                        ELSE ''''''
48:                        END
49:                   SELECT @insR = @insR + 1
50:              END
51:              SELECT @chvRow = @chvRowTemp
52:         END
53:         SELECT @chvExec = @chvExec + @chvRow + ''''
54:         --PRINT @chvExec
55:         EXEC(@chvExec)
56:         FETCH colname_cursor3 INTO @chvRow, @chvCol, @chvVal
57: END
```

Listing 13.20 shows the printed results for each update performed. Notice the relationship between the UPDATE statement here and the values shown in Listing 13.19. You use the three values in each row of the cursor to create and dynamically execute each individual UPDATE statement.

LISTING 13.20   A SAMPLE OF GENERATED UPDATE STATEMENTS

```
exec prcrosstab 'stor_id', 'ord_date', 'qty', 'sales', 1, 5

update dbo.crosstable set Year_1994 = 8 where  rowhead = '6380'
update dbo.crosstable set Year_1993 = 50 where  rowhead = '7066'
update dbo.crosstable set Year_1994 = 75 where  rowhead = '7066'
update dbo.crosstable set Year_1992 = 80 where  rowhead = '7067'
update dbo.crosstable set Year_1994 = 10 where  rowhead = '7067'
update dbo.crosstable set Year_1993 = 85 where  rowhead = '7131'
update dbo.crosstable set Year_1994 = 45 where  rowhead = '7131'
update dbo.crosstable set Year_1993 = 60 where  rowhead = '7896'
update dbo.crosstable set Year_1993 = 55 where  rowhead = '8042'
update dbo.crosstable set Year_1994 = 25 where  rowhead = '8042'
```

Listing 13.19 begins by starting a transaction and opening the cursor. The transaction helps speed the process and is committed only after the procedure is nearly done. Lines 7 through 22 once again take care of invalid column names. Line 23 defines the initial UPDATE statement. Lines 24 through 30 append the Set portion of the update and convert returned null values to 0 to stay consistent with the existing data in the table.

Lines 31 through 53 take care of the WHERE clause portion of the update. The row values are checked for single quotation marks in line 38; if any exist, lines 39 through 52 iterate through the value and add quotation marks, so the final string produces a valid statement. For example, if the WHERE clause were looking for the row with a value of O'Neil, the clause would have to look like this: where rowhead = 'O''Neil'. The two single quotation marks evaluate to a single quotation mark in the string, producing the desired search result.

Finally, line 55 executes the update, and the process continues until all updates have been performed. The only thing left to do is to return the results and clean up after yourself.

Finishing Touches

Listing 13.21 shows the last stage of the procedure. First, you close and deallocate the cursor, commit the open transaction, and set the NOCOUNT to off. One last dynamic execution is performed in lines 8 through 11. This returns your data back to the caller of the procedure. Finally, you drop all three tables used by the procedure.

LISTING 13.21   THE FINAL TOUCHES OF prCrosstab

```
1: CLOSE colname_cursor3
2: DEALLOCATE colname_cursor3
3: COMMIT TRAN
4:
5: /*  Send back the data from crosstable  */
6: SET NOCOUNT OFF
```

```
 7:
 8: SELECT @chvExec='select * from ' + USER_NAME() + '.crosstable'
 9:
10: --PRINT @chvExec
11: EXEC (@chvExec)
12:
13: /*  Drop the tables  */
14: DROP TABLE #colnames
15: DROP TABLE #rownames
16: DROP TABLE crosstable
```

The code in Listing 13.22 shows all the PRINT statement results (formatted for readability). This was achieved by removing all the inline comments(--) before each PRINT statement from the stored procedure. A simple set of data is chosen to keep the listing short, but larger tables can generate hundreds of lines to be executed. Lines 44 through 51 show the actual results from this crosstabulation. These results are easily retrievable from a Visual Basic application, or even Access.

LISTING 13.22 A SAMPLE OF ALL DYNAMIC EXECUTIONS AND RESULTS

```
 1: exec prcrosstab 'stor_id', 'ord_date', 'qty', 'sales', 1, 5 --The
    ➥executed procedure
 2:
 3: --The Print statement results (formatted for readability)
 4:
 5: insert #colnames
 6:     select col1, col2
 7:     from (select distinct col1 = 'Year_' + datename(year, ord_date),
 8:                   col2 = datepart(year, ord_date),
 9:                   col3 = datepart(year, ord_date)
10:         from sales) xyz
11:     order by col3
12:
13: insert #rownames select distinct  stor_id from sales
14:
15: alter table dbo.crosstable add Year_1992 smallint null
16: alter table dbo.crosstable add Year_1993 smallint null
17: alter table dbo.crosstable add Year_1994 smallint null
18:
19: insert dbo.crosstable (rowhead) select
20:     rowname from #rownames
21:
22: declare colname_cursor3 cursor for
23:     select stor_id,
24:             'Year_' + datename(year, ord_date),
25:             total = CONVERT(varchar(255),SUM(qty))
```

continues

13

CROSSTABULATION

LISTING 13.22   CONTINUED

```
26:      from sales
27:      group by stor_id, 'Year_' + datename(year, ord_date)
28:
29: update dbo.crosstable set Year_1994 = 8 where   rowhead = '6380'
30: update dbo.crosstable set Year_1993 = 50 where  rowhead = '7066'
31: update dbo.crosstable set Year_1994 = 75 where  rowhead = '7066'
32: update dbo.crosstable set Year_1992 = 80 where  rowhead = '7067'
33: update dbo.crosstable set Year_1994 = 10 where  rowhead = '7067'
34: update dbo.crosstable set Year_1993 = 85 where  rowhead = '7131'
35: update dbo.crosstable set Year_1994 = 45 where  rowhead = '7131'
36: update dbo.crosstable set Year_1993 = 60 where  rowhead = '7896'
37: update dbo.crosstable set Year_1993 = 55 where  rowhead = '8042'
38: update dbo.crosstable set Year_1994 = 25 where  rowhead = '8042'
39:
40: select * from dbo.crosstable
41:
42: --The data results
43:
44: rowhead   Year_1992 Year_1993 Year_1994
45: -------- --------- --------- ---------
46: 6380      0         0         8
47: 7066      0         50        75
48: 7067      80        0         10
49: 7131      0         85        45
50: 7896      0         60        0
51: 8042      0         55        25
```

Summary

If you're asking what else you can do, this book's job is done.

There are many things you could change about this procedure without affecting its final outcome. Experiment with variations, add features—have fun with it. If you find something that would enhance it or have actually coded the addition, please let me know. As I said, I'll keep an up-to-date version at www.milori.com.

All the techniques used in this stored procedure are common T-SQL abilities. The combination, however, is quite unique, and demonstrates the full potential of T-SQL to perform some fantastic feats. As you can see, this procedure would not have been possible without dynamic execution. It's the key. Although the CASE expression made life much easier, it all could be replaced using variable and IF statements.

SQL Server - Essential Information

PART

II

IN THIS PART

Writing Effective Code

In the course of database development, stored procedures are often employed. The trick is to make them effective and useful. This chapter will give you a foundation on which you can build your own procedures. I will discuss why stored procedures are used, show how to formulate a procedure, introduce several examples, talk briefly about optimization, illustrate how to make procedures easier to read, and discuss modularity and code reuse.

Simple, Effective Code Is Elegant Code

In this chapter, I will introduce you to the power and beauty of well-written stored procedures using Transact-SQL (T-SQL). The T-SQL language provides two distinct types of statements:

- Structured Query Language (SQL) statements
- Procedural constructs, such as flow control, data storage, and error-handling statements

The stored procedure author must supply the following:

- A clear definition of what the procedure will accomplish
- Efficient and concise SQL queries
- Some creative formatting

A combination of elements from the T-SQL language with an enlightened understanding of how best to use them results in stored procedures that are elegant in both function and form.

Keep to the Objectives

When you begin the task of writing one or more stored procedures, it's important to stay focused on your objectives. In this section I will discuss why stored procedures are used in database development. I'll also talk about some common functions that stored procedures perform. If you can answer the questions "Why am I writing a stored procedure?" and "What will my procedure accomplish?", that will help you stay focused on your objectives.

Why Write a Stored Procedure?

There are many good reasons for writing a stored procedure:

- Queries in a stored procedure run faster
- A common interface for data access
- Code modularity and reuse
- Security through data isolation
- Independence from an external programming language

Queries run faster in a stored procedure because the access plan used by the database engine is precompiled.

> **NOTE**
>
> SQL Server 7 has improved the caching scheme for stored procedures. After a procedure has been loaded into the cache, it's then shared by all connections. Formerly, each connection had its own copy of a procedure in the cache.

Stored procedures provide a common interface to underlying tables and the data they contain. Similar to a view in this respect, the additional benefit is that the data can be filtered, combined, and altered in complex ways before it's returned to the caller.

Modularity is achieved because stored procedures can be as small as you like, and several can be combined into larger functional units. This is because a stored procedure can call another stored procedure.

Ease of reuse results from the procedure being stored in the database itself; it's immediately available for use by any connection with execute permission. Therefore, the database serves as a central repository for code used to access and manipulate its data.

Security and integrity of underlying tables can be enhanced by using stored procedures. It's possible to deny a user direct access to a table, but grant execute privileges on a procedure that *does* have full access to the table. In this way, you can control exactly how a table is accessed, for both storage and retrieval operations.

Through stored procedures, the logical operations performed on the data in a database can sometimes be made independent from an external programming language. A common example is opening a cursor in a language such as Visual Basic, manipulating the records in some manner, and then closing the cursor. This type of processing can be accomplished completely within a stored procedure—you don't need the Visual Basic program at all. The benefit here is that such operations are not tied to a client application. The application, written in any language, simply has to call the stored procedure.

Stored procedures can be wonderful things, but if you don't need to satisfy one or more of these requirements, or you lack other compelling reasons I have not listed here, it might not be worth the extra effort to wrap a simple SQL query inside a stored procedure. To put it another way, try to spell out exactly why you are writing a stored procedure before you begin writing it. Doing this first adds to the quality of the end product and should make the task of writing the procedure easier and less prone to design or coding errors. The choice to write a procedure is yours, and you can, I hope, now make a more informed choice.

What Task Will the Procedure Accomplish?

Given that you have a good reason to implement a database function as a stored procedure, the other major objective to consider is the specific task that the procedure will perform. Many different types of tasks can be accomplished by stored procedures, such as those in the following categories:

- Data storage and retrieval
- Data archiving and deletion
- Record processing
- Business logic

Later in the chapter, I'll show you one or more examples from each of these categories. Along the way, I will discuss how each procedure is formulated, constructed, and tested.

Each example will use the ubiquitous pubs database that's installed automatically with SQL Server.

Before I get into the examples, let's briefly talk about the major logical components of a typical stored procedure, and then discuss the steps you should take to produce a polished, well-crafted procedure.

Major Components of a Stored Procedure

As you design your procedure, keep these areas in mind:

- Input/output parameters
- SQL queries
- Error handling
- Conditions, iterations, and other logical constructs

Most commonly, the input/output parameters will be matched one-to-one with fields in the tables being accessed. There is no special trick to this; just pick the fields of interest and turn them into parameters. It's also possible to have parameters that control how the procedure operates on data. These can be Boolean flags or range values, for example.

SQL queries are the heart and soul of a stored procedure. Depending on the problem being solved, you might already have a SQL query ready to incorporate into the procedure. Or you might have to create a new query to do what needs doing. I recommend that you open up a Query Analyzer window (formerly `isql/w`) and create/test your query outside the procedure first. When you have the query working correctly, you can cut and paste it into the body of your new procedure.

Error-handling schemes can be made fairly elaborate, if necessary. T-SQL gives you the ability to raise errors by using the same mechanism as the database engine. You can register custom error numbers and associated descriptions with the server by using the `sp_addmessage` system procedure, and fire off the error from within your own stored procedure.

The logical constructs, such as condition or iteration statements, provided by T-SQL round out the areas of interest to the procedure designer. These statements are described in Chapter 7, "Stored Procedures." Some examples are `IF ELSE`, `WHILE`, `BEGIN`, `END`, and `DECLARE`.

Steps to Completing a Procedure

The following steps take you from conception to a beautiful procedure suitable for framing:

1. State why you need or want a stored procedure.
2. Document what the procedure will do.
3. Identify or create the SQL query.
4. List the procedure parameters.
5. Decide on the type of error handling.
6. Write the procedure.
7. Test the procedure.

14

WRITING
EFFECTIVE CODE

You should be able to state one or more reasons why you are sitting down to write a stored procedure. It could be a design consideration, based on the benefits offered by a stored procedure. Or perhaps you are handed a design done by someone else, and one of the requirements is using stored procedures. In any case, knowing why is an important first step.

Document the specific task that the procedure will accomplish. One or two sentences stating what it does is enough. Doing this documentation should help keep your efforts focused on the problem at hand.

Type the SQL query you will use into a Query Analyzer window and run it. Make sure it does what you intend before incorporating it into your procedure.

Type up a list of parameters, with the correct data types. The parameters often correspond to columns in one or more tables.

> **TIP**
>
> One way to save time is to execute the `sp_help` system stored procedure, and then cut and paste the columns you want into your procedure editing window, along with their data types.

The level of error handling you use depends on who will be calling the procedure and how complex its function is. Don't spend too much time upfront on an elaborate error-handling scheme. You can always add it later if the need arises. However, there should *always* be some way for the caller to tell whether the procedure failed.

You have the SQL query and the parameters, so now it's time to write some code. Many text or code editors are available, and most people have a favorite. I encourage you try the Query Analyzer. This one tool gives you everything you need to develop and test your procedure. It even has syntax coloring!

> **NOTE**
>
> Don't confuse the Query Analyzer with the simple editor that Enterprise Manager shows you when you open a saved procedure in Enterprise Manager. This window is good only for viewing the procedure code, not modifying it. In fact, it's inferior to the equivalent window in version 6.5, which behaved like a specialized `isql/w` window.

After the procedure is written, it should be tested. Again, the best place I've found for doing this is in Query Analyzer. A suggestion for coding and testing is to create your procedure in one window and save it to a file. Use a second window for testing both the standalone query and the calling of your finished procedure. Save it to another file. You then have all your work in two files that you can reload into a Query Analyzer window at any time.

Thanks for being patient. You have arrived at the examples!

A Data Retrieval Example

In this first example, you want a procedure that reads records from the `titles` table. You need to read only the following columns:

```
title_id, title, pub_id, ytd_sales
```

Say that you want to read only the one record that has a given `title_id`. For `title_id` `'BU1032'`, for example, the query would look like this:

```
SELECT      title,
            pub_id,
            ytd_sales
FROM        titles
WHERE       title_id = 'BU1032'
```

Based on the fields of interest and the `WHERE` clause of the query, here are the parameter arguments you need:

```
@title_id       tid,
@title          varchar(80)     OUTPUT,
@pub_id         char(4)         OUTPUT,
@ytd_sales      int             OUTPUT
```

Notice the use of `tid` for the datatype of `@title_id`. It's a good idea to use exactly the same data type for a stored procedure parameter as the data type of the corresponding column in the table where the data comes from or goes to. If it's a custom data type, and the definition later changes, the stored procedure parameter is automatically updated if it's declared by using the custom data type.

Also, notice the use of the `OUTPUT` keyword with the last three parameters. As you might know, T-SQL requires this keyword for parameters that return a value to the caller. If you forget to add it, the procedure runs without error, but you never get the values you expect back from the call to the procedure!

Now try using the most basic of error-handling mechanisms—namely, if the query fails for any reason, including no record found, the values passed back in the output parameters are `NULL`.

Last, you don't have a need for conditional or iterative structure in this example.

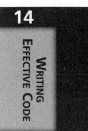

14

WRITING
EFFECTIVE CODE

The completed procedure is shown in Listing 14.1.

LISTING 14.1 Read_Title_Record.sql: A DATA RETRIEVAL EXAMPLE

```
CREATE PROCEDURE Read_Title_Record

        @title_id       tid,
        @title          varchar(80)  OUTPUT,
        @pub_id         char(4)      OUTPUT,
        @ytd_sales      int          OUTPUT
AS
BEGIN

        SELECT  @title = title,
                @pub_id = pub_id,
                @ytd_sales = ytd_sales
        FROM    titles
        WHERE   title_id = @title_id

END
GO
```

The query as it exists in the procedure is basically the same as the original query presented at the start of this example. It was plugged into the procedure by altering it to use the stored procedure parameters.

After you have a finished procedure, it must be tested. Again, the Query Analyzer comes to the rescue. It is fairly simple to set up the procedure parameters and call the procedure, as shown in Listing 14.2:

LISTING 14.2 Read_Title_Record_Test.sql: TESTING A COMPLETED PROCEDURE

```
DECLARE   @title        varchar(80),
          @pub_id       char(4),
          @ytd_sales    int

EXEC      ReadTitleRecord          'BU1032',
                          @title        OUTPUT,
                          @pub_id       OUTPUT,
                          @ytd_sales    OUTPUT

SELECT    'title' = @title,
          'pub_id' = @pub_id,
          'ytd_sales' = @ytd_sales
```

The results of running this test in Query Analyzer should look like those in Figure 14.1.

FIGURE **14.1**

Query Analyzer output after running Read_Title _Record_Test.sql.

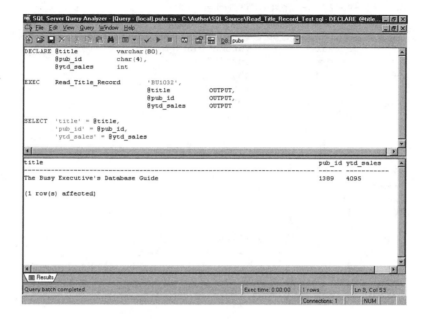

A Data Storage Example

This example shows how to write a record to the `titles` table. Say that a requirement is that the procedure will correctly handle trying to write a record whose key already exists in the table—it will update the existing record instead of inserting a new one.

From the requirements, you know that you need two separate queries. One will be an `INSERT` query, and the other an `UPDATE` query. For brevity these queries are not listed here.

Because you are storing an entire record, there must be one parameter for each column in the `titles` table.

There will be two SQL queries in this procedure. Often, when you have more than one query, you need some type of conditional statement to control which query is executed. In this case, if the record already exists, do one thing; otherwise, do something else.

Explicit error handling is not necessary in this example because the database engine generates errors if either of the queries fails. Listing 14.3 shows the completed procedure.

LISTING 14.3   Write_Title_Record.sql: A DATA STORAGE EXAMPLE

```
CREATE PROCEDURE Write_Title_Record

        @title_id       tid,
        @title          varchar(80),
        @type           char(12),
        @pub_id         char(4),
        @price          money,
        @advance        money,
        @royalty        int,
        @ytd_sales      int,
        @notes          varchar(200),
        @pubdate        datetime,
AS
BEGIN
        IF EXISTS
        (
                SELECT  *
                FROM    titles
                WHERE   title_id = @title_id
        )
        BEGIN
                UPDATE  titles
                SET     title = @title,
                        type = @type,
                        pub_id = @pub_id,
                        price = @price,
                        advance = @advance,
                        royalty = @royalty,
                        ytd_sales = @ytd_sales,
                        notes = @notes,
                        pubdate = @pubdate
                WHERE   title_id = @title_id
        END
        ELSE BEGIN
                INSERT  titles
                (
                        title_id,
                        title,
                        type,
                        pub_id,
                        price,
                        advance,
                        royalty,
                        ytd_sales,
                        notes,
                        pubdate
                )
                VALUES
                (
```

```
                              @title_id,
                              @title,
                              @type,
                              @pub_id,
                              @price,
                              @advance,
                              @royalty,
                              @ytd_sales,
                              @notes,
                              @pubdate
                  )
          END
END
GO
```

Here you are using the IF, ELSE statements to control which query is executed inside the procedure. The EXISTS statement is a powerful way to determine whether a record with a given key is already in a table. When the SQL Server query processor sees this keyword, it knows that it is checking for the existence of a record and does not actually fetch any rows.

A Data Archiving Example

The scenario for this example is that a title that goes out of print needs to have a record copied from the titles table into an archive table. So, you need to add a table to the pubs database, old_titles. It is a mirror image of the titles table, but will hold old titles that are no longer published. The file old_titles.sql on the CD-ROM accompanying this book contains the script to create this table.

For a title_id of 'BU1032', this is the query that will accomplish the archiving:

```
INSERT      old_titles
SELECT      *
FROM        titles
WHERE       title_id = 'BU1032'
```

The only parameter needed for this procedure is the @title_id of the title to be archived.

For error handling, I will introduce you to a simple mechanism used quite commonly in high-level programming languages (such as Visual Basic, C, Pascal, and so forth). Like functions in these languages, SQL Server stored procedures can have a return value that is essentially a special parameter. The caller of this procedure can look at the return value to determine whether the procedure succeeded. The procedure is shown in Listing 14.4.

14

WRITING
EFFECTIVE CODE

LISTING 14.4   `Archive_Old_Title.sql`: A DATA ARCHIVING EXAMPLE

```
CREATE PROCEDURE Archive_Old_Title

     @title_id  tid
AS
BEGIN

     DECLARE    @rows      int

     INSERT     old_titles
     SELECT     *
     FROM       titles
     WHERE      title_id = @title_id

     SELECT     @rows = @@ROWCOUNT

     IF @rows = 0 BEGIN

          RETURN -1
     END

     RETURN @rows

END
GO
```

The number of rows affected by a query is available at any point within a stored procedure in the @@ROWCOUNT global variable. This variable is constantly being updated after every query operation. If a T-SQL statement is not query related, @@ROWCOUNT is reset to zero. That's why you have to save the value immediately after the INSERT query. The IF statement below it resets @@ROWCOUNT to zero, so the second RETURN statement would never return the value you want, that is the number of rows affected by the insert.

The error-handling mechanism here is simple. If the title was not archived (because the title_id does not exist, for example) then a minus one (-1) is returned. The practice of returning a negative value to indicate an error is also quite common and works well for simple functions.

To test the procedure and its error-handling mechanism, you really need to create two scenarios, one positive and the other negative, as shown in Listing 14.5.

LISTING 14.5 ARCHIVE_OLD_TITLE_TEST.SQL: AN EXAMPLE OF A POSITIVE AND A NEGATIVE TEST

```
-- Positive test
DECLARE   @result    int
EXEC      @result = Archive_Old_Title   'BU1032'

SELECT    'result' = @result

-- Negative test
EXEC      @result = Archive_Old_Title   'BOGUS'

SELECT    'result' = @result
```

The results of running both the positive and negative test are shown in Figure 14.2.

FIGURE 14.2

Query Analyzer results after running Archive_Old_ Title_Test.sql.

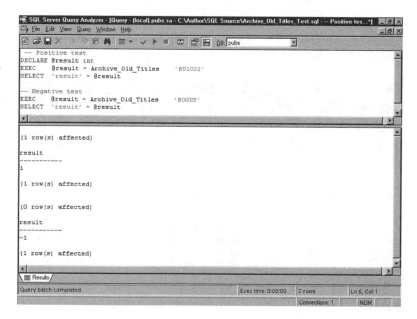

A Data Deletion Example

For this example, when a title goes out of print, you want to delete the records in the sales and roysched tables that correspond with the retired title.

The queries to accomplish the deletions are as follows for the 'BU1032' title:

```
DELETE
FROM    sales
WHERE   title_id = 'BU1032'
```

```
DELETE
FROM      roysched
WHERE     title_id = 'BU1032'
```

The only parameter needed is the `title_id` of the title you want to retire.

For error handling, an interesting situation occurs. You want both of the queries to be executed successfully. On the other hand, if one fails, you don't want to execute the other one. This is a job for a *transaction*. A good way to handle this, then, is to check for an error condition after each query and roll back the transaction if either one fails. Here is the code to accomplish that:

```
IF @@ERROR <> 0 BEGIN
     ROLLBACK TRANSACTION
     RAISERROR 50002 "Delete of sales record failed"
     RETURN -1
END
```

Inside the `IF` block, the transaction is rolled back, an error is raised, and a minus one is returned for good measure.

> **NOTE**
>
> SQL Server reserves error numbers 1–50000 for its own use. When you declare and raise your own errors, you should use numbers greater than 50000.

Listing 14.6 contains the completed procedure.

LISTING 14.6   `Retire_Title.sql`: A DATA DELETION EXAMPLE

```
CREATE PROCEDURE Retire_Title

     @title_id     tid
AS
BEGIN

     BEGIN TRANSACTION

     DELETE
     FROM      sales
     WHERE     title_id = @title_id

     IF @@ERROR <> 0 BEGIN
          ROLLBACK TRANSACTION
          RAISERROR 50002 "Delete of sales record failed"
          RETURN -1
     END
```

```
        DELETE
        FROM      roysched
        WHERE     title_id = @title_id

        IF @@ERROR <> 0 BEGIN
            ROLLBACK TRANSACTION
            RAISERROR 50003 "Delete of roysched record failed"
            RETURN -1
        END

        COMMIT TRANSACTION
        RETURN 0
END
GO
```

As described, a transaction is started before the queries are executed. If either query fails, the transaction is rolled back and an error is raised. Of course, if both queries succeed, you must explicitly commit the transaction that was started at the beginning of the procedure.

The code used to test the procedure is shown in Listing 14.7.

LISTING 14.7   Retire_Title_Test.sql: TESTING THE DELETION EXAMPLE

```
EXEC      Retire_Title     'BU1032'

SELECT    *
FROM      sales
WHERE     title_id = 'BU1032'

SELECT    *
FROM      roysched
WHERE     title_id = 'BU1032'
```

A Record Processing Example

Stored procedures can be used to perform *end of day*, or after hours, processing of records. For this example, say that there is a table of titles scheduled to be retired. During the day, records are added as the decision is made to retire a title. At some scheduled time (for example, on Friday evening at 11 p.m.), the titles in this table will actually be retired. A stored procedure is called by the SQL Executive to do the work.

Although it is grossly oversimplified for the sake of brevity, use the procedures you created in the previous two examples to do the following:

1. Archive the title.
2. Delete the active records no longer needed in ancillary tables.

The table of titles to be retired must be created. It's called `retired_titles` and its creation script is in a file called `Retired_Titles.sql` on the CD-ROM. It consists of a single column containing the `title_id`.

You don't need to create any new queries to do the work—the stored procedures from the previous two examples will do it for you.

There are no parameters required in this sample procedure.

Error handling will be a bit more elaborate than you've seen so far. You will respond to errors generated by the called subprocedures and write them out to a log file.

To accomplish the writing to a log file, Listing 14.8 shows a utility procedure you can reuse to write to any file.

LISTING 14.8   `Write_Log.sql`: A UTILITY PROCEDURE FOR WRITING TO A LOG FILE

```
CREATE PROCEDURE Write_Log

     @log_file      varchar(255),
     @msg           varchar(255)
AS
BEGIN

     DECLARE     @cmd_str      varchar(512)
     DECLARE     @date_str     varchar(30)

     SELECT      @date_str = CONVERT(varchar(24), GetDate())

     SELECT      @cmd_str = 'ECHO ' + @date_str + ' -- ' + @msg
     SELECT      @cmd_str = @cmd_str + '>>' + @log_file

     EXEC        master..xp_cmdshell @cmd_str
END
GO
```

Listing 14.9 shows the complete record-processing sample procedure.

LISTING 14.9 Write_Log.sql: A RECORD-PROCESSING EXAMPLE

```
CREATE PROCEDURE Process_Retired_Titles

AS
BEGIN

    DECLARE @title_id     tid,
            @result       int,
            @msg          varchar(255),
            @log_file     varchar(255)

    SELECT  @log_file = 'c:\logs\proc_ret_tit.log'

    DECLARE titles_cursor CURSOR
    FOR     SELECT    title_id
            FROM      retired_titles

    OPEN    titles_cursor

    FETCH NEXT FROM titles_cursor INTO @title_id

    WHILE @@FETCH_STATUS = 0 BEGIN

        EXEC    @result = Archive_Old_Title @title_id
        IF @result < 0 BEGIN
            SELECT  @msg = 'Failed to archive: ' + @title_id
            EXEC    Write_Log @log_file, @msg
        END

        EXEC    @result = Retire_Title @title_id
        IF @result < 0 BEGIN
            SELECT  @msg = 'Failed to delete: ' + @title_id
            EXEC    Write_Log @log_file, @msg
        END

        FETCH NEXT FROM titles_cursor INTO @title_id

    END

    DEALLOCATE titles_cursor
END
GO
```

This example is incomplete but serves to illustrate what you can accomplish with a stored procedure in the way of record processing.

A Business Logic Example

For the final example, I want to show how you can incorporate business rules right into a stored procedure. This sample procedure computes the total sales price of an order based on the titles selected, the discount type, the quantity ordered, and the title list price.

There will be several queries in the procedure, but for brevity's sake, I won't list them here.

The parameters will consist of the values needed to identify an order and the computed total sale: @stor_id, @ord_num, @discounttype, and @total_sale.

I'm going to leave out error handling to save space in this example. In the real world, however, you would probably want to include some error trapping in this procedure. Listing 14.10 shows the complete procedure.

LISTING 14.10   Write_Log.sql: A BUSINESS LOGIC EXAMPLE

```
CREATE PROCEDURE Compute_Price

    @stor_id      char(4),
    @ord_num      varchar(20),
    @discounttype varchar(40),
    @total_sale   money          OUTPUT
AS
BEGIN

    DECLARE @qty            smallint,
            @title_id       tid,
            @list_price     money,
            @discount       decimal(4,2),
            @curr_sale      money,
            @curr_discount  money

    SELECT  @total_sale = 0

    DECLARE order_cursor CURSOR
    FOR     SELECT  title_id,
                    qty
            FROM    sales
            WHERE   stor_id = @stor_id
            AND     ord_num = @ord_num

    OPEN    order_cursor

    FETCH NEXT FROM order_cursor INTO @title_id, @qty

    WHILE @@FETCH_STATUS = 0  BEGIN

        SELECT  @list_price = price
        FROM    titles
```

```
        WHERE      title_id = @title_id

        -- First attempt to get discount for this specific store based on
        -- the quantity ordered
        SELECT     @discount = discount
        FROM       discounts
        WHERE      stor_id = @stor_id
        AND        discounttype = @discounttype
        AND        @qty BETWEEN lowqty AND highqty

        -- If no discount exists for this store based on quantity, see if
        -- there is any discount at all for this store
        IF @discount IS NULL BEGIN
            SELECT   @discount = discount
            FROM     discounts
            WHERE    stor_id = @stor_id
            AND      discounttype = @discounttype
        END

        -- If there is no discount specific to this store, check for a
➥company
        -- wide generic discount based on quantity
        IF @discount IS NULL BEGIN
            SELECT   @discount = discount
            FROM     discounts
            WHERE    stor_id IS NULL
            AND      discounttype = @discounttype
            AND      @qty BETWEEN lowqty AND highqty
        END

        -- If there is no generic discount based on quantity, the final
➥chance
        -- for a discount depends on the discount type
        IF @discount IS NULL BEGIN
            SELECT   @discount = discount
            FROM     discounts
            WHERE    stor_id IS NULL
            AND      discounttype = @discounttype
        END

        SELECT @discount = ISNULL(@discount, 0.0000)
        SELECT @curr_discount = (@qty * @list_price * (@discount / 100))
        SELECT @curr_sale = @qty * @list_price - @curr_discount
        SELECT @total_sale = @total_sale + @curr_sale

        FETCH NEXT FROM order_cursor INTO @title_id, @qty
    END

    CLOSE order_cursor
    DEALLOCATE order_cursor
END
GO
```

14

WRITING
EFFECTIVE CODE

In this example, you see some fairly elaborate manipulation of data that rivals what you can do in most third-generation languages. With all the built-in functions, system and extended stored procedures, and T-SQL statements available, there's little you can't accomplish in a stored procedure.

I've tried to cover a lot of ground with these examples while keeping them simple. That's a good practice to follow when you write your own procedures, by the way. Excessively complex procedures are hard to design, code, and debug. Remember the "KISS" (Keep It Simple, Stupid) principle.

One powerful feature, not covered in the examples, is the use of a stored procedure to return one or more resultsets to the caller. Briefly, if you execute a query that returns multiple rows inside a stored procedure, these rows will be returned to the caller. A useful tactic for complex operations is to create a temporary table in the stored procedure, perform processing that results in records being stored in the temporary table, and then return all the records in the temporary table to the caller. Another is to return multiple resultsets to the caller; A client application can obtain data from several resultsets using a single call to a stored procedure. When a client application needs data from two or more related tables, this approach is sometimes better than creating one complex query that employs joins. Returning resultsets from stored procedures is an important topic, and I encourage you to experiment with the possibilities.

Another area I did not discuss is debugging. Again, this is an important topic when you go on to create more sophisticated procedures. The venerable `PRINT` statement and the `Write_Log` procedure I presented can be a big help for quick-and-dirty debugging.

An entire book could be dedicated to examples of stored procedures. I hope that those presented here have given you a sense of what you can do with stored procedures as well as how to go about writing one.

Methods of Optimization

There are times when you must optimize your stored procedures for critical operations. Generally, optimization of any executable program falls into two broad categories:

- Maximizing performance
- Minimizing resource requirements

These two types of optimization are sometimes mutually exclusive, and sometimes not.

With SQL Server 7.0, many optimizations that didn't exist or had to be done manually in previous releases are now done automatically by the Query Optimizer and storage engine. Be that as it may, there are still some important points to consider when you need a procedure tuned for speed or minimal overhead. Keep these points in mind:

- Network operations are costly.
- Set-oriented operations usually run faster than cursor operations.
- Indexes can be your best friend.
- SQL Server 7 now optionally provides parallel execution of some types of queries.
- Transactions are costly, but careful use of them can actually reduce resource requirements for queries involving high volumes of data.

Network operations are costly to performance. The details are beyond the scope of this chapter, but there are some things you can do to reduce the cost. First, move as much processing as possible to the server. For example, don't call ten different stored procedures from a client application when you could call one procedure, which in turn calls the other procedures on the server. Don't be afraid to create a procedure with many parameters, if that makes sense. The networking layer uses fixed length packets, so a procedure with one parameter or ten is going to take the same amount of time.

Set-oriented operations are usually faster (99.9% of the time!). For example, it is quicker to execute a mass UPDATE than it is to open a cursor on a table and then update each row individually. If you can't avoid using a cursor, a couple of things can help with performance. First, select only the columns you need when opening the cursor (SELECT *, for example, is bad). Second, forward-only and read-only cursors perform better than scrollable and or updatable cursors.

You hear about indexes a lot when working with a database. Use them often. It's perfectly okay to create an index specifically to improve the performance of a stored procedure. Yes, indexes require extra storage space and a small amount of overhead for write operations, but the gains exceed the costs by a mile for retrieval operations. Use them.

With SQL Server 7.0, you now have the option of executing queries in parallel. The details on this are covered elsewhere in the book, but please remember that you don't gain anything in absolute execution time using parallel queries unless the server hardware incorporates multiple processors.

On the one hand, wrapping your SQL queries inside a transaction increases the overhead needed to execute them, but there's an advantage to using explicit transactions because you can decide when to commit. An example is updating a large table. If you use the implicit transaction (which is started automatically for all storage queries), your UPDATE is going to continue to soak up more and more resources (such as locks and transaction log space) until the query is finished. If, on the other hand, you break up the query into ten sections or ranges, and explicitly start and commit your own transactions for each section, the resource requirements will be about one tenth as much.

14

WRITING
EFFECTIVE CODE

This is by no means a comprehensive coverage of optimization. Just remember that the methods you use to optimize SQL queries outside stored procedures are just as applicable inside a procedure.

Punctuation for Readability

This section covers some simple ways you can format your procedure code so that it is easily readable. Taking the extra time (a few minutes at best) to lay out your code in a logical structured way benefits anyone who has to read it, including you, the procedure author. Of course, the machine doesn't care how it's formatted as long as it's syntactically correct. People, however, are highly sensitive to visual cues—not surprising when you consider that about a third of the human brain is devoted to visual processing.

The T-SQL language is highly flexible, so it's easy to apply some creative formatting. One of the keys to proper formatting is the judicious use of whitespace (spaces, tabs, carriage returns, and so forth). Here is some T-SQL code that is hard to read because everything is bunched together:

```
if @somevalue is null begin select * from table
where @somecolumn = 'X' end
```

Here is the same code using whitespace to visually separate or combine related elements in a logical manner:

```
if @somevariable is null begin
    select  *
    from    table
    where   somecolumn = 'value'
end
```

With this formatting, you can see right away that you have a SELECT statement with a WHERE clause inside a conditional expression. It practically leaps out of the page. But you can do more. Because T-SQL is not case sensitive, you can use case as a tool to further organize the code into logical sections. It's somewhat of a de facto standard to capitalize T-SQL statements like so:

```
IF @somevariable IS NULL BEGIN
    SELECT  *
    FROM    table
    WHERE   somecolumn = 'value'
END
```

Now when you see a keyword in all caps, you know it is part of the T-SQL language. This is particularly beneficial for someone who is not an expert user. He or she can see the keywords in all caps and look up their meaning in the help files.

You can do more with case. Variable and column names are easier to read when the first character is capitalized. The capital letter says "This is the beginning of something." Because many variable and column names are compound names, you can capitalize the first letter of each word that makes up the name:

```
IF @SomeVariable IS NULL BEGIN
    SELECT    *
    FROM      Table
    WHERE     SomeColumn = 'value'
END
```

I usually take it one step further, and place an underscore between each word of the compound name:

```
IF @Some_Variable IS NULL BEGIN
    SELECT    *
    FROM      Table
    WHERE     Some_Column = 'value'
END
```

Here are some additional formatting templates you can use for various types of T-SQL statements:

```
INSERT    Table
(
    A
)
VALUES
(
    'A'
)

UPDATE    Table
SET       A = 'A'
WHERE     B = 'B'

SELECT    A
FROM      Table1
WHERE     B =
          (
                SELECT    B
                FROM      Table2
                WHERE     C = 'C'
          )
```

These are only suggestions, of course, designed to give you an idea of how you can break up your code to make it eye-friendly.

You might be wondering why I haven't mentioned comments. There's nothing wrong with comments, but well-written code should be largely self-documenting. Too many comments only serve to clutter things up. That said, there are a couple of places where comments are desirable. One is a banner comment at the top of a procedure. I suggest something like this:

```
/************************************************************
     Name:         My_Procedure
     Purpose:      To unlock the mysteries of the universe
     Author:       Yours Truly
     Date:         12/31/1999
     Dependencies: NONE

     Revision:     01/01/2000 YT  Added some code
************************************************************/
CREATE PROCEDURE My_Procedure

AS
BEGIN
```

The other is a line comment above a particularly complex series of statements, such as a WHILE loop:

```
-- The following loop calculates the gross national product
-- and performs a regression analysis
WHILE @More_To_Do BEGIN
```

You don't have to follow these suggestions to the letter. Impart your own style in formatting your code, but do remember that other people eventually have to read and understand what you wrote—count on it.

Modularity of Stored Procedures

The final topic of this chapter is concerned with the notion of code modules that can be "plugged together" and reused over and over again. As software systems become more and more complex and the demand for such systems increases, it becomes desirable to build the systems from "off the shelf" components. It's similar to the automobile industry. There is no way we would have the staggering number of automobiles we have on the road today unless the thousands of pieces used to build them were standardized.

Reusable software modules should have these qualities:

- The function they perform should be atomic.
- A naming convention should be established.
- Parameter types should be consistent and as generic as possible.

- Error handling should be robust.
- They should perform something of real value.
- Detailed documentation with examples should be included.

An *atomic* function is one that cannot easily be broken down into smaller pieces.

Reusable components generally belong in a *library*. Each procedure should be named so that the library it belongs to is easily discernible, such as the sp_ that's in front of the system procedures that come with SQL Server.

Part of what makes procedures reusable is that their parameters are designed to accept a wide range of values. For example, declare a varchar value as varchar(255) so that it can accept a wide variety of string sizes.

Because you don't know exactly how the reusable procedure will be used, and because the user does not want to debug your procedure, make sure the error handling is rock solid. The user should be able to tell exactly what's going wrong based on the type of errors your procedure throws.

It might seem obvious, but the reusable procedure should do something genuinely useful—something complex or tedious that the user would rather not have to code.

Document the procedure. It's likely that the user won't have you around to explain how the procedure works or what it does. A description and an example of its use will make the user very happy.

Listing 14.8 from the previous examples is a good illustration of a reusable stored procedure.

Summary

This chapter has explained why procedures are written, the types of things they commonly do, tips on optimizing them, and how to make them more readable for people. You also took a look at code modularity principles. I hope that by reading this chapter you have gotten the "procedure fever." If you are like me, you'll wonder how you ever did without them.

CHAPTER 15

Using Multiple Tiers and Client/Server Architecture

You've probably heard the term "n-tiered architecture" around the water cooler or some technical journal by now. So what does it mean and how does it affect you? Well, these and many more answers about the flexibility of multiple-tier architecture are unraveled in this chapter.

Understanding Client/Server Architectures

In developing an understanding of client/server architectures, it's useful to introduce three basic definitions:

- Client/server model
- Client/server application
- Client/server system

Client/Server Model

In its most basic form, the client/server model is *a concept for describing communications between service consumers (clients) and service providers (servers)*. The defining feature of this model is that a client initiates an interaction with a server by sending a message or by invoking an operation. Likewise, the response of the server is a message that is sent back to the client. Figure 15.1 is a basic graphical representation of this model.

FIGURE 15.1

Simple client/server model.

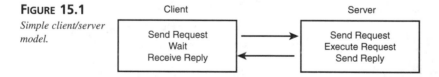

What is useful about this definition is that it's general enough to allow for a variety of computing architectures that can appropriately be designated as client/server. Examples include the following:

- Two processes running on the same machine, with one functioning as a client and the other functioning as a server (for example, a client application and an in-process COM server).
- A LAN in which clients can request file and print services from file and print servers.

- A peer-to-peer network in which a given node can function as both a client and a server (such as a Windows 95 network, with each workstation capable of requesting and offering file and print services for other workstations on the network).

- A complex multitier application in which application logic is distributed across multiple servers throughout the enterprise.

Client/Server Application

A client/server application can simply be described as *an application based on the client/server model*. Applications that satisfy this definition are characterized by *segmentation of application functionality* into roles that fit the definitions of a client and a server given earlier. How this segmentation is done can vary from application to application, but in each case the client and server roles involve processing designed to address one or more of the following functional needs:

- **Presentation services**   Application functionality that supports presenting data to and retrieving data from the end user.

- **Business logic**   Application functionality that supports enforcement of business rules.

- **Data services**   Application functionality that supports retrieving, adding, editing, and deleting the data managed by the application.

Client/Server System

A client/server system is *a computing system based on the client/server model*. In this context, clients and servers are usually (but not necessarily) defined in terms of the hardware (machines) that's performing these roles. These are the basic components that make up a system defined in this way:

- **Clients**   Consumers of services provided by servers.
- **Servers**   Providers of services requested by clients.
- **Middleware**   Technology that supports communication between clients and servers. Although middleware usually includes services provided by networking hardware and software, this may or may not be true in a given application.

15

MULTIPLE TIERS
AND
CLIENT/SERVER

Evolution of Client/Server Computing Architectures

When the basic definition of the client/server model is taken into consideration, it can be seen that client/server computing represents a specific case of *distributed cooperative processing*. In attempting to understand client/server computing, it's beneficial to consider several computing architectures that have contributed significantly to the current implementations of distributed computing. This is particularly true because most contemporary enterprise computing environments are a hybrid of these architectures.

Host-Based Systems

Host-based systems represent the most primitive architecture that was the precursor of today's modern distributed computing architectures. Host-based systems consist of a central CPU and attached unintelligent, or "dumb," terminals. As such, host-based systems have no distributed capability; all processing is done on one central CPU. Perhaps the most well-known example of the host-based architecture is the traditional mainframe computer with attached dumb terminals. Figure 15.2 illustrates the host-based architecture.

FIGURE 15.2
Host-based architecture.

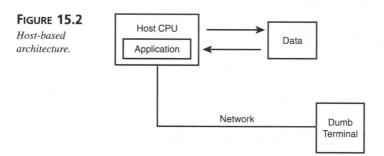

Despite assertions that client/server systems would "replace the mainframe," such claims have proved largely unfounded. Mainframe computers still constitute the central repository for a large portion of the legacy data in many organizations. This continues to be an important consideration when developing holistic, integrated enterprise computing environments, particularly as it relates to OLAP (Online Analytical Processing) applications, such as data warehouses.

Two-Tier Client/Server Architecture

The advent of inexpensive local area networking technologies paved the way for the first generation of client/server systems. These systems are called *two-tier* because of the simple client tier and server tier that are the basis of their design.

Initially, systems based on this architecture used a *shared-device model* to allow PCs connected to a LAN to share file and print resources located on other devices on the network. For many, this architecture has come to be synonymous with the term *LAN* (local area network).

Within this context, the devices that offer shared resources to network clients are referred to as *file servers* (those devices that provide shared-file resources) and *print servers* (those devices that provide shared-printer resources). This architecture is appropriately referred to as the "first generation" because it implements distributed processing (even if it's limited to file and printer I/O) and incorporates the basic components of any client/server system:

- Client
- Server
- Network

For many organizations, Novell networks based on this architecture represented the first foray into the world of network computing. To a large degree, Microsoft Windows NT networks have now become the platform of choice for the delivery of file and print services in the modern enterprise. Figure 15.3 illustrates the file and print server architecture.

FIGURE 15.3

Shared-device (file and print server) architecture.

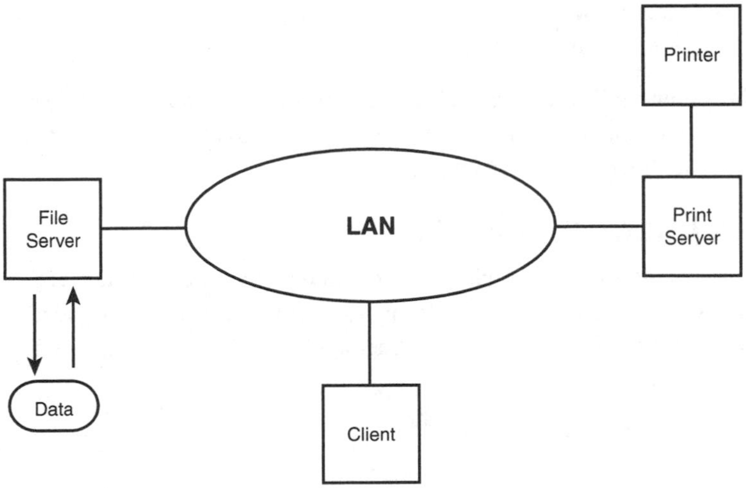

The next stage in the growth of two-tier client/server systems was realized with the pro-liferation of the robust RDBMSs (relational database management systems), which have become a standard feature of today's business computing environments. These systems use a *shared-processing model* to allow the logic of an application to be distributed between the *front-end* client application (typically implemented in the form of a Windows GUI application) and the *back-end* server application (typically implemented in the form of database stored procedures and triggers). Figure 15.4 illustrates the shared-processing architecture.

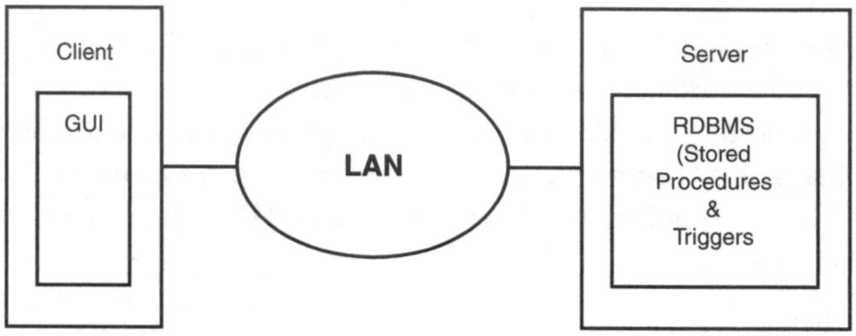

FIGURE 15.4
Shared-processing architecture.

As shared-processing architecture has become more prominent, application developers have seen fit to divide the processing requirements of an application into three areas of functional need:

- **Presentation services**   Processing that manages the presentation of data to, and interaction with, the end user.
- **Business logic**   Processing that manages the enforcement of business rules pri-marily through data validation.
- **Data services**   Processing that manages basic data operations (SELECT, INSERT, UPDATE, and DELETE)

The attempt to leverage the advantages of the distributed-processing architecture to meet these needs has given rise to two application design paradigms: fat client architecture and thin client (fat server) architecture.

Fat Client Architecture

As the name suggests, applications based on a fat client architecture locate the bulk of processing logic on the client (front-end). Both presentation services and enforcement of business rules are located in the client application, as illustrated by Figure 15.5.

FIGURE 15.5
Fat client architecture.

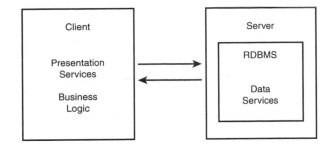

Thin Client (Fat Server) Architecture

Thin client (fat server) applications seek to relegate the client (front-end) to a stream-lined role of managing presentation services and target the server (back-end) for the role of enforcing business rules and providing data services, as illustrated by Figure 15.6.

FIGURE 15.6
Thin client architecture.

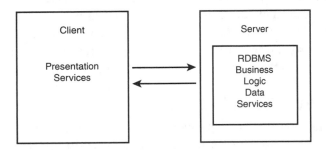

Peer-to-Peer Systems

Peer-to-peer systems traditionally represented a slight variation on the file and print server theme. In this architecture, clients can also assume the role of servers, and likewise, servers can assume the role of clients. A good example of this architecture is the Microsoft Windows for Workgroups network, which laid the groundwork for the peer-to-peer net-working capability that has become a standard feature of the Windows 95/98 and NT operating systems.

In this architecture a Windows 95 machine, for example, can take advantage of shared files and printers on other Windows 95 machines and at the same time share its files and printers with them. The role of a particular machine is defined by the nature of its com-munication with another machine. Figure 15.7 illustrates the peer-to-peer architecture.

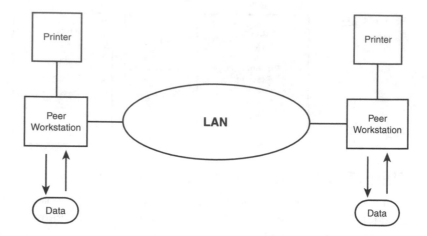

FIGURE 15.7
Peer-to-peer architecture.

Although the traditional perception of peer-to-peer processing can seem simple, that can be misleading. In point of fact, there are many indications that this architecture could figure prominently in state-of-the-art distributed applications. In such a scenario, business intelligence would be dispersed throughout the enterprise in intelligent components that are capable of requesting and providing services.

Three-Tier Client/Server

With the proliferation of two-tier client/server systems in business environments, several factors have become a source of increasing concern in the struggle to develop cost-effective solutions:

- **Scalability**   As the demands on an application change in terms of numbers of users and transactions, the application should scale to accommodate these changes. The extent to which initial investments in development can be leveraged to accommodate the growth of an application contributes significantly to its overall cost-effectiveness as a solution.

- **Maintainability**   The issue of maintainability becomes a particular concern with managing business rules in today's rapidly changing business environments. One of the problems that can be associated with two-tier, fat client applications results from the fact that business logic often resides in each client application. As the business grows and changes, the costs of maintaining application business logic to accommodate these changes can be staggering. The degree to which changes in business logic can be reduced to a central point of maintenance can dramatically reduce the costs of managing change within an organization.

- **Performance and reliability**   Increasingly, business users want more information and they want it faster. As businesses and their applications grow and change, the need for increased performance and reliability must be managed while keeping development costs to a minimum.

Three-tier client/server systems are gaining increasing popularity as a means of addressing these concerns. Continued reduction in the cost of hardware, accompanied by the availability of robust middleware products, Rapid Application Development (RAD) tools and component technologies have allowed the three-tier architecture to emerge as a practical option for application developers; previously, they had been little more than a theoretical ideal.

The tiers in the three-tier architecture are defined in terms of the following services:

- Presentation services
- Business services (business rules)
- Data services

Typically, these tiers (especially the business services and data services tiers) are implemented as components, which encapsulate the corresponding services and act as service providers to applications that require them, as shown in Figure 15.8.

FIGURE 15.8

Three-tier architecture.

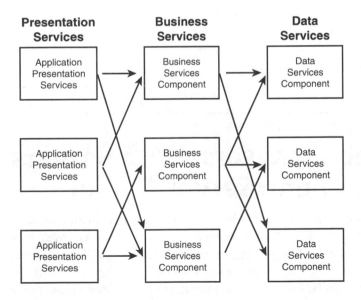

15

These three tiers serve as the *logical model* for the three-tier architecture and do not nec-essarily correspond to physical locations on the network. A distinct advantage of the three-tier architecture is the flexibility and scalability it allows in developing an application's physical implementation. After an application has been partitioned in this manner, it lends itself to a variety of physical implementations. Scaling the application to meet changing needs in the organization becomes simply a deployment issue, which requires no modifications to the application's source code.

When an application is developed using the three-tier architecture, presentation services are implemented in a thin client, and business services and data services are encapsulated in components. Table 15.1 shows some of the physical implementations of this logical model.

TABLE 15.1 COMPARING 1, 2, AND 3-TIER IMPLEMENTATIONS

	Fat Client	*Thin Client*	*Three-Tier (Physical)*
Client machine	Presentation services Business services Data services	Presentation services	Presentation services
Application server			Business services
Database server		Business services Data services	Data services

Web Browsers, Web Servers, and the Client/Server Model

Any discussion of Web technology and client/server computing should begin by stating clearly that the *World Wide Web is a client/server system*. The Web browser (client) assumes the role of managing presentation services. The Web server (server) assumes the role of servicing requests for content from the client browser. HTML pages stored on the server contain HTML code (which serves as the mechanism for defining the presentation modality) and the actual data to be presented.

Remember that managing presentation services is a function shared by the client and the server. The client browser assumes a streamlined role of executing HTML code. As such, it's very much a "thin client." The application-specific details of how presentation services are managed reside on the Web server in the form of HTML code, thus offering a central point of maintenance.

To the extent that the Web browser/Web server architecture is a client/server architecture, it lends itself to the two-tier and three-tier architectures mentioned previously.

Two-Tier Web Architecture

Two-tier Web architecture has been the traditional model used in Web site design. In this architecture, data is stored in HTML pages on the Web server. The client browser requests a Web page, which is returned by the server and presented to the user in the client browser (see Figure 15.9).

FIGURE 15.9
Simple Web browser/Web server architecture (two-tier).

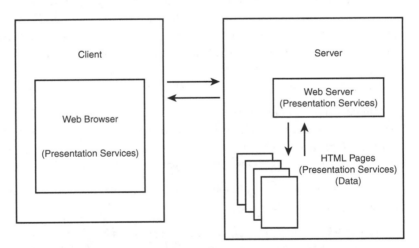

One of the limitations of this rudimentary model is that the data in the HTML pages is static. Furthermore, HTML as a language is geared primarily toward managing presentation services, so it doesn't lend itself to managing business rules data services.

NOTE

Static pre-existing HTML pages rarely prove to be a useful Web-based application. Most often we need some type of data to be generated dynamically.

15

MULTIPLE TIERS AND CLIENT/SERVER

Three-Tier Web Architecture

To address the limitations of two-tier Web architecture, three-tier Web architecture is based on the concept of *dynamic Web applications* as opposed to *static Web pages*. In a three-tier Web architecture, the Web server assumes the role of a middle-tier application server acting as a gateway to a back-end database server.

In one of its more popular implementations, this architecture uses a technology known as *server-side scripting* to enhance the level of services the Web server can offer. Server-side scripting technologies, such as Microsoft Active Server Pages (ASP), have been developed to allow developers to embed programmatic logic in Web pages using scripting languages, such as VBScript or JScript, with the added benefit that script programming is executed on the Web server before the content is delivered to the client for presentation to the user.

The basic architectural component of a server-side scripting model is the *server-side script page*. Server-side script pages, distinguished from standard HTML pages by their extension (.ASP which represents Active Server Pages), serve as containers for scripting to be executed on the Web server. When a client browser requests a server-side script page, the Web server identifies it by its extension and reads and executes the script. The resulting output (usually in the form of standard HTML) is then sent to the client.

In a three-tier Web model, server-side script pages are used to locate application logic on the Web server as it would be in a component on a middle-tier application server. Business logic and requests for back-end database services are implemented through server-side script pages. Figure 15.10 illustrates the three-tier Web architecture.

Although this model offers obvious improvements over the two-tier Web architecture, it can have certain disadvantages:

- The Web server can become a bottleneck because it is responsible for processing server-side scripts in addition to servicing requests from client browsers for content.

- Scripting is often not as robust as an actual programming language and can also be difficult to maintain.

NOTE

Keep in mind that ASP pages often contain several flavors of technologies, such as HTML, JavaScript, VBScript, and so on which adds to the difficulty in maintaining their code.

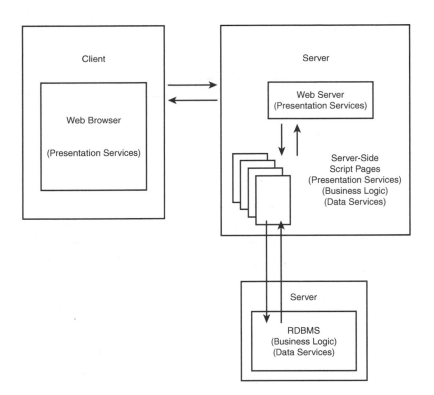

FIGURE 15.10

Three-tier Web architecture.

To address these potential limitations, some developers have extended the three-tier Web architecture to make use of components integrated with server-side scripting. In this model, components are used to encapsulate business logic and possibly data services. Server-side script pages are used to pass relevant information from the session of a client browser back to this component layer. All processing related to enforcing business logic and database access is performed within the component layer. Finally, data is returned to the calling server-side script pages, which manage presenting the data to the client browser. Figure 15.11 depicts this scenario.

The component-based three-tier Web architecture has several advantages over the basic three-tier Web model:

- Components developed in programming languages tend to be more robust than script pages in terms of overall functionality and error handling.
- Components tend to be easier to debug and maintain.
- Using components for encapsulation of business logic lends itself to scalability and code reuse better than script pages do.
- Components do not rely on the Web server for processing, thus eliminating it as a potential performance bottleneck.

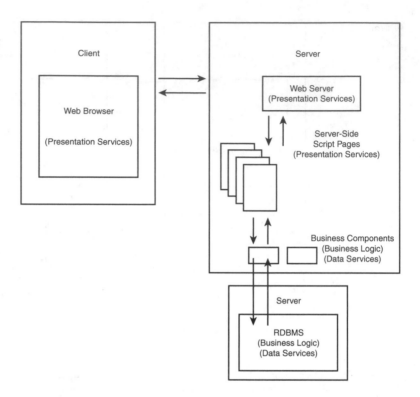

FIGURE 15.11
Component-based three-tier Web architecture.

Microsoft's Three-Tier Services Model

Microsoft's three-tier services model is formally known as Windows DNA (Distributed interNet Applications Architecture), which uses COM (Component Object Model) components as the means of making system and application services available. Windows DNA describes a three-tier architecture consisting of the following tiers:

- User services
- Business services
- Data services

Like the three-tier architecture described previously, Windows DNA tiers describe a logical model and do not necessarily correspond to the physical locations where they reside.

User Services

The user services tier of Windows DNA handles presenting information to and interacting with users. The user services tier generally corresponds to the client that is deployed on the user's desktop. Windows DNA defines four types of clients that can be used to implement the user services tier:

- **Browser-neutral client** This type of client relies on simple, page-based HTML to manage presentation of data and interaction with the user. This approach ensures compatibility with the broadest range of client browsers, although it might result in a compromise in the functionality and richness of the user interface.

- **Browser-enhanced client** The browser-enhanced client is designed to take advantage of technologies supported by a particular browser, such as Dynamic HTML (DHTML), scripting, and ActiveX controls, to maximize the richness and functionality of the user interface. This type of client is often well suited for applications such as corporate intranets, in which the organization has standardized on a particular browser.

- **Internet-reliant client** Unlike page-based applications run within the context of a browser, an Internet-reliant client is an actual Windows executable program. The Internet-reliant client is capable of integrating access to the Internet with access to operating system services on the client machine.

- **Internet-enhanced client** Internet-enhanced clients are written using the Microsoft Win32 application programming interface (API). Internet-enhanced clients use component technology to support access to Internet technologies in the Windows application platform from within a Win32 application. Microsoft Office 97 and Microsoft Visual Studio are both examples of Internet-enhanced clients.

Business Services

Applications based on Windows DNA rely on the business services tier to supply the bulk of the application's functionality and to enforce the application's business rules. The business services tier is implemented by integrating Microsoft server-based products with a runtime environment for customized COM components. According to the Microsoft DNA model, the following application services are located on the business services tier:

- **Web Services** (Microsoft Internet Information Server and Active Server Pages)
- **Transaction and Component Services** (Microsoft Transaction Server and COM)
- **Messaging Services** (Microsoft Message Queue Server)
- **Universal Data Access** (Microsoft Data Access Components)
- **Interoperability with Mainframe Environments** (Microsoft SNA Server)

15

MULTIPLE TIERS AND CLIENT/SERVER

Data Services

The data services tier of Windows DNA is made up of data in various types of data stores. These are the two most prominent types of data stores in this architecture:

- Microsoft SQL Server 7.0 databases
- Microsoft Exchange Server version 5.5 directories and information stores

N-Tier Applications Using RAD Development Tools

One of the factors that has contributed significantly to the feasibility of developing and deploying multitier applications in today's enterprise environments is the availability of Rapid Application Development (RAD) tools, such as Microsoft's Visual Studio. RAD tools allow developers to quickly design, develop, debug, and deploy multitier applications and to achieve the gains in performance, scalability, and maintainability that are becoming increasingly in demand.

At the core of Microsoft's technologies that contribute to the RAD process is COM. This is so for two reasons:

- Microsoft has adopted COM as a standard interface for exposing the services provided by most of its front-end and back-end applications. The use of the COM interface in this regard allows developers to easily leverage the strength of existing Microsoft applications and to integrate this functionality into their own applications. Furthermore, because of the proliferation of Microsoft operating systems on both clients and servers in today's business computing environments, many third-party suppliers of tools and middleware are opting to use the COM interface to expose the services offered by their products to developers of business applications.

- Microsoft has greatly reduced the complexity of developing customized COM components. Quick, easy COM component design, development, and implementation has emerged as a central feature of Microsoft Visual Studio's suite of development tools. In the same manner that Microsoft has used the COM interface as a "wrapper" to expose the features of its applications for easy reuse, developers can use the COM interface to encapsulate business functions, thus achieving significant gains in performance, scalability, maintainability, and code reuse.

COM and Microsoft Application Services

The ability to integrate the functionality of Microsoft applications and technologies into multitier applications contributes significantly to the RAD process. The COM interface allows business applications to access the features of a given application or technology *programatically* in the same way that business users access similar features *interactively*. Typically, application services are made available through COM components that take the form of *object libraries* containing classes with the various services in a particular application. The emergence of the COM interface as a standard for exposing application services allows developers to easily "mix and match" application services on an as-needed basis as part of their own applications.

Some of the Microsoft application services that are available to developers through COM object libraries include the following:

- Web services
- Transaction and component services
- Messaging services
- Universal Data Access

Web Services

As Web technology is playing a more important role in multitier applications, developers are increasingly in need of harnessing the capability of Microsoft Internet Information Server (and the technologies it supports, such as Active Server Pages) in multitier applications. Microsoft Internet Information Server (IIS) 4.0 functions as a gateway between business services and user services in a multitier application. IIS extends applications to the Web over a corporate intranet or the Internet.

The Web services object model includes the following objects:

> **NOTE**
>
> ASP contains 5 main objects: `Server`, `Application`, `Response`, `Request`, and `ObjectContext`. We'll discuss a few of these here but for more detail refer back to the Internet chapter.

15

MULTIPLE TIERS
AND
CLIENT/SERVER

- **Server object**   The Server object provides access to methods and properties on the server. Most of these methods and properties serve as utility functions. Most often, we use the Server object to create COM objects within ASPs using the following sample code:

```
set objMyObject = Server.CreateObject("BusinessServer.MyRuleObject")
```

- **Session object**   The Session object can be used to store information needed for a particular user session. Variables stored in the Session object are not discarded when the user jumps between pages in the application; instead, these variables persist for the entire user session. The Web server automatically creates an instance of a Session object when a Web page from the application is requested by a user who does not already have a session. The server destroys the Session object when the session expires or is abandoned. One common use for the Session object is to store user preferences. For example, if users indicate that they prefer not to view graphics, this information can be stored in the Session object.

> **NOTE**
>
> Try not to overuse Session variables because they are persistent data in a stateless world.

- **Application object**   The Application object can be used to share information among all users of a given application. An ASP-based application is defined as all the .asp files in a virtual directory and its subdirectories. Because the Application object can be shared by more than one user, there are Lock and Unlock methods to ensure that multiple users do not try to alter a property simultaneously.

- **Request object**   The Request object retrieves the values that the client browser passed to the server during an HTTP request.

- **Response object**   The Response object can be used to send output to the client.

Transactions and Component Services

When implementing support for transactions in an enterprise environment, it is often necessary to manage complex logical transactions that can span multiple databases and that require services provided by multiple business components. To ensure consistency in this type of processing, an application needs to manage the transaction as a single logical unit that can be rolled back or committed in its entirety. Microsoft Transaction Server (MTS) is a component-based transaction-processing system designed to meet such complex transaction-processing requirements.

Without MTS, developers would have to write components to manually track the requested changes and restore data if any changes failed. Using MTS, developers can declare components to require transactions and let MTS handle the coordination and execution of the transaction. Transaction processing under MTS applies to database access for databases supported by MTS. MTS cannot be used to roll back changes to the file system or changes to other, nontransactional resources. Currently, MTS supports SQL Server and any database that supports the XA protocol from the X/Open consortium.

MTS uses a COM interface to provide a number of services that can be used to develop custom COM components that encapsulate an application's business rules. These services include the following:

- Support for distributed transactions.
- Security services to control instancing and use of objects.
- Automatic management of processes and threads.
- Object instance management.
- Management of database connections (connection pooling).

> **NOTE**
>
> For more information on MTS and COM, see Chapter 27.

Messaging Services

Microsoft Message Queue Server (MSMQ) provides asynchronous communication services for applications. Message queueing is an integral part of Windows DNA because it enables reliable messaging when a user is disconnected from the network. It also allows for greater fault tolerance over unreliable networks.

After an MSMQ message is sent, the sender can go on to other work without waiting for the recipient to respond. The message goes into a queue located on the server until it receives a request from the recipient indicating that it's ready to receive the message. MSMQ bridges the business services tier and the data services tier of a distributed application because the message queues are considered unstructured storage, like the Microsoft Exchange Server database.

MSMQ provides automatic integration with MTS. This feature enables applications to participate in transaction processing without being connected to a network. An application can wrap an MSMQ message in MTS transactions, send it into a local queue on a portable computer, and then update a database, such as a customer account or a product inventory, when the network becomes available. When applications use MSMQ's transactional delivery mode, MSMQ makes sure that messages are delivered exactly one time and delivered in the order in which they were sent.

MSMQ differs from Microsoft Exchange Server in that Exchange enables *person-to-person messaging* and MSMQ provides *application-to-application messaging*. MSMQ can act as a MAPI (Messaging API) transport provider to allow MAPI-enabled applications to communicate with other applications using MSMQ. The MSMQ Exchange Connector enables MSMQ to act as a communications transport between computers running Microsoft Exchange Server and to MSMQ-enabled applications. For example, Microsoft Exchange Server users can receive email messages through MSMQ or send Microsoft Exchange forms that are received as messages by processing applications.

Universal Data Access

Universal Data Access is Microsoft's strategy for supplying access to information across the enterprise. In a Windows DNA multitier application, data access components cross the boundary between the business services tier and the data services tier. These components, such as ActiveX Data Objects (ADO), are called from the custom business objects that run in the Microsoft Transaction Server environment.

The Universal Data Access–based framework operates at two levels within an application. At the systems level, OLE DB defines an architecture specified as a set of COM-based interfaces that encapsulate database management system services. At the application level, ADO provides a high-level interface to enable developers to access data from any programming language.

The Microsoft Open Database Connectivity (ODBC) interface is an industry standard. The ODBC interface enables applications to access data from a variety of RDBMSs. ODBC permits maximum interoperability; an application can access data in diverse RDBMSs through a single interface. Furthermore, that application is independent of any database management system from which it accesses data. Users of the application can add software components, called *drivers*, that establish an interface between an application and a specific database management system.

ADO, OLE DB, and ODBC make up the Microsoft Data Access Components (MDAC).

COM and Business Application Services

In the same manner that the COM interface is used as a means of making the services of Microsoft applications available, it can also be used to access the services provided by custom application components.

Microsoft Visual Studio tools allow developers to quickly and easily develop object libraries implemented as COM components to expose business logic through classes that represent the relevant business objects. Components developed in this manner can then be reused by any applications that require the services they provide.

A typical object model is based on a class hierarchy consisting of a high-level administrative class and subordinate classes that model different business objects. Figure 15.12 illustrates this type of object model.

FIGURE 15.12
Typical business object model.

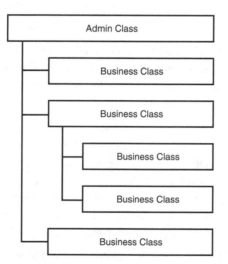

RAD and Project Life Cycle

One of the strengths of Microsoft Visual Studio as a RAD tool is its support for all phases of the application development project life cycle. These phases include the following:

- Design and modeling
- Development
- Deployment

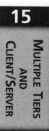

Design and Modeling

In traditional two-tier application development, modeling usually involved only the development of a database design. However, effective multitier application development requires thorough modeling of the entire application that takes into account the segmentation of application services and component architecture as well as the data model.

Microsoft Visual Studio has two tools that support this phase of the project life cycle:

- **Microsoft Visual Modeler**   Provides an easy-to-use interface for designing efficient application architectures. Microsoft Visual Modeler automatically generates code from the application design.

- **Enterprise Visual Database Tools**   Provides tools for designing data models for SQL Server and Oracle databases.

Development

Developing multitier applications based on the COM interface requires the ability to quickly code customized COM components and to easily track and reuse existing COM components. Some of the tools that Microsoft Visual Studio offers to support this phase of the project life cycle include the following:

- **Development tools**   Visual Basic, Visual C++, Microsoft J++, Microsoft Visual InterDev 6.0, and Visual FoxPro are integrated into Microsoft Visual Studio using a common IDE (Integrated Development Environment) look and feel. These tools allow developers to reduce development time by building components that can be easily reused across a wide range of business applications. Support for developing components based on the COM interface allows for seamless integration of components regardless of the specific programming language used to develop them.

- **Debugging support**   Provides visual debugging across languages and includes client- and server-side debugging, with point-and-click breakpoints, drag-and-drop watch windows, and multiple call stacks.

- **Visual Component Manager**   Improves team productivity by enabling developers to easily find, track, and catalog components as they are developed.

- **Query Designer**   Enables developers to quickly build, test, and integrate sophisticated SQL statements.

- **Visual Studio Analyzer**   A graphical performance analysis tool for analyzing distributed applications and improving application performance.

Deployment

Deploying multitier applications in a RAD environment requires the ability to easily manage the physical placement of application components. Microsoft Visual Studio offers the following features to support this phase of the project life cycle:

- **Package and Deployment Wizard**   Enables reducing deployment costs by supporting the automatic deployment of applications and components to both client and server computers.

> **NOTE**
>
> The Visual Basic Package and Deployment Wizard is a considerable improvement to its predecessors in that it now has a user-friendly interface that allows for packaging an application for Internet distribution.

- **MTS Integration**   Microsoft Management Console (MMC) snap-in allows easy administration of MTS components and applications, including security services to control instancing and use of objects.

Scalability and SQL Server

Scalability is a central theme in any discussion of multitiered client/server applications. The database is a major component of the client/server architecture, and its scalability is a significant concern. The database needs to provide for your current business needs without preventing future expansion and growth.

In the same manner that organizations standardize on desktop and server operating systems in an attempt to optimize cost and efficiency in support and maintenance, an organization can standardize on a particular RDBMS, too.

To this end, Microsoft is seeking to position SQL Server 7.0 as a one-stop shopping solution for an organization's database needs. SQL Server 7.0's scalability features include the following:

- Platform scalability
- Enhanced query processing
- Dynamic row-level locking
- Advanced replication
- Mobile computing support

Platform Scalability

SQL Server 7.0 uses a single database engine that can scale from mobile laptop computers to small business servers to very large databases (VLDB) having terabytes of data and thousands of users running on symmetric multiprocessor clusters. It is designed to integrate well with existing applications, particularly those that have been developed for Microsoft platforms and COM component technologies. In addition, it is tightly integrated with Microsoft Visual Studio, thus providing a cost-effective environment for designing, developing, and deploying new custom applications.

Enhanced Query Processing

SQL Server 7.0 includes several features to offer better support for query processing:

- **Query processor**   The query processor for SQL Server 7.0 has been redesigned to provide support for large databases and complex queries. One of the goals of redesigning the query processor is to make SQL Server a viable choice for high-end OLTP and data warehousing systems.

- **Parallel queries**   Support for intra-query parallelism allows running a single query across multiple processors. Steps in a single query are executed in parallel to optimize response time.

- **Joins**   SQL Server 7.0 uses hash and merge join strategies to improve performance for specific types of data retrieval. Multiple join types can be used within a single query, and the query processor is capable of recognizing common join types, such as star query joins, and optimizing for these specific join types.

Dynamic Row-Level Locking

One of the new features in SQL Server 7.0 is support for dynamic row-level locking, an essential feature for high-end OLTP and data warehousing systems. The lock manager is designed to dynamically adjust the resources it uses for larger databases, so the locks server configuration does not need to be adjusted manually.

Advanced Replication

SQL Server 7.0 replication features include merge replication with conflict resolution, which allows mobile and remote users to make changes to data and have their changes synchronize automatically when they connect to the network.

Mobile Computing Support

Telecommuting, sales force, and branch automation illustrate the need to support mobile computing. Mobile computing introduces a number of challenges, including offline application usage and automatic data synchronization.

In addition to the replication capability described previously, SQL Server 7.0 includes several features that are well-suited to the needs of mobile computing:

- **SQL Server Desktop**   SQL Server Desktop is a low footprint edition built on the same code base as SQL Server 7.0 and SQL Server 7.0 Enterprise Edition so that applications are fully compatible, from a laptop to symmetric multiprocessing (SMP) servers.
- **Auto tuning and zero administration features**   These features are targeted at eliminating administration requirements for common tasks.

Summary

Today's business world is a fast-paced, rapidly changing environment. Businesses are constantly looking to information technology as a means of meeting the challenges of this environment and gaining a competitive edge. At the same time, IT managers often face reductions in funding that essentially require them to do "more with less."

As businesses have grown and changed, client/server systems have grown to accommodate these changes. From basic, two-tier file and print server networks to complex, multitier, Web-based architectures, client/server computing has remained a central point of innovation in business computing technologies.

The latest advances in client/server systems and architecture offer businesses the opportunity to gain the competitive advantage they are looking for and to manage costs effectively. The emergence of Web technologies has virtually revolutionized the implications of how information can be harnessed to power business productivity.

As IT managers look to these technologies for answers, it's important to remember that client/server architectures are moving toward a more holistic, enterprise-scale computing environment. Benefits such as encapsulation of business logic, central points of maintenance, and code reuse derive from a vision of a highly integrated computing environment, where the entire enterprise is automated coherently.

15

MULTIPLE TIERS AND CLIENT/SERVER

Having a well-planned, enterprise-wide strategy for the development of business applications is one of keys to achieving the potential benefits of these new technologies. One of the challenges that many IT professionals face is how to justify the short-term cost of planning and designing systems based on these new architectures to gain a greater advantage in the long term.

When considering Microsoft's product offerings in client/server computing, it's clear Microsoft has recognized this challenge and is seeking to supply products geared toward meeting it. COM component technology represents a significant advance toward getting parts of the enterprise system "talking to one another." The complexity of implementing this technology has been greatly reduced and made far more accessible to the development community at large by RAD tools such as Microsoft Visual Studio.

SQL Server 7.0 represents one of the more important advances in Microsoft's overall client/server computing strategy. With features such as scalability from the laptop to the multiprocessor cluster, enhanced query processing, and support for mobile computing, SQL Server 7.0 seeks to resolve many of the limitations of its predecessors. SQL Server 7.0's tight integration with Microsoft Visual Studio makes designing, developing, and deploying client/server systems based on these new technologies that much easier.

Replication

CHAPTER 16

Birds do it. Bees do it. Even SQL Server does it. SQL Server's implementation of replication lets data reproduce and distribute itself without writing any code. It puts the power of distributed data into the hands of anyone using SQL Server version 6.x or above. Although version 7.0 adds distributed updates to the mix, some business problems require more than the out-of-the-box capabilities that replication has to offer. For these applications, Microsoft allows you to control replication through a rich application interface.

In SQL Server's documentation, Microsoft states that replication allows you to distribute and synchronize data across servers at different locations. If that was all it did, SQL Server replication would still be a very nice tool. To our benefit, the replication tools included with SQL Server are both flexible and extendable. A bit of design and development creativity, along with SQL Server's standard replication features, can solve some very complex business problems.

There is a dark side to using replication. Aspects of design, development, and administration become more complex. Data modeling entities and attributes develop multiple business roles. Backup and recovery issues give database administrators nightmares, if they can sleep at all. Accidental data modifications, dispersed to many databases, can clog network bandwidth and transaction logs and shut down databases. These problems are just specific instances of issues that plague all distributed applications, though, and most can be avoided if you have a good understanding of how replication works when you design your solution.

> **TIP**
>
> Replication is simple in theory, but in practice it gets complicated quickly. Careful planning is an absolute necessity with this or any other distributed infrastructure technology!

The built-in replication tools included with SQL Server provide a range of update options, primarily varying in the update latency and degree of consistency assured. If strict transactional control is required, you can use immediate-updating subscribers to immediately update the publisher when a subscriber updates a local copy. Unlike earlier versions of SQL Server, version 7 automatically manages a two-phase commit protocol using the Distributed Transaction Coordinator (MSDTC). On the other end of the spectrum, merge replication maintains wholly distributed data, bringing it together at specified intervals to merge and propagate changes to all subscribers.

The first section of the chapter reviews the terminology and mechanisms of SQL Server's built-in replication tools along with the different roles a database can play. This section also looks at two replication models and how they can be used to solve real-world problems. The second section discusses more advanced uses of replication, including ActiveX controls, SQL-DMO, stored procedures and replication, and replication over Windows NT Remote Access Services (RAS).

Replication Concepts for Programmers

We're taking a quick tour of replication, focusing on what programmers need to know to understand and design a system using it. There are plenty of books that explain how to set up and administer replication. This is not one of them. If you are interested in the setup and administration of servers and databases using replication, check out this book's companion publication, *Microsoft SQL Server 7.0 Unleashed*.

Replication Lingo

Microsoft uses a newspaper publishing analogy to describe its implementation of replication. Here is a list of those terms:

- A *publisher* is a database with the capability to replicate data.
- A *subscriber* is a database that can receive published data.
- A *distributor* is a database that collects published data from one or more publishers and distributes it to one or more subscribers.
- An *article* is a set of published data from a table.
- A *publication* is a collection of articles grouped together by a publisher.
- A *subscription* is the registration by a subscriber to receive a publication from a publisher.

Articles within publications can be subscribed to individually, without subscribing to the entire publication, but Microsoft states this is allowed only for backward compatibility with SQL Server 6.x. The GUI tools do not give you the ability to do this, and it may not be supported in later releases.

Do you have that all memorized? If not, you can refer to Figure 16.1 for an illustration of how the replication roles relate to one another.

FIGURE 16.1
Each real-world role maps to a role in SQL Server's replication model.

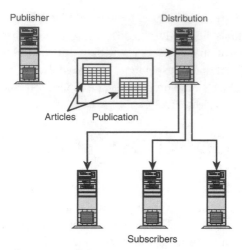

You can install publisher, distributor, and subscriber databases onto a single SQL Server. On the other hand, you can put each database on a separate server on a separate continent. Microsoft has given you plenty of flexibility when it comes to designing a distributed data system. Later in the chapter you look at some of the combinations of publishers, subscribers, and distributors as they apply to specific business scenarios.

Transactions

Transactions are the core of a SQL Server database. They give SQL Server its capability to recover from catastrophes that leave simple desktop databases in chaos. A transaction is started implicitly on a single SQL statement or explicitly by programmer definition on all inserts, updates, or deletes to a database. The transaction is committed when the modification is complete. If any part of the transaction fails prior to being committed, the entire transaction rolls back, as if it never happened. This is built into almost all data activity that occurs on a SQL Server database.

SQL Server replication makes use of transactional properties to ensure that data being replicated reaches its destination. If replication fails, SQL Server has notification capabilities that are quite powerful.

Transaction Properties

Before the transaction property of consistency is discussed, make sure you are familiar with the ACID properties of transactions. ACID is an acronym for atomicity, consistency, isolation, and durability. Because each property's full definition is lengthy and redundant, explaining their exact meanings has been left to the database theorists. Brief definitions of each one follow:

- Atomicity ensures that a transaction either completes perfectly or not at all. If a SQL statement is updating 20 rows and fails on any row, all rows are returned to their original state and the transaction is terminated.

- Consistency extends atomicity to include any applied logical/business rules as part of the success or failure of a transaction. In other words, a consistent transaction fails if any business rule is broken.

- Isolation keeps concurrent uncommitted transactions from interfering with each other. Data-locking strategies ensure correct data modification.

- Durability guarantees that a system failure will not affect committed transactions and will return uncommitted transactions to their last committed state prior to the system failure.

Loose Consistency

SQL Server replication provides what Microsoft calls Latent Guaranteed Consistency, or "loose" consistency, on transactions. *Loose consistency* is a replication model that allows a time lag between when the published data is altered and when the subscribing copies are altered. All copies of the data may not be the same at any point in time, and, particularly with merge publications, the final result may not be the same as it would be if all updates were performed at one site.

The loose consistency replication model does not meet the ACID requirements. Although errors are raised by the replication mechanisms if a failure occurs, the entire logical transaction cannot be undone because it is not being dealt with as a single atomic transaction. Sounds bad, doesn't it?

Not really. First of all, SQL Server has a great set of tools to set up and administer replication. This takes a huge workload off database administrators and developers, who don't have to reinvent the replication wheel. Adding a new subscriber is a point-and-click operation.

From the consistency standpoint, looseness is often exactly what you want when replicating data. For example, a traveling sales force with subscribed databases on its laptops cannot be constantly connected to the publishing database (at least not cost-effectively at the time of this writing) to be certain that every salesman always has identical data. Does every branch office of an insurance company need a client's new zip code the minute it is changed at the client's local branch? Probably not.

Another advantage of the loose consistency model is scalability. Adding a new subscriber is simple with the included replication management tools in SQL Server, and synchronization and updates can be applied on a scheduled basis when server loads are low, and do not require that high capacity connections between publisher and subscriber be available at all times.

Immediate Guaranteed Consistency and Two-Phase Commits

Two-phase commit (2PC) transactions fully comply with the ACID properties and supply what Microsoft terms Immediate Guaranteed Consistency. If any part of a transaction fails, the entire transaction fails, even over multiple databases in multiple locations. Replicating data using this data distribution model ensures that all copies are identical at all times. SQL Server provides a 2PC facility with distributed transactions and MSDTC for SQL code, and with Microsoft Transaction Server for ActiveX programming.

Financial transactions are the most common example of two-phase commit transactions. When money is transferred between accounts, it is required that both account balances be updated together or not at all. Deducting money from one account without adding it to the other would make money for the bank, temporarily, but would not keep customers coming back. This example of two-phase commit isn't technically replication because you are updating two different tables, not duplicating information to many places. It does illustrate the tight consistency ACID property that some transactions require.

There are a few restrictions when using a two-phase commit model. First, it requires that every copy of the data that is part of the transaction be available. If they're not, no changes can be made anywhere. If you implement an application that is distributed across five servers across the country, all must be available; one server crashing, or a failed telephone line, can halt data updates across your entire data infrastructure.

Second, data-locking requirements are rigid. Not only do all the members of the transaction have to be online, but all the rows affected in every copy have to be available to be updated. Imagine a zip code update failing in a branch office in Toledo because the Boise branch office is printing a customer report and has the customer table locked.

> **NOTE**
>
> In earlier versions of SQL Server, two-phase commit models could be code and administration intensive for application software; applications can be written to retrieve server names from tables for distributed transactions, but it can be cumbersome. With distributed transactions, the data are explicitly updated on multiple servers, named by the updating application, within the SQL that makes the update. This method bypasses replication in favor of updating all databases through code, and is applicable only when all locations must have updates immediately.

If strict consistency across sites is not required, a database can be replicated from a central publisher and updated at subscribers using the immediate update option on the subscription. On subscriptions with the immediate-update option set, a central database serves as the reference database, and updates from subscribers are immediately applied to the central database in a two-phase commit. Other subscribers will not reflect the changed data until their scheduled update time, and there is a penalty to be paid in resources used to update the master on every update at a subscriber. Still, this approach enables you to maintain consistency through the master server, and ensures it always contains the latest data.

How Replication Works

SQL Agent, an NT Service installed with SQL Server, controls all scheduled tasks for SQL Server; the replication mechanism uses it to control replication tasks. SQL Server automatically creates these tasks when databases are marked published, when publications are defined, and when subscribers are added. Look more closely at the function of these tasks in Figure 16.2. The log reader task reads the transaction log to generate SQL statements, which are copied to the distribution database. The distribution task then executes the SQL statements on each subscriber. Table 16.1 summarizes the more common replication tasks for you.

TABLE 16.1 SQL SERVER REPLICATION TASKS

Task	Purpose
Log reader	Monitors the publisher's transaction log and creates entries in the distribution database for transmission to subscribers
Distribution	Reads distribution entries and executes SQL on subscribers to replicate updates
Merge	Assembles updates and performs conflict resolution for contradictory or illegal updates
Clean-up	One or more tasks responsible for freeing resources, such as data files, when they are no longer needed for distribution

FIGURE 16.2

The log reader and distribution tasks, in a simple one publisher/ many subscriber replication model.

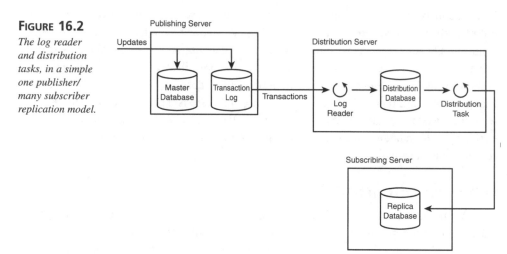

Replication Jobs

The log reader task is created when a database is marked as published. The log reader immediately begins to scan the database's transaction log for committed transactions. When qualifying transactions are found, it creates SQL statements to replicate the changes and puts them in the distribution database. A *qualifying transaction* is committed, published, and subscribed to. This task runs continuously by default.

When a publication is defined, a Snapshot Agent is created for that publication. Before a new subscription can begin receiving updates from the master server, it must have a complete and consistent copy of the data from the master. The synchronization job is scheduled as the administrator specifies to perform synchronization for new subscriptions. When it runs, it copies a snapshot of the published data to the distribution server and adds a distribution task to copy the data to subscribers.

For Merge publications, a Merge Agent is created to propagate changes among participating servers. This job assembles updates that have been made to data on publishers and subscribers, and resolves conflicts using either default resolution rules or with resolvers you supply.

On the distribution server, distribution and clean-up jobs handle propagating snapshots, updates, and disposing of supporting data when no longer needed. The distribution task executes the SQL statements from the distribution database for the subscriber in the order they occurred on the publisher. The SQL statements are grouped into jobs, which are submitted to the subscriber as a single transaction. By default, the distribution task runs continuously on the distribution database. Clean-up tasks are created on the distribution server to follow along behind other jobs and get rid of old data files and transactions; these are retained for a short period (three days by default) to aid in failure recovery.

> **TIP**
>
> Check replication status and task execution in SQL Enterprise Manager, under the Replication Monitor node of the database tree.

From a programming standpoint, each of these tasks can be controlled via custom applications developed using SQL-DMO and the Replication Distributor Interface. These techniques are described in more detail in the "Advanced Replication" section of this chapter.

Troubleshooting

Troubleshooting replication in older versions of SQL Server 6.5 could be painful at times. SQL Server 7.0 makes problem resolution easier both by making information more accessible to operators and by automating some management functions that can save a replication job.

> **TIP**
>
> If your SQL Servers have access to email, set up an email account for each server and use the account to allow the built-in alerting features to notify you if your replication tasks fail.

The following are some items you should keep in mind when designing and implementing a solution using replication:

- Pay attention to triggers and stored procedures. Replication will try to keep your data consistent, but it won't follow your dependencies around the world, nor can it resolve all of them. Furthermore, it is easy to create triggers on the publisher that are inappropriate on the client—Web publishing tasks created with the Web Assistant Wizard, for example.

- Consider transaction sizes when you update replicated databases. Although SQL Server 7.0 will grow the transaction log automatically (if so configured), it might not be able to if your subscribers don't have the same resources as the publisher. Even if they do, it is time consuming for the subscribing servers, can be a large waste of disk space, and can cause replication to fail. If you have a doubt about the resources that may be available after deployment, take precautionary measures when building your applications, such as partitioning updates into smaller jobs where possible or partitioning your data with tables or replication filters. For large repetitive updates, consider replicating stored procedure execution instead of just the data changes.

- Get your database backup and recovery plans in place, especially during development. Once you have a fair amount of data being replicated, it is very annoying, time-consuming, and costly to re-create it by hand. This is basic, but often ignored during the development phase of a project, and failure recovery in replicated data systems is *much* more complicated than it is in a single-server environment.

Replication Limitations

Every product has some limitations. Here are some of the shortcomings of SQL Server replication:

- Only data are replicated. This makes sense, because SQL Server performs replication by monitoring the publisher's transaction log and sending logged changes to the distributor. Because the system tables are not replicated, neither are changes to database objects—so don't expect a new stored procedure added to a publisher to appear on a subscriber using SQL Server replication. You have to write the code to do that yourself.

  The only exception to this rule is for published stored procedures. This doesn't replicate the procedures; publishing a stored procedure in a subscription tells SQL Server to distribute the fact of it having been run. The stored procedure will then be run on the subscriber server instead of applying the individual updates that resulted from its execution.

- On subscribed tables, user-defined data types (UDDT) are converted to their native data types, timestamps become `binary(8)`, and `identity` columns become plain `integer` data types. A UDDT is converted because it is defined in the database system table `systypes`, which is not replicated. In addition, non-SQL Server subscribers would not be able to use UDDTs. By definition, a timestamp value can only be created and modified by SQL Server. It is guaranteed to be a unique value within a database. If replication were allowed to change a timestamp value on a subscriber, non-unique values could be introduced into the subscribing database. For similar reasons, `identity` columns are converted to their base data types. If you use these special data types, your table definitions will differ between publishers and subscribers.

- It is important to emphasize that SQL Server replication is normally a high latency, loose consistency replication model. With most replication configurations, there is no time frame in which the data are guaranteed to be replicated to all subscribers and no guarantee that they ever will. SQL Server generates an error message eventually if something goes wrong, but not when the information is originally changed. Even if you use immediate updating subscribers, this will only ensure that the individual subscriber and the publishing database are up to date; other subscribers will not be updated until their scheduled replications, which may be too late for your application.

- Nonlogged operations such as bulk copying and text or image column changes are not automatically replicated. For bulk copying, you must make sure that bulk copying is being logged by having an index on the table importing data or by setting the database `SELECT INTO/BULK COPY` option to `false`. Both of these bulk copy settings slow data imports. You have to weigh the benefits and decide what is best for your application. For text and image replication, you must use the Transact-SQL commands `WRITETEXT` and `UPDATETEXT` with the `WITH LOG` option.

Replication Business Models

With the flexibility available from SQL Server there are many ways to combine the three replication roles (publisher, distributor, and subscriber) with one or more servers. This section illustrates two common replication models, along with how they might be used for business solutions. There are many other possible replication models.

> **NOTE**
>
> Are you easily confused by the many-to-many, *n*-tier, cascading complexity of replication options? Join the crowd. Here are the allowable combinations for replication scenarios. Each publisher can create many publications. Each publication can have many articles. Each subscriber can receive publications from many publishers via each publisher's single distributor. A publisher must have exactly one distributor. All these roles can be performed on a single server or on many servers.

Suppose you have a single database that is being used heavily for data entry and reporting. The problem is that a report that takes 15 minutes to run locks a table that 30 data-entry operators need to update. There they sit, waiting for their screens to refresh. With the model in Figure 16.3, you can replicate the tables needed for reporting to another database, allowing the first database to function as the OLTP (online transaction processing) database for the data-entry operators and the second database to function as the OLAP (online analysis processing) database for people who run reports. This can all be done on a single server or on separate physical servers. If a single server is chosen, replication is very fast and does not create network traffic.

FIGURE 16.3

Putting OLTP and OLAP together without the locking contention of a single database.

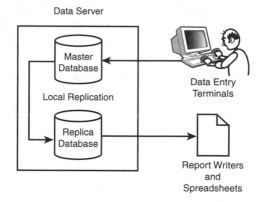

Another common SQL replication scenario is one central subscriber receiving data from many publishers. This scenario can apply to data warehousing applications or point-of-sale locations reporting back to a centralized database. Sharpen your Transact-SQL skills if you are doing a data warehousing project. Stored procedure replication, which is discussed more fully in the "Advanced Replication" section of this chapter, is a useful technique for data scrubbing. Figure 16.4 illustrates an example of this model.

TIP

Data scrubbing refers to the process of checking and (possibly) correcting data that enter your data warehouse. One of the problems involved in data warehousing is that it doesn't only provide good data to users who couldn't access the data before. It also propagates erroneous data, allowing many more people to make bad decisions based on it than previously. If you are bringing together data from separate or heterogeneous databases, you need to include either manual or automatic processes to clean up the data entering your warehouse.

FIGURE 16.4
A data warehouse replication model.

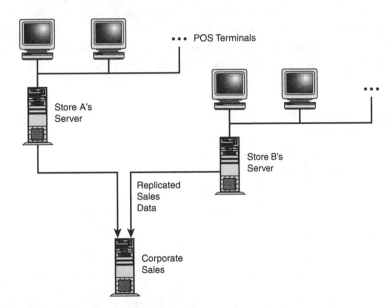

Advanced Replication

The point-and-click replication interface provided by SQL Server has much to offer. With it you can set up complex replication designs. What if that isn't enough? Synthesize your own solutions utilizing the replication mechanisms and tool sets in SQL Server. This chapter's following sections present some ideas to use when programming with replication.

Replication and SQL-DMO

Replication administration is normally managed using SQL Enterprise Manager. SQL-DMO can be used with a development language like Visual Basic or Visual C++ to develop your own replication management applications. Unfortunately, SQL-DMO applications written for SQL Server 6.5 will not work with version 7. Although replication itself is similar between the two versions, the architecture of the database and the processes it runs have changed. SQL-DMO for version 7 uses a new object library, appropriately named Microsoft SQLDMO Object Library, in place of the SQLOLE object library of version 6.x.

There are some interesting gotchas in porting to the new library, as well. One I ran into in updating this chapter to version 7 is the representation of dates. Instead of returning a variant date for times from the schedule, the SQLDMO library Schedule object returns dates packed into a Long data item. I used the function shown in Listing 16.1 to convert to a Visual Basic Date value.

LISTING 16.1   A SIMPLE VISUAL BASIC FUNCTION TO UNPACK CODED DATES USING STRING FUNCTIONS

```
Function LongToDate(ldate) As Date
    ' local strings we use for conversion
    Dim dstr, yr, mo, dy As String

    ' split year, month, day out of the integer value
    dstr = CStr(ldate)
    If Len(dstr) = 8 Then
        yr = Mid(dstr, 1, 4)
        mo = Mid(dstr, 5, 2)
        dy = Mid(dstr, 7, 2)

        ' send a string to the cdate function it will understand
        LongToDate = CDate(mo + "/" + dy + "/" + yr)
    Else
        LongToDate = 0
    End If

End Function
```

For simplicity, the function just converts the Long to a string and creates a new string with a date format that VB can understand.

The type library for SQL-DMO is distributed as a resource library called sqldmo.rll. The file is located under the `\mssql\binn\resources` directory where SQL Server is installed, in a subdirectory named for the numeric resource ID of your installation (for example, 1033). This file is needed to create SQL-DMO objects using Class Wizard in Visual C++, but for Visual Basic it isn't. In VB, you just add the Microsoft SQLDMO Object Library to your project references and away you go. If you need it, the SQL DMO type library's globally unique identifier (GUID) is {10010001-E260-11CF-AE68-00AA004A34D5}.

What can you do with SQL-DMO and replication? Say you are publishing from a central database to subscribing databases located on laptops that dial up to receive updates. Each laptop needs to dial up to the main server, start the replication process, and hang up when replication completes. As part of the laptop's database application, you could include a simple module that does the dialing, monitors the replication task, and hangs up when complete. This is possible using SQL-DMO and either a RAS ActiveX component or the RAS API. Take a look at Listing 16.2 for a simple Visual Basic example that runs a replication task using SQL-DMO. Although this example is running a distribution task, you can design an application that will run any task you have created in the database for SQLServerAgent.

LISTING 16.2 A VISUAL BASIC EXAMPLE USING SQL-DMO TO START AND MONITOR A REPLICATION TASK

```
'This goes in general declarations
'Windows system function
Private Declare Sub Sleep Lib "kernel32" (ByVal dwMilliseconds As Long)

'The rest goes into your form.  Or in a button.  Or wherever you see fit
Private Sub Form_Load()
    RunSQLExecTask
End Sub

Sub RunSQLExecTask()

    'declare the SQL-DMO objects
    Dim DMOSQLObject As SQLDMO.SQLServer
    Dim DMOSQLJobServer As SQLDMO.JobServer
    Dim DMOSQLJob As SQLDMO.Job

    'other misc. declarations
    Dim strTask As String           'name of the replication task to run
    Dim strErrorDesc As String      'minimalist error handler
    Dim dLastRunDate As Date        'when task last ran
    Dim dActiveEndDate As Date      'date when task becomes inactive
```

continues

LISTING 16.2 CONTINUED

```
Dim bTaskEnabled As Boolean      'indicates whether task is enabled
Dim lStatusNumber As Long        'status of task
Dim iCheckAgain As Integer       'loop counter
Dim iMaxRetries As Integer       'times to check status of task
Dim iSleepTime As Integer        'frequency of task status checks

On Error GoTo ErrorHandler 'enable error handler

'set number of times to check for completion of SQL task
'each retry waits for iSleepTime milliseconds
iMaxRetries = 100
iSleepTime = 1000

'initialize the server object
Set DMOSQLObject = CreateObject("SQLDMO.SQLServer")

' You must use sa as the login name to work with replication tasks
' unless using SQL Server mixed or integrated security.  In that
' case, just pass <servername> to the .Connect method.  If the
' user running the program has sufficient rights to the server,
' the connection will work.
'login to SQL Server <servername> , <login name>, <password>
DMOSQLObject.Connect "SOMESERV", "sa", ""

'instantiate the SQLServerAgent object
Set DMOSQLJobServer = DMOSQLObject.JobServer

'name of the task to run - you can get a collection of tasks from
'DMOSQLJobServer.Jobs for your UI.  I'm not doing that here.
strTask = "SOMESERV-InetLogDB-InetServerLog-ANOTHERSERV-InetlogRepl-
➥0"

'instantiate the SQL Server Agent task
Set DMOSQLJob = DMOSQLJobServer.Jobs(strTask)


'In this section we determine whether to run the task based on
'various attributes
'Check the SQL-DMO enum SQLDMO_JOBOUTCOME_TYPE for the values of
'constants such as SQLDMOJobOutcome_InProgress

'check to see if the task is running
If DMOSQLJob.LastRunOutcome <> SQLDMOJobOutcome_InProgress Then

    'get last run information about the task
    dLastRunDate = LongToDate(DMOSQLJob.LastRunDate)

    'get task's active end date from first schedule; if multiple
    ➥schedules
```

```
'are accommodated in your app, you must enumerate the JobSchedules
➥list.
dActiveEndDate =
➥LongToDate(DMOSQLJob.JobSchedules(1).Schedule.ActiveEndDate)

'find out whether the task has been disabled
bTaskEnabled = DMOSQLJob.Enabled

'check that task is enabled
If Not bTaskEnabled Then
    strErrorDesc = "Remote task is disabled in SQLServerAgent."
    GoTo ErrorHandler
End If

'check the end date
If dActiveEndDate <= Now Then
    strErrorDesc = "Task is no longer active."
    GoTo ErrorHandler
End If

'start the task
DMOSQLJob.Invoke

iCheckAgain = 0

'check the task's completion status every iSleepTime milliseconds
Do
    iCheckAgain = iCheckAgain + 1
    ' check every iSleepTime milliseconds for completion of tasks
    Sleep (iSleepTime)

    'Update the object
    DMOSQLJob.Refresh

    'see if task has finished
    If dLastRunDate < DMOSQLJob.LastRunDate Then
        lStatusNumber = DMOSQLJob.LastRunOutcome
        iCheckAgain = 0
    End If

Loop Until (iCheckAgain = 0 Or iCheckAgain = iMaxRetries)

If lStatusNumber <> SQLDMOJobOutcome_Succeeded Then
    MsgBox "Job execution failed. See the job history.", , "Job
    ➥failed"
ElseIf iCheckAgain = iMaxRetries Then
    strErrorDesc = "Maximum retries reached, exiting the
    ➥application."
```

continues

LISTING 16.2   CONTINUED

```
            GoTo ErrorHandler
        Else
            MsgBox "Job completed successfully.", , "Job succeeded"
        End If

    Else
        'task is already running
        strErrorDesc = "Task status indicates that it is already running"
        GoTo ErrorHandler
    End If

    'clean up and exit
    Set DMOSQLJob = Nothing
    Set DMOSQLJobServer = Nothing
    Set DMOSQLObject = Nothing
    Exit Sub

ErrorHandler:
    'do your error handling stuff
    Set DMOSQLJob = Nothing
    Set DMOSQLJobServer = Nothing
    Set DMOSQLObject = Nothing
    If strErrorDesc = "" Then
        strErrorDesc = "Unknown error"
    End If

    MsgBox strErrorDesc

End Sub
```

Another use for the SQL-DMO is writing small applications that allow a user or group of users to control replication task setup and scheduling, without giving them system administrator (sa) or database owner (dbo) authority. If you think the SQL Enterprise Manager interface could be improved, why wait for the next version? The SQL-DMO tool set gives you the power to write your own interface.

Stored Procedures

Replication stored procedures are one of the neatest features included with the SQL Server replication tools. They allow you to execute a stored procedure on a remote server based on data changes to a publishing database. In other words, you can use replication to run completely unrelated procedures on a remote server to do anything you want based on data changes on a local server. The SQL Server replication tasks use this mechanism to update subscribers, and it also allows you to replace the default code with your own.

Here's a good example: Say there is a remote warehouse running SQL Server with an inventory system. At the home office the accountants are looking for a way to get changes from inventory to the accounting system quickly and on a regular basis. Replication to the rescue! Publish the pertinent table on the inventory system, but instead of storing the data from inventory on the accounting system, update the accounting tables directly using a stored procedure. You can write a little application using SQL-DMO for the accountants that runs the distribution task whenever they want the latest warehouse information.

Setting up replication to trigger a stored procedure is easy. In fact, if you specify during article creation that all participating servers will be SQL Servers, the replication mechanism itself uses replication stored procedures to distribute changes.

1. Follow the normal process for setting up your publication using the Create and Manage Publications window in SQL Server Enterprise Manager.
2. After creating the publication, select the Articles tab on the publication's Properties dialog.
3. Click the ellipsis button next to the article you wish to modify. This opens the Manage Article window. Click the Scripts tab, and you see the screen shown in Figure 16.5.

FIGURE 16.5
This is where to set up the stored procedure replication mechanism.

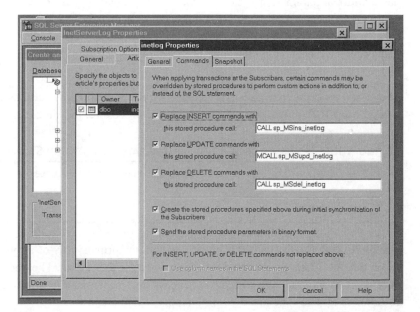

4. On the article Properties dialog, select the Commands page to modify the stored procedure to run.

You can set the replication procedure here for any replicated operation. To change the default for deletes, set the check box for Replace DELETE Commands with This Stored Procedure Call:. The text box to the right becomes active. To run a stored procedure other than the default, type the following:

```
CALL <remote stored procedure name>
```

To disable a default replication mechanism, type the following:

```
NONE
```

If you call a stored procedure using the replication mechanism, SQL Server does not check to see if it actually exists on the remote server. A missing stored procedure causes replication failure. The called stored procedure is not invoked until replication actually occurs. If this situation is likely, check the Create the Stored Procedures Specified... check box near the bottom of the article properties Commands tab.

There is nothing special about the replication stored procedures on the remote server. They can be used like any other stored procedure. However, they need to be written with parameters, so that there is one parameter for each column in the published article and one additional parameter for each column in the primary key of the article's table. These additional parameters allow the stored procedure to differentiate between the primary key prior to the data change and the primary key's new values. These additional parameter values can be discarded by the stored procedure if no changes were made to the primary key.

The stored procedures SQL Server generates for replication are useful as a demonstration. Listing 16.3 shows an example of a delete procedure, the simplest of the lot.

LISTING 16.3   EXAMPLE OF SQL SERVER-GENERATED REPLICATION STORED PROCEDURE

```
create procedure "sp_MSdel_inetlog" @pkc1 uniqueidentifier
as
delete "dbo"."inetlog"
where "eventId" = @pkc1
```

The replication facility calls this procedure with the primary key of a row that was deleted on the publisher, in order to delete the row on the subscriber. The update stored procedure is much more complex because it checks the flags passed in indicating which columns to update. The insert is, well, an insert statement.

Merge Replication

Merge replication is the mechanism Microsoft provides for implementing distributed updates to a database without requiring a high-speed connection between all servers, all the time. For databases that need to be used and updated at widely separated sites, the best solution would provide a "multiple master" architecture, where all participating sites shared ownership of the data and arbitrated updates to it on an ongoing basis. With SQL Server, multiple master replication doesn't exist per se, because in SQL Server replication there is always only one master copy of a database. The distinction is less critical than it could be, however, for though there is a hierarchical relationship between servers, updates may be accomplished at subscribers as well as at the publisher if replication is configured for immediate update subscribers or for merge replication.

In earlier versions of SQL Server, implementing such a solution was a complex and error-prone task. SQL Server 7 automates much of this for you now, but it still requires planning and careful design. For the effort, though, you gain two things:

- Once the data are synchronized across participating sites, the database's users can update data locally; as replication tasks distribute the updates, the data on other servers is gradually "converged" to include the changes.

- With merge replication, the master database does not have to be connected and updated in lockstep with the subscribers, as is the case with immediate update subscribers. Instead, the updates are propagated from the subscribers back to the publisher in a manner conceptually similar to that in which updates flow from the publisher out to the subscribers.

Unfortunately, merge replication is not perfect. Most importantly, updates to the data cannot be guaranteed to be consistent across all sites because they cannot be checked for consistency at the time of execution. Inherent in this architecture is the need for conflict resolution or a method of saying whose updates win. Someone's update gets thrown out if there is a conflict, so the resultant data set may or may not be the same as it would be if all updates were made on one server if precautions are not taken.

The most common method for dealing with this problem is through data partitioning. By divvying up subsets of the data so that each site gains access only to data it will need to update, you can keep conflicts from occurring at all. Your master sales database, for example, might be partitioned by sales region in replication to regional offices. With this approach, each region sees and can update only the data for which it is responsible. If it is feasible, this is an effective means of controlling distributed updates.

If partitioning is not an option, conflict resolution is necessary to maintain the integrity of the master database during merge updates. The default configuration used by SQL Server to detect conflicts checks updates column by column and does not call updates to different columns a conflict; updates to separate columns in the same row are combined to form the output row. The publication can be configured to treat two updates to the same row as a conflict, though, with the article properties dialog during setup. However conflicts are defined, the resolver can use the update time or a subscriber priority when deciding which update wins.

If the default resolver does not satisfy the needs of your application, you may decide to implement a custom resolver. A custom resolver is an external component that implements the `ICustomResolver` interface. The resolver is registered and used on the distribution server in the case of a push subscription, or on the subscriber in the case of a pull. SQL Server will query the resolver for the conflict types it is prepared to handle (such as updates), then will call the resolver to arbitrate when those types of change conflicts occur. Your best approach for implementing a custom resolver is to start from one of the examples provided with SQL Server in the `\devtools\samples\sqlrepl` directory and modify it to use your custom logic.

> **NOTE**
>
> `ICustomResolver` is a custom COM interface defined in the sqlres.h header supplied with SQL Server. In addition to the `IUnknown` methods, it defines `GetHandledStates` and `Reconcile` members. `GetHandledStates` is called by SQL Server after the object is instantiated to learn what conflict events the resolver can handle. `Reconcile` is called thereafter whenever one of the handled events occurs.

Replication Over Dial-Up Connections

Replication over dial-up lines is basically the same as replication over a LAN or WAN. However, it is slower, and there are sometimes network and security issues involved. There are several programming options to coordinate the dialing and replication tasks. One method is to write it using the SQL-DMO tools and the RAS API.

Another way is to write a batch file that uses the ISQL utility, which comes with SQL Server, to start the SQL replication tasks and the Windows NT rasdial.exe utility to connect to remote subscribers. Put it all in a batch file and automate it using NT's AT scheduling service. There are many options for automating replication.

Here are some issues to be aware of when setting up RAS replication:

- After the initial synchronization, the distribution task's schedule needs to be changed from running continuously to running only when requested. Then it can be controlled programmatically, allowing subscribers to dial in and pick up their replicated jobs on demand. Writing applications to do this is where the SQL-DMO tools come in handy.

- For two-way RAS replication, the RAS server has to be on the same server as the distribution database. If the distribution databases cannot directly connect, only one-way replication can be achieved. This makes sense because a RAS client sees the entire remote network. A machine on the network, however, doesn't see the RAS client on the network, which prevents replication from running.

- Unless you like working directly with the Win32 RAS API, get a RAS dialing control. Be sure to get one that allows you to connect synchronously or you'll be writing lots of code to handle your RAS connections.

- One way to avoid security problems is to give the Windows NT login used by SQL Agent the same login ID and password on all SQL Servers involved in replication and on all remote access server's phone books. This is useful when replicating across remote domains.

TIP

If you are going to attempt dial-up replication using RAS, you need to know this. RAS connection behavior changed between Windows NT versions 3.51 and 4.0. In version 3.51, dial-up RAS clients stay attached to a RAS server even after a user has logged off the RAS server. In NT 4.0, all RAS connections are disconnected when a user logs off the local machine. This is pretty tough on dial-up clients. See Microsoft Knowledge Base article Q158909, "How to Keep RAS Connections Active After Logging Off," for more details. The article says to modify the entry in NT 4.0, but in reality you have to add it yourself. To do it, log on as an administrator and use the NT registry editor to create a new value called `KeepRASConnections` with a data type of `REG_SZ` under `HKEY_LOCAL_MACHINE\SOFTWARE\Microsoft\Windows NT\CurrentVersion\WinLogon`.

Set the string to a value of 1 (`true`) to keep RAS connections active.

> **TIP**
>
> Purchase a two-way ring-down circuit if you are going to do any extensive RAS replication development. It is basically a phone company in a box the size of a small external modem. When two modems are plugged into it with RJ-11 connectors, the attached computers can emulate real phone lines. You can do performance testing without having to coordinate with a truly remote machine. They are manufactured by Viking Electronics, Inc. of Hudson, Wisconsin, but must be purchased from a local distributor. If you need one of these, you need it bad.

Summary

This chapter only touches on some of the capabilities of SQL Server replication. Here are the chapter's main points:

- There are three main roles in replication—publishing, distributing, and subscribing.
- SQL Server replication uses loose consistency on replicated data.
- Replication works by reading a published database's committed transaction log entries and converting them into SQL statements, which are executed on the subscribing database.
- SQL Agent jobs provide the mechanism for replication's operation. Controlling the tasks controls replication.
- Only data (and if published, stored procedure execution) are replicated by SQL Server.
- SQL-DMO can be used to programmatically control replication.
- Merge replication can be complex and must be designed to gracefully resolve conflicting updates.
- With some restrictions, RAS can be used for replication.

Migrating to SQL Server: Data Conversion and Integration

PART III

Outgrowing Access

CHAPTER 17

Welcome to Chapter 17, "Outgrowing Access." Finding yourself at this chapter more than likely means you fit into one of two categories: an individual who has made a commitment to move data from Access to SQL Server and is now looking for a method to make the actual move, or someone at a crossroads, still attempting to pick the right path—staying with Access or moving to SQL Server.

I have divided this chapter into two parts. In this first part, you look at the architecture of both databases to determine differences between the two. You examine how each feature of SQL Server compares with Access so you can determine whether SQL Server is truly right for you. In the second part, you review the actual migration of data from Access to SQL Server and a few methods of moving the data over.

Determining the Need to Move from Access to SQL Server

Now that your boss has posed the question "Should we move to this SQL Server?" you're running around trying to determine the answer. Well, one way to answer this question is to examine what benefits SQL Server has to offer over Access. Are those features right for you? Is it overkill to move to SQL Server?

In this section, you look at those features and the overall pros and cons of SQL Server. As a preface, I'll say that with the release of SQL Server 7.0, Microsoft has made the move to SQL Server even easier and, in many more cases, justifiable.

I will also touch on the subject of Enterprise Databases, a phrase tied to SQL Server, by explaining the requirements of an Enterprise Database and describing some of the environments where you find them running.

Requirements for an Enterprise Database

Before delving into a contrast and comparison discussion of Access and SQL server, you need to understand what makes a database an Enterprise Database.

In most instances, an Enterprise Database, when deployed in a corporate environment, tends to service thousands of users at a time. However, sometimes you find an Enterprise Database deployed in small corporate shops, not so much because of the user load, but because of the volume of transactions.

An Enterprise Database must meet the following minimum requirements:

- Be available 24 hours a day, 7 days a week.
- Take advantage of the native O/S, thus offering stability and performance.

- Offer built-in redundancy and allow users to recover from a disaster through built-in features such as transaction logs.

- Must be based on client/server architecture.

- User/Group-level security offered through the database.

- Capable of supporting very large databases, in the terabyte range.

- Ability to performance-tune the database.

Enterprise Databases tend to be dedicated to the one task of providing the back-end to many different applications. These applications could be developed in-house or be commercially available. Because of the Enterprise Database's features, many companies developing their own in-house applications can take advantage of greater storage capacity, intricate database locking, and better performance between the client and the server.

Here are a few examples of how Microsoft SQL Server can be deployed as an Enterprise Database server:

- The back-end to an e-commerce Internet site.

- The back-end to an accounting/finance package.

- A data warehousing solution.

- The database solution to a document management system.

- The database to BackOffice applications, such as SMS (Systems Management Server).

As you can see, SQL Server has a variety of uses when deployed as an Enterprise Database server. Many of these uses require a redundant, high-performance database to be available. In most cases, the increased use of Enterprise Databases is coming from the demand of the Internet and its use as a medium to publish and store information. Many Web sites have thousands of users accessing information at one time; for special events, the load has gone into the hundreds of thousands.

With an understanding of what's expected from an Enterprise Database, you should now have a clearer idea of SQL Server's capabilities.

Features of Access Versus SQL Server

Even though comparing features of SQL Server and Access is similar to comparing a server-class machine to a desktop machine, you still need to understand the differences between the two. A major difference could be the only reason you make the move to SQL Server. However, to justify the move to SQL Server, someone else might need several reasons to upsize.

Access is perfectly capable of completing the tasks it has been designed for, but it's restricted by being a desktop database designed to run on a desktop-class machine. This is not to say that Access is not a good product. Far from it—Access is good for what it has been designed for. Going through this section should help you determine whether your current needs require you to upsize from Access to SQL Server.

Keep in mind that you might find a justifiable reason to upsize, such as the need for greater capacity; however, there are pros and cons to moving up. At the end of this section, you will take a look at a few of them.

Client/Server Architecture

SQL Server is based on the client/server architecture, meaning that the server is freed from performing client-side tasks, such as handling screen updates and keystrokes. Access, however, is not based on the client/server architecture. In addition to handling the database tasks, Access must also split processor time between client-side activity.

This difference not only governs the type of applications you can develop for the database you choose, but also the type of hardware you must run at the desktop. The client/server architecture lets you run "thinner" clients at the desktop. With the push to run more and more applications at the server, thereby decreasing the amount of processing done at the desktop, SQL Server gives you the ability to follow suit.

Administration

SQL Server administrators have a variety of tools at their disposal to administer the server:

- **SQL Server Enterprise Manager**   Enterprise Manager (shown in Figure 17.1) offers the administrator the ability to manage not only the local SQL server, but also any SQL server that's part of the network. Several built-in wizards help administrators create and manage databases and their objects. With Enterprise Manager, an administrator can create scheduled tasks, alerts, and stored procedures.

- **SQL Server Performance Monitor**   SQL Server Performance Monitor is integrated into Windows NT Performance Monitor. An administrator can monitor performance variables, such as logins per second, user connections, or bulk copy rows per second.

FIGURE 17.1

In the SQL Server Enterprise Manager's easy-to-use interface, you can complete a variety of tasks.

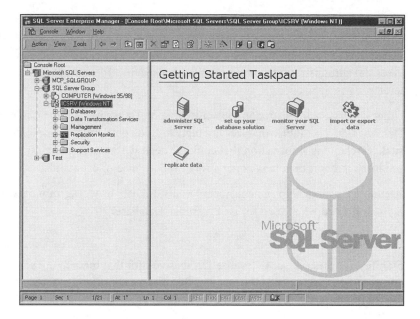

- **Programmable administration**　Using SQL Distributed Management Objects (SQL-DMO), an administrator can program applications to automatically administer a SQL server. Now, SQL Server can be embedded within applications transparently. Administrators can customize applications to handle the day-to-day tasks unique to their environment.

- **Database Maintenance Plan**　The Database Maintenance Plan Wizard allows an administrator to create a set of tasks that the SQL Server Agent can run on a regular basis. These tasks include backing up the database, updating statistics, and running integrity checks against the database.

The administrative tools offered in Access are limited. Several wizards are available, but they are used mainly to create databases, tables, and forms. Tasks such as backing up the database can't be done with Access. There are no tools to monitor database activity or create a maintenance plan. Database errors are not logged; alerts or scheduled tasks cannot be created. The tools offered in Access mainly reflect its capabilities—thus the limitation on administrative tools.

Access does have a built-in wizard for performance analysis, but you can run the performance analyzer only against tables, queries, forms, modules, or macros. The performance analyzer reports suggestions on how to improve the response of these objects. However, the tool can't produce real-time performance reports like those in SQL Server Performance Monitor.

With SQL Server, users can be limited to the objects they can administer. Access does allow you to restrict objects in the database with the User Level Security Wizard. This wizard lets the administrator restrict what objects a user can see. However, SQL Server gives the administrator the ability to be more specific about what objects can be administered.

Other database administration tools available in Access include the Table Analyzer and Documenter. The Table Analyzer attempts to find conflicting information in the table, such as repeating information that could be dealt with more efficiently. The Documenter produces a report on a table, query, form, report, macro, or module.

Again, these tools help cement Access as a valid user or workgroup database, but they are still limited when used for an Enterprise Database.

Stability

Stability is critical to an Enterprise Database or, for that matter, any server relied on companywide and on a 24/7 basis. For this reason, considering Access as the database of choice might not be wise if stability is a question.

Stability is governed by the database and by the operating system it runs on. If you try to share an Access database in Windows 95, the system is more likely to crash with a bigger load on the machine than if you were sharing the same database in Windows NT, simply because Windows NT is more stable than Windows 95 when sharing files. It doesn't mean that Access is taking advantage of any of the features in NT that SQL Server uses to increase overall stability. SQL Server takes advantage of and uses the multithreading capability available in Windows NT. So if you add additional processors to your server, SQL Server instantly takes advantage of them to run multiple processes at one time. This way, the server can process requests from multiple users or create additional data pages as needed, without forcing other tasks to wait.

SQL Server uses transaction logs. When a user attempts to make a change to a database, the changes are first written to the transaction log and then passed to the database. So if there's a database failure, it's possible to recover data from any point in time. If a user was writing to an Access database and corruption occurred at the database, you couldn't roll back from that transaction; the only way to recover would be to restore the entire database file from backup. You would end up losing whatever work you did after the last backup.

For backups, Microsoft SQL Server has built-in Backup and Restore capabilities. You can back up a database to file or tape and restore right from the tape device or file. In Access, an administrator must restore the database from the tape backup program, thus increasing the overall recovery period.

It's possible to execute incremental backups from within SQL Server. Instead of having to back up the entire database, an administrator can now back up only what's changed on the database. With Access, you have no choice but to back up the entire database.

When performing backups, Access users have to log out; it's not possible to back up the .mdb file while users are still in Access. SQL Server, however, doesn't require that users be logged out of the database when it's being backed up. This only enforces SQL Server's ability to be available 24 hours a day.

With rapidly increasing databases, the constant growth of the database file can be an issue. SQL Server 7.0 now supports the option to dynamically increase the size of a database in either fixed percentages or megabytes. This way, the daily operations of a company are not affected by downtime when the database needs more space.

Scalability

Microsoft SQL Server was designed from the outset as an Enterprise Database. The design team kept in mind the need for a scalable system, a database that could serve an entire company's needs—not just in the present, but in the future, too.

Earlier versions of SQL Server were designed to support 200MB–300MB databases, but version 7.0 has the capability of supporting terabyte databases. Another scalable aspect of SQL Server 7.0 is its ability to run the same database engine on a multitude of platforms. SQL Server 7.0 is supported on Windows 95/98, Windows NT Workstation, Windows NT Server, and Windows NT Enterprise Edition.

This scalability allows application developers more freedom when creating applications to work with SQL Server. The developer generally doesn't have to be concerned with the abilities of the O/S. There might be some performance limitations when running SQL Server on lower-end systems, such as Windows 95/98 or Windows NT Workstation.

Another new feature in SQL Server 7.0 is the server's ability to dynamically self-tune. This allows users to install SQL Server on laptops and desktops without having to tune the server for their particular type of machine.

Last, because SQL Server 7.0 database files reside on operating system files instead of logical devices, scalability has increased. SQL Server databases can now dynamically increase in size. The administrator can set the database to grow in set percentages or megabytes.

Access, on the other hand, suffers greatly from its lack of scalability. Even though the application itself can run on any of the Windows-based platforms, it can't take advantage of the more scalable operating systems, such as Windows NT Server. Adding more processors to the system won't necessarily make the Access database run any faster,

17

OUTGROWING
ACCESS

mostly because Access can't fully utilize the capabilities of the NT operating system. On the other hand, SQL Server can use the additional processors to run multiple process threads simultaneously. Now SQL Server can process multiple user requests at the same time without having to drop other tasks.

Capacity

The question of capacity alone can force an organization to switch from Access to SQL Server. According to Microsoft documentation, an Access database can grow up to 1.2GB. Realistically, however, an Access database has grown to its capacity by the time it reaches 500MB–700MB. After a certain point, you begin to see performance degradation with an Access database that has grown too large. On the other hand, SQL Server 7.0 is now capable of growing over several terabytes. If you expect your database to grow over the 1GB size, then the move to SQL Server is an easier decision to make.

Security

Microsoft SQL Server supports Windows NT Authentication and Mixed Mode security. Windows NT Authentication uses the Windows NT login information the user supplied when logging into the network. This simplifies security administration because an administrator needs to manage user/group information from only one location.

Mixed Mode security can take advantage of Windows NT Authentication, but if no Windows NT account information is supplied, SQL Server uses the SQL Server login. Using either method of security, an administrator can set restrictions on SQL Server databases and its objects. Access to triggers, views, and indexes can all be restricted according to security information.

Access has the ability to apply security restrictions on databases. However, because Access doesn't support objects such as views and triggers, there's no option to restrict security down to this level. User-level restriction in Access can be set to tables, forms, reports, macros, and modules.

When compared to SQL Server, there are many limitations to the security features in Access. There's no integration with Windows NT security, which would make administrators' lives easier and take advantage of the C2 level security offered with Windows NT.

A database that is being deployed to serve the purpose of an Enterprise Database must offer more restrictions than just denying access to the database or the tables in the database.

With Access, you can restrict someone from viewing a table or query, for example (see Figure 17.2). But what if you wanted them to see a certain part of the table or a particular view? In Access you would have to create a query or combine information from two different tables. With SQL Server, you can create a view to data and then go on to restrict who has access to this view.

FIGURE 17.2

Setting user and group permissions for database objects under Access 97.

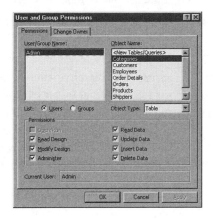

Multiple Users

The number of concurrent users who can connect to the database can be a decision-making factor, too. You can share an Access database by placing it in a shared folder; then up to 255 users can have access to the database.

SQL Server allows a maximum of 32,767 user connections. As you can see, the difference between Access and SQL Server in number of user connections is significant enough to justify a migration from Access to SQL Server.

Insert Locking

Environments that have multiple users accessing the database at one time face a number of problems with insert locking or blocking problems. *Blocking* occurs when multiple users try to add new rows to a table at the same time. There are two main reasons blocking occurs in Access. First, all new rows are added to the end of the table, and second, page locking causes a problem.

When a user places a new row in an Access table, the Jet engine locks the 2KB page where the new record resides while it's being written to the table. This process prevents any other rows from being added. You begin to see substantial blocking problems in an Access environment where more than 15 to 20 users are doing actual data entry.

SQL Server also uses page locking to help avoid conflicts. SQL Server locks are applied at different levels of granularity in the database. Locks can be acquired on rows, pages, keys, ranges of keys, indexes, tables, or databases. However, by using clustered indexes and a fill factor, SQL Server can alleviate this problem. *Clustered indexes* control the physical order of rows in a table. Only one clustered index can exist per table, but it can contain multiple columns. The *fill factor* is a definable number that controls how full a page can become before SQL Server creates a new one. By placing a clustered index on columns with many unique values and setting the fill factor to a number below 100, you can reduce the potential for blocking to happen during data entry.

In addition to clustered indexes and fill factors, SQL Server version 7.0 has enhanced row-level locking. Version 7.0 now supports full row-level locking for both data and index entries. The lock manager has now been optimized to finish lock requests faster, thus increasing the concurrency, particularly when applications append rows to tables and indexes. The lock manager chooses between page locking when operations are locking rows in many pages and row-level locking when you have fewer rows or rows scattered throughout a table.

Issues to Consider

For some of you, reading through the preceding section may have helped you conclude that you should upsize to SQL Server. However, before you take this step, you should consider a few more issues:

- The need for a dedicated SQL Server administrator—Unlike Access, SQL Server is a product that must be maintained and fine-tuned. It's an extremely complex product compared to Access. Bringing SQL Server in-house requires either hiring someone to administer the box or training someone currently on staff.

- Buying additional hardware—You must run SQL Server on a server-class machine. Even though version 7.0 is scalable, if you plan on using it to run a companywide database, you must look at running the product on a dedicated server. Along with installing a new server in your environment, you should consider the administration of the box, such as running daily backups, checking for the latest service packs for the operating system, checking for viruses, and so on. If you already have an in-house MIS staff, the transition of bringing up a new server isn't such a big issue. But if your company does not have a dedicated MIS staff, then you could face some problems.

- Overall cost—With the need to run SQL Server on a dedicated box, train or hire SQL Server administrators, and have the extra cost of maintaining an additional server, the question of whether to upsize might come down to money. If you're finding that Access is simply too slow, it might be more cost-effective to add a processor or memory to the box running the Access database.

What's Really Causing the Problem?

Maybe you have turned to this chapter in desperation. Your Access database isn't performing the way it should—at least, in your humble opinion, it isn't. You have tried everything from moving the database to a faster machine to redesigning the database to spending endless hours looking over the code of your front-end application.

If you have tried all the avenues you see as possible causes for your problems, you should consider running an evaluation of SQL Server before making the leap to it. Microsoft has evaluation copies of SQL Server available on its Web site. You can download the evaluation copy, load it on Windows 95, NT Workstation, or even NT Server, and port over your database. You haven't invested the dollars to buy the software to find out if it really makes a difference with SQL Server. Keep in mind that version 7.0 is scalable, so you can run it on a Windows 95 or an NT Workstation machine; you might not even have to invest the time and effort to prepare a dedicated server for the task.

If you're performing your evaluation to discover performance issues, you should remember to take advantage of ISQL statements to run queries against the database. Doing so can save you the time needed to build queries in Access against the SQL database or rewrite your front-end application. By using ISQL statements, you can see the response time of the query, thus eliminating possible causes of the problem.

Just remember that you could be facing a problem of additional capacity, better security, or more stability; for this situation, there's no other alternative but upsizing to SQL Server. It's important to understand your problem and know whether upsizing will truly solve it.

Making the Move from Access to SQL Server

When an organization takes on the task of moving its information from Access to SQL Server, there are some factors to consider, such as buying additional hardware, the status of front-end applications used as part of the Access database solution, and the methods of migrating to SQL Server.

Issues with Visual Basic, Access, and SQL Server

Many companies have taken advantage of Visual Basic (VB) and its ability to allow developers to create applications faster. Visual Basic has many built-in controls that tie in easily with Access databases. With these controls, a developer can create a front-end to an Access database that's more user-friendly than an Access forms interface. The other advantage of using a Visual Basic front-end rather than native Access front-ends is the application's wider range of capabilities. A Visual Basic developer can create a more reliable application that performs better.

However, if developers have created a Visual Basic front-end to Access, they could face a daunting task when trying to move their data from Access to SQL Server and keep the front-end fully functioning. A developer has two choices: attempt to migrate the front-end application or rewrite the application. I'll examine both choices to explain the pros and cons.

If a developer chooses to migrate the front-end application, much of the task depends on how the application was written and the database's new structure. Looking at this problem from a broad perspective, if data controls are used and the database structure remains the same, a developer can easily go into the application and update the data controls to point to SQL Server. From that point on, all data is retrieved from and written to SQL Server.

If the original application was not written using data controls, the developer faces a bigger challenge.

Another hurdle could arise if the database structure changes when it's imported into SQL Server. This change is a problem no matter what database you're importing data into, even if it's another Access database. Depending on how much of the structure changed, the application might need to be radically rewritten. In fact, it might be more cost-effective to rewrite the entire application from beginning to end. This rewrite could help the developer take advantage of the enhancements in Visual Basic, such as the new ActiveX Data Objects (ADO) control, for programming the SQL Server back-end.

ADO has been implemented to replace Data Access Objects (DAO) and Remote Data Objects (RDO). When using ADO to connect to a SQL Server database, the ADO makes as much of the SQL Server database available as possible with the fastest and most reliable connection of all three methods (ADO, RDO, and DAO). The ADO control also has many shortcuts for common operations when you're programming with SQL Server.

Another issue facing developers is data types. In Access, they are defined using Visual Basic specifications, but in SQL Server, they are based on C. A programmer must be extra sensitive to how the data types are defined in the application. Table 17.1 shows how the data types are converted.

TABLE 17.1 DATA TYPE CONVERSION BETWEEN MICROSOFT ACCESS AND MICROSOFT SQL SERVER

Access	SQL Server
Text	Varchar
Memo	Text
Byte	Smallint
Integer	Smallint
Long Integer	Int
Single	Real
Double	Float
Replication ID	Varbinary
Date/Time	Datetime
Currency	Money
Autonumber (Long Integer)	Int (Identity)
Yes/No	Bit
OLE Object	Image

NOTE

Be careful when you're selecting a data type to be used in SQL Server. You can change the data type for a field in Access; however, you can't change the data type in SQL Server. You have to create a new table so that data can be transferred to that table.

Finally, the option to migrate or rewrite the application is governed by the application's current status. If it was originally written as a 16-bit application, then a developer should rewrite it using a 32-bit version of Visual Basic to take full advantage of operating systems such as Win95 and NT.

On the other hand, if the application was written using a 32-bit version of Visual Basic and requires only minor updates to data controls, then it's worthwhile to simply migrate the application. Many reasons determine which option you should choose, but keep in mind which option will result in the most efficient application that can take advantage of SQL Server. Remember, you went to the lengths of upsizing to SQL Server, so take the extra step to refine your front-end application to walk and talk smoothly with SQL Server.

Using the DTS Import Wizard

The DTS Import Wizard is a new feature available in Microsoft SQL Server 7.0. Using the Data Transformation Services (DTS), an administrator can import and export data between multiple heterogeneous sources. The DTS wizard can be used to copy stored procedures, indexes, and other database objects between SQL Server 7.0 systems, and it can be used to copy schema and relational databases. The DTS wizard has other features, but in this section, I'm concentrating on using it to import Access databases into SQL Server.

Other than the DTS wizard, there are three additional methods of moving your data from Access to SQL Server. The following sections briefly cover each option, before delving back into the DTS wizard.

Linked Table Queries

As long as the tables already exist on SQL Server, you can link them directly to your Access database and then use queries to move the data over. The benefit of using Linked Table Queries when transferring data from Access to SQL Server is twofold. First, if the data you're moving is too large to be moved in one shot, you can move the data over systematically; second, Linked Table Queries are useful if the table structure differs between the two databases. Keep in mind, even though you have more control over the actual data being exported by using queries, only data can be transferred.

Bulk Copy Program

Similar to Linked Table Queries, Bulk Copy Program (BCP) can be used only to transfer data from Access to SQL Server. However, BCP does have its benefits when you need to transfer data over WANs or slow connections or use a floppy disk. To use the BCP option, you must first export data to a comma-delimited or tab-delimited file. You can then use the BCP utility to import the data into SQL Server.

Follow these steps to import an Access database into SQL Server with the BCP utility:

> **NOTE**
>
> In this example, it is assumed you're using Access 97. Also remember that you can only export data using the BCP utility; for that reason, you'll be exporting data from a single table to SQL Server.

1. Launch Access and open the database you want to import into SQL Server.
2. Select a table and right-click on it.
3. Choose Save As/Export from the pop-up menu.
4. Click OK to save the table to a file or database.
5. From the Save As Type drop-down list, select Text Files.
6. Type a filename in the text box.
7. Click Export to export the table.
8. The Export Text Wizard then launches. Click Next to continue.
9. Select comma for the delimiter option.
10. Click Next to continue, and click Finish to complete the task.

Copy the file you just created to a location on SQL Server, or you can copy it to a floppy disk, if it's not possible to copy directly to the SQL Server machine.

In SQL Server you must create the table that the data is being imported into by following these steps:

1. First, launch Enterprise Manager, and then expand the SQL Server machine where you want to create the table.
2. Expand the Databases folder, and expand the database where the table will be created.
3. Right-click on the Table icon and select New Table.
4. Type in a name for the new table.
5. Create the columns with the appropriate data types and lengths. Click the disk icon on the toolbar to save the table.
6. Close the window to exit.
7. From SQL Server, launch a command prompt and change to the MSSQL7\BINN directory. It's assumed that SQL Server 7.0 is installed in the MSSQL7 directory.

17

OUTGROWING ACCESS

8. Type in a command similar to this one:

```
bcp dbname..tablename in export.txt /fformat.fmt /Sservername /Usa
/Ppassword
```

In this command, *dbname* is the database name, *tablename* is the name of the table data is being imported into, *export.txt* is the file you saved when exporting the table, and the .fmt file is a formatter file you created before the procedure began.

This command differs depending on how you exported the file from Access and how you want to import it into SQL Server. For more information on the BCP utility, see SQL Server Books Online.

Access 97 Upsizing Wizard

The Upsizing Wizard is a free tool you can download from Microsoft's Web site. It's an easy-to-use tool that allows you to export your current Access databases to SQL Server. To run the Upsizing Wizard, you need to have a large enough database already created on the SQL Server.

In the following exercise, you will be exporting a database from Access into SQL Server. First, follow these steps to create a SQL Server database:

1. Launch Enterprise Manager.
2. Expand the SQL Server folder and expand the server where the database will be created.
3. Right-click the Databases folder and select New Database.
4. Type in a name for the database and change the size of the file for the database as needed. Remember to create the database so you have enough room for future expandability.
5. Select the Transaction Log tab to create a transaction log.
6. Click OK when done.

Next, launch the Upsizing Wizard so that you can actually export the database:

1. Launch Access 97 and open the database you want to export.
2. Choose Tools, Add-Ins, Upsize to SQL Server from the menu.
3. You're then prompted to pick between using an existing database or creating a new one. Select the option Use an Existing Database.

> **NOTE**
>
> You can't create a new database on a SQL Server 7.0 machine by using the Upsize Wizard. For this reason, you must create the database beforehand.

4. Click Next to continue. You're then prompted for a DSN name. Create a new data source and configure it to connect to the new database.

5. Select the new data source you just created and click OK.

6. Log into the SQL Server machine, and click OK.

7. In the Available Tables list, select the tables you want to export, and click Next (see Figure 17.3).

FIGURE 17.3

Using the Upsizing Wizard to select which tables to export to the SQL Server machine.

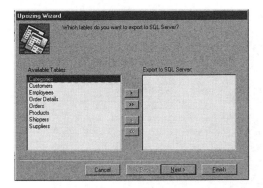

8. You can upsize particular table attributes, too, including indexes, validation rules, defaults, and table relationships.

9. You can create an upsizing report and/or click Finish when you're done.

The wizard then begins to upsize the database; errors encountered during the process are displayed onscreen. At the end of the process, the report is displayed, too, if you selected the option to run it.

Being able to use the Upsizing Wizard to export not only data, but also table attributes, makes it an excellent tool for upsizing your data.

DTS Import Wizard

Before using the DTS wizard, be sure to back up your Access database. You can simply copy the .mdb file to a secure location or back up the database to tape.

When importing data into the SQL Server machine, you need to specify the source and destination, so you must create the destination database beforehand.

To import an Access database, follow these steps:

1. Launch Enterprise Manager.

2. Expand the SQL Server Group and select the SQL Server machine.

3. Expand the SQL Server machine and select the database you're importing the information into.

4. Choose Tools, Data Transformation Services, Import Data from the menu.

5. When the DTS wizard opens, click Next to continue.

6. In the Source drop-down list, select Microsoft Access as your source (see Figure 17.4).

FIGURE 17.4

Selecting which Access database file to import into SQL Server using the Data Transformation Service wizard.

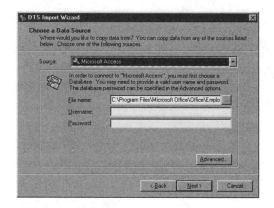

7. Enter the path for the location of the Access `.mdb` file in the File Name text box, and type in the username and password if necessary. Click Next to continue.

8. In the Destination box, confirm the database that the data is being imported into, and click Next to continue.

9. Select to copy the tables from the source, and click Next to continue.

10. Select the tables you want to import. Click the Preview button to view the data before it's exported. Click the Transform button to change Column Mappings and Transformations. Click Next to continue.

11. Select to option to run the task immediately, and click Next to continue.

12. Click Finish when done.

I have just discussed several methods of importing data into SQL Server from Access. Which method is best for you depends on the data you want to import into SQL Server. If you have only tables that need to be exported, then the DTS wizard is the best tool. However, if you want to bring over objects associated with the database, then you should consider the Upsizing Wizard, but using Linked Queries and the BCP utility might be enough to get the job done.

Summary

The decision to move from Access to SQL Server can come down to many factors or just one. On top of this, a database administrator looks at the decision differently than a developer does (by some miracle, they might occasionally agree with each other). What you need to keep in mind is what you expect from the database and what kind of down-time you can tolerate. What volume of transactions does your database have to support? Does your data have to be accessible through the Internet? All these factors play an important role in what you do. Now that you have reviewed some of the major differences between the two database management systems, I hope your decision has become easier to make.

17

OUTGROWING
ACCESS

Making the Switch from Sybase SQL Server

Starting with 7.0, the Roads Diverge

At one time, Sybase SQL Server and Microsoft SQL Server were practically the same product. Sybase and Microsoft had a relationship and the end result was a similar product marketed under two separate company names. By teaming up, Sybase and Microsoft were able to offer customers a multi-platform database solution covering the most popular UNIX platforms as well as a growing Windows NT platform. Right around the time that Sybase released System 10 and Microsoft released SQL Server version 6.0, the products began to take on a different look. This different look was the result of the partnership between the two companies drifting apart.

Following this split, Sybase continued to forge ahead with performance and reliability focused mainly on the enterprise market. Sybase was most interested in the biggest companies with the largest database requirements. Microsoft in version 6.0 and then onto version 6.5, on the other hand, focused primarily on a toolset upgrade and increased ease of manageability. Microsoft's new task scheduler, SQL Trace utility, and Enterprise Manager made managing the complex database easier. No longer was the Database Administrator (DBA) tied to the ISQL command-line database utility. DBAs could spend less time managing the database without learning complex system stored procedures and maintenance commands.

With SQL 7.0, the breakup is finally complete. In fact, Sybase went as far as renaming its flagship server product; as of version 11.5, it is called Sybase Adaptive Server. Microsoft held onto the SQL Server name and went from version 6.5 to the new 7.0. With SQL 7.0, Microsoft rebuilt and reengineered the entire product.

Looking Forward

Sybase recently released version 11.9.2 of Adaptive Server. In this release, Sybase implemented row-level locking and more advanced management tools to aid the DBA in managing the most complex databases. As new versions continue to develop, count on the similarities of these two products to dwindle down to mere separate products. As a programmer developing client/server applications, it will become increasingly more difficult to port applications between these databases. Each product with its latest releases has added additional data types, system stored procedures, Transact-SQL commands, and locking schemes. Although similar in functionality, these new features behave dissimilarly in each product. Basically, these products are not the same anymore. Porting between Sybase Adaptive Server and Microsoft SQL 7.0 should not be as difficult as porting a large application between PowerBuilder and Visual Basic, for example. However, porting databases between these products could take some work, depending on the features used and the code's complexity.

The Remaining Similarities

While Microsoft SQL Server and Sybase Adaptive Server continue to progress down different paths, there are a number of remaining similarities between the products. The overlap in feature sets will allow DBAs to remain familiar with some of the core administrative tasks while possibly running both versions in test/conversion modes. Many of the system procedures remain similar and the version of Transact-SQL in both products have a similar core set of instructions.

System Procedures

The underlying system stored procedures in both products still begin with *sp_*. They can still be called from your favorite query tool, and they even perform many of the same functions. The old favorites, such as sp_helpdb, sp_who, and sp_configure, still exist in both versions, but the code and results have changed slightly. For example, sp_helpdb in SQL 7.0 now has additional columns such as filegroup, max size, and growth to reflect the new storage mechanisms in SQL 7.0. These columns don't pertain to Sybase Adaptive Server, so they do not show up.

It is advisable to spend some extra time becoming familiar with the similarities and differences of favorite commands and functions you use in Sybase. Microsoft's Books Online is easy to install and use and offers an abundance of specific definitions and examples of stored procedure, commands, and functions. Take special note of any parameter, output, functionality, and compatibility differences specified. In addition to altering functionality in common stored procedures, both Microsoft and Sybase have added procedures and functions. These new procedures and functions are used to help administer and code new feature sets and functionality.

This chapter points out as many of the major differences as possible between the two products. There are, however, many more subtle "fine print" differences that aren't covered here, so thorough preparation and extensive testing should prevail. A major conversion such as this is not a project that should be rushed or treated lightly.

18

MAKING THE
SWITCH FROM
SYBASE

Microsoft Transact-SQL Versus Sybase Transact-SQL

Both Microsoft and Sybase have implemented a version of the ANSI SQL standard for their structured query language. Although neither company followed every aspect of the standard, the basics still exist in both products. SELECT, INSERT, UPDATE, and DELETE statements still perform the same. Many stored procedures written in either product still compile in both SQL 7.0 and Adaptive Server.

For instance, the syntax to create a new stored procedure is the same in both products as shown below:

```
CREATE PROCEDURE GetAuthors as
select * from pubs..Authors
```

Differences Between Microsoft SQL 7.0 and Sybase Adaptive Server

As Microsoft SQL Server and Sybase Adaptive Server have grown apart, the behavioral differences or application logic can affect the results of converted applications. Although some differences will be quite noticeable, such as a Sybase stored procedure that refuses to compile in SQL 7.0, other differences will be much more subtle. It will be necessary to heavily test the behavior and resultsets of all programming logic in script files and stored procedures prior to completing the conversion. This section will provide a set of core differences that must be explored during the critical planning stage.

Compatibility Modes

A temporary solution to some of the compatibility differences between SQL 7.0 and Sybase is to change the database's compatibility level. To make this change, use the sp_dbcmptlevel stored procedure, which can make a SQL 7.0 database mimic some of the behavior of a SQL 6.5 or SQL 6.0 database. This stored procedure could be important because some of the characteristics in the earlier versions of SQL Server match the same characteristics of Sybase Adaptive Server. For instance, in SQL Server 6.0 and 6.5, a query with a GROUP BY clause and no ORDER BY clause automatically sorted the result-set. In SQL 7.0, this behavior has changed and the resultset would no longer be sorted. This change in the order of the resultset could change the logic of an application that relied on sorted data returned from a GROUP BY query. In SQL 7.0, an ORDER BY clause would now be added to the data to get the same results. It won't take long for users to figure out that all the results in their drop-down list box are no longer sorted—so be prepared.

In addition to sorting the GROUP BY clauses, sp_dbcmptlevel helps the Sybase developer in other areas. Part of the migration process from Sybase Adaptive Server to Microsoft SQL 7.0 could be an interim SQL 7.0 converted database running the SQL 6.5 compatibility mode. This way, developers have more time to track down and test a full SQL 7.0 implementation. These settings are specific to the database. Therefore, two copies of the database can be migrated to the SQL 7.0 server, with one in each compatibility mode (6.5 and 7.0).

Other notable behaviors can be reproduced in SQL 7.0 to act more like a SQL 6.5 or Sybase server. The following statements and results are listed in Table 18.1 to show the difference in the versions.

TABLE 18.1 DATA COMPATIBILITY MODE BEHAVIOR

Statement	SQL 6.5 and Sybase 11.5.1	SQL 7.0 Native
SELECT au_fname FROM authors GROUP BY au_fname	All distinct au_fname in ascending order.	All distinct au_fname in inserted order.
UPDATE authors SET a.au_fname = "Betty"	au_fname in all rows updated to "Betty".	Error.
CREATE TABLE malls (ID int, test bit)	test column(bit) defaults to NOT NULL.	test column(bit) determined by session or database settings.
ALTER TABLE authors ALTER COLUMN au_lname varchar(60) NULL	Invalid syntax.	Changes the au_lname column from varchar(40) to varchar(60).
CREATE TRIGGER tu_authors on authors for update as print 'Update tu_authors' go CREATE TRIGGER tu_authors2 on authors for update as print 'Update tu_authors2' go	tu_authors2 overwrites tu_authors.	Both tu_authors and tu_authors2 are created and fire when the authors table is updated.

18

MAKING THE
SWITCH FROM
SYBASE

continues

TABLE 18.1 CONTINUED

Statement	SQL 6.5 and Sybase 11.5.1	SQL 7.0 Native
CREATE PROC test_proc as SELECT au_lname from #archive	Sybase—error if #archive does not exist; SQL 6.5—warning.	No warning.
SELECT DATALENGTH('')	Returns 1.	Returns 0.
SELECT DATALENGTH(N'')	Sybase—returns 1; SQL 6.5—returns 2.	Returns 0.
SELECT LTRIM(' ')	Returns NULL.	Returns an empty string.
select LTRIM(N' ')	Returns NULL.	Returns an empty string.
select REPLICATE ('123',0)	Returns NULL.	Returns an empty string.
select REPLICATE (N'123',0)	Returns NULL.	Returns an empty string.
select RIGHT(N'123',0)	Returns NULL.	Returns an empty string.
select RIGHT('123',0)	Returns NULL.	Returns an empty string.
select RIGHT('123',-1)	Returns NULL.	Error.
select RIGHT(N'123',-1)	Returns NULL.	Error.
select RTRIM(' ')	Returns NULL.	Returns an empty string.
select RTRIM(N' ')	Returns NULL.	Returns an empty string.
select space(0)	Returns NULL.	Returns an empty string.
select SUBSTRING ('123',1,0)	Returns NULL.	Returns an empty string.
select SUBSTRING (N'123',1,0)	Returns NULL.	Returns an empty string.
select CHARINDEX ('SQLServer',NULL)	Returns 0.	Returns NULL.
INSERT x SELECT 1 INTO y FROM authors	SQL 6.5—no error; Sybase—error.	Error.

In addition to the examples in Table 18.1, the differences in the compatibility levels extend to reserved words, too. When the compatibility mode is set to 70, the following words cannot be used for object names and identifiers: BACKUP, DENY, PERCENT, RESTORE, and TOP. When the compatibility mode is set to 65, the following words cannot be used for object names and identifiers: AUTHORIZATION, CASCASE, CROSS, DISTRIBUTED, ESCAPE, FULL, INNER, JOIN, LEFT, OUTER, PRIVILEGES, RESTRICT, RIGHT, SCHEMA, and WORK. If the compatibility mode is set to 60, all the preceding words can be used. For example, if the compatibility mode is set to 60, you can create a stored procedure named LEFT. This is *not* recommended, however, because the goal is to change the database to the 70 compatibility mode as soon as possible. If the mode is set to 60, it's in your best interest to rename any objects that have names with the keywords listed here. These specific keywords, however, refer only to the different compatibility modes of Microsoft SQL Server and do not directly apply to Sybase Adaptive Server. For more information on this topic, please see the "Reserved Words" section of this chapter.

Here is the syntax for sp_dbcmptlevel:

sp_dbcmptlevel [[@dbname=] *name***][,[@new_cmptlevel=]***version***]**

In this code, @dbname is the name of the database for checking or changing the compatibility level. For @new_cmptlevel, set it to 70, 65, or 60 with a default of NULL. This parameter decides which compatibility level the database is set at.

Let's take a look at this example:

sp_dbcmptlevel pubs

It returns the following:

```
The current compatibility level is 70.
```

Now take a look at another example:

sp_dbcmptlevel pubs, 65

It returns this:

```
DBCC execution completed. If DBCC printed error messages, contact your
➥system administrator.
```

At this point, you can rerun sp_dbcmptlevel to verify that the pubs database was changed correctly:

Sp_dbcmptlevel pubs

It returns the following:

```
The current compatibility level is 65.
```

It's important to note that sp_dbcmptlevel does not restore full backward compatibility. In some cases, the compatibility could not be reversed; only the SQL 7.0 functionality is available.

18

MAKING THE
SWITCH FROM
SYBASE

Transaction Management Modes

Both Microsoft SQL 7.0 and Sybase Adaptive Server support a mode of operation in which transactions are automatically started following any data retrieval or data modification statement. Although the functionality is the same, the syntax for enabling this mode is different for the two products. The two syntaxes are compared as shown:

Sybase	`set chained [ on ¦ off ]`
Microsoft	`set implicit_transactions [ on ¦ off ]`

It is important to update procedures that make changes to this setting. All occurrences of SET CHAINED [ON ¦ OFF] must be changed to SET IMPLICIT_TRANSACTION [ON ¦ OFF] before migrating to SQL 7.0. Drastic behavioral differences in transaction logic could be affected if it is not changed. The Sybase default is to run in unchained mode, in which all transactions must start with an explicit BEGIN TRANSACTION and finish with either a ROLLBACK TRANSACTION or a COMMIT TRANSACTION statement. OLE-DB, ODBC, and Microsoft DB-LIB connections default to implicit_transaction off, which is equivalent to Sybase's unchained mode. Therefore, if the modes are not changed, there's no need to worry. However, check all stored procedures, script files, and application code for this command and address the differences immediately.

To determine the current transaction mode in Sybase, use the following syntax:

```
select @@tranchained
go
```

A 0 indicates that the default unchained mode is being used. A 1 indicates that the connection is running in chained mode.

To determine whether implicit_transaction is on or off for your connection to SQL 7.0, use the following syntax:

```
IF (@@options & 2) > 0
  PRINT 'on'
ELSE
  PRINT 'off'
```

In addition, Sybase Adaptive Server allows stored procedures to be compiled with COMMIT TRANSACTION statements without matching BEGIN TRANSACTION statements if they were compiled in chained mode. Each COMMIT TRANSACTION has to match up with a BEGIN TRANSACTION if it is going to be successfully compiled into Microsoft SQL 7.0.

Isolation Levels

In a multithreaded application such as a relational database, it is important for the database engine to manage how data is isolated between running processes. For example, Fred begins a transaction and updates a row. There are settings in both database engines that carry rules for determining whether other users are able to read that data row before the transaction is either committed or rolled back. If Betty is able to read the updated row, she is allowed to perform a dirty read (because the data change may or may not be committed to the database) and the server is therefore set (in SQL 7.0) to READ UNCOMMITTED. If, on the contrary, Betty is unable to read this data row until Fred completes his transaction, the isolation level is set to READ COMMITTED.

Database locking performance and query results can be affected if this setting is not set the same for both versions. Therefore, it will be important to convert all Sybase syntax to the appropriate Microsoft syntax.

The syntax is different for Sybase and Microsoft when referring to the isolation levels with the SET statement. Sybase isolation levels can be set to 0, 1, 2, or 3. Isolation level 2 is new to Sybase Adaptive Server 11.9.2. To view the current isolation level in the Sybase environment, use the following syntax:

```
select @@isolation
go
```

Sybase defaults to a value of 1, which represents READ COMMITTED. Microsoft SQL 7.0 can be set to READ UNCOMMITTED, READ COMMITTED, REPEATABLE READ, and SERIALIZABLE. REPEATABLE READ is not a true implementation of isolation level 2 and behaves similarly to SERIALIZABLE. Before conversion, make sure each isolation level is the same on both servers.

Sybase	Microsoft
0	READ UNCOMMITTED
1	READ COMMITTED
2	REPEATABLE READ
3	SERIALIZABLE

Refer to the server documentation for a full explanation of the effects of different isolation levels.

Reserved Words

Both Sybase Adaptive Server and Microsoft SQL Server have lists of reserved words that cannot be used to name objects in the database. The lists for the two products are similar but not exactly the same. This becomes a problem in conversions if the names of any Sybase database object is a SQL 7.0 reserved word. For example, LEFT is a reserved word in SQL 7.0 but not in Sybase Adaptive Server, so if you try to create a stored procedure named LEFT in SQL 7.0, you get the following error:

```
create procedure LEFT as
select * from authors
go

Server: Msg 156, Level 15, State 1
Incorrect syntax near the keyword 'LEFT'.
```

This issue could make the conversion from Sybase to Microsoft a little more difficult because objects that could be created in Sybase might not be able to be created in SQL 7.0. The following is a list of SQL 7.0 reserved words that are not reserved words in Sybase. Any objects in your Sybase database with names in this list must be renamed before a SQL 7.0 conversion.

BACKUP	FREETEXT	REPEATABLE
COLUMN	FREETEXTTABLE	REPLICATION
COMMITTED	FULL	RESTORE
CONTAINS	IDENTITYCOL	RESTRICT
CONTAINSTABLE	INNER	RIGHT
CROSS	JOIN	ROWGUIDCOL
CURRENT_DATE	LEFT	SERIALIZABLE
CURRENT_TIME	NOCHECK	SESSION_USER
CURRENT_TIMESTAMP	OPENDATASOURCE	SYSTEMUSER
CURRENT_USER	OPENQUERY	TAPE
DENY	OPENROWSET	TOP
DISTRIBUTED	OUTER	UNCOMMITTED
FILE	PERCENT	UPDATETEXT
FLOPPY	PIPE	

Cursor Syntax

Creating and executing stored procedures in both products remain similar, but a few exceptions in the cursor statements should be noted when converting. In this area, the same stored procedure will not compile on both products. The following example is from a SQL 7.0 cursor. The main differences between the two are formatted in boldface. These changes are not show-stoppers, but they do represent some work to be done in the conversion process. In large applications, these subtle changes could take some time to locate and fix.

```
1   CREATE PROCEDURE sql_cursor AS

2   declare @lname char(20), @fname char(20)

3   DECLARE mycursor CURSOR FOR
4   select au_lname, au_fname from authors

5   OPEN mycursor

6   FETCH FROM mycursor INTO @lname, @fname

7   WHILE @@FETCH_STATUS /* Sybase uses @@SQLSTATUS
➥instead of @@FETCH_STATUS */ = 0
8   BEGIN
9   FETCH FROM mycursor INTO @lname, @fname
10  /*
11  **   SOME BUSINESS LOGIC GOES HERE
12  */
13  END

14 CLOSE mycursor
15 DEALLOCATE /* Sybase needs the word CURSOR right here */ mycursor
```

It's important to note that Microsoft uses @@FETCH_STATUS and Sybase uses @@SQLSTATUS in line 7. Both have a similar purpose, but they do not return the same error codes. Therefore, if your Sybase cursor syntax was written to trap return codes 1 or 2, the numbers must be changed. Table 18.2 shows the differences between the return codes. If your cursor was written to use the loop WHILE @@SQLSTATUS = 0, the only change for line 7 is changing the @@SQLSTATUS to @@FETCH_STATUS.

TABLE 18.2   CURSOR GLOBAL VARIABLE DIFFERENCES

	Sybase (@@SQLSTATUS)	*Microsoft* (@@FETCH_STATUS)
Fetch was successful	0	0
Fetch statement failed	1	-2
No more rows available	2	-1

In addition to the changes for the FETCH statement return code, it's necessary to remove the keyword CURSOR from line 15. A DEALLOCATE statement with the keyword cursor will fail if attempted in SQL 7.0.

For Sybase, this is the syntax for the DEALLOCATE statement:

```
DEALLOCATE cursor cursor_name
```

Here's the syntax for the DEALLOCATE statement in Microsoft SQL 7.0:

```
DEALLOCATE { { [GLOBAL] cursor_name } ¦ @cursor_variable_name}
```

Microsoft has also enhanced the cursors beyond Sybase's capabilities. Included with SQL 7.0 are scrollable cursors, which let you fetch the first or last row, the next or previous row, absolute and relative positioning from the current row, and even GLOBAL cursors, which can be used by processes that didn't create the cursor. Although this enhanced functionality makes cursor programming easier and more powerful, cursors should still be used sparingly. Both Sybase and Microsoft's database engines excel at processing sets of data. Server-side cursors, which process one row at a time, traditionally do not perform as well.

Rollback Trigger

Sybase Adaptive Server incorporates the ROLLBACK TRIGGER command. When issued within a trigger, this command rolls back all work done in the trigger as well as the statement that caused the trigger to fire. This command behaves differently from the standard ROLLBACK TRANSACTION command by halting the execution of the remainder of the trigger. The standard ROLLBACK TRANSACTION command in a trigger doesn't halt execution of the remainder of the trigger, but it does halt execution of the remainder of the batch. The ROLLBACK TRIGGER command halts the execution of the remainder of the trigger, rolls back the trigger, rolls back the statement that fired the trigger, and then continues with the remainder of the batch.

The ROLLBACK TRIGGER command does not exist in Microsoft SQL 7.0. All Sybase stored procedures that incorporate the ROLLBACK TRIGGER command must be converted before a successful migration to SQL 7.0. You might need to reconsider using the ROLLBACK TRIGGER. By using the ROLLBACK TRIGGER command, it could be misleading when modifying data in tables with triggers. A single ROLLBACK TRIGGER rolls back only the trigger and the modification that fired the trigger. The remainder of the transaction continues and, if committed, is written to the database without the single command that was rolled back. Therefore, all statements in the transaction might not have completed successfully, but the data was committed anyway.

Rewriting the stored procedures that use ROLLBACK TRIGGER to work in Microsoft SQL 7.0 requires nested triggers with savepoints. Here's a sample trigger using ROLLBACK TRIGGER in Sybase Adaptive Server:

```
1  create table table1 (a int, b int)
2  go

3  create trigger trigger1 on table1 for INSERT
4  as

5  if exists (select 1 from inserted where a = 100)
6  begin
7    rollback trigger with raiserror 50000
➥'Invalid value for column a'
8  end

9  insert into table2
10 select a, getdate() from inserted

11 return
12 go
```

In this code, all inserts into table1 also insert an audit row into table2 unless a = 100. If a = 100, the ROLLBACK TRIGGER command is fired and the INSERT in line 9 is *not* fired. The rest of the batch continues, and a raiserror occurs, stating that there was an error in one of the INSERT commands. The INSERT commands are shown here:

```
1  begin tran
2  insert into table1 values (1, 1)
3  insert into table1 values (100, 2)
4  insert into table1 values (3, 3)
5  go
6  select * from table1
```

18

MAKING THE
SWITCH FROM
SYBASE

After issuing these commands, `table1` and `table2` each have two rows. `table1` has the values `1,1` and `3,3` and the second `INSERT` isn't committed because of the `ROLLBACK TRIGGER`. `table2` has the values `1,(currentdate)` and `3,(currentdate)` and the `100` isn't inserted because all processing in the trigger halts when `a = 100` and the `ROLLBACK TRIGGER` is fired. Mimicking this behavior in Microsoft SQL 7.0 requires some additional code. The outer transaction must now be accompanied with savepoints, as shown here:

```
1   create trigger1 on table1 for INSERT
2   as

3   save tran trigger1

4   if exists (select * from inserted where a = 100)
5   begin
6   rollback tran trigger1
7   raiserror 50000 'Rollback'
8   end

9   /* if a = 100 this statement will not fire */
10  insert into table2
11  select a, getdate() from inserted
12  go
```

This trigger now begins with a savepoint (line 3) and the `ROLLBACK TRANSACTION` rolls back only the trigger logic, not the entire transaction (which is similar to Sybase's `ROLLBACK TRIGGER` statement). The changes to the batch job are shown here:

```
begin tran

save tran save1
insert into table1 values (1, 1)
if @@error = 50000
  rollback tran save1

save tran save2
insert into table1 values (100, 2)
if @@error = 50000
  rollback tran save2

save tran save3
insert into table1 values (3, 3)
if @@error = 50000
  rollback tran save3

commit tran
```

As you can see, the changes are not trivial. Because the ROLLBACK TRIGGER command can allow any single batch statement to fail, the additional logic must be included in the migrated Microsoft SQL 7.0 stored procedure code. Depending on the use of ROLLBACK TRIGGER, this could be a big, but necessary, job. There are no shortcuts here. The behavior of the trigger changes if all the ROLLBACK TRIGGER statements are changed to ROLLBACK TRANSACTION after converting, so be careful.

Optimizer Hints

Optimizer hints allow the developer to override the plan that the SQL Server Optimizer has chosen for a particular query. Microsoft SQL 7.0 allows for optimizer hints on SELECT, INSERT, UPDATE, and DELETE statements, but Sybase Adaptive Server allows optimizer hints only on SELECT statements. Should you use optimizer hints? Sometimes. Should it take an act of Congress to put an optimizer hint into production? *Yes.* Optimizer hints are like a double-edged sword. You might be able to speed up a query by using an optimizer hint, but the same optimizer hint could hurt you when the data changes.

The syntax for each version is compared here. Each query uses the following table and indexes:

```
create table orders (order_id int, customer_id int, amount money)
go
create index ind_orders on orders(order_id)
go

select customer_id from orders where order_id = '55555'
```

If showplan reports that the ind_orders index isn't being used on the SELECT query, both Sybase and Microsoft allow you to override the Optimizer's decision and force it to use the index. Again, be careful. In complex queries, you might beat the optimizer at its own game and successfully speed up your query when there are only 1,000 rows in the table, for example. However, before putting the optimizer hint in production, find out how big the table could become. If the size change will be drastic, any hints must be revisited periodically. It's important to clearly document where all hints are used and assign someone to periodically revisit the hint and determine whether it's still the best choice. The Optimizer reevaluates the query plan based on the latest statistics every time the query is run unless it is overwritten with a hint. Here's the Sybase syntax to force the use of the ind_orders index:

```
select customer_id from orders (index ind_orders)
where order_id = '55555'
```

18

MAKING THE
SWITCH FROM
SYBASE

The Microsoft SQL 7.0 syntax is as follows:

```
select customer_id from orders (index = ind_orders)
where order_id = '55555'
```

It is important to know that hints in Sybase Adaptive Server can also use prefetch sizes (2KB, 4KB, 8KB, or 16KB) and I/O strategies (LRU or MRU). These choices do not exist in Microsoft, so any references to them in an optimizer hint must be removed. Here's an example:

```
select customer_id from orders (index ind_orders prefetch 16 lru)
where order_id = '55555'
```

This Sybase query forces the optimizer to use large I/O (16KB) and to use the LRU replacement strategy. The prefetch 16 lru portion of the query would have to be removed to work in Microsoft SQL 7.0.

Optimizing Query Plans

The fastest processors, chip sets, and hard drives make database servers perform well, but nothing in database tuning is more important than optimized queries. The bottom line is that reducing I/Os in queries reduces work on the server. Even the simplest queries can be written to put unnecessary loads on the server. For example, if a query is run to return a resultset to the user that performs 100,000 I/Os, the server must perform 100,000 units of work. What if you could add an index and then run the same query with only 1,000 I/Os? Which query would allow the server and the application to scale better? The easy answer is the optimized query that performs only 1,000 I/Os per call. Sure, you can throw more hardware at this database server and make it perform 100,000 I/Os faster, but why not reduce the work the server has to do by a scale of 100 with adding a simple index, for example? Yes, indexes do have overhead on INSERT, UPDATE, and DELETE commands, but that overhead comes at a small price for big benefits.

The Sybase/Microsoft SQL Server 6.5 Approach

Sybase servers use a text-based query analysis tool called SHOWPLAN; it was designed to let the DBA or developer take a peek at how the Optimizer was performing the query passed to it. Here is the command to enable SHOWPLAN from within the ISQL application:

```
1>  set showplan on
2>  go
```

All queries sent after SHOWPLAN is enabled return with additional information that explains the query plan and reports which indexes were used, what I/O sizes were used (Sybase), what worktables were created, and so forth. With this tool, developers and DBAs can determine whether the overhead of certain indexes is necessary.

The SQL 7.0 GUI Approach

Microsoft SQL Server 6.5 has a similar SHOWPLAN tool. However, in SQL 7.0, Microsoft added the SQL Query Analyzer, which offers a graphical representation of the query plans. This tool will become a valuable addition to the SQL programmer's toolbox. The SET SHOWPLAN ON in Sybase and Microsoft SQL 6.0 and 6.5 has now been changed to either SET SHOWPLAN_TEXT or SET SHOWPLAN_ALL in Microsoft SQL 7.0. The output of the new SHOWPLAN command does not even resemble the output from the old SHOWPLAN.

> **NOTE**
>
> The examples in this section use the pubs database installed on Microsoft SQL Server 7.0 and the pubs2 database installed from the instpb2 script that comes with Sybase Adaptive Server 11.5 for Windows NT.

This first example demonstrates a simple SELECT statement against the authors table in the pubs database. The actual query is as follows:

```
SELECT au_lname from authors
```

This is the output in Sybase:

```
1> select * from authors
2> go

3 QUERY PLAN FOR STATEMENT 1 (at line 1)


4       STEP 1
5           The type of query is SELECT

6           FROM TABLE
7               authors
8           Nested iteration
9           Table Scan
10          Ascending scan
11          Positioning at start of table
12          Using I/O Size 2 Kbytes
13          With LRU Buffer Replacement Strategy
```

As you can see, the query plan from Sybase tells a little story about how the query was executed. From this example, I can tell that a table scan was issued (line 9) and the scan began at the start of the table (line 11). It also tells me that it retrieved the data using 2KB of I/O at a time (line 12) and used the LRU (Least Recently Used) portion of the buffer cache (line 13). The last two lines of the SHOWPLAN output are unique to Sybase because Sybase allows 2KB, 4KB, 8KB, and 16KB I/Os to the database and uses them depending on the server setup and the costs associated.

The Microsoft SQL 7.0 SET SHOWPLAN_ALL output is much more complex and even much too wide to display in this book. In addition, the SET SHOWPLAN_ALL command does not execute the query as Sybase Adaptive Server does; it uses estimates of resource requirements. Here are a few of the columns to pay attention to when analyzing SET SHOWPLAN_ALL in SQL 7.0:

PhysicalOp	This is important to see if an index was used.
EstimatedRows	The number of rows SQL Server thinks satisfy the query.
EstimatedIO	The estimated I/O cost.
EstimatedCPU	The estimated CPU cost.
Warnings	SQL 7.0 might provide warnings about the query if, for example, the Optimizer had to guess about a query plan because there were no valid statistics. This column is important to look at when troubleshooting performance problems. No stats = no performance.

The new SQL Server Query Analyzer produces comparable information as the Sybase Adaptive Server SHOWPLAN. Although the information is similar, the presentation is very different. The following query was run in the Microsoft SQL Server Query Analyzer. This query was chosen because it contains a GROUP BY clause, a WHERE clause, and an aggregate (count(*)).

From this example, I can immediately tell that an index was used when accessing both the stores and the sales tables. This is seen on the far right from reading the beginning of the index name immediately after the table name. Next, moving right to left, the rows retrieved by the stores table are sorted (Sort icon). The resultset is then joined (Nested Loops/Inner Join) and passed to the Stream Aggregate portion for processing the count(*) aggregate. As you can see, a picture is worth 1,000 words. When reading the output of this tool becomes second nature, you will find it easy to write efficient and effective stored procedures.

Temporary Table Names

Table 18.3 shows the maximum lengths for both permanent and temporary table names in Microsoft SQL 7.0 and Sybase Adaptive Server. Temporary tables in both servers begin with a single pound sign (#). As you can see, you aren't forced to shorten your temporary table names when converting to SQL 7.0. Note that the maximum length of a temporary table name in both Sybase and Microsoft is shorter than the maximum length of a permanent table. This is because both products add a unique identifier onto the end of the temporary table name. This way, multiple users can create temporary table names in `tempdb` without naming conflicts.

TABLE 18.3 TABLE NAME LENGTHS

Type of Table Name	Maximum Length
Sybase table name	30
Sybase temporary table name	13
Microsoft table name	128
Microsoft temporary table name	116

The `RAISERROR` Statement

Sybase Adaptive Server's `RAISERROR` statements allow you to send messages back to the client application. Here's an example of the `RAISERROR` statement:

```
if @rate < 0
  RAISERROR 20000 "The rate cannot be less than zero"
```

If `@rate` is less than zero, an error message is sent to the client application with an error number of `20000` and the text message `"The rate cannot be less than zero"`. Code that must be changed in a basic `RAISERROR` statement like this one will be the error number. Microsoft `RAISERROR` statements want the error number to be `50000` or greater. If you try to issue the `RAISERROR` as shown here in SQL 7.0, you get the following error:

```
Server: Msg 2732, Level 16, State 1
User error number 20000 is invalid.
The number must be between 20001 and 2147483647.
```

SQL 7.0 lets you change the error code to `20001`, but Microsoft documentation recommends that you start at `50000`.

18

MAKING THE
SWITCH FROM
SYBASE

Data Types

The number of system data types has been expanded in Microsoft SQL 7.0. This expansion is a direct result of the increase in page size from 2KB to 8KB. Table 18.4 compares the maximum widths of similar data types.

TABLE 18.4 DATA TYPE WIDTHS

Data Type	Sybase (Maximum width)	Microsoft (Maximum width)
char(n)	255	8000
varchar(n)	255	8000
nchar(n)	255	4000
nvarchar(n)	255	4000
binary	255	8000
varbinary	255	8000

In addition, note that the bit data type in SQL 7.0 can be set to 0, 1, or null, but the bit data type in Sybase does not allow nulls.

Identity Columns

Identity columns are similar in Sybase and Microsoft. However, you now have more data type choices when converting to Microsoft SQL 7.0. Sybase identity columns can only be data type numeric(x,0), but Microsoft identity data types can be either tinyint, smallint, int, decimal(x,0), or numeric(x,0).

PRINT Syntax

The PRINT statement in SQL 7.0 does not support substitution syntax like the print statement in Sybase Adaptive Server. All PRINT statements that use substitution syntax must be changed to RAISERROR statements during the conversion process.

Here's a sample PRINT statement in Sybase:

```
print "The table '%1!' is not owned by the user '%2!'.",
@tabname, @username
```

In this example, %1 and %2 are substituted for the @tabname and the @username variables when returned to the user application. Because Microsoft does not support this syntax, it recommends converting PRINT statements that use substitution syntax to RAISERROR statements. Because each RAISERROR has a severity attached, it is necessary to use a lower severity lever (less than 10) because the command is only intended to provide information to the user application. Full RAISERROR syntax in SQL 7.0 is displayed in Books Online.

Summary

Converting a Sybase Adaptive Server to Microsoft SQL 7.0 is a feat that can be accomplished, but there are a number of differences between the two products that must be addressed. Depending on the size of your application, this conversion could turn into a lengthy process. You don't have to rewrite the whole application, but there are a fair amount of show-stoppers. However, look at the bright side: I can't think of an easier conversion between two major database packages than this one, and a successful conversion is highly probable because of the products' many similarities. Most changes appear to be syntactical, so the entire application shouldn't have to be rewritten. Good luck!

CHAPTER 19

Optimizing ODBC Using Visual C++

Open database connectivity (ODBC) is the standard data access facility included in all Microsoft Windows operating systems. Introduced with Windows 3.1, it's one of the longest-lived and most stable features offered on Microsoft desktops. Although some interfaces have come and gone, and other technologies are positioned to supersede it, ODBC remains an effective solution for database access in both client and server components. This chapter describes the architecture and function of ODBC in the Windows environment, examines the pros and cons of applying ODBC in your application, and then demonstrates in detail the two primary methods for using ODBC in Microsoft Visual C++ 6.. I'm assuming you're familiar with constructing applications using Visual C++ and conversant in normal database concepts. This chapter focuses only on the specifics of ODBC in Visual C++, not general client/server database issues.

For application developers, ODBC is a functional data access interface based on the X/Open (now the Open Group) Structured Query Language Call-Level Interface (SQL CLI). With this pedigree, it's no surprise that it shares many attributes with the embedded SQL model. The principal advantage of ODBC is its ability to target different vendors' databases through the same API and SQL grammar. With ODBC, you don't need to preprocess your code with vendor-specific tools, as in the case of embedded SQL, or build versions of your client for every version of SQL database you need to support.

ODBC is the most widely supported database interface in existence, and hundreds of thousands of pages of documentation are available from various sources. Strangely, however, few documents describe it start to finish so that you can see how the pieces work together. Although I can't give you the whole of ODBC here, I *can* give you that end-to-end view in enough detail for you to effectively apply the technology.

I'll start with a discussion of the ODBC database and application model. Following that, you walk through the details of the database operations you're likely to use with the standard ODBC API. I then round out the discussion with the information you need in order to use the Microsoft Foundation Classes' ODBC classes to reduce some of the complexity inherent in CLI database access. If you follow along, you will be well prepared to develop or maintain database applications using ODBC.

ODBC Architecture

First, I must describe the model. To achieve its vendor independence, ODBC uses a four-layer architecture consisting of the client, the driver manager, the database driver, and the database server itself. These components form a pipeline through which commands are passed from the client to the server and status reports and data return to the client, as shown in Figure 19.1.

FIGURE **19.1**

*ODBC architec-
tural layers.*

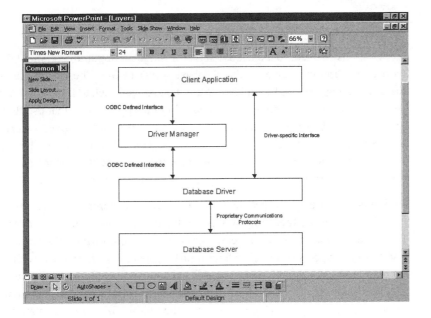

The *client* is usually your code and generates the SQL commands that the server executes on its behalf. It could be a client application interacting with the user or a server
process that requires database services in its operation, but to the server, they are the
same. The database *server*, of course, is the database manager that processes SQL
queries. In between is ODBC, its two components connecting and translating between
the client and the server.

The *driver manager* is the traffic marshal of ODBC. When an application requests a connection to a data source, it's the driver manager that reads the description of the data
source, locates and loads the correct driver, and manages the application's connections to
drivers. It also provides a limited trace facility for debugging. The driver manager is
implemented as dynamic link libraries (DLLs) loaded by the client.

The database vendor usually supplies the *database driver*, which implements whatever
translation and communications features are necessary to translate ODBC SQL grammar
to server-specific SQL, communicate the query to the server, and retrieve result data and
status information. Any vendor-specific functions, such as SQL Server's Tabular Data
Stream communications protocol or Oracle's SQL*Net, are implemented or called by the
driver component. The database drivers are also implemented as DLLs in the client's
process space, although they can make calls to other processes or libraries the client
application is unaware of.

19

OPTIMIZING
ODBC USING
VISUAL C++

Database Abstraction

Applications connect to a database server through a *data source name*, DSN, which is a named description of an available database server or file. These DSNs are configured on the client computers individually and can be changed, deleted, or pointed to different servers or types of servers without modifying the applications that use them. One of my products, a Web-based application that uses an ODBC data source, uses Access97 or SQL Server as the backing database, depending on the installation. The application source code makes no special allowance for the database it's connected to, and the only difference in installations is which type of database is specified in the DSN.

As hinted previously, the problem of connecting to different databases with the same code involves more than simply isolating the connection behind a standard API. Database vendors, for various reasons, implement SQL differently. I will not debate the good or bad aspects of this situation; it just exists and must be dealt with. ODBC's remedy is to define a single SQL grammar, based on ANSI SQL-92, and define layers of compliance for drivers based on how completely they implement this grammar. For details on driver conformance levels, please consult the ODBC SDK documentation.

Applications can issue their queries in this version of SQL to different databases, and the driver is responsible for translating, if necessary, from the standard SQL query to what's required by the database server. Any constructs not recognized by the driver, or those that need no translation, are passed through directly. By passing them along instead of enforcing adherence to ODBC SQL, applications that are expected to use only one brand of database server can use that server's query language to the fullest.

Why Use ODBC?

In 1997 and 1998, Microsoft changed its emphasis from DB-Library to OLE DB and from ODBC to ADO. Because ODBC's days seem limited, why in the world would you continue to use it in your applications? Well, ODBC is not quite dead, and it still has advantages that warrant consideration. ODBC might not be your access method of choice for COM applications, but if you have an application with ODBC interfaces in place, or if your new application uses a conventional architecture, you should consider ODBC for your data access solution. In fact, the SQL Server administrative and client tools themselves use ODBC.

ODBC is a low-level, tightly focused API. As such, it's lean compared to ADO and provides greater control over the database interface. In exchange for some greater complexity, programmers are free to implement their connections and manipulate data in precisely the manner they need, without conforming to a larger object model. For functional programmers, programmers new to Windows and COM, or those with a background in other database libraries, ODBC is a comparatively quick technology to learn and put into practice. For experienced developers (and development leaders), it's an established standard with broad industry support and developer expertise.

Describing the connection and support advantages of ODBC might read like a testimonial to ODBC, but that's not the intent. In the end, you should choose the technology based on the same cost-to-benefit questions you would use in any other technology selection. I find the two largest issues in the selection of ODBC to be its capability to connect to any data source on the planet and the broad availability of ODBC tools, developers, and applications.

Universal Connectivity

When developing COM-based component applications, ADO fits in with the rest of the application as an object-based service for accessing your data. The additional instantiation and communication overhead for applications is generally not an issue because interactive applications are generally unaffected and server programs can be designed to minimize its effects. In the grand scheme of things, the technological infrastructure shared by ADO with other newer Microsoft facilities (such as Active Directory) makes ADO a strong choice for COM-based efforts.

ADO cannot claim the level of support that ODBC enjoys, though; every major database vendor supplies an ODBC interface, and some nondatabase applications have ODBC drivers that provide a table-flavored view of their data. There are even third-party vendors of ODBC drivers, if the database supplier's drivers don't suit your needs. When accessing data for which an OLE DB provider does not exist, ADO must use the ODBC interface anyway, and the additional level of indirection is another detail to manage and another potential point of failure. For all these reasons, ODBC remains the most efficient, simplest, and best-supported technology, and it is a highly effective integration path in heterogeneous data environments.

Established Technology

Probably the most compelling argument for ODBC is its long track record and wide availability. Although some vendors have better drivers than others, ODBC is overall a simple, effective, efficient, and supportable technology that usually works when you ask it to. As *the* ubiquitous database interface, ODBC has gained support from most database development tools, even those created by database vendors whose preferred interface is their own. General database development tools that used to ship with a raft of custom database interface libraries now need only the ability to connect to ODBC.

For the same reason, most developers of database applications for Windows have experience with ODBC. Using data sources with ODBC is largely the same regardless of the backing database, as compared to the nightmare of learning each proprietary client library from each database vendor. Sybase and Oracle, for example, use their own connection protocols behind the ODBC driver, and you still have to manage their network libraries. Hoever, developers can build applications using familiar tools and similar procedures and call sequences without regard for those issues. For typical software projects, which begin development behind schedule and over budget, any improvement in ease of implementation is a good thing.

Legacy applications with database connections are another place where ODBC will have a continuing role. Although ADO can be the best choice for new development, rewriting an application's ODBC code using ADO just does not make sense. Because the code is there and must be maintained, as a programmer or designer, you need to keep ODBC in your back pocket.

Finally, delivery into the workplace is usually not marred by problems in implementing the database connection. Network connectivity or client configuration can be a problem with any client interface, but the necessary ODBC drivers often already exist on the target machine; if not, they are easily installed from the redistribution kit supplied by Microsoft or the vendor. Database connection settings can be distributed as file data sources in corporate products, so the user need not even see the fact of the database connection. These files can be updated centrally with software management packages so that data location and connectivity are no longer user concerns.

Security Issues in ODBC

There is one inherent security issue in ODBC that I know of, but physical and human problems remain the greatest threats to corporate data. On the one hand, if one has access to the hardware, networks and media are so easily compromised that physical security should be prominent on any company's list. On the other hand, more data has been lost by simple theft or employee defection than has ever been hacked. Still, computer security should be addressed in deploying this or any other technology that provides access to your or your customer's corporate data stores.

On the database itself, SQL Server has two database authentication methods: native and NT-based. You can choose to use the standard user ID and password authentication method, but for several reasons, it's probably not the best choice for large installations. First, every time a user has to type a password, there is an additional opportunity to compromise it. Second, with this method you implement two different security domains: your normal NT security accounts and your SQL Server accounts. They must be administered separately, and at the end of the day, you will find that one of them becomes out of date, usually the one in SQL Server. If you will be fielding your solution in a large environment, your DBAs should walk hand in hand with the SAs in implementing a security strategy that unifies the database security controls with the general network. In NT and SQL Server environments, this means using trusted connections in your ODBC applications and granting access to NT groups and users in your database server. If you create appropriate NT groups and control access based on group membership, not only will you simplify your security model, but you will also position yourself better for migrating to Windows 2000.

An easy way to steal your corporate data is to listen to your network traffic (although not as easy as copying your data to a floppy and walking out with it). If your data is worth any security measures, do not use clear protocols on your network, and don't even consider allowing customers on the Internet to connect to your supposedly secure servers using clear IP connections. Use SQL Server's multiprotocol configuration and encrypt your data streams. If you send clear data over your network, anyone with a laptop can plug into an unattended hub and capture your livelihood to disk, but even a simple encryption scheme will deter many would-be crackers.

Network sniffs are difficult to decipher, though. A much easier way to gain access to your databases is to compromise passwords, and it turns out to be simple with mismanaged file DSNs. I mentioned earlier that file DSNs were an excellent tool for managing end users' connections to databases, and they are, but they are also the only real security problem I have found in ODBC. The problem is that you can store more than just the connection information in a DSN file; you can also save the user ID and password. Worse still, the DSN file is a plain text file that anyone can view.

This is your DSN file:

```
[ODBC]
DRIVER=SQL Server
Trusted_Connection=Yes
DATABASE=accounting
SERVER=ACCT002
```

This is your DSN file with a red-flashing-light security hole:

```
[ODBC]
DRIVER=SQL Server
UID=someuserid
PWD=mypassword
DATABASE=accounting
SERVER=ACCT002
```

Anyone who can read this file can access any data in the database that is referenced by the DSN, and any other data this user has access to. Thankfully, the check box to store passwords in file DSNs seems to have been removed in the current version of the ODBC administrator, but that won't stop a knowing user from creating a file data source with a text editor. The only effective counter to this problem, of which I am aware, is education.

Methods of Connecting with ODBC

Installing ODBC and setting up data sources is almost pedestrian. For busy system administrators, it's a prime candidate for automation or allowing users to download an installation pack. I'll walk through the installation procedure here, but if you were able to set up your sound card, you can set up ODBC while playing solitaire and sampling a new latte.

Installing the Drivers

As usual with a new version of SQL Server, the Enterprise Manager applications do not work across versions by default. Thankfully, another trend has continued: ODBC applications continue to enjoy connectivity to SQL Server 7 with existing drivers, as well as using new versions without modification.

SQL Server 7's ODBC drivers are supplied as part of a separately installed package called Microsoft Data Access Components (MDAC). In this release, the driver kit is located in the CDROM:\MSEQ\x86 directory in a single self-extracting file called mdac_typ.exe. According to Microsoft, the drivers are Level 2 compliant under the ODBC version 3.51 specification. Further, they still operate correctly with SQL Server 6.5 while making version 7's new features available. If you're adding application features that need the new bulk copy capability, or you're distributing a previously single-hosted server, you need to update your drivers.

If you're just upgrading the server and don't want to change the clients, the ODBC drivers for SQL Server 6.5 also work well with SQL 7. You can't use the new features version 7 gives to clients until you update the drivers, but you shouldn't encounter any problems with existing code.

> **TIP**
>
> I do advise that you update to the latest version of MDAC if it's feasible in your environment. Earlier versions of MDAC have been varied and variously dependable, so synchronizing to the current version will probably be to your advantage. Version 2.1 also adds connection pooling in the Driver Manager. Check `http://www.microsoft.com/data/download.htm` for the newest version of MDAC. The usual precautions still hold: Apply the latest service packs first, and test the software in your environment before deploying.

To install the drivers on a client, you can use the distribution CD-ROM or make the install file (`mdac_typ.exe`) available on a network share. You must be administrator (or have administrative privileges) on Windows NT to install the software, but installation on Windows 95 or Windows 98 requires no special account. Windows 95 users must install the DCOM for Windows 95 update (`DCOM95.exe`, available from Microsoft at `http://www.microsoft.com/dcom`) before installing MDAC 2.1.

Starting the MDAC install file on the client produces the standard Microsoft software license dialog; please read the agreement and click Yes to continue (if, of course, you do agree to its terms). The next dialog advises you to close all running applications before continuing. If you have client applications that are using data services, you should exit them here. Continue when you're ready.

The next dialog is the main installation fork; you can either take the default and install everything or choose a custom installation and load only specific components. Unless disk space is at an absolute premium, the default installation is probably the easiest way to remain consistent with all your clients. This choice installs the current ODBC drivers and OLE DB providers for SQL Server, Access (Microsoft Jet), Visual FoxPro (for Xbase files), and Oracle.

19

OPTIMIZING
ODBC USING
VISUAL C++

> **TIP**
>
> The SQL*Net protocol used by Oracle RDBMSs is proprietary and must be licensed from Oracle. The ODBC driver and OLE DB provider Microsoft distributes do not contain the SQL*Net protocol, but instead provide an ODBC interface on top of an existing Oracle client; you still have to install and maintain the Oracle network software (SQL*Net version 2.3 or later).
>
> You might still want to use the Microsoft drivers. I recently built a Visual C++ application that needed to store binary objects in an Oracle server through the MFC ODBC library. Although the Oracle-supplied drivers would not insert the BLOBs into the database, the drivers from Microsoft worked correctly.

If you choose the custom installation, the next dialog is the one shown in Figure 19.2.

FIGURE 19.2

The custom installation for Microsoft Data Access 2.1.

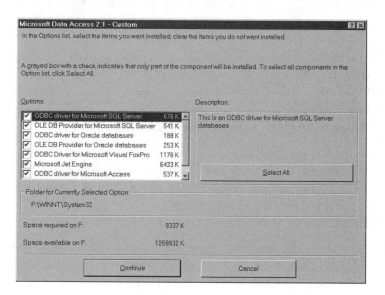

All you can do to customize the installation is deselect any drivers or providers for installation. Note that if you want to install the Access driver or provider, you should also update the Jet engine. If you're going to be working only with ODBC applications, you can deselect the OLE DB providers. When you're satisfied with your selection, click Continue.

After the drivers are installed, reboot your computer. On Windows NT, log in using the same account you were using for installation so that the install program can update some other goodies. You're done.

Working with Data Sources

Earlier I mentioned data sources without really getting into what they are and how to work with them. This section discusses the different types of data sources, why you would use each type, and the mechanics of creating them.

What Is a Data Source?

To connect to a database server, ODBC must have certain information; the specifics of what information is needed vary among drivers, but the driver manager must have at least the type of driver to load and the location of the data. The driver often requires a machine name and database or schema to log in to the connection, although the application can change these as it sees fit. In Windows, the settings required to connect to the database server are stored as named records in odbc.ini, in the Registry under the keys HKEY_LOCAL_MACHINE\SOFTWARE\ODBC\ODBC.INI and HKEY_CURRENT_USER\SOFTWARE\ODBC\ODBC.INI, or in a file with a .dsn extension.

The data source name is a textual key used to identify which record of connection settings an application is going to use. The term *DSN* is often applied to the record of the settings themselves, too. All the parameters in the DSN can be overridden by the application when it connects to the server, but generally this is not the best idea. If the information is hard-coded into the application, it can be changed only with a recompilation and redistribution of the software. If it's stored outside the application, it's an additional function to maintain, and a duplicative one; ODBC DSNs already provide this function. All that being said, I will note that a DSN is not required to connect with ODBC; an application can supply a full connection string and connect directly to the database without a DSN.

There are three types of DSNs—file-based, system, and user—and each is appropriate for a different application. The most common of them is the *system DSN*. Stored in HKEY_LOCAL_MACHINE\SOFTWARE\ODBC\ODBC.INI, a system DSN is available to any user on the computer by default, although in Windows NT you can change the permissions on its Registry key to control access. A system DSN is useful for an application used by several users on the same machine or on a server because you set the connection up once for all users. Under the odbc.ini Registry branch, each data source is its own key containing named strings (REG_SZ) for each of the connection attributes specified in the DSN. For the server parameter on the Accounting DSN, for example, you would have a value like this:

```
SOFTWARE\ODBC\ODBC.INI\Accounting\Server: REG_SZ: ACCT002
```

19

OPTIMIZING
ODBC USING
VISUAL C++

On the other hand, users often want to connect to a database for data they are going to use in their own analysis, but that isn't necessarily useful for another user. For this case, a *user DSN* is appropriate. These are stored in HKEY_CURRENT_USER\SOFTWARE\ODBC\ODBC.INI. Because the HKEY hive is specific to the logged-in user, these DSNs are available only to the user who created them. The user typically manages these data sources.

Finally, *file DSN*s are data sources whose information is stored in files. In Windows NT 4.0 and Windows 98, the files are usually located in the c:\Program Files\Common Files\Odbc\Data Sources directory. In Windows 95, they are usually placed in the c:\Windows\odbc\Data Sources directory. These are just defaults, however; the files can be stored anywhere on the computer or on an attached network drive, and these defaults can vary with your system configuration.

The file DSN is a plain text file in the Windows INI file format, in which each line has a connection attribute name, an equals sign, and a value for the connection attribute. The following is an example:

```
[ODBC]
DRIVER=SQL Server
Trusted_Connection=Yes
DATABASE=accounting
SERVER=ACCT002
```

This DSN connects a user to a SQL Server database on the mythical \\ACCT002 server using NT integrated authentication and then sets the default database context to the accounting database. File DSNs have little advantage over Registry-based DSNs when defined and used on a single machine, but when distributing software in a corporate environment, they can be used to distribute connection information along with your client/server application package. Used in this fashion, file DSNs allow your application to be up and ready to connect as soon as it's installed, and the DSN can be maintained centrally to simplify network management. Registry-based (system and user) DSNs, although they can be managed and distributed centrally, require reinstallation on the client whenever they are updated, which is not necessary with file DSNs.

Managing Systemwide Characteristics

Data sources and other functions of ODBC are managed with the ODBC Administrator. You start the ODBC Administrator from the Control Panel by double-clicking on the ODBC Data Sources applet. The ODBC Data Source Administrator interface is shown in Figure 19.3.

FIGURE 19.3

The ODBC Data Source Administrator.

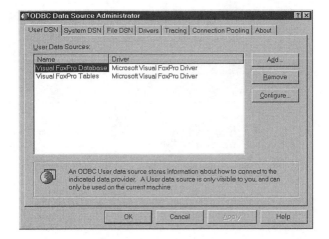

The ODBC Administrator window has seven tabs. The first three, where data sources are configured, are discussed when you set up data sources later. The remaining four are systemwide and perform the functions listed in Table 19.1.

TABLE 19.1 ODBC System-Level Administration Tabs

Tab Name	Functions Exposed
Drivers	View the filename, vendor, and versions of installed drivers
Tracing	Control the ODBC tracing feature (useful for debugging)
Connection Pooling	Enable or disable connection pooling for drivers, and set time-out values for pool connections and server retries
About	Display the path and versions for global ODBC components

The Drivers tab displays all the drivers installed on your system that the ODBC Administrator is aware of. This information is useful for working with the driver vendor's technical support staff. You can also use this information in a corporate setting to verify that a particular workstation has the correct drivers for the applications you need.

Tracing, shown in Figure 19.4, controls the ODBC trace facility. This feature is extremely useful for debugging or performance tuning. On this panel, you can specify a log file into which ODBC records a text description of every command sent by any application to the driver manager or a database driver.

19

OPTIMIZING
ODBC USING
VISUAL C++

FIGURE 19.4

The ODBC Data Source Administrator's Tracing tab.

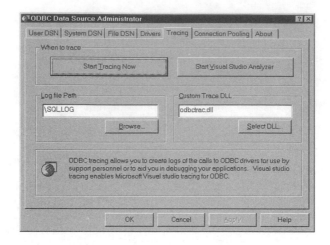

Connection pooling (see Figure 19.5), a new feature in ODBC 3.51 (MDAC 2.1), refers to reusing database connections from a client application (but not across multiple, separate programs). This capability can significantly increase performance if a user application connects and disconnects repeatedly to the same server. Pooling is a double-edged sword, however, because each open connection to the database takes up resources on both the client and the server. If the client makes infrequent use of the database, but keeps the connection alive, it continues to take up server resources (not to mention a client access license!) to no avail. On the other hand, if a single connection is constantly reused and kept alive by the driver manager, the server's resources aren't wasted in constantly setting up and breaking down client connections. You should monitor license usage, server activity, and the ODBC connection pooling counters in performance monitor to decide what the best setup is in your environment.

FIGURE 19.5

The ODBC Data Source Administrator's Connection Pooling tab.

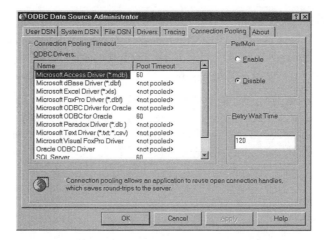

Settings on the Connection Pooling tab in the ODBC Administrator enable pooling and set pool timeout values for database drivers, turn performance monitoring on and off, and configure the server retry interval. To enable pooling on a driver type or set its timeout, double-click on the driver type. In the Set Connection Pooling Attributes dialog (see Figure 19.6), select the option Pool Connections to This Driver to turn on pooling. The time setting is the amount of time after the application requests disconnection before ODBC actually disconnects it from the server. Until the timeout expires, the connection is held open.

FIGURE 19.6

The Set Connection Pooling Attributes dialog.

In the PerfMon area of the Connection Pooling tab, you can turn on and off Performance Monitor counters for monitoring connection pooling performance; because this feature depends on the Windows NT performance monitoring interface, the Enable selection is disabled in Windows 95 and Windows 98. The Retry Wait Time value is the amount of time, in seconds, the driver manager waits before retrying a failed server connection.

The last tab, About, lists the paths and versions of the core ODBC components. They include the Administrator, the Driver Manager, Control Panel applets, and the Cursor Library, which simulates cursors, if possible, on data sources that don't support them directly.

Registry-Based Data Sources

Configuring data sources (the subject of the remaining tabs) is similar for user and system DSNs, but file DSNs are a little different. This section covers system and user DSNs, and the differences in file DSNs are described in the following section.

Selecting the User DSN or System DSN tabs and then clicking the Add button produce the Create New Data Source dialog. Here you select the database driver to use to connect the data source you're creating. You will, of course, always select the SQL Server driver (who would use any other database?) and click Finish. This doesn't really finish anything; it just moves you to the next dialog box.

19

Actually, you will use several types of data sources in your work with ODBC, but the dialogs that follow the Create New Data Source window are driver specific. As mentioned before, each type of driver requires different information to connect to its particular flavor of database server or database file, and the configuration interface reflects these differences.

The first pane of the Create a New Data Source to SQL Server Wizard (see Figure 19.7) takes the DSN record name, a user-friendly description, and the name of the host to connect. This last can be any name that NetBIOS can resolve, including bare TCP/IP addresses if necessary; enter this information carefully because you won't find out until two screens later if you misspell it. You can specify just the source name and server hostname and then click the Finish button to accept the ODBC defaults for the connection, and exit. If you would rather have finer control over the connection defaults (and make sure that the DSN will work), click Next instead.

FIGURE 19.7

Create a New Data Source to SQL Server, step 1.

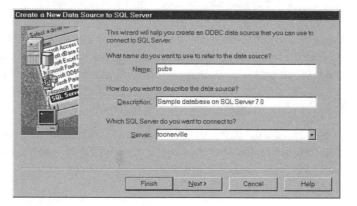

After clicking Next, the second pane (see Figure 19.8) asks you to set the authentication method and asks whether you want to connect to SQL Server to retrieve values for later steps. The client configuration tab normally need not be changed, but you can modify the server NetBIOS naming and select a particular network library, if you choose. If installed, ODBC will use the Multiprotocol library by default, which is probably what you want. It's generally easier to allow ODBC to connect to the server for defaults because it lets you point and shoot options such as the database name in later steps. Set this check box, and click Next.

FIGURE 19.8

*Create a New
Data Source to
SQL Server, step 2.*

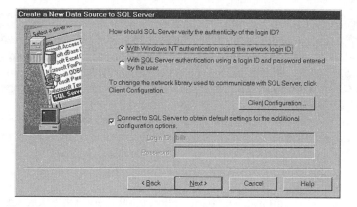

Step 3, shown in Figure 19.9, sets some common options on the server-side environment
in which queries on this DSN are processed. Setting the default database to a particular
database on the server is a useful option; in this example, you set the default to pubs so
that you don't have to set the catalog (current database) on connection. The Attach
Database Filename option is used in SQL Server 7 to attach a database file to the server;
if a file is specified here, it's attached at connection time and becomes the default context for the connection.

The Create Temporary Stored Procedures... option is relevant only for 6.5 and earlier
servers. In older versions, a significant performance penalty was incurred with applications using high-level access libraries (such as MFC or ADO) that prepared statements
with no replaceable parameters that were issued only once. Microsoft has adjusted the
interaction between ODBC and SQL Server 7 to stop this situation from developing, so
the option is grayed out when you're connecting to version 7.

FIGURE 19.9

*Create a New
Data Source to
SQL Server, step 3.*

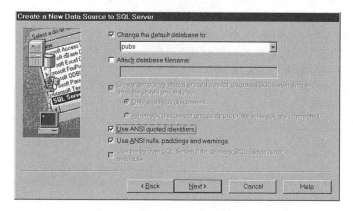

19

**OPTIMIZING
ODBC USING
VISUAL C++**

> **TIP**
>
> The additional overhead from ODBC creating and dropping stored procedures for prepared statements was responsible for about 75% of the execution time for a 6.5-based server application I worked on. When tuning performance of ODBC applications using older servers, use SQL Trace to look for excessive creation of temporary stored procedures named #odbc#* containing fully specified SQL queries (that is, no parameters). If they are prevalent, turn off the Create Temporary Stored Procedures... option in step 3.

The Use ANSI Quoted Identifiers option allows SQL Server to enforce ANSI rules for quoting. Simply put, double quotes go around identifiers, single quotes go around strings, and that's it. The Use ANSI Nulls, Paddings and Warnings option is a similar compatibility setting, aligning the behavior of SQL Server more closely with SQL-92. If you have problems with an application that was originally developed for an older version of SQL Server, particularly 6.0 or earlier, you can try turning off the ANSI Null handling.

The last configuration item is whether to use a standby server if the primary one is unavailable. If the server does not have this capability, as mine does not, this option is grayed out. This option does not affect operations of clustered servers (where Microsoft Cluster Server controls failover).

Step 4 contains less used, but still useful, options for language support and performance information. To switch to any supported language, use the option Change the Language of SQL Server System Messages To. If needed, you can disable automatic character translation between the server's character set and the client's. The Use Regional Settings When Outputting Currency, Numbers, Dates and Times option is useful if applications only display the information, but should not be used if the data is to be manipulated. The last two settings allow you to collect dynamic information on query times and database usage in disk files that you can later use as input for tuning your data environment. The Save Long Running Queries to the Log File option logs queries that take longer than the time you specify to a file; the option Log ODBC Driver Statistics to the Log File stores both raw counted statistics and execution times for each connection used across the data source.

When you click Finish in this last step, you have configured the data source. A dialog box (see Figure 19.10) appears that summarizes the settings you have chosen and allows you to test the data source to make sure that it works.

FIGURE 19.10

The ODBC Microsoft SQL Server Setup dialog for finishing DSN configuration.

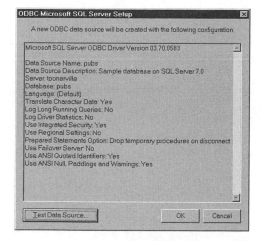

Click Test Data Source to check the connection. If all is well, you'll see the display in Figure 19.11 indicating successful configuration.

FIGURE 19.11

The message indicating that the SQL Server ODBC data source test was successful.

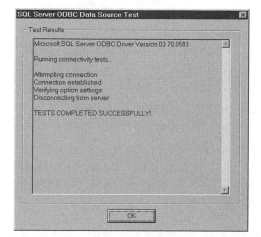

That's all there is to creating system and user DSNs. On the User DSN and System DSN tabs, there are additional buttons to remove or configure a data source. Configuring an existing data source is identical to creating a new one, but the options you specified previously are displayed instead of the driver's defaults.

File-Based Data Sources

Creating a file DSN is similar to user or system DSNs, but with a few changes for file locations and names. Figure 19.12 shows the File DSN tab of the ODBC Administrator.

FIGURE **19.12**

The ODBC Data Source Administrator's File DSN tab.

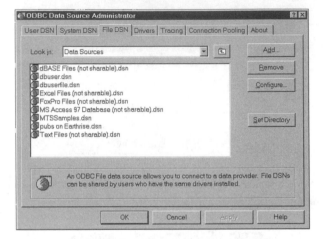

The Add, Remove, and Configure buttons function similarly to their counterparts on the User and System DSN tabs, but above the list of available file DSNs is a new control, a standard Windows directory selection box. This control allows you to browse other directories for DSN files that are not in the default location. If you want, you can change the default location for DSNs by setting a different path in this drop-down list and then clicking the Set Directory button. This is a systemwide setting, so change it with care.

Otherwise, the only difference in creating a file DSN than creating any other type is that after you pick the database driver, you're prompted for the name of the file in which to store the DSN. This name serves as the name in the driver configuration dialog and is used by applications to open the data source.

TIP

SQL Server comes with a neat little utility for testing data sources. ODBCPING.EXE takes the name of the data source or a server hostname, and optionally a user ID and password, and attempts to connect to a SQL Server on the host or DSN provided. If it succeeds, it prints the version information for the server (similar to the DBMS_VER attribute from the sp_server_info stored procedure) and returns to the command prompt. You can use a client application such as MSQuery to test a data source, but ODBCPING is a lot quicker!

Call-Level Interface

ODBC—specified before object-oriented programming took over the world and pushed back year-2000 repairs even further— is inevitably a functional interface. In this section you will find the real meat of this discussion—the bare ODBC API. I'll begin with a discussion of the sequence of events in programming ODBC, followed by detailed discussion of each step in the process, and wrap it all up with the Microsoft Foundation Classes' support for ODBC, which provides an abstraction that, although thin, is of great help.

When connecting to an ODBC data source, an application follows a predetermined series of steps to set up and establish the connection, use it to manipulate data and databases, and release the connection and the resources allocated for it. The ODBC engine's dynamics are described in a set of *state transition tables* (*STTs*), in addition to the usual description of procedures and function interfaces. The STTs may be of use to developers writing ODBC drivers, but for your purposes, a summary of the operation of the interface from an application's perspective should be sufficient (and easier to read).

The principal entities in the application interface are the `Environment`, the `Connection`, the `Statement`, and `Parameters`, both in and out. At a very high level, the application allocates an `Environment` within which it can allocate one or more `Connections`. These connections can then be bound to a data source (DSN), and then zero or more `Statements` can be created and executed in the connection to manipulate or retrieve data through the data source.

When the application is done with the database, it must deallocate each of the allocated objects in reverse order. Attempting to free a connection in which one or more statements are still allocated, for example, will produce the dreaded `HY010, Function sequence error`.

Table 19.2 is an abbreviated description of the sequence of events and the functions called by the application to effect each operation. Down the left column are the normal steps taken by the application in interacting with ODBC. The right column contains the most common operations available at each point and the API calls you need to use to perform them (to conserve space, the functions are listed only with the first instance of an operation in the table).

When working in your own application, you might find Table 19.2 useful in deciding where to go next; I advise you to read in the ODBC SDK documentation the description of each API call listed here. All of them are used in almost every application you work with, and it's worth your while to know them well.

TABLE 19.2   HIGH-LEVEL ODBC FUNCTION SEQUENCES

When the Application...	Then It Can...
Starts	Allocate an environment (`SQLAllocHandle`) or set environment attributes (`SQLSetEnvAttr`).
Allocates an environment	Set environment attributes, allocate a connection (`SQLAllocHandle`), set connection attributes (`SQLSetConnectAttr`), or deallocate the environment (`SQLFreeHandle`).
Allocates a connection	Modify some connection attributes, connect to a data source (`SQLConnect`, `SQLDriverConnect`, or `SQLBrowseConnect`), or deallocate the connection (`SQLFreeHandle`).
Connects to a data source	Still modify some connection attributes, set statement attributes (`SQLSetStmtAttr`), or allocate a statement (`SQLAllocHandle`).
Allocates a statement	Prepare a statement (`SQLPrepare`), set statement attributes, execute the statement directly (`SQLExecDirect`), or deallocate the statement (`SQLFreeHandle`).
Prepares a statement (optional)	Bind parameters to the statement (`SQLBindParameter`), set statement attributes, execute it (`SQLExecute`), or deallocate the statement.
Binds parameters to a statement (optional)	Place data in the buffers it has bound preparatory to executing the statement, set statement attributes, or deallocate the statement.
Executes a statement	Bind buffers into which to retrieve result columns (`SQLBindCol`); if the driver is not expecting data or executing the statement asynchronously after this call, the application can deallocate the statement.
Binds result columns (optional)	Fetch data from the statement's rowset (`SQLFetch`), end the retrieval with `SQLCloseCursor`, or deallocate the statement.
Deallocates all statements in a connection	Disconnect the connection from the data source (`SQLDisconnect`).
Disconnects from the data source	Deallocate the connection.
Deallocates all connections on the environment	Deallocate the environment.

The examples run against the pubs sample database in the SQL Server distribution; most SQL Server developers should be familiar with this database, and it keeps you from having to build another toy database.

Because you're working with SQL Server 7, I'm assuming that you have the MDAC 2.1 components installed on your computer. Many of the interfaces in the 2.x versions of ODBC are deprecated in 3.x, so you're going to stay with the current versions of these functions. If you're using the ODBC 2.x SDK, you still gain value from the demonstration code, but you have to substitute some older API calls to compile it. The sequence of events is the same, but some functions have been combined or modified somewhat (for example, the version 1.0/2.0 SQLAllocEnv has been combined with the other allocators into SQLAllocHandle).

The application I used to test the code samples is an MFC-based Win32 program in Microsoft Visual C++ 6. For simplicity, I built a dialog-based application with no other connections or facilities bound in and then, I hooked up buttons to each test case I wanted to run. If you would like to try the samples, you will find this an easy way to run the code and observe the effect of different options.

Basics

ODBC programs are structurally simple. There are three libraries and six C header files you should know. For general client applications, ODBC32.LIB must be linked into your executable. This is the import library for the driver manager, and it provides entry definitions for the bulk of the ODBC API. The second library, which you might never use, is ODBCCP32.LIB. It contains the programmatic interface to the ODBC Administrator (ODBCCP32.DLL, for ODBC Control Panel, 32-bit, I suppose). You can use this interface to create, remove, and modify data sources or to set any of the other global data access options available through the ODBC Data Sources Administrator Control Panel applet. The last is ODBCBCP.LIB, which links SQL Server–specific functions.

The headers you use to interact with these libraries are SQL.h, SQLTYPES.h, SQLEXT.h, ODBCSS.H, and possibly ODBCINST.h or SQLUCODE.h. SQL Server 7 includes the additional file ODBCSS.H, which defines SQL Server's extensions to ODBC. All these files and their contents are summarized in Table 19.3.

TABLE **19.3** ODBC HEADER FILES FOR VISUAL C++

Header	Library	Purpose
SQL.h	ODBC32.LIB	Definitions of standard CLI API for ODBC, including data access and manipulation API definitions for ODBC32.LIB; also imports SQLTYPES.h
SQLTYPES.h	All	Definitions of standard types used in ODBC (for example, SQLINTEGER, SQLFLOAT)
SQLEXT.h	ODBC32.LIB	Microsoft extensions to the CLI environment that deviate from the standard CLI API; includes concurrency, data mapping and other functions specific to ODBC; includes SQLUCODE.h
ODBCINST.h	ODBCCP32.LIB	Interfaces for manipulating data sources, database driver registration, and other parameters of the host's global ODBC configuration
SQLUCODE.h	ODBC32.LIB	Unicode features; need be explicitly addressed only if you are targeting a different locale from that in which you develop your application
ODBCSS.H	ODBCBCP.LIB	SQL Server 7–specific ODBC extensions

NOTE

In Visual C++ 6, which has development libraries updated to version 3.51 of ODBC, there are minor differences in the headers from the version 3.5 SDK. They mostly involve updates to version numbers and some tuning of conditional include directives regulating what symbols are included for the version of ODBC you're targeting. By defining ODBCVER in your compiler directives to the hexadecimal constants 0x0250, 0x0300, 0x0350, or 0x0351, you can tailor the symbols defined for the ODBC API. Beyond these small changes, SQLEXT.h also has some additional API calls for interacting with the Visual Studio Analyzer, and some Unicode definitions have been touched up.

For Win32 applications, particularly those developed in Visual C++, you should encounter no unique build requirements. If you're building a non-MFC application, you need to include the ODBC import libraries (ODBC32.LIB, ODBCCP32.LIB, and/or ODBCBCP.LIB) for whatever feature set you use. Include the headers for whatever functions you are using, as described in the table, and you're off and running.

In an MFC application, add the following statement to your StdAfx.h header file:

```
#include <afxdb.h>     // MFC support for ODBC.
```

This statement includes the C and C++ declarations for MFC-based database development (including the SQL* headers) and directives instructing VC to link the relevant ODBC import libraries. There's no need for include statements in your source files other than StdAfx.h.

Before you start using ODBC, you need to address error detection. Most ODBC functions return a value of type SQLRETURN that can take on the values described in Table 19.4.

TABLE 19.4   SQLRETURN VALUES

Return Code	Meaning
SQL_SUCCESS	The operation succeeded.
SQL_SUCCESS_WITH_INFO	The operation succeeded and recorded possibly useful information.
SQL_NO_DATA	No information is available to satisfy the request (for example, an update does not affect any rows in the database).
SQL_ERROR	The operation failed
SQL_INVALID_HANDLE	The handle passed to a function call was not valid or was not valid for that operation.
SQL_NEED_DATA	More data is necessary to satisfy the request (such as when inserting or updating a long field using SQLPutData).
SQL_STILL_EXECUTING	An operation was attempted while a previous asynchronous operation was still.outstanding

Status reporting in ODBC 3.x is accessed through the SQLGetDiagRec and SQLGetDiagField functions. ODBC maintains a list of zero or more information records pertaining to the *last ODBC function executed*, from which you can retrieve error, warning, or simple status information. SQLGetDiagRec retrieves some commonly useful fields from a single record in this list, but cannot access the entire record; SQLGetDiagField retrieves only one field at a time, but has access to all data in the status records. All the return codes in Table 19.4, except SQL_SUCCESS, imply that the function called has recorded a list of status records for SQLGetDiagRec or SQLGetDiagField.

NOTE

When you're calling ODBC functions, you probably want to treat SQL_SUCCESS_WITH_INFO the same as you would SQL_SUCCESS. Although the information returned from the driver is sometimes interesting, it's normally not useful to the application or the user. ODBC defines a macro named SQL_SUCCEEDED, which evaluates to TRUE if its parameter is either SQL_SUCCESS or SQL_SUCCESS_WITH_INFO.

SQLGetDiagRec takes as input parameters an object handle, the handle type, the one-based index number of the record to retrieve, and the addresses of output buffers. ODBC fills those storage locations with the client (ODBC) status code, the database server's native status code, a human-readable text message, and the length of the message in the buffer. Listing 19.1 is a simple function to retrieve and display error messages in a dialog box; it assumes that a return value indicated a problem, so it complains if no records are available (without this assumption, you could make the loop a simple WHILE). Data passed into this function includes the handle on which the error occurred, the type code for the handle passed in (SQL_HANDLE_ENV, SQL_HANDLE_DBC, or SQL_HANDLE_STMT), and a window handle to be the parent of the message box. The function has *auto* variables for the out parameters from SQLGetDiagRec, which it displays in a message box.

LISTING 19.1 A C++ FUNCTION TO RETRIEVE AND DISPLAY DIAGNOSTIC RECORDS

```
void    ShowSQLInfo( SQLHANDLE hnd, SQLSMALLINT htType,
                     HWND hWnd = NULL )
{
    SQLCHAR       SqlState[6];      // ODBC status code
    SQLINTEGER    SqlNativeCode;    // native status code
    SQLCHAR       SqlMessage[256];  // text message
    SQLSMALLINT   SqlMessageLen;    // length of message
                                    // in SqlMessage
    SQLRETURN     diagCode;
    SQLSMALLINT   recordNumber = 1;

    diagCode = SQLGetDiagRec( htType, hnd, recordNumber,
        SqlState, &SqlNativeCode, SqlMessage,
        sizeof( SqlMessage ), &SqlMessageLen );
    if ( SQL_SUCCEEDED(diagCode) )
    {
        do
        {
            MessageBox ( hWnd, (LPCTSTR)SqlMessage,
                "SQL Information Message",
```

```
                MB_ICONINFORMATION ¦ MB_OK );
            recordNumber++;
            diagCode = SQLGetDiagRec( htType, hnd,
                recordNumber, SqlState, &SqlNativeCode,
                SqlMessage, sizeof( SqlMessage ),
                &SqlMessageLen );
        }
        while ( SQL_SUCCEEDED(diagCode) );
    }
    else
    {
        // tried to display information, but none found.
        MessageBox( hWnd, "ODBC reported an error, but " \
                " cannot explain it.", "Unexpected error",
                MB_ICONEXCLAMATION ¦ MB_OK );
    }
}
```

Later examples use the `ShowSQLInfo` function in the following manner:

```
if ( SQL_SUCCEEDED(sqlVal) )
{
    // do more processing
}
else
    ShowSQLInfo( ctx.hEnv, SQL_HANDLE_ENV );
```

`SQLGetDiagField` works similarly to `SQLGetDiagRec`, but with a number of additional capabilities. On the downside, of course, you have to call the function for each individual data value you want to retrieve. `SQLGetDiagField` can retrieve either `header` fields or `record` fields (`SQLGetDiagRec` retrieves only `record` fields). The `header` fields include information on the type of function just executed, the number of rows contained in the current cursor (on a statement), the number of rows affected by an operation, and the number of status records available for retrieval. When retrieving header fields, the `RecNumber` parameter (parameter 3) is ignored.

For example, instead of iterating over the status records until you reach the end of the list (the method used in Listing 19.1), you could use the following code to retrieve the number of records ahead of time (assuming type definitions as in Listing 19.1):

```
SQLINTEGER   recsAvailable;

DiagCode = SQLGetDiagField( SQL_HANDLE_STMT,
    hnd, 1, SQL_DIAG_NUMBER, &recsAvailable,
    SQL_IS_INTEGER, NULL );
```

19

OPTIMIZING
ODBC USING
VISUAL C++

For most cases, SQLGetDiagRec gives you enough status information because your most common need is finding out what went wrong when an error occurred. SQLGetDiag Field can provide additional information, although the most useful—row counts for statements—can be retrieved with the much simpler SQLRowCount.

Connecting to a Database

Probably the most complicated part of using ODBC, from an API perspective, is the connection process. It's unfortunate that this should be so because the connection setup defines the environment and subsequent operation of your application's data access code. I'll try to present the connection process here as straightforwardly as possible so that you can concentrate on more important things.

Connection Strings: Not Just for Paper Cups Anymore

The *connection string* is a textual statement containing attribute-value pairs, separated by semicolons, that the application uses to tell the driver manager what to connect and how to connect it. Although not all connection methods use a connect string, I'll discuss them here because of their broad application in programming for ODBC in all languages, not just C++.

Table 19.5 lists the ODBC-defined keywords that can be included. They generally correspond to the parameters specified in the first two steps of creating a data source.

TABLE 19.5   ODBC-DEFINED CONNECTION KEYWORDS

Keyword	Purpose
DSN	Identifies the data source name to connect (used with system and user DSNs)
DRIVER	Specifies a driver to connect with that is used when a DSN is not specified
FILEDSN	Identifies a file DSN to connect
PWD	Gives the password to use in standard authentication (not saved to a log file when logging is enabled)
SAVEFILE	Names a file in which the parameters to the connection are stored after the connection is established
UID	Holds the user ID to use in connecting with standard authentication

In addition to the keywords in Table 19.5, the SQL Server ODBC driver recognizes the parameters shown in Table 19.6. These driver-specific values correspond to the values specified in the SQL Server–specific dialogs in the data source setup.

TABLE 19.6   SQL SERVER–SPECIFIC CONNECTION STRING KEYWORDS

Keyword	Purpose
ADDRESS	Network address of the server to connect
ANSINPW	Turns on or off ANSI Null handling, padding, and warnings
APP sp_who	Sets the name displayed for the application when someone runs
ATTACHDBFILENAME	Database file to attach (SQL Server 7 only)
AUTOTRANSLATE	Turns character translation on or off
DATABASE	Names the default database to use on the server
FALLBACK	Determines whether to attempt connection to a fallback server if the primary connect fails
LANGUAGE	Language used for SQL Server messages
NETWORK	Network library to use
SERVER	Hostname of the server to connect to
QUERYLOGFILE	File in which long-running queries are logged
QUERYLOG_ON	Indicates whether to log long-running queries
QUERYLOGTIME	Threshold (milliseconds) over which a query is logged
QUOTEDID	If yes, enables SQL-92 rules for quoting
REGIONAL	Tells SQL Server to use client locale when returning date, time, and currency values as text
STATSLOGFILE	Names the file in which ODBC interface statistics are logged
STATSLOG_ON	Turns on statistics logging
TRUSTED_CONNECTION	Enables using NT integrated authentication to the database server
USEPROCFORPREPARE	Instructs the driver whether to use temporary stored procedures for prepared statements (6.5 and earlier)
WSID	Specifies the workstation shown by administration queries

19

OPTIMIZING
ODBC USING
VISUAL C++

The connection string is formed by stringing together a keyword, an equals sign, and the value for the parameter identified by the keyword. If multiple keyword-value pairs are specified, they are separated by semicolons. A minimal connection string using standard authentication specifies the DSN, the user ID, and the user's password, as in `"DSN=pubs;UID=pubsuser;PWD=pubsuser"`. To use NT integrated authentication for the same connection, the connection string would be `"DSN=pubs;Trusted_Connection=yes"`.

It's also possible to establish a "DSN-less" connection. To do so, you must specify the driver, enclosed in braces, and supply the driver-specific information the driver needs to connect to its host. For SQL Server, the user ID and password (or trusted connection) and the host name must be included; such a connection would look like this:

```
"DRIVER={SQL
➥Server};SERVER=toonerville;Trusted_Connection=yes;DATABASE=pubs"
```

The ODBC Environment

For its first step in using ODBC, your application has to set up its ODBC environment. This process has two parts: setting environment options and requesting the environment itself. Environment options govern the operation of the ODBC interface with the application and are not driver specific; they can't be because a driver is not loaded until long after the environment is fixed. Only two basic environment attributes are supported in ODBC 3.5: connection pooling and ODBC version conformance.

Set environment attributes with SQLSetEnvAttr. This function takes parameters of the environment handle, the integer attribute identifier, and the attribute value. The fourth parameter is largely irrelevant; it's intended to carry the length of the string, if the third parameter is a pointer to a string, but there are no string-valued environment attributes. Listing 19.2 demonstrates setting up the ODBC environment as described in the following paragraphs.

LISTING 19.2 INITIALIZING THE ODBC ENVIRONMENT

```
bool
OpenEnvironment( SQLHENV & hEnv )
{
    bool    retval = (SQLSetEnvAttr( NULL,
                        SQL_ATTR_CONNECTION_POOLING,
                        SQLPOINTER(SQL_CP_ONE_PER_DRIVER),
                        0 ) == SQL_SUCCESS );

    // Allocate handle and set default connection attributes
    // to 3.x behavior
    if ( retval )
    {
        retval = ( SQLAllocHandle(SQL_HANDLE_ENV,
                    SQL_NULL_HANDLE, &hEnv) == SQL_SUCCESS );

        // Now that the environment is allocated, set
        // conformance to what you want for this application.
        // Note the dual use of the pointer value (argument
        // 3); requires casting for integer (non-pointer)
        // information.
```

```
        if ( retval )
        {
            // set ODBC 3.x conventions
            retval = (SQLSetEnvAttr( hEnv,
                SQL_ATTR_ODBC_VERSION,
                SQLPOINTER(SQL_OV_ODBC3), 0) == SQL_SUCCESS);
        }
    }
    return retval;
}
```

Whether and how to use connection pooling is set with the `SQL_ATTR_CONNECTION_POOL-ING` attribute flag to `SQL_CP_OFF`, `SQL_CP_ONE_PER_HENV`, or `SQL_CP_ONE_PER_DRIVER`. They disable connection pooling, pool connections on each environment, or pool connections on each driver, respectively. This option must be set before the environment is allocated with `SQLAllocHandle`, and the environment handle passed to `SQLSetEnvAttr` should be a null pointer. For most applications, the question of allocating pools per environment or per driver doesn't affect operation because programs normally use one environment and connect to one database with one driver. If you're working with multiple databases from multiple vendors, it might be advantageous to use per-driver pooling, but in other cases, per-environment suffices equally well.

Setting the `SQL_ATTR_CP_MATCH` attribute to `SQL_CP_STRICT_MATCH` or `SQL_CP_RELAXED_MATCH` controls the criteria used by the driver manager to match connection requests to an available connection in the pool. The default, `strict`, requires that all options and attributes requested for the connection must match the candidate connection from the pool before it is reused. `Relaxed` matching requires only that the keywords in the connection string match, but doesn't require other options to match. Changing this attribute to `relaxed` matching might gain an infinitesimal performance increase if you know it's safe, but you won't need to touch it in normal situations. The example does not modify this attribute.

After the environment is allocated, you must set ODBC version conformance before going any further. Trying to take any action on the environment before setting the conformance version produces a `Function sequence error`. In most cases, use `SQL_OV_ODBC3` to specify version 3.x behavior, but you can specify version 2.x to maintain compatibility with legacy code.

19

OPTIMIZING
ODBC USING
VISUAL C++

Setting Up the Connection

Making a connection to the database involves two steps: allocating a connection and then connecting it to the server. Attributes are set using SQLSetConnectAttr, and the application can retrieve them by using SQLGetConnectAttr. Default attributes are enough for many applications, but you can specify several options to modify the behaviors of the connection and statements executed on the connection. As always, there are connection attributes that are ODBC-defined and not necessarily supported by SQL Server, and SQL Server-specific attributes that are supported *only* by SQL Server. To complicate matters, some connection attributes can be set on a connection before it's connected to a data source, some only after it's connected, and others at any time you like, if a statement is not in the process of retrieving data.

Table 19.7 lists some common ODBC-defined connection attributes and when they can be set. Table 19.8 contains SQL Server-defined attributes. To use the SQL Server definitions, you must include ODBCSS.h in your application source.

TABLE 19.7   ODBC-DEFINED CONNECTION ATTRIBUTES

Attribute	Set When	Purpose
SQL_ATTR_ACCCESS_MODE	Any time	Sets read-only or read-write access (default: read-write)
SQL_ATTR_ASYNC_ENABLE	Any time	Enables asynchronous statement execution (default: off)
SQL_ATTR_AUTOCOMMIT	Any time	Sets whether transactions must be manually committed with SQLEndTran() (default: auto)
SQL_ATTR_CURRENT_CATALOG	Anytime	In SQL Server, sets the current database (default: use server default)
SQL_ATTR_ODBC_CURSORS	Before	Sets whether the connection driver manager will load and use the ODBC cursor library (client cursors) (default: uses driver native capability)
SQL_ATTR_QUIET_MODE	Any time	Sets the window handle used by the driver as parent for dialogs; doesn't affect login dialogs from SQLDriverConnect (default: NULL, and the driver does not display dialogs)

Attribute	Set When	Purpose
SQL_ATTR_TRACE	Any time	Turns tracing on and off (default: off)
SQL_ATTR_TRACEFILE	Any time	Sets the file that receives trace messages
SQL_ATTR_TXN_ISOLATION	Any time	Sets transaction isolation levels (default: SQL_READ_COMMITTED)

An additional read-only attribute you might find useful is SQL_ATTR_CONNECTION_DEAD, which you can use to tell whether the connection has been disrupted. You can retrieve this value by using SQLGetConnectAttr, but you may not set it.

> **NOTE**
>
> Asynchronous execution, turned on with SQL_ATTR_ASYNC_ENABLE, is rarely necessary in the present Microsoft Data Access environment. Originally, it was needed to allow your application to continue processing messages and respond to the user while a database transaction was progressing. Using Win32 threads is much simpler and easier and should be used instead of asynchronous ODBC when possible. Asynchronous execution makes sense only if you have legacy code that uses it or the database driver you have to use is not thread-safe.

TABLE 19.8 COMMON SQL SERVER–SPECIFIC CONNECTION ATTRIBUTES

Attribute	Set When	Purpose
SQL_COPT_SS_ANSI_NPW	Before connection	Enable ANSI Nulls, padding, and warnings (default: on)
SQL_COPT_SS_BCP	Before connection	Allow BCP operations on this connection (default: false)
SQL_COPT_SS_ENLIST IN_DTC	After connection	In applications using the Microsoft Distributed Transaction Controller (MS DTC), places this statement under the control of an open DTC transaction (default: transactions are not distributed)

19

OPTIMIZING
ODBC USING
VISUAL C++

continues

TABLE 19.8   CONTINUED

Attribute	Set When	Purpose
SQL_COPT_SS_PRESERVE CURSORS	Before connection	Determines whether server cursors are closed when a transaction is committed or rolled back (default: cursors are closed)
SQL_COPT_SS_QUOTED IDENT	Anytime	Determines whether to enforce ANSI rules for quoting (default: yes)

Connecting to the Server

With the environment in hand, you can connect to the database. In these code examples, use the following structure to pass ODBC context information to the functions used to demonstrate each topic:

```
typedef struct
{
    SQLHENV    hEnv;  // odbc environment handle
    SQLHDBC    hConn; // odbc connection
    SQLHSTMT   hStmt; // odbc statement on this connection
} ODBCContext;
```

This structure saves having to pass individual parameters and helps keep associated objects together.

You will use one of three functions to connect to the database: SQLConnect, SQLDriverConnect, and SQLBrowseConnect. The simplest of the lot, SQLConnect, is also the oldest. It allows only the conventional style of database connection, using a DSN, user ID, and password. Listing 19.3 demonstrates connecting with SQLConnect.

LISTING 19.3   A SIMPLE CONNECTION TO A DATABASE USING A DSN, USER ID, AND PASSWORD

```
bool
NormalConnect( ODBCContext & ctx, UCHAR * szConnect,
               UCHAR * szUser, UCHAR * szPassword  )
{
    bool       retval;
    SQLRETURN  sqlVal;

    // allocate a connection
    retval = ( SQLAllocHandle( SQL_HANDLE_DBC, ctx.hEnv,
        &ctx.hConn ) == SQL_SUCCESS );
```

```
    // set "before connection" attributes here

    // connect to the DSN
    if ( retval )
    {
        sqlVal = SQLConnect(ctx.hConn,
                    szConnect, lstrlen( (LPCSTR)szConnect ),
                    szUser, lstrlen( (LPCSTR)szUser ),
                    szPassword, lstrlen( (LPCSTR)szPassword ) );
        if ( SQL_SUCCEEDED(sqlVal) )
        {
            // set "after connection" attributes here
            retval = true;
        }
        else
            ShowSQLInfo( ctx.hConn, SQL_HANDLE_DBC );
    }
    else
        ShowSQLInfo( ctx.hEnv, SQL_HANDLE_ENV );

    return retval;
}
```

In many applications, SQLConnect is all you ever need. It depends on you to manage getting a DSN, user ID, and password, but in trade it offers the simplest of the three connection functions.

SQLDriverConnect: A Little More Caffeine, Please

If you need more flexibility, or you want to use a connection string to more fully specify the connection method, move up to SQLDriverConnect. It's your function of choice for anything but simple connections, and in applications that need to set extensive options on connection, it's a far easier path than using SQLSetConnectAttr to specify them individually.

SQLDriverConnect takes eight parameters to establish a connection, but don't worry—they all make sense. The first, of course, is the connection handle. This parameter is followed by a window handle to serve as a parent to dialog boxes put up by the driver; you can pass NULL if you don't want driver dialogs. The next two are a pointer to the connection string you want to connect with and the length of that string. You next supply a pointer to, and the size of, a buffer in which the driver returns the final connection string; ODBC fills in the length of this string in the SQLSMALLINT pointed to by the seventh parameter. The last item is the completion flag, discussed in the next paragraph.

Listing 19.4 is the same function as in the SQLConnect example, but modified to use SQLDriverConnect. The window handle in the example is retrieved with the MFC function AfxGetMainWnd and passed to the driver so that it can raise connection dialogs if necessary. The call to SQLDriverConnect uses SQL_DRIVER_COMPLETE as the completion flag, so if the caller supplies a fully specified connection, the connection is made without any interaction. If something is missing, such as a password, the user is prompted and the connection made before SQLDriverConnect returns to the caller.

LISTING 19.4 CONNECTING WITH SQLDriverConnect

```
// connects to the dsn
bool
NormalConnect( ODBCContext & ctx,
➥UCHAR * szConnect, UCHAR * szUser, UCHAR * szPassword  )
{
        bool       retval = false;
        SQLRETURN  sqlVal = SQL_SUCCESS;
static  UCHAR      connString[2048] = "";
static  UCHAR      outConnString[2048] = "";
static  SQLSMALLINT outConnStringLength = 0;
        HWND       windowHandle = AfxGetMainWnd()->m_hWnd;

    // allocate a connection
    retval = ( SQLAllocHandle( SQL_HANDLE_DBC, ctx.hEnv,
                            &ctx.hConn ) == SQL_SUCCESS );

    // connect to the DSN
    if ( retval )
    {
        // DSN connection
        if ( outConnStringLength == 0 )
            sprintf( (LPSTR)connString, "DSN=%s;UID=%s;PWD=%s",
                szConnect, szUser, szPassword );
        else
            lstrcpyn( (LPSTR)connString, (LPSTR)outConnString,
                                outConnStringLength + 1 );

        sqlVal = SQLDriverConnect(
            ctx.hConn,                // allocated connection
            windowHandle,             // parent window for dialogs
            connString,               // connection string
            SQLSMALLINT(lstrlen( (LPCSTR)connString)),
                                      //length of connect string
            outConnString,            // connect string that the
                                      // driver completes
            sizeof(outConnString),    // max size of output string
            &outConnStringLength,     // num characters returned
                                      // in outConnString
            SQL_DRIVER_COMPLETE );    // connect type flag

        if ( SQL_SUCCEEDED(sqlVal) )
```

```
    {
        retval = true;
    }
    else
    {
        outConnStringLength = 0;
        ShowSQLInfo( ctx.hConn, SQL_HANDLE_DBC );
    }
    }
    else
        ShowSQLInfo( ctx.hEnv, SQL_HANDLE_ENV );

    return retval;
}
```

If the input connection string is fully specified and the connection succeeds, the driver creates a new connection string with all the defaults that are applied on the connection. This string is copied into the output buffer you supplied (outConnString), and the number of characters put into the buffer returned in the next-to-last parameter (outConnStringLength).

If the input string is not fully specified, the driver manager takes action based on the value you sent in the last parameter; these flags and the behavior they create are summarized in Table 19.9. *If connection pooling is enabled, only SQL_DRIVER_NOPROMPT is allowed; ODBC cannot prompt the user for information on a pooled connection!*

In the example, the function copies the completed string supplied by the driver to the input string buffer when the connection succeeds. If you're using SQL_DRIVER_PROMPT to ask the user for information, but want to release the connection when you're not using it, saving the complete string and reusing it keeps the user from being prompted every time you reconnect.

TABLE 19.9   PROMPT CONSTANT VALUES AND THEIR RESULTS

Value	Effect
SQL_PROMPT	The user is presented with dialogs to verify the connection even if the information in the DSN and connect strings is sufficient to connect to the server.
SQL_DRIVER_COMPLETE	The driver prompts the user for information only if the information in the DSN and connect strings is insufficient to complete the connection.
SQL_DRIVER_COMPLETE_REQUIRED	Similar to SQL_DRIVER_COMPLETE, but the user can set only information that is required to connect.
SQL_DRIVER_NOPROMPT	The user is not prompted for any information; if the connection cannot be established, the function returns an error.

If a user ID is specified in the connect string, but no password, and the data source is configured to use trusted connections, the UID parameter of the connect string is disregarded, and the login is authenticated using the security context within which the program is running—usually that of the user who ran the program.

In the out buffer, ODBC reports back to you all the connection attributes that were filled in by the driver, including the user ID and password. The returned string looks something like this:

```
DSN=pubs;Description="Sample database on SQL Server 7.0;
➥SERVER=toonerville;UID=pubsuser;PWD=pubspasswd;APP=ODBC
Application;WSID=mystation;DATABASE=pubs;TranslationDLL=Yes
```

Notice that the user ID and password are returned as clear text to the application. This is no more risky than the previous SQLConnect example, where the application was manipulating this information all along, but you should be aware that even using SQLDriverConnect, an application will have access to user passwords.

SQLBrowseConnect: Let the User Decide

SQLDriverConnect is enough for just about any situation you encounter in C++ client applications; in fact, the MFC classes for database access use it for their connections. In certain rare situations, you might need to construct the entire connection setup on the fly, and this is where SQLBrowseConnect comes into play. Using SQLBrowseConnect, you can find valid servers and get what information you need to give the driver to log in and use them.

SQLBrowseConnect is necessary when the parameter values necessary for a connection aren't known and the list of parameters is unknown, too. With SQLBrowseConnect, you start by calling the driver with the values you *do* have, and it tells you what else it needs. As long as you give it valid, but insufficient, connection information, it returns SQL_NEED_DATA and fills in the output string with information to help you ask the user for additional input.

You can see this by changing the SQLDriverConnect example to use the following connection code instead:

```
// fill in connString with the name of a DSN
lstrcpy( (LPSTR)connString,
        "DRIVER={SQL Server};Trusted_Connection=yes;" );

// now find out what you don't know
sqlVal = SQLBrowseConnect(
            ctx.hConn,
            connString, lstrlen( (LPSTR)connString),
            outConnString, sizeof(outConnString),
            &outConnStringLength );
```

(I used the SQL Server driver explicitly; you could also use SQLDrivers to retrieve a list of available drivers and present that as your first selection.) If you run this code in the Visual C++ debugger, you'll see that after the call to SQLBrowseConnect, ODBC has filled in outConnString with something like this:

```
"SERVER:Server={toonerville, (local)};UID:Login ID=?;
➥PWD:Password=?;*APP:AppName=?:*WSID:WorkStation ID=?"
```

This string contains a list of the required and optional connect string parameters for connecting to a SQL Server database. Similar to a connection string in construction, each parameter has three parts: the keyword to use for the parameter, a user-friendly name for the parameter to use in prompting the user, and either a question mark or, in the case of the SERVER parameter, a list of available servers. Optional parameters are marked with a leading asterisk, which should be removed from the keyword value before using it.

To prompt a user dynamically for connection information, you would parse the output string, use the friendly names to prompt the user for each value, and then add the values supplied to the connection string you originally sent to the driver. Finally, you would call SQLBrowseConnect again with the new information. As long as the function returns SQL_NEED_DATA, you continue the process until you have connected to a database or the driver returns an error value.

With the variance in functionality between drivers in supporting this function, it's difficult to predict a specific response to SQLBrowseConnect, so you must be as general as possible. Compared to the previous example, the Microsoft Oracle driver returned `"UID:User Name=?;PWD:Password=?;SERVER:Oracle Server Name=?;"` for an equivalent query, although the local TNSNAMES.ORA has several connects that could be presented as options for the server name. You should not expect any particular behavior from a driver.

Statements: Manipulating SQL Server Data

ODBC applications get their work done by using statements. A *statement* is any SQL query you execute against the database. The statement can insert or update rows, or it can generate a resultset that can then be processed by the application. All the preparatory operations for setting up the environment and connecting to the database set the stage for executing statements.

The SQL statement itself can be of whatever legal form you choose. If portability is unimportant to you, you can write your SQL using straight Transact-SQL with only a few necessary concessions to ODBC. If you want to preserve the ability to change database servers, if you must work with multiple databases in your application, or if you need a common SQL grammar for any reason, you should write your application using the ODBC grammar. SQL Server supports much of SQL-92 directly, by the way, so there is little translation overhead. This choice is wholly dependent on your objectives, and no definitive, general rule applies in all cases. Theoretically, the more portable the better, but if you have no need for portability, concentrating on SQL Server can simplify your effort.

Just as with queries typed in Query Analyzer, the SQL may or may not return data to you; updates, inserts, and deletes do not, but selects do. Stored procedures may or may not, depending on their purpose. Data definition queries (such as CREATE TABLE) do not return resultsets. The ODBC statement model is flexible enough to accommodate all these types of query execution.

The Simplest ODBC Statement

Before tackling the details of ODBC statement execution with SQL Server, take a look at a simple example with the absolute minimum required to run a query on the database. This is a statement that executes against the database and returns no data.

In ODBC, an application allocates a statement handle on a connection the same way a connection is allocated on an environment, with SQLAllocHandle:

```
sqlVal = SQLAllocHandle( SQL_HANDLE_STMT, ctx.hConn,
                         &ctx.hStmt );
```

When allocating a statement, the parent object handle is the connection handle, and the target type is SQL_HANDLE_STMT. After the statement has been allocated, any attributes can be set on the statement up to the point at which it's prepared. Some attributes can be set after it's prepared, but before it's executed. However, after it's executed and a resultset potentially created for it, there's little that can be done to change its behavior without closing the resultset and reissuing the statement.

After the statement is allocated, if all you want to do is execute it, you use SQLExecDirect as in the following example:

```
SQLCHAR simpSQL[] = "UPDATE authors " \
                    "SET au_lname = 'Jones'" \
                    "WHERE au_id='123-45-6789'";

void
SimpleStatement( ODBCContext & ctx )
{
    SQLRETURN sqlVal = SQLAllocHandle(
                            SQL_HANDLE_STMT,
                            ctx.hConn,
                            &ctx.hStmt );
```

```
    if ( sqlVal == SQL_SUCCESS )
    {
        sqlVal = SQLExecDirect( ctx.hStmt,
                                simpSQL,
                                SQL_NTS );

        if ( !SQL_SUCCEEDED( sqlVal ) &&
                sqlVal != SQL_NO_DATA )
            ShowSQLInfo( ctx.hStmt, SQL_HANDLE_STMT );
        SQLFreeHandle( SQL_HANDLE_STMT, ctx.hStmt );
    }
    else
        ShowSQLInfo( ctx.hStmt, SQL_HANDLE_STMT );
    // If an error occurred, let the user know.
}
```

Assuming the environment and connection have been established, this example executes a simple update statement against the authors table and then checks and reports if any errors occur.

Statement Details

The model used by ODBC includes the statement, its parameters, zero or more resultsets returned by the server in response to the statement's execution, and the status, success, or failure of the statement's execution. Although a much more detailed classification is possible, within ODBC the most pertinent separation of statements is according to whether they return results to the caller.

You saw an example of a resultless statement already. They are both simpler than statements with results and eons faster. The order of events (and I will go into them in more detail, of course) is as follows:

1. The application allocates a statement.
2. For a statement that is repeated (such as multiple inserts to the same table), it calls SQLPrepare to preprocess the query and set up a cached query plan on the server.
3. It binds input parameter buffers to the statement, if appropriate.
4. For statements with parameters, the application places data in them for this execution of the statement.
5. The application calls either SQLExecDirect for unprepared statements or SQLExecute for prepared statements.
6. For each additional execution, it loops to step 4.

For statements that do return results, a bit more complexity is involved. A simple retrieval would perform the following steps:

1. Allocate a statement as before.
2. Prepare the statement, if you want.
3. If needed, bind statement parameters.
4. Set parameter data.
5. Execute the statement.
6. Bind a set of column buffers to the statement to retrieve single rows of data.
7. Use SQLFetch to retrieve result columns into column variables.
8. Perform whatever processing is needed on the data.
9. To fetch the next row, loop to step 7 until the fetch returns SQL_NO_DATA;
10. When all needed results have been processed, call SQLCloseCursor with the statement handle to close the cursor and free the statement for another SQL query, or call SQLFreeHandle to dispose of the statement altogether.

When a statement's execution produces data for the client, a resultset is created. With SQL Server, the default resultset is a static, temporary snapshot of the data. The data received by the application is the data as it was when the query was executed (it does not change as other applications update the data). By default, SQL Server instantiates a forward-only cursor to traverse the resultset, and the application must scan to the end or call SQLCloseCursor before performing another operation on the connection. No user intervention is necessary to create the cursor.

Some simplifications are hidden in the preceding list of steps. First, the program uses the default cursor behavior; this is not true for all applications. The second assumption is that there is only one resultset returned by the statement. Finally, the code must know the resultset's characteristics (number of columns, type), or it becomes much more complicated quickly. If you need to build your code in a generic fashion and handle any results you receive from an SQL query, the following is more accurate:

1. Allocate a statement as before.
2. Set the cursor attributes to be used in returning results to the client, such as its concurrency, updatability, and sensitivity/locking behavior.
3. Prepare the statement, if desired.
4. If needed, bind statement parameters.
5. Set parameter data.
6. Execute the statement.

7. If the characteristics of the resultset are not known, use ODBC metadata functions (SQLNumResultCols, SQLDescribeCol, and SQLColAttribute) to determine the number, type, and sizes of the results.

8. Bind a set of column buffers to the statement to retrieve single rows of data, or bind arrays of row or column buffers to the statement to retrieve a number of rows at a time.

9. Use SQLFetch or SQLFetchScroll to retrieve result columns into column variables.

10. Perform whatever processing you like with the data, including updating the data with a different statement or SQLSetPos, if the driver supports positioned updates (as SQL Server 7 does).

11. To fetch the next row or set of rows, loop to step 9 until the fetch returns SQL_NO_DATA.

12. Call SQLMoreResults to discover whether another resultset is available from the same statements, and prepare to process it if so; if SQLMoreResults returns SQL_SUCCESS, loop to step 7 to process the next resultset.

13. To execute the statement again with different parameters, loop to step 5.

14. When all needed results have been processed, call SQLCloseCursor with the statement handle to close the cursor and free the statement for another SQL query, or call SQLFreeHandle to dispose of the statement altogether.

Truly, now, ODBC programming isn't as complicated as it's made out to be, is it?

Although ODBC is reputed to be horribly complicated, the first retrieval scenario is much more likely than the second. Only general analytic and database management tools need to be able to manipulate any data in the server on demand, so discovering the form of result columns at runtime is not going to be a normal part of your life. If your design is reasonably well specified, your application will know in advance what data it manipulates and how it is retrieved. If this is true, the need to dynamically describe the form of the query results is removed.

19

> **TIP**
>
> Don't retrieve data unless you have to! Unless you have serious concerns about your database server's load, retrieving data to the client should be the last option you consider when working with databases. SQL is a powerful language for manipulating relational data, and you can realize huge savings in resources across the board if you can use an SQL query for a manipulation instead of processing the data on the client.

In reality, your code will fall somewhere between the two extremes. If you start from the simple and add only those additional operations you need, you should find a good balance between oversimplifying and using every feature in ODBC.

Statement Attributes

Statement attributes can be set by using SQLSetStmtAttr and queried with SQLGetStmtAttr; as with connections, there are ODBC-defined and SQL Server–specific statement attributes, although the latter are few at the statement level. As with connection attributes, you cannot set statement attributes while a statement is executing, and you cannot set cursor or concurrency control after the statement has been prepared.

SQLSetStmtAttr operates in the same fashion as SQLSetConnectAttr; it takes a statement handle, the ID of the attribute to change, and either the integer value to set or a pointer to the value and the size. Table 19.10 shows commonly used ODBC-defined attributes for statements. For SQL Server, the two attributes of greatest interest are SQL_SOPT_SS_CURSOR_OPTIONS and SQL_SOPT_SS_TEXTPTR_LOGGING. The former can be used to set automatic first row fetching or a special read-only, fast-forward cursor optimized for forward-only resultset scans. SQL_SOPT_SS_TEXTPTR_LOGGING is used to turn off text and image field logging to boost performance by not copying large binary fields to the transaction log.

TABLE 19.10   COMMON ODBC STATEMENT ATTRIBUTES

Attribute	Purpose
SQL_ATTR_ASYNC_ENABLE	Enables or disables asynchronous execution (default: off)
SQL_ATTR_CONCURRENCY	Controls update and locking behavior of cursors (default: read-only cursors)
SQL_ATTR_CURSOR_SCROLLABLE	Determines whether a cursor generated for the statement is forward-only or scrollable (default: forward-only)
SQL_ATTR_CURSOR_SENSITIVITY	Controls whether the rows retrieved by the cursor are affected by subsequent updates outside the cursor (ODBC default is unspecified, but SQL Server cursors by default are sensitive to other cursors within the same transaction)
SQL_ATTR_CURSOR_TYPE	Sets the cursor type used for resultsets (default: static, forward-only)
SQL_ATTR_MAX_LENGTH	Sets maximum number of bytes returned on the statement
SQL_ATTR_MAX_ROWS	Sets maximum number of rows returned on the statement
SQL_ATTR_METADATA_ID	Same effect as the connection attribute of the same name

Attribute	*Purpose*
SQL_ATTR_NOSCAN	Disables ODBC driver scanning for escape sequences
SQL_ATTR_QUERY_TIMEOUT	Maximum execution time for statement
SQL_ATTR_ROW_NUMBER	Retrieves the current row position of a cursor (read-only)
SQL_ATTR_ROW_BIND_TYPE	Sets column-wise or row-wise binding, location for block cursors

Data Conversions Between SQL Server, ODBC, and the Client

Database vendors can store data in any form they choose. When data is retrieved and transmitted over the network, it's via a *custom protocol* (usually), which means that the data arrives at the client in any form the designer sees fit. ODBC and client programs must have a means of mapping server data types to a standard format (an ODBC data type) that the client can then retrieve into its native type (the host language type). ODBC defines the mapping between host languages and ODBC, and the driver defines the mapping from ODBC types to the native database types. Whenever you send data to or receive data from ODBC, you must specify how the data is to be interpreted. Further, you must verify that the data types you specify are compatible with the data types used to store the data in the database. Table 19.11 lists common C types and useful mappings to ODBC and SQL Server types.

TABLE 19.11 COMMON C TYPES AND ODBC CANONICAL TYPES

C Type	*C Typedef*	*ODBC Type ID*	*SQL Server*
unsigned char	SQLCHAR	SQL_C_CHAR	char, varchar
short (16 bit)	SQLSMALLINT	SQL_C_SHORT	smallint
long (32 bit)	SQLINTEGER	SQL_C_LONG	int
double	SQLDOUBLE	SQL_C_DOUBLE	float
unsigned char *	SQLCHAR *	SQL_C_CHAR	varchar
	SQL_LONGVARBINARY	SQL_C_BINARY	image
	SQL_LONGVARCHAR	SQL_C_CHAR	text
DATE_STRUCT	SQL_DATE_STRUCT	SQL_C_TYPE_DATE	datetime
TIME_STRUCT	SQL_TIME_STRUCT	SQL_C_TYPE_TIME	datetime
TIMESTAMP_STRUCT	SQL_TIMESTAMP_STRUCT	SQL_C_TYPE_TIMESTAMP	datetime

19

OPTIMIZING
ODBC USING
VISUAL C++

The type conversions in Table 19.11 are only a sample of possible conversions; there are far too many combinations to list here. For the full set of conversions between ODBC and C types, you should see the "Data Types" topic in the ODBC SDK documentation; for SQL Server to ODBC types, see the "Mapping Data Types" topic in SQL Server 7 Books Online.

Each variable you send or receive is accompanied by an SQLINTEGER variable called an *indicator*. This variable is used to tell ODBC the size of the data sent or for ODBC to tell you. In some cases, when you transmit data, the indicator size value can be replaced with one of the "magic" values from Table 19.12. An additional macro for creating this value, SQL_LEN_DATA_AT_EXEC(size), is discussed in the section "Working with Large Data Items" later in this chapter.

TABLE 19.12   MAGIC NUMBERS FOR INDICATOR VARIABLES

Value	Meaning
SQL_NTS	The character parameter is a null-terminated string.
SQL_NULL_DATA	The parameter is NULL.
SQL_DEFAULT_PARAM	In calling a stored procedure, use the default for the given parameter.

ODBC uses internal data structures, called *descriptors*, to maintain complete information on parameters and result columns. The preceding discussion presents ODBC data types as simply as possible, but for ultimate control over type management, you can allocate your own descriptors and then manipulate and associate them to data as you see fit. Because this fine-grained control over conversions is rarely needed, I prefer to let ODBC handle them.

Parameters

A SQL statement in ODBC can be fully specified in the query itself, or it can be written to take replaceable parameters. A fully specified SQL statement could be written thus:

```
SELECT au_lname FROM authors WHERE au_id='123-45-6789'
```

This is the same sort of query you might execute from a Query Analyzer or an ISQL prompt to retrieve the author information for a single author. It's perfectly adequate if you're always going to execute the same SQL with the same parameters (for example, the literal in the WHERE clause in the example). Usually, this is not the case. For example, a member function of a C++ class that stores its persistent state in the database needs to fill the data values in an insert or update with the values of its member data.

ODBC allows you to create your SQL with embedded parameter markers (the ? character) and bind program variables to each parameter using SQLBindParameter. If you have a character buffer containing the author ID in question, instead of the preceding statement, you use the following SQL:

```
SELECT au_lname FROM authors WHERE au_id=?
```

Then use SQLBindParameter to tell ODBC where to find the value for each parameter (in this case, only one) by providing a pointer and type information, as in the following:

```
char        au_id[13];
SQLINTEGER cbAuId = SQL_NTS;
sqlVal = SQLBindParameter( ctx.hStmt, 1,
    SQL_PARAM_INPUT, SQL_C_CHAR, SQL_CHAR,
    lstrlen(au_id ), 0,
    au_id, sizeof( au_id ),
    &cbAuId);
```

In this example, au_id is a simple C character array of the appropriate size to hold an author ID. The parameters to SQLBindParameter are described in Table 19.13.

TABLE 19.13 PARAMETERS FOR SQLBindParameter

Parameter	Description
Statement	Handle of the statement on which the parameters are bound
Parameter number	Number of the parameter being bound, from left to right starting with one
Parameter direction	In, out, or in/out
Variable type	C type of the program variable
SQL type	SQL type into which the C variable is formatted before it's sent to the server
Size/precision	Size of the input parameter
Precision/scale	For decimal types, the scale (exact/inexact); usually set to zero
Variable address	Address of program variable containing the parameter's data
Variable size	Size of buffer; number of bytes ODBC is allowed to write in an out parameter
Pointer to indicator/type code	Points to a variable that contains the length of the parameter data or a type code; this variable receives the indicator value for output or in/out parameters

19

OPTIMIZING
ODBC USING
VISUAL C++

In the example, you pass the handle to the statement, and then 1 to indicate that you are binding the first parameter. The parameter direction is SQL_PARAM_INPUT because the parameter is the criterion value and receives no data from the statement. The C data type is SQL_C_CHAR (a C character buffer), which is converted to a SQL_CHAR string in the statement. The size in bytes is the length of the string in this case, and because the parameter is character data, the precision value is irrelevant (passed as a zero in the example). The variable pointer is simply the address of the array, and the size is supplied with the sizeof operator.

The last parameter is declared only because it has to be passed as a pointer for this case. Because the parameter is input only, an indicator variable is not strictly necessary, but it's declared and set to the value SQL_NTS to indicate that the value in au_id is a null-terminated string.

When you use replaceable parameters, you do not include delimiters (for example, single quotes for string values). Changing the sample statement to the following causes it to fail:

```
SELECT au_lname FROM authors WHERE au_id='?'
```

You must introduce another structure, which in these and later examples will hold the author information you retrieve or send to the database. Listing 19.5 shows its definition.

LISTING 19.5 THE AuthorInformation STRUCTURE

```
typedef    struct
{
    char    au_id[12];      // UDT id(varchar) picture is SSAN.
    long    ind_au_id;      // indicator; on return from retrieve,
                            // holds length of data in its
                            // companion variable, sans
                            // terminating NULL.

    char    au_lname[41]; // varchar(40)
    long    ind_au_lname; // indicator

    char    au_fname[21]; // varchar(20)
    long    ind_au_fname; // indicator

    char    phone[13];    // varchar(12)
    long    ind_phone;    // indicator

    char    address[41];  // varchar(40)
    long    ind_address;  // indicator

    char    city[21];     // varchar(20)
    long    ind_city;     // indicator
```

```
    char    state[3];     // char(2)
    long    ind_state;    // indicator

    char    zip[6];       // varchar(5)
    long    ind_zip;      // indicator

    bool    contract;     // bit; bool reflects semantics of
                     // data.
    long    ind_contract; // indicator

} AuthorInformation;
```

Listing 19.6 demonstrates using a bound parameter to query the database instead of literal SQL. This example plans to use the au_id member of the AuthorInformation structure to hold the input parameter (the author ID you will query for), so use a SQL statement with one parameter in the WHERE clause and bind the au_id variable to it. I'll also sneak in a demonstration of preparing a statement for execution, even though I don't discuss it until the next section.

LISTING 19.6   A BOUND PARAMETER FOR QUERY CRITERION

```
SQLCHAR    sSQL[] =     "SELECT au_lname, au_fname, phone, " \
                   "address, city, state, zip, contract " \
                   "FROM authors WHERE au_id = ?";

bool
PrepareQuery( ODBCContext & ctx, AuthorInformation & auInfo)
{
    bool       retval = false;
    SQLRETURN  sqlVal = SQLAllocHandle( SQL_HANDLE_STMT,
                                ctx.hConn, &ctx.hStmt );
    // prepare the statement if you got one
    if ( SQL_SUCCEEDED(sqlVal) )
    {
        sqlVal = SQLPrepare( ctx.hStmt, sSQL,
                            lstrlen((LPCTSTR) sSQL) );
        if ( SQL_SUCCEEDED(sqlVal) )
        {
            auInfo.ind_au_id = SQL_NTS; // magic indicator
            sqlVal = SQLBindParameter( ctx.hStmt, 1,
                        SQL_PARAM_INPUT, SQL_C_CHAR, SQL_CHAR,
                        lstrlen(auInfo.au_id), 0,
                        auInfo.au_id, sizeof( auInfo.au_id ),
                        &auInfo.ind_au_id);
            if ( SQL_SUCCEEDED(sqlVal) )
            {
```

continues

19

OPTIMIZING ODBC USING VISUAL C++

LISTING **19.6**   CONTINUED

```
            sqlVal = SQLExecute( ctx.hStmt );
            if ( SQL_SUCCEEDED(sqlVal) )
            {
                // success
                retval = true;
            }
        }
    }
    if ( !SQL_SUCCEEDED( sqlVal ) )
        ShowSQLInfo( ctx.hStmt, SQL_HANDLE_STMT );
}
else
    ShowSQLInfo( ctx.hConn, SQL_HANDLE_DBC );

return retval;
}
```

Execution Modes: Prepared Versus Direct

When the query is sent to the server, it passes through a compilation phase, when the statement is parsed, and then an optimization phase that constructs a plan for its execution aimed at accomplishing the requested operations using the least resources (processor, disk, memory, and so forth). This preparation process happens for every statement that is executed.

The simplest query method is *direct execution*, which sends the query to the server and retrieves results in one step. Preparation occurs when the statement is submitted for execution, and can be repeated each time the query is submitted. With *prepared execution*, the client sends the query to the server in a preliminary step so that the server can prepare the query ahead of time. The client then sends a command to the server to execute the query as a second step, with whatever parameters are needed. If the statement is to be executed many times with different parameters, the query plan can be reused instead of parsing and planning the statement each time. In SQL Server 7, the execution plans are shared across the server, so similar requests from multiple users can reuse the same execution plan.

In SQL Server 6.5, preparing a statement in ODBC created a stored procedure on the server that contained the SQL in the query and took the same parameters as were marked in the statement. This stored procedure was useful only on the statement it was prepared with, however. Because these stored procedures were created into tempdb, with all the overhead that involves, a server trying to work with prepared statements from a large client pool quickly ran into problems as the statements' procedures were written to disk.

SQL Server 7 supports prepared execution directly to remove this performance penalty. By not writing temporary procedures to `tempdb`, the overhead involved with prepared statements is significantly lower.

Although these points make a good case for prepared execution in SQL Server 7, direct execution still has a place. Most significant is that the query plans shared among prepared statements are also shared with directly executed statements in version 7. With direct execution, the statement must still be parsed when it's sent to the server. However, after it's parsed, if it matches an existing, cached query plan, it's executed without the additional planning step. Also, prepared statements cannot be shared; although the execution plan is, each statement must be parsed before an appropriate plan can be selected. If a query is prepared, but not reused, preparing the statement degrades performance, not improves it. Microsoft advises that with SQL Server 7, prepared execution is most appropriate if the statement is executed at least three times. With less reuse, network overhead can dominate performance because prepared execution requires two roundtrips to the server instead of the one required for direct execution.

Fetching Data

After you have executed a statement that returns results, you should retrieve the data from the resultset. You use either `SQLFetch` or `SQLFetchScroll` to retrieve data, in a process that's essentially the reverse of sending parameters (actually, at just a little lower abstraction, it *is* identical).

`SELECT` statements and stored procedure calls can create resultsets. With SQL Server 7, there is really no way to tell whether any data was retrieved without trying to fetch a row; if no data was retrieved, the first fetch returns `SQL_NO_DATA`. Neither `SQLRowCount` nor `SQLNumResultCols` can be used on the SQL Server to test this condition. `SQLRowCount` is valid only on `UPDATES` or `DELETES`, and `SQLNumResultCols` always returns the number of columns that would occur if there were data.

Retrieving one row of data at a time requires binding a column buffer to each column with `SQLBindCol` and calling `SQLFetch` to fill in the buffer. Data type specifications similar to those used with `SQLBindParameter` tell ODBC what type to convert the data from the server into when filling in the buffers.

Continuing the example from Listing 19.6, which prepares a statement using a bound parameter, the code in Listing 19.7 binds columns to the resultset created by that statement and then retrieves a row of data from the resultset.

LISTING 19.7   BINDING PROGRAM VARIABLES AND RETRIEVING COLUMN DATA

```
// retrieves the information from the author SELECT statement.
bool
GetData( ODBCContext & ctx, AuthorInformation & auInfo )
{
    SQLRETURN    sqlVal;
    bool         retval = false;

    // bind result cols
    sqlVal = SQLBindCol( ctx.hStmt, 1, SQL_C_CHAR,
        auInfo.au_lname, sizeof( auInfo.au_lname),
        &auInfo.ind_au_lname );
    if ( sqlVal == SQL_SUCCESS )
        sqlVal = SQLBindCol( ctx.hStmt, 2, SQL_C_CHAR,
            auInfo.au_fname, sizeof( auInfo.au_fname),
            &auInfo.ind_au_fname );
    if ( sqlVal == SQL_SUCCESS )
        sqlVal = SQLBindCol( ctx.hStmt, 3, SQL_C_CHAR,
            auInfo.phone, sizeof( auInfo.phone),
            &auInfo.ind_phone );
    if ( sqlVal == SQL_SUCCESS )
        sqlVal = SQLBindCol( ctx.hStmt, 4, SQL_C_CHAR,
            auInfo.address, sizeof( auInfo.address),
            &auInfo.ind_address );
    if ( sqlVal == SQL_SUCCESS )
        sqlVal = SQLBindCol( ctx.hStmt, 5, SQL_C_CHAR,
            auInfo.city, sizeof( auInfo.city),
            &auInfo.ind_city );
    if ( sqlVal == SQL_SUCCESS )
        sqlVal = SQLBindCol( ctx.hStmt, 6, SQL_C_CHAR,
            auInfo.state, sizeof( auInfo.state),
            &auInfo.ind_state );
    if ( sqlVal == SQL_SUCCESS )
        sqlVal = SQLBindCol( ctx.hStmt, 7, SQL_C_CHAR,
            auInfo.zip, sizeof( auInfo.zip),
            &auInfo.ind_zip );
    if ( sqlVal == SQL_SUCCESS )
        sqlVal = SQLBindCol( ctx.hStmt, 8, SQL_C_BIT,
            &auInfo.contract, sizeof( auInfo.contract ),
            &auInfo.ind_contract );

    if ( sqlVal == SQL_SUCCESS ) // no success with info
    {
        // now that the columns are bound, fetch data
        sqlVal = SQLFetch( ctx.hStmt );

        if ( SQL_SUCCEEDED(sqlVal) )
        {
            retval = TRUE;
        }
```

```
        if ( sqlVal != SQL_SUCCESS )
        {
            if ( sqlVal == SQL_NO_DATA )
                MessageBox( NULL,
                    "No data returned from SQLFetch()",
                    "Data not found", MB_OK );
            else
                ShowSQLInfo( ctx.hStmt, SQL_HANDLE_STMT );
        }
    }
    else    // bindcol failed
        ShowSQLInfo( ctx.hStmt, SQL_HANDLE_STMT );

    return retval;
}
```

Notice the similarity of `SQLBindCol` to `SQLBindParameter`? If you can use one, you can use the other. In the example, because you are going to retrieve all the data, you bind the columns in the same order they are going to be returned. Always specify your data; if you retrieve only specific columns, you will save yourself a lot of trouble. In the query, the columns are all listed explicitly; a `"SELECT * FROM...,"` leaves you wide open for trouble if *a)* you don't get the column order just right, *b)* someone adds a column later, or *c)* a data transfer changes the columns' natural order in the database.

On the other hand, you don't have to use all the data listed in the query. Only the data you bind is retrieved, and you have to bind only data you need. Of course, there's a catch—the data you bind has to go from left to right—that is, you can bind column 1, columns 1 and 2, or columns 1, 2, and 3, but you can't bind columns 1, 2, and 11. By ordering your parameters from most to least used, particularly if you have image or text columns on the end, you can cut your traffic by retrieving only the data you need. Not binding a column does not mean you can't retrieve it, by the way; unbound columns can still be retrieved using `SQLGetData`. As with statement parameters, statement result columns remain in effect until the statement is freed or the binding is replaced by another with `SQLBindCol` using the same column number.

Cursors

Retrieving more than one row requires a cursor. You have experienced cursor effects already, but now you need to address them specifically. In simplest terms, a *cursor* is a window that reveals your current position (often, one row) in a resultset. Cursors have three major attributes of concern: sensitivity, transfer (rowset) size, and scrollability. The flexibility afforded by the varying types of cursors yields a complex variety of choices, but for each application, the appropriate mix of dynamics and transfer size is usually obvious.

Cursor Sensitivity

Sensitivity refers to whether the data returned through a cursor is constant over the life of the cursor; do you see the same data as everyone else, or are you isolated from other users' changes while you work with the cursor?

Conceptually, when you create a *static* cursor, everything about its resultset is fixed, including the membership of rows and the data retrieved for columns in those rows. No updates that are made while you have the cursor open will show up in the data you see. A dynamic cursor, on the other hand, can be more or less sensitive to changes in the data from which it's drawn, either in membership or data.

When it's created, a *keyset-driven* cursor stores the list of rows that match the query that created it. Unlike a static cursor, it retrieves the data for each row as the client fetches the row. Membership in the cursor is fixed because the IDs of rows are stored only once, but the data values in the rows retrieved can change during the cursor's lifetime and are seen when the rows are fetched.

A fully *dynamic* cursor is exactly that; both the data in rows and their membership in the resultset can change on the fly. This gives you the most up-to-date view of the data, but it would be impossible to run an expense report from it! Contrary to what you might think, a fully dynamic cursor is rarely what you need because there is little assurance of what you might be seeing. You use a dynamic cursor most when you have specific information you need (not a large resultset), but you need it to be the latest data.

A compromise between keyset and dynamic cursors, which SQL Server does *not* support, is the mixed cursor. By setting the rowset size to some fraction of the expected number of rows, you set a locality in which the membership is fixed, as is characteristic of the keyset-driven cursor. When you seek beyond that keyset, the database is requeried to retrieve the keys for the new locale. The new set of keys is retrieved from the current state of the database and is thus fully dynamic. By tuning the size of the keyset, you can vary the behavior of this type of cursor between the two ends of the spectrum.

The type of cursor used on the statement, whether static, dynamic, or keyset driven, is set by using the statement attribute SQL_ATTR_CURSOR_TYPE. This attribute must be set before the statement is prepared or executed.

Block Cursors and Rowsets

Listing 19.7 demonstrated the default static, *forward-only* cursor retrieving a single row at a time into a set of column buffers. A *block* cursor retrieves multiple rows (a *rowset*) in one fetch if you need to process a large number of rows from a statement. You can increase the number of rows retrieved per fetch to an arbitrary size using an array of rows (a rowset buffer). First, declare a structure that holds the data and indicators for the individual columns; coincidentally, the `AuthorInformation` structure has just the right elements for this use. Decide on the size you want the rowset to be, and allocate an array of row structures containing the correct number of elements. Then, set statement attributes to tell ODBC how many elements and which way (row- or column-wise) to fill them in. Finally, bind the *first* column variable in each column to tell ODBC where to start each column. Listing 19.8 demonstrates a row-wise block fetch.

LISTING 19.8   RETRIEVING A ROWSET WITH A BLOCK CURSOR

```
SQLCHAR allSQL[] = "SELECT au_id, au_lname, au_fname, phone," \
                   " address, city, state, zip, contract" \
                   " FROM Authors";
#define    au_array_size    30

// use block cursor to retrieve a block of data at a time.
bool
BlockCursor( ODBCContext & ctx )
{
    bool               retval = false;
    AuthorInformation auInfo[au_array_size];
    SQLUINTEGER        auRowsFetched = 0;

    // Set size of elements in the row array
    sqlVal = SQLSetStmtAttr (ctx.hStmt,
            SQL_ATTR_ROW_BIND_TYPE,
            SQLPOINTER(sizeof(AuthorInformation)), 0 );
    if ( SQL_SUCCEEDED( sqlVal ) )
        sqlVal = SQLSetStmtAttr ( ctx.hStmt,
            SQL_ATTR_ROW_ARRAY_SIZE,
            SQLPOINTER(au_array_size), 0 );

    // tell driver to put number of rows fetched in
    // the auRowsFetched variable
    if ( SQL_SUCCEEDED( sqlVal ) )
        sqlVal = SQLSetStmtAttr ( ctx.hStmt,
            SQL_ATTR_ROWS_FETCHED_PTR,
            SQLPOINTER(&auRowsFetched), 0 );

    if ( SQL_SUCCEEDED( sqlVal ) )
    {
        // bind columns
        sqlVal = SQLBindCol( ctx.hStmt, 1, SQL_C_CHAR,
                auInfo[0].au_id, sizeof( auInfo[0].au_id ),
                &auInfo[0].ind_au_id );
        if ( sqlVal == SQL_SUCCESS )
            sqlVal = SQLBindCol( ctx.hStmt, 2, SQL_C_CHAR,
                        auInfo[0].au_lname,
```

continues

LISTING **19.8**   CONTINUED

```c
                            sizeof( auInfo[0].au_lname),
                            &auInfo[0].ind_au_lname );
    if ( sqlVal == SQL_SUCCESS )
        sqlVal = SQLBindCol( ctx.hStmt, 3, SQL_C_CHAR,
                            auInfo[0].au_fname,
                            sizeof( auInfo[0].au_fname),
                            &auInfo[0].ind_au_fname );
    if ( sqlVal == SQL_SUCCESS )
        sqlVal = SQLBindCol( ctx.hStmt, 4, SQL_C_CHAR,
                            auInfo[0].phone,
                            sizeof( auInfo[0].phone),
                            &auInfo[0].ind_phone );
    if ( sqlVal == SQL_SUCCESS )
        sqlVal = SQLBindCol( ctx.hStmt, 5, SQL_C_CHAR,
                            auInfo[0].address,
                            sizeof( auInfo[0].address),
                            &auInfo[0].ind_address );
    if ( sqlVal == SQL_SUCCESS )
        sqlVal = SQLBindCol( ctx.hStmt, 6, SQL_C_CHAR,
                            auInfo[0].city,
                            sizeof( auInfo[0].city),
                            &auInfo[0].ind_city );
    if ( sqlVal == SQL_SUCCESS )
        sqlVal = SQLBindCol( ctx.hStmt, 7, SQL_C_CHAR,
                            auInfo[0].state,
                            sizeof( auInfo[0].state),
                            &auInfo[0].ind_state );
    if ( sqlVal == SQL_SUCCESS )
        sqlVal = SQLBindCol( ctx.hStmt, 8, SQL_C_CHAR,
                            auInfo[0].zip,
                            sizeof( auInfo[0].zip),
                            &auInfo[0].ind_zip );
    if ( sqlVal == SQL_SUCCESS )
        sqlVal = SQLBindCol( ctx.hStmt, 9, SQL_C_BIT,
                            &auInfo[0].contract,
                            sizeof( auInfo[0].contract ),
                            &auInfo[0].ind_contract );

    if ( sqlVal == SQL_SUCCESS )
        sqlVal = SQLExecDirect( ctx.hStmt, allSQL, SQL_NTS );

    if ( sqlVal == SQL_SUCCESS )
    {
        // now that the resultset exists, fetch data
        sqlVal = SQLFetch( ctx.hStmt );

        if ( SQL_SUCCEEDED(sqlVal) )
        {
            // Number of rows fetched is in auRowsFetched
```

```
                // Do whatever processing you need to here.
                retval = TRUE;
            }

            if ( sqlVal != SQL_SUCCESS )
            {
                if ( sqlVal == SQL_NO_DATA )
                    MessageBox( NULL,
                        "No data returned from SQLFetch()",
                        "Data not found", MB_OK );
            }
        }
    }

    if ( !SQL_SUCCEEDED( sqlVal ) && (sqlVal != SQL_NO_DATA) )
        ShowSQLInfo( ctx.hStmt, SQL_HANDLE_STMT );

    return retval;
}
```

In this example, you are filling the elements in row-major form. Hoever, to fill a column-major buffer, you could declare column buffers (arrays of column elements, instead of arrays of rows), and for the SQL_ATTR_ROW_BIND_TYPE, you would specify SQL_BIND_BY_COLUMN. Unlike row buffers, column buffers don't have to be contiguous, column to column.

Scrolling Cursors

The last cursor aspect to discuss is scrollability. With a little additional effort, you can make cursors scrollable, so you can seek to any record and move backward as well as forward.

You have to start with a fresh HSTMT; you can't use SQLCloseCursor on a statement and then start over. With a fresh handle, the following code does the trick:

```
// use a scrollable cursor
sqlVal = SQLSetStmtAttr ( ctx.hStmt,
                SQL_ATTR_CURSOR_SCROLLABLE,
                SQLPOINTER(SQL_SCROLLABLE), 0 );
```

After you set this attribute, all other operations work the same; in fact, if you just use SQLFetch as usual, it behaves just like your old forward-only cursor. If you use SQLFetchScroll, though, you can go anywhere on the resultset:

```
// jump to the first record
SQLFetchScroll( ctx.hStmt, SQL_FETCH_FIRST, 0 );
```

Pretty easy, but you have some more options you can use. The SQL_FETCH_FIRST says that the last parameter is ignored and the cursor jumps to the first record in the resultset. Your other choices include SQL_FETCH_NEXT and SQL_FETCH_PRIOR, which get the next and previous rows, respectively, and SQL_FETCH_RELATIVE and SQL_FETCH_ABSOLUTE, which retrieve a specified number from the current record or from the first record. SQL_FETCH_LAST is the counterpart to SQL_FETCH_FIRST.

Before you make all your cursors scrollable, remember that a forward-only cursor is going to be much, much faster, if only because caching it is trivial (locality is always the next record). Use a scrollable cursor only for live views that have to move around, and use the default to scan results from start to finish.

End to End: Debugging ODBC Code

You cannot develop ODBC applications effectively without being aware of and using a number of tools effectively. You will take a quick look at some of them here, but the best way for you to learn where each is appropriate is to experiment with your code and monitor each portion of the link between your application and the database. There are five tools for peering inside each layer of ODBC and your SQL Server: the Visual C++ debugger, the ODBC trace facility, the Network Monitor, the SQL Profiler, and the Windows NT Performance Monitor.

The Visual C++ debugger is the obvious place to start. I always advise those who are looking at efficiency and reliability questions to first use the debugger to watch what the program is doing. Step through critical routines and look at data structures at each step in the program. Look at decision points in the code. Set breakpoints at each flow of control statement and look at the variables in scope at the time. Are any of them off the wall? Could a variable adopt a value that would cause the decision to fail? If you allocate a data structure and return it to the caller, look at the structure just before the function returns. Are any members not initialized? For database accesses, look at the parameters. Are all the parameters in the statement accounted for when you issue a query? A common error is not binding all the parameter columns, causing ODBC to return SQL_NEED_DATA from a SQLExecute or SQLExecDirect. When the statement is executed, is there other data in scope that could be used to tighten the query search criteria? Another error is to search too broadly and then use repeated fetches to find the data the program really needs. If you have criterion values, put them in the query so that the server has to send you only the data you really want.

You can watch the interface between your application and the ODBC driver manager and driver with the ODBC trace facility. If you're working with a complex application and get errors you can't pin down, such as function sequence problems, try tracing while stepping through with the debugger. The trace facility allows you to see all ODBC function calls and parameters, including pointer values. By correlating them to the state of the program at the time the error occurs, you can usually figure out why you're sending bad data to the server.

Another useful tool, although not always installed, is Windows NT's Network Monitor. A network sniffer with restricted function, in interactive mode you can use it to follow all the correspondence between your computer and another machine. This tool lets you follow network statistics, inspect packet data, and assess the interaction between your application and SQL Server. It's not the most accessible information (it takes a fair amount of knowledge to interpret the results), but it's indispensable if you suspect network problems or load-related performance degradation.

Anyone building applications against SQL Server has to run the Profiler. Profiler shows you the database interaction with the driver. I have worked with several other servers, and this tool makes me want to build software on SQL Server. If you even suspect that a problem might lurk in the way you're using the database server, bring up this program and find out for sure.

Need I say it? If you have a performance problem, open up Performance Monitor. Monitor CPU, working set, virtual memory pages/sec, and network packets, both on your client and on the database server. Look for overutilized resources, and then adjust your monitored parameters to explore potential trouble spots in more detail. If you have a copy of the Windows NT 3.5 Resource Kit, you're in luck; the volume *Optimizing Windows NT* has the most comprehensive discussion of NT performance debugging I've ever seen (and a lot of it is still useful). Adding to the comprehensive system-monitoring capability you have in NT, SQL Server has a number of performance counters you can use to inspect its internal operation.

These tools let you dissect your ODBC connection and inspect its activities at every layer between the user and the database file on the server. I recommend you try them even if you aren't having problems; seeing how the software works together is valuable in its own right. You might need to use other tools to analyze the results because with most of these tools you capture a lot of raw data. However, a little persistence brings a handsome return on your time investment. Please refer to the section, "Monitoring SQL Server Performance and Activity" in the "Administering SQL Server" chapter of Books Online for more information on tuning SQL Servers.

19

OPTIMIZING
ODBC USING
VISUAL C++

Working with Large Data Items

SQL Server can store large data items collectively known as *binary large objects (BLOBs)*, in addition to the familiar text and numeric items. This has advantages over what's often the alternative—storing large objects in files and the path to them in the database. Storing binary data in files is sometimes simpler and reduces the load on the database server program if images are retrieved often, but it complicates your system installation and requires that those paths never, ever change during the lifetime of the rows that reference them. There is no simple way to enforce referential integrity on the path columns in the tables, either. If you store these items in the database, on the other hand, backups of the database include *all* the data, the database can enforce your integrity rules, and the database can be transferred to other servers (or your existing server can be reconfigured) without breaking file path references.

The data types SQL Server supplies to handle large data are the text and image types. Storing these data is a little more complex than atomic data items, mainly because it's not at all certain that the entire object can be transferred in one operation. Because SQL Server 7 allows objects up to 2GB, you need to use a different method to retrieve and insert images.

Use `SQLGetData` and `SQLPutData` to transfer large data. Although these functions can be used to retrieve any unbound columns (and bound columns, too, with some drivers), it's usually clearer to bind any fixed columns you're going to use. The best approach is to place all small data at the head of the SELECT list, with the large object or objects at the end, and then bind all the small columns while leaving the large data unbound. This is the method demonstrated in Listing 19.9, which retrieves a photo from the Northwind sample's `Employees` table.

LISTING 19.9   RETRIEVING LARGE DATA WITH SQLGetData

```
SQLCHAR    photoSQL[] = "SELECT EmployeeID,
➥Photo FROM Employees WHERE EmployeeID = 6";
const    photoSize = 262144;    // 256K bytes

void
GetPhoto( ODBCContext & ctx )
{
    bool        retval = false;
    SQLRETURN    sqlVal = SQL_SUCCESS;
    // copy of context
    ODBCContext ctx2;

    // table data variables
    void *      empPhoto = new BYTE[photoSize];
```

```
    SQLINTEGER   photoBytes;
    SQLINTEGER   empId;

/*
 * conection code elided
 *
 */
    // ctx2 is connected to Northwind; make a statement
    sqlVal = SQLAllocHandle( SQL_HANDLE_STMT, ctx2.hConn,
                             &ctx2.hStmt );

    if ( SQL_SUCCEEDED( sqlVal ) )
    {
        // Bind the integer return value from SQLBindCol;
        // use SQLGetData for the image information.
        SQLBindCol( ctx2.hStmt, 1, SQL_C_LONG, &empId,
                    SQL_IS_INTEGER, NULL );

        sqlVal = SQLExecDirect( ctx2.hStmt, photoSQL, SQL_NTS );

        if ( SQL_SUCCEEDED( sqlVal ) )
            sqlVal = SQLFetch( ctx2.hStmt );

        if ( SQL_SUCCEEDED( sqlVal ) )
        {
            // retrieve data until you don't get any or until
            // the buffer only fills partially or no data
            do
            {
                sqlVal = SQLGetData( ctx2.hStmt, 2, SQL_C_CHAR,
                                     empPhoto, photoSize,
                                     &photoBytes );

                if ( SQL_SUCCEEDED(sqlVal) &&
                     (photoBytes != SQL_NULL_DATA) )
                {
                    ; // put the data somewhere, process it, and so on
                }
            }
            while ( SQL_SUCCEEDED(sqlVal) &&
                    (photoBytes >= photoSize) );
        }

        if ( !SQL_SUCCEEDED(sqlVal) && (sqlVal != SQL_NO_DATA) )
            ShowSQLInfo( ctx2.hStmt, SQL_HANDLE_STMT );

        SQLCloseCursor( ctx2.hStmt );
        SQLFreeHandle( SQL_HANDLE_STMT, ctx2.hStmt );
    }
    else
```

19

OPTIMIZING
ODBC USING
VISUAL C++

continues

LISTING 19.9   CONTINUED

```
        ShowSQLInfo( ctx.hConn, SQL_HANDLE_DBC );

/*
 * shutdown code elided
 *
 */
    if ( empPhoto )
        delete [] empPhoto;
}
```

For this example, you use an explicit SELECT string to simplify the code. Retrieving the employee ID and photo from the database, you bind the empID variable to the ID column, an integer, but leave the image column unbound. You execute the statement and issue a fetch to retrieve the matching row, and then you retrieve the image's data in the DO...WHILE loop (the fetch retrieves bound columns immediately). SQLGetData retrieves up to the size of the buffer into the buffer you provide. While there is more data waiting, it returns the total size of the image in the indicator variable you pass by reference in the last parameter. When it has fetched the last block, it reports the number of bytes in the buffer from the last block. While more data remains, the function returns SQL_SUCCESS_WITH_INFO, with a SQLSTATE value of 01004 indicating that the data block was right-truncated.

Uploading data into the database isn't much more complex. You bind the image buffer as an input parameter in the same manner as the small data items. However, in the indicator for the column parameter, you store the SQL_LEN_DATA_AT_EXEC(datasize) macro's return value, to tell the driver how much data it gets for the BLOB parameter. In this case, the parameter data pointer need not be a pointer to a buffer; you can pass anything you like in this position, usually a value that indicates to your code where the data should come from.

When you execute the insert or update statement, the driver returns SQL_NEED_DATA to tell you to start sending blocks of data. Because you might need to send more than one column of BLOB data, you call SQLParamData now to ask the driver which column it's waiting for; you get back the value you passed to SQLBindParameter as the data pointer. Using this value to identify which column to send if you have more than one, you then call SQLPutData, repeatedly if necessary, until you have sent all the data you need to send for the column. To complete the operation, you call SQLParamData again, which tells the driver the column data has all been transferred and queries whether the driver is waiting for any other columns. The driver returns SQL_NEED_DATA again for the next column if it exists, and then you repeat the sending loop to send that data. If all columns have been sent, `SQLParamData` returns `SQL_SUCCESS` or `SQL_SUCCESS_WITH_INFO`, or whatever other `SQLRETURN` is appropriate if an error occurred. The code in Listing 19.10 follows these steps to create a new Employee record in Northwind and upload a photo. Note that, contrary to the examples you see in the online documentation, you can not pass a zero value for the `Column Size` parameter to `SQLBindParameter`. From empirical results, it seems that any nonzero value is acceptable, but passing zero causes an error with SQL Server.

LISTING 19.10 SENDING AN IMAGE TO THE Employee TABLE WITH `SQLPutData`

```
char      empLname[] = "Smith";
char      empFname[] = "John";
SQLCHAR empInsertSQL[] = "INSERT INTO Employees( " \
                         "FirstName, LastName, Photo ) " \
                         "VALUES( ?, ?, ? )";
void
InsertPhoto( ODBCContext & ctx )
{
    // insert a bitmap into the employees table in Northwind.
    SQLRETURN       sqlVal;

    HANDLE       hFile, rxFile; // handle we set,
                                // handle we get back from ODBC
    BYTE         buffer[8192];  // 8K transfer buffer
    long         fileSize;
    ULONG        bytesIread;
    SQLINTEGER photoInd = 0, fnameInd = 0, lnameInd = 0;

    // open the file
    hFile = CreateFile( "photo.bmp", GENERIC_READ, 0, NULL,
                        OPEN_EXISTING, FILE_FLAG_SEQUENTIAL_SCAN,
                        NULL );

    if ( hFile && (hFile != INVALID_HANDLE_VALUE) )
    {
        // get how much data to send
        fileSize = GetFileSize( hFile, NULL );

        // establish the database connection
        // *** connect code removed ***

        sqlVal = SQLPrepare( ctx.hStmt, empInsertSQL, SQL_NTS );

        fnameInd = lstrlen( empFname );
        lnameInd = lstrlen( empLname );

        // have to define this variable even though it's
        // never used for anything
```

continues

19

OPTIMIZING
ODBC USING
VISUAL C++

LISTING 19.10   CONTINUED

```
// but to pass the last value to SQLBindParameter
photoInd = SQL_LEN_DATA_AT_EXEC(fileSize);

SQLBindParameter( ctx.hStmt, 1,
                  SQL_PARAM_INPUT,
                  SQL_C_CHAR, SQL_CHAR,
                  lstrlen( empFname ), 0,
                  empFname, sizeof( empFname ),
                  &fnameInd );

if ( SQL_SUCCEEDED(sqlVal) )
    sqlVal = SQLBindParameter( ctx.hStmt, 2,
                  SQL_PARAM_INPUT,
                  SQL_C_CHAR, SQL_CHAR,
                  lstrlen( empLname ), 0,
                  empLname, sizeof( empLname ),
                  &lnameInd );

if ( SQL_SUCCEEDED(sqlVal) )
    sqlVal = SQLBindParameter( ctx.hStmt, 3,
                  SQL_PARAM_INPUT,
                  SQL_C_BINARY, SQL_LONGVARBINARY,
                  sizeof( buffer ), 0, hFile, 0,
                  &photoInd );

if ( SQL_SUCCEEDED(sqlVal) )
    sqlVal = SQLExecute( ctx.hStmt );

if ( sqlVal == SQL_NEED_DATA )
{
    sqlVal = SQLParamData( ctx.hStmt, &rxFile );
    ASSERT( rxFile == hFile );

    do
    {
        ReadFile( hFile, buffer, sizeof( buffer ),
                  &bytesIread, NULL );
        sqlVal = SQLPutData( ctx.hStmt, buffer,
                             bytesIread );
    }
    while ( SQL_SUCCEEDED( sqlVal ) &&
            (bytesIread == sizeof(buffer)) );

    sqlVal = SQLParamData( ctx.hStmt, &rxFile );

} // end if statement executed okay and need more input

if ( !SQL_SUCCEEDED(sqlVal) )
    ShowSQLInfo( ctx.hStmt, SQL_HANDLE_STMT );
```

```
    // *** database cleanup removed ***

    CloseHandle( hFile );
  } // end if file open worked
}
```

Simplifying ODBC with Microsoft Foundation Classes

Well, you braved the depths of ODBC and came out unscathed (if a little muddy). Now you can step back a little from the API and discuss the Microsoft Foundation Classes' support for ODBC. In terms of object-oriented abstraction, MFC does only a moderate amount to isolate you from the complexities of ODBC, but what little it does has a huge impact.

MFC simplifies database access by modeling it as two items: a database and a recordset. With these two items, the entirety of an SQL database is made available. The abstraction, however, is deceptively simple; with the knowledge you have gained of ODBC, these two items can be made to perform nearly as well as raw ODBC code, with a significant reduction in the complexity of your client code. As in any program element, reduced complexity usually means fewer bugs and easier maintenance.

Object Model

The objects in the MFC database interface give you a thin layer over the ODBC API, but they add considerable value by bringing along a large body of code for moving, translating, and presenting data to your application. The CDatabase class encapsulates the data source connection, and a statement and resultset are combined into the CRecordset class. This is much better than the profligate array of objects, functions, types, and so forth, a beginner must master to use the CLI.

The classes I'll discuss that relate to database access are summarized in Table 19.14.

TABLE 19.14 MFC ODBC CLASSES

Class	Purpose
CDatabase	Contains the environment and connection to the database; maintains connection-level options and above
CDBException	Cexception subclass that provides database state variables along with exception data

continues

TABLE 19.14 CONTINUED

Class	Purpose
CFieldExchange	Contains constant definitions and data for record field exchange
CLongBinary, CByteArray	Classes for manipulating BLOB data
CRecordset	Contains data on ODBC statement and its resultset/cursor

The entire example of connecting to a database with CDatabase, executing a query, and then disconnecting is contained in Listing 19.11. This is as simple as database access gets in C++; the CRecordset-derived CAuthors class is missing because you don't write that. You're going to look first at the code in the example, and then I'll talk about creating the CAuthors recordset.

The code in Listing 19.11 receives an author ID as an input parameter and an auInfo structure for an in/out parameter, into which it places information for the author identified by the id parameter. To retrieve the information, it creates a CDatabase object that it connects to the pubs DSN with CDatabase::OpenEx. It then creates a CRecordset-derived CAuthors object on the database object it just created. To query for the author in question, the program sets the recordset's filter string to the WHERE criterion desired, au_id = '<the value passed in>', and then it opens the recordset. In the Open member function, the recordset's query is executed and the first record fetched from the database. In this case, because you're searching on an exact match for the primary key, this is also the *only* record in the resultset. If a record was found, the information from it is copied to the auInfo variable, and the function returns true.

LISTING 19.11 THE CODE SAMPLE FOR A SIMPLE DATABASE OPERATION

```
#include "Authors.h"     // CAuthors recordset

bool
MFCQuery( const char * au_id, AuthorInformation & auInfo )
{
    bool    retval = false;
    CDatabase    db;    // connection to the database

     try
    {
        db.OpenEx( "DSN=pubs;Trusted_Connection=TRUE",
                  CDatabase::noOdbcDialog );

        // retrieve the data using the CAuthors class,
        // which is built on the authors table in pubs.
```

```
        CAuthors    auRS( &db );

        // set the WHERE criteria
        auRS.m_strFilter.Format( "au_id = '%s'", au_id );

        auRS.Open();

        if ( !auRS.IsEOF() )
        {
            // got the record, copy out the information.
            strcpy( auInfo.au_lname, auRS.m_au_lname );
            strcpy( auInfo.au_fname, auRS.m_au_fname );
            strcpy( auInfo.phone, auRS.m_phone );
            strcpy( auInfo.address, auRS.m_address );
            strcpy( auInfo.city, auRS.m_city );
            strcpy( auInfo.state, auRS.m_state );
            strcpy( auInfo.zip, auRS.m_zip );
            auInfo.contract = auRS.m_contract != 0;
        }
        else
            MessageBox( NULL,
                    "No data matched the supplied id",
                    "Retrieve failed", MB_OK );

        auRS.Close();

        retval = true;      // if you get here, you're ok.
    }
    catch( CDBException * dbe )
    {
        dbe->ReportError();
    }
    catch( ... )
    {
        MessageBox( NULL, "Unknown exception encountered",
            "MFCQuery error", MB_ICONEXCLAMATION );
        throw;
    }

    if ( db.IsOpen() )
        db.Close();

    return retval;
}
```

CDatabase

Connecting to the database is as simple as declaring a CDatabase and calling its Open or OpenEx member function with a connection string. There are two main differences between Open and OpenEx: the parameters on the connection you can set and the formulation of the connection string.

With Open, you can specify the name of the DSN and/or a connection string, and one of three flags: exclusive open, read-only open, and whether to use the ODBC Cursor Library. I suppose the exclusive flag is supplied for compatibility, but the version 6.0 MFC library does not support it at all. The connection string you pass to Open must start with ODBC; a, la Visual Basic; the connection string you give OpenEx, on the other hand, cannot have this keyword on the string, but the function adds it to the m_strConnect variable it saves to reconnect! Strange but true...

With OpenEx, your options are much simpler than Open; you pass it the connection string and an or-connected list of the database options you want set. The option list is not the ODBC option values, but an enumeration in the declaration of CDatabase. Table 19.15 lists these options and their effect.

TABLE 19.15 LEGAL VALUES FOR THE dwOptions PARAMETER TO CDatabase::Open

Option	Effect
CDatabase::openExclusive	Connection failure; this option is not supported.
CDatabase::openReadOnly	Prohibits updating the database on this connection.
CDatabase::useCursorLib	Use the cursor library to simulate cursors.
CDatabase::noOdbcDialog	Do not display connection dialogs at all; uses SQL_DRIVER_NOPROMPT.
CDatabase::forceOdbcDialog	Always display the connection dialog; uses SQL_DRI-VER_PROMPT.

The example uses the OpenEx function with a connect string to go ahead and connect to the database without further ado. If you'd rather, you can use the following to connect with the defaults:

```
db.Open( "pubs" );
```

If you have the pubs data source set up to use a trusted connection, it connects to the server without delay; if the DSN is set to use standard authentication, the user is prompted for a user ID and password. Because this method connects using the default of SQL_DRIVER_COMPLETE, it cannot be used on a connection that has connection pooling turned on, but the OpenEx in the example functions correctly.

CRecordset

The CRecordset class uses the CDatabase class to keep track of the environment and connection handles, as well as a list of the CRecordset instances that are allocated on the connection. CRecordset does not, however, use the CDatabase object to issue queries; it has its own operations to take care of manipulating table data with the assistance of the CFieldExchange class. The bulk of the statement-related code is maintained in the CRecordset, and CFieldExchange handles field-related operations, such as parameter and column bindings.

CRecordset follows the same high-level operations as ADO recordsets for data updates, but it has quite a bit of additional capability to retrieve and manipulate characteristics of its ODBC behavior. With MFC, though, you access them only if you need to; it's not required with MFC and Visual Studio.

Errors in the MFC ODBC classes are usually propagated by using exceptions of type CDBException. This class contains, in addition to the CException class's methods, the return code from the ODBC function that failed (m_nRetCode), the ODBC-defined error message (m_strError), and the native database error message (m_strStateNativeOrigin).

NOTE

The ODBC database classes are thread-safe, but the same problems with threading are present here as in any other application. Consider what synchronization is necessary when you design your application; if you want to avoid most problems easily without additional programming, then share a CDatabase object among threads, but not CRecordset objects. Because the ODBC database driver is a DLL loaded in the program's process space, it must be thread-safe, too (SQL Server's is).

When starting your thread, remember to use the Visual C++ runtime function _beginthread(ex) so that the new thread's runtime library is set up correctly. I do not know of an upper limit on the number of connections you can have in your program in theory. In practice, while testing software for this chapter, I

continues

19

OPTIMIZING
ODBC USING
VISUAL C++

> observed a maximum of about 1,300–1,400 threads on a machine with 96MB of RAM. After the kernel ran out of memory, the system simply hung any further calls to Win32's `CreateThread` until an existing thread exited.
>
> Much higher throughput resulted, by the way, when new connections were offset by as little as 19 milliseconds, compared to just dumping a bunch of threads out.

As Simple As It Gets: Using Recordsets and Class Wizard

Using recordsets is so easy it might make you wonder why I didn't cut to the chase and skip talking about the functional interface to ODBC. The answer is that right underneath the surface of the `CDatabase` and `CRecordset` classes is the ODBC CLI API. As soon as you want to do anything more complicated than just looking up a record, or if you start wondering about performance, you have to know how to program ODBC, or you'll never find out. Without the information that precedes this section, the MFC ODBC classes are a sharp knife, but with only one blade. With that knowledge, you get the screwdriver, the nail file, and the funny little spring-loaded scissors.

With a recordset, you can find, retrieve, update, and delete records in the database using a very small number of commands. Compared to the code in the introductory example, relatively well-organized C code using ODBC was more than 400 lines. You can retrieve BLOBs from the database almost as easily as simple character data with MFC, but ODBC's complexity balloons upward when you begin using large data. When you create a recordset, all the low-level code is generated or copied from code that already works, so you can be pretty sure that yours will, too (although you can still have performance or concurrency items to deal with). If you start to think that it's wiser to use MFC for ODBC than program the interface directly, you're probably right. In some specific instances, you'll have to do bare-metal ODBC, but those situations are few.

Subclassing `CRecordset` with Class Wizard

To get started with a recordset, open Visual C++ and either open or create a project in which to place your recordset. You're going to use Class Wizard to create your recordsets most of the time. The New Class Wizard walks you all the way through, selecting a database, a table, and which columns to include in the data you use. The first step is to make the target project active and then choose Insert, New Class from the menu to produce the dialog shown in Figure 19.13.

FIGURE 19.13

The New Class dialog.

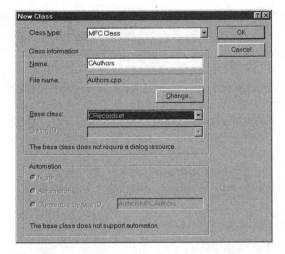

Leave the class type as MFC Class, and then type a name for the class (I followed the MFC convention in the example, calling the class CAuthors). The wizard defaults the filenames to <*classname*>.h and <*classname*>.cpp, but you can change these assignments by clicking the Change button and typing the filenames you prefer. Select CRecordset from the Base Class drop-down list to set the parent class for CAuthors, and the Automation area grays out. When you're satisfied with what you have filled in, click OK. Be sure that you get this right; if you want to change any of this information later, it's not fun and quite prone to error.

The next display (shown in Figure 19.14) lets you hook up the data class to a data source. This sets the default connection for the recordset and lets Class Wizard query the database for schema information so that it can create the class with correct data types and mappings to columns. On this screen you can use the drop-down list to select a data source name from which Class Wizard gets the information it needs. In the Recordset Type area, select either a snapshot or dynaset, terms originating in Visual Basic that essentially mean that the recordset will use a static, forward-only cursor (for the Snapshot option) or a keyset-driven cursor (for the Dynaset option). Finally, you can choose to bind all columns in the table (VC6 lets you create recordsets on views, too) or not; if you choose not to, you need to use Class Wizard after the recordset has been created to bind database columns.

19

OPTIMIZING
ODBC USING
VISUAL C++

> **TIP**
>
> The Visual C++ Class Wizard doesn't allow you to specify Dynamic for a cursor type when creating a recordset, but you can set it in your code after it's created by Class Wizard. Open the class's `.cpp` file, go to the constructor for the class, and change the line `m_nDefaultType = snapshot;` to `m_nDefaultType = dynamic;`, and it's done.

FIGURE 19.14

Database options in the New Class Wizard.

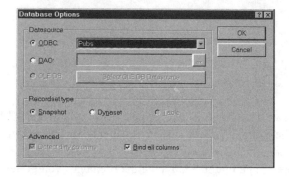

Click OK, and you can pick your table or view from a list of those in the database (see Figure 19.15). You can select more than one table here, although by default they are not correlated in the resultset. I'll get to that, though, so for now just pick the `authors` table and click OK to proceed.

FIGURE 19.15

The Select Database Tables dialog in the New Class Wizard.

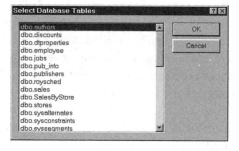

After you pick the tables and click OK, Class Wizard creates the C++ files to implement the recordset with the names and characteristics you indicated. From the options used for this example, you get a recordset that is instantiated as in Listings 19.12 and 19.13. Basic use of this `CRecordset`-derived class is demonstrated in the introductory sample.

LISTING 19.12 THE Authors RECORDSET HEADER CREATED BY CLASS WIZARD

```
#if !defined(AFX_AUTHORS_H__3B8A14C3_..._INCLUDED_)
#define AFX_AUTHORS_H__3B8A14C3_..._INCLUDED_

#if _MSC_VER > 1000
#pragma once
#endif // _MSC_VER > 1000
// Authors.h : header file
//

/////////////////////////////////////////////////////////
// CAuthors recordset

class CAuthors : public CRecordset
{
public:
    CAuthors(CDatabase* pDatabase = NULL);
    DECLARE_DYNAMIC(CAuthors)

// Field/Param Data
    //{{AFX_FIELD(CAuthors, CRecordset)
    CString    m_au_id;
    CString    m_au_lname;
    CString    m_au_fname;
    CString    m_phone;
    CString    m_address;
    CString    m_city;
    CString    m_state;
    CString    m_zip;
    BOOL    m_contract;
    //}}AFX_FIELD


// Overrides
    // ClassWizard generated virtual function overrides
    //{{AFX_VIRTUAL(CAuthors)
    public:
    virtual CString GetDefaultConnect();
                                // Default connection string
    virtual CString GetDefaultSQL();
                                // Default SQL for Recordset
    virtual void DoFieldExchange(CFieldExchange* pFX);
                                // RFX support

    //}}AFX_VIRTUAL

// Implementation
#ifdef _DEBUG
```

continues

LISTING 19.12 CONTINUED

```cpp
    virtual void AssertValid() const;
    virtual void Dump(CDumpContext& dc) const;
#endif
};


//{{AFX_INSERT_LOCATION}}
// Microsoft Visual C++ will insert additional
        declarations immediately before the previous line.

#endif // !defined(AFX_AUTHORS_H__3B8A14C3_..._INCLUDED_)
```

LISTING 19.13 THE Authors RECORDSET IMPLEMENTATION CREATED BY CLASS WIZARD

```cpp
// Authors.cpp : implementation file
//

#include "stdafx.h"
#include "ODBC.h"
#include "Authors.h"

#ifdef _DEBUG
#define new DEBUG_NEW
#undef THIS_FILE
static char THIS_FILE[] = __FILE__;
#endif


/////////////////////////////////////////////////////////
// CAuthors

IMPLEMENT_DYNAMIC(CAuthors, CRecordset)

CAuthors::CAuthors(CDatabase* pdb)
    : CRecordset(pdb)
{
    //{{AFX_FIELD_INIT(CAuthors)
    m_au_id = _T("");
    m_au_lname = _T("");
    m_au_fname = _T("");
    m_phone = _T("");
    m_address = _T("");
    m_city = _T("");
    m_state = _T("");
    m_zip = _T("");
    m_contract = FALSE;
    m_nFields = 9;
    //}}AFX_FIELD_INIT
    m_nDefaultType = dynaset;
}
```

```
CString CAuthors::GetDefaultConnect()
{
    return _T("ODBC;DSN=Pubs");
}

CString CAuthors::GetDefaultSQL()
{
    return _T("[dbo].[authors]");
}

void CAuthors::DoFieldExchange(CFieldExchange* pFX)
{
    //{{AFX_FIELD_MAP(CAuthors)
    pFX->SetFieldType(CFieldExchange::outputColumn);
    RFX_Text(pFX, _T("[au_id]"), m_au_id);
    RFX_Text(pFX, _T("[au_lname]"), m_au_lname);
    RFX_Text(pFX, _T("[au_fname]"), m_au_fname);
    RFX_Text(pFX, _T("[phone]"), m_phone);
    RFX_Text(pFX, _T("[address]"), m_address);
    RFX_Text(pFX, _T("[city]"), m_city);
    RFX_Text(pFX, _T("[state]"), m_state);
    RFX_Text(pFX, _T("[zip]"), m_zip);
    RFX_Bool(pFX, _T("[contract]"), m_contract);
    //}}AFX_FIELD_MAP
}

/////////////////////////////////////////////////////////
// CAuthors diagnostics

#ifdef _DEBUG
void CAuthors::AssertValid() const
{
    CRecordset::AssertValid();
}

void CAuthors::Dump(CDumpContext& dc) const
{
    CRecordset::Dump(dc);
}
#endif //_DEBUG
```

The CRecordset subclass that Class Wizard creates has member data for each column you bind, either by selecting the Bind All Columns check box when you create it or specifying it on the Member Variables tab in Class Wizard. It also writes five member functions with the following roles:

- GetDefaultConnect—Returns a connect string with only the DSN used to create the recordset

- GetDefaultSQL—Returns a string containing the ODBC SQL name for the source of the data within the DSN (in this case, the authors table)

- DoFieldExchange—Distributes Record Field Exchange messages to transfer column and parameter data between ODBC and the object's member variables

- AssertValid—Should perform an internal self-check per MFC conventions, but default behavior defers to the superclass

- Dump—Should serialize debug text about the recordset's state to the dump context provided; default refers upward to CRecordset

Operations on the CRecordset Subclass

The four standard operations (create, retrieve, update, and delete) are simple using recordsets. The original sample already demonstrates the retrieve (SELECT) operation; to filter a query, you set the m_strFilter string to the criteria that should follow the keyword WHERE in a SELECT statement. In the example, you used CString's member function Format to construct a filter with the author ID passed into the function.

The CRecordset object has two data members you use to specify what data it retrieves:

- m_strFilter   The criterion string that is placed after the WHERE when the query is constructed to retrieve the recordset's resultset

- m_strSort   The sort criteria placed after the ORDER BY in the query

The recordset issues the statement on which it's based when opened, creating the resultset and cursor it will use, so it can fill its member variables with the data from the first retrieved row. Therefore, setting either of these values after you call Open has no effect.

You have already seen the use of the m_strFilter string to retrieve data. Creating a record is just as simple as retrieving one. After opening the recordset, you call the AddNew() member to create a new record. Assign the values that should be placed in the new record to the appropriate member variables in the recordset, and then call Update to commit the change, as in Listing 19.14.

LISTING 19.14 INSERTING A RECORD USING A RECORDSET

```
CAuthors    auRS( &db );

// set the WHERE criteria
auRS.m_strFilter = "NOT (au_id = au_id)";

auRS.Open();

auRS.AddNew();
    // got the record, copy out the information.
    auRS.m_au_id = "123-45-6789";
    auRS.m_au_lname = "Robison";
    auRS.m_au_fname = "William";
    auRS.m_phone = "408-555-1212";
    auRS.m_address = "1234 Main Street";
    auRS.m_city = "Redwood Shores";
    auRS.m_state = "CA";
    auRS.m_zip = "20104";
    auRS.m_contract = 1;
auRS.Update();

auRS.Close();
```

Pay attention to the `m_strFilter` expression explicitly set to a criterion that can never be true. If there is a large amount of data in the table, this keeps SQL Server 6.5 from creating a large resultset when the recordset is opened. This is another performance killer.

With a recordset, an update is simply a matter of seeking to the record you want to update, calling the recordset's `Edit` function, and then calling `Update` to commit the changes. The code in Listing 19.15 changes an author's first name to "Aristotle."

LISTING 19.15 UPDATING A RECORD USING A `CRecordset`

```
CAuthors    auRS( &db );

// set the WHERE criteria
auRS.m_strFilter = "au_id = '123-45-6789'";

auRS.Open();

if ( !auRS.IsEOF() )
{
    auRS.Edit();
        // got the record, update the information.
        auRS.m_au_fname = "Aristotle";
    auRS.Update()
}

auRS.Close();
```

Deleting a record is identical to updating it, but you call the `CRecordset::Delete` function after the cursor is positioned on the record to delete. The record is immediately deleted; you should not call `Updates` as with `AddNew` and `Edit`.

Recordset Navigation

For nonsearched updates (that is, using client-side scans) or iteration over a resultset (fetches), `CRecordset` includes navigation functions consistent with other data access technologies from Microsoft. Table 19.16 lists the navigation functions and their effects. Keep in mind that navigation is restricted by the underlying resultset's cursor type, so trying to `MovePrev` on a default snapshot recordset (which is based on a static, forward-only cursor) would fail.

TABLE 19.16   CRecordset NAVIGATION MEMBERS

Member Name	Purpose
MoveFirst	Sets the cursor position to the first row in the resultset
MoveLast	Sets the cursor position to the last row in the resultset
MoveNext	Moves the cursor to the next row in the resultset
MovePrev	Moves the cursor to the previous row in the resultset
Move	Moves the cursor position a specified number of rows in one operation
IsBOF	Returns TRUE if the cursor is positioned on the first row in the resultset
IsEOF	Returns TRUE if the cursor is positioned on the last row in the resultset

Connecting to SQL Server from Visual Basic

IN THIS CHAPTER

This chapter describes designing and developing MS Visual Basic 6.0 applications that access a SQL Server 7.0 database. First, the chapter focuses on discussing the three-tier model of software systems and different implementations of the model. When designing the system, a user also needs an understanding of the programming interfaces a Visual Basic program can use to access SQL Server data. This chapter explains details of using both ODBC (open database connectivity) call-level interface and object interfaces, such as Data Access Objects (DAO) and Remote Data Objects (RDO).

Developing Efficient Visual Basic Applications for SQL Server

Designing and programming large complex systems for SQL Server can be a challenge for a software developer, who must choose programming languages and tools, make a proper database design, select algorithms and data structures, and design the graphical user interface and the application interface. One of the most important decisions in the software design is the location of the applications. In other words, the designer has to specify where such parts of the system as data, business rules, data entry programs, and other pieces of the running code are going to be located.

MS Visual Basic supports a few program interfaces to database management systems, particularly to SQL Server. Call-level interfaces include ODBC and DB-Library interfaces, object interfaces include Data Access Objects (DAO), Remote Data Objects (RDO), OLE DB, and ActiveX Data Objects (ADO). There is also a special SQL Distributed Management Objects (SQL-DMO) interface for SQL Server administration tasks. The right choice of the interface can drastically change both the performance of the entire system and the speed of development.

Three-Tier Application Model: Choosing an Implementation

Designing a big data warehousing system needs the proper selection of the application model. The traditional client/server model was recently improved by adding a middle layer to the model that made it a three-tier model. The three-tier approach divides the system into three logical components, as shown in Figure 20.1.

FIGURE 20.1
Three-tier architecture.

The details of this model are discussed in the following list. Each tier of the model is responsible for providing services.

- **Data Services**   Data services maintain data and operations on data, such as adding, modifying, deleting, and archiving. These services maintain data relationships and integrity, support backup, and restore operations. Usually the data services are represented by a database management system.

- **Business Services**   Business services contain business rules and data processing logic, such as data validation rules, transaction processing support, and record archiving logic. The main purpose of these services is to apply the logic of data maintenance specific to the application.

- **Presentation (or User) Services**   Presentation services support a user interface and handle user data input and data presentation (output).

> **NOTE**
>
> In client/server terminology, sometimes presentation services are defined as a *client* (or a *front-end*), data services as a *server* (or a *back-end*), and business services as a *middle layer*. However, it's important to understand that each two pieces can represent the communication between a client and a server. For example, the middle layer can be a server for the front-end.

The physical implementation of the system can be done in a number of different ways. I'll discuss details of the following three implementations of the logical three-tier model:

- Fat client implementation
- Thin client implementation
- Multitier implementation

20

CONNECTING TO
SQL SERVER
FROM VB

Fat Client Implementation

One of the implementation options for the three-tier model is running business and pre-sentation services on the client. This is possibly the most popular approach to writing Visual Basic applications for SQL Server. This implementation physically has only two tiers, in which the server supports only data services, as shown in Figure 20.2.

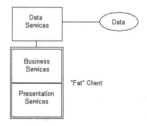

There are a couple of disadvantages to this approach. First, by increasing the application code on the client computer, the client computer has to be more powerful, which increases the system cost because you usually consider systems with many clients. When the system should work with hundreds and thousands of clients, this approach can become too expensive.

Another disadvantage of the fat client implementation is the possible increase of maintenance costs. Every change of the validation logic and the business rules in the system results in upgrading the client programs. It could become a problem if the system has a considerable number of clients.

The primary advantage of the fat client implementation is in decreasing the network traffic if the validation and business rules can be specified without referring to the database. In this case, only the data that passed the validation is transferred to the server. As an example of input data validation, say you have small tables, such as a country names table, residing on the client computer. If the data entry module checks the local table instead of comparing the country name against the main database, that would certainly decrease the network traffic.

Another important consideration is the process of the system development. If the developers of the front-end are limited in their access to the back-end and, for example, can't validate the input against the data in the database, this approach enables them to process the data correctly.

Thin Client Implementation

In the thin client implementation, the business services are located on the server. The business logic is usually represented with stored procedures. For SQL Server databases, the stored procedures are coded in Transact-SQL. This implementation, like the fat client implementation, physically has two tiers also, as shown in Figure 20.3.

FIGURE 20.3

*Thin client imple-
mentation.*

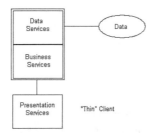

The advantage of this approach is decreasing the system cost because the thin client needs fewer system resources, which is important for a system with many clients. Also, the maintenance cost might be lower than in systems with fat clients because the code is concentrated on the server side.

If the business rules depend on the data in the database, the thin client approach decreases the network traffic.

The major disadvantage of this approach is lack of flexibility of the stored procedures. Visual Basic offers much more programming power than Transact-SQL.

> **NOTE**
>
> The thin client physical implementation of the three-tier model is sometimes called the *fat server model* to avoid confusion with the thin client/server computing model, which refers to a thin client hardware device and a technology such as Citrix.

Multitier Implementation

The simplest multitier implementation is a three-tier one, one of the many possible physical implementations of the three-tier model. In this implementation, business services run as a separate process. This process can be configured to run on the same server where the data services are located, or it can be located on a different server.

20

CONNECTING TO
SQL SERVER
FROM VB

The key distinction of this implementation is that data services, business services, and presentation services can run as separate processes on different computers. The three-tier implementation is shown in Figure 20.4.

FIGURE 20.4

Three-tier imple-mentation.

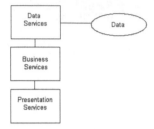

The Internet has added a new flavor to the three-tier models. Web technology splits presentation services into a browser client and the Web server. Increasing the number of clients has also resulted in using tools such as Microsoft Transaction Server (MTS), which is designed to increase the middle tier's flexibility by using COM objects. Splitting presentation services or adding COM components to the middle layer results in additional tiers in the physical implementation.

The advantage of this approach is that the multitier systems are more scalable and more flexible. If the business rules consume too many computer resources, it might be advantageous to separate the middle tier from the data services and run the code on a separate computer. However, this solution increases the network traffic and can slow the system down if the traffic becomes too intensive.

Choosing a Physical Implementation

When making a decision about the physical implementation of the three-tier model, you have to take into consideration a few features of the system:

- **Amount of data**   If the database is huge, you have to separate the data services and might even run them on a separate computer (or computers).
- **A complexity of business rules**   If the business rules are too complex or are going to grow, it might be advantageous to separate the business rules into one process or into a set of COM objects.
- **Reusability of the code**   If you want to use the business rules with different front ends, it is also a good idea to separate them in a set of COM objects.
- **Maintenance issues**   In a system with many clients, maintenance and support are cheaper if the client program is thin.

- **Network traffic**   In distributed systems, particularly in Internet-based systems, the traffic issues become very important. If the business rules are data driven, they should reside as close to the data services as possible.

Call-Level and Object Interfaces: Choosing an Interface

When developing a Visual Basic application that accesses SQL Server data, it's important to correctly choose a programming interface. There are several call-level and object interfaces that allow access to SQL Server data.

Call-Level Interfaces

A *call-level interface* is an Application Programming Interface (API) that supplies a set of function calls for accessing the data. This type of interface was the only choice for developers a few years ago. APIs usually come in the form of dynamic link libraries (DLLs) and can be accessed from Visual Basic.

The common problem with APIs in a Windows environment is that Visual Basic applications sometimes can't provide the data types that the APIs specified for input parameters. In this case, a developer has to write a mapping layer between the Visual Basic application and the API. Fortunately, both interfaces discussed in this chapter were written in a standard way that supports calls from a Visual Basic program.

SQL Server offers two call-level interfaces to a Visual Basic programmer:

- DB-Library
- Open database connectivity (ODBC)

DB-Library is an API developed by Microsoft to provide function calls to SQL Server. Therefore, the DB-Library is SQL Server specific and cannot be used with another database management system. For a few years, the DB-Library interface was preferred to SQL Server. However, with the invention of other interfaces, DB-Library has become obsolete.

ODBC is an industry standard that supports SQL requests to relational databases. A database management system provider usually distributes an ODBC driver, a layer that translates a SQL statement to the access function of the particular database. Using ODBC for development is more convenient than DB-Library: DB-Library has more functions than ODBC (approximately 150 versus 50 in ODBC), but ODBC is easier to learn and can also be used for other database management systems.

Object Interfaces

With the evolution of object-oriented programming, API-type interfaces are being replaced with object interfaces. In such interfaces, objects are created to access a database instead of using direct function calls. You can set and get an object property or call a method. The programming code becomes cleaner and simpler to develop and maintain.

Microsoft uses several object interfaces to access data in a database management system such as SQL Server:

- Data Access Objects (DAO)
- Remote Data Objects (RDO)
- OLE DB
- ActiveX Data Objects

The DAO interface was developed to access local databases through the Jet database engine that comes with MS Visual Basic or MS Access. DAO is optimized for Jet databases, so it's probably not the right choice if the application has to access only SQL Server databases. However, DAO can join data from multiple data sources, which can be considered a big advantage of this interface.

RDO is closely tied to ODBC and works considerably faster than DAO when accessing SQL Server databases. It was developed to access server rather than local databases. The RDO functionality is similar to DAO, so it's preferable to DAO in SQL Server applications. However, RDO doesn't allow joining data sources or accessing Jet database.

An important feature of RDO is that it returns an ODBC handle to a Visual Basic program, therefore giving you the ability to use ODBC features that aren't supported in RDO.

OLE DB can be thought of as a successor or an object version of the ODBC API. ADO is definitely a successor of DAO and RDO. Both OLE DB and ADO work faster than DAO and RDO. ADO is also accessible from scripting languages such as VBScript, which could make it a new industry standard.

Figure 20.5 shows the results of comparing the speeds of different data access interfaces.

In this list of different data models ADO is rapidly becoming the most popular one. The basics of ADO are covered in Chapter 23. The ease of use and learning certainly will make it more popular than ADO or RDO. The possibility of using ADO along with ODBC or OLE DB makes it even more attractive to software developers. However, currently, not every OLE DB provider supports all ADO features. Therefore, the idea of using ADO as a universal interface is still not working.

FIGURE 20.5

Comparing the speed of SQL Server data access from a Visual Basic program.

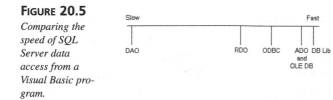

Using Open Database Connectivity (ODBC)

SQL Server ODBC Driver: ODBC Overview and Setup

The SQL Server ODBC driver provides a communication layer between client applications and the database server. There is a rumor in the database developers' community that the ODBC driver seriously slows data processing down, compared with the DB-Library. The rumor is based on ODBC drivers usually being implemented as an additional layer on top of the native database management system API. However, the implementation of the SQL Server ODBC is quite different. In fact, the ODBC driver replaced SQL Server's native API—DB-Library. Tests have shown that the performance of an ODBC-based SQL Server application is approximately the same as the performance of a DB-Library–based application.

Table 20.1 shows the transport architecture for the ODBC client communication to the SQL Server machine.

TABLE 20.1   ODBC AND SQL SERVER COMMUNICATION ARCHITECTURE

TCP/IP	*Novell*
Windows 32-Bit Application	**Windows 32-Bit Application**
ODBC Driver Manager (odbc32.dll)	ODBC Driver Manager (odbc32.dll)
SQL Server ODBC driver (sqlsrv32.dll)	SQL Server ODBC driver (sqlsrv32.dll)
Client network library (dbmssocn.dll)	Client network library (dbmsspxn.dll)

continues

TABLE 20.1 CONTINUED

TCP/IP	*Novell*
Windows 32-Bit Application	**Windows 32-Bit Application**
TCP/IP protocol	Novell protocol
Server network library (ssmssocn.dll)	Server network library (ssmsspxn.dll)
Open Data Services	Open Data Services
SQL Server	SQL Server

This architecture consists of the following components:

- **Client Application**   The application calls the ODBC API and passes SQL statements to be executed on the server.

- **ODBC Driver Manager**   The ODBC Driver Manager manages the communication between the application and the ODBC drivers. This very thin layer analyzes the program request, loads the driver, and passes the request to the driver. The driver manager for 32-bit Windows operating systems, `odbc32.dll`, is located by default in the system folder.

- **SQL Server ODBC Driver**   The SQL Server ODBC driver for 32-bit Windows operating systems, `sqlsrv32.dll`, is located by default in the system folder. The driver is responsible for handling the calls from the client application. If necessary, the driver translates the ANSI or ODBC SQL statements into the Transact-SQL syntax and passes them to the SQL Server machine.

- **SQL Server Network Transport**   The driver communicates with the SQL Server via the network libraries using the TDS (Tabular Data Stream) protocol. The network protocol stack, which resides on both the client and the server, transfers the data from the clients to the SQL Server and back. The Server Net-Library resides on the server and provides the transport connection to the SQL Server machine. There are different Net-Libraries for TCP/IP Windows Sockets, named pipes, Novell SPX/IPX, Banyan VINES, and so forth.

- **Open Data Services**   This part of the system supports an API for accessing the server. Open Data Services receives the TDS packets and transfers them to SQL Server.

- **SQL Server**   This is the main server engine that processes all requests from the SQL Server clients and directly accesses the data.

Setting Up a Data Source

In this section, you're going to write an application to access the database for a travel agency. By means of the SQL Server Enterprise Manager, I created the Travel database and added the Hotel table to it. Figure 20.6 shows the SQL Server 7.0 Enterprise Manager screen with the Travel data dictionary.

FIGURE 20.6

The Travel database viewed by SQL Server Enterprise Manager.

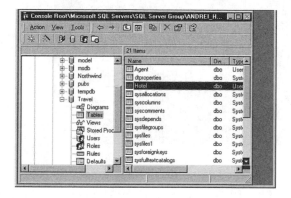

To set up a new data source, you have to run the ODBC Data Source Administrator program on the client computer. You can find it under the name "ODBC Data Sources" in Windows NT or "32-bit ODBC" in Windows 95 in the system's Control Panel. Figure 20.7 shows the icon for this program.

FIGURE 20.7

The ODBC Data Source Administrator icon.

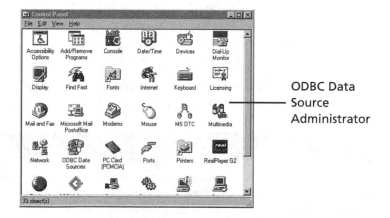

ODBC Data
Source
Administrator

A double-click on this icon brings up the ODBC Data Source Administrator screen. To set up the ODBC data source, follow theses steps:

1. Select the System DSN tab on the main screen. Other users will be able to use this DSN as well.

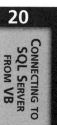

2. Click the Add button. The ODBC Data Source Administrator brings up a list of installed ODBC drivers. The SQL Server driver is included in several Microsoft packages. You can install it, for example, from the MS Visual Studio CD-ROM.

3. Select the SQL Server driver. Figure 20.8 shows the resulting screen.

FIGURE 20.8

Creating an ODBC data source.

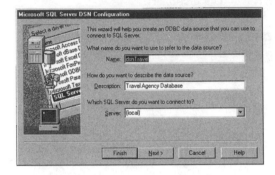

4. Click the Finish button and follow the dialogs.

5. Enter the name of the data source in the Name text box. For this example, use `dsnTravel` for the name in your ODBC connection.

6. Enter the description of the data source in the Description text box. The description is needed for information purposes only.

7. Enter the name of the SQL Server machine in the Server text box.

8. In the next few screens, it's important to set up the default database. You should change it to the Travel database.

9. For all other parameters, you can use the default values. To change the Net-Library configuration, you might want to talk to your network administrator.

After the setup is done, the new data source name, `dsnTravel`, appears in the list of DSNs. Now you can use this name in all ODBC connections in your program.

NOTE

It's important that SQL Server allows access to the database for applications running on the client computer. If the access rights are not correctly set, the ODBC Data Source Administrator will not connect to SQL Server, giving you an error message.

Connecting to the ODBC Data Source

The ODBC API function resides in the `odbc.dll` file. To declare the functions in your Visual Basic program, you have to add the `odbc32.txt` file to the project. The file includes ODBC functions and a constants declaration. If you don't have the file in your installation of Visual Basic, you can download it from the Microsoft Web site.

The following code establishes a connection with the `dsnTravel` data source:

```
Dim strDSN As String, strUID As String, strPWD As String

Dim hen As Long        ' environment handle
Dim hdbc As Long       ' connect handle
Dim hstmt As Long      ' statement handle
Dim intRc As Integer   ' return value

intRc = SQLAllocEnv(hen)         ' allocate environment handle
intRc = SQLAllocConnect(ByVal hen, hdbc)   ' allocate connection

strDSN = "dsnTravel"
strUID = "admin"
strPWD = ""
intRc = SQLConnect(hdbc, strDSN, Len(strDSN), strUID, _
                   Len(strUID), strPWD, Len(strPWD))
```

To establish the connection, you have to make a few ODBC API calls:

1. The first call to the `SQLAllocEnv` function allocates an environment handle. If successful, the function returns 0:

   ```
   intRc = SQLAllocEnv(hen)         ' allocate environment handle
   ```

   The function was replaced with the `SQLAllocHandle` in ODBC v3. However, the `odbc32.txt` file that supports Visual Basic calls does not have the constants declaration for using this new function.

2. The second call to the `SQLAllocConnect` function allocates the connection handle. As a first parameter passed By Val, the function uses the created environment handle and returns 0 if successful:

   ```
   intRc = SQLAllocConnect(ByVal hen, _
           hdbc) ' allocate connection
   ```

3. The third call to the `SQLConnect` function establishes the connection to the ODBC driver and to the data source. The function accepts the following parameters:
   - Allocated connection handle
   - Data source name
   - Data source name length

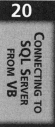

- Username
- Username length
- Password name
- Password name length

Certain data sources need more parameters. In that case, you have to use the SQLDriverConnect function.

Executing SQL Statements: Processing Queries

The ODBC standard has two models for executing a SQL statement. The first model uses the SQLExecDirect function to execute a statement. This model is useful if you want to execute the statement just once or twice. In this case, the database engine compiles the execution plan, executes the plan, and returns the results to the application.

If you don't want to compile the plan every time you pass a statement, which definitely increases the program overhead, you can use the SQLPrepare/SQLExecute model.

Consider the travel agency application. You want to fix a few problems in the Travel database that appeared because of an error in data entry. For example, you want to change the Country field to AUSTRALIA in all records of the Hotel table where the City field is SYDNEY. The following code does this database update:

```
Dim sQuery As String        ' sql statement      ' Run query
    sQuery = "update hotel set country='AUSTRALIA' " + _
             "where city='SYDNEY'"
    intRc = SQLAllocStmt(hdbc, hstmt)
    intRc = SQLExecDirect(hstmt, sQuery, Len(sQuery))
intRc = SQLFreeStmt(hstmt, SQL_CLOSE)
```

The code calls three ODBC functions:

- The SQLAllocStmt function allocates a statement handle. If successful, the function returns 0:

  ```
  intRc = SQLAllocStmt(hdbc, hstmt)          ' allocate environment
  handle
  ```

  The function was replaced with the SQLAllocHandle in ODBC v3. However, the odbc32.txt file that supports Visual Basic calls does not have the constant declarations for using this new function.

- The second call to the SQLExecDirect processes the sQuery query. The function accepts the statement handle, the string with the query, and the length of the string.

- The third function, SQLFreeStmt, stops processing the statement, closes all associated cursors, and frees other resources.

Resultsets

The ODBC standard does not make a distinction between a cursor and a resultset, assuming that a cursor is opened on each resultset. In the ODBC model, all SQL statements return a resultset within a cursor. To retrieve the rows, an application has to call the SQLFetch or SQLExtendedFetch functions.

The following example shows how an application can work with the resultsets.

Creating the New Project

In this section, you'll create a program that shows certain fields of the Hotel table in the Travel database. First, I created a new project with one form, named Form1, and added the odbc32.txt file to it. I renamed the form to frmODBC (to do that, select the form, press F4 to show the Properties window, and change the name of the form) and renamed the project to ODBCtest.

I also added one new module to the project and renamed it modODBC. In the General Declarations section, I added the following code:

```
Option Explicit

'Specify handles
Public henv As Long
Public hConnect As Long
Public hstmt As Long

'Declare system functions
Declare Sub CopyMemory Lib "Kernel32" Alias "RtlMoveMemory" ( _
         hpvDest As Any, hpvSource As Any, ByVal cbCopy As Long)
Declare Function GlobalAlloc Lib "Kernel32" _
         (ByVal wFlags As Integer, _
         ByVal dwBytes As Long) As Integer
Declare Function GlobalLock Lib "Kernel32" _
         (ByVal hMem As Integer) As Long
Declare Function GlobalUnlock Lib "Kernel32" _
           (ByVal hMem As Integer) As Integer
Declare Function GlobalFree Lib "Kernel32" _
           (ByVal hMem As Integer) As Integer
Public Const GMEM_FIXED = &H0
Public Const GMEM_MOVEABLE = &H2
```

This code declares an environment handle, henv, a connection handle, hConnect, and a statement handle, hstmt. Also, I declared memory allocation functions to use in the code and constants for use with the functions.

20

CONNECTING TO SQL SERVER FROM VB

Establishing a Connection

To show the ODBC functionality, you want to get the recordset and show certain fields on the frmODBC form. To provide this functionality, I added three text boxes to the form and named them txtHotelName, txtCity, and txtCountry. I also added a command button, which has the Command1 name by default.

To the Form_Load event I added the code that initializes and establishes the connection:

```
Private Sub Form_Load()

  Dim icbConnStrOut  As Integer

  Dim sConnectStr    As String
  Dim sConnectBuffer As String
  Dim intRc As Integer

  sConnectStr = ""
  sConnectBuffer = Space$(255)
  sConnectStr = "odbc;database=Travel;dsn=dsnTravel;"

  intRc = SQLAllocEnv(henv)
  intRc = SQLAllocConnect(henv, hConnect)
  intRc = SQLDriverConnect(hConnect, Me.hWnd, _
                      sConnectStr, Len(sConnectStr), _
    sConnectBuffer, Len(sConnectBuffer), icbConnStrOut, _
    SQL_DRIVER_NOPROMPT)

End Sub
```

In this connection, use the dsnTravel data source that you set up before.

Getting the Recordset

Now you're ready to get and process the recordset. To execute the SQL statement and get the recordset back, you have to add a little more code to the Form_Load event:

```
Dim sQuery As String
  ' Specify and run the query
  sQuery = "select HotelName, Country, City From Hotel"
  intRc = SQLAllocStmt(hConnect, hstmt)
  intRc = SQLExecDirect(hstmt, sQuery, Len(sQuery))
```

This code declares the sQuery string to hold the simple SQL select statement. The statement selects three fields from the Hotel table and then allocates the statement handle and executes the query.

After the SQLExecDirect function is executed successfully, the recordset is returned to the client computer. To make it usable in the Visual Basic application, you have to allocate the memory, provide the variables for the data, and do some C-like programming.

First, declare the variables for the memory support in the form's Declaration section:

```
' lenth of column data
  Dim lHotelLen As Long, lCityLen As Long, lCountryLen As Long
  ' pointers to fields in the memory
  Dim lpHotel As Long, lpCountry As Long, lpCity As Long
  ' memory handles
  Dim hMemHotel As Integer,
hMemCountry As Integer, hMemCity As Integer
```

The following code allocates the memory, binds the columns to the allocated memory, and fetches the data from the recordset to the memory:

```
If intRc = SQL_SUCCESS Or intRc = SQL_SUCCESS_WITH_INFO Then
    ' allocate memory and get ptr to it for each column
    hMemHotel = GlobalAlloc(GMEM_MOVEABLE, 30)
    lpHotel = GlobalLock(hMemHotel)
    hMemCountry = GlobalAlloc(GMEM_MOVEABLE, 30)
    lpCountry = GlobalLock(hMemCountry)
    hMemCity = GlobalAlloc(GMEM_MOVEABLE, 30)
    lpCity = GlobalLock(hMemCity)
    ' bind the columns to the allocated memory.
    intRc = SQLBindCol(hstmt, 1, SQL_C_CHAR, ByVal lpHotel, 30, _
            lHotelLen)
    intRc = SQLBindCol(hstmt, 2, SQL_C_CHAR, ByVal lpCountry, 30, _
            lCountryLen)
    intRc = SQLBindCol(hstmt, 3, SQL_C_CHAR, ByVal lpCity, 30, __
            lCityLen)
    ' fetch the first record into memory
    intRc = SQLFetch(hstmt)
  Else
    MsgBox ("Error getting data")
  End If
```

This code contains two new ODBC functions: SQLBindCol and SQLFetch. The SQLBindCol function binds the application data buffers to the columns in the recordset. The function accepts the following parameters:

- **Statement handle**   This parameter is the handle created by the SQL AllocStmt function.

- **Column number**   Specifies the column in the recordset.

- **Target type**   Specifies the type of memory buffer. In this program, it's specified as SQL_C_CHAR (character string).

- **Target**   Specifies the buffer where the column value will be copied. Note that you pass the ByVal parameter.

- **Buffer length**   Defines the length of the buffer.

- **String length**   Specifies the variable that will accept the length of the string.

20

CONNECTING TO
SQL SERVER
FROM VB

The `SQLFetch` function returns the rowset to the application. Because the columns are bound, it returns the data in these columns.

Getting the Fields

To show the fields in the recordset, add some code to the `Click` event of the command button:

```
Private Sub Command1_Click()

  ' strings for data fields
  Dim sHotel As String, sCountry As String, sCity As String

  Static intRc As Integer

  If (intRc = SQL_SUCCESS Or intRc = SQL_SUCCESS_WITH_INFO) Then

        ' initialize string space                 '
        sHotel = String$(30, " ")
        sCountry = String$(30, " ")
        sCity = String$(30, " ")

        ' copy the string from memory to a VB string              '
        Call CopyMemory(ByVal sCountry, ByVal lpCountry, lCountryLen)
        Call CopyMemory(ByVal sHotel, ByVal lpHotel, lHotelLen)
        Call CopyMemory(ByVal sCity, ByVal lpCity, lCityLen)
        txtHotelName.Text = sHotel
        txtCountry.Text = sCountry
        txtCity.Text = sCity
        intRc = SQLFetch(hstmt)
  Else
    Exit Sub
  End If

End Sub
```

The code copies the `Hotel`, `Country`, and `City` values to the corresponding text boxes, and then executes the `SQLFetch` function to get the next record.

Closing the Connection

Finally, you have to close the connection and release the memory variables. This code is created in the `Unload` event of the `frmODBC`:

```
Private Sub Form_Unload(Cancel As Integer)
    Dim intRc
```

```
   ' unbind columns and free memory          '
   intRc = SQLFreeStmt(hstmt, SQL_UNBIND)

   intRc = GlobalUnlock(hMemCity)
   intRc = GlobalUnlock(hMemHotel)
   intRc = GlobalUnlock(hMemCountry)
   intRc = GlobalFree(hMemCity)
   intRc = GlobalFree(hMemHotel)
   intRc = GlobalFree(hMemCountry)
   ' free statement handle       '
   intRc = SQLFreeStmt(hstmt, SQL_CLOSE)

End Sub
```

Data Access Objects

Data Access Objects (DAO) is an object interface to data sources. It's represented by a set of hierarchically designed objects that describe different levels of data.

Visual Basic 6.0 comes with DAO version 3.51 and the DAO 2.5/3.51 compatibility library. DAO is the object interface that was created to work with the Microsoft Jet data engine. DAO is optimized for local Jet databases, which are originally Access databases.

Previously, every program that accessed SQL Server or another database through DAO needed the Jet engine to run. Starting from version 3.5, DAO has had a connection mode called ODBCDirect. This mode establishes a connection to an ODBC data source without loading MS Jet in the computer's memory. Therefore, the VB application becomes faster and more efficient.

Another advantage of using ODBCDirect is that you can use ODBC's special capabilities, such as *batch updates* (sending a few statements at the same time to the server) or *asynchronous query* (executing a query asynchronously).

Creating and Modifying Databases: Data Definition Language Operations

DAO versions 3.5 and higher come with two models of database access. The first model traditionally works with the Jet engine; the second model accesses ODBC sources directly. Tables 20.2 and 20.3 show the upper levels of the object hierarchy for both models. For the full description of the objects, you might want to read the Visual Basic reference manual.

20

CONNECTING TO
SQL SERVER
FROM VB

TABLE 20.2 OBJECT HIERARCHY FOR MICROSOFT JET WORKSPACE

Collections	*Objects*
Level 1: DBEngine	
Errors Collection	-> Error
WorkSpaces Collection	-> Workspace
Level 2: Workspace	
Databases Collection	-> Database
Groups Collection	-> Group
Users Collection	-> User
Level 3: Databases	
QueryDefs Collection	-> QueryDef
Recordsets Collection	-> Recordset
Relations Collection	-> Relation
Containers Collection	-> Container
TableDefs Collection	-> TableDef

TABLE 20.3 OBJECT HIERARCHY FOR THE ODBCDIRECT WORKSPACE

Level 1: DBEngine	
Errors Collection	-> Errors
WorkSpaces Collection	-> Workspace
Level 2: Workspace	
Connections Collection	-> Connection
Databases Collection	-> Database
Level 3: Connection	
QueryDefs Collection	-> QueryDef
Recordsets Collection	-> Recordset
Level 3: Databases	
Recordsets Collection	-> Recordset

All DAO objects are derived from the DBEngine object, .which is located at the very top of the DAO objects hierarchy. You can't create more than one DBEngine object. To specify the model to access a data source, you have to create a *workspace,* a database environment that determines the means of the database access. It's a non-persistent object that means workspaces are not stored in the database. In this section, you're going to write a

VB procedure that converts a SQL Server database to an encrypted Access database. This example assumes that the Access database does not exist, so you have to create it.

> **NOTE**
>
> Even before writing code for DAO, make sure that Microsoft DAO 3.51 Object Library (in VB 6.0) is selected in the references of your project. To do that, choose Project, References from the menu, and then select the library from the list and click OK.

Creating Workspaces

First, you have to specify workspaces. To take advantage of the features of each type of workspace, create the MS Jet workspace for accessing the Access database and the ODBCDirect workspace for the SQL Server database. There are a few reasons for this selection. First, Jet is adjusted for Access databases, so the program has better performance with this approach. On the other hand, ODBCDirect was developed specifically for accessing remote data, so it works better with SQL Server. Second, ODBCDirect functionality does not provide table definitions and the ability to create tables using DAO objects.

To create workspaces, use the `CreateWorkspace` method of the `DBEngine` object:

```
Dim wrkJetA As Workspace
Dim wrkJetS As Workspace
Set wrkJetA = DBEngine.CreateWorkspace("", "admin", "", dbUseJet)
Set wrkJetS = DBEngine.CreateWorkspace("", "admin", "", dbUseODBC)
```

When you finish processing data, you can close workspaces to free the objects in memory:

```
rstAccess.Close
rstSQLServer.Close
```

In DAO 3.5, the `CreateWorkspace` method got the fourth parameter, which specifies the type of workspace. The parameter can be `dbUseJet` or `dbUseODBC`. If the fourth parameter is not specified, the Jet workspace is created by default.

Creating a Database

To create a database, you use Data Definition Language (DDL) operations specific to Microsoft Jet. The first method you're going to use is `CreateDatabase`:

```
Set dbsAccess = wrkJetA.CreateDatabase("Travel.mdb", _

                  dbLangGeneral, dbEncrypt)
```

The first parameter specifies the database filename; the second parameter specifies a collating order for creating the database. The last parameter can specify the version of the data format or force the data encryption. Use the `dbEncrypt` parameter for encrypting the database.

Now you have to create a table definition. In this example, you'll create the Hotel table with fairly common fields:

```
Dim tdfNew As TableDef
Set tdfNew = dbsAccess.CreateTableDef("Hotel")
  With tdfNew
    .Fields.Append .CreateField("HotelID", dbInteger)
    .Fields.Append .CreateField("HotelName", dbText)
    .Fields.Append .CreateField("Country", dbText)
    .Fields.Append .CreateField("State", dbText)
    .Fields.Append .CreateField("City", dbText)
    .Fields.Append .CreateField("Address", dbText)
    .Fields.Append .CreateField("Zip", dbText)
    .Fields.Append .CreateField("PhoneNo", dbText)
    .Fields.Append .CreateField("FaxNo", dbText)
    .Fields.Append .CreateField("ContactName", dbText)
  End With
  dbsAccess.TableDefs.Append tdfNew
```

This code uses the `tdfNew` object of the type `TableDef` and a collection of table definitions. First, create a table definition object in the `dbsAccess` database using the `CreateTableDef` method. Then create fields in this table definition and append them to the `Fields` collection of the table definition. Finally, append the `tdfNew` object to the collection of table definitions.

> **NOTE**
>
> The `CreateField` method can accept three parameters: field name, field type, and field size. Please read your Visual Basic manual for the list of correct field types.

To create indexes in the table, use a collection of indexes as you used a collection of fields. The procedure of creating an index is quite simple. You create and index, and then specify fields in the index. Finally, add the index to the collection of indexes. To use the index in the rest of the code, you have to apply the `Refresh` method:

```
With tdfNew
Dim idxHotel As Index
    Set idxHotel = .CreateIndex("Hotel")
    With idxHotel
```

```
      .Fields.Append .CreateField("HotelName")
      .Fields.Append .CreateField("Country")
   End With
   .Indexes.Append idxHotel
   .Indexes.Refresh

End With
```

> **NOTE**
>
> To remove an index or a field from the table definition, use the `Delete` method, which you can apply to both indexes and fields collections. You can also delete a tabledef with this method. In that case, you delete both the table definition and the data in the table.

As mentioned, ODBCDirect doesn't have the ability to create tables using DDL specific to DAO. However, you can create a table using SQL data definition language.

For the same travel agency application, you'll create a new SQL Server table named Agent. However, before designing the table, I'm going to discuss a connection to the database.

Connecting to SQL Server Database

In ODBCDirect you can use two types of objects: the `Connection` object and the `Database` object. The `Connection` object is supposed to work with remote database connectivity; it is adjusted for this type of data access instead of for local databases. The `Connection` object can run asynchronous operations and access server-specific functionality (such as specifying parameter values for stored procedures).

What is the reason for using the `Database` object? The main reason is the ability to switch the data (from Microsoft SQL Server to Microsoft Jet) without changing the programming code.

> **TIP**
>
> In an application that mixes the `Connection` and `Database` objects, you might find the `Connection` property of the `Database` object and the `Database` property of the `Connection` object to be useful.

The following code establishes a connection to the SQL Server Travel database by using the `dsnTravel` data source set up in the beginning of this chapter:

```
Dim wrkJetS As Workspace
Dim dbsSQLServer As Connection

  Set wrkJetS = DBEngine.CreateWorkspace("", "admin", "", dbUseODBC)
  Set dbsSQLServer = wrkJetS.OpenConnection("", _
      dbDriverNoPrompt, False, _
      "odbc;database=Travel;dsn=dsnTravel;")
```

The `OpenConnection` method accepts four parameters: `name`, `options`, `readonly`, and `connect`. The `name` parameter provides the name property for the `Connection` object. However, if the `connect` parameter does not supply a valid ODBC connect string, the `name` parameter can refer to a valid DSN. Otherwise, the ODBC Driver Manager prompts you to specify the connection. The `options` parameter specifies what type of prompt you would like to use.

Using SQL Server Data Definition Language

Now you're ready to create an Agent table in the Travel database by using the CREATE TABLE Transact-SQL statement:

```
Dim SQLCommand As String
SQLCommand = "Create Table Agent ("
  SQLCommand = SQLCommand + "AgentID int,"
  SQLCommand = SQLCommand + "AgentName varchar(40),"
  SQLCommand = SQLCommand + "Country varchar(40),"
  SQLCommand = SQLCommand + "State char(2),"
  SQLCommand = SQLCommand + "City varchar(30),"
  SQLCommand = SQLCommand + "Address varchar(40),"
  SQLCommand = SQLCommand + "Zip varchar(10),"
  SQLCommand = SQLCommand + "PhoneNo varchar(30),"
  SQLCommand = SQLCommand + "FaxNo varchar(30),"
  SQLCommand = SQLCommand + "ContactName varchar(40)"
  SQLCommand = SQLCommand + ")"

dbsSQLServer.Execute (SQLCommand)
```

This code prepares the CREATE TABLE command and executes it with the `Execute` method. This method can have a second parameter, too. The parameters are described in the Table 20.4.

TABLE 20.4 OPTIONAL PARAMETERS FOR THE *Execute* METHOD OF THE ODBC Connection OBJECT

`dbRunAsync`	Executes the query asynchronously.
`dbExecDirect`	Executes the statement without first calling the `SQLPrepare` ODBC API function.

The same technique is used to execute other data definition language statements, such as ALTER TABLE, DROP TABLE, CREATE INDEX, DROP INDEX, and so forth.

Working with Recordsets: Data Manipulation Language Operations

In this section, you're going to develop a small VB application that converts the Hotel table of the SQL Server database to the Access table.

Recordsets

The project consists of the modMain module with two procedures—Main and ConvertS2A—and a form that displays the progress of the conversion. The Main procedure is the starting point of the project:

```
Public Sub Main()
  Load frmCounter
  frmCounter.Show vbModeless

  Call ConvertS2A
  Unload frmCounter
End Sub
```

The Main procedure loads the frmCounter form that shows the number of the processed records, as shown on Figure 20.9.

FIGURE 20.9
Counter of processed records.

It's important that the frmCounter form has a label named lblCounter. The program changes the caption of the label every time the next record is processed. The form is shown as modeless, which enables further code execution.

The Main procedure calls the ConvertS2A procedure, which is shown in Listing 20.1.

LISTING 20.1 THE Convert S2A PROCEDURE

```
Public Sub ConvertS2A()

'*** DAO objects definition
  Dim wrkJetA As Workspace
  Dim wrkJetS As Workspace
  Dim dbsAccess As Database
  Dim dbsSQLServer As Connection
```

continues

LISTING 20.1   CONTINUED

```
  Dim rstAccess As Recordset
  Dim rstSQLServer As Recordset

'*** Record counter
  Dim iCounter

'*** Prepare to the data coonversion
On Error GoTo ErrLabel
  Set wrkJetA = DBEngine.CreateWorkspace("", "admin", "", dbUseJet)
  Set wrkJetS = DBEngine.CreateWorkspace("", "admin", "", dbUseODBC)
  Set dbsAccess = wrkJetA.OpenDatabase("Travel.mdb", True)
  Set dbsSQLServer = wrkJetS.OpenConnection("", _
      dbDriverNoPrompt, False, _
      "odbc;database=Travel;dsn=dsnTravel;")
  Set rstAccess = dbsAccess.OpenRecordset("Hotel", dbOpenDynaset)
  Set rstSQLServer = dbsSQLServer.OpenRecordset("Hotel", _
                    dbOpenDynamic, dbExecDirect, dbOptimistic)

On Error Resume Next
  iCounter = 0

'*** Convert the table record by record
  With rstSQLServer
    .MoveFirst
    Do While Not .EOF
      iCounter = iCounter + 1
      rstAccess.AddNew
      rstAccess.Fields("HotelID") = Val(.Fields("HotelID"))
      rstAccess.Fields("HotelName") = .Fields("HotelName")
      rstAccess.Fields("Country") = .Fields("Country")
      rstAccess.Fields("State") = .Fields("State")
      rstAccess.Fields("City") = .Fields("City")
      rstAccess.Fields("Address") = .Fields("Address")
      rstAccess.Fields("Zip") = .Fields("Zip")
      rstAccess.Fields("PhoneNo") = .Fields("PhoneNo")
      rstAccess.Fields("FaxNo") = .Fields("FaxNo")
      rstAccess.Fields("ContactName") = .Fields("ContactName")

      If Err.Number = 0 Then
        rstAccess.Update
      Else
        rstAccess.CancelUpdate
      End If

      .MoveNext
      frmCounter.lblCounter.Caption = Str(iCounter)
      frmCounter.Refresh
    Loop
```

```
   End With

'*** Release DAO objects
   rstAccess.Close
   rstSQLServer.Close
   dbsAccess.Close
   dbsSQLServer.Close
   wrkJetS.Close
   wrkJetA.Close

Exit Sub

'*** Error handling
ErrLabel:
   MsgBox ("Error: " + Err.Description)

End Sub
```

The beginning of the program defines DAO objects, such as workspaces, databases, connections, and recordsets. The program then creates the workspaces and opens the database and the connection. Now you're ready to open recordsets. A recordset is similar to an ODBC cursor, and you can specify the cursor type as the second parameter of the method. The available recordset types are shown in Table 20.5.

TABLE 20.5 RECORDSET TYPES SUPPORTED FOR ODBCDirect

Recordset Type	Description
dbOpenDynamic	Similar to dynamic cursor
dbOpenDynaset	Similar to keyset cursor
dbOpenSnapshot	Similar to static cursor
dbOpenForwardOnly	Forward-only scrolling type of recordset

> **NOTE**
>
> The dbOpenTable cursor is supported only for Jet workspaces.

A table name, query name, or SQL statement that returns records can specify the recordset. For example, you could use the SQL SELECT statement to get the same result:

```
Set rstSQLServer = _
    dbsSQLServer.OpenRecordset("select * from Hotel", _
        dbOpenDynamic, dbExecDirect, dbOptimistic)
```

The last parameter specifies the type of locking for the recordset. ODBCDirect allows five values for the locking type, as shown in Table 20.6.

TABLE 20.6   RECORDSET LOCKING TYPES FOR ODBCDirect

Locking Type	Description
dbOptimistic	For optimistic locking, the page containing the record is not locked until the Update method is executed.
dbPessimistic	For pessimistic locking, the page containing the record is locked as soon as the Edit or AddNew method is executed.
dbOptimisticValue	Uses optimistic concurrency based on row values.
dbOptimisticBatch	The updating rows are buffered locally, and then the program issues the batch update.
dbReadOnly	Prevents users from changing records (default for ODBCDirect workspaces).

The rest of the program is quite simple. You run the loop until the end of the recordset is encountered. During the loop, you use MoveNext, AddNew, Update, or CancelUpdate methods. The following section discusses the data manipulation language operations with recordsets.

Operations with Recordsets

This section describes the operations which can be done with recordsets.

- **Navigation operations**   MoveFirst, MoveLast, MoveNext, and MovePrevious methods work exactly as you'd expect. They move to the first, last, next, or previous record in the recordset and make that record the current one. Two properties, BOF and EOF, are closely related to these methods. Consequently, executing MoveNext results in reaching the end of the recordset and sets the EOF property to true. Executing MovePrevious results in reaching the end of the recordset and sets the BOF property to true.

  The Move method with the rows parameter moves the current position the specified number of rows forward or backward (if the number is negative). As the second parameter, you can specify a bookmarked position by saving the recordset's Bookmark property in a variable.

  FindFirst, FindLast, FindNext, and FindPrevious locate the first, last, next, or previous record of a dynaset or a snapshot that satisfy certain criteria. The criteria are specified as a parameter for methods of the String type. The syntax of the string is similar to the WHERE clause in a SQL statement, but without the word WHERE. For example, the string can be "HotelId=5".

- **Adding, editing, deleting, and updating operations** You can use the Delete method to delete the current record in the recordset. The AddNew method creates a new record for an updatable recordset, and the Edit method copies the current record from an updatable recordset to the edit buffer. After the record is modified, save the changes using the Update method or cancel the changes using the CancelUpdate method.

Working with ODBCDirect QueryDef Objects

The ODBCDirect QueryDef objects are quite different from the MS Jet ones. Two main features distinguish these QueryDef objects. ODBCDirect QueryDef objects support asynchronous operations, unlike Jet QueryDef objects. The second major difference is that Jet QueryDef objects are typically saved in the database, and the ODBCDirect QueryDef objects are always temporary.

Possibly the most common use of QueryDef objects in the ODBCDirect workspace is the execution of stored procedures. For example, here's how to create a Visual Basic program that creates and then uses a stored procedure to get the recordset that contains all the hotels in a certain city:

```
Public Sub QDExample()

  Dim wrkJetS As Workspace
  Dim dbsSQLServer As Connection
  Dim qdf As QueryDef
  Dim StoredString As String
  Dim rstHotels As Recordset

  Set wrkJetS = DBEngine.CreateWorkspace("", "admin", "", dbUseODBC)
  Set dbsSQLServer = wrkJetS.OpenConnection("", _
      dbDriverNoPrompt, False, _
      "odbc;database=Travel;dsn=dsnTravel;")

'Create the stored procedure
  StoredString = "create proc GetHotels " & _
              "(@City varchar(30)) " & _
              "as select * from Hotel " & _
              "where City = @City"

  dbsSQLServer.Execute StoredString

'Execute the query
  Set qdf = dbsSQLServer.CreateQueryDef("GetQ", _
          "{call GetHotels (?)}")

  qdf.Parameters(0) = "SYDNEY"
```

```
Set rstHotels = qdf.OpenRecordset()
MsgBox rstHotels.Fields("Address")

rstHotels.Close
dbsSQLServer.Close
wrkJetS.Close
End Sub
```

The program declares the objects, as usual, and then creates an ODBCDirect workspace and opens a connection. Then the program creates the stored procedure using Transact-SQL. The procedure selects records from the Hotel table in which the City field is equal to the argument of the procedure. The Transact-SQL statement is stored in the StoredString variable.

Creating the stored procedure on the server is as simple as applying the Execute method to the connection:

```
dbsSQLServer.Execute StoredString
```

Then create a QueryDef with one parameter, and name the QueryDef GetQ:

```
Set qdf = dbsSQLServer.CreateQueryDef("GetQ", _
            "{call GetHotels (?)}")
```

Now you can select records in the database that have a certain value in the City field. To specify the field, you have to set up the parameter of the QueryDef. For this example, select SYDNEY:

```
qdf.Parameters(0) = "SYDNEY"
```

To create the recordset that consists of all records with SYDNEY in the City field, apply the OpenRecordset method:

```
Set rstHotels = qdf.OpenRecordset()
  MsgBox rstHotels.Fields("Address")
```

The message box shows you the address of the first record in the recordset and verifies the program's correctness.

DAO was a very popular data model during a few years. However, it was designed specifically for Jet databases, and it lost its significance with new data models.

Remote Data Objects (RDO)

RDO appeared on the scene at the time when developers started to pay more attention to accessing databases remotely. RDO did not replace DAO completely but became another important tool in database development.

RDO Compared to DAO

There's a big difference in the functionality of these two object interfaces. Basically, they were designed for different purposes. DAO was designed for accessing local databases, specifically Access databases; RDO was designed for accessing data remotely in such databases as SQL Server and Oracle.

Table 20.7 compares the functionality of DAO and RDO.

TABLE 20.7   COMPARISON OF THE FUNCTIONALITY OF DAO AND RDO

DAO with MS Jet Workspaces	*RDO*
Tuned up for local Access databases.	Tuned up for accessing data on remote servers.
Uses Microsoft Jet, which produces a huge overhead, so it needs a more powerful computer.	Doesn't use Jet; uses a very thin layer instead. Can run on computers with minimal configuration.
Does not have access to server-side cursors.	Has access to server-side cursors.
Does not support asynchronous access (except ODBCDirect QueryDef objects).	Supports asynchronous queries.
DAO 2.5 works on 16-bit operating systems; higher versions work on 32-bit operating systems only.	Works on 32-bit operating systems only.

There's always a bit of a challenge to move from one data model to another. For programmers who got used to DAO, it would be simpler to move from the Jet workspace model to the ODBCDirect workspace model. The functionality of the ODBCDirect model is very similar to RDO; however, RDO is more advanced. For example, RDO support events, which helps in developing asynchronous data access.

Table 20.8 lists some of the DAO objects and the equivalent RDO objects to help DAO programmers transfer code more quickly to the RDO data model.

TABLE 20.8   DAO AND RDO OBJECTS

DAO with MS Jet Workspaces	RDO
DBEngine	rdoEngine
User, Group	Not implemented
Workspace	rdoEnvironment
Database	rdoConnection
TableDef	rdoTable
Index	Not implemented
Recordset	rdoResultset
Table	Not implemented
Dynaset	Keyset
	Static
Field	rdoColumn
QueryDef	rdoPreparedStatement
Parameter	rdoParameter

Probably, the difference in programming with RDO and with DAO is a result of the models' design. DAO was designed for ISAM (Index Sequential Access Method) databases such as Access; RDO was designed for relational databases. DAO supports the creation and modification of the data dictionary; RDO relies on the server tools and utilities. However, you can run queries that create, modify, and delete tables and databases.

RDO Hierarchy and the `rdoEngine` Object

Table 20.9 shows the upper level of the RDO object hierarchy. For a full description of the objects, you might want to read the Visual Basic reference manual.

TABLE 20.9   OBJECT HIERARCHY FOR MICROSOFT JET WORKSPACE

Level 1: `rdoEngine`	
rdoErrors Collection	-> rdoError
rdoEnvironments Collection	-> rdoEnvironment
Level 2: `rdoEnvironment`	
rdoConnections Collection	-> rdoConnection

Level 3: `rdoConnection`

`rdoQueries` Collection	-> `rdoQuery`
`rdoResultsets` Collection	-> `rdoResultset`
`rdoTables` Collection	-> `rdoTable`

Level 4: `rdoQuery`

`rdoColumns` Collection	-> `rdoColumn`
`rdoParameters` Collection	-> `rdoParameter`

Level 4: `rdoResultset`

`rdoColumns` Collection	-> `rdoColumn`

Level 4: `rdoTable`

`rdoColumns` Collection	-> `rdoColumn`

Like the `DBEngine` object in DAO, the `rdoEngine` object is located at the top of the object hierarchy. It represents the remote data source, and you can't create additional `rdoEngine` objects.

The `rdoEngine` object supports two methods: the `rdoRegisterDataSource` method, which allows registering a new ODBC data source in the system Registry, and the `rdoCreateEnviroment` method, which creates a new `rdoEnvironment` object.

The `rdoEnvironment` Object

The `rdoEnvironment` object defines a logical set of connections—both open and allocated but unopened—and defines a transaction scope and security context for data manipulation language operations. The `rdoEnvironment` object is similar to DAO's workspace object.

The default `rdoEnvironment` object is created when the first RDO object is referenced in the code. The default `rdoEnvironment` object is the number 0 object in the collection of these objects. The name of the default object is `Default_Environment`; the username and the password for this object are both empty strings. However, you can change the default name and password by assigning new values to the `rdoDefaultUser` and `rdoDefaultPassword` properties of the `rdoEngine` object.

Instead of using the default `rdoEnvironment` object, you can create a new one using the `rdoCreateEnvironment` method of the `rdoEngine` object. Every new environment created with this method is automatically appended to the `rdoEnvironments` collection. The following statements create a new RDO environment:

20

```
Dim myEnvironment As rdoEnvironment
  Set myEnvironment = rdoEngine.rdoCreateEnvironment("myEnv", _
                        "admin", "SecretWord")
```

This code creates a new environment named myEnv for the admin user. The password for this object is defined as SecretWord. The username and the password are used when establishing a connection if no other values are supplied.

The rdoEnvironment object also specifies the transaction scope. The BeginTrans, CommitTrans, and RollbackTrans methods work within this scope.

> **NOTE**
>
> One rdoEnvironment object defines one transaction scope regardless how many connections are open in this environment. Therefore, if you use a BeginTrans method against one of the databases and perform transactions that affect several databases, the RollbackTrans method rolls back all of them.

The rdoEnvironment object supports the following methods:

- The Add and Remove methods enable adding items to and removing items from the rdoEnvironments collection.
- The BeginTrans, CommitTrans, and RollbackTrans methods manage transaction processing:

  BeginTrans starts the transaction.

  CommitTrans ends the current transaction and saves the changes.

  RollbackTrans ends the current transaction and restores the database statuses without saving them.
- The Close method closes the environment.
- The OpenConnection method opens a connection to an ODBC data source.

Establishing an RDO Connection

Connecting to a remote data source in RDO is very similar to the procedure in the ODBCDirect workspace of DAO; you have to apply the OpenConnection method of the environment object. The following code establishes a connection to the SQL Server Travel database, using the dsnTravel data source set up at the beginning of this chapter:

```
Dim myEnvironment As rdoEnvironment
Dim myConnection As rdoConnection
```

```
Set myEnvironment = rdoEngine.rdoCreateEnvironment("myEnv", _
                    "admin", "SecretWord")
Set myConnection = myEnvironment.OpenConnection("", _
                 rdDriverNoPrompt, False, _
                 "odbc;database=Travel;dsn=dsnTravel;")
'*******
' here the transaction code comes
'*******

  myConnection.Close
  myEnvironment.Close
```

The `OpenConnection` method accepts four parameters: `name`, `prompt`, `readonly`, `connect`, and `options`. The `name` parameter supplies the name property for the `Connection` object. However, if the `connect` parameter doesn't provide a valid ODBC connect string, the `name` parameter can refer to a valid DSN. Otherwise, the ODBC driver manager prompts you to specify the connection, unless the `rdDriverNoPrompt` is specified. The `prompt` parameter indicates what type of prompt you would like to use. There's only one value available for the `options` parameter: `rdAsyncEnable`. Setting this parameter means setting up asynchronous access to data.

If the process is asynchronous, you can check the `rdoConnection` object's `StillConnecting` property, which returns `false` if the connection operation is complete.

> **NOTE**
>
> All RDO methods support named arguments. You can specify them by using the *argument:=* syntax. For example, the connection in this section can be coded as follows:
>
> ```
> CString = "odbc;database=Travel;dsn=dsnTravel;"
> Set myConnection = myEnvironment.OpenConnection(_
>                 prompt:=rdDriverNoPrompt, _
>                 readonly:=False, _
>                 connect:=Cstring)
> ```

Cursors and Resultsets

Now you're going to create a Visual Basic application that views the Hotel table of the Travel database. Assume that the DSN settings remain the same, and you can create a connection that was explained previously.

Creating a Project

First, create a standard Visual Basic project with one form. Change the default name of the project to rdoEx. To do that, choose Project, Properties from the menu. Click OK to save the changes. Then open the form and press F4 to get the Properties window. Change the Name property to rdoExample.

To use RDO, you have to add the corresponding library to the project. Choose Project, References from the menu, and then add Microsoft Remote Data Object 2.0 to the list of references. Click OK.

Setting Up an Interface

The Travel database has 10 fields: HotelID, HotelName, Address, City, State, Zip, Country, PhoneNo, FaxNo, and ContactName. You're going to create the appropriate interface so they can be seen. Create 10 text boxes on the form with the following names: txtHotelID, txtHotelName, txtAddress, txtCity, txtState, txtZip, txtCountry, txtPhoneNo, txtFaxNo, and txtContactName. Add the corresponding labels beside the text boxes.

To display the list of hotels, use the listview control. To add the control to the project, choose Project, Components from the menu, and then check the check box beside Microsoft Windows Common Controls 6.0. The common controls come with Visual Basic 6.0. Several new control icons appear on the Visual Basic toolbox. Select the listview control and drag and drop it onto the form.

Change the name of the control to lvHotels. Right-click and select the report type of view on the tab. Then click on the Column Headers tab and add the following items: Hotel Name, Address, City, State, Zip, Country, Phone No, Fax No, and Contact Name. You can make certain columns invisible by assigning their width to 0.

You want to show the full list of the hotels in the listview control and the individual elements in the text boxes. Adding the ShowItem procedure to the form will show the items from the listview control:

```
Public Sub ShowItem()
  txtHotelID.Text = Mid(lvHotels.SelectedItem.Key, 4)
  txtHotelName.Text = lvHotels.SelectedItem.Text
  txtAddress.Text = lvHotels.SelectedItem.SubItems(1)
  txtCity.Text = lvHotels.SelectedItem.SubItems(2)
  txtState.Text = lvHotels.SelectedItem.SubItems(3)
  txtZip.Text = lvHotels.SelectedItem.SubItems(4)
  txtCountry.Text = lvHotels.SelectedItem.SubItems(5)
  txtPhoneNo.Text = lvHotels.SelectedItem.SubItems(6)
```

```
txtFaxNo.Text = lvHotels.SelectedItem.SubItems(7)
txtContactName.Text = lvHotels.SelectedItem.SubItems(8)

End Sub
```

The procedure shows fields in a selected row of the `listview` control in the corresponding text boxes. If you need more information about Windows Common Controls, refer to your Visual Basic manual.

Setting Up the Resultset

Now you're going to fill the `listview` control and the text boxes with the data on the `Form_Load` event.

First, you have to create an RDO environment and open a connection, as described previously:

```
Dim myEnvironment As rdoEnvironment
Dim myConnection As rdoConnection
  Set myEnvironment = rdoEngine.rdoCreateEnvironment("myEnv", _
                      "admin", "SecretWord")
  Set myConnection = myEnvironment.OpenConnection("", _
                     rdDriverNoPrompt, False, _
                     "odbc;database=Travel;dsn=dsnTravel;")
```

This code creates the `myConnection` connection. To create a resultset, use the `OpenResultset` method of the connection. The `OpenResultset` method has the following parameters:

- **Name** This parameter can be the name of an `rdoQuery`, the name of an `rdoTable`, or a SQL statement that returns rows. Queries are discussed later in this chapter.

- **Type** This parameter specifies the type of resultset.

- **Locktype** This parameter specifies the lock type.

- **Options** You can use the following constants for this parameter: `rdAsyncEnable` specifies the asynchronous execution, `rdExecDirect` specifies using `SQLExecDirect` instead of `SQLPrepare` and `SQLExecute`.

There are four types of resultsets and corresponding values of the `type` parameter in the `OpenResultset` function:

- **rdOpenForwardOnly** You can use this type if you want to retrieve the data quickly and don't want to create an overhead. You can only move to the next row in this type of resultset.

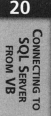

- **rdOpenKeySet**   The `keyset` type of cursor is similar to the Jet `dynaset` recordset. A key is built for each row and used to fetch the data quickly. After the keyset is fully populated, the membership is frozen. It means that appends or updates do not affect the cursor until it is rebuilt.

- **rdOpenDynamic**   This type is similar to the `keyset` type except the membership is not frozen. This type carries the biggest overhead.

- **rdOpenStatic**   The static type of cursor is similar to the Jet `snapshot` recordset. Not all changes are detected by the cursor until it is closed and reopened.

In this example, you want to populate the `listview` control and close the resultset, so select the forward-only type of resultset:

```
SQlString = "select * from Hotel"
  Set myResultset = myConnection.OpenResultset(SQlString,
  ➥rdOpenForwardOnly, , rdExecDirect)
```

Resultsets have a group of methods much like those in Jet recordsets. The first group enables navigation in the recordset. There are five methods that move the current row in the recordset: `Move`, `MoveNext`, `MovePrevious`, `MoveFirst`, and `MoveLast`.

- The `Move` method accepts two parameters: `rows` and `start`. The first parameter specifies the number of rows the position will move. The second parameter specifies the bookmark, which could be generated by using the `Bookmark` property and then used as a start position for the move.

- The `MoveNext`, `MovePrevious`, `MoveFirst`, and `MoveLast` methods move the current row to the corresponding position in the resultset. The `MoveLast` method can accept an `rdAsyncEnable` parameter that forces the operation to run asynchronously.

Moving within a resultset can change an `EOF` (end of resultset) or a `BOF` (beginning of resultset) property. For more information, refer to your Visual Basic manual.

- Another important group of methods enables editing a resultset. You can start an operation by using the `AddNew` or `Edit` method. The `AddNew` method appends a blank row to the resultset, and the `Edit` method creates a buffer to edit the resultset. To update the resultset, you have to execute the `Update` method; to cancel it, you have to execute the `CancelUpdate` method. You can use the `Delete` method to delete rows from the resultset.

The following code continues processing the resultset for the Hotel table. The code populates the listview control and the text boxes on the form.

```
Do While Not myResultset.EOF
 On Error Resume Next
    Set itmA = lvHotels.ListItems.Add()
    itmA.Key = "Key" & myResultset!HotelID
    itmA.Text = myResultset!HotelName
    itmA.SubItems(1) = IIf(IsNull(myResultset!Address), _
                           " ", myResultset!Address)
    itmA.SubItems(2) = myResultset!City
    itmA.SubItems(3) = IIf(IsNull(myResultset!State), _
                           " ", myResultset!State)
    itmA.SubItems(4) = IIf(IsNull(myResultset!Zip), _
                           " ", myResultset!Zip)
    itmA.SubItems(5) = myResultset!Country
    itmA.SubItems(6) = IIf(IsNull(myResultset!PhoneNo), _
                           " ", myResultset!PhoneNo)
    itmA.SubItems(7) = IIf(IsNull(myResultset!FaxNo), _
                           " ", myResultset!FaxNo)
    itmA.SubItems(8) = IIf(IsNull(myResultset!ContactName), _
                           " ", myResultset!ContactName)

    On Error GoTo 0
    myResultset.MoveNext
 Loop

 lvHotels.ListItems(1).Selected = True
 Call ShowItem
```

Finally, you have to close the objects:

```
myResultset.Close
myConnection.Close
myEnvironment.Close
```

To enable navigating in the listview control, call the ShowItem procedure in the lvHotels_ItemClick event code:

```
Private Sub lvHotels_ItemClick(ByVal Item As MSComctlLib.ListItem)
  Call ShowItem

End Sub
```

The output interface of the program is shown in Figure 20.10.

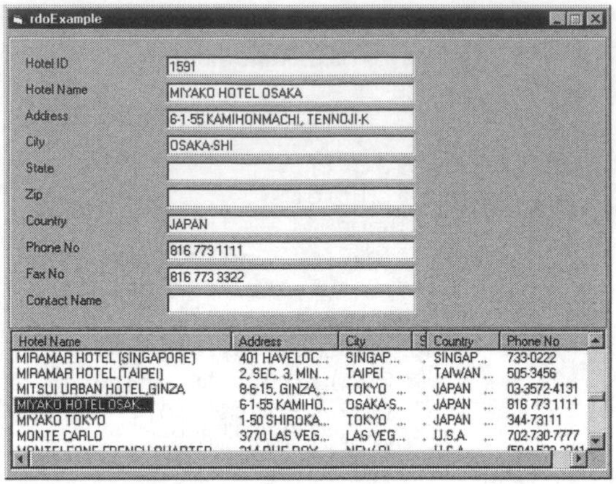

FIGURE 20.10

The SQL table viewer program.

Managing Lock Types

The `OpenResult` method can use the `LockType` parameter. The parameter accepts the following values:

- **`rdConcurReadOnly`**   The resultset is created as read-only. No updates are permitted.

- **`rdConcurLock`**   Specifies the pessimistic concurrency.

- **`rdConcurRowVer`**   Specifies the optimistic concurrency based on row ID.

- **`rdConcurValues`**   Specifies the optimistic concurrency based on row values.

- **`rdConcurBatch`**   Specifies the optimistic concurrency using batch mode updates.

Submitting Queries

Instead of creating a resultset on the client side and using methods such as `AddNew`, `Delete`, or `Edit`, you can use queries with the `INSERT`, `DELETE`, or `UPDATE` SQL statements.

To create a query, you have to execute the `CreateQuery` method of the `Connection` object. First, you have to declare an `rdoQuery`, for example

```
Dim myQuery as rdoQuery
```

Then you can create a query:

```
Set myQuery = myConnection.CreateQuery(Qname, SQLString)
```

The first parameter, `Qname`, is a string that specifies the query's name property. The second parameter is optional and specifies the SQL statement for the query. You can specify the SQL statement later with the `SQL` property of the `rdoQuery`.

The following example deletes all records from the Hotel table in which the `Country` field is equal to `AUSTRALIA`.

```
Dim myEnvironment As rdoEnvironment
Dim myConnection As rdoConnection
Dim myQuery As New rdoQuery

Dim SqlString As String

  Set myEnvironment = rdoEngine.rdoCreateEnvironment("myEnv", _
                        "admin", "SecretWord")
  Set myConnection = myEnvironment.OpenConnection("", _
                      rdDriverNoPrompt, False, _
                      "odbc;database=Travel;dsn=dsnTravel;")

  SqlString = "delete from hotel where country='AUSTRALIA'"

  myQuery.Name = "testName"
  myQuery.SQL = SqlString
  myQuery.RowsetSize = 1

  Set myQuery.ActiveConnection = myConnection
  myQuery.Execute

  myConnection.Close
  myEnvironment.Close
```

Query Parameters

In the previous example, you might want to pass a parameter to the query that specifies the country. To do that, change the SQL statement as follows:

```
SqlString = "delete from hotel where country= ? "
```

The question mark (?) is a placeholder for the query argument. To pass parameters to a query, you have to access the `rdoParameters` collection in the query object. Numbers in the collection start with 0, so you have to write the statement as follows if you want to delete all records with hotels in Canada:

```
myQuery.Parameters(0) = 'CANADA'
```

Extending RDO with ODBC

You can extend RDO's capabilities by using it along with ODBC. Table 20.10 shows ODBC handles that are available in RDO.

TABLE 20.10 ODBC HANDLES AND CORRESPONDING RDO OBJECT PROPERTIES

rdoEnvironment.hEnv	SQLAllocEnv
rdoConnection.hDbc	SQLAllocConnect, SQLDriverConnect
rdoResultset.hStmt	SQLAllocStmt
rdoQuery.hStmt	SQLAllocStmt
rdoPreparedStatement.hStmt	SQLAllocStmt

> **WARNING**
>
> The MSDN library for Visual Studio 6.0 warns you that using RDO and ODBC can cause unpredictable problems. For example, if you close connections or deallocate any of those handles using ODBC, RDO's behavior is unpredictable.

Summary

There are several different approaches to access data in database development. This chapter discusses their pros and contras in detail. This chapter describes object and call-level interfaces and a few different data models. Starting with a description of ODBC, the chapter continues with object models such as DAO and RDO. The latest data model, ADO is discussed in Chapter 24.

CHAPTER 21

Using SQL-DMO via Visual Basic to Manage SQL Server

SQL Server is well endowed with powerful functions to manage and administer it. Graphical administration tools such as Microsoft Management Console enable the SQL Server administrator to quickly and easily control all aspects of a server or servers. These tools use Microsoft's *Data Management Objects* (DMO) library, which exposes this powerful functionality. SQL-DMO is a mature, well-defined library that enables developers to harness this rich functionality through code in their applications.

DMO is implemented as a dual-interface, in-process server; this means it can be used by any OLE Automation controller (such as Microsoft's Visual Basic), or as a COM object by a C/C++ application. This chapter focuses on using DMO from Visual Basic because this is the tool of choice for most developers building this style of application. But first, you'll need to know some fundamental Visual Basic syntax to understand the examples.

In this chapter, you'll see exactly what SQL-DMO is and look at some real-world examples to use in your own projects immediately. The chapter starts by clearing up some misconceptions about DMO and then discusses the concepts behind DMO. Next comes a detailed discussion of the object model covering the most important objects, methods, and properties. Then you'll move on to several practical examples of using SQL-DMO from Visual Basic. Finally, you'll get some guidelines for developing your own SQL-DMO applications.

DMO Concepts

To best use DMO in your applications, you first need to understand it. Because SQL Server offers many types of functionality, let's first examine what SQL-DMO actually is.

What It Is, What It Isn't

You've probably heard of open database connectivity (ODBC), Data Access Objects (DAO), Remote Database Objects (RDO), DB Library, and possibly even ActiveX Data Objects (ADO). You might have used one or more of these technologies as the basis of your client/server applications. All these technologies are used to access data stored in databases such as SQL Server. Applications based on these technologies can execute queries and insert, modify, and delete information stored in SQL Server.

DMO shares only one thing with these technologies: It is another TLA (three-letter acronym). In fact, SQL-DMO is not concerned with the information databases can store; instead, it is occupied with the structure and maintenance of the databases themselves, as well as with the operation of the SQL Servers that contain the databases. For example, programmers often use SQL-DMO to automate an interface to perform database administration (DBA) tasks, such as backups, database replication, and ad-hoc performance reporting. SQL-DMO is not another new data access technology.

Accessing SQL-DMO Objects from Visual Basic

Before you can use SQL-DMO in your Visual Basic projects, you need to create a reference to the SQL-DMO OLE Automation component. However, before you can do this, you need to install the SQL Server client utilities on the development machine(s). This includes the SQL-DMO dynamic link library (DLL). You then can add a project reference to SQL-DMO. To do this, open your project in Visual Basic. Then choose Project, References. The References dialog box appears, as shown in Figure 21.1.

FIGURE 21.1

Adding a project reference to the SQL-DMO library.

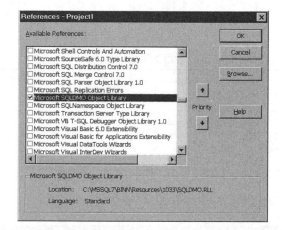

Check the Microsoft SQLDMO Object Library check box and click OK. Having added a reference to SQL-DMO in your Visual Basic project, you can now access all the objects available in SQL-DMO by using native Visual Basic syntax for creating objects, calling methods, and setting properties.

Implementing SQL-DMO Objects

The SQL-DMO object model contains several types of objects:

- Creatable objects
- Noncreatable objects
- Collections
- Lists

This section gives you some simple examples of using SQL-DMO objects.

Creating SQL-DMO Objects

Creatable objects are objects that can be instantiated by using the New keyword:

```
Dim objMyDB As New SQLDMO.Database
```

Or you can use this syntax:

```
Dim objMyDB as SQLDMO.Database
Set objMyDB = New SQLDMO.Database
```

After the object is instantiated, you can set its properties and call its methods, as Listing 21.1 shows.

LISTING 21.1 CALLING SQL-DMO OBJECT METHODS

```
' set Name property of database object
objMyDB.Name = "SouthWind"
Set objMySvr = New SQLDMO.SQLServer
' call Connect method of SQLServer object
objMySvr.Connect "HIGH5", "sa", "password"
objMySvr.Databases.Add objMyDB
objMySvr.DisConnect
```

The methods used in this example are explained later in the chapter.

> **CAUTION**
>
> Always remember to disconnect the SQL Server object before the object variable goes out of scope. This will ensure that server resources are properly released before the client object is destroyed.

Noncreatable Objects

Noncreatable objects are objects that cannot be instantiated by the user. These objects can be returned only as the result of a method call or as a property of another object. The JobServer object is noncreatable, for example; it cannot be instantiated by using the New keyword. The JobServer object is returned as a property of the SQLServer object:

```
' get reference to JobServer
Set objJobSvr = objMySvr.JobServer
intNumJobs = objJobSvr.Jobs.Count
MsgBox "The job server contains " & CStr(intNumJobs) & " jobs."

Private WithEvents mobjMySvr As SQLDMO.SQLServer
```

```
Private Function mobjMySvr_ConnectionBroken _
                (ByVal Message As String) As Boolean
    Select Case MsgBox(Message, vbRetryCancel+vbExclamation, _
                    "Connection Broken")
    Case vbRetry
        ' tell DMO to attempt to re-connect
        mobjMySvr_ConnectionBroken = True
    Case vbCancel
        mobjMySvr_ConnectionBroken = False
    End Select
End Function
```

Here, the ConnectionBroken event is raised when a network or server error causes the client's connection to the specific SQL Server represented by the SQLServer object to break.

Collections

Collections are essentially containers of objects of a similar type. Many objects contain collections of other objects. Objects within a collection can be referenced through the Item method, using a numeric index or a key string. You can add objects to or remove them from a collection by using that collection's Add and Remove methods. The Databases collection of the SQLServer object is an example of a collection.

List Objects

A *list* is a special type of collection (SQLObjectList) with a fixed membership—that is, you can't add members to or remove members from the collection. Lists expose the Count property and the Item and Refresh methods. Examples of methods that return SQLObjectList objects are the ListKeys method of the Column object and the ListPermissions method of the StoredProcedure object.

Using SQL-DMO to Manage Databases

You can use DMO to manage all aspects of database structure. Tables, columns, indexes, and keys can be created, set, modified, and dropped using SQL-DMO. A developer can use the Table object to create new tables or modify existing tables. You can add new columns to a table by creating a Column object and setting its properties. After you set the column properties, the column is added to the table's Columns collection. Listing 21.2 shows how to add a column to an existing table.

LISTING 21.2   ADDING A NEW COLUMN TO AN EXISTING TABLE

```
Dim objMySvr As SQLDMO.SQLServer
Dim objMyDB as SQLDMO.Database
Dim objCustTbl As SQLDMO.Table
Dim objNewCol As SQLDMO.Column

' connect to server
Set objMySvr = New SQLDMO.SQLServer
objMySvr.Connect "HIGH5", "sa", ""

' get reference to Customers table
Set objMyDB = objMySvr.Databases("NorthWind")
Set objCustTbl = objMyDB.Tables("Customers")

' create new column for Email address
Set objNewCol = New SQLDMO.Column
objNewCol.Name = "Email"
objNewCol.Datatype = "nvarchar"
objNewCol.Length =
objNewCol.AllowsNulls = True

' add column to table
objCustTbl.Columns.Add objNewCol

objMySvr.DisConnect
```

Some of the more frequently used objects for managing databases follow:

- `Database`   Contains collections of other objects, such as `Tables`, `Views`, `StoredProcedures`, `Defaults`, `Users`, and others. You can create and add databases to a `SQLServer` object.

- `Table`   Contains collections of other objects, such as `Columns`, `Index`, `Keys`, `Triggers`, `Checks`, and others. You can create and add tables to a `Database` object.

- `FileGroup`   Contains one or more `DBFile` objects, which represent the physical files containing a database's data storage, transaction log, and indexes. A `Database` can have several `FileGroup` objects.

Using SQL-DMO to Manage Servers

The true power of SQL-DMO is evident in its rich object model for managing servers and server-related activity. You can do the following with SQL-DMO:

- Dynamically configure servers.
- Create and manage SQL Server Agent tasks.

- Manage database replication tasks in fine detail.

- Transfer databases in whole or in part from one server to another.

- Import and export data from various sources, such as flat files.

Some objects frequently used to manage servers follow:

SQLServer   One of the most fundamental objects in the SQL-DMO object model, this is the parent of most of the major objects in the model (including the Databases collection). The Configuration object enables you to dynamically configure a particular SQL Server. The BackupDevice object exposes the standard SQL Server backup and restore functions. You can register RemoteServers with the server.

Replication   Contains many objects used to replicate databases across SQL Servers in various configurations. It contains Distributor, Publisher, and Subscriber objects, as well as many subordinate objects that provide this functionality.

JobServer   Carries out the functions provided by the SQL Server Agent. You can create and schedule tasks using the Job object. You can define operators, and they can be the recipients of alerts.

BulkCopy   Represents the SQL Server bulk insert capability, as provided by the command-line BCP program. It is a standalone object used as an argument to the Table object's ImportData and ExportData methods.

Exploring the SQL-DMO Object Model

Now that you've had a taste of SQL-DMO, you can take a look at this topic in a bit more detail. First you'll look at the entire object model. Then you'll learn about the major objects and the object hierarchies under them.

SQL-DMO Object Model

Figure 21.2 shows the entire SQL-DMO object hierarchy.

The Application Object

The Application object is the top object in the SQL-DMO hierarchy. It contains properties—such as VersionMajor, VersionMinor, and ODBCVersionString—that return the SQL Server and ODBC version information. This information can be used to check for compliance at the start of a SQL-DMO application.

FIGURE 21.2

*The SQL-DMO
object hierarchy.*

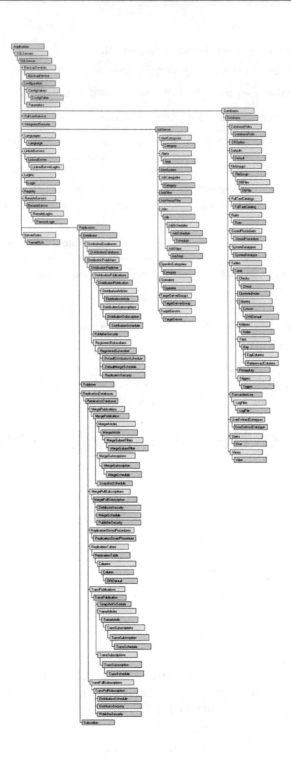

LISTING 21.3   SEARCHING FOR AN AVAILABLE SERVER

```
Dim objApp As SQLDMO.Application
Dim objAvailSvrs As SQLDMO.NameList ' a "super" collection
Dim objSvr As SQLDMO.SQLServer
Dim strMsg As String

' get reference to Application object
Set objApp = New SQLDMO.Application
Set objAvailSvrs = objApp.ListAvailableSQLServers
strMsg = "No. of servers: " & CStr(objAvailSvrs.Count)

' get list of available servers
If objAvailSvrs.Count > 0 Then
    For Each objSvr In objAvailSvrs
        strMsg = strMsg & vbCrLf & "    " & objSvr.NetName
    Next
End If
If objAvailSvrs.FindName("HIGH5") = 0 Then
    strMsg = strMsg & vbCrLf & "HIGH5 is not available."
Else
    strMsg = strMsg & vbCrLf & "HIGH5 is available."
End If
MsgBox strMsg, vbInformation, App.Title

Set objSvr = Nothing
Set objAvailSvrs = Nothing
objApp.Quit
```

The Application object also contains the ServerGroups collection, which manages a registry-based catalog of SQL Servers. In this way, servers can be categorized according to function, region, version, or any other property. Such RegisteredServers can exist in more than one ServerGroup. To register a server, create a RegisteredServer object, set its properties, and then add it to a ServerGroup object. If it's a new ServerGroup, add it to the Application object's ServerGroups collection. Listing 21.4 provides a generic routine for registering a server in a specified server group.

LISTING 21.4   REGISTERING A SERVER IN A SERVER GROUP

```
Public Sub RegisterServer(ByVal vstrGroup As String, _
                          ByVal vstrServer As String)
On Error GoTo ERR_HANDLER

Dim objApp As SQLDMO.Application
Dim objGroup As SQLDMO.ServerGroup
Dim objRegSvr As RegisteredServer
Dim booNewGroup As Boolean
```

continues

LISTING 21.4   CONTINUED

```
' get reference to Application object
Set objApp = New SQLDMO.Application

' check to see if group already exists
On Error Resume Next
Set objGroup = objApp.ServerGroups(vstrGroup)
If Err Then
    ' create new group
    Set objGroup = New SQLDMO.ServerGroup
    objGroup.Name = vstrGroup
    objApp.ServerGroups.Add objGroup
    booNewGroup = True
End If

' check to see if server already exists in group
On Error Resume Next
Set objRegSvr = objGroup.RegisteredServers(vstrServer)
If Err Then
    ' create new server and add to RegisteredServers collection
    Set objRegSvr = New SQLDMO.RegisteredServer
    objRegSvr.Name = vstrServer
    objGroup.RegisteredServers.Add objRegSvr
End If

' if this was a new group, then add it
' to the Application object
If booNewGroup Then
    objApp.ServerGroups.Add objGroup
End If

Cleanup:
Set objSvr = Nothing
Set objAvailSvrs = Nothing
objApp.Quit
Exit Sub

ERR_HANDLER:
MsgBox Err.Description, vbCritical, App.Title
Resume Cleanup
End Sub
```

Finally, the Application object contains the SQLServers collection, which simply lists
the connected servers in the currently running SQL-DMO application:

```
Set objApp = New SQLDMO.Application
MsgBox objApp.SQLServers.Count      ' should be
Set objSvr = New SQLDMO.SQLServer
objSvr.Connect "HIGH5", "sa", ""
MsgBox objApp.SQLServers.Count      ' should be
```

The SQLServer Object

The SQLServer object, one of the most important objects in SQL-DMO, is often the hub of most SQL-DMO development efforts. Table 21.1 lists the more commonly used properties and methods:

TABLE 21.1   COMMONLY USED PROPERTIES AND METHODS

Property or Method	Description
Databases method	Returns a reference to a Databases collection representing the databases available on the server.
JobServer method	Returns a reference to a JobServer object which exposes the functionality provided by the SQL Server Agent.
Replication method	Returns a reference to a Replication object which makes SQL Server's database replication functionality available.
BackupDevices method	Returns a reference to a BackupDevices collection which lists the different media devices used by the database's Backup object. You can check the status of BackupDevice objects and add new devices to the collection.
Logins method	Returns a reference to a Logins collection which manages the user login records used by SQL Server to authenticate users; alternatively, used by Windows NT authentication to map against users.
ServerRoles method	SQL Server has a number of predefined user groups with similar security levels for the purpose of restricting access to the functionality of the SQL Server installation. These groups are known as *server roles* and are represented by a fixed number of ServerRole objects contained in the ServerRoles collection. User membership of these roles can be controlled. Users can be added to the sysadmin role, for example, giving them the same rights as the sa login.
LinkedServers method	SQL Server can maintain a list of nonlocal, heterogeneous OLE DB data providers against which it can run distributed Transact-SQL queries. These data providers are registered as a collection of LinkedServer objects. The LinkedServers collection is persisted in the database. Data provider definitions are thus visible to all SQL Server users.

continues

TABLE 21.1 CONTINUED

Property or Method	Description
RemoteServers method	Gives SQL Server a means of maintaining authentication information for a list of remote SQL Servers from which it will accept, and to which it can initiate, remote connections for the purposes of executing Transact-SQL queries against databases on the remote server (or on the local server, if accepting a connection).

The Database, Jobserver, and Replication objects are described in more detail in the following sections. Now you'll take a look at a few of the more interesting items contained in the SQLServer object.

Logins

SQL Server has two basic security modes:

- **Windows NT authentication**   Maps SQL Server logins to Windows NT users.
- **SQL Server authentication**   Requires SQL Server to maintain lists of logins and passwords that are unrelated to any external operating system security. In this mode, users are required to log in to SQL Server specifically.

A third security mode, mixed security, directs SQL Server to accept either type of login.

SQL-DMO manages SQL Server logins via the Logins collection. To add a new login, create a Login object, set its Name and Database properties, and call the SetPassword method to set the password (if using SQL Server authentication). Finally, add the Login object to the Logins collection. Listing 21.5 demonstrates this process.

LISTING 21.5 ADDING A NEW LOGIN

```
Dim objSvr As SQLDMO.SQLServer
Dim objLogin As SQLDMO.Login

' connect to server
Set objSvr = New SQLDMO.SQLServer
objSvr.Connect "HIGH5", "sa", ""

' create new login
Set objLogin = New SQLDMO.Login
objLogin.Name = "Mike"  ' Must be unique!!!
objLogin.Database = "Northwind"
objLogin.SetPassword "", strPassword
```

```
' add to logins collection
objSvr.Logins.Add objLogin
objSvr.DisConnect
```

> **WARNING**
>
> Embedding any plain-text password in an application is a bad, bad idea! This is done in the examples only for simplicity's sake. A better approach would be to prompt the user for the required password at run time.

The `ServerRole` Object

You can get a specific `ServerRole` object from the `ServerRoles` collection by specifying the role name in the key. You can make certain users members of a particular server role by calling the `AddMember` method of the given `ServerRole` object and specifying a valid SQL Server login name. Calling the `DropMember` method deletes members from a role. You can get a list of role members by calling the `EnumServerRoleMember` method. This returns a `QueryResult` object, which is the SQL-DMO equivalent of a Visual Basic resultset. `EnumServerRolePermission` returns a list of the execution privileges of the role. Listing 21.6 shows how to list the members of a role.

LISTING 21.6   LISTING MEMBERS OF A SERVER ROLE

```
Dim objSvr As SQLDMO.SQLServer
Dim objRole As SQLDMO.ServerRole
Dim objMembers As SQLDMO.QueryResults
Dim intIdx As Integer

' connect to database
Set objSvr = New SQLDMO.SQLServer
objSvr.Connect "(local)", "sa", ""
' get sysadmin role
Set objRole = objSvr.ServerRoles("sysadmin")
Set objMembers = objRole.EnumServerRoleMember
' enumerate members
For intIdx = 1 To objMembers.Rows
    Debug.Print objMembers.GetColumnString(intIdx, 1)
Next intIdx
objSvr.DisConnect
```

The `LinkedServer` Object

Linked servers are a powerful way of linking to data in non[nd]SQL Server data stores via OLE DB. Data in linked servers can be queried from SQL Server via Transact-SQL statements. This forms a good basis for executing distributed transactions against heterogeneous data sources, such as a mixed SQL Server/Oracle environment. SQL Server client applications do not need to know about different data sources they might need. The data they need can be accessed through SQL Server. In addition, when using Microsoft OLE DB Provider for ODBC, just about any data source with an ODBC driver can be accessed from SQL Server.

To create a linked server using SQL-DMO, create a new `LinkedServer` object, set its `Name` property to a unique value (this is how it will be referenced in Transact-SQL queries), set its `ProviderName` property, and optionally, set its `DataSource` or `ProviderString` property. You should set `ProviderName` to the OLE DB simple provider name. Table 21.2 lists provider names for various OLE DB providers.

TABLE 21.2   OLE DB DATA PROVIDERS

OLE DB Source	Provider Name	Data Source	ProviderData String
SQL Server	`SQLOLEDB`	Network name of SQL Server	N/A
Oracle	`MSDAORA`	SQL*Net alias for Oracle database	N/A
Access/Jet	`Microsoft.Jet.OLEDB.4.0`	Full path of `MDB` file	N/A
ODBC	`MSDASQL`	System DSN (DSN_less) string	ODBC connection (DSN-less) string
Excel spreadsheet	`Microsoft.Jet.OLEDB.4.0`	Full path of Excel file	Excel 5.0

The `Database` Object

The methods and properties of the `Database` object are the primary means by which you manage databases in SQL Server. You saw in Listing 21.1 how to create a database by appending a `Database` object to the server's `Databases` collection. You can get a reference to an existing database by referencing an item in this collection with the database name as a key.

Using a `Database` object, you can add or remove tables, views, stored procedures, rules, and other items using the appropriate collections. Here are some of the more commonly used collections:

- `Tables`
- `Views`
- `StoredProcedures`
- `UserDefinedDatatypes`
- `Defaults` Lists the column defaults—default values—that have been defined for tables in this database.
- `Users` Lists the users of the database; SQL Server logins can map to specific users for each database.
- `DatabaseRoles` Similar to the `ServerRoles` collection of the `SQLServer` object. Database users can be added to the membership of specific system or user-defined database roles. By default, users belong to the `public` role when they are created.

Listing 21.7 shows an example of adding a stored procedure to a database.

LISTING 21.7 ADDING A STORED PROCEDURE TO A DATABASE

```
Dim objMySvr As SQLDMO.SQLServer
Dim objDB As SQLDMO.Database
Dim objProc As SQLDMO.StoredProcedure
Dim strName As String

' connect to server
Set objMySvr = New SQLDMO.SQLServer
objMySvr.Connect "(local)", "sa", ""

' create new stored procedure
Set objProc = New SQLDMO.StoredProcedure
strName = "TenLeastExpensiveProducts"
objProc.Name = strName
```

continues

LISTING 21.7   CONTINUED

```
objProc.Text = "create procedure " & strName & " AS" & vbCrLf _
    & "SET ROWCOUNT 10 " & vbCrLf _
    & "SELECT Products.ProductName, Products.UnitPrice" & vbCrLf _
    & "From Products ORDER BY Products.UnitPrice ASC"

' add procedure to database
Set objDB = objMySvr.Databases("Northwind")
objDB.StoredProcedures.Add objProc

objMySvr.DisConnect
Set objProc = Nothing
Set objDB = Nothing
Set objMySvr = Nothing
```

In addition to adding objects to or removing them from your database by using collections, you can perform maintenance actions on the database using its methods. Table 21.3 lists some of these methods.

TABLE 21.3   COMMONLY USED DATABASE METHODS

Method	*Description*
CheckTables([*repair type*])	Performs an integrity test on the pages that store the tables and indexes of the specified database. This is the equivalent of executing the Transact-SQL command DBCC CHECKDB. This method returns a string containing any error information.
ExecuteImmediate(command [,*executiontype*][,*length*])	Executes the Transact-SQL batch specified in the command parameter. This method has a couple of siblings: ExecuteWithResults and ExecuteWithResultsAndMessages. This method is useful for running administrative scripts against the specified database.
Grant(privilege, granteenames), Deny	Grants or denies database privileges to the specified users or roles.
IsUser(user)	Returns True if the specified user is a valid user of this database.
Shrink(newsize, truncateflag)	Attempts to shrink the size of the physical files implementing a database in order to recover lost disk space. Specifying a number between 1 and 100 for newsize denotes a target as a percentage of existing database size. Specifying any negative number causes the server to attempt to shrink the database as much as possible.

Method	Description
`Transfer(transferobject)`	Takes a single parameter specifying a `Transfer` object. Calling this method causes part or all of the specified database to be transferred to another database (possibly on another server).
`UpdateIndexStatistics`	Updates the data distribution statistics used by all indexes on user-defined tables in the specified database.

The `Database` object contains many more interesting methods and properties. Unfortunately, a discussion of them would cause this already weighty tome to swell to twice its size, making it even harder to lift than it already is!

The `Table` Object

The `Table` object is exposed through the `Tables` collection of the `Database` object. Referencing the `Tables` collection using the SQL Server table name as a key returns a useable `Table` object. You can use the `Table` object to directly manipulate the metadata in your database. That is, you can create, alter, or tweak tables, thereby changing their structure. You can create or modify indexes to improve the performance of queries, and you can use methods to import data to and export data from your tables.

Table 21.4 lists some of the more important collections that belong to the `Table` object.

TABLE 21.4 Table OBJECT COLLECTIONS

Collection	Description
`Columns`	Contains `Column` objects representing the actual columns of the table. Each `Column` object fully describes the corresponding table column's properties, including name, data type, and size. You can add or remove columns from the `Columns` collection to perform the corresponding action on the underlying table. (Refer to Listing 21.2 for an example of adding a column to an existing table.)
`Keys`	Lists the primary and foreign key constraints defined for the table. As with other collections you have examined so far, adding or removing `Key` objects has an associated effect on the table being manipulated. Creating a key is a case of setting the `Key.Type` property to `SQLDMOKey_Primary` or `SQLDMOKey_Foreign`, and then add participating column names to the `KeyColumnsNames` collection. And, you can optionally set the `ReferencedTable` property and `ReferencedColumnsNames`

continues

TABLE 21.4   CONTINUED

Collection	Description
	collection (if this is a foreign key). If the Name property of a key is not specified before the key is created, SQL Server generates the key name.
Indexes	Operates much like the Keys collection. Set the Name, Type, and IndexedColumns properties of an Index object before you add it to an existing table's Indexes collection.
Checks	Contains Check objects that reflect the SQL Server CHECK constraints that exist on the specified table. You can add and remove checks in a manner consistent with indexes and keys. A check is defined by its Text property, which is just the SQL Server Transact-SQL definition of the constraint.
Triggers	Operates much like the Checks collection. Trigger objects are created, their Text property is set, and the objects are added to an existing table's Triggers collection.

CAUTION

Always remember to call the Table object's BeginAlter method before you make multiple changes to a table. This call must be matched with a corresponding DoAlter method call immediately after the changes. Outside a BeginAlter ... DoAlter block, any change causes a discrete ALTER TABLE command to be issued. Within the block, the changes are grouped.

Listing 21.8 shows the addition of a new index and a trigger to an existing table in the Northwind sample database provided with SQL Server.

LISTING 21.8   ADDING AN INDEX AND A TRIGGER TO AN EXISTING TABLE

```
Dim objMySvr As SQLDMO.SQLServer
Dim objTbl As SQLDMO.Table
Dim objIdx As SQLDMO.Index
Dim objTrigger As SQLDMO.Trigger
Dim strName As String

' connect to server
```

```
Set objMySvr = New SQLDMO.SQLServer
objMySvr.Connect "(local)", "sa", ""

' get reference to Orders table
Set objTbl = objMySvr.Databases("Northwind").Tables("Orders")

' create new index
Set objIdx = New SQLDMO.Index
objIdx.Name = "IX_ShipCity"
objIdx.Type = SQLDMOIndex_Default
objIdx.IndexedColumns = "ShipCity"

' create new trigger
' purpose of trigger is to force a specific
' courier for overseas orders.
Set objTrigger = New SQLDMO.Trigger
strName = "Orders_Ins"
With objTrigger
    .Name = strName
    .Text = "CREATE TRIGGER " & strName _
        & " ON Orders FOR INSERT AS" & vbCrLf _
        & " IF (SELECT ShipCountry FROM inserted)" _
        & " <> 'USA'" & vbCrLf _
        & " UPDATE Orders SET ShipVia = 1" & vbCrLf _
        & " FROM Orders o, Inserted i" & vbCrLf _
        & " WHERE o.OrderID = i.OrderID"
End With

' make changes to table
objTbl.BeginAlter
objTbl.Indexes.Add objIdx
objTbl.Triggers.Add objTrigger
objTbl.DoAlter

objMySvr.DisConnect
Set objTbl = Nothing
Set objIdx = Nothing
Set objTrigger = Nothing
```

The JobServer (Executive) Object

The JobServer object is an important part of the SQL Server SQL-DMO hierarchy. Through this object and its subordinates, the entire functionality of the SQL Server Agent is exposed. The prime focus of JobServer is to coordinate the running of jobs. Each job consists of one or more JobSteps that define the discrete commands to be carried out by the job server at the time the job is scheduled.

The JobServer object is also responsible for notifying specified operators of alerts that occur as a response to SQL Server errors that match defined criteria. Some of the more important collections of the JobServer object follow:

- Jobs   Contains the Job objects corresponding to jobs scheduled to run on this SQL Server.

- Alerts   Contains the Alert objects that have been defined by the user. Each Alert object acts as a filter designed to respond to SQL Server errors of a defined severity, or to particular error message numbers. In addition, alerts can be restricted to respond to error conditions arising in specific databases.

- Operators   Contains a number of Operator objects that correspond to SQL Server operators. An *operator* is basically a recipient of alerts and job status notification messages. An operator is defined by the email and network name addresses (EmailAddress and NetSendAddress properties) that act as a destination for SQL Server messages, and by the list of notifications for which this operator will be the recipient. Use the AddNotification and RemoveNotification methods of the Operator object to control which messages an operator sees.

- TargetServers   Contains TargetServer objects that correspond to a list of SQL Servers that have been enlisted to act as job execution targets. In SQL Server 7.0, the SQL Server Agent can direct the job execution of multiple servers.

The JobServer object also exposes the following methods and properties that control its operation and/or provide status information:

- Start, Stop methods   Start and stop the SQL Server Agent service.

- Status property   Returns a value specifying the operational state of the SQL Server Agent service. This is a read-only property.

- EnumJobs(*[JobFilter]*)   Returns a QueryResults object method listing information on all the jobs currently defined in the SQL Server Agent. The method takes an optional JobFilter object, which restricts the resultset.

- EnumJobHistory   Returns a QueryResults object (*[JobFilter]*) method listing the historical results of all jobs run on the server since the last time the job history was purged (PurgeJobHistory method). The optional JobFilter object restricts the resultset.

- Refresh method   Updates the collections and properties of the JobServer object with the current values from the SQL Server Agent.

The Replication Object

The `Replication` object contains a rich object hierarchy almost as complex as the rest of the SQL-DMO hierarchy. It encapsulates the functionality of SQL Server that allows data to be replicated from server to server. Although replication is a topic too complex to cover in a couple of pages (see Chapter 16, "Replication," for a more thorough treatment of the subject), this section briefly discusses the SQL-DMO objects used to manage replication functions.

Recall that SQL Server replication is based on the concept of publishers offering *articles* (data from tables or stored procedures) for replication. Subscribers are the recipients of this data. Replication comes in three types: snapshot, transactional, and merge. Finally, subscriptions can be *push* (the act of publishing and subscribing are one and the same) or *pull* (the subscriber controls the receipt of data). In addition, multiple remote servers can act as distributors of the published information.

The following list covers some of the more pertinent methods, objects, and collections in the `Replication` object hierarchy:

- **ConfigureReplication method**   When called, this method enables (or disables) replication on the server by adding the appropriate replication components (stored procedures and system tables supporting replication).

- **Distributor object**   With this object, a local distributor can be installed or removed from the local SQL Server. Each distributor can maintain one or more `DistributionDatabases` and `DistributionPublishers`. The `DistributionPublishers` collection represents publishers that are using this distributor for replication.

- **ReplicationDatabases collection**   This collection represents the user databases on the server that can participate in replication. Each `ReplicationDatabase` object exposes the following collections for managing the publication or subscription of replicated databases:

  - `MergePublications` and `TransPublications` collections.   Adding `MergePublications` and `TransPublication` objects to their respective collections is the way data is published using either merge or transactional replication. In addition, each publication object contains `MergeArticles` and `MergeSubscriptions`, and `TransArticles` and `TransSubscriptions`, respectively. The articles correspond to tables being published for replication, and the subscriptions correspond to the push subscriptions made from the publisher.

- MergePullSubscriptions and TransPullSubscriptions collections. Subscribers can initiate a pull of data from a publisher by creating new MergePullSubscription or TransPullSubscription objects (as appropriate), setting some properties (Publisher, PublicationDB, Publication, SubscriptionType, and SecurityMode), and adding the object to the appropriate collection.

Common Practical Uses of SQL-DMO

This section gives some Visual Basic examples of using SQL-DMO in real-life scenarios. Although these examples are not complete standalone programs, every effort has been made to make the code generic enough to be used with little modification in your own programs. The examples take the form of generic, useful (hopefully) procedures.

User Administration Example

You can use the procedures shown in Listing 21.9 in a typical user administration program. These examples are part of a hypothetical program that manages users of the Southwind database. The procedures assume the existence of two module-level object variables called mobjSvr (representing a SQL Server called HIGH5) and mobjDB (representing the Southwind database on that server). The following procedures are included:

- ListUsers
- AddNewUser
- ChangeUserPassword
- ListUserRoles
- AddUserRole
- RemoveUserRole

LISTING 21.9 ROUTINES FOR MANAGING USERS AND ASSIGNING ROLES

```
Private mobjSvr As SQLDMO.SQLServer
Private mobjDB As SQLDMO.Database

Public Function ConnectDB() As Boolean
    ' connect to database
    Set mobjSvr = New SQLDMO.SQLServer
    mobjSvr.Connect "HIGH5", "sa", ""
    ' get reference to Southwind database
    Set mobjDB = mobjSvr.Databases("Southwind")
```

```
        ConnectDB = True
End Function

Public Sub DisconnectDB()
    Set mobjDB = Nothing
    mobjSvr.Disconnect
    Set mobjSvr = Nothing
End Sub

' The following routine lists current users
' of the Southwind database
Public Sub ListUsers(ByRef rlisUsers As ListBox)
    Dim i As Integer
    Dim objQry As QueryResults
    rlisUsers.Clear
    Set objQry = mobjDB.EnumLoginMappings
    With objQry
        For i = 1 To .Rows
            rlisUsers.AddItem .GetColumnString(i, 1)
        Next i
    End With
    Set objQry = Nothing
End Sub
' The following routine adds a new user
' to the Southwind database
Public Function AddNewUser _
                (ByVal vstrUser As String) As Boolean
    On Error GoTo ERR_HANDLER
    Dim objLogin As SQLDMO.Login
    Dim objUser As SQLDMO.User
    ' create new login and default to our database
    ' NB: initially password is empty
    Set objLogin = New SQLDMO.Login
    objLogin.Name = vstrUser
    objLogin.Database = mobjDB.Name
    ' create similarly named db user
    Set objUser = New SQLDMO.User
    objUser.Name = vstrUser
    objUser.Login = vstrUser
    ' add to appropriate collections
    mobjSvr.Logins.Add objLogin
    mobjDB.Users.Add objUser
    AddNewUser = True
    Exit Function
ERR_HANDLER:
    AddNewUser = False
End Function
' The following routine is used to change a user's password
' in the Southwind database
```

continues

LISTING 21.9   CONTINUED

```
Public Function ChangeUserPassword _
                (ByVal vstrUser As String, _
                 ByVal vstrOldPwd As String, _
                 ByVal vstrNewPwd As String) As Boolean
    On Error Resume Next
    ChangeUserPassword = True
    With mobjSvr.Logins(vstrUser)
        .SetPassword vstrOldPwd, vstrNewPwd
    End With
    If Err Then ChangeUserPassword = False
End Function
' The following routine lists user roles for a
' specified user of the Southwind database
Public Sub ListUserRoles _
                (ByVal vstrUser As String, _
                 ByRef rlisRoles As ListBox)
    Dim i As Integer
    Dim strDBU As String
    rlisRoles.Clear
    ' get DB username equivalent of login user
    strDBU = mobjSvr.Logins(vstrUser).GetUserName(mobjDB.Name)
    With mobjDB.Users(strDBU)
        For i = 1 To .ListMembers.Count
            rlisRoles.AddItem .ListMembers(i)
        Next i
    End With
End Sub
' The following routine adds a new tole to a
' specified user of the Southwind database.
Public Function AddUserRole _
                (ByVal vstrUser As String, _
                 ByVal vstrRole As String) As Boolean
    Dim strDBU As String
    On Error Resume Next
    ' get DB username equivalent of login user
    strDBU = mobjSvr.Logins(vstrUser).GetUserName(mobjDB.Name)
    AddUserRole = True
    mobjDB.DatabaseRoles(vstrRole).AddMember strDBU
    If Err Then AddUserRole = False
End Function
' The following routine removes a user role from the
' specified user of the Southwind database.
Public Function RemoveUserRole _
                (ByVal vstrUser As String, _
                 ByVal vstrRole As String) As Boolean
    Dim strDBU As String
    On Error Resume Next
    ' get DB username equivalent of login user
    strDBU = mobjSvr.Logins(vstrUser).GetUserName(mobjDB.Name)
```

```
        RemoveUserRole = True
        mobjDB.DatabaseRoles(vstrRole).DropMember strDBU
        If Err Then RemoveUserRole = False
End Function
```

Flat File Import/Export Example

This example shows how the user can use the BulkCopy object to import or export data to or from tables in SQL Server. In Listing 21.10, the FileImportExport routine provides a generic interface for importing or exporting a tab-delimited file into a specified table. The routine is placed in a form containing two Label controls (lblNumRows and lblStatus) that are updated in the RowsCopied event of the BulkCopy object. The user can abort the operation by clicking the cmdAbort command button. Before using this for your own database, note that this example truncates any existing data in a table when an import operation is specified.

LISTING 21.10 IMPORTING AND EXPORTING DATA FROM A SQL SERVER TABLE

```
Private WithEvents mobjBC As SQLDMO.BulkCopy

Public Enum IEX_ENUM
    iexImport
    iexExport
End Enum

Private Sub cmdAbort_Click()
    ' abort bulkcopy operation
    mobjBC.Abort
End Sub

Private Sub mobjBC_RowsCopied(ByVal Message As String, ByVal Rows As Long)
    ' update status as bulkcopy progresses.
    lblNumRows.Caption = Rows
    lblStatus.Caption = Message
End Sub

Public Sub FileImportExport(ByVal vstrDB As String, _
                            ByVal vstrTable As String, _
                            ByVal vstrFile As String, _
                            ByVal vImpExpFlag As IEX_ENUM)

    Dim objSvr As New SQLDMO.SQLServer

    ' connect to server
    objSvr.Connect "(local)", "sa", ""
    ' set bulkcopy object properties
```

continues

LISTING **21.10**   CONTINUED

```
Set mobjBC = New SQLDMO.BulkCopy
With mobjBC
    .DataFileType = SQLDMODataFile_TabDelimitedChar
    .ColumnDelimiter = vbTab
    .RowDelimiter = vbCrLf
    .DataFilePath = vstrFile
End With

With objSvr.Databases(vstrDB).Tables(vstrTable)
    If vImpExpFlag = iexExport Then
        ' if exporting then...
        ' delete existing file
        Kill vstrFile
        ' export data
        .ExportData mobjBC
    Else
        ' if importing then...
        ' set BC options supporting non-logged operation
        mobjBC.SuspendIndexing = True
        mobjBC.UseBulkCopyOption = True
        ' delete existing data from table (non-logged)
        .TruncateData
        ' import data
        .ImportData mobjBC
    End If
End With

objSvr.DisConnect
Set objSvr = Nothing

End Sub
```

Remote Database Synchronization Example

This example shows how a remote client may create anonymous pull subscriptions to a server over the Internet. In Listing 21.11, a remote SQL Server application can call the CreateSubscription procedure to create a merge-type pull subscription to a specified publication of a database that has been published on an Internet server. The subscription in this example is scheduled to run weekly.

LISTING 21.11   CREATING A SUBSCRIPTION TO A TABLE PUBLISHED OVER THE INTERNET

```
Public Sub CreateSubscription(ByVal vstrRemoteDB As String, _
                              ByVal vstrDBName As String, _
                              ByVal vstrPub As String, _
                              ByVal vstrPubPwd As String, _
                              ByVal vstrDistPwd As String)

    Dim objSub As New SQLDMO.MergePullSubscription

    ' Firstly, we set the object to point to the publisher
    ' and publication that we will be replicating from.
    With objSub
        .Publisher = vstrRemoteDB
        .PublicationDB = vstrDBName
        .Publication = vstrPub
        .SubscriberType = SQLDMOMergeSubscriber_Anonymous
        With .DistributorSecurity
            .SecurityMode = SQLDMOReplSecurity_Normal
            .StandardLogin = "sa"
            .StandardPassword = vstrDistPwd
        End With
        With .PublisherSecurity
            .SecurityMode = SQLDMOReplSecurity_Normal
            .StandardLogin = "sa"
            .StandardPassword = vstrPubPwd
        End With
        ' This subscription is to be run weekly.
        With .MergeSchedule
            .FrequencyType = SQLDMOFreq_Weekly
            .ActiveStartDate = CLng(Format$(Now, "yyyymmdd"))
        End With
    End With
    ' Then, we add this object to the MergePullSubscriptions
    ' collection of our replicated database.
    mobjSvr.Replication.ReplicationDatabases(vstrDBName) _
        .MergePullSubscriptions.Add objSub
    Set objSub = Nothing

End Sub
```

Building Database Management Tools

I hope you've now gained some insight into the new, improved SQL-DMO in SQL Server 7.0. This chapter closes with a few pointers for developing your own SQL-DMO applications.

Guidelines for Building Your Own Database Management Tools

The most important thing to remember when using SQL-DMO is to keep in mind what you are trying to achieve with your code. Although using SQL-DMO to completely rebuild the SQL Server Enterprise Manager *is* possible given enough time, it is probably a waste of time (unless you really, really don't like the Microsoft Management Console!). Keep your use of SQL-DMO objects function-driven.

- Do your users need to periodically import data from a text file sourced from a dusty FORTRAN application on some ancient mainframe? Use the `BulkCopy` object.

- Does the setup program for your nifty Internet shopping application need to create some pull subscriptions for the catalog and pricing information it needs to obtain from `www.shoptillyadrop.com`? Use the `Replication` objects.

- Does the customer for your new n-tier, bleeding-edge client/server application insist on using SQL Server authentication and demand that you provide users with an easy way to change their passwords? Use the `Login` object.

Summary

In spite of the cautions mentioned in this chapter, don't be afraid to experiment and play around. The SQL-DMO hierarchy is a rich command set that puts the full power of SQL Server at your fingertips. You'll be surprised at what riches lurk within its labyrinthine structure. Unlike data access object models such as ADO, with SQL-DMO you get to play SQL Server god. Just be careful that you don't grant too many godlike powers to your users. Your manager or customer might never forgive you!

CHAPTER 22

Automating Web Publication of SQL Server Data

The order comes down from above: "Put the database up on the Web. Now." It's up to you to decide the best way to do it. When choosing a solution, you have to balance your priorities. Is development speed the top priority? Or are you more concerned about the quality of the Web pages, and how they incorporate into your overall Web strategy? How important is maintainability? Are you willing to let this "one time" assignment become a permanent chore?

This chapter explores the Web Assistant, a wizard that creates HTML files that you can publish onto the Web. This is different than having an HTML page "pull" data from the datbase into another dynamically created HTML page. Chapter 24, "SQL Server, ADO, and the Web," covers more in-depth methods for publishing to the Web that you can use to customize or refine Web pages you create with the Web Assistant.

Components of the Web Assistant

When should you use Web Assistant? The short answer is to use it when you want publish something in a hurry without having to agonize over how it looks.

The Web Assistant is nice little tool, but it's not the only way to publish data. Like all wizards, the Web Assistant has its limitations. This chapter explains what the Web Assistant can and can't do. When you implement your solution, you might need to enhance the solutions with additional programming as demonstrated in Chapter 24. However, the Web Assistant makes creating and updating Web pages a relatively simple matter by using built-in SQL Server stored and extended procedures.

Web Assistant generates HTML (Hypertext Markup Language) files based on SQL Server 7 data.

I use *Web Assistant* as the umbrella term for the components that make up this technology. Here is a summary of the items:

Term	*Description*
Web Assistant DLL	Xpweb70.dll, normally located in the ..\MSSQL7\BINN folder.
xp_makewebtask	Extended stored procedure that is called by sp_makewebtask and calls xpweb70.dll.
sp_makewebtask	Stored procedure that can be called either manually or through the Web Assistant Wizard.
Web Assistant Wizard	Wizard with dialog boxes that in the end calls sp_makewebtask.

The standard approach is to run the Web Assistant Wizard and step through all the dialog boxes until, at the end, you have generated your HTML file.

Using the Web Assistant Wizard

The Web Assistant Wizard is just one of many wizards that come with SQL Server 7. Although this wizard has the highest profile in Microsoft's literature, in the egalitarian kingdom of Enterprise Manager, it receives no special menu item or button. By the way, it seems to me that *assistant* and *wizard* mean pretty much the same thing. Why not just call it Web Wizard? I think part of the reason might be that it was called Web Assistant in 6.5, and Microsoft didn't want to rename it. Not that Microsoft has shown any previous qualms over renaming products and tools...

22

AUTOMATING WEB PUBLICATION OF SQL SERVER

> **NOTE**
>
> To run the wizard, you need execute permission for xp_makewebtask and sp_makewebtask. You will also need the permission for the database objects upon which you want to run the wizard.

To run the wizard, follow these steps:

1. Start Enterprise Manager.
2. In the left pane, select the server that has the database whose data you want to publish.
3. Choose Tools, Wizards from the menu.
4. The Select Wizard dialog box then appears. The Web Assistant Wizard is located under the Management heading. Double-click on Management or click on the plus sign next to Management.
5. Select Web Assistant Wizard and then click OK, or simply double-click it.

There's another way to get to the Web Assistant Wizard. In the left pane, under your server, there's a folder called Management. If you open that folder, one of the items is Web Publishing. When it's selected, you can create a new Web Assistant Job by choosing Action, New. If you are displaying the snap-in buttons, you can click the New button as well (it kind of like a yellow asterisk).

At this point, you can step your way through the screens because they're pretty self-explanatory. What I'm going to do instead is discuss xp_makewebtask and sp_makewebtask.

Using `xp_makewebtask` and `sp_makewebtask`

Think of Web Assistant Wizard as the manager who goes in front of the client with his slideshow presentation, and of `xp_makewebtask` and `sp_makewebtask` as the person who's really doing the work. We all know which person you need to talk to understand what's really going on.

`Sp_makewebtask` is the stored procedure that calls the extended stored procedure `xp_makewebtask`, which is located in `xpweb7.dll`. All `sp_makewebtask` does is call `xp_makewebtask`, so `xp_makewebtask` is really doing all the work. Microsoft does not want developers to worry about extended stored procedures. They prefer to provide developers with a regular stored procedure as a front end.

Frankly, I don't have a problem with that, except for some extended stored procedures (say, `xp_regread`, which allows you to read the registry of the computer upon which that SQL Server is running), its philosophy is "Don't worry your pretty head about it. We could give you a stored procedure to wrap around it, but we're either too busy, or we simply don't want you to run it. As for documentation, no way."

Then there are extended stored procedures such as `xp_readmail` (allows you to read a mail message from the SQL Server mail inbox), which has documentation and is designed to be called directly. Go figure.

All extended stored procedures are located in the master database. There's a special category called "Extended Stored Procedures" that isn't in any other database.

Using Enterprise Manager with the Stored Procedures

Just for kicks, let's look at what Enterprise Manager is willing to tell us about `xp_makewebtask`:

1. Start Enterprise Manager.
2. Double-click on your server's name.
3. Double-click on Databases.
4. Double-click on Master.

5. Click on Extended Stored Procedures. In the right pane, you'll see a long list of extended stored procedure names. Note that several of them start with "sp" as opposed to "xp".

6. Scroll down until you see xp_makewebtask. Double-click on it to display its properties.

As you can see from Figure 22.1, there isn't a whole lot of information. You get the DLL name and a button that allows you to set permissions for the extended stored procedure. Whee.

FIGURE 22.1

The properties for
xp_makewebtask.

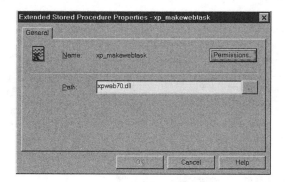

Let's try our luck with sp_makewebtask. This is a "regular" stored procedure, or at least as "regular" as a stored procedure can be that's located in the master database. That is to say, it's a stored procedure that Microsoft wrote and included with SQL Server 7, not some stored procedure you wrote for your database.

1. While still in Enterprise Manager, with the Master database selected, click on Stored Procedures in the left pane.

2. In the right pane, scroll through the list of stored procedures until you find sp_makewebtask. Select it and then double-click on it.

You can see the properties for sp_makewebtask—primarily its code is shown—in Figure 22.2.

FIGURE 22.2
The properties for
sp_makewebtask.

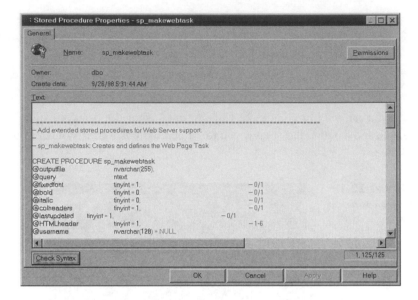

Refining Web Pages with sp_makewebtask and xp_makewebtask

The results in Figure 22.2 are more encouraging for using straight code rather than the interface for using these stored procedures. Listing 22.1 shows all the code for sp_makewebtask. As you can see, it really doesn't do too much other than make a call to xp_makewebtask. It has 33 parameters, and it passes each directly to a call to xp_makewebtask. The exceptions to this are @dbname, @procname, and @username, which, if empty, have values generated for them.

> **NOTE**
>
> Here are just a couple of reminders when looking at the code. In Transact-SQL, parameters and variable names start with the @ sign. Unicode variable types start with an n, such as nvarchar. Similarly, literal strings that are to be assigned Unicode variables have an N in front of them.

LISTING 22.1   sp_makewebtask

```
--====================================================================
-- Add extended stored procedures for Web Server support.
--
-- sp_makewebtask: Creates and defines the Web Page Task

CREATE PROCEDURE sp_makewebtask
@outputfile        nvarchar(255),
@query             ntext,
@fixedfont         tinyint = 1,                    -- 0/1
@bold              tinyint = 0,                  -- 0/1
@italic            tinyint = 0,                    -- 0/1
@colheaders        tinyint = 1,                    -- 0/1
@lastupdated     tinyint = 1,                 -- 0/1
@HTMLheader        tinyint = 1,                    -- 1-6
@username          nvarchar(128) = NULL,
@dbname            nvarchar(128) = NULL,
@templatefile      nvarchar(255) = NULL,
@webpagetitle      nvarchar(255) = NULL,
@resultstitle      nvarchar(255) = NULL,
@URL             nvarchar(255) = NULL,
@reftext           nvarchar(255) = NULL,
@table_urls        tinyint = 0,                    -- 0/1;
➥1=use table of URLs
@url_query         nvarchar(255) = NULL,
@whentype          tinyint = 1,
                          -- 1=now, 2=later, 3=every xday
                          -- 4=every n units of time
@targetdate        int = 0,                      -- yyyymmdd as int
@targettime        int = 0,                      -- hhnnss as int
@dayflags          tinyint = 1,              -- powers
➥of 2 for days of week
@numunits          tinyint = 1,
@unittype          tinyint = 1,      -- 1=hours, 2=days, 3=weeks, 4=minutes
@procname          nvarchar(128) = NULL,    -- name to use when making
                   -- the task and the wrapper/condenser stored procs
@maketask          int = 2,              -- 0=create unencrypted sproc,
➥no task
                   -- 1=encrypted sproc and task 2=unencrypted sproc
➥and task
@rowcnt            int = 0,          -- max no of rows to display
@tabborder         tinyint = 1,        -- borders around the results table
@singlerow         tinyint = 0,        -- Single row per page
@blobfmt         ntext = NULL,        -- Formatting for text and image
fields
@nrowsperpage      int = 0,      -- Results displayed in multiple pages of
                          -- n rows per page
@datachg         ntext = NULL, --Table and column names for a trigger
```

continues

22
AUTOMATING
WEB PUBLICATION
OF SQL SERVER

LISTING 22.1   CONTINUED

```
@charset        nvarchar(25) = N'utf-8', -- Universal character set
                                         -- is the default
@codepage       int = 65001     -- utf-8 (universal) code page
                                -- is the default

AS
BEGIN

    DECLARE @suid smallint
    DECLARE @yearchar nvarchar(4)
    DECLARE @monthchar nvarchar(2)
    DECLARE @daychar nvarchar(2)
    DECLARE @hourchar nvarchar(2)
    DECLARE @minchar nvarchar(2)
    DECLARE @secchar nvarchar(2)
    DECLARE @currdate datetime
    DECLARE  @retval int


-- Check for valid @dbname if supplied
    IF (@dbname is NOT NULL)
       IF (NOT(exists(SELECT
➡* FROM master..sysdatabases WHERE name = @dbname)))
       BEGIN
            RAISERROR(16854,11,1)
            RETURN (9)
       END

-- IF not supplied, determine the user executing this procedure
    SET @username = suser_sname()

    IF ( (charindex ('\',@username) > 0) OR (@username is NULL) )
    BEGIN
        SELECT @username = N'dbo'
    END

-- If not supplied, determine the database currently active
    IF (@dbname is NULL)
    BEGIN
        SELECT @dbname = d.name
          FROM master..sysdatabases d,
               master..sysprocesses p
         WHERE d.dbid  = p.dbid
           AND spid    = @@spid

    END

-- Generate @procname if not supplied
IF (@procname is NULL)
```

```
BEGIN

  SET @currdate = getdate()

  SET @yearchar = convert(nvarchar(4), year(@currdate))
  SET @monthchar =
      right('0' + rtrim(convert(nvarchar(2),
                                month(@currdate))),2)
  SET @daychar =
      right('0' + rtrim(convert(nvarchar(2),
                                day(@currdate))),2)
  SET @hourchar =
      right('0' + rtrim(convert(nvarchar(2),
                                datepart(hh,@currdate))),2)
  SET @minchar =
      right('0' + rtrim(convert(nvarchar(2),
                                datepart(mi,@currdate))),2)
  SET @secchar =
      right('0' + rtrim(convert(nvarchar(2),
                                datepart(ss,@currdate))),2)

  -- Get default procname if not supplied
  SET @procname = N'web_'
                  + convert(nchar(14), @yearchar
                                       + @monthchar
                                       + @daychar
                                       + @hourchar
                                       + @minchar
                                       + @secchar)
                + convert(nvarchar(20), @@spid)
                + right(rtrim(convert(VARCHAR(25), RAND())),
                        4)
    END

  SET @retval = 0

-- Create the Web task
  EXECUTE @retval =
    master..xp_makewebtask  @outputfile,
                            @query,
                            @username,
                            @procname,
                            @dbname,
                            @fixedfont,
                            @bold,
                            @italic,
                            @colheaders,
                            @lastupdated,
                            @HTMLheader,
```

continues

LISTING 22.1   CONTINUED

```
                          @templatefile,
                          @webpagetitle,
                          @resultstitle,
                          @URL,
                          @reftext,
                          @table_urls,
                          @url_query,
                          @whentype,
                          @targetdate,
                          @targettime,
                          @dayflags,
                          @numunits,
                          @unittype,
                          @rowcnt,
                          @maketask,
                          @tabborder,
                          @singlerow,
                          @blobfmt,
                          @nrowsperpage,
                          @datachg,
                          @charset,
                          @codepage

    IF (@retval <> 0)
        BEGIN
            SET @procname = 'xp_makewebtask'
            RAISERROR(@retval, 11, 1, @procname)
        END

    RETURN @retval

END
```

The procedure sp_makewebtask has 33 parameters. Fortunately, you don't need to specify all of them to get results. In fact, only two parameters are required: @outputfile and @query. Other parameters let you specify aesthetics of the Web page's appearance as well as automation option.

Required and Basic Parameters for sp_makewebtask

Let's take sp_makewebtask out for a spin. First, create a folder named "Pubs HTML," where the HTML files will be generated.

Next, start Query Analyzer, which is in your Microsoft SQL Server 7.0 program folder. After logging in, type the following in the query window:

```
EXECUTE sp_makewebtask
            @outputfile = N'C:\Pubs HTML\Titles.htm',
            @query=N'Select title From titles',
            @dbname=N'pubs'
```

This code generates the file `C:\Pubs HTML\Titles.htm`. Because it's an HTML file, it looks different in a browser than it does in an ASCII editor such as Notepad. To view the file in a browser, open Microsoft Internet Explorer, and type **C:\Pubs HTML\Titles.htm** in the address bar. The result should look something like Figure 22.3.

FIGURE 22.3

The file generated by sp_makewebtask.

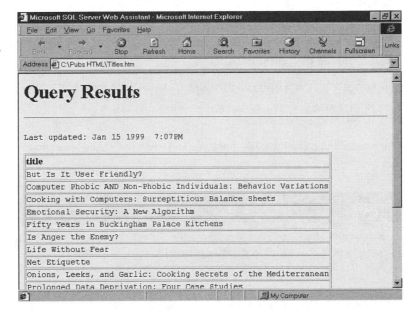

To view the HTML code for the file, choose View, View Source from the Internet Explorer menu.

@outputfile

Let's examine the parameters used to generate the file. The `@outputfile` parameter specifies the name of the file that will be generated. If it already exists, it's overwritten without any warning.

The file extension can be anything, or you could omit it altogether. Keep in mind, however, that Internet Explorer 4.0 on NT 4.0 (and probably other versions as well) uses a file's extension to determine how local files should be viewed. So, if you save the file as `Titles.whatever`, it brings up a dialog box asking you to associate the file with an application. Microsoft has already associated `.htm` files with Internet Explorer. Note that this is not a problem with Netscape Communicator 4.5 (and probably not a problem with other versions of Netscape, either).

If the file path is incorrect (say, the folder doesn't exist), you get an error message, and the file isn't generated.

@query

The `@query` parameter is simply your query. In this case, you just have a simple `SELECT` statement: `Select title From titles`. The results of this query are displayed in the file specified in `@outputfile`.

Suppose you give it a query that returns no rows, for example:

```
@query=N'Select title From titles where title =
     ➥ ''Slartibartfast'''
```

The result is that the table has only one row with the value `"The specified statement did not generate any data"`.

> **NOTE**
>
> Note that you need to put two single quotes next right next to each other when you have a single quote embedded within a string.

If the query is syntactically incorrect, you get an error message, and no file is generated.

You can, if you're feeling rambunctious, put a non-`SELECT` statement into the query. Here the query is an insert statement:

```
@query=N'Insert Into Titles(Title_ID, Title) Values
     ➥ (''102030'', ''Yippity Skippity'')'
```

Remarkably, the `INSERT` statement is actually executed, and the row is inserted into the table. The HTML file generated simply contains the cryptic message `More results can be found in:`. That's it. The same is true if you use a `DELETE` statement, and probably for similar statements. For the other parameters described here, this phrase precedes links to other pages. I'm guessing that the stored procedure wasn't expecting to have to handle data modification statements, which is certainly excusable.

You can also call stored procedures in your query. For example, to run the `byroyalty` stored procedure, with the `@percentage` parameter equal to `30`, you would set the `@query` parameter like this:

```
@query=N'exec byroyalty @percentage=30'
```

@dbname

The `@dbname` parameter is simply the name of the database from which the query will be run. If it is omitted, the current database is used. An error occurs if the database used is invalid.

@username

The `@username` parameter is optional because `sp_makewebtask` defaults to the current user. If you're not the sa or the dbo, this parameter doesn't really help because you can't use alternative usernames, anyway.

Page Formatting Parameters

The next parameters I discuss affect what the exported page looks like. They're nothing terribly fancy, but you're likely to use them frequently.

- The `@fixedfont` parameter must be `0` or `1`. The default is `1`. If it's `0`, the text is proportional, meaning that `iiii` is narrower than `WWWW`. If the parameter's value is `1`, `iiii` and `WWWW` are the same width. The default is `1` because about 25% of browsers don't handle proportional fonts. The HTML tag that is being added or left out is `<TT>`.

- The `@bold` parameter must be `0` or `1`. The default is `0`. If it's `0`, the data isn't **bold**; if it's `1`, it is. The HTML tag that's being added or left out is `<B>`.

- The `@colheaders` parameter must be `0` or `1`. The default is `1`. If it's `0`, the table has no column headers. If it's `1`, there are column headers.

- The `@lastupdated` parameter must be `0` or `1`. The default is `1`. If it's `0`, the "Last Updated" phrase is absent from the Web page. It it's `1`, the phrase is there.

- The `@HTMLheader` parameter must be `1–6`. The default is `1`. This parameter specifies the size of the caption above the header, with `1` being the biggest and `6` the smallest.

- The `@webpagetitle` parameter specifies the title of the Web page. The title is what shows up on the browser's title bar and is the default name when you bookmark a page. This parameter's a little strange because if you leave it blank or set it to one space, the title is `Microsoft SQL Server Web Assistant`. However, if you set this parameter to two spaces, the Web page has no title.

> **NOTE**
>
> By the way, the documentation helpfully suggests that another way of removing the title is to manually edit the Web page and take out the <TITLE> </TITLE> tags and the text between them. I don't really understand why you would do that instead of setting the @webpagetitle parameter to two blank spaces.

- The @resultstitle parameter sets the caption above the table of data. The default value is Query Results.

- The @tabborder parameter must be 0 or 1. The default is 1. If it's 0, there's no border; if it's 1, there is.

- The @charset parameter describes the name of the character set used by the page, which is recognized by the browser. The value is set in the <META> tag value of charset. The default is N'utf-8. You might want to change it if you are working with different alphabets. To see the list of available character sets on your computer, type **Exec sp_enumcodepages** in Query Analyzer.

- The @codepage parameter is the numeric value for the codepage to be used by the browser. The default is 65001. To see the list of available character sets on your computer, type **Exec sp_enumcodepages**.

Link-Related Parameters

The next four parameters allow you to put a link at the bottom of the page.

The @URL parameter and the @reftext parameter work together. The @URL parameter specifies the uniform resource locator (URL) of the link (for example, http://www.yahoo.com). The @reftext parameter specifies what the link looks like on the page, such as Click here to go to Yahoo.

If you want more than a list of automatically generated links, you need to use the @table_urls and @url_query parameters. The @table_urls parameter must be either 0 (the default) or 1. If it's 0, it means that you're not going to have a list of links; it's 1, it means you will. If it is 1, you can't use the @URL and @reftext parameters.

The @url_query parameter works only if the @table_urls parameter is set to 1, and @URL and @reftext is blank. This parameter should contain a query that when executed returns two columns. The first column should contain the URL, and the second should contain the description of the URL that will appear on the page.

You don't have a table to generate such a query. For example, the following will work:

```
@url_query='
Select ''http://www.hotbot.com'' As URL,
            ''HotBot'' As Descr
Union
Select ''http://www.lycos.com'' As URL,
            ''Lycos'' As Descr
Union
Select ''http://www.yahoo.com'' As URL,
            ''Yahoo'' As Descr'
```

Unfortunately, because this parameter is nvarchar(255), you are limited to the size of the query. Of course, you could create a stored procedure that executes a longer SELECT statement. Note that it doesn't matter to sp_makewebtask what the names of the columns are for your query.

Rows per Page Parameters

The following parameters affect how many rows are shown on the generated Web page.

@rowsperpage

The @rowsperpage parameter specifies how many items can be shown on a page. If the number of rows that are to be returned is greater than the @rowsperpage value, multiple files are generated. Each page ends with a number specifying its order. (The first file's name ends with 1, the second with 2, and so forth.) Links are provided at the bottom of each page to the other pages. So, for example, suppose you made the following call:

```
EXECUTE sp_makewebtask @outputfile =
EXECUTE sp_makewebtask @outputfile =
    ➥ N'C:\Pubs HTML\Titles Rows Per Page Options.htm',
@query=N'SELECT title FROM titles',
                    @dbname=N'pubs',
                    @nrowsperpage=4
```

The query returns 18 rows. The result is that five files are generated: Titles Rows Per Page Options1.htm, Titles Rows Per Page Options2.htm through Titles Rows Per Page Options5.htm. Note that Titles Rows Per Page Options.htm (no number) is *not* generated. Figure 22.4 shows what the second page looks like.

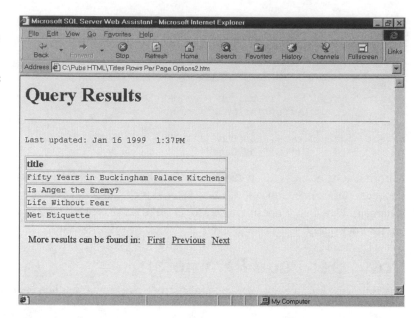

> **NOTE**
>
> Notice the `More results can be found in:` phrase, which mysteriously showed up when you put an `INSERT` statement into the query parameter.

@singlerow

The @singlerow must have a value of 0 or 1. When the value is 0, the parameter is ignored. When the value is 1, only one row is displayed per page. Additionally, @nrowsperpage doesn't work when @singlerow is set to 1. The fact is that this parameter is kind of pointless, considering that @nrowsperpage can be set to 1.

@rowcnt

The @rowcnt parameter sets how many rows appear on the page. The default is 0, which is interpreted to mean there's no limit to the rows returned. Setting this parameter to 5 limits the page to five rows. Note that the remaining items are lost and that they're not put on another page.

> **TIP**
>
> The cool way to limit a query, however, is to use the new TOP keyword in your query, as shown here:
>
> ```
> @query='Select Top 5 titles from title
> ```

Even if you refuse to be cool, you could get the same effect by setting @nrowsperpage=5, and then just keep the first page, but you'd still have to delete the Next link at the bottom of the page.

Template Parameters

You can create an HTML file with your own formatting preferences, and you can specify the following:

- The location of a table of data
- The location of columns within a table

Listing 22.2 is a sample template file named Template Example.tmp.txt that simply specifies where a table of data should be located with the <%insert_data_here%> tag. The tag is replaced with a table when the stored procedure is run.

LISTING 22.2   USING TAGS TO INSERT DATA IN A TEMPLATE FILE

```
<HTML>
<HEAD>
<META content="text/html; charset=utf-8" http-equiv=Content-Type>
<TITLE>Microsoft SQL Server Web Assistant</TITLE>
</HEAD>
<BODY>
<H1>Query Results</H1>
<HR>
Template Dude was here!
<P>
<%insert_data_here%>
<HR>
</BODY>
</HTML>
```

The @templatefile parameter is used to take advantage of this file. Here is the call to sp_makewebtask:

```
EXECUTE sp_makewebtask
    @outputfile = 'C:\Pubs HTML\Template Example.HTM',
    @query = N'SELECT pub_name, city, state, country FROM ➡
publishers',
    @dbname = N'pubs',
    @templatefile = 'C:\Pubs HTML\Template Example.tmp.txt'
```

The results of this call are shown in Figure 22.5.

FIGURE 22.5

The results of using the basic template.

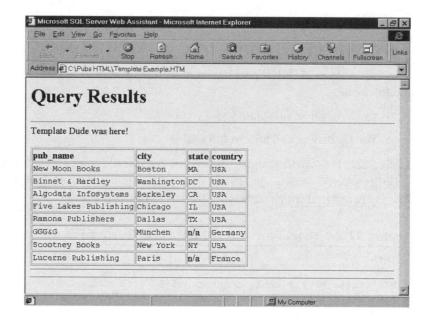

You can specify column level insertion points in a template, too. To do so, put a <%begindetail%> tag before the second row of a table and a <%enddetail%> at the end of the row. Within the row for each cell, you put <%insert_data_here%> where each column should go. Listing 22.3 shows the Template Example Detail.tmp.txt file that uses this method.

LISTING 22.3   USING BEGIN AND END DETAIL TAGS

```
<HR>
Template Detail Dude was here!
<P>
<P><TABLE BORDER=1>
<TR><TH ALIGN=LEFT>pub_name</TH>
    <TH ALIGN=LEFT>city</TH>
```

```
    <TH ALIGN=LEFT>state</TH>
    <TH ALIGN=LEFT>country</TH>
</TR>
<%begindetail%>
<TR><TD><TT>* <%insert_data_here%> *</TT></TD>
    <TD><TT>@ <%insert_data_here%> @</TT></TD>
    <TD><TT># <%insert_data_here%> #</TT></TD>
    <TD><TT>% <%insert_data_here%> %</TT></TD>
</TR>
<%enddetail%>
<HR>
```

The results of this call are shown in Figure 22.6.

FIGURE 22.6

The results of using the detailed template.

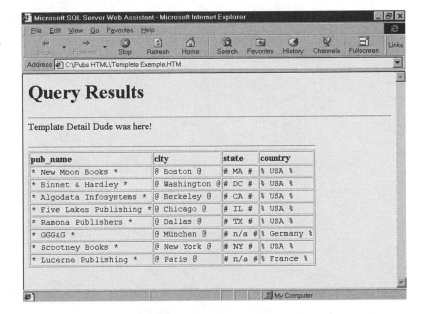

@blobfmt

The @blobfmt parameter is extremely interesting. It's designed to more easily look at text and image columns, but its functionality works with all data types.

The following is a call with @blobfmt:

```
EXECUTE sp_makewebtask @outputfile =
        'C:\Pubs HTML\blobfmt.HTM',
                    @query =
N'SELECT pub_name, city, state,
      country, logo, ''Click here to see logo''
```

```
From pub_info Inner  Join publishers
  On pub_info.pub_id = publishers.pub_id',
                   @dbname = N'pubs',
                   @blobfmt = '%5%
              FILE=C:\Pubs HTML\blobfmt Detail Logo.GIF'
```

Figure 22.7 shows the results of the call. Note that in the SELECT statement, the Logo is the fifth column, but that it isn't on the screen. On the other hand, the sixth column, the string "Click here to see logo" is a link. When you click on the first row's link, the logo is shown, which is shown in Figure 22.8.

FIGURE 22.7

The results of the call to sp_makewebtask.

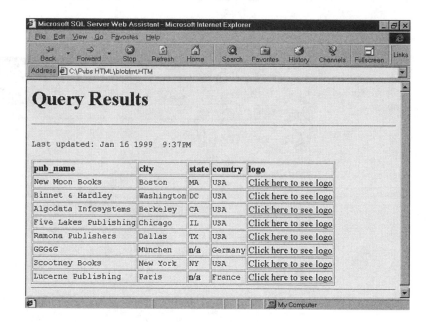

So the Logo column was written to another file and the column that followed it (in this case, the string Click here to see logo links to it.

Here's how it works. The @blobfmt parameter has its own structure:

%ColumnNumber% FILE=ColumnFilename TPLT=TemplateFilename URL=URLFilename

In this example, there are two parts to @blobfmt:

'%5% FILE=C:\Pubs HTML\blobfmt Detail Logo.GIF'

FIGURE 22.8

The results of clicking on the Click here to see logo *link.*

The contents of the fifth column, Logo, are written to C:\Pubs HTML\blobfmt Detail Logo.gif. Well, almost. Actually, the logo for the first row has the value C:\Pubs HTML\blobfmt Detail Logo1.gif, the second row has C:\Pubs HTML\blobfmt Detail Logo2.gif, and so forth.

The structure of %ColumnNumber% FILE=ColumnFilename can be repeated for several columns.

The TPLT portion specifies an optional template file to be used for the filename specified by the FILE= part. This is a template for the column only, not for the page with the links. You still use the @templatefile parameter for that.

The URL= allows you to specify the URL link address for the file. If you set URL=http://www.yahoo.com/index.html, the links to the column page will be http://www.yahoo.com/index1.html, http://www.yahoo.com/index2.html, and so on.

The name of the parameter is @blobfmt; blob stands for *binary large object*, which in SQL Server is image and text data types. However, this parameter works the same for all data types. Its functionality allows you to link to a page that contains one column of one row on a separate page. It just so happens that image and text columns are usually the only ones in which one row, one column would be interesting, but now varchar columns can be 8,000 characters long, so they might be able to benefit from this. For example, let's say you have a column defined as Varchar(8000), and it contains large amounts of text. You could use this technique to display the contents of the column on a separate page.

Conceivably, you could come up with a way to take advantage of having links generated within the data table, regardless of any files that might have been generated along the way. With the `url` portion of the parameter, you could specify link addresses that have nothing to do with any data at all. Unfortunately, the links generated all follow the pattern of having the row number attached at the end. Theoretically, however, you could create pages through some other means that match what the links say. Finally, there's nothing stopping you from manually editing the HTML files and setting the links to what you want them to be.

Automating Web Publishing with Job-Related Parameters

So far, these page-creating examples have been a one-time affair. Web Assistant, however, has the ability to create a job that generates Web pages at specified times. It can even specify that they're generated whenever the data changes.

Let me state an important point: Until now, the examples I showed you did not create any Web Assistant jobs. A Web Assistant job is created only when you specify that the Web page should be generated at a time other than the present. Unfortunately, as near as I can tell, this little nugget of information isn't in any of the documentation.

@whentype

The `@whentype` parameter allows you to schedule when the Web page will be generated. There are ten different settings (1 through 10) for this parameter, and practically each value depends on other parameters, with their different possible values. The specific details for each value can be found under `sp_makewebtask` in Books Online. (I know I just criticized the documentation in the previous paragraph, but generally it's accurate.) The settings you're most likely to use are the default for creating a page right away, (1); at times specified in `targetdate` and `targettime` (2); and, for data that's relatively static, `10`, which creates the page immediately and upon changes in the data. Other options let you specify creation by days, hours, or upon request.

The following code is a call to `sp_makewebtask` that generates a Web Assistant job you can run at any time. The `@whentype` parameter is set to 5. The `@procname` parameter is the name of the stored procedure and the job that will be created.

```
EXECUTE sp_makewebtask @outputfile =
                       'C:\Pubs HTML\Titles for the Web.HTM',
                       @query = N'Select title from titles',
                       @dbname = N'pubs',
                       @procname = 'TitlesWeb',
                       @whentype = 5
```

After this call is made, the Web page still hasn't been generated. The following call to sp_runwebtask does that:

```
sp_runwebtask @procname = 'TitlesWeb'
```

In Figure 22.9, you can see the new job in the Management folder under Web Publishing. If you double-click on the job, you see something like what's shown in Figure 22.10.

FIGURE 22.9

The TitlesWeb job in the Web Publishing folder.

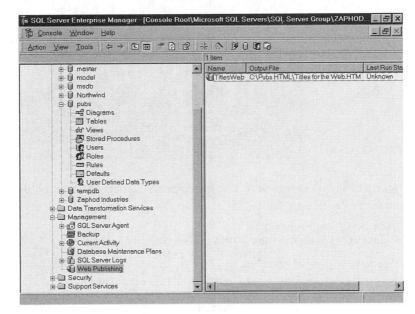

A stored procedure with the name TitlesWeb was also created when you ran the call to sp_makewebtask. For some reason, this stored procedure isn't visible unless you right-click on Stored Procedures and select Refresh. Here are the contents of the stored procedure:

```
CREATE PROCEDURE [TitlesWeb]  AS Select title from titles
```

It seems pretty pointless for SQL Server to have created a stored procedure just for this job. But the simple fact is that your TitlesWeb Web Assistant job simply won't work without it.

22

AUTOMATING
WEB PUBLICATION
OF SQL SERVER

FIGURE 22.10

*The TitlesWeb
job's properties.*

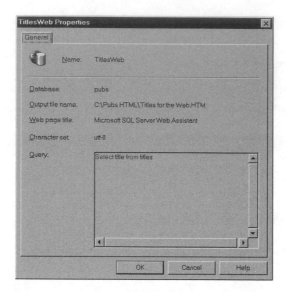

Next, run sp_makewebtask so that it creates a SQL Server Agent job that's scheduled to run every day. Here's the call:

```
EXECUTE sp_makewebtask
➡@outputfile = 'C:\Pubs HTML\Titles for the Web.HTM',
                    @query = N'Select title from titles',
                    @dbname = N'pubs',
                    @procname = 'TitlesWebEveryDay',
                    @whentype = 4,
                    @targetdate=19990117,
                    @numunits=1,
                    @unittype=2
```

When @whentype = 4, the page is generated periodically, based on the values of @targetdate, @numunits, and @unittype. The @targetdate is 1/17/1998, the @unittype=2, which is days, and the @numunits=1, which means the job runs once every day. The @targettime parameter is missing, which means the task is run at midnight.

A look at the SQL Server Agent folder under the Management folder shows that you have a job for TitlesWebEveryDay (see Figure 22.11).

FIGURE 22.11

The TitlesWeb
EveryDay *SQL
Server Agent job.*

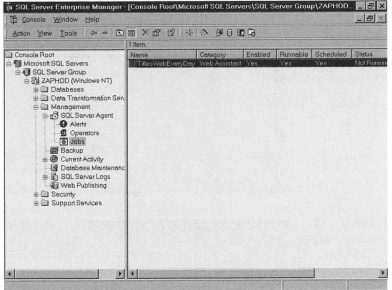

If you double-click on the job, you can see its properties. Figure 22.12 shows the
General tab's properties, and Figure 22.13 shows the Steps tab's properties. If you click
the Edit button, you can see the command in the job step, shown in Figure 22.14. Not
surprisingly, it's a call to sp_runwebtask. Figure 22.15 shows the schedule for the task,
which is daily at midnight.

FIGURE 22.12

*The General tab of
the* TitlesWeb
EveryDay *SQL
Server Agent Job's
properties dialog.*

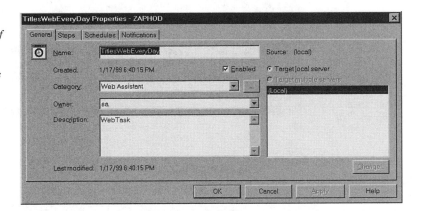

FIGURE 22.13

The Steps tab of the TitlesWeb EveryDay *SQL Server Agent Job's properties dialog.*

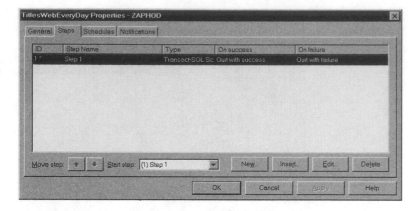

FIGURE 22.14

The Edit Job Step dialog for the TitlesWebEveryDay *SQL Server Agent Job.*

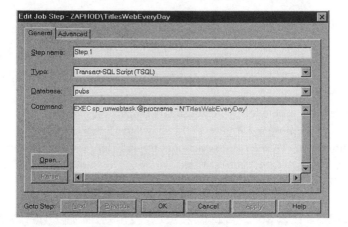

FIGURE 22.15

The Schedules tab of the TitlesWeb EveryDay *SQL Server Agent Job's properties dialog.*

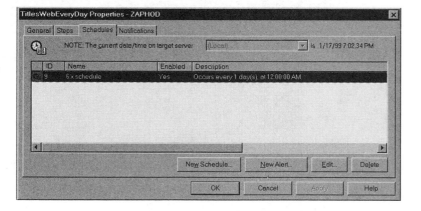

Finally, in this example a page is generated each time the data changes. The call to use is shown here:

```
EXECUTE sp_makewebtask
        @outputfile = 'C:\Pubs HTML\Titles All the Time.HTM',
        @query      = N'Select title from titles',
        @dbname     = N'pubs',
        @procname   = 'Titles All The Time',
        @whentype   = 10,
        @datachg    = 'TABLE=titles'
```

Here, @whentype is set to 10, which basically indicates that the page is to be generated once now, and then again whenever the data changes. The @datachg parameter indicates in which table the triggers are created. You can specify multiple tables and columns as well, using the format TABLE=name[*Column=name*].

This command simply creates insert, update, and delete triggers on the titles table. Here's the Insert trigger:

```
CREATE TRIGGER [Titles All The Time_1]
            ON [titles]
 FOR INSERT AS
   BEGIN
     EXEC sp_runwebtask @procname =  N'Titles All The Time'
   END
```

It's simply a call to sp_runwebtask. The update and delete triggers are the same. To see the triggers for yourself, follow these steps:

1. In Enterprise Manager, select Databases, Pubs, and Tables in the left pane.

2. Select the titles table, and right-click on it. Choose Design Table.

3. Click the Triggers button (the button right after the Set Primary Key button).

4. Click in the Name combo box and select one of the four triggers: [Titles All The Time_1], [Titles All The Time_2], and [Titles All The Time_4].

Figure 22.16 is the trigger screen, showing the [Titles All The Time_1] trigger.

22

AUTOMATING WEB PUBLICATION OF SQL SERVER

FIGURE 22.16

The [Titles All The Time_1] *trigger in the* titles *table.*

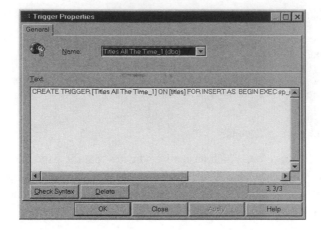

Summary

As you have seen, a lot of the Web Assistant's extended functionality is really the clever use of the SQL Server Agent and triggers. This is a good thing. Think of Web Assistant as a showcase for the advanced features of SQL Server 7.0.

CHAPTER 23

SQL Server, ADO, and the Web

The Evolution of Data Access

In the early days of the Internet, it was difficult at best to present Web pages that derived from databases. By itself, static HTML was hardly the answer to the problem. To bridge the gap between the data harbored in relational databases and the Web, Microsoft introduced Active Server Pages (ASP). With ASP, developers can create dynamic Web pages that present data from a relational database.

During the time of the Web's evolution, Microsoft was progressing through Data Access Objects (DAO) and Remote Data Objects (RDO). Both DAO and RDO are tools that permit developers to communicate with an ODBC-compliant database. However, neither DAO nor RDO is best suited for the stateless and thin client world of Web development. This is where ActiveX Data Objects (ADO) comes in.

This chapter discusses the merits of using ADO within Active Server Pages to develop Web applications against SQL Server. First, I'll lay the basis for the chapter by reviewing the objects in the ADO object model, and then review the `Connection` object and its properties and methods, followed by the `Command` object and its features. The `Command` object can be useful for executing stored procedures in SQL Server. Then I'll move into the `Recordset` object and its nuances, including a discussion of stateless, disconnected recordsets. Finally, I'll rap up with an explanation of how ADO can be moved from the Web server to the client browser by using Remote Data Services (RDS).

The ADO Object Model

ADO solves the problem of accessing data in non-relational data sources by using OLE DB, a new technology that gives applications uniform access to data stored in diverse information sources. What does this mean to you? That means you can now access data in text files, non-relational databases, Index Server, and Active Directory Service (ADS), as well as data in RDBMSs (relational database management systems) such as Oracle and SQL Server. No longer are you limited to ODBC-compliant data sources.

Besides access to a wider range of data sources, ADO's other primary benefits are its ease of use, tremendous feature set, high speed, and low memory overhead. Among its list of features, ADO's recordsets support a stateless environment and simple access to stored procedures, making ADO the tool of choice when accessing SQL Server.

One huge advantage ADO has over RDO and DAO is its ease of use. The object models of DAO and RDO are vastly larger than ADO's object model. The ADO object model, as shown in Figure 23.1, contains three main objects: `Connection`, `Command`, and `Recordset`. These main objects can be independently created and used to access a data source. In addition to these main objects, there are the `Error`, `Parameter`, `Field`, and `Property` objects. These auxiliary objects are used to support the functionality of the three main objects.

FIGURE 23.1

The ADO object model.

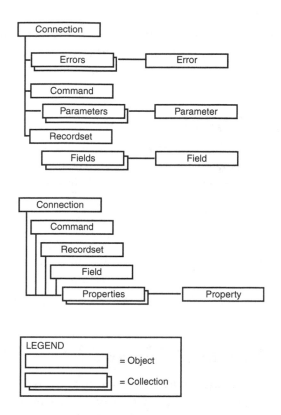

A brief explanation of each of the objects in the ADO object model follows. Even though you're concentrating on the `Command` object throughout this chapter and its use with stored procedures, you need to understand how the other objects work with each other first.

Main ADO Objects

The `Connection` object is used to make the link to the data source—SQL Server in this case—through OLE DB. A `Connection` object represents a single link with SQL Server. You can check or set values of the `Connection` object such as the default database to use its transactional methods, such as `BeginTrans`, `CommitTrans`, and `RollbackTrans`.

The Command object is used mainly to access stored procedures in SQL Server, although it can be used to further manipulate a recordset. Mostly, you use the Command object when you need to execute a stored procedure with (or without) parameters and/or return values.

The Recordset object is used to retrieve a dataset from the data source. After the data set is retrieved, the features of the Recordset object can be used to navigate, edit, add, or delete its records. The Recordset object always refers to a single record within a dataset as the current record.

Auxiliary ADO Objects

The Errors collection contains zero or more Error objects. The Error object has information about the most recently raised errors that occurred on the existing Connection object. Any operation involving ADO objects can generate one or more provider errors. When an error occurs, one or more Error objects are placed in the Errors collection of the Connection object.

The Parameters collection contains zero or more Parameter objects. The Parameter object represents an argument associated with parameterized queries or the arguments and the return values of stored procedures. Some OLE DB providers don't support parameterized queries and/or stored procedures. The Parameter object doesn't work with those providers.

The Connection Object

Before ADO 2.0, you needed to use an ODBC data source to connect to SQL Server. You could use a data source name created through the ODBC Data Source Administrator (see Listing 23.1) or use a DSN-less connection string (see Listing 23.2). Either way, you're using ODBC to connect to SQL Server.

LISTING 23.1   CONNECTING TO SQL SERVER VIA A DSN

```
<%
set objConn = Server.CreateObject("ADODB.Connection")
objConn.Open "pubs"
%>
```

LISTING 23.2 CONNECTING TO SQL SERVER VIA AN ODBC (DSN-LESS) CONNECTION STRING

```
<%
set objConn = Server.CreateObject("ADODB.Connection")
objConn.Open "Driver={SQL Server};Server=papanotebook;" & _
    "Uid=sa;Pwd=;Database=pubs"
%>
```

The code above creates a connection to the server named "papanotebook" and accesses the database named "pubs" using the username "sa" with no password.

ADO 1.5 introduces you to the concept of OLE DB providers and connecting to databases with them. This method is supposed to be faster and more flexible, allowing you to reach a wider range of back-ends. Everything sounds great, right? The only problem is that with ADO 1.5, the only OLE DB provider that existed at the time was the provider for ODBC. This sounds a bit confusing, so examine it a little closer.

In ODBC, if you wanted to connect to SQL Server from your ASP, you had to go through ODBC, then through the ODBC driver for SQL Server, and on to SQL Server itself (see Figure 23.2). However, with the OLE DB provider for ODBC, you had to go through OLE DB to the OLE DB provider for ODBC, then through ODBC on through the ODBC driver for SQL Server on to SQL Server itself (see Figure 23.3).

FIGURE 23.2

Accessing SQL Server through ODBC.

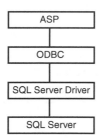

With ADO 2.0 and the Microsoft Data Access Components (MDAC), there are several new OLE DB providers, including one for SQL Server. Using this new OLE DB provider for SQL Server, you can now access SQL Server directly through OLE DB instead of having to go around and through ODBC, too. Listing 23.3 shows how you can access SQL Server through its OLE DB provider in ADO 2.0.

FIGURE 23.3
Accessing SQL Server through OLE DB's ODBC provider.

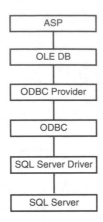

LISTING 23.3   CONNECTING TO SQL SERVER VIA AN OLE DB CONNECTION STRING

```
<%
set objConn = Server.CreateObject("ADODB.Connection")
objConn.Open "Provider=SQLOLEDB.1;User ID=sa;Password=;" & _
    "Initial Catalog=pubs;Data Source=papanotebook"
%>
```

Of course, instead of passing this long parameter to the `Connection.Open` method, you can store the connection string in the `Application` object within the `global.asa` file (see Listing 23.4).

LISTING 23.4   STORING THE CONNECTION STRING IN THE Application OBJECT

```
Application("ConnString") = "Provider=SQLOLEDB.1;User ID=sa;" & _
    "Password=;Initial Catalog=pubs;Data Source=papanotebook"
```

After you have stored the connection string in an `Application` object variable, you can simply use it to open your connections, as shown in Listing 23.5.

LISTING 23.5   OPENING A CONNECTION USING THE Application OBJECT

```
Set objConn = Server.CreateObject("ADODB.Connection")
ObjConn.Open Application("ConnString")
```

Transaction Management

The `Connection` object is used for more than connecting to databases—managing database transactions, for example. The `BeginTrans` method initiates a transaction with the data source, and `CommitTrans` and `RollbackTrans` complete a transaction. `RollbackTrans` ends the transaction and cancels all changes made since the beginning of the transaction. `CommitTrans` ends the transaction and applies all changes made since the beginning of the transaction. Listing 23.6 shows a transaction that commits its changes unless a business rules has been violated.

LISTING 23.6   A BUSINESS RULE THAT CONTROLS A TRANSACTION

```
'--- Open the connection and begin a transaction.
Set objConn = Server.CreateObject("ADODB.Connection")
ObjConn.Open Application("ConnString")
ObjConn.BeginTrans
'--- Perform database changes as per the business rules.
ObjConn.Execute "UPDATE titles SET price = price * 1.1"
ObjConn.Execute "UPDATE roysched SET royalty = royalty * 1.2"
'--- Perform other business logic ...
'---
'--- Based on a specific business rule,
'--- determine whether to commit or rollback.
If booDoIt then
    ObjConn.CommitTrans
Else
    ObjConn.RollbackTrans
End If
```

The code in Listing 23.6 opens a transaction and makes some database changes. Then, depending on a business rule, you set a variable called `booDoIt`. This variable is then used to decide whether you commit or abort the changes.

Transaction Considerations

When dealing with transactions, there are some special considerations for tweaking your code to get its maximum performance. Transactions hold locks open on the data source. Therefore, it's prudent to keep the transactions as short as possible so other users can access the data. Remember, as long as the transaction is open, concurrent users can't access the data locked by the transaction. However, you can use the `IsolationLevel` property to bend that rule. If you set the `Connection` object's `IsolationLevel` property to `adXactReadUncommitted`, then concurrent users can read the data used in the transaction but can't edit it.

> **NOTE**
>
> Keep in mind that you should not close the `Connection` object in the middle of a transaction. Also, avoid refreshing a `Recordset` that uses a `Connection` object within a transaction. Either of these actions causes different, but troublesome, errors.

Connection Pooling

The old school of thought suggested that you open your connections at the beginning of your application and close them at the end. This suggestion made sense because opening and closing connections is a resource-expensive process. However, problems arise when the connection is disrupted or merely by the sheer resource burden it places on the server. ADO takes advantage of a relatively new feature known as "connection pooling" to tackle this problem.

Connection pooling is a resource management tool that recycles unused database connections. When a connection is closed by code, it's thrown into a pool for a default of 60 seconds. If another connection is requested by a user, the pool is checked to see if there are any connections available. If a connection is available in the pool, it's allocated to the new user. Otherwise, a new connection is created for the user.

Connection pooling draws a lot of debate because it violates the very premise of the way programmers coded for years: Keep your connections open throughout the application. However, as long as you adhere to one simple rule, connection pooling is well worth the effort. That rule is to open the connection right before you need it, perform your SQL, and then close the connection. You should follow this rule even if it means you have to open and close a connection several times in a single ASP (see Listing 23.7). The reasoning behind this rule is that the connection is not being held when it's not needed and there's a minimal resource load on reopening and closing the connection. Of course, without pooling, this rule wouldn't float.

LISTING 23.7 HOW TO CODE TAKING ADVANTAGE OF CONNECTION POOLING

```
Set objConn = Server.CreateObject("ADODB.Connection")
'--- Open a connection.
ObjConn.Open Application("ConnString")
'--- Perform database changes.
ObjConn.Execute strSQL1
ObjConn.Execute strSQL2
'--- Close the connection.
```

```
ObjConn.Close
'--- Perform business rules, calculations, validation, etc.
'--- (Anything without needing a connection.)
x = y + z
a = b * x
'--- Open a connection again.
ObjConn.Open Application("ConnString")
'--- Perform database changes.
ObjConn.Execute strSQL3
ObjConn.Execute strSQL4
'--- Close the connection again.
ObjConn.Close
```

Executing SQL

In addition to handling more intricate features such as transaction management and connection pooling, the `Connection` object can also handle everyday tasks, such as executing SQL. The `Execute` method of the `Connection` object can be used to execute a SQL statement and optionally return a `Recordset` object (see Listing 23.8).

LISTING 23.8   EXECUTING SQL VIA THE `Connection` OBJECT

```
Set objConn = Server.CreateObject("ADODB.Connection")
ObjConn.Open Application("ConnString")
ObjConn.Execute "UPDATE titles SET price = price * 1.1"
```

The code in Listing 23.8 executes the SQL and appears not to return a `Recordset` object. This is where ADO 1.5 differs from ADO 2.0: ADO 1.5 returns a `Recordset` object, whether or not there were any results returned to the application. In ADO 2.0, you can eliminate the returned `Recordset` by setting a parameter on the `Execute` method. To use this feature, simply add the value of `adExecuteNoRecords` to the value being passed to the `Options` parameter of the `Execute` method (see Listing 23.9).

The `Execute` method of the `Connection` object has 3 arguments as shown below:

```
Connection.Execute CommandText, RecordsAffected, Options
```

The `CommandText` can be the SQL, table name, or stored procedure to execute (open in the case of a table). The `RecordsAffected` is a by value argument that returns the number of records affected by the `CommandText`. If any action query was executed, this argument would return the number of rows affected by that action query. The `Options` argument lets you specify a variety of options such as fetching asynchronously or what the `CommandText` represents.

23

SQL SERVER, ADO, AND THE WEB

LISTING 23.9   EXECUTING SQL VIA THE Connection OBJECT

```
Set objConn = Server.CreateObject("ADODB.Connection")
ObjConn.Open Application("ConnString")
StrSQL = "UPDATE titles SET price = price * 1.1"
ObjConn.Execute strSQL,, adCmdText + adExecuteNoRecords
```

> **NOTE**
>
> Keep in mind that adExecuteNoRecords applies only to adCmdStoredProc and adCmdText command types. The other command types are meant to return results.

Of course, if you want a Recordset to be returned, you can always store it in a variable, as shown in Listing 23.10.

LISTING 23.10   RETURNING A Recordset FROM A Connection OBJECT

```
set objConn = Server.CreateObject("ADODB.Connection")
set objRS = Server.CreateObject("ADODB.Recordset")
objConn.Open Application("ConnString")
strSQL = "SELECT * FROM titles"
set objRS = objConn.Execute(strSQL)
```

Using Stored Procedures with the Command Object

Like the Connection object, the Command object can also be used to execute SQL and return a Recordset (see Listing 23.11). However, the main advantage of using a Command object is its capacity to pass parameters to and from stored procedures. In addition to returning a return value, SQL Server stored procedures can have input, output, and inputoutput parameters. With the ADO Command object, you can use all these types of parameters with a SQL Server stored procedure.

LISTING 23.11   RETURNING A Recordset FROM A Command OBJECT

```
set objConn = Server.CreateObject("ADODB.Connection")
set objCmd = Server.CreateObject("ADODB.Command")
set objRS = Server.CreateObject("ADODB.Recordset")
objConn.Open Application("ConnString")
set objCmd.ActiveConnection = objConn
```

```
strSQL = "SELECT * FROM titles"
set objRS = objCmd.Execute(strSQL)
```

Passing Parameters

Listing 23.12 shows how you can retrieve a recordset from the ByRoyalty stored procedure by using ADO. This stored procedure retrieves a dataset of all authors who make more than a specified royalty percentage. You specify that percentage by passing a value for the percentage parameter.

LISTING 23.12 EXECUTING A STORED PROCEDURE WITH PARAMETERS

```
set objConn = Server.CreateObject("ADODB.Connection")
set objCmd = Server.CreateObject("ADODB.Command")
set objRS = Server.CreateObject("ADODB.Recordset")
objConn.Open Application("ConnString")
set objCmd.ActiveConnection = objConn
objCmd.CommandText = "ByRoyalty"
objCmd.CommandType = adCmdStoredProc
objCmd.Parameters.Append objCmd.CreateParameter("percentage", _
    adInteger, adParamInput,,50)
set objRS = objCmd.Execute
```

Let's take this code apart so you can examine its working parts. First, the code creates the three objects you require: the Connection object to communicate to the database, the Command object to execute the stored procedure, and the Recordset object to hold the returned dataset. Then you open the Connection object and associate it with the Command object by setting the Command object's ActiveConnection property.

Now that the preliminary code is written, specify the name of the stored procedure that the Command object should execute by setting the CommandText property. Because a Command object can execute SQL, open tables, and execute stored procedures, you need to tell the Command object what you want it to do. In this example, you do that setting the CommandType property to adCmdStoredProc.

You have specified the value for the stored procedure's parameter, but before you can do that, you need to consider that the Command object's Parameters collection is still empty. There are two ways to fill the Parameters collection: using the Refresh method or creating the parameter(s) and adding them to the collection by using the Command object's CreateParameter method and the Parameters collection's Append method. Using the Refresh method requires the least amount of code, as shown in Listing 23.13. However, the Refresh method puts the burden on the data provider to determine the number of parameters, their names, data types, sizes, and directions (that is, Input, Output,

23

SQL SERVER,
ADO, AND THE
WEB

InputOutput, or Return). The problem with making the data provider do the work for you is that this process requires significant resources. Basically, it's just like anything else in this world: The shortest way isn't always the best way.

LISTING 23.13 REQUESTING THE DATA PROVIDER TO FURNISH THE STORED PROCEDURE'S PARAMETER LIST

```
objCmd.Parameters.Refresh
```

The alternative to using the Refresh method is to create the parameters one by one and add them to the Parameters collection manually. This way, you have to specify the name of the parameter, its datatype and size, the direction, and the value (if it's an Input or InputOutput parameter). This might seem like a lot of work, but it pays off because it should increase your code's performance. The syntax of the Command.CreateParameter method and the Command object's Parameters.Append method is shown in Listing 23.14.

LISTING 23.14 EXECUTING A STORED PROCEDURE WITH PARAMETERS

```
Set objParm = ObjCmd.CreateParameter(param_name, _
    datatype, direction, size, value)
ObjCmd.Parameters.Append objParm
```

The param_name is the name of the parameter as it is known to SQL Server, and the datatype is the type of data the parameter requires. The direction is one of the following: adParamInput, adParamOutput, adParamInputOutput, or adParamReturnValue. Finally, the size refers to the length of the character-based data types, and the value is where you pass in a value for Input or InputOutput parameters. After the parameter has been created and stored in the objParm variable, you can add it to the Parameters collection by using the Append method, as shown in Listing 23.12. And don't forget that after you have set the properties of the Command object and its parameters, you can retrieve a Recordset object from the Command object's Execute method, as shown in Listing 23.11.

The Recordset Object

Retrieving data in ADO is as simple as writing a SQL statement, calling a stored procedure, and specifying a single table or the name of a data file. In Listing 23.10, you saw how to specify a SQL SELECT statement to request a dataset from the Connection object. More recently, you have seen how to retrieve a dataset from a stored procedure via a Command object. However, there are other ways to retrieve a Recordset object using ADO.

Retrieving an Entire Table

You can retrieve all the columns and rows of data from a table by using ADO. Simply specify the name of a table as the source of a `Recordset` object and set the `Options` parameter of the `Open` method to `adCmdTable` (see Listing 23.15).

LISTING 23.15 OPENING A TABLE INTO A `Recordset`

```
objRS.Open "authors", objConn, adOpenForwardOnly, _
    adLockReadOnly, adCmdTable
```

The `Open` method of the `Recordset` object has 5 arguments as shown in Listing 23.15. The first argument represents the data source for the `Recordset`. In Listing 23.15 we specified the authors table. The second argument lets us specify the `Connection` object to use. The third argument indicates the type of cursor to use. We chose to use a forward-only cursor, which allows us to scroll forward one record at a time or go to the first record (for other cursor types, see the ADO reference material in MSDN). The fourth argument specifies the type of locking strategy used on the `Recordset`. We chose to make the recordset's data read-only in Listing 25.14. Finally, the fifth argument specifies the options for the recordset. Here we indicated that we wanted to open a table, as opposed to running SQL, a file or a stored proc.

You can also open a table into a `Recordset` by using the `Command` object, as shown in Listing 23.16. Either method is acceptable; however, in this case, there's slightly more flexibility in using the `Command` object because the `Recordset` object lacks a `CommandType` property, as opposed to the `Command` object. Therefore, you must set the `Options` parameter of the `Recordset`'s `Open` method if you decide not to use the `Command` object.

LISTING 23.16 OPENING A TABLE USING A `Command` OBJECT

```
objCmd.CommandText = "authors"
objCmd.CommandType = adCmdTable
set objRS = objCmd.Execute
```

Recordset Basics

Before you go any further, you need to review some of the basic features of a `Recordset` object. Before you can open a `Recordset`, you need to specify the type of cursor, the location of the cursor, and the type of locking. After the cursor is opened, you can add new records, edit or delete the data, or simply navigate the recordset. Then, of course, there are the miscellaneous features, such as sorting, finding, and indexing a `Recordset`. Let's start by examining the types of cursors.

Types of Cursors

The `CursorType` property can be set to one of the following constant values: `adOpenStatic`, `adOpenForwardOnly`, `adOpenDynamic`, or `adOpenKeyset`. Forward-only cursors, the default type, allow you to move only one record forward at a time or move directly to the first record by using the `MoveNext` and `MoveFirst` methods.

`Static` cursors allow you to navigate throughout the `Recordset` by using all the `Move` methods and the bookmarking features. However, this cursor type does not permit you to see changes by other users without requerying the database.

`Keyset` cursors, however, do allow you to notice data changes and deleted data rows made by other users, as long as you use the `Resync` method to request that you see the changes. You can't see newly added rows with a `keyset` cursor, though. For this, you must use a `dynamic` cursor, which can see all changes, deletions, and additions to the underlying data when using the `Resync` method.

Server-Side or Client-Side Cursors?

You set the `CursorLocation` property to one of the following constant values: `adUseClient` and `adUseServer`. Server-side cursors are the default, and they specify that the cursor exists within, and is managed by, the data provider. Server-side cursors allow for additional sensitivity to changes others make to the data source. However, some features you would prefer to take advantage of (such as disconnected recordsets, sorting, and temporary recordset indexing) are not supported by server-side cursors. In these cases, you need to use client-side cursors (see Listing 23.17), which specify that the Microsoft Client Cursor Provider should manage the cursor.

LISTING 23.17 SETTING THE CURSOR LOCATION TO BE CLIENT-SIDE

```
ObjRS.CursorLocation = adUseClient
```

Locking Types

In addition to the location of the cursor and the type of cursor, you need to specify the type of lock you want to enforce on the cursor by setting the `LockType` property of the `Recordset` object to one of the following: `adLockReadOnly`, `adLockPessimistic`, `adLockOptimistic`, or `adLockBatchOptimistic`. Pessimistic locks hold a lock on the data page that the recordset's current row is on while the record is being edited. That means as soon as any field's value in the record is changed, the lock is enforced. Only then, not until the Recordset's Update method is called on that record, is the lock released.

Pessimistic locks differ from optimistic locks, which only enforce the lock while the record is being updated (while the Update method is being issued). The final type of lock is a batch optimistic lock, used for updating batches of records at one time. This type becomes vital when you get into disconnected recordsets later in this chapter.

Editing Data

Editing data in SQL Server is rather simple using ADO. To add a new record to a table, just use the AddNew method of the Recordset object, as shown in Listing 23.18. After you call this method, you can set the values of the fields and then follow it up with a call to the Update method, which saves the changes.

LISTING 23.18 ADDING A NEW RECORD TO A TABLE

```
set objConn = Server.CreateObject("ADODB.Connection")
set objCmd = Server.CreateObject("ADODB.Command")
set objRS = Server.CreateObject("ADODB.Recordset")
objConn.Open "Provider=SQLOLEDB.1;User ID=sa;" & _
    "Password=;Initial Catalog=pubs;Data Source=papanotebook"
set objCmd.ActiveConnection = objConn
objCmd.CreateParameter("percentage",adInteger, adParamInput,,50)
objCmd.CommandText = "authors"
objRS.Open objCmd, , adOpenStatic, adLockOptimistic
objRS.AddNew
objRS("au_id") = "123-45-6789"
objRS("au_lname") = "Papa"
objRS("au_fname") = "Colleen"
objRS("phone") = "919 555-1234"
objRS("address") = "1 Lois Lane"
objRS("city") = "Metropolis"
objRS("state") = "NY"
objRS("zip") = "12345"
objRS("contract") = False
objRS.Update
```

23

SQL SERVER,
ADO, AND THE
WEB

Updating data values is as easy as going to the record and the field you want to change, setting the value, and then issuing the Update method. Unlike other data access tools, ADO does not require the developer to execute an Edit method to begin editing a record. Rather, as soon as you change a value of a field, ADO recognizes that the developer is editing the record so it issues an implicit edit for you. Listing 23.19 shows how you can edit data with ADO.

LISTING 23.19   EDITING AN EXISTING RECORD IN A TABLE

```
set objConn = Server.CreateObject("ADODB.Connection")
set objCmd = Server.CreateObject("ADODB.Command")
set objRS = Server.CreateObject("ADODB.Recordset")
objConn.Open "Provider=SQLOLEDB.1;User ID=sa;" & _
    "Password=;Initial Catalog=pubs;Data Source=papanotebook"
set objCmd.ActiveConnection = objConn
objCmd.CommandText = "SELECT * FROM authors WHERE au_lname = 'Papa'"
objRS.Open objCmd, , adOpenStatic, adLockOptimistic
objRS("phone") = "919 555-5000"
objRS.Update
```

Deleting records from a table is even simpler. All you need to do is find the record you want to remove and issue the Delete method. Listing 23.20 shows the Delete method in action.

LISTING 23.20   DELETING AN EXISTING RECORD IN A TABLE

```
set objConn = Server.CreateObject("ADODB.Connection")
set objCmd = Server.CreateObject("ADODB.Command")
set objRS = Server.CreateObject("ADODB.Recordset")
objConn.Open "Provider=SQLOLEDB.1;User ID=sa;" & _
    "Password=;Initial Catalog=pubs;Data Source=papanotebook"
set objCmd.ActiveConnection = objConn
objCmd.CommandText = "SELECT * FROM authors WHERE au_lname = 'Papa'"
objRS.Open objCmd, , adOpenStatic, adLockOptimistic
objRS.Delete
```

Batch Updates

If you need to make several changes to a recordset, you are better off sending the changes in a single group to the database. In ADO, this method can be interpreted as doing batch updates. SQL Server responds much faster if, for example, you send six updates in one shot instead of six updates in individual batches. Batch updates really become useful when you get into disconnected recordsets later in this chapter, as you can make several changes to a recordset without keeping a connection open to the database.

Batch updating requires that you set the LockType property appropriately, as shown in Listing 23.21. Then you open the recordset as usual, make your changes to the fields, and issue the Update method. This is where the difference comes in: The Update method changes the value of the fields in the recordset, but not in the underlying database. This way, you can make several updates (deletes or inserts) and save them to the ADO recordset, and later send them to the database in a single shot by issuing the UpdateBatch method (again, see Listing 23.21).

LISTING 23.21 ADDING A NEW RECORD TO A TABLE

```
set objConn = Server.CreateObject("ADODB.Connection")
set objCmd = Server.CreateObject("ADODB.Command")
set objRS = Server.CreateObject("ADODB.Recordset")
objConn.Open "Provider=SQLOLEDB.1;User ID=sa;" & _
    Password=;Initial Catalog=pubs;Data Source=papanotebook"
set objCmd.ActiveConnection = objConn
objCmd.CommandText = "authors"
objRS.Open objCmd, , adOpenStatic, adLockBatchOptimistic
objRS.MoveNext
objRS("phone") = "555 555-5555"
objRS.Update
objRS.MoveNext
objRS("phone") = "555 555-4444"
objRS.Update
objRS.AddNew
objRS("au_id") = "123-45-0000"
objRS("au_lname") = "Papa"
objRS("au_fname") = "Colleen"
objRS("phone") = "919 555-1234"
objRS("address") = "1 Lois Lane"
objRS("city") = "Metropolis"
objRS("state") = "NY"
objRS("zip") = "12345"
objRS("contract") = False
objRS.Update
objRS.UpdateBatch
```

So when would you want to use this technique? Say you have several Web pages of information that all pertain to a single topic, such as pages of a survey. There might be five pages of information on the survey, but they all need to be saved to a single table in SQL Server called survey. Using batch updating, you can store the recordset in a Session object variable and make the final batch update when the user finishes with the last survey page. Even though this is a single record, it's an opportunity for batch updating to make life easier.

23

SQL SERVER,
ADO, AND THE
WEB

Another common situation for batch updating is when you want to allow a user to edit several records on a single Web page within a table or a grid. In this case, you let the user make several changes, and then you save them all at once by using the `UpdateBatch` method.

Temporary Indexing

You know that an index can improve the performance of your SQL statements, but what's less well known is that you can also use indexes to enhance the performance of the operations that find or sort values in an ADO `Recordset`. ADO 2.0 introduces the ability to place an index on a field in your recordset. Keep in mind that the index is temporary, in that it exists only within the ADO recordset and ceases to exist when the recordset is closed.

To create an index on a field in a recordset, you must set the value of the `Optimize` property within the field's `Properties` collection. The `Optimize` property is dynamic as it exists in the `Properties` collection only if the `CursorLocation` property is set to `adUseClient`. You simply need to set this property to `True` to create the index (see Listing 23.22) and `False` to remove the index.

LISTING 23.22 CREATING AN INDEX ON THE City FIELD

```
set objConn = Server.CreateObject("ADODB.Connection")
set objRS = Server.CreateObject("ADODB.Recordset")
objConn.Open "Provider=SQLOLEDB.1;User ID=sa;Password=;" & _
    Initial Catalog=pubs;Data Source=papanotebook"
strSQL = "SELECT * FROM authors"
objRS.CursorLocation = adUseClient
objRS.Open strSQL, objConn, adOpenStatic
objRS("city").Properties("Optimize") = True
```

You can then search a particular field for values much faster now that the index has been created on the recordset. What else does this buy you? Well, how about finding a particular record in a recordset? Or what about sorting a recordset without requerying the database with a new sort order? These features were conspicuously absent in previous versions of ADO.

Sorting a Recordset

The reason you can now sort a recordset is because indexing is possible. Consider how a sorting routine would work for a recordset without indexing. The entire recordset (not just a single field) would have to be physically moved within the recordset to accomplish the sorting algorithm, which would have caused tremendous performance concerns. With the advent of indexing in ADO 2.0, sorting is achieved by creating a series of pointers (indexes) to each record in its sorted order. This way, the data in the recordset does not have to be physically relocated, thus saving resources.

Now that you know how it works, let's see how you use it. To sort a recordset, simply set the Sort property to the name of a field and the type of sort (that is, ascending or descending). You can also list several fields to extend the sort order, separating them by commas, as shown in Listing 23.23.

LISTING 23.23 SORTING THE AUTHORS BY STATE AND CITY

```
set objConn = Server.CreateObject("ADODB.Connection")
set objRS = Server.CreateObject("ADODB.Recordset")
objConn.Open "Provider=SQLOLEDB.1;User ID=sa;Password=;" & _
    Initial Catalog=pubs;Data Source=papanotebook"
strSQL = "SELECT * FROM authors"
objRS.CursorLocation = adUseClient
objRS.Open strSQL, objConn, adOpenStatic
objRS.Sort = "state asc, city desc"
```

Finding a Specific Record

Another feature new to ADO 2.0 is finding a specific record. To do this you use the new Find method, as shown in Listing 23.24.

LISTING 23.24 Find METHOD SYNTAX

```
recordset.Find criteria, skipRows, searchDirection, start
```

The criteria specifies the rows you're searching for. This can be a string expression that's basically a SQL WHERE clause without the WHERE keyword. Listing 23.25 shows the Find method in action using the criteria. The start parameter designates a bookmark of the row in the recordset to begin the search at. The skipRows parameter specifies which row in relation to the starting point to begin searching. The default is the current row, or 0. In other words, skipRows is the offset applied to the start parameter. Finally, the searchDirection specifies which direction search for the criteria: forward or backward.

LISTING 23.25 FINDING A SPECIFIC RECORD

```
set objConn = Server.CreateObject("ADODB.Connection")
set objRS = Server.CreateObject("ADODB.Recordset")
objConn.Open "Provider=SQLOLEDB.1;User ID=sa;" & _
    "Password=;Initial Catalog=pubs;Data Source=papanotebook"
strSQL = "SELECT * FROM authors"
objRS.CursorLocation = adUseClient
objRS.Open strSQL, objConn, adOpenStatic
objRS.Find "state = 'NC'"
```

If several rows meet your criteria, you can reissue the Find method and its parameters, changing only the skipRows parameter. You simply change this value to 1, so it begins its search after the current row.

Taking Advantage of Disconnected Recordsets

Throughout this chapter, I have been alluding to how you can use several features of ADO in implementing disconnected recordsets. In this section, you see how the features of ADO all come together, but first, let's see why disconnected recordsets are so cool.

Remember back to the section on batch updates where you had an application with a five-page survey. The survey data all came from a single table in a SQL Server database, and you stored the recordset in the session. Part of the solution to this application involves disconnecting the recordset from the database after you have the original data. Then you pass the disconnected recordset from page to page using the session so you can accumulate all the changes. To accomplish this task, you need to disconnect the record-set, which involves a few key lines of code.

First, the CursorLocation must be set to client-side (adUseClient). This makes sense if you consider that after the database is disconnected from the recordset, the recordset has no way of communicating with SQL Server to access a server-side cursor. Next, you want to set the LockType to allow for batch updating (adLockBatchOptimistic). This is required so you can send all intermediate changes (changes made while disconnected) to the database in one shot when you reconnect. Finally, after the recordset is opened for the first time, you must set the ActiveConnection to Nothing. Listing 23.26 shows the ASP to store the disconnected recordset in the session.

LISTING 23.26   RETRIEVING/STORING THE DISCONNECTED RECORDSET IN THE SESSION

```
if isobject(session("RS")) then
    '--- Retrieve the stored disconnected recordset
    '--- from the session object.
    set objRS = session("RS")
else
    set objConn = Server.CreateObject("ADODB.Connection")
    set objRS = Server.CreateObject("ADODB.Recordset")
    '--- Open the connection and create the recordset.
    strConn = "Provider=SQLOLEDB.1;User ID=sa;Initial"
    strConn = strConn & " Catalog=pubs;Data Source=papanotebook"
    objConn.Open strConn
    strSQL = "SELECT * FROM authors"
    '--- Use a client-side cursor since we want to disconnect.
    objRS.CursorLocation = adUseClient
    '--- Open the recordset.
    objRS.Open strSQL, objConn, adOpenStatic, adLockBatchOptimistic
```

```
'--- Disconnect from the connection and the database.
    set objRS.ActiveConnection = nothing
    set session("RS") = objRS
end if
```

Notice that the first thing you do is check whether the recordset is in the session yet. If it is, you simply retrieve it. Otherwise, you create the recordset, disconnect it, and store it in the session. After that, you can let your users edit the data in the disconnected recordset without affecting the database (by issuing the Update method). To save the changes back to the database, you need to reconnect to SQL Server and issue a batch update, as shown in Listing 23.27.

LISTING 23.27   OPENING THE CONNECTION TO THE PUBS DATABASE

```
set objRS = session("RS")
set objConn = Server.CreateObject("ADODB.Connection")
'--- Open the connection and create the recordset.
objConn.Open "Provider=SQLOLEDB.1;User ID=sa;" & _
    "Password=;Initial Catalog=pubs;Data Source=papanotebook"
set objRS.ActiveConnection = objConn
objRS.UpdateBatch
```

This code sends all the changes made while disconnected to SQL Server. If any changes were unsuccessful, you can check them by setting the Filter property to adFilterConflictingRecords. This setting seemingly reduces the recordset to the records that caused the error when applied to SQL Server.

If you want to see what changes have been made before the UpdateBatch method is called, you can apply yet a different filter. Setting the Filter property to adFilterPendingRecords shows you the records that have been changes with the Update method but have not yet been saved to the SQL Server database.

The Filter property is very powerful, especially when associated with disconnected recordsets. When you set the Filter property, it automatically screens out records in the Recordset object. The filtered Recordset becomes the current cursor, but you can retrieve the original recordset data by setting the filter to adFilterNone.

RDS: Moving ADO to the Browser

One of the downfalls of server-side processing (ASP) is that the control must go back to the Web server to process the user's actions. For example, the user wants to see all the sales for this month by product, but only 10 products per page. Using ADO within an ASP, every time the user wanted to go to another page, the control would go back to the

Web server to process the request, re-create the page with the new data, and render it back to the client's browser.

With RDS, you don't have to make round trips anymore. In this same scenario, control would not go back to the server to process the request. Rather, the Internet Explorer browser would accept the request and render the page with the new data. RDS can do this because it stores the ADO recordset within the client browser when it first gets the data from the Web server.

> **NOTE**
>
> RDS is a wonderful technology, but because it downloads the data to the browser, it may yield a performance hit up front. Because of this, you may want to defer using RDS for large recordsets. You'll have to test your recordset size over your Internet connection to determine its viability.

Before you get too excited, keep in mind that the full feature set of RDS works only in Internet Explorer (IE) 4.0 or higher. So if you are targeting the Internet at large, RDS is probably not your solution. However, if you're building an application for your intranet, RDS is viable as long as your company standard is IE 4.01 with Service Pack 1 or higher.

RDS retrieves a recordset across the Internet by using HTTP (Hypertext Transfer Protocol). Formerly, you could transfer data through objects only by using DCOM or remote automation. However, RDS takes advantage of the Web and HTTP to allow you to pass an ADO recordset across the Internet. The end result: You can store data in the client IE browser.

RDS requires a minimum of three parameters to retrieve a recordset to the IE browser: `server`, `connect`, and `sql`. The `server` parameter simply points to the Web server's address. The `connect` parameter should be set to a connection string that the Web server can process. This can be an ODBC data source, an ODBC DSN-less connection string, or an OLE DB connection string. Finally, the `sql` parameter should be set to the SELECT statement used to retrieve the data. Listing 23.28 shows all these properties at work to render the list of authors on an HTML page.

LISTING 23.28   DISPLAYING AUTHOR INFORMATION TO A BROWSER USING RDS

```
<HTML>
<HEAD>
```

```
<!-- RDS DataControl -->
<object classid="clsid:bd96c556-65a3-11d0-983a-00c04fc29e33"
id="objRS" width="0" height="0">
<param name="server" value="http://papanotebook">
<param name="sql" value="select au_fname, au_lname,
    city, state from authors order by au_lname, au_fname">
<param name="connect" value="Provider=SQLOLEDB.1;
    User ID=sa;Password=;Initial Catalog=pubs;Data Source=papanotebook">
</object>

<TITLE>Authors</TITLE>
</HEAD>
<BODY>
<Center>
<h2>Authors</h2>

<table border="0" width="640">
    <tr align="CENTER">
        <td width="25%" nowrap><b>First Name</b></td>
        <td width="25%" nowrap><b>Last Name</b></td>
        <td width="25%" nowrap><b>City</b></td>
        <td width="25%" nowrap><b>State</b></td>
    </tr>
</table>
<table border="0" datasrc="#objRS" width="640">
    <tr align="CENTER">
        <td> <input size=15 name=first datafld="au_fname"></td>
        <td> <input size=15 name=last datafld="au_lname"></td>
        <td> <input size=15 name=city datafld="city"></td>
        <td> <input size=15 name=state datafld="state"></td>
    </tr>
</table>
</center>
</BODY>
</HTML>
```

23

SQL SERVER, ADO, AND THE WEB

To use the RDS DataControl, you must first create the RDS DataControl object, as shown here:

```
<object classid="clsid:bd96c556-65a3-11d0-983a-00c04fc29e33"
id="objRS" width="0" height="0">
</object>
```

Be sure to give the RDS DataControl object a unique ID to refer to it, such as objRS. You'll use it to refer to the returned recordset. The properties of the RDS DataControl can be set with the <param> tags. Notice these tags and the property settings shown in Listing 23.28.

You can bind the data from an RDS `DataControl` to an HTML table by placing a `datas-rc` property in the table tag and setting it to the ID of the RDS `DataControl`. (Just be sure to prefix the ID in the property with a # character.) Finally, you need to bind the data columns to columns in the HTML table. You can do this by putting text boxes in the table and setting the `datafld` property of the text box to the column name. Refer to Listing 23.28 for a complete listing of the HTML used to render the author data to an IE 4 browser using RDS.

Summary

ADO 2.0 introduces several new features such as indexing, sorting, and finding and enhances some existing features. For access to a SQL Server database, ADO is the best choice because of its speed, small resource burden, and ease of use. Executing stored procedures, issuing batch updates, and using remote recordsets with RDS are only a few of the ADO features you can integrate with SQL Server.

As you port more applications to a Web environment, ADO becomes more important to the development process. Because of ADO's advantage over other data access techniques (speed, size, ease of use), it makes it the perfect choice for data access over the Web. If you need to be concerned about transferring too much data back and forth between the client browser and the Web server, RDS allows you to bring an ADO recordset right to the browser so you can reduce your round trips. Any way you look at it, ADO is the way to go with enterprise databases.

CHAPTER 24

Microsoft's COM/DCOM

Randy Morin

IN THIS CHAPTER

When discussing COM (Component Object Model) and DCOM (Distributed COM) in such broad terms, as I do in this chapter, I usually get two specific questions from the confused listeners and readers. What is COM? And what is the difference between COM and DCOM? I'll start with a definition of COM.

COM is a protocol that defines how object servers interact with object consumers. In this definition, *object servers* are modules that implement COM classes and *object consumers* are modules that use COM objects.

Before DCOM was introduced, a COM object server could be in two locations in relation to the object consumer. They could be in the same process as the object consumer or in a process different from the object consumer.

DCOM Architecture

When object servers exist in the same process as an object consumer, the object method calls are bound directly to the method implementations (see Figure 24.1). Object servers that exist in the same process as the object consumer are often referred to as *in-process COM servers*.

FIGURE 24.1

In-process COM objects.

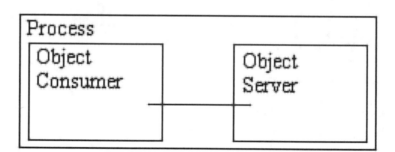

When object servers exist in a separate process from the object consumer, the object method calls are bound to a proxy method implementation (see Figure 24.2). The call to the proxy is forwarded by the COM runtime using Remote Procedure Calls (RPC) to the method implementation in a second process. Object servers that exist in a separate process from the object consumer are often called *local COM servers*.

FIGURE 24.2

Local COM objects.

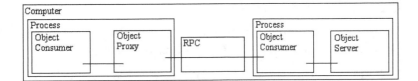

Next, what is the difference between COM and DCOM? *DCOM* extends the COM protocol by enabling object servers to exist on a separate computer from the object consumer.

When the object server exists on a separate computer, the COM runtime forwards the method calls using RPC from the proxy in one process on one computer to the implementation in a second process on a second computer (see Figure 24.3). Object servers that exist on a separate machine from the object consumer are called *remote COM servers*.

FIGURE 24.3

Remote COM objects.

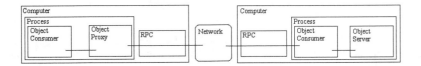

CORBA

DCOM is not the only distributed object protocol. There are at least as many distributed object protocols as there are programmers in Silicon Valley, probably more. The most popular of these competing protocols is CORBA. Several differences exist in the implementation of CORBA and DCOM that could favor either protocol.

CORBA has been around for years and has been implemented and well tested on almost every major platform. DCOM has also been around for years, but has existed only on Win32 machines until just recently. DCOM as implemented on Win32 has many usable services, including connection points, events, automation, the NT Event Log, the NT Service Control Manager, and so on. CORBA has some usable services, but lacks the quality and quantity of services available in Win32 DCOM.

I won't dive into any more detail about CORBA versus DCOM because it's not the topic of this chapter. But I'll leave you with one thought: Do you live in Bill's world?

24

MICROSOFT'S
COM/DCOM

DCE RPC and IDL

COM was not built from scratch. Microsoft used DCE RPC (Distributed Computing Environment Remote Procedure Call) as a major building block in the design of COM.

DCE RPC is a protocol that enables procedures (not objects) to be called on a remote machine. COM is Microsoft's object-oriented implementation of DCE RPC and is built completely on top of Microsoft RPC (Microsoft's implementation of DCE RPC).

DCE RPC defines its interfaces with interface definition language (IDL). COM also defines its interfaces using IDL, but COM's IDL is an object-oriented implementation of IDL. Listing 24.1 is an example of a COM IDL file.

LISTING 24.1 SAMPLE COM IDL FILE

```
// localserver.idl : IDL source for localserver.dll
//

// This file will be processed by the MIDL tool to
// produce the type library (localserver.tlb) and marshalling code.

import "oaidl.idl";
import "ocidl.idl";

    [
        object,
        uuid(C5278593-9EB0-11D2-9C2B-B86D06C10000),
        dual,
        helpstring("Itestobject2 Interface"),
        pointer_default(unique)
    ]
    interface Itestobject2 : IDispatch
    {
        [id(1), helpstring("method Hello")] HRESULT Hello();
    };
[
    uuid(C5278584-9EB0-11D2-9C2B-B86D06C10000),
    version(1.0),
    helpstring("localserver 1.0 Type Library")
]
library LOCALSERVERLib
{
    importlib("stdole32.tlb");
    importlib("stdole2.tlb");

    [
        uuid(C5278594-9EB0-11D2-9C2B-B86D06C10000),
        helpstring("testobject2 Class")
    ]
```

```
    coclass testobject2
    {
        [default] interface Itestobject2;
    };
};
```

> **NOTE**
>
> It is a common misperception that IDL is C++. This is not true. Although IDL is
> syntactically similar to C++, IDL is not C++ code.

There are three elements to this IDL file. It has an interface definition, a library (aka type
library) definition, and a class definition. All IDL elements have two parts: the element
attributes and the element body.

Our interface definition has five attributes. The first two attributes (object and uuid) are
required for COM objects. The object attribute identifies the interface as an OLE interface. If this attribute were not present, the interface would be an RPC interface. The uuid
attributes assigned a unique ID to the interface. The body of the interface definition specifies the name of the interface; that is, Itestobject2 inherits the IDispatch interface
and all of its methods. The Itestobject2 interface also defines one additional method
named Hello() that does not take any parameters.

LISTING 24.2 SAMPLE INTERFACE DEFINITION

```
[
    object,
    uuid(C5278593-9EB0-11D2-9C2B-B86D06C10000),
    dual,
    helpstring("Itestobject2 Interface"),
    pointer_default(unique)
]
interface Itestobject2 : IDispatch
{
    [id(1), helpstring("method Hello")] HRESULT Hello();
};
```

Our library definition has three attributes. You'll recognize the uuid attribute; it is similar to the uuid attribute that was in our interface definition. The body of a library definition may contain any number of interface and class definitions. These interface and class
definitions will be part of the library.

24

MICROSOFT'S
COM/DCOM

LISTING 24.3 SAMPLE LIBRARY DEFINITION

```
[
    uuid(C5278584-9EB0-11D2-9C2B-B86D06C10000),
    version(1.0),
    helpstring("localserver 1.0 Type Library")
]
library LOCALSERVERLib
{
    importlib("stdole32.tlb");
    importlib("stdole2.tlb");

    ...
};
```

Our class definition also has the uuid attribute. The body of our class definition defines the name of our class as testobject2 and enumerates all of the supported interfaces. Our class only supports one interface: the Itestobject2 interface that we defined earlier in the IDL file.

LISTING 24.4 SAMPLE CLASS DEFINITION

```
[
    uuid(C5278594-9EB0-11D2-9C2B-B86D06C10000),
    helpstring("testobject2 Class")
]
coclass testobject2
{
    [default] interface Itestobject2;
};
```

IDL is considered language-neutral because you can develop your interfaces in IDL and implement them in a variety of languages, including C++, Java, Visual Basic, and Pascal. You can even write your first implementation of an object in one language and decide later to reimplement it in another language. Because IDL is language-neutral, object consumers can use the same interface without having to consider which language the class was implemented with.

Another advantage of language neutrality is that object consumers can be implemented in a language different from the object server's language. In a multitier application, the client could be written in a GUI RAD tool such as Visual Basic, and the mid-tier could be written in a powerful application tool such as Visual C++.

Distributed Object

So COM binds object servers and object consumers in the same process, in separate processes, and on separate machines. But does COM do it well? COM does many things well, making life much easier for the programmer. For example, COM performs location transparency and marshaling quite well.

Location Transparency

COM provides for location transparency by making object creation and manipulation of objects almost identical, no matter how far the object consumer is from the object server. That means the object consumers do not need to know if the object server is an in-process, a local, or a remote server.

Location transparency has several clear advantages. An object consumer can be created to use an object server without requiring knowledge of the server's location. The server can then be moved during production to get performance benefits.

> **NOTE**
>
> The object consumer can be programmed to use a remote application object. The system operator might realize during production that the remoteness of the application object is causing a performance problem. The application object can be moved to the local machine without having to rewrite any code. It can even be moved to the local process without having to rewrite the object consumer. When moving object servers from out-of-process to in-process, the object server might have to be rewritten.

Threading and Marshaling

An important part of implementing distributed objects is marshaling objects across the thread, process, and computer boundaries. So you can fully understand what I mean by *marshaling*, I should explain where the term originated. The word originally described the process of arranging soldiers in preparation for battle.

A similar definition is used when defining marshaling as it pertains to moving data across thread, process, and computer boundaries. *Marshaling* is the process of packaging data into packets before transferring the data across the thread, process, or computer boundary. *Unmarshaling* is unpacking the data after transferring it across the boundary.

It might be obvious why COM must marshal data between computers and processes, but it's not always obvious why COM marshals data between threads. When a COM method is invoked, the parameters are placed on the threads stack. If a COM method is called across threads, the parameters must be moved to the thread stack of the called COM object.

Apartments

To perform the marshaling, COM objects exist in a container similar to a thread called an *apartment*. Whenever COM objects are moved across apartment boundaries, the object is marshaled. In early versions of 32-bit COM, there was only one type of apartment that was later named a *single threaded apartment* (*STA*). All threads existed in only one apartment, and all apartments contained exactly one thread. If a process had two threads that shared a COM object, the object had to be marshaled between the two threads.

When object methods were invoked in an STA, the marshaling was serialized through a Windows message queue. This ensured that two calls from two separate client apartments would be properly serialized.

Later, a second type of apartment was introduced called the *multithreaded apartment* (*MTA*). All threads still existed in only one apartment, but MTAs could contain one or more threads. Another difference between STAs and MTAs is that a process can contain zero or more STAs, but at most only one MTA.

When object methods are invoked in an MTA, the marshaling is not serialized on a Windows message queue. That means COM objects existing in an MTA could have concurrency issues. Two client calls coming in simultaneously will execute simultaneously on two separate threads.

Marshaling

You can accomplish marshaling in COM in one of three ways: type library marshaling, standard marshaling, or custom marshaling. The three types of marshaling came about as marshaling evolved.

Custom marshaling is the basic marshaling mechanism that gives the programmer direct control over how the COM objects are marshaled. Not many COM objects use custom marshaling because it's not the easiest concept to grasp, never mind implement.

Standard marshaling is the next step up the ladder of marshaling. It enables programmers to specify the interface in IDL. The IDL can be compiled by a compiler called *MIDL* to generate the code necessary to build a marshaling proxy-stub.

> **NOTE**
>
> The first time you use standard marshaling across computer boundaries, you'll probably have to register the proxy-stub DLL on both the client and server machines. You can register the proxy-stub DLL with the REGSVR32.EXE utility.

Type library marshaling is the current top-of-the-ladder method for marshaling your objects. If your COM interface is tagged as an automation compatible interface, MIDL generates a type library (.tlb) file. Some languages, such as Visual Basic, bypass IDL and embed the type library directly in the target module, which makes type library marshaling completely transparent to the programmer—I mean *really* transparent.

> **NO TYPE LIBRARY**
>
> One of the most asked categories of questions on NetNews is about marshaling Visual Basic interfaces between computers. If you create a Visual Basic ActiveX EXE, the type library gets embedded within the EXE, so you can install the single component quite easily on the server. However, there's a problem when you want to install the type library on the remote client machine. The type library is embedded in the EXE. Do you have to install the server EXE on the client machine? You don't and shouldn't. Installing the type library has become the source of nightmares. So how do you install the type library on the client machine? It's not easy.
>
> From your VB IDE, go to Project Properties and check the Remote Server Files check box (see Figure 24.4).
>
> When you make your EXE, VB generates a .vbr and .tlb file. Then you use the CLIREG32.EXE registration utility to register the type library on the client machine.

When COM attempts to marshal an interface that uses type library marshaling, the proxy-stub for OLE automation performs the marshaling by interpreting the type library, which leads me to the disadvantages of using type library marshaling.

24

MICROSOFT'S
COM/DCOM

FIGURE 24.4

The Remote Server Files check box in Visual Basic's Project Properties dialog.

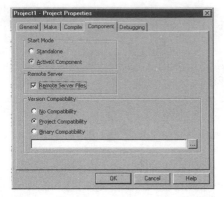

> **TIP**
>
> Registering a type library is quite a manual process. I am unaware of any readily available tools that register type libraries. But what I've done is create a small utility called RegTypeLib that does exactly that. Listing 24.5 gives you the source code.

LISTING 24.5   REGTYPELIB SOURCE CODE

```cpp
#include <windows.h>
#include <io.h>
#include <sstream>

inline std::wstring AnsiToWide(const std::string & str)
{
  WCHAR * sz = new WCHAR[str.length()+1];
  ::MultiByteToWideChar(CP_ACP, 0, str.c_str(), -1,
                        sz, str.length()+1);
  std::wstring ws = sz;
  delete[] sz;
  return ws;
}

int WINAPI WinMain( HINSTANCE hInstance,
          HINSTANCE hPrevInstance,
          LPSTR lpCmdLine,
          int nCmdShow)
{
  ::CoInitialize(NULL);
  try
  {
    if ( ( lpCmdLine == NULL ) ||
         ( ::lstrlen(lpCmdLine) == 0) ||
```

```
            ( _access( lpCmdLine, 0 ) == -1 ) )
    {
      ::MessageBox(NULL, "Usage: REGTLB.EXE yourtlb.tlb",
                   "Type library does not exist", MB_OK+MB_ICONERROR);
      throw 0;
    }

    ITypeLib * typelib;
    HRESULT hresult = ::LoadTypeLibEx(AnsiToWide(lpCmdLine).c_str(),
                                      REGKIND_REGISTER, &typelib);
    if ( FAILED(hresult) )
    {
      std::stringstream ss;
      ss << "File = " << lpCmdLine << ". HRESULT = " << hresult;
      ::MessageBox(NULL, ss.str().c_str(),
                   "Error while registering type library",
                   MB_OK+MB_ICONERROR);
      throw 0;
    }
    typelib->Release();
  }
  catch(...)
  {
  }
  ::CoUninitialize();

  return 0;
};
```

You can also run RegTypeLib from Windows Explorer by adding the entries in Listing 24.6 to your Windows NT Registry. To do that, copy the contents of Listing 24.6 into a .reg file and open the file from Windows Explorer.

LISTING 24.6   CONFIGURE REGISTRY FOR REGISTRATION OF TYPE LIBRARIES

```
REGEDIT4

[HKEY_CLASSES_ROOT\.tlb]
@="tlbfile"

[HKEY_CLASSES_ROOT\tlbfile]
@="Type Library"

[HKEY_CLASSES_ROOT\tlbfile\shell\Register Type Library\command]
@="REGTYPELIB.EXE %1"
```

24

MICROSOFT'S COM/DCOM

> **TIP**
>
> You'll have to compile the RegTypeLib executable and place it in the executable path before you can actually use this technique.
>
> After you've added Registry entries, built the RegTypeLib executable, and placed it in the executable path, you can simply right-click on a type library file to get a menu that includes the option to register the file.

The automation marshaler abstracts the process of marshaling objects. The abstraction that makes type library marshaling easier also makes the marshaling slower. Type library marshaling is slower than standard marshaling.

Beyond the ability to bind object servers and consumers that exist in different locations in relation to each other, COM automatically provides for two important services: threading and security.

DCOM Security

COM inherently provides for security by using the Security Support Provider Interface (SSPI) to manage the security of its objects. *SSPI* is a protocol used across all of Microsoft's technologies to authenticate a user. Because SSPI is only a protocol and not an implementation, the security provider can be readily switched without having to rewrite all your security.

Because COM uses SSPI, it can use any security provider that exports such an interface, including NT security (NTLM). Windows NT 4.0 and previous versions use the NTLM authentication protocol.

Windows NT 5.0 will implement a new default authentication protocol—Kerberos. Because COM accesses its security provider using SSPI, the transition to Kerberos will be nearly transparent. A third important security service is SChannel (secure channel) security. This security server is already implemented in Windows NT 4.0 and provides for the SSL/PCT protocols.

Microsoft has an online DCOM security FAQ that I've found quite valuable. You might want to visit the following Web page when you have a potential DCOM security problem:

```
http://support.microsoft.com/support/kb/articles/Q158/5/08.asp
```

Activation and Call Security

COM has two categories of security: activation security and call security. *Activation security* describes which clients are permitted to launch which COM servers. *Call security* indicates which clients are permitted to invoke methods on which COM classes.

Machine-Wide, Process-Wide, and Programmatic Security

A COM object can choose to implement security using machine-wide, process-wide, or programmatic security. COM objects that do not implement their own security and legacy objects that were written before DCOM use the machine-wide security default. Machine-wide security defaults are saved in the Registry key `HKEY_LOCAL_MACHINE\Software\Microsoft\OLE`. The security values for both launch and access permissions are saved as self-relative security descriptors.

Self-relative security descriptors are a flat structure that describes a set of security permissions. Unless you really need to know your security, I suggest you ignore these structures and manipulate the Registry settings using a configuration utility such as DCOMCNFG, which is described later in the chapter in the section titled "DCOMCNFG."

COM objects can also be implemented using process-wide security. These security settings are configured in the Windows Registry under the COM server's AppId, that is, `HKEY_CLASSES_ROOT\AppId\{AppId-as-GUID}`.

The most flexible method of implementing COM security is using programmatic security, which is done by calling the `CoInitializeSecurity()` function or by manipulating the `IClientSecurity` or `IServerSecurity` interfaces.

Authentication Levels

COM offers different levels of authentication security.

- No Authentication
- Connection
- Call
- Packet
- Packet Integrity
- Packet Privacy

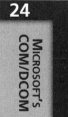

24

MICROSOFT'S
COM/DCOM

The lowest level of security is no authentication. The next level is connection-level authentication, which authenticates the client only when it first connects. This authentication level is available only to protocols that are connection based. This includes TPC/IP but not UDP/IP.

Call-level authentication authenticates the client before every remote call. Packet-level authentication authenticates the client for every packet received. Packet-level authentication with data integrity and packet-level authentication with encryption also authenticate the client for every packet received, and both authentication levels also verify that the packets were not modified during transmission. In addition, packet-level authentication with encryption encrypts the packet before transmitting.

Impersonation

Another important feature of COM is that COM servers have the ability to impersonate their callers. Impersonation enables COM servers to limit and extend its security privileges to match that of the client. I won't discuss all the impersonation levels; they are more appropriate for an advanced DCOM book such as the Sams book *COM/DCOM Unleashed*.

Common Techniques

With the advent of the three-tier client/server architecture, application servers (the middle tier) have become a breading ground of ingenuity. These application servers require four important characteristics:

- The ability to be remotely launched, monitored, and stopped
- The ability to be easily configured
- The ability to scale
- The ability to fail safely

In the next few sections, I describe how you can incorporate these four characteristics into your application servers.

DCOM Services

A powerful feature of DCOM is the ability to remotely launch COM servers. All COM servers have this innate ability. If you create a COM object on a remote machine, the DCOM service control manager (SCM) on the remote machine automatically launches the COM server and makes its COM objects available for use.

In fact, the SCM managers on both machines also try to manage the lifetime of the COM server. That is, when all references to a remote object are released and no other clients have references to any objects of the COM server, the SCM takes the steps to unload the COM server.

This is not always desirable behavior. Loading, unloading, and reloading a COM server is a taxing operation. Sometimes you want a COM server to be loaded all the time, so that any new incoming object requests do not incur the penalty of having to reload the COM server. This type of behavior can be easily accomplished by making your COM server into a Windows NT service. The service can be configured to automatically load when the computer is first started and unloaded only when the computer is shut down.

NT Security Versus Mixed Security

It's important to note when you are implementing an application server as an NT service connected to a SQL Server database that services typically run under the local system user account. This user account has no privileges beyond the boundaries of the single machine. That means the service can't connect to a SQL Server database using integrated NT security.

The workaround is to run the service under another user account or use SQL Server's standard or mixed authentication. You can run a service under an alternative user account with the Service Control Manager Control Panel applet (see Figure 24.5). To get this dialog, go to the Control Panel. Double-click the Services icon. Select the service you want to configure, and click the Startup button.

FIGURE 24.5

The Service dialog allows logging on as a different user.

Configuration

A common problem inexperienced COM programmers have is installing COM servers. Unlike regular DLLs and EXEs, it is not enough to just copy the module to the appropriate directory and run the program. COM servers must be registered in the Windows NT Registry.

The common practice for COM DLLs is to export two functions, `DllRegisterServer()` and `DllUnregisterServer()`, from the DLL. You can then use a utility called `REGSVR32.EXE` that invokes these exported functions to install and uninstall the DLL COM server.

The common practice for COM EXEs is to parse the command line when the server is first started. If the command line includes the `/REGSERVER` or `/UNREGSERVER` command-line parameters, the executable installs or uninstalls itself and exits.

> **TIP**
>
> If you add the values in Listing 24.7 to your Windows NT Registry, you should be able to right-click on a COM DLL or EXE in Windows Explorer and easily invoke the registration and unregistration. You can add these values by simply saved Listing 24.7 as a `.reg` file and opening it in Windows Explorer.

LISTING 24.7 CONFIGURE REGISTRY FOR SELF-REGISTRATION

```
REGEDIT4

[HKEY_CLASSES_ROOT\.dll]
@="dllfile"

[HKEY_CLASSES_ROOT\dllfile]
@="Application Extension"

[HKEY_CLASSES_ROOT\dllfile\shell\Register COM server\command]
@="REGSVR32.EXE %1"

[HKEY_CLASSES_ROOT\dllfile\shell\Unregister COM server\command]
@="REGSVR32.EXE /u %1"

[HKEY_CLASSES_ROOT\.exe]
@="exefile"

[HKEY_CLASSES_ROOT\exefile]
@="Application"
```

```
[HKEY_CLASSES_ROOT\exefile\shell\Register COM server\command]
@="%1 /REGSERVER"

[HKEY_CLASSES_ROOT\exefile\shell\Unregister COM server\command]
@="%1 /UNREGSERVER"
```

As discussed earlier in this chapter, DCOM provides for both machine-wide and process-wide security, but these settings are saved as self-relative security descriptors. As I mentioned, self-relative security descriptors are not important because there are many configuration utilities that can read and write them for you from the Registry. Two such utilities are DCOMCNFG and OLEVIEW.

DCOMCNFG

DCOMCNFG is installed with nearly every DCOM installation. This makes the utility convenient because you're assured that it can be installed almost everywhere.

> **NOTE**
>
> At the time of this writing, there are at least two versions of DCOMCNFG. The first version did not have any of the protocol tabs mentioned in the following paragraphs, nor did it have a check box to enable COM Internet services.

You can start DCOMCNFG by choosing Start, Run from the Windows taskbar. Type DCOMCNFG and click OK to open the main dialog of DCOMCNFG (see Figure 24.6).

FIGURE 24.6

The DCOMCNFG Applications tab.

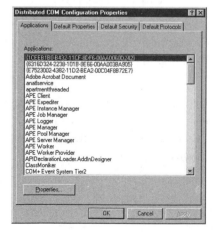

Select the Default Properties tab from the main dialog. This switches you to a property page where you can enable and disable DCOM and set default security authentication and identity (see Figure 24.7).

FIGURE 24.7

The DCOMCNFG Default Properties tab.

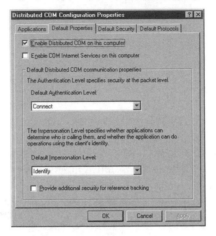

If you wanted to disable DCOM on your computer, you could uncheck the Enable Distributed COM on This Computer check box. By "disable DCOM," I mean disable COM from sending data between computers. This option does not disable in-process or local COM servers.

If you check Enable COM Internet Services on This Computer, you can configure your local copy of IIS (Internet Information Server) Web server to use the ISAPI RPC proxy, so that remote DCOM clients can use HTTP to talk to DCOM servers on the IIS server.

If a COM server doesn't specify an authentication level or impersonation level, COM automatically uses the values specified in the Default Authentication Level and Default Impersonation Level combo boxes. I described the different authentication levels earlier in the section "Authentication Levels."

The Provide Additional Security for Reference Tracking check box enables tracking calls to `IUnknown::AddRef()` and `IUnknown::Release()`. The tracking adds additional security so COM consumers don't maliciously decrement the reference count. The additional tracking does slow calls to these methods, however.

> **NOTE**
>
> The IUnknown interface is the base interface that all COM interfaces are derived from, either directly or in-directly. The AddRef() and Release() methods control the lifespan of the object. The normal behavior of these methods is that each time the methods are called the reference count increases or descreases by one. When the reference count reaches zero, the object is normally destroyed.

Select the Default Security tab. This third tab configures the default access, launch, and configuration permissions (see Figure 24.8).

FIGURE 24.8

The DCOMCNFG Default Security tab.

In the Default Access Permissions section, you can define which clients are permitted to access COM objects. The Default Launch Permissions, determine which clients are permitted to launch COM servers. Use the Default Configuration Permissions section to define which clients are permitted to configure these settings.

24

MICROSOFT'S COM/DCOM

> **CAUTION**
>
> The next paragraph is from NetNews and is completely self-explanatory. To configure the default configuration permissions, you need write permissions. It's a cyclical thing. Be very careful when modifying the configuration permissions.
>
> "Using DCOMCNFG.EXE, I accidentally set one of my servers to use the default configuration permissions. Unfortunately, the default permissions were read only. The administrator does not have permissions to change this. Does anybody know how to get full control back?"

These default permissions apply when a COM object server does not override the default settings.

Select the Default Protocols tab (see Figure 24.9). This tab specifies the different network protocols used by DCOM.

FIGURE 24.9

The DCOMCNFG Default Protocols tab.

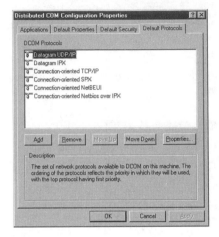

If you return to the Applications tab, you can configure an individual COM server. Simply select the COM server from the Applications list box and click the Properties button. The Object Properties dialog is displayed (see Figure 24.10).

FIGURE 24.10

The DCOMCNFG Object Properties dialog.

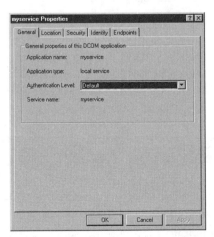

In the General tab, the only property you currently are allowed to modify is the authentication level. This authentication level overrides the level specified in the Default Properties tab (refer to Figure 24.7).

Select the Location tab (see Figure 24.11) to configure where the COM server will be run. If you want to run a COM server on a remote machine, check the Run Application on the Following Computer check box and specify the computer name in the text box.

FIGURE 24.11

The DCOMCNFG Location tab.

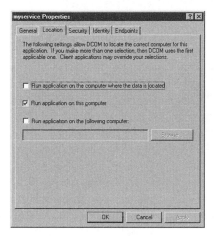

Select the Security tab (see Figure 24.12). This tab configures who can launch, access, and configure the COM server. These permissions are identical to those in the Default Security tab (refer to Figure 24.8), except that they apply only to the selected COM server. If any of the three group boxes specify to use default permissions, the permissions configured in the Default Security tab are used.

FIGURE 24.12

The DCOMCNFG Security tab.

24

MICROSOFT'S COM/DCOM

Select the Identity tab (see Figure 24.13) to specify the security account used to launch
and run the COM server.

FIGURE 24.13

*The DCOMCNFG
Identity tab.*

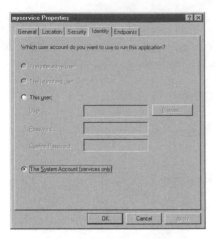

You are given four possible user accounts. The interactive user is the local user logged
on to the workstation. The launching user is the one who initially launches the COM
server. You can also launch a DCOM server by using a specific user account.

The System Account can be used only when a COM server is launched as a service. Also
known as the local system account, this account has no privileges beyond the boundaries
of the local workstation, but it does have all rights necessary to access resources on the
local computer. Therefore, a COM server running as the local system account can never
access resources on a remote computer because the local system account does not exist
on remote machines, so it cannot be authenticated.

Select the Endpoints tab (see Figure 24.14). This last tab specifies the network protocols
that can be used to access this DCOM server.

If you were to configure a COM server to be accessible or to be accessed using HTTP to
bypass a firewall that permits only HTTP transaction, you would add the Tunneling
TCP/IP protocol.

OLEVIEW

OLEVIEW, a utility similar to DCOMCNFG, allows you to configure a DCOM object
server (see Figure 24.15). I won't go into detail on its workings, but I've mentioned it
here so that you're aware of its existence.

24

MICROSOFT'S
COM/DCOM

FIGURE 24.14
*The DCOMCNFG
Endpoints tab.*

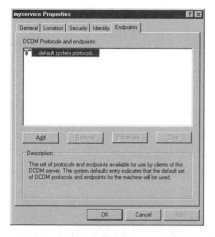

FIGURE 24.15
*The OLEVIEW
utility.*

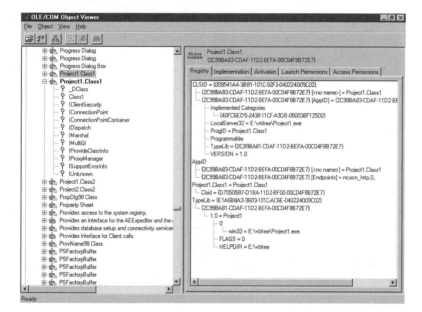

OLEVIEW has some advantages over DCOMCNFG; specifically, it allows you to view
an object's type library. This in itself is reason enough to add this tool to your toolbox.
Unfortunately, OLEVIEW has many disadvantages. The primary one is that OLEVIEW
is not installed on many computer systems. To use OLEVIEW on most computers, you'll
likely have to install it. This has discouraged me from using it because it's too easy to
fall back to old faithful, DCOMCNFG.

You can download a copy of the latest OLEVIEW installation from Microsoft at
`http://www.microsoft.com/oledev/`.

Scalability

Scalability is sometimes defined as the ability of a system to incur greater and greater
loads. I break a system's ability to scale into two levels:

- The first level of scaling is the ability to add users without affecting performance
  or having to add additional application servers.
- The second level of scaling is the ability to add users without affecting performance by adding additional application servers.

The first level of scaling is the simplest. Can your server bash through enough transactions to allow for more clients? This type of scaling usually allows for hundreds of
simultaneous users. Eventually, adding that nth user begins degrading performance.

The second level of scaling is where the action is. By providing for the ability to add
more and more application servers (or mid-tier servers), the application can be scaled
almost endlessly. Eventually, you will reach a saturation point, where adding new application servers no longer allows you to add more clients. The higher this saturation point,
the more scalable the application.

With one application server, you might be able to attain x transactions per second. When
you add a second application server, you should be able to attain between one-and-a-half
and two times x transactions per second. A third application server should increase performance to between two and three times x transaction per second, and so on.

Now the problem becomes how you distribute the client transactions among your two or
more application servers. If you distribute too many transactions to any one-application
server, performance will not be optimized. The action of balancing distribution of transactions between servers is called *load balancing*. DCOM makes it quite easy to provide
for two types of load balancing known as static and dynamic load balancing.

Static Load Balancing

Static load balancing is easy to implement; you simply configure each client system to
direct all calls to one specific application server. If you configure half the clients to use
one application server and half to use a second application server, you have achieved a
form of load balancing.

Static load balancing can be accomplished with DCOM by setting the remote machine name with DCOMCNFG or by writing the remote machine name in the Registry during setup.

As I previously explained, you can configure the computer so that an object is created using DCOMCNFG. From the DCOMCNFG main dialog, select the application name and click Properties. From the Location tab (refer to Figure 24.11), check the Run Application on the Following Computer check box and type the remote computer name in the text box.

Static load balancing is easy to implement, but it is not optimal. It is highly probable that at some point in time a large percentage of active clients could be connected to one application server. Although all clients are evenly distributed between the two servers, this does not ensure that all active clients are distributed evenly between the two servers.

Dynamic Load Balancing

A solution that better distributes the load between two application servers is *dynamic load balancing*. Instead of configuring during setup for a client machine to use a application server, the application server name can be passed to the client when the client application starts. Under this scenario, a broker (or referral component) accepts the initial connection from the client application. The broker determines which application server has the lowest load and passes a reference to the server back to the client application. The broker component can either create the interface pointer and return it to the client application, or the broker component can simply pass back the IP address or computer name of the application machine.

Failures

An important feature of COM is its ability to deal with failures. What happens after you have created a few dozen remote objects and the network fails? What happens when failures occur in a COM server?

Network Failure and Garbage Collection

Your client application creates a remote object on your application server, but the network fails. Fortunately, all COM method returns an error code known as an HRESULT. When the network fails between the client and server, method calls return RPC errors indicating that the connection object is no longer valid. This makes it easy to recover from such faults. The client application can test the error code and act accordingly when failures occur.

For mission-critical application servers, a common redundancy mechanism is to instantiate two remote application servers on two unique computers when the application is initially loaded. If during normal processing the primary application server fails, calls to the application server return HRESULTs indicating the type of failure. When these HRESULTs are received, application processing can easily continue on the secondary application server.

COM also performs automatic garbage collection on the server machine to ensure recovery from network failures that break the connection between the client and server. The COM subsystem pings clients that have references to local COM objects. If a client fails to respond to three successive ping attempts with an interval of two minutes between pings, the COM subsystem assumes the client is dead and deallocates any references the client might have had on the COM objects.

Performance

After you've implemented your first DCOM server and you've gathered some experience with the technologies that surround DCOM, you'll probably begin to realize that performance can be taxing on an application if you don't properly implement your DCOM objects.

The most important performance consideration in distributed objects is the same consideration we often use when developing database applications: round-trips. Round-trips are the number of times a client application must send data to a server and receive response data from the server. This is important because the client application typically blocks after the data is sent and until the response is received.

Application performance can be accurately estimated as the amount of round-trips multiplied by a constant amount of time plus a small variance. These same rules apply in DCOM. If you have a remote object with four properties and you set each of the properties individually, you will have exhausted four round-trips. On the other hand, if you made one function that took four parameters that had the same effect as setting the four properties individually, you will have reduced your round-trips to one.

Summary

In finishing this chapter, I'd like to remind you of the virtues of COM/DCOM:

- **Language neutrality**   The ability to freely switch between languages
- **Location transparency**   The ability to make the location of the object servers transparent to the object consumer

- **Marshaling**   The ability to pack and unpack your objects for transmission between thread, process, and computer boundaries
- **Security**   The ability to configure who can launch, access, and configure your COM components
- **Configuration**   The ability to easily configure your COM components in a variety of ways

If you are interested in reading further, I suggest you start with the following COM/DCOM URLs:

- COM home: `http://www.microsoft.com/com/default.asp`
- A technical overview of COM:
  `http://www.microsoft.com/com/wpaper/Com_modl.asp`
- Microsoft's DCOM mailing list archive:
  `http://discuss.microsoft.com/archives/dcom.html`

So that's COM/DCOM in less than 6,000 words. I didn't really do COM justice—I have another 6,000 words I'd like to say about it. This book is about SQL Server, however, so I'll let you get back on your way to learning SQL Server.

24

**MICROSOFT'S
COM/DCOM**

Why the Future Is Microsoft Transaction Server

IN THIS CHAPTER

A critical key to the success of an enterprise is the dissemination of its corporate data. After all, data is the lifeblood of business. For the last few years, application development has been building on the concept of client/server programming. This type of programming involves a distinct separation of the client and an interface to the database from this client. The client/server concept led to advances in multitiered system designs that, when coupled with the Internet, enabled enterprises to increase their capabilities to meet growing demands. As the trend of "componentized" development and distributed systems has grown, the need for a common implementation context has become paramount.

In 1996, Microsoft debuted its implementation of a COM-compliant wrapper for components to share information, provide for object pooling, support connection pooling, and participate in cross-system transactions. With this technology, developers can focus on the business logic at hand instead of the complex details involved in communicating across processes or machines.

As distributed computing increases in scope and the general public accesses your applications in droves via the Internet, the need to increase scalability and to gracefully handle these heavy resource requests will only continue to grow. *Microsoft Transaction Server* (MTS) can help bridge the gap between your burgeoning user base and the resources available to you on your servers.

Using Three-Tiered Architecture with the Internet

The Web has caused us to view our applications design from new angles because of the unique challenges it presents. With an ever-increasing base of users, our applications must be able to scale dramatically. Microsoft Transaction Server assists us by brokering objects in a way that maximizes their scalability. This section explores three-tiered architecture as it applies to Internet applications; you'll see where MTS fits in and how it works. You'll also examine the programming considerations for a COM object intended for use with MTS to maximize the benefits to your application, and you'll look at the steps to deploy these components in MTS when you're ready for production. The examples here use Visual Basic and *Internet Information Server* (IIS) for clarity but apply to any language that can create a COM object.

The Client Tier

In an Internet application, the client is the Web browser. It replaces the standard executable in traditional client/server development as the interface to the business logic of the application. Today, the browser can provide rich user experience without all the headaches of deployment. You can make changes to the application from the servers in your corporation's Web farm instead of having to compile new executables and deliver them to the user.

To reach a broad base of users, you should write your HTML in a generic fashion to run on any browser. If you have the luxury of dictating the browser, you can use more advanced interfaces. If you require the application to use Internet Explorer, for example, you can use ActiveX controls to provide more functionality. There are tradeoffs, though, even if you specify the browser. When using ActiveX, you still must install controls and code on the client (although the browser handles it for you), and you have to deal with potential incompatibility issues.

The Business Logic Tier

The browser calls the business logic layer for everything it must do. This layer acts as the bridge from the client to access the databases involved in the system. Client calls are made to a Web server that can delegate tasks to components—whether locally with COM or on other application servers using DCOM. Using DCOM requires special programming considerations because a great deal of overhead is involved in a call to a remote machine rather than a local one.

DCOM uses a proxy object on the calling server to access a stub on the application server where the component is running. Each call to any property or method must be packaged from the client sent across the wire (marshaled) and unpackaged on the remote machine; the same process happens in reverse for the call back. Components rich in object structure (those having many properties and methods for each call) do not scale well because of the overhead involved in this proxy/stub conversation. If you are using DCOM, it is best to have a few methods that accept many parameters and include the information sought by the return value of the method; or you should use parameters that pass through the method and are read on the other side. Flattening an object model this way provides for infinitely better performance than setting many properties and then calling methods that act on those properties.

COM calls objects that already reside on the local machine, so the overhead is far less because method and property calls are really happening in the same process space as the caller. A disadvantage of using COM for the business logic tier is that if things go horribly wrong, you could bring down the Web server because both types of calls are on the same machine.

Usually a combination of the COM and DCOM approach is best. A verbose and easy-to-program-against COM object model residing on the Web server can internally call DCOM components remotely. This way the packing and unpacking is done in the local object, and the developer building Active Server Pages is shielded from this complexity.

The Data Tier

The last tier in the architecture is the data tier. It resides on a separate machine from the Web server and interacts with business objects from the middle tier. The database can reside on one or more machines and is accessed by *open database connectivity* (ODBC), an object linking and embedding database (OLE DB), or whatever data access engine you prefer.

All data access in this type of architecture is designed to go through the business layer to perform its tasks, ensuring the integrity of the database by not allowing users to directly interact with a corporation's database.

Understanding MTS

Microsoft Transaction Sever is meant to run on the Web server and the application server. On the Web server, MTS provides its runtime environment to IIS and its objects (`Request`, `Response`, `Server`, and so on). These, in turn, call COM or DCOM components, which pass the context of the relationship along to the application server. On the application server, MTS houses the application's components and brokers objects between the Web server and any other application servers.

MTS provides a context wrapper around COM objects that intercept incoming calls and broker objects appropriately. When you deploy on a server for use in MTS, you don't need to register the components on the client machine. This is because the traditional calls to your objects are actually calls into MTS. MTS then forwards the call to your component. The additional overhead of this wrapper is minimal and is balanced out by the fact that your components can be kept loaded, ready to receive incoming calls.

MTS's main components are `ObjectControl` and `ObjectContext`. When you want to explicitly use MTS's functionality, you must implement the `ObjectControl` interface.

In Visual Basic, this implementation occurs in a class module, usually one designed for `MultiUse`, as shown here:

```
Implements ObjectControl
Private pobjContext as ObjectContext
```

The variable defined in this example is module level in scope and will house the context wrapper reference that will be used throughout the class.

By implementing this interface, you get a new object in the object's drop-down menu and three methods of this object. Descriptions of the three methods follow.

ObjectControl_Activate

This method fires when the component is initialized and fires after the
`Class_Initialize` event. This is a good place to get the object context that you will use
in the class. Using one of the new global functions given to you by the implementation
of the `ObjectControl`, you set the module-level variable you created to point to the context wrapper.

```
Sub ObjectControl_Activate
    Set pobjContext = GetObjectContext()
End Sub
```

ObjectControl_Deactivate

This subroutine mimics the `Class_Terminate` event and is a good place to explicitly
release the context wrapper.

```
Sub ObjectControl_Deactivate
    Set pobjContext = Nothing
End Sub
```

ObjectControl_CanBePooled

```
Function ObjectControl_CanBePooled as Boolean
    ObjectControl_CanBePooled = False
End Function
```

This is not functional in MTS 2.0 and will be implemented in a later version. When
adding code to this interface, it is important to understand what will happen when this
function is active down the road. If you set the return value of this function to `True`, you
must be sure to reinitialize all your module-level variables. In the future, this property
will tell MTS whether to destroy the object, even when it is out of scope. If set to `True`,
it will simply fire the `Initialize` event again, effectively recycling the object rather
than creating a new one. Therefore, you must be prepared to return it to a state where it
will be ready to make clean method calls and so that no variables are left lingering.

The system requires that if you implement `ObjectControl`, you must add code to each of
three subroutines that it adds. I've found that you can get away with just adding a blank
line to the routine to satisfy the compiler.

When you are running under the context wrapper, you will want to use the
`CreateInstance` method of the context object instead of using the traditional system-
level `CreateObject` call or setting.

```
'As 'New'

 'Assuming 'Customer' is the name of a class in the project.
'Pre MTS  call to create an instance of the object
```

```
Dim objCustomer as Customer
Set objCustomer = New Customer

'or

Dim objCustomer as Object
Set objCustomer = CreateObject("MyDll.Customer")

' An MTS enabled call

Dim objCustomer as Object
' or a specific object type..
Dim objCustomer as Customer

Set objCustomer = pobjContext.CreateInstance("MyDll.Customer")
```

> **NOTE**
>
> While developing your component, you can make it more robust by accounting for the off chance that someone will deploy your component without using MTS. In the event that someone fires `Revsvr32.exe` on your DLL and doesn't create an MTS package for it, your code can degrade gracefully if you check for the existence of the context object before firing methods against it. (You therefore avoid an `Object or With Variable Not Set` error.)
>
> To do this, test for a valid object reference before a method or property is set:
> ```
> Dim objCustomer as Customer
>
> If pobjContext Is Nothing Then
>     Set objCustomer = New Customer
> Else
> Set objCustomer pobjContext.CreateInstance("MyDll.Customer")
> End If
> ```

By using the context object's `CreateInstance` method, you can carry all the transactional state and role information to the new object. Of course, the `Customer` object must also implement `ObjectControl` and get a reference to the object context.

Programming MTS Transactions

The transactional engine MTS uses is the *Distributed Transaction Coordinator* (DTC). The DTC uses a two-phase commit standard specified by the X/Open DTP group. Your programs may explicitly tell the DTC that a `Commit` or `Rollback` is needed across components and machines.

You can set transaction settings for classes in Visual Basic 6.0 in the Properties dialog box or on a package after it is deployed in MTS. Here are the possible settings for each class:

- **Requires a Transaction:** This class cannot be created outside the context of a transaction. If this object is created and the context wrapper is not in the process of a transaction, a new transaction is created.

- **Requires a New Transaction:** A new transaction is created when this class is initialized.

- **Supports Transactions:** This class participates in any existing transactions that are in place when the class is initialized. If there are no active transactions, no action is taken by the class to create one.

- **Does Not Support Transactions:** The class exists beyond the scope of any existing transactions.

When an object that requires a transaction ('requires' or 'requires a new') is instantiated and an active transaction is not in the scope of the object context, a new transaction is created. The object that originates a transaction is called the *root* object. The root object is the one that ultimately decides the fate of a transaction. The components it calls along the way simply indicate whether their part succeeded or failed. These settings ultimately roll back up to the root object, which then decides, based on the calls made by its subordinate objects, whether the transaction was a success.

While writing code that is to be included in the scope of a transaction, you can specify the outcome of the call in a particular method and report it to the object that created it.

In the following example, a method call reports its transactional value upon method completion:

```
Function MyFunction as Boolean

    On Error Goto Errhandler

' If something good happens then....
If SomethingGoodHappens Then
    If Not(pobjContext Is Nothing) Then pobjContext.SetComplete
    Else
If Not(pobjContext Is Nothing) Then pobjContext.Abort
    End If

Exit Function
Errhandler:
' Also we can tell MTS to abort the transaction if an error is trapped
    If Not(pobjContext Is Nothing) Then pobjContext.SetAbort

End Function
```

25

MICROSOFT
TRANSACTION
SERVER

Calling `SetComplete` or `SetAbort` tells the MTS transaction manager that this object is done and is ready to be deactivated, reporting what it thinks about the state of the transaction on its way out.

If the object is not ready to be terminated and is in the scope of a transaction, you can keep the class alive by calling `EnableCommit` or `DisableCommit`. When one of these two methods is called, the root object on the next level up in the hierarchy is told that the object is currently in the state of succeeding or failing. The calling object is not quite through with the class and may yet call other properties and methods that may further affect the state of the transaction. Calling `SetAbort` tells the caller "I will never succeed under these circumstances and this transaction will fail," but calling `DisableCommit` isn't as binding. `DisableCommit` tells its creator that things have gone wrong but may be repaired to a state that will allow the transaction to succeed.

After the root receives the call back from its subordinates, it can call `SetComplete` or `SetAbort`. When a subordinate method fails and calls `SetAbort`, this must somehow be communicated to the caller (root). There are many ways to do this. One method is to have the subordinate object return a value of `False` when `SetAbort` is called inside of it.

Code in the root class looks like this:

```
Implements ObjectControl
Private pobjContext as ObjectContext

Sub ObjectControl_Activate
    Set pobjContext = GetObjectContext()
End Sub

Sub MyTransactionalRootCall
    Dim objSubordinate as Object

    If pobjContext Is Nothing Then
    Set objSubordinate = CreateObject("MyDll.SubordinateClass")
    Else
Set objSubordinate = _
pobjContext.CreateInstance("MyDll.SubordinateClass")
    End If

    If objSubordinate.MyTransactionalFunction Then
        If Not(pobjContext Is Nothing) Then pobjContext.SetComplete
    Else
        If Not(pobjContext Is Nothing) Then pobjContext.SetAbort
    End If
End Sub
```

In the subordinate class, the code looks like this:

```
Implements ObjectControl
Private pobjContext as ObjectContext

Sub ObjectControl_Activate
    Set pobjContext = GetObjectContext()
End Sub

Public Function MyTransactionalFunction as Boolean
    On Error Goto errhandler

' We're happy
    If Not(pobjContext is Nothing) Then pobjContext.EnableCommit
Exit Function
    Errhandler:
'We're not happy
    If Not(pobjContext is Nothing) Then pobjContext.DisableCommit End
    ➥Function
```

Code can be written to handle the "Rollback" and undo work done up to the point of the transaction's failure.

Deploying MTS Components

To deploy your components in MTS, there is no need to register your component your-self, as you do with a tool such as Regsvr32.exe. The package you create is considered the entry point into the component. MTS is a snap-in that runs in the *Microsoft Management Console* (MMC).

Drilling down through the menus to get to your installed packages reveals the systems that are currently transaction-server aware on the machine.

Each transaction server package usually represents a component. The package can be one or more DLLs; MTS cannot use EXEs because they cannot be loaded into the caller's process. You can view the interfaces of your package by selecting the Components node in the package.

Each creatable object's ProgID appears in the list view on the right of the screen. When one (or more) of these objects is in use, the green ball spins to indicate that the interface is loaded and active. By selecting the Status View button, you can see the number of objects loaded and active, as well as the number of components currently in call. The component counters do not appear for an interface inside your component if you create objects using the New keyword. The preferred method of creating objects in an MTS sce-nario is to use the object context's CreateInstance method. If you use CreateObject, however, your interface counters will appear.

25

MICROSOFT
TRANSACTION
SERVER

To create a new package, right-click on the Packages Installed folder and choose New, Package.

Select the Create New Package option, and then give your component a name. You are taken to the Set Package Identity screen.

Here you can set the NT account under which you want your component to run. If you choose the interactive user, you are telling MTS to run the component as though it is the currently logged-in individual. This option can cause problems when your component goes into production if the DLL makes calls that require permissions that the interactive user may not have. It is best to run the component under a specific account. MTS provides an account for you that is convenient to use to ensure that your application has the permissions it requires. The MTSSA account is the service account for MTS and is added to the system when you install the Windows NT Option Pack.

This shows a package with the name New Package. To set more detailed properties of the package, right-click on the new package and choose Properties.

You can specify that the component use a security model for access to various functions by enabling the Enable Authorization Checking check box and specifying the authentication level of calls. This feature enables you to use a role-based model for accessing your component's functionality.

There are a few ways to drop your component into MTS. Probably the easiest is to select the Components tab and drag and drop the DLL into the view pane. This method enumerates through your DLL and finds all the creatable interfaces.

And that's all there is to it. MTS enables you to use as much or as little of its benefits as you want. You gain the benefits of object pooling simply by dropping your components into the MTS system with no special code required on the part of the developer. On the other hand, you can allow your objects to be aware of the context in which they are running and share information among other objects running in the same context.

The need for this kind of increased scalability will provide a fruitful future for MTS's technology.

The Importance of Stateless Environments

In simple terms, when we maintain state we are *stateful* and when we don't, we are *stateless.* Suppose that between each request a user performs, you remember who the user is and what that user did. You would be *maintaining state.* If between each request a user performs, you don't remember or track what that user did and all of the pertinent data passed in to get to the next part of the process, you are stateless. In other words, a stateless object does not retain any information from one method call to the next. A stateful object has an internal storage mechanism that enables it to retain information across multiple method calls.

Suppose a user logs on to your system. Each time he requests his airline itinerary, you display it to him without using cookies or client-side tokens. The system knows the client's user ID and airline itinerary ID. With this scenario, you are using Web server resources to track what the client does, who he is, and where he goes on the server. This is a stateful environment, and it limits your scalability.

On the other hand, suppose that each time a user requests her airline itinerary, she must pass in her user ID and airline itinerary ID. The system does not have any knowledge of the client's IDs until that information is entered. With this scenario, Web server resources are not tracking what the client does, who she is, and where she goes on the server. This is a stateless environment.

Limiting Scalability by Maintaining State

Maintaining state on the Web server can lead to resource starvation, which limits your ability to scale and overall performance. However, other areas of your model can be affected by this stateful design.

It is common programming practice in a single-user environment to think of an object as being active as long as you need it. Method calls are simple because the object remembers information from one call to the next. However, stateful objects can impact the scalability of an application. State can consume server resources such as memory, disk space, and database connections. And because state is often client specific, it holds the resources until the client releases the object. You must balance the decision to hold resources (either locally in a stateful object or not) against the other requirements of your application.

Now consider the airline itinerary again. Suppose that every time you need to add or delete a segment from your flight itinerary, you interact with a COM component that talks to a back-end database. Initially, when you instantiated the component, you passed it a user ID. Each time you want to update or delete something in conjunction with that itinerary, you pass the new flight information or which segment to delete. Because the Web server maintains the user ID and airline itinerary ID you gave it earlier, it can make those changes to your existing itinerary.

25

MICROSOFT
TRANSACTION
SERVER

In general, try to avoid maintaining state that consumes scarce or expensive resources. Holding database connections consumes scarce resources, for example. This can reduce your scalability because a limited number of database connections can be allocated and used connections cannot be pooled.

Now you can make your system more efficient: When you instantiate the component, a SQL Server database connection is also created. This could theoretically save you some time instead of causing your system to take performance hits by creating connections each time you interact with the component. This model would appear efficient with 5 to 10, or maybe even 100 users. Now what happens when you need to have 5,000 users connected at once? Using this approach, you would have 5,000 COM components and 5,000 database connections. Clearly you can see the pitfalls if you scaled up to 100,000 or 1 million users. This isn't a good design because it, too, is stateful.

A better approach would be to use stateless components and connection pooling. This isn't difficult to implement, and the scalability and performance increases are tremendous. If you change your COM component so that each time you pass update or delete criteria for your itinerary you also pass it the user ID and airline itinerary ID, it can still return updated itinerary information. The difference is that it can be released as soon as you are done using it, thereby freeing precious system resources. Instead of managing your connections and devising a connection-pooling framework, you could host your component in MTS and take advantage of *just-in-time* (JIT) and connection pooling. Making these slight changes gives you a way to scale to more than 10,000 simultaneous users.

Using Just-in-Time Activation

Just-in-time (JIT) activation helps reduce consumption of precious system resources by recycling objects when they are finished with their work. JIT activation also helps ensure the isolation of transactions so that information from one transaction is not carried into the next transaction. Through JIT activation, MTS activates the component when the client actually calls a method in the object. This frees the clients from having to track when an instance of an object should be created in relation to when it is used. The client can create this instance and hold it as long as it wants before using it because MTS will not create and activate the object until it is needed. This feature is very important in methods that are called quite frequently and deal with many transactions.

When a client calls a method of an object, MTS activates the object by creating it and allowing the method call to go through to the object. When the object is finished and it returns from the method call, MTS deactivates the object to free its resources for use by other objects. Later, when the client calls another method, the object is activated again.

MTS deactivates an object by releasing all references to it, which effectively destroys the object. When the object is destroyed, it loses all its local state, such as local variables, and properties. However, MTS manages the client pointer so that it remains valid. When the client calls a method on the deactivated object, MTS activates it by re-creating it and allowing the method call to go through. MTS manages the client's pointer to the object in such a way that the client is unaware that the object has been destroyed and re-created. However, the object's local state is reset, and it does not remember anything from the previous activation.

After an object is activated, it can be deactivated in one of three ways. Deactivating an object is different from destroying it. The object can request deactivation through the ObjectContext interface by calling SetAbort or SetComplete. If the object is participating in a transaction, and that transaction is committed or aborted, the object is deactivated after the processing in the transaction is complete. Finally, if all the clients that are accessing the object release their references to that object, it is deactivated. When an object is deactivated, MTS can use the resources that were allocated to it for other objects. This means that any information that was stored inside the object is lost. The recently deactivated object could also be recycled if MTS detects another client requesting the same object.

```
Function GetData() As Boolean
    Dim objData As New DataObject
    Dim strSQL As String
    Dim objRS As Recordset
    Dim strConnect As String

    On Error GoTo errhandler
    strConnect= UID=Acct;PWD=pass;Database=MyData;
➥Server=Jabba;DRIVER={SQL SERVER};DSN='' "
strConnect= " UID=Acct;PWD=pass;Database=MyData;Server=Jabba;
➥DRIVER={SQL SERVER};DSN='' "
    strSQL = "EXEC sp_DNU_sel"
    With objData
        If .OpenConnection(strConnect) Then
            If .OpenRecordSet(strSQL) Then
                Do Until .RecordSetObject.EOF
strMessage = strMessage & Trim(.RecordSetObject("sentence"))
.RecordSetObject.MoveNext
                Loop

                Set objRS = .RecordSetObject.NextRecordset
                pstrMessage = strMessage
                Call PresentData(strMessage)

            End If
        Else
```

```
        GetNews = False
    End If
    End With

    Set objData = Nothing
    Set objNews = Nothing
    If Not (pobjContext Is Nothing) Then pobjContext.SetComplete
    GetNews = True

    Exit Function
errhandler:
    Set objData = Nothing
    Set objNews = Nothing
    If Not (pobjContext Is Nothing) Then pobjContext.SetAbort
    Call errorhandler(Err, "GetNews")
End Function
```

When an object decides to become stateful, MTS no longer has the capability to use its resources for any other objects. An object will become stateful if it does not call `SetAbort` or `SetComplete` when it finishes its processing. The stateful object has, in effect, locked a portion of the resources with which MTS has to work. MTS relies on its capability to dynamically manage resources to allow applications to effectively scale. Therefore, if a system is using a large number of stateful objects, it will be much less efficient when scaling.

NOTE

It is important to remember that an object is not deactivated when it calls `EnableCommit` or `DisableCommit`, or neglects to call any context object methods. Also, an object is not deactivated when the transaction ends—for example, when the transaction times out. An object is only deactivated when it calls `SetAbort` or `SetComplete` and returns from the method call.

Also with respect to stateful objects, MTS gains its efficiency from being able to automatically activate and then quickly deactivate objects. Remember that when an object deactivates, it loses all information stored inside of it. In order for an object to be stateful, it must maintain internal information, which means it cannot be deactivated. If a stateful object is deactivated, it loses all its state, thus becoming a stateless object.

Determining State in MTS

The MTS runtime environment manages all the threads for you. MTS components need not—and, in fact, should not—create threads. It is important to note that components must never terminate a thread that calls into a DLL.

Every MTS component has a `ThreadingModel` Registry attribute, which you can specify when you develop the component. This attribute determines how the component's objects are assigned to threads for method execution. The possible values are `Single`, `Apartment`, and `Both`.

All objects of a single-threaded component execute on the main thread. This is compatible with the default COM threading model, which is used for components that do not have a `ThreadingModel` Registry attribute.

The main threading model provides compatibility with COM components that are not reentrant. Because objects always execute on the main thread, method execution is serialized across all objects in the component. In fact, method execution is serialized across all components in a process that uses this policy. This allows components to use libraries that are not reentrant, but it has very limited scalability.

Single-threaded, `stateful` components are prone to deadlocks. You can eliminate this problem by using stateless objects and calling `SetComplete` before returning from any method.

Each object of an apartment-threaded component is assigned to a thread in its apartment for the life of the object; however, multiple threads can be used for multiple objects. This is a standard COM concurrency model. Each apartment is tied to a specific thread and has a Windows message pump.

The apartment-threading model provides significant concurrency improvements over the main threading model. Activities determine apartment boundaries; two objects can execute concurrently as long as they are in different activities. These objects may be in the same component or in different components.

As a general rule, MTS objects should be stateless. Using stateless objects provides the following benefits:

- Stateless objects help ensure transaction isolation and database consistency by not introducing data from one transaction to another.
- They reduce the server load by not storing data indefinitely.
- They improve scalability because of the reduced server load and because there are fewer internal data dependencies in the stateless object.

25

MICROSOFT
TRANSACTION
SERVER

Maximizing Performance with MTS

You can improve the efficiency of the objects you manage by using MTS in a number of ways:

- Avoid passing or returning objects. Passing object references across process and network boundaries wastes time.

- Pass arguments by value (ByVal) whenever possible. The ByVal keyword minimizes trips across networks.

- When making updates, keep resources locked for as short a time as possible. This method maximizes the availability of resources to other objects.

- Avoid creating database cursors. Cursors create a large amount of overhead. Whenever you create a Recordset object, *ActiveX Data Objects* (ADO) create a cursor. Instead of creating Recordset objects, run SQL commands whenever possible.

- Use methods that accept all the property values as arguments. Avoid exposing object properties. Each time a client accesses an object property, it makes at least one round-trip call across the network.

- Enable MTS to run simultaneous client requests through objects by making them apartment threaded. In Visual Basic 6, you make objects apartment threaded by selecting the Apartment Threaded option in the Project Properties dialog box. (Because these are typically server-based objects, you'll also want to select the Unattended Execution option.)

Deciding Whether to Deactivate or Terminate

Components built with Visual Basic have Initialize and Terminate events that you can use to implement startup and shutdown code for each class.

However, the context object is not available in the Initialize and Terminate events. If you need to read security credentials in the Initialize event, for example, you cannot get that information. Also, because of JIT activation, the Initialize and Terminate events get called many times during a user session even though the client is not releasing its pointer to the object. This can be confusing to programmers who implement these events.

To use the context object during initialization or shutdown, implement the
`IObjectControl` interface in your class. `IObjectControl` has three methods: `Activate`,
`Deactivate`, and `CanBePooled`. MTS calls the `Activate` and `Deactivate` methods when
your object is activated and deactivated. You can add startup and shutdown code to these
methods to handle activation and deactivation more appropriately; in addition, you have
access to the context object within these methods.

```
Implements ObjectControl
Private pobjContext As ObjectContext

Private Sub ObjectControl_Activate()
    Set pobjContext = GetObjectContext
End Sub

Private Function ObjectControl_CanBePooled() As Boolean
    ObjectControl_CanBePooled = True
End Function

Private Sub ObjectControl_Deactivate()
    Set pobjContext = Nothing
End Sub
```

Providing Statelessness for Your Web Farm

When sitting around in a designing session, someone will invariably ask, "Does this system
have to be 24 by 7?" The answer is always "Yes." Which is followed up with, "Do we need
to interact with mainframes or legacy systems?" The answer here too is "Yes, of course."

I then ask, "Do your back-end systems ever go down for maintenance?" I usually get
something to the effect of "Every Friday at midnight."

You may have already guessed my next question: "So how can we be 24 by 7 if the back-
end system goes down for maintenance Friday at midnight and we need to rely on it?"

This is usually followed by a lot of head scratching.

If you take a look at your load-balancing situation in the earlier airline itinerary example,
you can take advantage of the same approach to provide statelessness for the Web farm.
You can use client-side cookies, HTML forms, or pass your user ID and airline itinerary
ID as part of a URL string. You can now enable the load-balancing mechanism to route
you to any available server on the Web farm.

Employing this stateless model for both your Web servers and components removes all
reliance on a specific server. Think of what would occur in a stateful design if Client A
were directed to Server 1 and Server 1 crashed between requests. Upon the second
request, Client A would get an error message. If your model were stateless, the

load-balancing mechanism would remove Server 1 from its routing table and redirect Client A to another server. Because your model is stateless, you also can deal with the increase in traffic that the rest of the farm must deal with because the first server is down. So being stateless buys you the capability to scale, as well as higher availability and simple, effective fault tolerance.

Using these techniques in your design and development should provide you and your team with untold scalability. But in the end, you will have a much more flexible and scalable design that enables you to take advantage of every last system resource.

CHAPTER 26

Other Development Clients and SQL Server Connectivity

Unless you work in an all-Microsoft, all-the-time shop, you will invariably need to connect to and retrieve data from SQL Server into other development environments. How this is done and how easily depend entirely on the development environment.

This chapter takes a look at two such environments: Borland's Delphi and Sybase's PowerBuilder. This is by no means an exhaustive examination of the database capabilities of these two programming systems, but is designed to give the SQL Server programmer an overview of their capabilities to help make an initial determination of which environment is the right one for the individual programmer. For each environment, you will examine how it

- Connects to the database in development mode
- Handles bound controls
- Assists you in developing SQL statements
- Connects to the database in runtime mode

Delphi's Database Models

Delphi is a graphical programming environment much like Visual Basic. Visual Basic is based on the BASIC language, but Delphi is based on Pascal, a language that is popular as a teaching tool in many universities and programming certification courses.

Also, unlike Visual Basic, Delphi was built from the ground up to be a database programming language. Data access was built in to the environment instead of being added a couple of versions after the initial release.

Delphi provides database support for many file-based databases (such as dBASE and Paradox) and, via ODBC, access to a wide range of traditional client/server databases. Support for MS SQL Server is provided through the use of ODBC.

Programming Databases in Delphi

Like Visual Basic, two sets of controls give you access to databases in Delphi. The first set is the data access controls located on the Data Access tab shown in Figure 26.1.

FIGURE 26.1

*Delphi's Data
Access toolbar.*

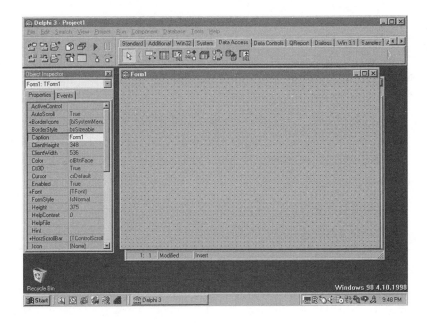

These controls manage the connection between your Delphi code and the data-aware
objects included in Delphi and the database.

The second set of controls are the data controls located on the Data Controls tab shown
in Figure 26.2.

FIGURE 26.2

*Delphi's Data
Controls toolbar.*

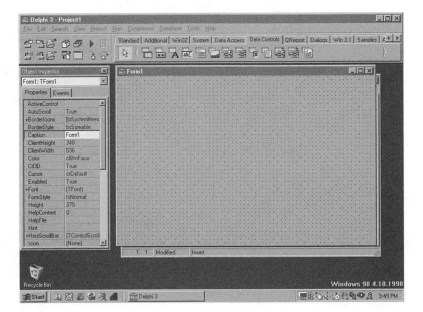

The data controls are the interface design elements you use to communicate through the Data Access Objects (DAO) with the SQL Server database.

To begin examining Delphi's SQL Server programming capabilities, you'll start by reviewing these controls and their uses in the following sections.

Using the Database Access Controls

Before you can use any of the bound controls on a form, you must first enable database access using one or more of the database access controls. These controls are described in the following sections.

DataSource

The DataSource component exists to connect multiple data-aware controls with one dataset. In other words, the DataSource component is the link between a control, such as a text edit field, and another database access component, such as a table.

You link a DataSource object to a table or query component by setting its DataSet property. To demonstrate this, place a table component and a DataSource component on a single form. The Properties dialog for the DataSource has a list of all available database access components, shown in Figure 26.3. You can select only one such component as the dataset of your DataSource.

FIGURE 26.3

The DataSource *Properties dialog.*

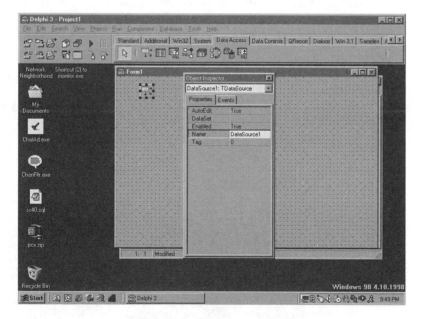

Table

Table objects are the easiest way to display data in your Delphi application. They are used to display the contents of a single table when linked to data-aware controls. Two properties are of primary concern when using a Table object: the DataBaseName property and the TableName property.

The DataBaseName property is set to the name of the alias you want to use (*alias* is the word Delphi uses to refer to the ODBC DataSource name).

After you have set the DataBaseName property, you can select from a list of tables in the specified database to set the TableName property.

Query

The Query object is similar to the Table object except that it does not link to a specific table with the TableName property. Rather, it has a SQL property, which contains a SQL statement that, when executed, builds the resultset for the object. SQL statements can be set dynamically at runtime or by editing the SQL property at design time.

StoredProc

Of more interest to the SQL Server programmer is the Stored Procedure object. This object is similar to the Query object except that the SQL property of the Query object is replaced by the StoredProcName property, which holds the name of the procedure to be executed. The resultset of the procedure is the dataset of the Stored Procedure object and is treated as though it were a table.

Database

The Database object is used for transaction control. Normally, you use a Database object to connect to the database and then use that connection as the transport vehicle for the other controls. This allows you to maintain only one connection to the database rather than a separate connection for different data access controls.

Session

The Session control is used to maintain a global list of all databases the application is connected to and provides an event to help you with database login.

BatchMove

The BatchMove object is used to perform bulk copy operations. It's of marginal use for the SQL Server programmer because other mechanisms are available to perform this task more efficiently. The BatchMove object is useful when you need to programmatically provide this feature in the absence of the more appropriate methods.

Update SQL

The Update SQL object is similar to the Query object except that the SQL statement used is one that updates the database.

Data Controls

The databound controls are how the Delphi programmer visually displays data on a form. They include all the standard user interface elements, such as text fields and list boxes.

The first thing that the Visual Basic programmer looking at Delphi will notice is that the controls look and act much like the Visual Basic data-aware controls. Each has properties that link it to a data source and allow you to determine the column or columns displayed in the individual control. What follows is a brief overview of each of the controls and how it can be used.

DBGrid

This control is used to display the contents of a table in grid form. The table's colums make up the columns of the grid and the rows make up the rows. DBGrid controls are used most often to provide database browse functionality to display summarized data; the user can drill down through this summary to see detailed data.

DBEdit

The DBEdit control allows the user to view and edit the contents of a single database column.

DBMemo

The DBMemo control allows the user to view and edit larger text columns. It works exactly like the DBEdit control except that it can display the data in a multiline format.

DBImage

DBImage controls are used to display database BLOB columns that contain images.

DBListBox and DBComboBox

The DBListBox and DBComboBox controls allow the user to select single values from a displayed resultset. You will rarely use these components because they have been superseded by DBLookupListBox and DBLookupCombo. They are included in Delphi's current release to maintain backward compatibility with Delphi 1.0.

Other Development Clients and SQL Server Connectivity

CHAPTER 26

737

26

DEVELOPMENT
CLIENTS AND SQL
CONNECTIVITY

DBLookupListBox and DBLookupComboBox

The DBLookupListBox and DBLookupComboBox controls allow you to build a list based on the contents of a column in the database. These controls are useful when you're restricting the user's entry in a field to a predefined list of values. The benefit of these controls is that the values can be stored in a database table where they can be easily changed without forcing a program's recompile and redistribution.

DBCheckBox

DBCheckBox controls are used to allow the user to toggle an On/Off option. These single-column controls are most often used when the column's data type is bit.

DBRadioGroup

The DBRadioGroup control is similar to the DBCheckBox except that it allows the user to select from a group of mutually exclusive choices. Use this one when the column's data type is char(1) or bit, allowing each button to represent one value to be viewed or edited in the case of char data types, or 0 or 1 for bit data types.

DBRichEdit

DBRichEdit controls allow the user to edit formatted text. The text can come from a database column or a file. Formatting is performed according to the standard for rich text files.

DBChart

DBChart controls allow the user to graph data.

DBCtrlGrid

This control is a multirecord grid control that can contain other data-aware controls. You can use it to build more sophisticated data manipulation interfaces than you can by using the individual controls on a form. The controls you place in the DBCtrlGrid are duplicated for every row in the database.

Using the Controls on a Form

As with Visual Basic, using the data controls on a form is just a matter of placing the controls on the form and setting their properties to construct the desired resultset. This process usually consists of a minimum of packing a DataSource control and a Table or Query control on the form. Then you place the display controls you want, such as DBEdit and DBLookupListBox controls, on the form and set their DataSource and DataField properties. Delphi handles the rest.

This process works in almost the same manner as Visual Basic's data-aware controls, so you don't need to examine the details here.

The Form Wizard

Delphi gives you an easier method of creating simple database-aware forms—the Form Wizard. This wizard automates the task of selecting the proper controls and setting their properties for database access. Because you can use the Form Wizard as an initial form-generation tool to create layouts you can refine later, it's worth taking a closer look at this wizard.

Unlike other form generations in Delphi, you do not access the Database Form Wizard by choosing File, New from the menu. Rather, you access it by choosing Database, Form Wizard to invoke the wizard and display its first page, shown in Figure 26.4.

FIGURE 26.4

The Database Form Wizard entry page.

On this page you tell the wizard what the form's layout should be and what data access control (`Table` or `Query`) you want to use to retrieve the resultset from the database. Remember, you can always change the data access control later to a `Stored Procedure` or `Update SQL`.

The next page of the wizard, shown in Figure 26.5, allows you to select the database alias and table from which the data is retrieved.

Next, the wizard asks you to specify which columns from the resultset you want to display, as shown in Figure 26.6.

Other Development Clients and SQL Server Connectivity

CHAPTER 26

739

26

DEVELOPMENT
CLIENTS AND SQL
CONNECTIVITY

FIGURE 26.5

*The Database
Form Wizard
information page.*

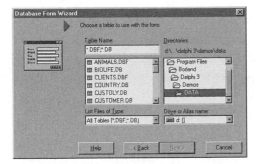

FIGURE 26.6

*Specifying the
columns.*

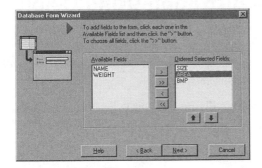

Then you're asked to specify a presentation layout. There are three choices: Horizontal and Vertical freeform layouts and Grid style layout.

Finishing up, the wizard generates a form using the settings you selected along the way, as shown in Figure 26.7.

FIGURE 26.7

*A wizard-
generated form.*

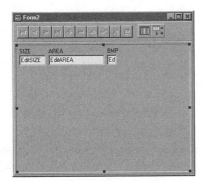

Accessing the Database Through Code

Of course, it's also possible to manipulate each of the data access controls at runtime to change or set their connection properties as the user interacts with the application. For example, you can switch the table to which a `Table` object is connected by using the following code:

```
Table1.TableName := "authors";
Table1.CreateTable;
Table1.Open;
```

Database Administration Using Delphi

Delphi offers the programmer a set of basic database administration tools for creating tables and other database objects and for entering and editing data in the database. Before moving on to show you how to program Delphi database applications, this section gives you an overview of this capability.

The Database Explorer, shown in Figure 26.8, provides primary support for database administration in Delphi.

FIGURE 26.8

The Database Explorer dialog.

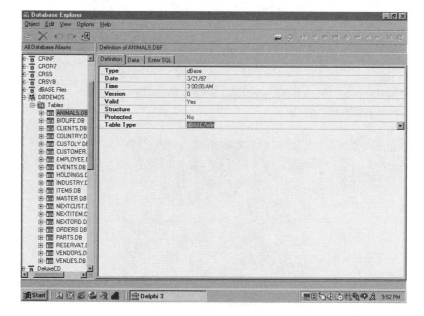

Other Development Clients and SQL Server Connectivity

CHAPTER 26

741

26

DEVELOPMENT
CLIENTS AND SQL
CONNECTIVITY

This dialog is divided into two panes. The pane on the left is a simple tree view that lists all ODBC DataSource names defined in the development system. In Delphi-speak, they are called *database aliases*.

The right pane shows information about the currently selected item. As you can see, what's actually displayed in the right pane changes, depending on the type of object selected in the left pane. For example, selecting a Table object causes the right pane to display a tabbed area where you can select from Table Definition, Data View, or SQL mode.

Each of these provides basic services, and you will probably use the tools that ship with SQL Server for most tasks. However, when you need to quickly look up a column name while writing code, this little built-in tool is a lifesaver.

PowerBuilder and Microsoft SQL Server

Sybase's PowerBuilder is one of the most widely used environments for developing client/server database applications. Microsoft SQL Server is well supported by PowerBuilder with the inclusion of native drivers in the high-end versions and ODBC connectivity in all versions.

In the sections that follow, you will take a look at

- How to connect PowerBuilder to SQL Server in the development and runtime environments
- The DataWindow object
- PowerBuilder's support for embedded SQL
- Database administration using PowerBuilder

Connecting to the Database

PowerBuilder offers two ways to connect to the Microsoft SQL Server database: native drivers and ODBC. Each offers advantages and disadvantages, which are explored in this section. Deciding which driver to use is a matter of balancing the functionality needed for the application with the driver's capabilities and making the best decision for each given situation.

PowerBuilder ships in three versions, and the one you use depends on the type of development you're doing. For desktop database development, there is PowerBuilder Desktop, which ships with a limited number of ODBC drivers to support the most popular desktop databases, such as Microsoft Access, FoxPro, and Sybase SQL Anywhere. It has not shipped with ODBC drivers for the traditional server-based databases, such as Microsoft SQL Server or Oracle (even the desktop version).

For that reason, to connect to Microsoft SQL Server 7 (even the new desktop version), you need one of the other two versions of PowerBuilder—Professional or Enterprise. These two versions are functionally identical, giving you the ability to access server-based databases and desktop databases. The Professional version limits access to ODBC drivers only, but the Enterprise version allows access using either the native drivers or ODBC. Which version you use depends on the individual project.

ODBC Versus Native Drivers: Which to Use

The first decision facing a PowerBuilder developer writing an application that accesses Microsoft SQL Server is which type of driver to use. The PowerBuilder native drivers have the reputation of allowing fast database access. ODBC drivers have traditionally been slower, although the latest drivers perform better than their predecessors. If the application involves moving large amounts of data between the server and the client, you're better off choosing the native driver to benefit from the performance boost. If this is not the case, the decision is a little less clear.

One advantage of the ODBC driver is that it's almost certainly installed on the target system if that system is set up to access SQL Server. Using the ODBC driver will not require installing any additional driver DLLs. If size of the installation package is a factor, go with the ODBC driver.

An advantage of the native driver is that it does not require any modifications to the system Registry or the odbc.ini file to create an ODBC DSN. This reduces the complexity of the installation routine, so there's one less thing to go wrong (such as a user deleting the DSN or the odbc.ini file).

After you weigh all the factors, you will most likely decide in favor of the native driver. The ease of setup and maintenance outweighs the benefits of ODBC's wide availability, and you get the full benefit of the native driver's speed whether your application moves large amounts of data or not.

Connecting to the Database

To develop SQL Server applications, you must be able to make a database connection from the development machine to the database. This connection requires that the development machine have the SQL Server client installed from the SQL Server CD-ROM. Without that installation, PowerBuilder can't properly connect.

After the client is installed, you need to take steps to identify your target database to the PowerBuilder environment. This process is known as *creating a profile*. The following section demonstrates how to create a profile using both the ODBC driver and the native PowerBuilder driver.

Creating a Profile to Use an ODBC Driver

To create a profile to use an ODBC driver, you must first set up an ODBC data source name (DSN) that accesses the database you want to connect to in one of two ways—using the Windows Control Panel applet to create the DSN or using PowerBuilder's built-in ODBC configuration utility. This section shows you how to use PowerBuilder's built-in utility to create the DSN.

You open the utility by clicking the Configure ODBC icon on the PowerBuilder toolbar. This displays the first configuration dialog, as shown in Figure 26.9.

FIGURE 26.9

Configuring ODBC from within PowerBuilder.

This dialog displays all the installed ODBC drivers in the upper list box, Installed Drivers, and the DSNs already configured for the selected driver in the lower list box, Data Sources for Selected Drivers. This particular dialog shows four DSNs configured for the SQL Server driver on this system.

To create a new driver, all you need to do is to click the Create button to launch the DSN Configuration Wizard shown in Figure 26.10. Note that this wizard is not a PowerBuilder implementation; it's launched by the ODBC driver selected. If you were to create a DSN for one of the other installed databases, the steps you take after this point would be different.

FIGURE 26.10

The DSN Configuration Wizard.

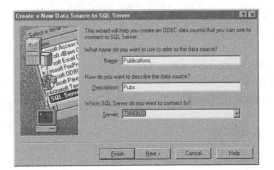

The first page of the wizard asks you for information on the name you want to create and the name of the server where the target database resides. After you have supplied that information, click Next to go to the wizard's second page, shown in Figure 26.11.

FIGURE 26.11

Setting SQL Server security options.

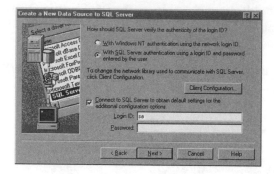

Here you select what type of security to use when connecting to the database—NT's built-in username and password security or SQL Server's security system. If you elect to use SQL Server security, you must specify a username and password; if you don't, you're prompted for them each time the development environment connects to the database.

You can also click the Client Configuration button to select which protocol the client uses to communicate with the database, as shown in Figure 26.12. Normally, you can use the defaults.

FIGURE 26.12

Configuring the client communication protocol.

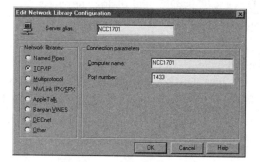

Next, you specify which database on your server you want to switch to when you connect and specify how SQL Server handles temporary stored procedures. Other than entering the target database name, you usually leave the dialog unchanged (see Figure 26.13).

FIGURE 26.13

*Optional SQL
Server parameters.*

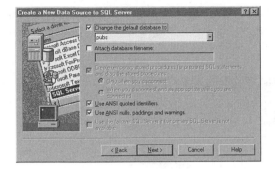

The final step is to select any logging options you want to use when connecting, as shown in Figure 26.14. Normally you don't need to log unless you're troubleshooting a problem.

FIGURE 26.14

Logging options.

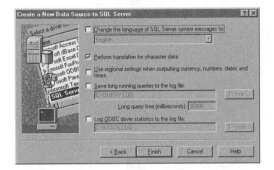

Clicking Finish shows you the settings you have selected along the way and gives you an opportunity to test the connection (see Figure 26.15).

FIGURE 26.15

*Reviewing the
settings.*

Now that you have a DSN, you need to create a PowerBuilder profile that uses the DSN
to connect PowerBuilder to the database. You do this by invoking the Profile utility from
the toolbar, as shown in Figure 26.16.

FIGURE 26.16

*The Database
Profiles dialog.*

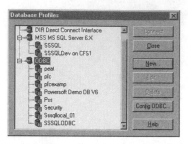

To create an ODBC profile, click on the ODBC section and then click the New button to
open the profile configuration dialog, shown in Figure 26.17.

FIGURE 26.17

*Creating a new
profile.*

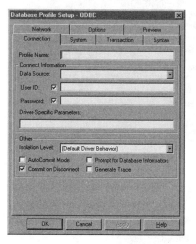

The only tab on this dialog that requires information to be entered to create the profile is
the Connection tab. Here you enter the profile name—the name that PowerBuilder uses
internally to refer to the profile, the DSN—selected from the Data Source drop-down list
of all defined DSNs for the system, and the username and password used to connect.
After you enter this information, click OK and PowerBuilder creates the profile. It then
appears in the profile list under ODBC.

The final step is testing the connection. To do this, click the Connect button in the
Database Profiles dialog. If no error messages appear, you're properly connected. You
can then click on the database icon on the toolbar to work directly with the database, as
discussed later in this chapter.

Other Development Clients and SQL Server Connectivity

CHAPTER 26

747

26

DEVELOPMENT
CLIENTS AND SQL
CONNECTIVITY

Creating a Profile: Using the Native Driver

Creating a profile using a native driver is an easier task because the native driver does not use a DSN to connect, so you can skip all the steps needed to create a DSN. To create a native driver profile, go directly to the Database Profiles dialog. There you select the Microsoft SQL Server driver and click the New button to create the profile.

The Database Profile Setup dialog appears again, but with some different options shown on the Connection tab (see Figure 26.18).

FIGURE 26.18

The Database Profile Setup dialog for a native driver.

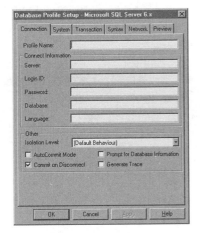

After all the settings are in place, click OK and then test the connection as explained previously.

The rest of the PowerBuilder interface looks and acts the same whether you're using a native or ODBC driver; PowerBuilder insulates you from any differences in the method of connection.

Database Administration Using PowerBuilder

Like Delphi, one of the things you can do with PowerBuilder is administer your database, although in a limited fashion. Because you will likely use the tools provided by Microsoft for database administration, you need only a cursory look at PowerBuilder's capabilities in this area before moving on to see how to actually write database applications in PowerBuilder.

Database administration in PowerBuilder is done with the Database Painter, invoked by using the icon on the toolbar. This opens the Painter, establishes a connection to the database whose profile is currently active, and displays a list of tables in the database, shown in Figure 26.19.

FIGURE 26.19

The table list in the Database Painter.

From here, you can select a set of tables you want to work with. When you have selected the tables, click Open and PowerBuilder builds a display showing the tables, their columns, and information such as the relationships defined among the tables and the key and indexes defined, as shown in Figure 26.20.

FIGURE 26.20

Table properties.

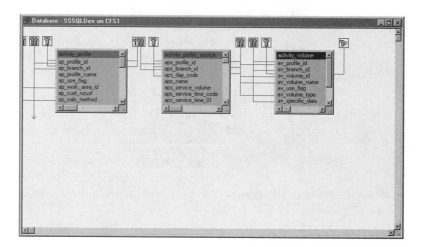

From here, you can perform a variety of tasks. For example, you can select a table and alter its definition by right-clicking the title bar and choosing Alter Table, which opens the Alter Table dialog shown in Figure 26.21.

26

FIGURE 26.21

The Alter Table dialog.

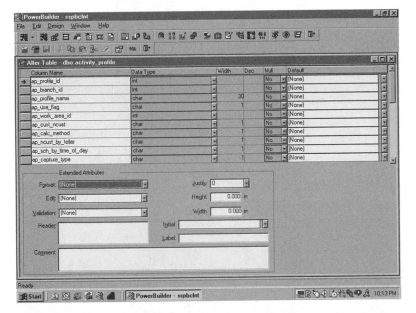

The most advantageous part of this dialog is at the bottom, where you edit PowerBuilder's extended attributes.

In every database accessed by the PowerBuilder development environment, PowerBuilder builds a special set of system tables. These tables store information that PowerBuilder uses to control how data in a particular column is displayed when it's used in a DataWindow. DataWindows are discussed in more detail later in this chapter.

Using the extended attributes, you can determine display information such as the label or header information, font, field size, validation, and default values. This information takes a little time to set up, but you'll save time later when you build your application.

Another useful thing you can do in the Database Painter is manipulate data. To do this, select a table and click one of the data manipulation icons on the toolbar. You can manipulate data using grid, tabular, or freeform views. Figure 26.22 shows the grid view.

FIGURE 26.22

Displaying data in grid view.

When displaying data in any view, you can edit, insert, or delete data.

Finally, you can use a built-in SQL editor, called Database Administration, to send SQL statements to the database (see Figure 26.23). To enter the SQL editor, choose Design, Database Administration from the Database Painter menu.

FIGURE 26.23

The Database Administration window.

You can also execute stored procedures from this window by using the EXECUTE command. Any SQL executed here displays its resultset in a data manipulation grid window, as discussed earlier.

As you can see, these are fairly rudimentary database administration capabilities that PowerBuilder includes as a convenience. Any heavy-duty tasks are better left to other tools.

PowerBuilder Database Objects

The heart of database programming in PowerBuilder is in the objects it provides for that purpose. PowerBuilder has two main objects: the DataWindow and the Pipeline. The following sections discuss those two objects and demonstrate their use.

The DataWindow Object

The most important factor behind PowerBuilder's popularity as a programming language is the DataWindow object, which allows the developer to easily turn SQL syntax into a visual object, ready to use on any window in the application. Unlike Delphi or Visual Basic, in which you use individual controls bound to a particular column in the database, in PowerBuilder you create a single object that contains all the individual column-bound objects you want to use.

There are four steps to creating and using a DataWindow:

1. Define the presentation style—what the DataWindow looks like. Will it be grid, tabular, freeform, or one of the other styles?

2. Define the SQL syntax used to create the DataWindow.

3. Refine the object from its generated state to how you want it to appear in your application.

4. Place the object in a DataWindow control on a window and write some code to enable its functionality.

The first thing you see when you enter the DataWindow Painter is the Select DataWindow dialog shown in Figure 26.24.

Here you can select an existing object to work with or elect to create a new object. When you click the New button to create a new object, you see the New DataWindow dialog, shown in Figure 26.25.

FIGURE 26.24

*The Select
DataWindow
dialog.*

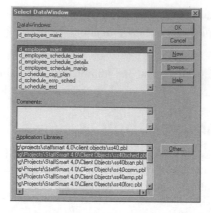

FIGURE 26.25

DataWindow *styles
and sources.*

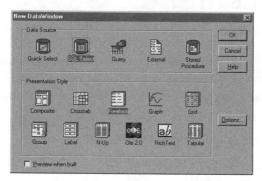

Use the upper set of icons in this dialog to select a data source type for the DataWindow,
which specifies where the data you want to display in the DataWindow comes from.
Possible choices depend on what database engine your current profile connects to. For
Microsoft SQL Server, these are the possible choices:.

1. *Quick Select*   Allows you to quickly build a SELECT statement. Use this choice
   when your SQL statement does not contain complex joins or retrieval arguments.

2. *SQL Select*   Allows you to write any valid SQL statement to act as the data source
   of the DataWindow. This is the choice used most often and is the basis of what
   you see in this chapter. You have the choice of creating the syntax graphically or
   simply entering a SQL statement in much the same way as using the Database
   Administration tool in the Database Painter.

3. *Query*   Allows you to use a saved PowerBuilder Query object as the data source
   for your DataWindow.

4. *External*   Allows you to define a resultset that you later populate manually. Using external `DataWindow` objects gives you a great deal of flexibility at the cost of requiring you to write additional code to create the resultset and display the data.

5. *Stored Procedure*   Allows you to use an existing stored procedure for the data source of the `DataWindow`.

Each selection takes you into a different version of the next window. For purposes of this discussion, I will create a `DataWindow` using the SQL Select option and a Grid presentation style. These selections display the dialog shown in Figure 26.26, which is much like the Select Tables dialog in the Database Painter.

FIGURE 26.26

Selecting tables for a `DataWindow`.

Select the table or tables you want to use in the SQL statement and click OK; you can also click Cancel to enter the SELECT statement manually with the SQL editor.

After you have selected a set of tables, you see a view that shows you the tables selected, their columns, and the default joins (if PowerBuilder can detect them) between the tables (see Figure 26.27).

FIGURE 26.27

Multitable joins in the Database Painter.

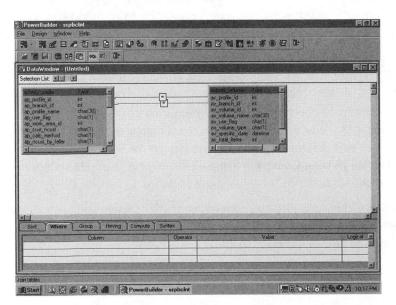

If you need to edit how the tables are joined, you can click on the box on the line between the two tables. This allows you to define outer joins or otherwise modify the resultset, as in Figure 26.28.

FIGURE 26.28

Creating or modifying joins.

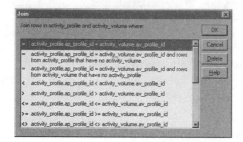

To create the DataWindow, select the columns from each table that you want to see in the finished object, and then use the tabbed section at the bottom to define the WHERE clause or any special clauses (HAVING, GROUP BY, and so forth) you want to build into the SQL statement.

NOTE

For any WHERE clause that needs a variable substituted at runtime, you must define a retrieval argument. For example, if you want your WHERE clause to retrieve only rows where the primary key column is equal to a specific value, you need a retrieval argument defined to act as a placeholder for the specific value. You would think that you could specify the placeholder in the Value column of the Database Painter's WHERE clause section, but this is not enough. You must also choose Design, Retrieval Arguments from the menu and enter them there. When you issue a Retrieve() command to the control at runtime, you must pass in the values in the order in which the arguments are defined here.

If you want to check the generated syntax, you can do so in one of two ways. If all you want to do is edit the syntax, use the Syntax tab at the bottom of the Painter. If you want to edit the syntax, you must first convert the DataWindow view to Syntax by choosing Design, Convert to Syntax. This invokes the syntax editor and allows you to edit the syntax.

When you have the syntax as you want it, click Design and uncheck the Data Source item. This takes you to another view, where you can check the format of the generated object, as shown in Figure 26.29.

Other Development Clients and SQL Server Connectivity

CHAPTER 26

755

26

DEVELOPMENT
CLIENTS AND SQL
CONNECTIVITY

FIGURE 26.29

The DataWindow *design mode.*

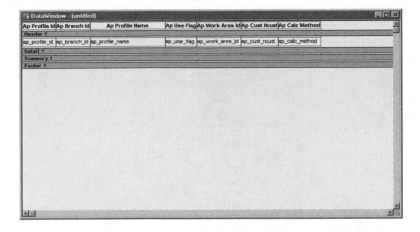

You can make changes to the formatting. Here's where the time spent setting up the PowerBuilder extended attributes saves you programming time now. The DataWindow is generated using the values specified in the extended attributes. If you do not set up extended attributes, PowerBuilder generates the object using defaults, which are guaranteed to be less pleasing than you want and require extra work to correct.

To view the object as it will appear with data, click the Preview icon on the toolbar. This retrieves data into the object by executing the SQL statement that underlies the object. It's also a good method to use to check the syntax's validity and make sure that it retrieves what you want it to retrieve.

When everything is the way you want it, save the object for later use.

Using the DataWindow Object in a Window

Now it's time to use your DataWindow in a window. To do this, use the Window Painter to create the window (I won't go into the details of that process here), and then place a DataWindow control on the window to contain the DataWindow object you just created.

The DataWindow control is different from the DataWindow object. It serves only as a container for the objects created in the DataWindow Painter and gives them an interface to use for writing program code.

To use a DataWindow control, place it on the window and then double-click it to display the properties dialog, shown in Figure 26.30.

FIGURE 26.30

The DataWindow *control's proper-ties.*

In the DataWindow Object Name field, enter the name you gave the object. You can also set some display options, such as whether the control will use scrollbars when needed. When everything is as you want, click OK. Figure 26.31 shows a Window object with a DataWindow control displaying a DataWindow object.

FIGURE 26.31

A DataWindow *object within a* DataWindow *control.*

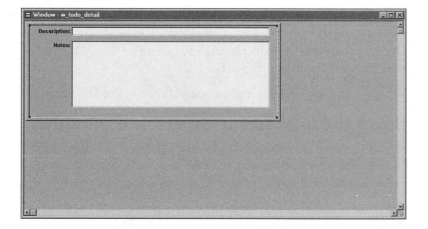

To make the DataWindow work at runtime, you must now write some code. Specifically, you must do two things:

1. Connect the DataWindow control to a transaction object.
2. Retrieve data into the DataWindow object.

Other Development Clients and SQL Server Connectivity

CHAPTER 26

757

26

DEVELOPMENT
CLIENTS AND SQL
CONNECTIVITY

A *transaction object* is how PowerBuilder code connects to the database. PowerBuilder supplies one global transaction object called SQLCA. This object is populated with information needed to establish the connection to the database. This information includes the server name, database name, user ID, and password. Listing 26.1 shows the code needed to set up SQLCA to connect to a Microsoft SQL Server database.

LISTING 26.1

```
// Profile SSSQL
SQLCA.DBMS = "MSS Microsoft SQL Server 6.x"
SQLCA.Database = "sssql"
SQLCA.ServerName = "NCC1701"
SQLCA.LogId = "sa"
SQLCA.LogPass = ""
SQLCA.AutoCommit = False
SQLCA.DBParm = ""
```

Place this code in the Open event of your application or window and then add the code shown in Listing 26.2.

LISTING 26.2

```
CONNECT USING SQLCA;
IF SQLCA.SQLCode <> 0 then
    MessageBox("Connect Error", "Failed to Connect to Database")
End if
```

Now, in the Open event of the Window object that contains your DataWindow, place the code in Listing 26.3.

LISTING 26.3

```
Dw_1.SetTransObject(SQLCA)
Dw_1.Retrieve()
```

Remember that you need to pass any arguments you defined in the DataWindow object to the Retrieve() function, as follows:

```
Dw_1.Retrieve(arg1,arg2)
```

In this line, arg_1 and arg_2 represent the values you want to be passed.

If you now run your application and open the window, you see your DataWindow filled with data. PowerBuilder hides all the nuts and bolts, enabling you to spend most of your time on other coding tasks.

Pipeline Objects

PowerBuilder also has one other database object you should be aware of: the Pipeline object, which allows you to move data between databases or objects within a single database. It basically creates two sets of SQL statements, one to select the data to be moved and one to insert the data into the target.

There are many better ways to perform this task using Microsoft SQL Server, and you rarely use pipelines when programming SQL Server databases. The most basic use of pipelines is for moving small amounts of data from other databases into SQL Server when methods such as Bulk Copy or Import are not available.

Connecting Through PowerScript

PowerScript is the language of PowerBuilder and it, too, supports database operations. It does so in the form of embedded SQL. Almost any command that can be run from an ISQL window can be executed by using embedded SQL, including SELECT and UPDATE statements. You can declare cursors, fetch their results, and run stored procedures.

Embedded SQL is executed with the same transaction object as DataWindow SQL. Normally, you use SQLCA for this purpose. Listings 27.4–27.7 show how to execute the four main types of SQL statements in PowerScript. Each assumes that SQLCA has been populated and is connected to the target database.

LISTING 26.4   THE SELECT STATEMENT

```
String  s_branch_name
Long        l_branch_id
Long        passed_value

Passed_value = 123456

SELECT      branch_id,
        branch_name
INTO        :l_branch_id,
        :s_branch_name
FROM        branches
WHERE branch_id = :passed_value
USING SQLCA;
```

LISTING 26.5   THE UPDATE STATEMENT

```
String  s_branch_name
Long        passed_value

S_branch_name = "New Branch Name"
```

```
UPDATE branches
SET         branch_name = :s_branch_name
WHERE branch_id = :passed_value
USING SQLCA;
```

LISTING 26.6   DECLARING AND FETCHING A CURSOR

```
Long profile_id
String profile_name

DECLARE     VOLUME_CURSOR CURSOR FOR

SELECT          ap_profile_id,
            ap_profile_name
FROM        ACTIVITY_PROFILE
USING SQLCA;

OPEN VOLUME_CURSOR;

DO UNTIL SQLCA.SQLCode <> 0

FETCH       VOLUME_CURSOR
 INTO          :Profile_ID,
        :Profile_Name

Loop
```

LISTING 26.7   EXECUTING STORED PROCEDURES

```
String employee_name
String employee_address
String employee_phone

Employee_name = "Karen"

DECLARE Emp_proc procedure for sp_GetEmployeeName
@emp_name = :Employee_name
USING SQLCA;

Execute emp_proc;

Do Until SQLCA.SQLCode <> 0
    Fetch sp_GetEmployeeName
INTO :employee_address
    :employee_phone
Loop
```

As you can see from these listings, using embedded SQL in PowerScript is a simple proposition.

Delphi Versus PowerBuilder: Which Should I Use?

Now that you have looked at the different ways Delphi and PowerBuilder handle database access, let's finish with a comparison of the two environments to help you decide which one is right for you. This is no easy task. Each environment has its fans, each of whom swears that his or her favorite is so far ahead of the competition that to choose the other would be foolhardy.

However, most developers know that this is not the case. Each environment has strengths and weaknesses that must be weighed when making a decision about which is right for you.

Delphi is similar to some versions of Visual Basic in both layout and manner of operation. PowerBuilder has its own paradigm. If you're a Visual Basic programmer, you might have better initial results using Delphi.

On the other hand, PowerBuilder does one thing very well—handle database access. If you're already familiar with PowerBuilder and are ahead of its learning curve (reputed to be steep), you should use PowerBuilder.

CHAPTER 27

Integrating SQL with Other Microsoft Products

Microsoft's strategy of *product integration* is so prevalent these days that even the United States government has sat up and taken notice: Across its different product segments, the line between product boundaries has blurred to the degree that it's hard to tell where one product ends and another begins. SQL Server 7.0, developed during the transition to this product integration nirvana, is no different. It was designed from the outset to integrate closely with the operating system itself—especially with the upcoming Windows 2000—and with other Microsoft application products. SQL Server's OS integration comes in the form of its Enterprise Manager MMC snap-in, its system services, and its support of such OS-specific features as clustering and fail-over support.

Product integration, in general, allows users and programmers to access SQL Server in environments they are, perhaps, more comfortable with. For example, although the MMC-hosted Enterprise Manager provides a consistent look and feel with other MMC snap-ins, the millions of Microsoft Access users might be overwhelmed by such an interface. By supplying numerous hooks into SQL Server that other application programs and servers can access, Microsoft has made SQL Server a portable tool that more users can use.

This chapter looks at the integration of SQL Server with several other Microsoft products, including Microsoft Access and other Office applications, as well as Web integration on the server- and client-side with Internet Information Server (IIS) and Internet Explorer. Programmatically, SQL Server also integrates with all of Microsoft's Visual Tools, including Visual Basic, Visual C++, and Visual InterDev. Details of using Microsoft's Visual Tools with SQL Server 7 are provided elsewhere in this book (for example, see Chapter 1, "Taking Advantage of the New Tools").

Using Access as a Front-End to SQL Server 7.0

Microsoft's flagship desktop database product, Microsoft Access, has been available as a front-end tool to SQL Server for years. Because of its own integration with the Microsoft Office suite, MS Access offers a simplified user interface that relies heavily on menus and toolbars consistent with other Office applications. This made MS Access a suitable choice for roaming users and programmers who needed to operate on lower-end machines, such as laptops and Windows 9x desktops. Because MS Access is part of the best-selling Office suite, millions of users are familiar with the product.

Microsoft's native Access file format (*.mdb) uses the Jet database engine, an operating system component that determines how data access systems store their data in a disk-based file. The Jet engine, introduced with MS Access 1.0 and Visual Basic 3.0, was designed to handle small databases. Although it's been improved over the years and is still supported in Access 2000, Microsoft has recently started moving users toward OLE DB and SQL Server–based databases. In Office 2000, users can work natively with files in SQL Server file format (*.mdf) as well as its own MDB format. Users of previous versions of Access, however, can still work remotely with SQL Server databases by using an ODBC connection, but this is a weak form of product integration because you're simply linking MS Access to the actual database.

In this section, you get a tour of the features in MS Access that allow you to use these desktop database products with SQL Server 7.

With Access 2000, SQL Server integration is brought to a new level. Access 2000 supports the use of SQL Server 7 as a *back-end store* that works with a new *Access Project* format to create a true client-server solution. An Access Project (which has an *.adp file extension) contains forms, reports, macros, modules, and the new *Data Access Pages* (see the following section "Creating an Access Project"). This type of project doesn't directly contain tables or queries; rather, it's connected directly to a SQL Server (the back-end store) that can contain database objects, such as tables, stored procedures, views, and database diagrams. What's important to note here is that there are separate client (Access) and server (SQL Server) components. The separation of user interface and data components (business rules) is an important part of client-server/n-tier development.

Microsoft Access 2000 ships with a special personal edition of SQL Server 7 that can be used as the back-end store. If you have the full SQL Server 7 product, however, you should install that instead. Regardless, you can integrate SQL Server 7 and Access on any Windows 95, Windows 98, or Windows NT 4.0+ machine, making it a viable solution for any developer or user. It's worth noting that the version of SQL Server 7 that ships with Access has no user interface elements at all (such as Enterprise Manager). This is not a problem, however, because Access offers an excellent visual interface that you will be using here. Furthermore, should you decide to work with both Access 2000 and SQL Server 7, it's likely you will decide to use Access as a front-end anyway. Unlike Enterprise Manager, Access has a consistent and friendly user interface (UI) that's appropriate for many types of users.

> **TIP**
>
> If you are using Access and its integrated, UI-less version of SQL Server 7.0 on Windows NT 4.0, you need to install Service Pack 4 first. This service pack ships on the Office 2000 and Access 2000 CD-ROMs.

Creating an Access Project

To create an Access Project that uses a SQL Server 7.0 database as a back-end store, simply start Access and choose Access Database Wizards, Pages, and Projects from the dialog that appears. This choice opens the New dialog, where you can select one of the following options from the General tab:

- **Database**   Creates a new Access database (MDB file).
- **Data Access Page**   Creates a new Data Access Page, a Microsoft Internet Explorer 5.0–specific Web page that uses client-side data binding to connect to live, remote data.
- **Project (Existing Database)**   Opens an Access Project you've previously created.
- **Project (New Database)**   Creates a new Access Project (ADP file).

For purposes of this introduction, you'll create a new Access Project that connects to the Pubs database. Select the option for Project (Existing Database) and navigate to the folder where you'd like to save your project (*.adp) file. An OLE DB Data Link Properties dialog appears when you pick a name for the project. This dialog box guides you through connecting to a SQL Server database.

Microsoft introduced the concept of a *data link* with Windows 2000 and Office 2000. A data link is the OLE DB equivalent of an ODBC File Data Source Name (DSN): It allows you to connect clients, such as ASP (Active Server Pages) Web pages, Visual Basic programs, and the like to OLE DB–compatible data sources. Typically, these data sources are databases, but OLE DB extends ODBC by supporting other kinds of documents, such as spreadsheets and email. In any event, using a data link is similar to using an ODBC DSN: Simply connect to the correct SQL Server and supply the needed login information.

The Access 2000 Data Link Properties dialog also asks you which database you'd like to connect to. For purposes of this example, you are connecting to the Pubs SQL Server 7.0 database that exists on the same machine as Access, so you can supply the machine name, or `local`, as the name of SQL Server. When you finish the dialog, Access displays your Access Project, complete with the tables, stored procedures, and database diagrams that Pubs has to offer.

The advantage of using an Access Project is that it makes working with a SQL Server database as seamless as working with any native MDB file. Access users will appreciate the way SQL Server databases appear identical to their MDB document counterparts, and SQL Server users will probably find the Access interface superior to that provided by Enterprise Manager and the other SQL Server tools. In the following section, you take a look at some of the SQL Server features offered by Access.

Using an Access Project

The most obvious benefit to using Access as a SQL Server front-end is that Access provides an uncluttered view of your database. In Enterprise Manager, you are confronted with a bewildering array of nodes in the tree view, including lots of options that are not of interest to the developer. Not everyone needs—or wants—to administer SQL Server. As developers who need to get work done, we typically deal with individual SQL Server databases, not the myriad of administrative options provided by Enterprise Manager.

Access, however, gives you a database-level view of the information you need, and the tools you need to get your job done. Virtually everything you need to do, from creating views and stored procedures to creating database diagrams that visually represent tables and their dependencies, is easier in Access. For many developers, the full version of SQL Server is optional (although still desirable) because of the rich features available in Access. But because you are affecting the underlying SQL Server database from Access, any changes you make from Access automatically show up in Enterprise Manager (and vice versa): You are not dealing with a local copy of the database, but with the master database itself.

The tasks described in the following sections are available in Access 2000.

Working with Tables

You can create, open, design, delete, and modify SQL Server tables from Access. Working with SQL Server tables in Access is similar to working with Jet-based tables, and the look and feel of SQL Server table windows are much like their Access counterparts: Both Design and Datasheet views are available. The Design view allows you design the structure of the fields in each table, although field properties are harder to get to; for Jet-based MDB databases, a Field Properties section is added to the bottom of the Design view window so that you can easily change the data type, format, and other attributes of the current field. For SQL Server tables, however, you need to access these attributes from a separate Properties window or with the drop-down list boxes supplied with each field in the window. It's not more difficult—just different. It is, however, more consistent with the Design Table view in Enterprise Manager, and I suspect it was created with that functionality in mind.

Working with Triggers

Like triggers in Enterprise Manager, you can create, modify, and delete triggers from the Tables view in Access as well. The trigger editor in Access is similar to the one in Enterprise Manager, although, sadly, Access lacks the Check Syntax option from Enterprise Manager.

Working with Views

Accessing Views in Access is virtually identical to performing the same action in Enterprise Manager. The View Designer window, which was first introduced in Visual Studio 97, has been ported to and updated for Access 2000, SQL Server 7.0, and Visual Studio 6.0, so anyone familiar with these tools can work interchangeably with the others. There is one difference, however: In other tools, the View Designer features four panes where you can view table diagrams, field grids, raw SQL, and the results of the query that forms the view. Because of the Design/Datasheet modes used in Access, only the first three of these panes are available. The fourth choice can be seen by switching from Design to Datasheet view.

Working with Database Diagrams

This is another case in which the Access 2000 feature basically duplicates the functionality of the same feature in Enterprise Manager. Database diagrams, which give you a view of your data similar to the Web site diagrams you'd get in tools such as Visual InterDev and FrontPage, are the simplest way to view databases with complex interconnected tables. Dependencies are clearly shown, and Access can generate SQL scripts for you that perform the actions you undertake in this visual environment.

Working with Stored Procedures

Stored procedures are, of course, a mainstay of any SQL developer's toolbox and the Stored Procedure "designer" in Access 2000 is simply a color-coded editor similar to what you see in Enterprise Manager or Visual Studio 6.0. Executing stored procedures in Access is similar to Enterprise Manager as well. If your stored procedure requires any parameters, Access prompts you for test values in a dialog before running the procedure, which is a nice touch.

Working with Forms

Access forms don't really have a one-to-one relationship with any objects in Enterprise Manager. If you're familiar with Access, you know that Access applications are typically designed with these forms, which give you a way to create a front-end to your database with a Visual Basic–style form designer or a wizard that steps you through the basic building blocks needed to get a form working. Access has a library of form styles that add visual niceties, such as fonts, colors, and background images. Because Access forms don't have a corresponding object in SQL Server, any forms you create will not be available from Enterprise Manager.

If you've ever used Visual Basic, or the Visual Basic for Applications (VBA) editor that comes with Microsoft Office, you'll be right at home with Access forms. What you get, essentially, is an environment where you can place controls on a form window and hook those controls—such as command buttons, text boxes, check boxes, and the like—to the underlying structures in the database. When your form is complete, it provides a front-end for *users* of the database, giving them a customized and (generally) simple way to view and modify data. From a programmer's perspective, this is, perhaps, one of the best reasons to use Access with SQL Server. In the past, forms could be used only with Access databases, but with the current level of integration, you can now use them with SQL Server databases, too.

Working with Reports

Like Access forms, reports are another feature unique to Access. And like forms, reports can be created by using a step-by-step wizard or by designing them by hand in a Visual Basic–like environment. A report is used to generate an executive summary of information in your database that's appropriate for users and management. It would be almost impossible to create such a report using the tools included with SQL Server, although enterprising SQL coders have been creating their own reports with Visual Basic and other tools for years. If you have access to—ahem—Access, you should consider using its Report feature instead.

Working with Data Access Pages

Data Access Pages is, perhaps, one of the most exciting new features in Access 2000. It requires that users have Internet Explorer 5.0, which comes with Access 2000/Office 2000, because it uses client-side data binding that's available only to that browser. Essentially, a Data Access Page is a client-side (rather than ASP-based, server-side) HTML document that includes Dynamic HTML scripting code and Microsoft Design-Time ActiveX Controls (DTCs) to provide an Access form–like Web-based application. In fact, Data Access Pages can be made to look practically identical to forms, although they can run in a Web browser. This way, clients can access them over the Internet or a local intranet and not need to have Access running on their machines. Data Access Pages are secure, too: Your database login and password are not part of the HTML codes that make up the page.

The Data Access Pages feature doesn't correspond to any of the Web-enabled features in SQL Server 7.0, but rather complements and expands on them. Data Access Pages, for one thing, require Internet Explorer 5.0, but the Web pages generated by the SQL Server Web Assistant should work in almost any Web browser. Data Access Pages is covered in the next section.

Using Data Access Pages

To create a Data Access Page, you need to have an Access Project open and linked to an open SQL Server database such as Pubs. In the database window, an option called Pages appears in the list of objects you can work with. This option allows you to create new Data Access Pages using the wizard or Design View window. You can also edit an existing Data Access Page.

Using the Data Access Pages Wizard

The Data Access Pages Wizard is the easiest way to create a data-bound Web page. Simply select the option Create Data Access Page by Using Wizard and work through the steps in the wizard, which is similar to the View Wizard mentioned earlier. Although you can use the resulting Data Access Page right in the Access environment, Access also saves the HTML file and its associated support files (including XML data, image files, and the like) to your My Documents folder. You can also publish the resulting files to a Web server and allow users to access the page over the Internet using the new Office 2000 Web folder feature.

Using Design View to Create a Data Access Page

Design view requires some familiarity with the design view editor, which, like the forms editor, is similar to Visual Basic. In essence, you must add controls to a gridded form and bind those controls to objects in the database. It's pretty monotonous compared to using the wizard, but you can, of course, achieve a level of customization impossible with the wizard. One recommendation is to use the wizard and then edit in Design view if you feel the need to customize the form. It's generally just too much work to start a Data Access Page from scratch using Design view, unless you've got a pretty simple database.

Bidirectional Replication with Microsoft SQL Server

In Access 97, you can replicate data from an Access database to SQL Server, but it's impossible to replicate data from SQL Server back to Access. This unidirectional replication, from a SQL Server *publisher* to a Jet-based Access *subscriber*, has been improved in Access 2000. Now, you can perform complete bidirectional replication between Access and SQL Server: Changes in SQL Server can be replicated to Access and vice versa.

> **NOTE**
>
> Of course, there are limitations to this feature. Only actual data such as tables can be replicated. Forms, reports, and other non-data objects cannot be replicated.

Interestingly, replication conflicts between Access 2000 and SQL Server 7.0 are now resolved by using the SQL Server Conflict Resolution Wizard. This wizard is part of SQL Server, not Access. The Conflict Resolution Wizard uses a conflict table to store those changes that aren't propagated to the server. It decides which changes can and can't be made based on an internal set of priority-based conflict resolution algorithms.

Using Excel with SQL Server 7

Beginning with Excel 2000, it's possible to use SQL Server (as well as a variety of other databases) as a data source for a PivotTable or PivotChart. A PivotTable allows you to dynamically filter large amounts of data so that the display changes in real-time as you manipulate it. PivotTables are especially useful when you need to compare a large group of related datasets. A PivotChart provides the same functionality graphically, so that large amounts of related data can be manipulated with graphs and charts. Although it's possible to create a PivotTable without an associated PivotChart, PivotCharts are always associated with a PivotTable that must reside in the same Excel workbook.

Creating an Excel PivotTable

To create a PivotTable, navigate to the appropriate workbook in Excel and choose Data, PivotTable and PivotChart Report from the menu. This launches the PivotTable and PivotChart Wizard, which asks you for the type of data you'll be using. There are four possibilities:

- Microsoft Excel list or database
- External data source
- Multiple consolidation ranges
- Another PivotTable or PivotChart (available only if you've already created one)

To use SQL Server, you need to select External Data Source. The second step of this wizard asks you to find the data source using Microsoft Query (which must be installed for this function to work). The Choose Data Source dialog allows you to select a previously created ODBC Data Source Name (DSN), create a new DSN, or construct an ad-hoc query. If you need to create a new DSN, you're walked through a step-by-step wizard to do so. For this example, you'll be creating a DSN called "northwind" that points to the Northwind SQL Server database.

From here, you're prompted to select the columns of data to include in the query. This gives you a list of the tables in the Northwind database, including Categories, Category Sales for 1997, and the like. When you've selected the fields you'd like to display, the wizard prompts you to pick the worksheet location for the PivotTable, or, if you've chosen fields from a variety of tables that aren't linked, the Microsoft Query program launches so you can make manual links. If you get to Microsoft Query, it's generally a good idea to go back and rethink things because it's hard to generate a logical table based on unrelated data.

From here, it's just a simple matter of dragging and dropping page fields, column fields, row fields, and data items into the PivotTable because Excel works with this PivotTable in the same way it would if you had been working with native Excel data.

Using SQL Server with Internet Information Server and Internet Explorer

As a key product in Microsoft's BackOffice suite of Windows-based servers, SQL Server integrates nicely with other Microsoft server products, including the Internet Information Server (IIS) 4.0 Web server (which will be renamed Internet Information Services in Windows 2000, incidentally). One of the key concepts of Microsoft's Windows DNA strategy involves distributed applications, and IIS is currently the most logical way to deploy these applications: by using the World Wide Web.

The Web introduces an interesting dilemma for the SQL Server developer. It's now possible, using Microsoft technologies, to deliver applications to clients in two basic ways. With the more common server-side approach, you can use technologies such as Active Server Pages to target any kind of browser running on any kind of operating system, leaving the proprietary logic on the server. Conversely, Internet Explorer 5.0 users can work with client-side database logic, relieving some of the stress on the server. Both approaches have their pros and cons.

Accessing Databases on the Server Side

In today's Web, you can rely on only a small set of common functionalities across clients. Different Web browsers running on different operating systems (perhaps on different hardware platforms) offer different levels of functionality. For this reason, Microsoft developed ASP, an IIS add-in that allows Web developers to perform database access and other functions from the server and transmit plain text to the browser. Because the information sent to the browser is text, any Web browser will do, and the developer doesn't need to worry about compatibility issues. For example, most ASP code is written in VBScript, which is not compatible with Netscape Navigator. No matter—by the time the Web page hits the browser, no traces of VBScript remain.

Client-Side Database Access with Internet Explorer

On the other hand, when you can guarantee that each of your clients is using Internet Explorer 5.0 (or, to a lesser extent, IE 4.01 with Service Pack 1), a whole new set of functionality becomes available because of the client-side data-binding features in this browser. Giving the client the ability to work with live data frees the server from processing overhead and gives the user a more powerful, dynamic experience.

Of course, it's rare when you can be sure that all your users are working with a particular browser. Currently, it makes sense to use client-side data binding only on intranets that use Internet Explorer as a standard.

> **NOTE**
>
> The concept of client-side data binding technologies was first introduced with IE 4.0. The first technology that used this concept was Remote Data Service (RDS). With the release of Visual Studio 98, another technology that made use of the same concept was introduced. This technology is the Design Time Controls.

Integration with Microsoft Transaction Server

Microsoft Transaction Server (MTS) is a component of Internet Information Server (IIS), Microsoft's Web server. You can access the MTS API to develop your own software components (DLL files) that can separate business logic into *transactions*, a concept that should be immediately familiar to any SQL Server developer. Transaction Server transactions, like their SQL Server equivalents, are atomic operations that succeed or fail as a single unit. Consider the classic Transaction Server example of a bank balance transfer. There are two distinct operations here: a withdrawal and a deposit. For the transfer transaction to be considered successful, however, both operations need to occur. If either one fails, the transaction is rolled back and neither occurs.

> **NOTE**
>
> In Windows 2000, Microsoft Transaction Server is renamed to Component Services to more accurately reflect the purpose of this technology. Component Services is a key administration tool for COM+/Windows DNA.

In the days before Transaction Server, programmers had to implement this behavior manually. Database developers often create transactions in SQL Server by using the BEGIN TRANSACTION and COMMIT TRANSACTION Transact-SQL commands inside stored procedures. These SQL Server–based transactions can be rolled back if one of the operations in the transaction fails. SQL Server transactions can also be rolled forward if needed.

> **TIP**
>
> If you aren't familiar with SQL Server transactions, please refer to Chapter 3, "Optimizing Queries," for a detailed discussion.

Microsoft Transaction Server takes the theory of SQL Server transactions and applies it to other technologies. Like SQL Server, Transaction Server interacts with the Microsoft Distributed Transaction Coordinator (MSDTC) to ensure that its transactions meet the ACID (Atomicity, Consistency, Isolatation, and Durability) test.

MTS is integrated with Internet Information Server and most commonly associated with it because the Web offers a stateless environment to developers. Typically, a Web client connects to a remote resource, such as a Web page (or, perhaps, a remote database that is accessed through a Web page), and the connection is broken as soon as all data is transferred. The Web relies on this sort of discontinuous connection to keep things running at an acceptable speed. If Web clients remained connected to Web servers continually, more and larger servers would be needed, and the infrastructure of the Internet itself would need to be beefed up.

With Transaction Server, you can circumvent the stateless nature of the Web and ensure that groups of operations—transactions—occur without error. When an operation in an MTS transaction fails, the whole operation fails, as with a SQL Server transaction. Most important, this capability is built into MTS for you, so you won't need to create and deploy your own custom solution.

MTS Transactions and IIS

With IIS 4.0, Active Server Pages (ASP) server-side scripting can access MTS features for the first time (in IIS 3.0, scripts could not access MTS features). This allows Web developers to create multitier (or *n-tier*) client/server Web applications. A multitier Web application generally consists of the following three layers:

- **Presentation**   The HTML- or DHTML-based user interface. The Web browser–based user interface provides ways for the user to interact with the Web application through rich Web forms and controls.

- **Business logic**   Rules that determine *how* the application processes. Business logic is used to connect the presentation layer with a data store, such as SQL Server.

- **Data services** Typically a structured data store, such as SQL Server or Oracle. Multiple data services can serve a single Web application, and this service is managed by MTS components in the middle (business logic) layer.

Using a three-tier approach such as this one isolates data from presentation. MTS components or scripts, working between these two layers, offer a logical place to provide this isolation and determine how the other two layers interact. Microsoft's strategy for combining this approach to client/server development with Web development is known as Windows Distributed InterNet Application Architecture (Windows DNA). Windows DNA uses HTML, Dynamic HTML (DHTML), and Active Server Pages to present the first (presentation) layer to the user. Microsoft Transaction Server and components that use MTS, such as IIS, IIS/ASP components, and ASP scripting, occupy the middle (business logic) layer. SQL Server usually occupies the data services layer, although other tools, such as Oracle, Microsoft Access, or an Exchange Server mail store, can be used as well, with some caveats. To integrate with MTS, the data store must support the XA protocol as specified by the X/Open Consortium. SQL Server is, of course, the premier database for use with MTS.

> **NOTE**
>
> XA is a two-phase commit protocol defined by the X/Open DTP group. This protocol allows for the coordination of transactions among multiple database servers, treating the transactions on these servers as one transaction. This implementation guarantees that either all the databases on the participating servers are updated, or none of them are. The XA protocol is natively supported by many Unix databases, including Oracle, Informix, and DB2.

Programming Active Server Pages with MTS

You can write Active Server Pages scripts that take advantage of MTS by using the ASP @TRANSACTION=REQUIRED directive along with the Transfer and Execute methods of the ASP Server object. The following block of skeleton code shows how a transaction is initiated in an ASP page:

```
<%@ TRANSACTION=REQUIRED %>

<%
' Begin transaction
'
' Code that must occur in a transaction
'
' End transaction
%>
```

A few notes about this block of code: The code here represents an entire ASP page. The `TRANSACTION` directive should be the first line of code on the page; it tells the ASP compiler that all the ASP code and components that the code might access are part of the same transaction. The `TRANSACTION` directive takes the form `<%@TRANSACTION=value%>`; *value* is a string that can be set to one of the values shown in Table 27.1.

TABLE 27.1   POSSIBLE VALUES FOR THE TRANSACTION ASP DIRECTIVE

Value	*Effect*
Required	Script following the directive initiates an MTS transaction.
Requires_New	Script following the directive initiates an MTS transaction.
Supported	Script following the directive doesn't initiate an MTS transaction.
Not_Supported	Script following the directive doesn't initiate an MTS transaction.

An ASP page containing an MTS transaction is called from another ASP page by using the `Server.Transfer` or `Server.Execute` methods. The `Transfer` method literally transfers control of the current session to another ASP page. Any variables and objects that were created on the first ASP page are carried over to the second ASP page. The `Transfer` method takes the following form:

```
Server.Transfer("path")
```

In this code, *path* is the absolute or relative path to the second ASP file. When using a transactional ASP page (one that begins with the `TRANSACTION` directive), you typically use the `Transfer` method to call the transactional page. When the transactional page has finished running, control is returned to the calling page.

You can also use the `Server` object's `Execute` method. The `Execute` method executes an ASP page without passing any variables or objects over to the second page. The `Execute` method is called just like the `Transfer` method:

```
Server.Execute("path")
```

The same rules apply to *path*. Regardless of whether you use `Server.Transfer` or `Server.Execute`, the second (called) ASP file includes the `TRANSACTION` directive as its first line. Then, when the code in that file has executed, it returns control to the calling page using the same style of redirection (`Transfer` or `Execute`) that called the page.

27

INTEGRATING SQL
WITH MICROSOFT
PRODUCTS

One final note on the use of transactional ASP: The transacted ASP page (the file that begins with the TRANSACTION directive) can handle two Transaction Server events: OnTransactionAbort and OnTransactionCommit. Which event handler executes depends, of course, on whether the transaction was completed successfully.

Here, then, is a simple code sample for an ASP page (transact1.asp) that calls a transacted page named transact2.asp:

```
<%@ Language=VBScript %>
<HTML>
<HEAD>
<TITLE>Test transaction</TITLE>
</HEAD>
<BODY>

<H1>Test transaction</H1>

<%
Server.Execute ("transact2.asp")
%>

<P>This appears after the transaction is complete.

</BODY>

</HTML>
```

The page that it calls is shown here:

```
<%@ TRANSACTION=REQUIRED %>

<%
Response.Write "<H2>This comes to you from within a transaction</H2>"

Sub OnTransactionAbort
    Response.Write "Transaction unsuccessful."
End Sub

Sub OnTransactionCommit
    Response.Write "Transaction successful."
End Sub
%>
```

The resulting output first renders the phrase Test transaction using a Heading One style, as denoted in transact1.asp. Then control shifts to the transacted page, transact2. This prints a phrase using the Heading Two style and then, depending on whether the transaction was successful, a success message. Control is then returned to the calling file (transact1.asp) where the phrase This appears after the transaction is complete. is printed.

Obviously, most of the transactional code you write will be more complicated than this, but the general structure will still be the same. In the following section, the use of ASP, SQL Server, and MTS is discussed.

MTS Transactions and SQL Server

If SQL Server provides for transactions, why bother using MTS in the Web pages that access SQL Server? Remember that SQL Server can auto-commit transactions only on a Transact-SQL line-by-line basis. If you want to explicitly enforce the use of transactions, you need to use Transact-SQL code with BEGIN TRANSACTION, COMMIT TRANSACTION, and ROLLBACK TRANSACTION to make sure that your code runs properly and, if not, that the changes can be rolled back. When you program for SQL Server with Active Server Pages and ActiveX Data Objects (ADO) as discussed in Chapter 25, "Accessing SQL Server Through OLE-DB and ADO," however, you typically use the objects in the ADO object model to manipulate data, not Transact-SQL code. For example, you might use an INSERT Transact-SQL statement to add a new row to a table or view using ADO, but it is more efficient to use the AddNew method of the Recordset object, as shown here:

```
<%
MyRS.AddNew
MyRS("fieldname") = value
MyRS("fieldname") = value
MyRS("fieldname") = value
...
MyRS.Update
%>
```

Operations such as this one, including row deletions, modifications, and additions, are obvious places to use a transactional ASP page. Otherwise, you'd be reduced to writing overly complex Transact-SQL code, which is unnecessary when you can use Transaction Server and ADO to do the hard work for you behind the scenes. There's no reason for any developer to waste time explicitly creating transactional code when Microsoft has given you a tool that will do it for you. This code, then, could be placed in a transactional ASP page that would resemble the following code:

```
<%@TRANSACTION-REQUIRED%>
<%
MyRS.AddNew
MyRS("fieldname") = value
MyRS("fieldname") = value
MyRS("fieldname") = value
...
MyRS.Update
Sub OnTransactionAbort
    Response.Write "New record was NOT written."
```

```
End Sub

Sub OnTransactionCommit
    Response.Write "New record created."
End Sub
%>
```

Enforcing Distributed Transactions

Interestingly, you can also force SQL Server 7.0 to seamlessly use the built-in services of Transaction Server. This option can be found by opening Enterprise Manager, right-clicking on the server you want to modify, and choosing Properties. In the dialog that appears, navigate to the Connections tab and check Enforce Distributed Transactions (MTS). If Microsoft Transaction Server is not available to SQL Server, this option is disabled.

MTS Transactions and the Visual Programming Tools

Microsoft Transaction Server can also be accessed from the Microsoft Visual programming tools, such as Visual Basic, Visual C++, and Visual J++. In fact, it's far more common and efficient for developers to wrap business logic into MTS components written in Visual Basic, Visual C++, or Visual J++ than to do so using transactional ASP pages. Of course, this is beyond the scope of this chapter, but a true Windows DNA Web application should use MTS components for the middle, business logic tier that act as middlemen between the client (which can be a Web browser or a true Win32 application) and the SQL Server data source. By wrapping your data access components into Transaction Server, you can ensure that they will be automatically scalable as the needs of your network grow.

Summary

In this chapter, you learned how to use Microsoft Access 2000 with SQL Server 7. The integration between these two products has been greatly improved, especially with the easy connection and the bidirectional replication. You also learned how to create Excel Pivot Tables based on SQL Server data. You also saw how SQL Server can be used as the data tier in Web applications using IIS as the Web server. Finally, you learned how SQL Server can be used with MTS to control distributed transactions and make sure data is consistent across multiple servers.

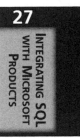

CHAPTER 28

Scheduling Jobs and Using ActiveX Servers to Implement Business Solutions

Microsoft made a major overhaul to the scheduling features of SQL Server 7.0. The new features now allow developers much more flexibility and power in scheduling jobs to run automatically. In this chapter we will discuss these new features and show you how we can use them to accomplish business goals in mission-critical situations.

Using the SQL Server Agent

Remember the last time you developed an enterprise solution for a major client? Did that client have a nightly job stream, possibly cascaded down from the system's former mainframe days? And did the client have any tasks that needed to be executed periodically throughout the day? And did the client ask you to port existing automated tasks into the new system? If you answered yes to any of these questions, you will definitely be interested in this chapter.

SQL Server 6.5 introduced a process of automating tasks through its SQL Executive service. The tasks could be scheduled to run once, hourly, daily, weekly, and so on. These tasks could be created to run an assortment of Transact-SQL scripts and subsequently run stored procedures. You could even notify people via email or pagers when a task failed or succeeded. In fact, the tasks you could create in SQL Server 6.5 were quite useful in implementing nightly job streams.

However, there were limitations with the scheduled tasks before SQL Server 7.0. Writing jobs in T-SQL, for example, was troublesome at best. T-SQL is a great language for short dataset-based actions; however, it is not a language geared toward enterprise solutions. Further, debugging T-SQL is difficult, and its interaction with ActiveX Servers is crude. Then along comes SQL Server 7.0.

SQL Server 7.0 enhances the scheduling tools in the successor to the SQL Executive service, the SQL Server Agent. You can still schedule tasks (now called jobs) using T-SQL and execute ActiveX Servers from T-SQL scripts, but now you can also create tasks by using scripting languages. Limited only by the capabilities of VBScript or JavaScript, you can create robust tasks. You can even create individual steps within a job, order them, and specify what should happen should a step fail.

But getting back to the original question, if you have ever used a scheduling utility in the past, you'll be thrilled with the new jobs offered by SQL Server 7.0's SQL Server Agent. This chapter explains what jobs are, what they can do, and how you can use them. After you've gotten a little background on jobs, then you can see how to implement them in T-SQL and in VBScript.

Implementing Jobs

SQL Server Agent, the successor to SQL Executive, supports scheduling periodic tasks and/or notifying system administrators of problems that have occurred. SQL Server 7.0 does a better job of configuring itself to meet processing demands than did previous versions of SQL Server. Scheduled jobs are still the best feature for implementing recurring tasks, such as nightly job streams, data backup procedures, and hourly inventory replenishments.

SQL Server Agent allows you to design and execute jobs consisting of one or more steps, which are usually T-SQL or VBScript statements that can be executed and scheduled. How often can you run these jobs? Well, as often as you like or on demand. The idea is that you can create jobs to define a business rule once. Then the SQL Server Agent executes it one or more times and monitors for success or failure.

What's in a Job Anyway?

The first step in implementing a job is to define it. Before you create a job, you need to determine what the job is intended to do, when it should do it, and what should happen if success or failure results. First, you must give the job a name to identify it by. When you're deciding on the job's name, keep in mind that it can contain spaces, but can't be longer than 128 characters.

After you've decided on the job name, you should consider what tasks the jobs should accomplish. Should the job have multiple steps, each contingent on the successful completion of the last? To answer this question, you must break down your job into the individual steps that define it. In the same scope, you need to decide which language will accomplish the task. Will T-SQL suffice, or should you use VBScript? And what do you want to happen if the step succeeds? Or what if it fails? Do you want it to go on to the next step when it fails or possibly skip to a specific step? What about retry attempts? Do you want the step to try again if it fails? Although previous versions of SQL Server lacked some of this functionality, all these issues can be configured using SQL Server 7.0.

28

SCHEDULING JOBS
AND USING
ACTIVEX SERVER

> **NOTE**
>
> In SQL Server 6.5, you could not schedule separate steps within a task. In fact, you often had to get around that by putting all the steps in a single task. Each step was a rule within an ActiveX Server, called by using T-SQL (you'll see how
>
> *continues*

> this is done a little later in this chapter). However, calling ActiveX Servers from within a single task by using T-SQL occurs asynchronously. Therefore, if you call three steps from three methods of an ActiveX Server in a single task, the second step doesn't wait for the first step to finish. This is one of the advantages of using VBScript to schedule tasks in SQL Server 7.0. However, in previous versions of SQL Server 7.0, you could have put all three steps within a single method of an ActiveX Server to get around this problem, but why should you have to?

T-SQL Jobs

Okay, enough background; time to move on to creating a job. Assume that the job requires you to order more product for any items that have fallen below their reorder level. You'll use the Northwind database's Product table to walk through this example.

Start by opening SQL Server Enterprise Manager and navigating to the SQL Server Agent node. After you have opened SQL Server Enterprise Manager, open the SQL Server Group and the local SQL Server that you'll use. Then, open the SQL Server Agent node and click on the Jobs node (as shown in Figure 28.1).

FIGURE 28.1

The SQL Server Enterprise Manager showing the SQL Server Agent's jobs (currently, none exist).

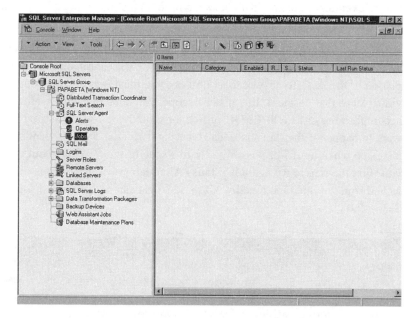

Right-click on Jobs, and then choose New Job to see the screen for setting up a new job. In the New Job Properties dialog box and on the General tab, enter a name for the job in the Name box. Then enter a description, not exceeding 512 characters, for the job in the Description box (as shown in Figure 28.2).

FIGURE 28.2

The New Job Properties dialog box for the new inventory replenishment job.

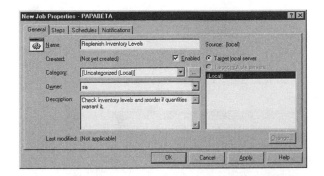

Then select the Steps tab and click New to create a new step. Keep in mind that every job must have at least one step. A *step* defines an individual and distinct unit of work that will be performed. For example, a job could have steps to create the invoices, send them to the billing clients, and then create a summary of the day's transactions.

But getting back to the example, you should now see a screen for creating a new step for the job. This step will order more items for those products that have fallen below the reorder level, so enter the name `Order More` in the Step Name box. Then select Transact-SQL Script (TSQL) from the Type drop-down list because you'll write this code in T-SQL. Then specify the database as Northwind and enter the T-SQL code, as shown in Listing 28.1, in the Command box. At this point, your screen should look similar to Figure 28.3.

28

SCHEDULING JOBS
AND USING
ACTIVEX SERVER

LISTING 28.1 THE T-SQL THAT DISPLAYS THE PRODUCTS BEFORE AND AFTER THE
REORDER LEVEL HAS BEEN CHANGED

```
SELECT ProductID, UnitsInStock, UnitsOnOrder, ReorderLevel
FROM Products ORDER BY ProductID

UPDATE Products
SET  UnitsOnOrder = (ReorderLevel - (UnitsInStock + UnitsOnOrder)) + 10
WHERE (UnitsInStock + UnitsOnOrder) <= ReorderLevel

SELECT ProductID, UnitsInStock, UnitsOnOrder, ReorderLevel
FROM Products ORDER BY ProductID
```

FIGURE 28.3

*The code for the
Order More step.*

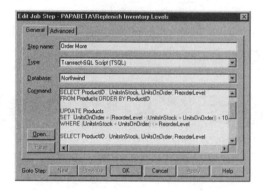

When you're done, you can click the Parse button to check your syntax. If you don't get
a successful message, SQL Server tries to tell you what the problem was. Next, select the
Advanced tab, where you can set some features you didn't have in previous versions of
SQL Server. For example, you can create an output file from this step by specifying the
name of the file in the Output File box. For this example, use c:\output.txt and enable
the Overwrite option button to overwrite it. (You can also select appending to the file.)

Then check the Append Output to Step History check box so that the output from the
step is saved to the job's history, too. You might have noticed the two SELECT statements
in Listing 28.1. Those statements display the data in the Products table before and after
the data is updated. If you didn't save this output to a file, you couldn't check the
changes to the data.

> **TIP**
>
> It's a good idea to save the output to a file if there are several rows of output.
> The job history log stores only a partial snapshot of the output, so if you want
> to check data, as you do in this case, then you should save the output to a file.

In previous versions of SQL Server, you could not specify which task to run next very easily (especially if you wanted to perform different tasks depending on the success or failure of a previous step). Well, no more problems in this version of SQL Server! You can tell the job what to do next when the step ends with success or failure. For this example, stick with the defaults, as shown in Figure 28.4.

FIGURE 28.4

Setting the step's advanced properties.

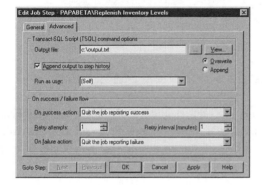

Here are the options you have for telling the step what to do next:

- Tell the step to quit reporting failure.
- Tell the step to quit reporting success.
- Tell the step to go to the next step.
- Tell the step to go to a specific step.

Finally, use the Retry Attempts spin box to set the retry attempts to 1, just in case, and then save your changes by clicking OK, and then clicking OK again.

Now that you have a job with a purpose, tell it when to run. Select the Schedules tab and click the New Schedule button. (Keep in mind that you can create multiple schedules for a single job.) Name the schedule for this job `Hourly Inventory Replenishments` in the Name box provided. Make sure the schedule type is Recurring, and then click the Change button to set the recurring schedule.

Set this job to run every hour, on the hour, during business hours (8:00 a.m. to 6:00 p.m.) on business days (Monday through Friday). To do that, select the Weekly option in the Occurs section and check off the weekdays on the check boxes provided in the Weekly section. Then, in the Daily Frequency section, select the Occurs Every option button, and set the frequency to occur every hour, starting at 8:00 a.m. and ending at 6:00 p.m. After you've applied the changes, your screen should look similar to Figure 28.5.

FIGURE 28.5

Setting the job's hourly schedule.

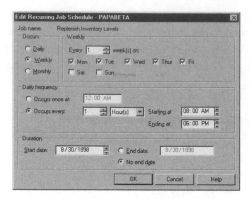

Now that you have set up the job's duties and its schedule, save your changes and get back to viewing the jobs in the SQL Server Agent. From there, right-click on the Replenish Inventory Levels job and choose Refresh Job to update the display with the job's current statistics.

Now let's get down to business! Run the job by right-clicking on it and choosing Start. It shouldn't take long, so check what happened by looking at the job's history. Right-click on the job again, but this time choose Job History (see Figure 28.6).

FIGURE 28.6

Checking the job's history.

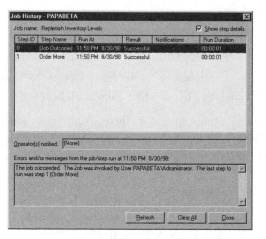

Notice that the job ran successfully. (If it didn't run successfully for you, look at the error messages displayed in the box at the bottom of this dialog window.) If you click on the 1 choice in the Step ID column, you should see the output results in the bottom box. Notice that there's only a partial look at these results because of limited space. To check the actual results, you can look in the output file you created. Using Notepad or another text editor, open the output file you created earlier (c:\output.txt). You will notice the time the step started and the output of both SELECT statements.

You could have broken this step into three steps: first, display the data; second, update it; and third, display the data again. You might want to try this on your own because you will undoubtedly want to include multiple steps in a job somewhere down the line. However, you're probably wondering how much you can accomplish using T-SQL right now.

Running ActiveX Servers Through VBScript Jobs

Well, what if you want to run a job in an ActiveX Server? You can run methods of ActiveX Servers by using the sp_OA system stored procedures. This method of running ActiveX Servers from SQL Server batches has been outdated in SQL Server 7.0. However, you might want to keep backward compatibility with former versions of SQL Server. Basically, these stored procedures can create, call methods of, set properties of, and destroy ActiveX Servers from a T-SQL script. They are sp_OACreate, sp_OAMethod, sp_OASetProperty, and sp_OADestroy, respectively. You can also read properties with sp_OAGetProperty and read error information from ActiveX Server with sp_OAGetErrorInfo.

If you've had any experience with these stored procedures, you know they can be somewhat difficult to figure out. Thankfully, SQL Server 7.0 has followed the lead of Web environments by allowing you to take advantage of scripting languages such as VBScript and JavaScript. Through these scripting languages, you can create ActiveX Servers and use more complex business logic built into the scripting languages.

Try modifying the job you just created to use VBScript instead of T-SQL. Right-click on the job and choose Properties from the shortcut menu. Then select the Steps tab and click the Edit button to modify the step. Now select Active Script in the Type drop-down list and Visual Basic Script in the Language drop-down list. Finally, enter the code from Listing 28.2 in the Command box.

LISTING 28.2 UPDATING THE INVENTORY WITH VBSCRIPT

```
set objConn = CreateObject("ADODB.Connection")
objConn.Open "Provider=SQLOLEDB.1;Persist Security Info=False;" & _
    "User ID=sa;Initial Catalog=Northwind;Data Source=papabeta"
strSQL = "UPDATE Products"
```

continues

LISTING 28.2 CONTINUED

```
strSQL = strSQL & " SET  UnitsOnOrder = "
strSQL = strSQL & " (ReorderLevel - (UnitsInStock + UnitsOnOrder)) + 10"
strSQL = strSQL & " WHERE (UnitsInStock + UnitsOnOrder) <= ReorderLevel"
objConn.Execute strSQL
objConn.Close
set objConn = Nothing
```

This code creates an ActiveX Server (the ADO `Connection` object) and issues the UPDATE statement to replenish the appropriate inventory.

Notice that if you select the Advanced tab, there are no options for saving the output of the VBScript. This really doesn't apply to VBScript (see Figure 28.7). (However, you could write your own code to do this through an ActiveX Server.)

FIGURE 28.7

Checking the step's advanced options.

Of course, if you want to see the results, you can create a step that simply selects all data from the Products table, and save the output to a file. Then create another step that does the same thing, except this step appends to the output file. That way, you have both outputs in the same file. Figure 28.8 shows the steps, in order, in the Job Properties dialog box.

FIGURE 28.8

Checking the job's steps.

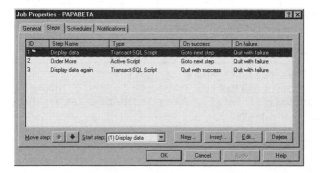

Be careful to have the correct step specified in the Start Step combo box at the bottom of the window. The starting step is easily identifiable by its green flag in the ID column (as shown in Figure 28.8).

> **WARNING**
>
> If you created a step in the past and are now adding new steps to the same job, you will want to double-check the On Success actions. For example, the On Success action does not change from Quit Reporting Success when you add a new step. So make sure your steps are in the correct order and the actions confirm that order. SQL Server tries to let you know when it believes you have a step out of order. For example, if you specified the second of three steps to quit regardless, SQL Server would tell you that the third step can never be run this way.

Putting It All Together

The benefit of running VBScript from within a job is that you get all the features of VBScript, and VBScript is much easier to code (and debug) than T-SQL for the majority of developers. What's even better is that you can run your own ActiveX Servers through a job by using VBScript. For example, you could have written an ActiveX Server in Visual Basic to replenish the inventory and called that from your job. The ActiveX Server in Visual Basic could have simply executed the same code that was in Listing 28.2, but it would be compiled into a DLL. Then you could execute this DLL from a job by using the code in Listing 28.3.

LISTING 28.3 UPDATING THE INVENTORY BY CALLING A VISUAL BASIC ACTIVEX SERVER FROM A VBSCRIPT JOB

```
set objInventory = CreateObject("MyRules.Inventory")
objInventory.Replenish
set objInventory = Nothing
```

This way, you can call any ActiveX Server's logic, keeping the job syntax simple and hiding the complexity of the rules in the ActiveX Server. You can also take advantage of any existing rules in ActiveX Server more readily by using VBScript. With new features such as steps, contingencies, and VBScript, the SQL Server Agent is a superb tool for implementing enterprise business solutions.

28

SCHEDULING JOBS AND USING ACTIVEX SERVER

Summary

This chapter has shown you some ways to schedule jobs using SQL Server Agent and Transact-SQL. You can also use code to work with ActiveX servers to execute the jobs you want to run, which offers you some advantages in the timing of their execution. Keep in mind, though, that T-SQL is more efficient than writing VBScript or VB ActiveX server code when manipulating data through SQL. This is true since T-SQL exists within SQL Server and is optimized for SQL Server's database engine. VB ActiveX servers are optimal when we need to perform additional tasks that include database interaction but are not limited to SQL calls.

Programming a Line-of-Business Solution

The purpose of this chapter is to provide guidelines, ideas, and suggestions for developing a SQL Server business application. Several topics on the development life cycle of a SQL Server application are touched on, but none are reviewed in depth. Each suggestion is based on experiences, both positive and negative, in developing SQL Server applications.

Infrastructure

When developing database applications, there are several infrastructure requirements. Computers for developing the application, the development software, a network, and the database are the basic requirements.

The Development Database

First is a development database, which should be a standalone server with resources, such as memory and disk space, that are adequate to develop the database application. Also, the database should be running the same version of Windows NT and SQL Server that the production database is running.

I have had clients who insisted that the development database run on the same server as the production file server. Invariably during development, a runaway query uses up all the resources on the server, causing the server to lock up. Expect the occasional runaway query, particularly if the developers are relatively inexperienced. Even experienced developers will, on occasion, inadvertently write a Cartesian product against million-row tables. Insist on a standalone development server even if it is a converted desktop computer.

Source Code Management

Source code management for database objects is not as easy as it is for client or middle-tier development tools, such as Visual Basic or PowerBuilder. There are some third-party tools for maintaining checkin and checkout capabilities for stored procedures. However, there aren't any automated source code management options for maintaining server-side source code management for table definitions. Although preferred, source code management does not have to be automated.

Simple management schemes using limited database permissions that allow creating objects under the login name of the developer can be used to prevent developers from overwriting one another's table and procedure definitions. However, this method does not prevent developers from inadvertently overwriting their own code, nor does it keep track of versions. It does require a lot of coordination between developers in reconciling versions of database objects and client code. This technique works better as a way to test changes of database objects without affecting other developers.

A better method of managing this source code is to keep all database code and definitions in text files. Often you can use change scripts generated by SQL 7 or by other third-party tools. The change scripts are the text files that contain your changes to the database. These change scripts can be managed using conventional source code management tools, such as PVCS Version Manager, that you might already be using to manage your client-side application code. Don't forget to include all database scripts in your management scheme. For example, insert statements for code tables should be part of your source code management scheme.

Using change scripts instead of going through the GUI tools to add tables, columns, and so forth, is more effective because it gives you the ability to test the implementation. It also supplies a tracking history of changes that have been made. Often, the developers have authority only in development databases to make table changes. By developing these change scripts, the developer can hand over the scripts to the database administrator for review, testing, and implementation.

Database Requirements

Database requirements for an application include performance requirements and up-time requirements. Questions include How many hours in a day does the database have to be available? How many days per week does it have to be available? How fast does the database have to respond to a particular request? Seconds? Minutes? These questions and their underlying requirements must be identified as part of the requirements-gathering phase of a project. They are used to identify the size and type of hardware needed for production use to the application, the backup schedule required, and the design of the batch, reporting, and online processes of your application.

In developing a database application, you must be aware of the application's projected size. Size is measured not only in gigabytes, but also in numbers of rows and numbers of users. A large application requires more performance testing and tuning. An application with a hundred users requires more performance tuning than an application with five users. Likewise, a 5GB database application requires more performance tuning than a 50MB database application.

The application's rate of growth must also be determined and planned for. For instance, you can retrieve all rows from a table for display to a user. This might be fine when there are only a few hundred rows, but as the table grows to thousands of rows, the application's performance will degrade.

These processes also have response-time requirements at the individual process level. Determine these database requirements and include them in the application design requirements.

The size of the application also includes the number of simultaneous users. Large numbers of users generally means there is a higher concurrency requirement. Find out what each class of user typically does during a "heavy" processing day.

Design and Development

The database design must be done before the application programming starts. If the database design changes after coding has been started, the code will most likely have to change. A good database design will allow for future enhancements without major changes to existing database objects. Normalization and primary key selection are the two most important database design considerations.

Normalization

The physical table design must always be the responsibility of the technical designers. End users should be able to offer guidance only on the logical design.

I have occasionally had nontechnical users mandate particular design elements in the database. In one case, they specified a table's "primary" key to be a single column of data type real. This key was to be generated from the current date plus a daily incrementing number as the number to the left of the decimal place. To the right of the decimal place was the foreign key reference to the entity this table was dependent on.

It is important in these circumstances to meet the clients' exact functional requirements. However, this does not mean that you have to forego a good database design; rather, it means that you have to present the logical design with the criteria that has been specified. The physical design should still be normalized, with additional views that give the clients the structures they want. In cases like the one I described, the physical table should be normalized, with a view built that provides the client with what he or she wants.

Primary Keys

The primary key is used to uniquely identify a row in a table. Although every table should have a primary key, SQL Server does not enforce this requirement. In designing the database, you need to determine whether your primary keys will be natural keys or surrogate keys. After that's determined, you should remain consistent across all tables.

A *natural key* is based on actual attributes of the entity (table). An example of a natural key for a table of people is a Social Security number, which uniquely identifies a person. Benefits of natural keys are that they are easy for users to understand and there is no space wasted in storing an extra column as there is when using surrogate keys.

A *surrogate key* is a generated value used only to uniquely identify the row. Generally, it's a serialized number. The identity property is used specifically for this purpose. SQL Server generates the values of the surrogate key for you.

I recommend using surrogate keys for a number of reasons:

- Surrogate keys guarantee uniqueness within a table. The Social Security number example doesn't take into account that not everyone has a Social Security number. A surrogate key allows this exception to occur.

- Another benefit to using surrogate keys is that normally the value never changes because it is generated rather than captured as application data. If the primary key value were to change, all related tables must have their foreign key values changed as well. For example, if the Social Security number captured in your application needed to be changed, every foreign key that references it would have to change, too. This requirement could involve updates across many tables, depending on the size of the database. If surrogate keys were used, only one column in one table would need to be changed.

- One of the biggest arguments for using natural keys over surrogate keys is the space saved by not having another column in the table. However, with the cost of disk space so relatively inexpensive, the benefits of using surrogate keys usually outweighs the drawbacks.

A primary key may be a composite key. A *composite key* is a key made up of two or more of the columns of the table. An intersection table that represents a many-to-many relationship normally has a composite primary key made up of the foreign keys of the intersecting tables. An example of this is the `titleauthor` table in the `pubs` database where the primary key is a composite of the `au_id` and `title_id` columns.

Null Constraint

For non-key data elements, you must decide whether a column allows null values. For data that you do not have absolute control over, you have to decide whether to allow the data into your system if it is not complete.

One of my clients processes large amounts of file transmissions with their customers. Some customers have implemented the file transmission logic worse than others have. Often, the transmitted data is incomplete or invalid. Instead of rejecting the file or particular records within the file, as much of the data as possible is salvaged and saved in the database. By not rejecting the data from the database, the customer order is at least initiated. By designing the database to allow for null data, the application can store incomplete records, which is a benefit to the customers.

Allowing null data elements into your database does present some challenges to your development effort. Null never equals anything including null. Therefore, using a column that allows null values presents the possibility that rows will be excluded from the result-set unless outer joins are used. Be aware that operations on a null value produce a null result. For string concatenation, this is different in SQL 7 than in earlier versions. Thus, SELECT 'A' + NULL results in NULL in SQL 7 whereas in SQL 6.5 it yields 'A'.

Programming for Performance

Consider a database application as three dependent pieces. SQL Server is one part, the application program (including both client and middle-tier) is another part, and the network is the last part. If any part fails, the application will not work. If any part is over-burdened, the application will not perform well.

Developers have the least ability to affect system performance through the network. This is usually the last place to look for performance enhancements in the application.

The database server provides more capability to enhance application performance, usually through better indexing and statistics updates.

In developing your database application, it is important to remember that a client application is making the requests to the database server through the network. In some cases, this client application is actually working through a middle-tier such as Microsoft MTS. The application that is responsible for communicating to the database has the most responsibility for locking, processing, and I/O burden. Most performance problems are caused by how the client and middle-tier applications are written and therefore should be the starting points for investigating performance issues.

Reduce Data Transmissions

When writing queries to retrieve data back to the client, always use the server to filter out rows that are not needed. Never do the filtering on the client. Also, retrieve only those columns that are required.

You can use top and percent to limit the retrieval of a particular query to the top *n* rows or the top *n* percent. This technique is particularly good for searches where wildcards can be used. For example, you can allow searches on last name with wildcards. If the WHERE clause of a SQL statement contains Like 'S%', the resulting number of records might be in the thousands. By using the top keyword in the SELECT statement, you can limit the number returned to a reasonable amount.

For a session limit, you can use SET ROWCOUNT to limit operations to the given number of rows. However, using SET ROWCOUNT is not recommended because it affects all operations, including updates and deletes, so it might have unintended consequences.

Always have SET NOCOUNT on for your connections. This statement stops the database from reporting back to the client how many rows were affected by the last SQL statement. In larger stored procedures, it can produce a significant savings because every SQL statement in the stored procedure would have sent back the row counts. Also, check your stored procedures for SELECT statements and PRINT statements that might have been added for debugging purposes and not removed.

Never Allow User Input Within a Transaction

Transactions need to be as short as possible. Open transactions hold locks on database resources, which prevents other users from having access to the resources. Collect all your data first and then begin your transaction. If an error is encountered during the transaction, immediately roll back the transaction and then display and/or log the error. If no error was encountered, immediately commit the transaction.

Never display a dialog box that waits for user input while a transaction is open. A user could start a process and then get a call (telephone, nature, or so forth). If the application is waiting for user input and the transaction is open, other processes could be blocked until the dialog box is responded to and the open transaction is cleared.

Prevent Deadlocks

In SQL 7, deadlock occurrences should drop because of the row-level locking capability. However, they can still occur, so you should code to minimize it as much as possible. Deadlocking affects performance because every time a deadlock occurs, the sacrificial transaction is immediately rolled back. Any work the victim has performed will be lost and have to be retried.

Always code your transactions to update tables in the same exact order throughout the application. Update order of the tables is critical because deadlocks occur when two processes are updating two or more of the same tables but in different orders. The first process has a lock on one table and is waiting on the second process to release its lock on another table. At the same time the second process is waiting for the first process to release its lock.

Updating the tables in the same order will, in most cases, fix the deadlocking problems. It might not be possible in some applications, however, if triggers are used to update one or more tables.

Avoid long-running transactions. The longer the transaction is running, the more likely a deadlock will happen. Certainly, it will cause blocking problems while it is running.

Even with row-level locking and maintaining a table update order, your application might still encounter deadlocks. Generally, the best way of dealing with a deadlock is to trap for the deadlock error 1205 and then immediately retry the transaction. Retry only a few times, maybe three or four, because you don't want the application retrying forever. Log this error even if the application was successful on the next try. This is important because if you know there is a deadlocking problem, you might be able to fix it.

As a last resort, you can specify some parts of your application as more likely to be a deadlock victim. By setting SET DEADLOCK_PRIORITY to LOW for a particular connection, that connection will more likely be chosen as the victim. This can be set during runtime depending on what part of the application the user is in. For example, you might prefer that a report generation process be a deadlock victim instead of a data entry process. You can set the deadlock priority to low before the report runs and then, after the report has finished, set the priority back to normal.

Don't Mix OLTP and OLAP

The heavy-duty reporting and querying typical of OLAP and decision support systems generally use extensive system resources and hold shared locks for long periods while the queries run. This makes for incompatibility with an OLTP system that generally has short queries and transactions with exclusive locks. To avoid this, use different database servers for the OLTP and OLAP requirements of your application. A side benefit to this is that you can use the SQL Server data transformation capabilities to flatten out your OLTP table structures for more efficient reporting. This can significantly improve performance for your reporting application.

Avoid Long-Running Queries

Usually, an application has reporting and search components that allow users to enter criteria for querying. A typical criterion is a date range. Allowing a user to enter a date range that spans too long a time could start a query that performs table scans of a huge table. At best, it causes the user to wait a very long time; at worst, it can use up the entire tempdb database.

Within your application, you can limit the type and ranges of query criteria. This type of approach is often used, but it can be difficult to determine a reasonable set of limits. For reporting, you can have the heavier reporting deferred until a time of light system usage, such as the evening. A reporting subsystem that supports a scheduler could be integrated into the application.

Testing the Database Application

Testing a database application involves more than ensuring that the processing on the inputs generates the correct outputs. It also must perform well. The response time must be measured and compared with the specified response time from the requirements. This involves testing the system under simulated loads with the number of simultaneous users running typical processes such as online updates, reports, and batch processes.

Determining how well the application performs can be difficult when developing a new application. Often, the amount of data available to test with is relatively small and does not give a good indication of how the system will perform after the application has been in a production environment for several months. Determining a method for generating an amount of data representative of production levels of data is important for a good performance test. If the application is replacing an existing application, and the existing application's data must be ported over into the new application, you already have a source of test data. Build your data-porting routines as early as possible so that the programmers and testers both have access to the data.

Testing the Performance

Look for system choke points. Move the database off the local area network, and access it over an analog modem. If your application performs well in this environment, it should not have network-related problems when it scales to many users.

Use the profiling tools in SQL Server. By running the Profiler to capture trace data on system usage, you can perform an index analysis for your overall application usage. You might be able to improve throughput with the suggested indexing schemes.

29

PROGRAMMING A LINE-OF-BUSINESS SOLUTION

The performance of an application means more than just running a particular process as fast as possible. You must also test for concurrent user access that mimics the use of the database in the production environment. Every application is different and is affected by the online, batch, and reporting processes that typically make up a line-of-business application.

In particular, some batch jobs might have to be rewritten to slow down the job and consequently allow for better concurrent access to database resources. For example, a stored procedure batch process that I had written worked correctly and was highly tuned for performance in that it ran in a relatively fast 20 minutes. However, it locked everyone out of the tables it was accessing. Because this batch process had to run during the day when online users were accessing the database, this was a problem, so I slowed the process by using the `waitfor` command after every SQL statement in the batch process. Now the process takes an extra 15 minutes to run, but when it does run, it doesn't noticeably affect the overall system performance.

Modifying Third-Party SQL Server Applications

Many SQL Server applications are available as "out of the box" solutions. Accounting, contact management, and other types of applications can be purchased rather than written in-house. Often they provide most but not all of the functionality required. In these cases, the application can be modified to fit the organization's business requirements.

Applications that provide source code require consideration when modifying the code. If the application vendor periodically updates the application, changes have to be done more carefully. The concern is that the vendor's update will overwrite your changes and that your changes will prevent the update from working properly.

If the client and/or middle-tier code are written in an object-oriented language, such as PowerBuilder, Java, or C++, making the modifications might be easier to maintain through version changes of the base applications.

Modifications to the SQL Server code or tables, however, can be much more difficult to maintain through version changes. You should document your changes within the code, as well as in change documents, with the actual location of the code changes.

Add columns carefully. Do not reuse an existing column for a purpose other than the one intended by the application vendor. When a new column is required, consider creating a separate table with the new column instead of just adding the column to the existing table. By isolating the change to a separate table, there is less chance of a problem when the application is upgraded. For example, your application vendor might drop and re-create a table during the upgrade process. If this is done to a table on which you have added a column, the added column will be lost during the upgrade process.

Summary

When developing a SQL Server application, having the right tools and a good database design is critical in getting the system to work. Also, knowing about issues, such as deadlocks, that are particular to database systems and how to prevent them will help reduce problems that don't surface until many users are actively using the application. These guidelines will help your application succeed.

Data Warehousing and Online Transaction Processing (OLTP)

Designing a database is certainly a difficult, and often badly done, part of a global information system project, but it's more difficult to create a universal database, one that accepts long-running complex queries and quick small transactions. My purpose is not, of course, to show you how to perform such a miracle, but just give you the right steps for creating a Decision Support System (DSS) database, based on a data warehouse, or an Online Transaction Processing (OLTP) database.

Usually, the database that allows for intensive transaction processing is not the same database that allows for Online Analytical Processing (OLAP). To optimize query performance, tables need to be denormalized, which produces a new database that can take a large amount of data and allow for relatively fast retrieval of the embedded information. Such databases are called *data warehouses*. Although data warehouses are designed to accommodate large amounts of data, the data is not expected to change much. You can safely assume that the data in a data warehouse is almost static. For the data to be transferred from the OLTP to the OLAP or DSS system, it needs to be scrubbed and handled in a special way. This is where the Data Transformation Services (DTS) play an important role.

This chapter has three major goals: first, to show you how to create a data warehouse and DSS system; second, to discuss transaction systems; and third, to give you hints on how to create these two types of applications. Of course, it is important for you to be familiar with SQL Server, indexing and locking issues, and creating stored procedures and remote stored procedures. If these subjects are not clear enough for you, you'll miss the point, so hurry up and go back to the first part of this book. For those who are fine with these subjects, let's go.

SQL Server as a Data Warehouse

As I was writing the outline of this chapter, I faced a major "chicken and egg"–like dilemma. I didn't know how to start, and I changed my mind probably ten times just finding good reasons to start with so and so, but finding other good reasons five minutes later. So I made a decision to do things as I do in the real world.

So first I give you a broad definition and the main issues of a data warehouse. Then you discover how to create a good warehouse, considering necessary software and hardware configurations. The main problem begins then: How will you fill your warehouse? You learn how to use a good fill-up strategy, mixing stored procedures, data importation, and replication.

What Is a Data Warehouse?

As its name implies, a *data warehouse* is a huge set of different data stored in one place. Although the name appeared a few years ago, the concept is older. The main purpose of a data warehouse is to hold almost all a company's data. Once a company's critical data has been stored in a data warehouse, the data warehouse becomes an integral part of the company's decision support system.

Assume you have a data warehouse holding all the sales records for the past three years, along with the order amount, product name, the store's name and address, and the customer's age and city. With this simple data, you can find trends and make decisions on the progress of sales in the three-year period. The problem is writing the right queries and finding the answer as fast as possible.

To get an answer quickly, the database must be well designed, and that's the main point of a data warehouse: being huge and fast. SQL Server has all the necessary features to create good data warehouses. Many of these features were enhanced in SQL Server 7.0. The following are some of the enhancements that make SQL Server a strong contender for building large data warehouses:

- New join algorithms make retrieving data from the data warehouse faster.
- The storage engine has been optimized for VLDBs (very large databases). It can theoretically support databases up to 1 million terabytes (TB).
- There are new utilities specifically for handling large databases.
- The enhanced parallel query engine allows running a query on multiple processors, which increases its speed in retrieving the needed data.
- The new replication features support handling VLDBs.

Implementing a Data Warehouse

First of all, it is important to design your warehouse well. With an efficient database architecture, you can achieve excellent performance. Some points in this section are not specific to SQL Server, especially the ones about normal forms, but they are here to remind you of the virtues of denormalization. For those who are familiar with these concepts of normal forms and denormalization, feel free to skip this small section.

Designing a data warehouse in SQL Server 7.0 involves the following steps:

- Determining the requirements from the user's, business's, and technical points of view.
- Designing and building the database.

- Loading data into the data warehouse, which might require extracting it from existing OLTP systems using the new DTS services.
- Designing and processing aggregations using OLAP tools.
- Querying and maintaining the data warehouse and OLAP databases.

Some of these issues—the requirements and database design—are covered in this section. The other issues are covered in the following sections.

Determining the Requirements

Entire chapters could be written to discuss collecting requirements for designing a computer business solution. Gathering these requirements is essential for the success of any software project. In this section, I will briefly discuss the outline of this issue without delving into it. The requirements fall in three major categories: user, business, and technical.

User Requirements

The end user should have a great deal of input when you're gathering the requirements for a business solution. Therefore, it is important to talk to the people who will be using the system when collecting such information. With data warehouses, the end user could be a manager or a CEO who wants to get sales reports that are timely and accurate. The end user could also be a shareholder who wants reports about the performance of the company she is investing in.

In any case, user requirements start by identifying the users, dividing them in categories, talking to them, and actually knowing what functionality they are looking for.

Business Requirements

The business requirements are usually an extension of the user requirements. It is important for business growth to know the current standing for performance and establish a future outlook. Such information can be based on previous data collected and stored in a data warehouse. Adequate querying of the data warehouse supplies a wealth of information that can be used for future planning.

Gathering business requirements leads to building the right reports and queries against the data warehouse, and can also lead to a better design of the data warehouse.

Technical Requirements

The technical requirements usually follow the determinations of the user and business requirements. After you know how the data warehouse can support the user and business needs, you can start designing it. In the process, you collect the needed technical information about the hardware and DTS implementation to best support those needs.

Designing and Building the Database

Size is among the differences between a DSS and an OLTP database. A DSS database can be huge, probably many terabytes, and cannot fit in memory.

Nevertheless, a user querying that database should not have to wait hours for results. Otherwise, he will soon forget this invaluable tool, and all your efforts will be lost. It's vital to offer your users good performance in terms of throughput and speed. One of the keys for good performance is having the right hardware. For example, don't expect to support a few hundred users when your database server does not have enough memory. You should use the right hardware, so which brings us to the physical design in the following section.

Physical Design

When you create your database, you need to think about creating the physical data files. In SQL Server 7.0, you can use as many data files as you need for your database. This improvement makes it easy to allow your database to span multiple disks.

Of course, I won't talk here about the transaction log files. They shouldn't be a major subject of concern in a data warehouse, except for when the data is loaded in the data warehouse, but I'll talk about them later in this chapter. Ideally, in a standard warehouse, all the data is read-only, so there's no need to use the transaction logs. I will focus only on reading data from disk to cache.

SQL Server and Windows NT offer two I/O improvement solutions:

- RAID 0: Disk stripe set
- RAID 5: Disk stripe set with parity

SQL Server offers one automatic read I/O improvement: read ahead.

> **NOTE**
>
> To use the SQL Server and Windows NT improved I/O features, you need to have at least two disks. Also, RAID is not available on Windows 9x.

The previous version of SQL Server allowed creating database segments to enhance I/O performance. These segments are no longer supported in SQL Server 7.0 because they

30

DATA WAREHOUSING AND OLTP

will always be less efficient than a RAID solution. Also, the new SQL Server 7.0 architecture is based on data files, which may allow you to simulate the benefits of the database segments.

It is important to pay close attention to physical design of the database. Imagine you have a table of 100,000 products, and you have a picture of almost all your products. If you store these pictures along with your data, the table will be quite big, and you take the risk of fragmenting data and mixing binary information (pictures) and character/numeric information. It is more interesting to split the table in two, with a one-to-one relationship enforced by a foreign key constraint, than to store the "picture table" on a separate disk, as shown in Figure 30.1.

FIGURE 30.1

Splitting a table into two tables can increase the overall throughput.

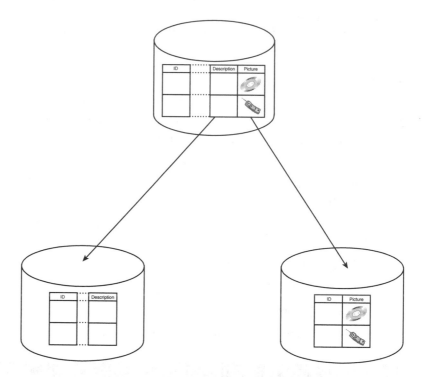

> **NOTE**
>
> Concerning the disk organization in RAID, a hardware solution is always better than a software one. However, if you don't have a RAID disk controller, you can easily take advantage of the software RAID solutions of Windows NT.

With a RAID 0 or 5 array, like the one shown in Figure 30.2, the throughput is increased.

FIGURE 30.2

*A RAID array
increases the data
output.*

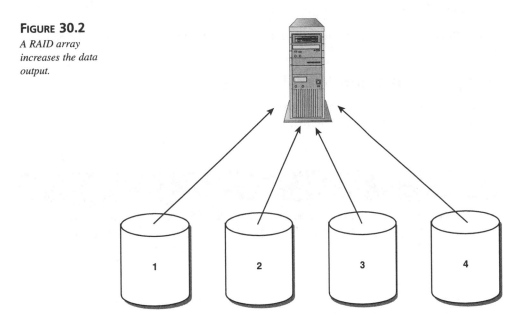

You can use the following enhanced SQL Server configuration options to improve disk I/O operations:

- `Max async io`: Indicates the maximum number of asynchronous I/O requests that a computer can issue against a data file. The default value is 32, but this value can be increased to 64 or higher in complex systems with many disks and controllers. As a rule of thumb, this value should be inversely proportional to the amount of disk activity on the server.

  It is recommended that this value be left at default if disks are not striped, spanning multiple drives, or using an intelligent controller.

- `Recovery interval`: This option controls when SQL Server issues a checkpoint in each database. Usually, SQL Server dynamically selects the best value for highest performance. However, you can monitor the disk activity using the Windows NT performance monitor and accordingly set a value for this option.

It's important to consider your database's physical design because it can have a dramatic impact on performance and transform a failure into success. As a quick summary, in order of importance, consider the following points before implementing your warehouse:

- Use a disk array, with a RAID 5 controller.
- Use a disk array, with software RAID 5.

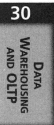

30

DATA
WAREHOUSING
AND OLTP

- Use a disk array, with a RAID 0 controller.
- Use a disk array, with software RAID 0.

After you have chosen a possible and affordable solution, let's come back to the conceptual design.

Normal Forms and Warehousing

I won't go into the normal forms discussion here; I assume you already know how to design your database in third normal form. Instead, I'll focus on the benefits of denormalization.

> **TIP**
>
> If normalization is not quite clear, you should read *Handbook of Relational Database Design* by Candace C. Fleming and Barbara Von Halle (Addison-Wesley, 1989).

Data warehouses must be prepared for long-running complex queries. Normally, the more joins, the slower the query (this is not always true, but I'll explain indexing the warehouse in the next section), so be prepared to denormalize your data. This operation is particularly important if you intend to create datacubes (see the section "How to Scrub (Prepare) Data for Warehouses").

For the moment, say you have been asked to create a data warehouse for a bank. You need information on customers and their accounts. You create the logical design shown in Figure 30.3.

FIGURE 30.3

Logical design in third normal form.

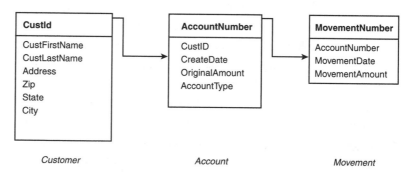

This bank has 100,000 customers, each of them with an average of 2.5 accounts (so a total of 250,000 accounts) and an average of 1 movement a day per account (365 × 250,000 = 91,250,000 total movements per year). With this figure, each join can cause a tremendous burden on input/output. Now, one of the main queries done on that system is calculating each account balance at the end of the year. The query to do that is shown in Listing 30.1.

LISTING 30.1 CALCULATING THE ACCOUNT BALANCE WITH THREE TABLES

```
SELECT C.Cust_ID, A.AccountNumber, Balance = Sum(MovementAmount)
FROM Customer AS C JOIN
     (Account AS A ON C.Cust_ID=A.Cust_ID) JOIN
     (Movement AS M ON A.AccountNumber=M.AccountNumber)
GROUP BY C.CustID, A.AccountNumber
```

That query can be a long-running one, even if it is simple (in fact, I made it simpler by ignoring the opening balance for each account). If you are in a hurry, you'd better change your design. In fact, because the optimizer is using nested iteration, even if you have good indexes, SQL Server will scan the account table 100,000 times—once for each customer—and the movement table (remember the number of lines) 250,000 times—once for each account.

And this query is a simple one! Some are much more complex and long-running. Even with a simple example, you can stall your server. What about a really complex one, with ORDER BY clauses, more tables, more calculations? Think about it—and decide to denormalize your database, as shown in Figure 30.4.

FIGURE 30.4
Denormalized logical design.

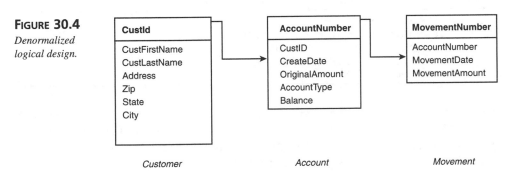

CustId
CustFirstName
CustLastName
Address
Zip
State
City

Customer

AccountNumber
CustID
CreateDate
OriginalAmount
AccountType
Balance

Account

MovementNumber
AccountNumber
MovementDate
MovementAmount

Movement

Listing 30.2 shows the new query after denormalization.

LISTING 30.2   CALCULATING THE ACCOUNT BALANCE WITH TWO TABLES

```
SELECT C.Cust_ID, A.AccountNumber, Balance
FROM Customer AS C JOIN
     (Account AS A ON C.Cust_ID=A.Cust_ID)
ORDER BY C.Cust_ID, A.AccountNumber
```

You don't have to calculate the balance for each account because it has already been calculated and maintained up to date, either by a trigger or by weekly batches (I talk about maintaining a denormalized model in the section "How to Scrub (Prepare) Data for Warehouses").

This approach decreases the number of I/O operations, so the query runs faster. You have what you wanted. The join is the feature to omit when you write a DSS query. Keep that rule in mind: Lowering the number of joins can be painful, but is almost always a win in big recordsets. Another way to improve query performance is, of course, using indexes in a smart fashion.

Row Width and I/O Speed

Another concern is the number of records per page. Remember, SQL Server uses 8KB pages to store table data. When you are working with a data warehouse, you should keep in mind that space management could be your enemy or your ally.

Let's return to the account balance example. At the end of the year, you have 91,250,000 movements. Listing 30.3 shows one way to create the movement table.

LISTING 30.3   CREATING AN OPTIMISTIC MOVEMENT TABLE

```
CREATE TABLE Movement
     (MovementNumber    Int NOT NULL IDENTITY(1,1),
      AccountNUmber     Int NOT NULL,
      MovementDate      Datetime NOT NULL,
      MovementAmount    Money NOT NULL)
```

The row length is 24 bytes (4+4+8+8). The amount of data that can be stored in one data page in SQL Server 7.0 is 8,060 bytes—that is, 335 records (the offset table takes 1 byte per record at the end of the page). Therefore, the movement table, set up as shown in Listing 30.4, needs 271,578 pages (2.07GB).

LISTING 30.4   CREATING A PESSIMISTIC BUT COMPACT MOVEMENT TABLE

```
CREATE TABLE Movement
    (MovementNumber    Int NOT NULL IDENTITY(1,1),
     AccountNUmber     Int NOT NULL,
     MovementDate      SmallDatetime NOT NULL,
     MovementAmount    SmallMoney NOT NULL)
```

The row length is 16 bytes (4+4+4+4); 503 records can be stored on a page, so the movement table needs 18,694 pages (1.379GB). You can see that changing two data types on a quite narrow table can have a dramatic effect on the physical storage (you spare more than 704MB).

> **NOTE**
>
> In the preceding calculations, conversions were based on 1GB = 1,024MB and 1MB = 1,024KB.

Of course, physical disk space is cheap. Buying a new 2GB disk is generally no problem, but what about transferring more than 700MB from disk to RAM? Even if you have very fast I/O disks, it can take a few seconds. Spare it! The more space you spare, the quicker your queries because of the reduction in I/O.

> **NOTE**
>
> If more than one foreign key existed in a table, chances are more duplicate data will exist in a single row. Foreign keys usually make rows smaller. For instance, instead of including the department name (varchar(32)), we include a department ID (integer), which requires less space to store. Therefore, with more foreign keys, the rows will be shorter. Also, foreign keys allow for redundant data. For instance, you can have multiple rows in the employee table belonging to the same department. The smaller row, along with the redundancies caused by the foreign keys, make I/O perform better.

In calculating the number of pages, I did not take into account the index pages. If your query uses indexes, remember the index pages need to be transferred into RAM to be used. If you redo the calculations of the needed disk space between the two scenarios discussed above (based on the data types), you will find that taking index pages into account will improve the savings with the smaller data types even more.

30

DATA
WAREHOUSING
AND OLTP

Indexing the Database

Indexes play a major role in data warehouses, and they are particularly effective with data warehouses because the database does not undergo many changes.

But before creating a large number of indexes, you need to thoroughly understand their different types (if you don't feel comfortable with indexes, go back to Chapter 3, "Optimizing Queries"). I will give you here a few hints on how to use indexes in the VLDB environment, which you encounter in data warehouses.

Clustered Indexes

The purpose of a data warehouse is to store a huge amount of data (if you're thinking I already said that, you are right, but I think you should keep this point in mind). Choosing the right field for your clustered index is very important, given that you can only use one such index on a table.

Here are clustered index choices you should think twice about:

- Primary key
- Unique column searched frequently on a single value

In a DSS system, you'll probably have more than one index on each table, so it's a good idea to choose cases other than the two listed here for the clustered index.

The difference between a clustered and a non-clustered index on highly selective columns (few to no duplicates) is so tiny (generally one page) that you should always choose a non-clustered index. The only exception to that rule is when you have an ORDER BY or a GROUP BY clause, when clustered indexes become a great help.

If you need to sort your query on that columns, a clustered index will be helpful (if it is chosen by the Optimizer, instead of another strategy) because the data are already sorted. However, you can use that method on only one group of columns.

> **TIP**
>
> Remember covering indexes? They are what I call non-clustered indexes—a query using only the columns defined in a non-clustered index (no other columns for the table) "covers" the index. The Optimizer doesn't need to read the data pages because all the necessary data is on the index leaf level.

Now that I've told you the bad choices, I am going to talk about the good ones:

- Columns used in range queries (BETWEEN...AND, >, <, >=, <=)
- Columns sorted or grouped
- Foreign key

For the first two choices, I don't think you have any problems understanding the reasons. For the third one, the reason is obvious, too, if you have a one-to-many relationship. Remember the account balance example? If you create a clustered index on the Movement.AccountNumber column, you can be sure all the movement for a specific account will be on the same page or on contiguous pages, which decreases the amount of I/O.

Non-Clustered Indexes

From what I have just told you about clustered indexes, you probably imagine that choosing non-clustered indexes is an easy task. Don't fool yourself, though. Deciding is always difficult.

Nevertheless, deciding on a non-clustered index is always easier than a clustered index. Be careful, however; an index does not always enhance performance. Say you're running a stored procedure named find_cust_city on your data warehouse:

```
SELECT * FROM customer WHERE city = @strCityName
```

If the variable @strCityName equals Shoshone and out of 100,000 customers, only three live in Shoshone, California, a non-clustered index on City can be useful because of the value's selectivity. If the variable equals Los Angeles and 30% (30,000) of your customers live in Los Angeles, however, a table scan will be used instead of the index.

Everything depends on the selectivity of the data in the column. Non-clustered indexes are useful when the selectivity is under 15% (that means the query can eliminate more than 85% of the records). With a parameter in a stored procedure, however, the selectivity is not calculated, but read in the distribution page. In the Shoshone versus Los Angeles situation, the table's selectivity would have been too high to select the index, even for Shoshone.

So when choosing a non-clustered index, monitor your creation. Make sure you have many distinct values in the indexed field, and use the Query Analyzer or the command DBCC SHOW_STATISTICS to see whether your index is being used.

Overindexing the Databases

Since not many updates are expected to take place in a data warehouse, you have a better chance to play with indexes.

> **WARNING**
>
> Don't read the previous sentence too quickly and create indexes all over the table. You need to update your database from time to time, and the more indexes you have, the longer it takes. Also, indexes consume physical storage; the more indexes, the more disk space you use.

Assuming that we are not updating data in a data warehouse, over-indexing can lead to good results. With more indexes, the optimizer can do a better choice because it has more indexes to select from to perform a given SQL statement.

> **NOTE**
>
> Remember that SQL Server uses only one clustered index per table (except with certain OR queries), so having a lot of different indexes increases your chance of using at least one of these indexes when executing a SQL statement.

Many people are using tools such as Business Objects or Microsoft Access to query data. The problem with these tools is that you don't know what queries users are going to write. Overindexing the tables increases the the chance that an index will be used when the SQL statement is executed. However, it is better to know in advance what kind of query they will be writing (sometimes, they run the same WHERE clause or query the same cubes).

Another area you need to be careful with when indexing your table is the column order. The column order is important in deciding which index will be used by the Optimizer. Assume you created the following index:

```
CREATE INDEX ncLastFirst ON customer(Lastname, Firstname)
```

If you query the table as shown here, the ncLastFirst index will probably be used:

```
SELECT * FROM Customers WHERE Firstname='John' AND LastName='Doe'
```

Of course, if you run the query as follows, the ncLastFirst index probably won't be used because the WHERE clause does not include both fields in the index:

```
SELECT * FROM Customers WHERE Firstname='John'
```

Now if you had created the following index, the second SELECT query could have used it:

```
CREATE INDEX ncFirstLast ON customer(Firstname, Lastname)
```

It all depends on the selectivity. If the selectivity factor is 2% for John and 10% for Doe when you are looking for John Doe, the ncFirstLast index is more selective than the ncLastFirst index.

This is another example of the index's selectivity. As you can see, overindexing the tables can have surprising consequences. When you are implementing your data warehouse, always keep in mind this maxim: Increasing the number of indexes increases the Optimizer's number of choices and increases the chances you have to decrease the amount of I/O.

How to Scrub (Prepare) Data for Warehouses

Creating the physical structure must be done before loading the data. SQL Server offers many ways to load data in the data warehouse.

SQL Server 7.0 introduced a host of new services, called *Data Transformation Services* (*DTS*). DTS allows for transferring data between different data sources and a SQL Server 7.0 database using an OLE DB–based architecture. These services have wizards that make the transfer process easy and manageable. In this section, I will be briefly discussing DTS, while discussing the old ways used with SQL Server 6.5 that can still be used with the new version 7.0. Here are the different data loading transformation and/or loading methods

- The Data Transformation Services (DTS) import/export
- Bulk copy program
- INSERT and INSERT...SELECT
- Replication
- CUBE and ROLLUP
- Online triggers and batches
- ActiveX scripting

Each solution has its virtues, explained in the following sections.

Using the Data Transformation Services (DTS)

Data Transformation Services (DTS) allows you to import and export data between multiple heterogeneous sources using an OLE DB–based architecture. DTS can also be used to transform data to build a data warehouse from an OLTP system.

30

DATA
WAREHOUSING
AND OLTP

> **NOTE**
>
> DTS does not only allow you to transfer tabular data, but also allows you to transfer database objects, such as indexes and stored procedures, between different machines running Microsoft SQL Server 7.0.

Transforming the data involves three operations:

- Data import/export
- Data transformation
- Transferring data objects

The following sections cover the first two operations: data import/export and data transformation and scrubbing.

Importing and Exporting Data

The export and import wizards allow for transferring data between any data source and SQL Server 7.0, and vice versa. These wizards can also be used to transfer database objects between databases. You can access these wizards by choosing Tools, Wizards from the menu in Enterprise Manager or by clicking the Run a Wizard button on the MMC toolbar.

Transforming Data

A *transformation* is the set of operations applied to source data before it is stored at the destination. For example, DTS allows calculating new values from one or more source columns, or even breaking a single column into multiple values to be stored in separate destination columns.

Transformations make it easy to implement complex data validation, scrubbing, and enhancement during import and export.

Please refer to Books Online for detailed discussions of the DTS utilities and services.

Loading Data with bcp

The bcp tool is probably the first one you use to load data from a heterogeneous source, either alone or with DTS. The only advantage of this solution is its speed.

TIP

If you intend to regularly load data with bcp, drop all the indexes first (don't forget primary key and unique constraints), load the data, and then re-create all the indexes (beginning with the clustered index). Just to give you an idea of the speed gain: Loading 1 million records in a table with three indexes (on a height-processor parallel Sequent computer) took me 26 hours. Doing the same thing in a script, dropping the indexes, loading the data, and then re-creating indexes took me two hours!

I won't go into bcp details here; Books Online has all the necessary information for you to run bcp and learn all its case-sensitive parameters. Let's go on to more modern solutions.

Loading Data with Stored Procedures

It's possible to create stored procedure containing INSERT or SELECT...INTO statements to fill the table, either in a trigger or in a batch procedure. But the results and constraints are different whether you are on the same server or on different servers. Obviously, it is faster if you are loading data on a server with the stored procedure on the server itself than it would be if such procedures were on a different server.

Loading a Warehouse Situated on the OLTP Server

If you want to fill a table named Customer in the Warehouse database from the Customer table in the Sales database, you can use the procedure fill_warehouse_customer shown in Listing 30.4.

LISTING 30.4   CREATING A PROCEDURE FILLING A TABLE FROM ANOTHER TABLE

```
CREATE PROC fill_warehouse_customer
AS
INSERT INTO Warehouse..Customer
   SELECT * FROM Sales..Customer
   WHERE cust_insert_date = GETDATE()
```

This procedure is convenient and easy to set up, but you can do better with SQL Server 7.0. The INSERT...EXECUTE statement can be used to load a table from the result of a stored procedure. Listing 30.5 shows how to create the procedure in the Sales database.

30

DATA
WAREHOUSING
AND OLTP

LISTING 30.5 CREATING A PROCEDURE JUST BY SELECTING DATA

```
CREATE PROC select_today_customer
AS
SELECT * FROM Sales..Customer
WHERE cust_insert_date = GETDATE()
```

Now you can use this procedure from the data warehouse database, as shown in Listing 30.6.

LISTING 30.6 CALLING A PROCEDURE TO INSERT ITS RESULT IN ANOTHER TABLE

```
INSERT Warehouse..Customer
   EXECUTE Sales..select_today_customer
```

Of course, it is possible to launch this statement during off-hours or use Optimizer hints to avoid blocking problems (later on, I discuss the blocking issues between OLTP and DSS databases).

One of the main advantage of this way of loading data is that you can use it from another server with the remote stored procedure.

Loading a Data Warehouse Situated on Another Server

A remote stored procedure offers the possibility of running a procedure on another server, so you can insert the result of a stored procedure in a local server.

The only thing you need to do is configure the remote servers by choosing Server, Remote Servers from the menu. To configure Server1 and Server2 (see Figure 30.5), use the following steps.

FIGURE 30.5

Inserting locally remote results.

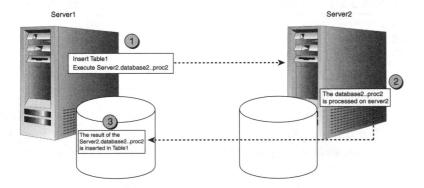

1. On Server1, declare Server2 as the remote server, either with SQL Enterprise Manager or with `sp_addlinkedserver 'server2'`.

2. On Server1, declare Server1 as the local server, either with SQL Enterprise Manager or with `sp_addlinkedserver 'server1', local`.

3. On Server2, declare Server1 as the remote server, either with SQL Enterprise Manager or with `sp_addlinkedserver 'server1'`.

4. On Server2, declare Server2 as the local server, either with SQL Enterprise Manager or with `sp_addlinkedserver 'server2', local`.

5. On Server2, map the necessary server1 logins on server2 logins. In order to do this you have to log on Server 2 with the built-in sysadmin privilege.

You can now run stored procedures (if you have the necessary rights) on Server2 from Server1.

> **WARNING**
>
> Watch the case! If you installed your server with a case-sensitive sort order (such as binary, for instance), you must declare the server names with the correct case.

> **NOTE**
>
> The stored procedure `sp_addserver` was kept in version 7.0 for backward compatibility. It is recommended that you use the new `sp_addlinkedserver` system stored procedure instead.

After you've done these operations, you can then run an INSERT...EXECUTE statement. If your Sales database is on the SalesManagement server, and your Warehouse database is on the DSS server, you can load your customer table with the query in Listing 30.6.

LISTING 30.6   CALLING A REMOTE STORED PROCEDURE TO INSERT ITS RESULT IN ANOTHER TABLE

```
INSERT Warehouse..Customer
    EXECUTE SalesManagement.Sales..select_today_customer
```

You can schedule this statement to be executed on a daily or weekly basis with SQL Executive. Nevertheless, this method has its own drawbacks. For example, how can you

30

DATA WAREHOUSING AND OLTP

update your data? Unfortunately, there is no way to use UPDATE...EXECUTE or DELETE...EXECUTE. One solution lies in replication, however.

Loading Data with Replication

Replication is probably the simplest way to regularly maintain a perfect copy of your OLTP server. Of course, a data warehouse will not fully synchronize with your OLTP databases, but usually this is not a big problem. The warehouse is generally there to help you find long-term trends, not to react to a sudden modification of data.

Replication is a perfect tool to duplicate data quickly and efficiently. The SQL Server replication is based on a publisher-subscriber metaphor. In this case, a warehouse is the subscriber of one or many publishers, as shown in Figure 30.6.

FIGURE 30.6

One subscriber (data warehouse) and many publishers.

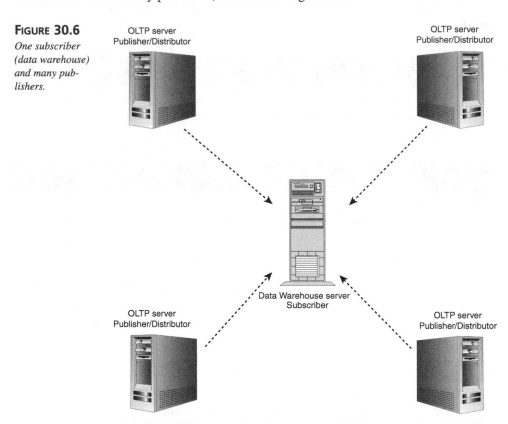

OLTP server
Publisher/Distributor

OLTP server
Publisher/Distributor

Data Warehouse server
Subscriber

OLTP server
Publisher/Distributor

OLTP server
Publisher/Distributor

The first step is scheduling replication tasks when you need them. Instead of covering the details of setting up a replication model (refer to Chapter 16, "Replication"), I'll focus on the important role the developer has in replication.

Normally, you replicate the same modification—that is, if an insert occurs on the publisher, the same insert occurs on the subscriber. Sometimes, however, the data models in the OLTP database and the warehouse are not the same. In this case, stored procedures can be effective.

It's possible to modify the original INSERT, UPDATE, and DELETE statements into stored procedures, so let's take a quick look at an example of what you can do.

When you insert a new customer in your Sales..Customer table (see Figure 30.7), you want to use replication to deal with three tables on your warehouse.

FIGURE 30.7

The
Sales..Customer
table.

CustId
CustFirstName
CustLasrMane
Address
Zip
State
City
Sex
Birth Date

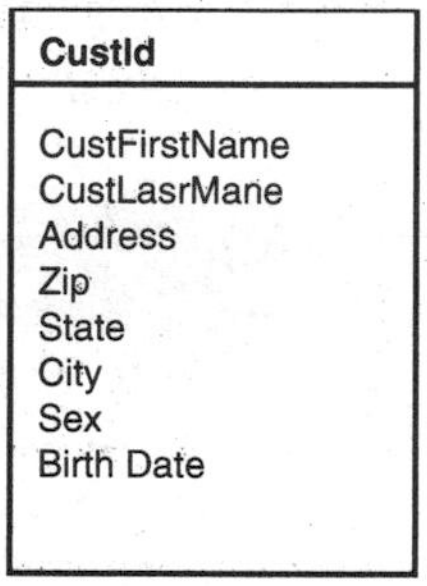

You need to dynamically calculate statistics on your customer's gender, age, and city of residence. It is possible to calculate that information when you need it (see *hypercubes* in the next section) or take advantage of stored procedures to do the operation dynamically on the subscriber.

On the subscriber side, you have the tables shown in Figure 30.8.

FIGURE 30.8

The three aggregate tables.

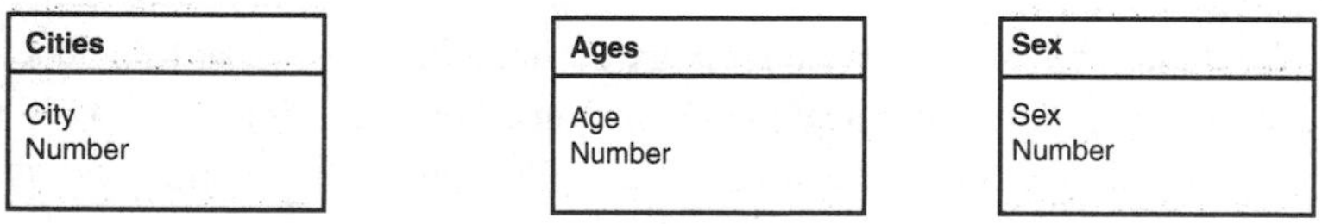

Cities		Ages		Sex
City		Age		Sex
Number		Number		Number

If you want to replicate these three tables, you can write the stored procedure shown in Listing 30.7 to update these three tables from the Sales..Customer table.

LISTING 30.7 REPLICATION STORED PROCEDURE

```
CREATE PROCEDURE update_aggregate_tables
@chvfname varchar(40), @chvlname varchar(40), @chvadd varchar(50),
@chrzip char(5),
@chrstate char(2), @chrcity varchar(20), @bitsex char(1),
```

continues

30

LISTING 30.7 CONTINUED

```
@datbirth smalldatime, @intcustid int
AS
BEGIN TRAN
    UPDATE cities
        SET number = number +1
        WHERE city = @chrcity
    UPDATE sex
        SET number = number +1
        WHERE sex = @bitsex
    UPDATE ages
        SET number = number +1
        WHERE BirthYear = RIGHT(CONVERT(char(10), @datbirth, 101),7)
COMMIT TRAN
```

> **TIP**
>
> I used the CONVERT function with the 101 parameter (a century using four digits). Remember that in a few months we change centuries. Calculating dates with two digits should be prohibited in all your programs; otherwise, you'll certainly have date-calculation problems.

This procedure has to be created in the subscriber database because it is executed on the subscriber machine.

After you've done that, in the article definition, tell SQL Server to replicate the INSERT statement with the article properties window or with the system stored procedures sp_helparticle and sp_changearticle.

Of course, you can apply the strategy outlined in this section to delete and update, too, and perform more complicated calculations. You are going to see how to perform complicated calculations in the simplest possible way with the CUBE and ROLLUP operators.

CUBE and ROLLUP Operators

The CUBE operator generates a multidimensional representation of detail and summary data in the database in the form of a multidimensional cube. A *cube* consists of a data source, dimensions, measures, and partitions. Cubes are designed based on the analytical requirements of users. The ROLLUP operator is useful in generating reports that have totals and subtotals. The resultset generated by the ROLLUP operator is similar to that generated by the CUBE operator.

The example in the previous section was a simple one because you knew how many men or women you have in your database or how many customers live in Los Angeles. If you want to know the sales for 26-year-old women living in Los Angeles, however, the task is impossible with the simple warehouse you have, so let's create a cube.

Creating the Cube

With the GROUP BY query shown in Listing 30.8, you can get a great deal of information, including data about sales for 26-year-old Los Angeles women (query results are shown in Listing 30.9).

LISTING 30.8 THE CLASSIC GROUP BY QUERY

```
SELECT city, BirthYear = RIGHT(CONVERT(char(10), BirthDate, 101),4),
            sex, Sum_sales=SUM(sales)
FROM Customer C JOIN Sales S ON C.Cust_ID = S.Cust_ID
GROUP BY city, RIGHT(CONVERT(char(10), BirthDate, 101),4), sex
```

LISTING 30.9 PARTIAL RESULTS FROM THE PRECEDING QUERY

```
city                 BirthYear sex Sum_sales
-------------------- --------- --- -------------------------
Ann Arbor            1938      0   389,78
Berkeley             1949      1   410,05
Berkeley             1965      0   413,04
Covelo               1978      1   457,90
Lawrence             1971      1   386,12
Los Angeles          1939      0   360,21
Los Angeles          1940      0   481,80
Los Angeles          1949      0   535,63
Los Angeles          1956      1   414,69
Los Angeles          1971      0   433,97
Menlo Park           1972      1   352,24
Nashville            1956      0   406,05
Oakland              1936      1   362,19
```

Fine, but what about the sales for a particular city (without birth year and sex)? You might say "Run another query," but the answer lies in Listing 30.10.

LISTING 30.10 A CUBE GROUP BY QUERY

```
SELECT city, BirthYear = RIGHT(CONVERT(char(10), BirthDate, 101),4),
      sex, Sum_sales=SUM(sales)
FROM Customer C JOIN Sales S ON C.Cust_ID = S.Cust_ID
GROUP BY city, RIGHT(CONVERT(char(10), BirthDate, 101),4), sex
WITH CUBE
```

30

DATA
WAREHOUSING
AND OLTP

The results of the query in Listing 30.10 are shown in Listing 30.11 below.

LISTING 30.11 PARTIAL RESULTS FROM THE PRECEDING QUERY

```
city                 BirthYear sex Sum_sales
-------------------- --------- --- ----------------------
Ann Arbor            1938      0    389,78
Ann Arbor            1938      (nul389,78
Ann Arbor            (null)    (nul389,78
Berkeley             (null)    1    410,05
Berkeley             (null)    (nul410,05
Berkeley             1965      0    413,04
Berkeley             1965      (nul413,04
Berkeley             (null)    (nul823,08
Covelo               1978      1    457,90
Covelo               1978      (nul457,90
Covelo               (null)    (nul457,90
Lawrence             1971      1    386,12
Lawrence             1971      (nul386,12
Lawrence             (null)    (nul386,12
Los Angeles          1939      0    360,21
Los Angeles          1939      (nul360,21
Los Angeles          1940      0    481,80
Los Angeles          1940      (nul481,80
...
Los Angeles          (null)    1    414,69
Menlo Park           (null)    1    352,24
Oakland              (null)    1    801,81
Salt Lake City       (null)    1    408,06
San Jose             (null)    1    337,29
Shoshone             (null)    1    463,55
Walnut Creek         (null)    1    894,83
(null)               (null)    1    4 926,54
```

Okay, the result is rather confusing because of the NULL values. You learned how to handle NULL values in Chapter 1, "Taking Advantage of the New Tools," but here you can have two types of NULL values. For example, if you read the third line of results in Listing 30.11, the two NULL values represent an aggregate. That line is the result of the average sales for all sales in the city of Ann Arbor. But look at the second and fifth lines for Berkeley. It seems these lines are identical. In fact, the first one represents a sale for a customer whose birthdate has not been inserted, so this birthdate is NULL (the BirthDate column accepts NULL values).

This can be rather confusing when you read the results, so you can slightly modify the query by using the GROUPING function, as shown in Listing 30.12.

LISTING 30.12 A GROUPING CUBE QUERY

```
SELECT city,
       BirthYear = RIGHT(CONVERT(char(10), BirthDate, 101),4),
       RealNull=GROUPING(RIGHT(CONVERT(char(10), BirthDate, 101),4)),
       sex, Sum_sales=SUM(sales)
FROM Customer C JOIN Sales S ON C.Cust_ID = S.Cust_ID
GROUP BY city, RIGHT(CONVERT(char(10), BirthDate, 101),4), sex
WITH CUBE
```

The results of the query in Listing 30.12 are presented in Listing 30.13 below.

LISTING 30.13 PARTIAL RESULTS FROM A GROUPING CUBE QUERY

city	BirthYear	RealNull	sex	Sum_sales
Ann Arbor	1938	0	0	389,78
Ann Arbor	1938	0	(nul	389,78
Ann Arbor	(null)	1	(nul	389,78
Berkeley	(null)	0	1	410,05
Berkeley	(null)	0	(nul	410,05
Berkeley	1965	0	0	413,04
Berkeley	1965	0	(nul	413,04
Berkeley	(null)	1	(nul	823,08
Covelo	1978	0	1	457,90
Covelo	1978	0	(nul	457,90
Covelo	(null)	1	(nul	457,90
Lawrence	1971	0	1	386,12
Lawrence	1971	0	(nul	386,12
Lawrence	(null)	1	(nul	386,12
Los Angeles	1939	0	0	360,21
Los Angeles	1939	0	(nul	360,21
Los Angeles	1940	0	0	481,80
Los Angeles	1940	0	(nul	481,80
...				
Los Angeles	(null)	1	1	414,69
Menlo Park	(null)	1	1	352,24
Oakland	(null)	1	1	801,81
Salt Lake City	(null)	1	1	408,06
San Jose	(null)	1	1	337,29
Shoshone	(null)	1	1	463,55
Walnut Creek	(null)	1	1	894,83
(null)	(null)	1	1	4 926,54

The result of the GROUPING function is 1 if the NULL value represents an aggregate and 0 if it's a real NULL value in the data. Now you know how to tell the difference between real NULL values and aggregate NULL values. A major problem remains, however; you are doing this job to create a warehouse, but who will use that warehouse? Probably not power users, but simple users, with little knowledge (or maybe none) about NULL values.

Therefore, you have to use other functions to create a readable cube. Take a look at the one in Listing 30.14 (the results of this query are presented in Listing 30.15).

LISTING 30.14   A READABLE DATACUBE

```
SELECT
City=CASE WHEN (GROUPING(city)=1) THEN 'All'
     ELSE ISNULL(city, 'Unknown')
     END,
BirthYear = CASE WHEN (GROUPING(BirthDate)=1) THEN 'All'
     ELSE ISNULL(RIGHT(CONVERT(char(10), BirthDate, 101),4),'Unknown')
     END ,
Sex = CASE WHEN (GROUPING(sex)=1) THEN 'All'
     ELSE ISNULL(sex, 'Unknown')
     END,
Sum_Sales=SUM(sales)
FROM Customer C JOIN Sales S ON C.Cust_ID = S.Cust_ID
GROUP BY city, BirthDate, sex
WITH CUBE
```

LISTING 30.15   PARTIAL RESULTS FROM THE READABLE DATACUBE

City	BirthYear	Sex	Sum_Sales
Ann Arbor	1938	0	389,78
Ann Arbor	1938	All	389,78
Ann Arbor	All	All	389,78
Berkeley	Unknown	1	410,05
Berkeley	Unknown	All	410,05
Berkeley	1965	0	413,04
Berkeley	1965	All	413,04
Berkeley	All	All	823,08
Covelo	1978	1	457,90
Covelo	1978	All	457,90
Covelo	All	All	457,90
Lawrence	1971	1	386,12
Lawrence	1971	All	386,12
Lawrence	All	All	386,12
Los Angeles	1939	0	360,21
Los Angeles	1939	All	360,21
Los Angeles	1940	0	481,80
Los Angeles	1940	All	481,80
...			
Los Angeles	All	1	414,69
Menlo Park	All	1	352,24
Oakland	All	1	801,81
Salt Lake City	All	1	408,06
San Jose	All	1	337,29
Shoshone	All	1	463,55
Walnut Creek	All	1	894,83
All	All	1	4 926,54

As you can see, you can now clearly differentiate between grouping and standard NULL values.

You can also create a stored cube with a SELECT INTO instead of a normal SELECT statement. With the new table—call it sales_cube—you can find all the sales for 26-year old women living in Los Angeles, as shown in Listing 30.16 and the results of the query in Listing 30.17.

LISTING 30.16   QUERYING THE CUBE

```
SELECT * FROM sales_cube
WHERE sex='0'
AND Birthyear=convert(char(4),DATEPART(yy, GETDATE())-26)
AND city='Los Angeles'
```

LISTING 30.17   RESULTS FROM THE PREVIOUS QUERY

City	BirthYear	Sex	Sum_Sales
Los Angeles	1971	0	433,97

Creating the cube is no problem. The problem is keeping the cube up-to-date.

Maintaining the Cube

The previous cube is a static one. If you want to update it, you need to execute the same query again, or you can maintain it. In fact, it should be updated if you update the sales table. For example, if you insert a new sale, you run the procedure shown in Listing 30.17 on the replicated INSERT statement.

LISTING 30.17   UPDATING THE CUBE IF YOU INSERT A NEW SALE

```
CREATE PROCEDURE Update_Sales_Cube @intcustid int, @mnysales money
AS
UPDATE sales_Cube SC
SET sum_sales = sum_sales + @mnysales
WHERE
 (city=ISNULL((SELECT city FROM customers WHERE cust_id=@intcustid),
 ➥'Unknown')
 OR city='All') AND
 (sex=ISNULL((SELECT sex FROM customers WHERE cust_id=@intcustid),
 ➥'Unknown')
 OR sex='All') AND
 (BirthYear=ISNULL((SELECT RIGHT(CONVERT(char(10), BirthDate, 101),7)
 FROM customers WHERE cust_id=@intcustid), 'Unknown')
 OR BirthYear='All')
```

30

DATA
WAREHOUSING
AND OLTP

This stored procedure must be created in the subscription database and used instead of the typical replicated INSERT statement. You can do the same thing for DELETE and UPDATE statements, too.

Batch Processing

The last, but not least, possibility for manipulating data in the data warehouse is using batch jobs to perform inserts, deletes, or updates. Using bcp or standard scripts is not that difficult. When you know how to use the SQL Server Agent, everything goes smoothly.

The major problem with data warehouses is the time spent to run queries, so I'll focus on that subject in the following sections to show how to transform your queries into "rocket-style" queries.

Large Queries and Performance Optimization

After you create your warehouse and set up all the necessary update procedures, people are going to start using it—which is probably the toughest part of all.

A lot of companies do not create a special querying application; instead, they use a standard tool such as business objects or Microsoft Access. The problem comes about because you do not know what data is going to be queried. It becomes important to create access paths with views or stored procedure, but you should be aware of what happens when you use them.

> **NOTE**
>
> Business Objects is a third-party tool used to perform online analytical processing (OLAP) of data in the data warehouse. Microsoft Access is a desktop database program with a graphical user interface (GUI) that allows you to produce summary reports. However, Microsoft Access cannot handle the amount of data available in large data warehouses, so it is not recommended for this purpose.

> **NOTE**
>
> Microsoft SQL Server 7.0 includes the Pivot Table service used in Microsoft Excel as part of the OLAP services. It can be used to provide offline data analysis, cube building, and data manipulation. This service also provides connectivity to OLE DB–compliant providers and non-OLAP relational data sources. The Pivot Table service can be used with SQL Server 7.0 and 6.5, and with MS Access and Oracle 7.x and 8.x.

Querying Data

In the previous section, you saw how to create the warehouse and datacubes. When users try to query these data, you want to avoid having them wait hours and hours for the results.

Analyzing the Query

The Query Analyzer gives you vital information for deciding which indexes to use. Chapter 3, "Optimizing Queries," has a good overview of what can be done with the Optimizer. When it comes to data warehouses, it's important to know the limits and optimize your query manually.

I won't talk about index choices here (go back a few pages to the "Indexing the Database" section), but about table order. The Optimizer is optimizing join order with four-table groups. Let's say, for instance, that you have the following query:

```
SELECT C1, C2, C3, C4
FROM T1, T2, T3, T4, T5
WHERE ...
```

With this query, the system optimizes the join between tables T1, T2, T3, and T4 and then optimizes the results of the previous join with T5. As far as large volume sets are concerned, that can be a catastrophe.

Take a look at an example of what to do. In your warehouse, you have five tables: customers, sales, sales_details, products, and suppliers. One of your users needs to query these five tables to find a possible correlation between the product suppliers and the city your customers live in.

The WHERE clause is city='Los Angeles' and product_name='New P1'. In the FROM clause, the user declares the tables in this order: customers, suppliers, sales, sales_details, products. The Optimizer chooses to join the first four tables, and then joins the results with the products table.

However, the products table is referenced in the WHERE clause. With that order, the system extracts the customers, suppliers, and sales information for the city of Los Angeles (that can result in a lot of information), and then joins that result with the products table.

If you write the FROM clause as customers, products, suppliers, sales, sales_details, the Optimizer reduces the number of rows for the first four-table join because of the WHERE clause. The query will be quicker, and the user more satisfied.

So when analyzing a query with the Show Query Plan check box enabled in the Connection Options dialog box (see Figure 30.9), have a look at the table order and try to change it to more than four tables. With fewer than four tables, don't bother with it.

FIGURE 30.9

The current Connection Options dialog box in the Query Analyzer.

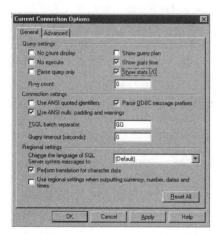

You can also enable the SET FORCEPLAN option to force the table order, but this isn't a good technique. Nobody knows data distribution better than SQL Server (if the statistics are up-to-date, of course), so it is better to disable that option and create a four-table group function with the WHERE clause.

Optimizer Hints

Optimizer hints are modifications you can make to the Optimizer's behavior for choosing indexes, selecting locks, and getting the first row quickly. These hints are done in the SQL code. Because little update activity usually goes on in the data warehouse, update hints aren't discussed here.

> **TIP**
>
> If you want to speed your SELECT query, you shouldn't use locks. You have three ways to do that: use the NOLOCK option, specify TRANSACTION ISOLATION LEVEL READ UNCOMMITTED, or set the database to read-only. Remember, though, that this tip applies just to read-only data warehouses.

In a warehouse, you are mainly concerned with crucial index choices and getting the first row as fast as possible.

INDEX (index1, index2, ...)

The INDEX hint is used to force the Optimizer to use a specific index or a table scan. Normally, the Optimizer knows its job, but sometimes this hint can be useful because the Optimizer can occasionally make mistakes. Nevertheless, always check your choice with STATISTICS IO and STATISTICS TIME which will give you useful information on the execution path of the query and which indexes, if any, have been used.

Option (Fast n)

In SQL Server 6.5, the FASTFIRSTROW hint allowed using the non-clustered index to find the first row quickly, even with a clustered index on your table. Although it's left in SQL Server 7.0 for backward compatibility, Microsoft recommends porting the code that uses it to the new SELECT option: (fast n).

Views

You can use views like tables to take advantage of Optimizer hints on complex queries. Views are particularly useful with more than four-table queries or with datacubes. Take a look at the view used in Listing 30.18.

LISTING 30.18   VIEW OF A DATACUBE

```
CREATE VIEW Sales_cube
AS
SELECT
CASE WHEN (GROUPING(city)=1) THEN 'All'
    ELSE ISNULL(city, 'Unknown')
    END,
BirthYear = CASE WHEN (GROUPING(BirthDate)=1) THEN 'All'
    ELSE ISNULL(RIGHT(CONVERT(char(10), BirthDate, 101),4),'Unknown')
    END ,
```

continues

30

DATA
WAREHOUSING
AND OLTP

LISTING 30.18 CONTINUED

```
CASE WHEN (GROUPING(sex)=1) THEN 'All'
     ELSE ISNULL(sex, 'Unknown')
     END,
Sum_Sales=SUM(sales)
FROM Customer C JOIN Sales S ON C.Cust_ID = S.Cust_ID
GROUP BY city, BirthDate, sex
WITH CUBE
```

This view is equivalent to the the last cube you built. You could use Optimizer hints to speed up the selection of data.

Stored Procedures

For querying warehouses, stored procedures can be used to create complicated SELECT queries, with or without cursors. The main point is to get fast results, and sometimes a quick recompilation is necessary.

Parameters and Recompilation

The recompilation of stored procedures i should be carefully considered with warehouses because of the huge amount of data. Imagine that the customer table has 10 million rows and a non-clustered index on the column Cust_id; you then create the procedure in Listing 30.19.

LISTING 30.19 A PROCEDURE THAT NEEDS TO BE RECOMPILED

```
CREATE PROCEDURE List_Customers @intcustid int
AS
SELECT * FROM Customer
WHERE Cust_id > @intcustid
```

If the first user runs the procedure with @intcustid = 9,999,999, the execution plan in the procedure cache uses the non-clustered index, and the answer is fast. If the second user runs the procedure with @intcustid = 100, he or she will use the plan created for the first user. In that case, however, a table scan would have been smarter and would have been calculated if the procedure had been recompiled.

Remember, the recompilation concerns only the optimization and the creation of the execution plan. In a data warehouse, because the number of manipulated rows is generally important, you should test your procedure with different values of parameters and with SET SHOWPLAN ALL or SET SHOWPLAN TEXT, to see whether a different execution plan can be generated. If so, then create your procedure by using the WITH RECOMPILE option.

> **TIP**
>
> Use the WITH RECOMPILE option when stored procedures take parameters that vary widely in value between executions, which might result in varying execution plans each time.

> **CAUTION**
>
> Always use the WITH COMPILE option with care. Using it forces stored procedures to be recompiled every time they are run, which results in slower execution time.

Warehouse Maintenance Tasks

A data warehouse is, first of all, a database, so you need to program maintenance tasks to have a fully secure and optimized system. I recommend programming the following tasks:

- Create all indexes by using the REPLACE EXISTING option of the CREATE INDEX statement every week.

- Run UPDATE STATISTICS every day, especially after loading data in the data warehouse.

- Run the system stored procedure sp_recompile for all the user's stored procedures and triggers every day, after running UPDATE STATISTICS.

- Perform DUMP TRANSACTION every day (if you dynamically update the database with replication or remote stored procedures).

- Perform the DBCC commands DBCC CHECKDB, NEWALLOC, and CHECKCATALOG every day.

- Perform DUMP DATABASE every week.

All these tasks have already been described in detail in other chapters. Nevertheless, the first two are particularly important on a huge dataset because if your indexes are not up-to-date, you can't expect good performances.

This section ends the discussion of data warehouses in SQL Server 7.0. However, there is still a great deal of information to cover. Actually, you could write a book on the new OLAP, DTS, and data warehousing features in SQL Server 7.0, but let's move on to a more dynamic topic: online transaction systems.

30

DATA WAREHOUSING AND OLTP

SQL Server and OLTP Systems

An OLTP (online transaction processing) system is characterized by many transactions per second. The Transaction Processing Council (TPC at: www.tpc.org) offers benchmarks for transaction systems. According to these benchmarks, SQL Server is now one of the fastest and cheapest transaction systems.

OLTP Issues

The main characteristics of an OLTP system are the following:

- Small, fast transactions
- A large number of transactions per second
- Very selective queries
- Fastest possible response time and best possible throughput

Of course, what a developer should have in mind while developing such a system is creating queries that are as fast as possible. Remember to write down the expected response times and throughput. Developers should have a comparison scale. Saying "as fast as possible" is not specific enough, but "less than half a second" is measurable.

Creating the Database

An OLTP database is generally quite different from a DSS database. Generally, that kind of database is in third normal form because you try to update, insert, or delete data, not read huge amounts of it.

In the following sections, therefore, you're going to see examples of normalized versus denormalized transactional databases and study the impact of row width on I/O and updating speed.

Normal Forms and OLTP

When you put your database in third normal form, you don't have data redundancy, so updating data has to be done in only one place.

In the database example in Figure 30.3, you don't need to make other updates if you have to insert a new movement. The insert operation has the chance to be fast. If you denormalize the database for DSS purposes, as in Figure 30.3, for each insert operation, you need to calculate the balance for each account if you want the data to be consistent. The insert operation, then, is slowed down by updating the account table, even if the table is updated by a trigger.

Of course, unless the database has to be operational on a 24/7 basis, this update can be done during an off-hour batch operation. In that case, the denormalization is not painful for transaction operations, but users should be aware that some data are updated off-hours, so they might encounter temporary inconsistencies.

For example, say the balance for account #101 is $1,000, and you credit $1,000 more to this account. If the balance is updated off-hours, the balance is still $1,000, not $2,000, as it should have been if it were updated immediately.

The first rule of an OLTP system is to minimize the length of transactions. Following this rule will minimize the impact of locks.

Row Width and Page Splitting

It seems as though if a row is small, the insert is quicker than for a large row. This is not always true, however, because it depends on the type of update/insert operation.

Unlike DSS systems, the row width has little influence on the speed of the transaction because the extracted recordsets are relatively small. However, like DSS systems, the impact of row width on page splitting remains in OLTP systems.

> **NOTE**
>
> Page splitting happens when a new row has to be inserted and there is not enough space on a non-clustered index page to accommodate the new entry. In this case, half the rows in the full index page move to a new page to make room for the new entry. Page splitting can have adverse performance implications and cause table fragmentation. It is important to note that data pages splitting is seldom in SQL Server 7.0 due to the larger page size (8KB).

If you have a clustered index and all the inserts are done at the end of the database, you don't need to be concerned with page splitting. But what happens if you have a non-clustered index and inserts or updates take place all over the table? The answer is that pages split.

When inserting a new record, if there is not enough space in the page for this record, the page splits; half the record stays in one place, and the other half goes to the new page.

The page allocation can take a long time, especially if the page has to be allocated on a new extent, so it is a good idea to try to avoid it. To do so, create a clustered index with a fill factor. If you had created the table with a clustered index and a fill factor value of 50, there would have been space in the page to insert the new row without splitting the page.

The second rule of an OLTP database, therefore, is to leave space in the pages by using a fill factor during indexing and reindexing the table to avoid page splitting.

Indexing the Database

Indexing an OLTP database is an important part of creating an application. Too many indexes slow down the updates, inserts, and deletes, but too few of them slow down selections. You have to find a compromise.

Clustered Indexes

Remember, with data warehouses, you can have only one clustered index per page, so choose it carefully. Usually, your worst enemy in an OLTP application is a clustered index, but you can come to consider it your best friend.

The clustered index is sorting data physically. If your data is equally spread among the table and equally inserted in the table, you'll probably see page splitting. If your inserts come only at the end of the table, however, everything runs smoothly. I have not said that all inserts should be done at the end of the table, but it's a good rule of thumb. The clustered index should be reserved for foreign keys and/or columns used in range queries. You can reduce page splitting by using the fill factor, especially because hard disk space is now cheaper than ever. That means you can avoid page splitting even in non-leaf index pages, so why bother with reserving your clustered index to insert rows at the end of the table?

Of course, if you are always inserting at the end of the table without any updates at all (as in accounting applications, SAP/R3, or BAAN), create your clustered index with a fill factor of 100.

Non-Clustered Indexes

Updating a non-clustered is more expensive than a clustered index because of the number of levels involved. It's interesting to set STATISTICS IO to ON during your test to see the number of pages accessed and updated by your statement. In fact, the more indexes you have, the more updates have to be done.

Reserve your non-clustered indexes for exact queries on unique (or almost unique) values and for primary keys. If you can avoid non-clustered indexes, you'll speed the update operations.

Right-Indexing the Databases

Right-indexing an OLTP database, as I have said, is a difficult task, but you should make a precise CRUD analysis to determine how useful the indexing will be. In fact, for each stored procedure you are going to write (you should always use stored procedures in OLTP applications, as explained in the section "Transactions," later in this chapter), you should follow these steps to test the usefulness of indexes:

> **NOTE**
>
> CRUD analysis is an acronym used to refer to analysis done using Create, Read, Update, and Delete queries. The purpose of such analysis is usually to study performance and locking issues.

1. Write down the results of logical reads for your procedure.

2. Study the search arguments and the join arguments of your query and create indexes on each of them. Overindex if you feel it is necessary (even create different indexes on the same columns).

3. Run your procedure, and write down the number of logical reads and the indexes used.

4. Drop all the unused indexes.

5. Run your procedure again, and check that the number of logical reads is less than the number you got in the first step.

6. Check the effect of the new indexes on all the other stored procedures. If they slowed the other procedures down dramatically, decide whether to drop them.

Of course, these steps are long and arduous, but that's the price you pay for a good design of your indexes. Nevertheless, an OLTP application is a compromise, but the first goal to reach is excellent response time and throughput.

So the third rule for OLTP applications is create only useful indexes and drop all the others.

Transactions

Transactions are the muscle of your OLTP application! If your transactions are well written on a well-designed database, your project will be a complete success.

I won't go into details on writing transactions (refer back to Chapter 3), but in the following sections will focus on special transaction traps you can encounter while developing an OLTP application.

Writing Efficient Transactions

First of all, always remember the fourth rule of OLTP applications: Keep transactions short—the shorter, the better. What do I mean by short? The amount of time between a BEGIN TRAN and the associated COMMIT or ROLLBACK, not necessarily the number of lines. For instance, a single update on 10 million rows is longer than 10 updates on one row (the locking and isolation level can have a noticeable effect on transactions, which I will discuss in a moment).

As a rule of thumb, remember that keeping your transaction as short as possible is the first step to writing efficient transactions.

Nested Transactions

SQL Server offers the possibility of nesting transactions. You can create up to 16 levels of transactions.

> **WARNING**
>
> Remember that triggers can count in the number of nested transactions. Therefore, you should know precisely what triggers you have and whether they increase the number of nested transactions.

Nested transactions can be useful because you can develop small, fast transactions, nesting them to create larger transactions. Take a look at the stored procedure in Listing 30.20, for example.

LISTING 30.20 A CLASSIC UPDATING STORED PROCEDURE

```
CREATE PROCEDURE update_customer
@intcustid integer, @chvcity varchar(25)
AS
DECLARE @chvoldcity varchar(25)
BEGIN TRAN
    SELECT @chvoldcity=city FROM customers WHERE cust_id=@intcustid
    UPDATE customer SET city=@chvcity WHERE cust_id=@intcustid
    UPDATE cities SET number=number-1 WHERE city=@chvoldcity
    UPDATE cities SET number=number+1 WHERE city=@chvcity
COMMIT TRAN
```

You can then run the script shown in Listing 30.21.

LISTING 30.21 NESTING PROCEDURE IN A TRANSACTION

```
BEGIN TRAN
     EXEC update_customer 12234, 'Walnut Creek'
     INSERT sales DEFAULT VALUES
COMMIT TRAN
```

This is a convenient way to do update/insert/delete operations. What seemed a short transaction in Listing 30.21 is in fact longer because of the nested transaction in the stored procedure. The nesting can cause the system to slow down. If that happens, there's a way to track problems, covered in the following section.

Correcting Slow Transactions

What I call a slow transaction is one that doesn't complete in the time requested. If the user asks for one to finish in less than half a second and it takes more than two seconds to run, it's a slow transaction.

The first step to correct that slowness is to identify whether locks are involved. To do that, set the `single user` option on and then run the transaction. You should notice whether it is faster. If not, this transaction doesn't have a locking or concurrency problem. If it is as fast as lighting, it is probably a locking problem.

For the moment, it is important to know what's happening. Unfortunately, SQL Server doesn't offer a procedure call stack, so you have to track the different procedure calls with the `PRINT` statement.

TIP

The following stored procedure can be used to calculate the number of minutes, seconds, and milliseconds between two `datetime` variables (this function is not totally accurate to the millisecond, but it gives you a fairly accurate idea of execution time):

```
CREATE PROCEDURE MinSecMil @start datetime, @end datetime,
     @chvresults varchar(9) OUTPUT

AS
DECLARE @intmin int, @intsec int, @intmil int, @intint int
SELECT @intint=DATEDIFF(ms, @start, @end)
SELECT @intmil= @intint % 1000
SELECT @intsec= ((@intint-@intmil)/1000) % 60
SELECT @intmin= (@intint-@intmil-(@intsec*1000))/60000
SELECT @chvresults=CONVERT(varchar(2), @intmin) + ":" + CONVERT
➥(varchar(2), @intsec) + ":" + CONVERT(varchar(3), @intmil)
```

30

DATA WAREHOUSING AND OLTP

The statements in Listing 30.22 can be inserted in procedures and triggers while debugging.

LISTING 30.22 DEBUGGING STATEMENTS

```
DECLARE @dtmstart datetime, @chvduration varchar(9)
PRINT "Entering procedure¦trigger procname"
PRINT "Transaction count: "
PRINT convert(varchar(2), @@TRANCOUNT)
SELECT @dtmstart=GETDATE()
…
EXEC MinSecMil @dtmstart, GETDATE(), @chvduration OUTPUT
PRINT @chvduration
PRINT "Exiting procedure¦trigger procname"
```

After you know all the procedure and trigger calls for a single procedure, you can test each procedure or trigger individually with STATISTICS IO and STATISTICS TIME turned on, and find the weakest one.

In all the cases I encountered and audited, the problem was not the number of nested transactions, but a slow transaction caused by lack of indexing. Adding or modifying an existing index has always been the solution. In some cases, however, you need to consider the database's design.

Distributed Transactions

Distributed computing is an important and complex subject. When we talk about distributed transactions, we generally refer to a two-phase commit.

Chapter 4, "Advanced Transact-SQL Statements," introduced distributed transactions and the Distributed Transaction Coordinator (DTC). One important benefit of distributed transaction with SQL Server 7.0 is the great ease in performing tasks. All you need to know is how to call a remote stored procedure and to use BEGIN DISTRIBUTED TRAN instead of BEGIN TRAN.

DTC was an interesting concept that has been the basis of Microsoft Transaction Server (MTS). A entire book could be written on Microsoft Transaction Server, but what you need to know about it is the incredible simplicity of creating distributed transactions. In fact, if you know how to create an ActiveX DLL, you almost know how to write a Transaction Server package.

Microsoft Transaction Server is the cornerstone for three-tier multi-database provider applications. If this product interests you, I suggest you surf the www.microsoft.com\transactions Web site. Also, refer back to Chapter 26, "Microsoft Transaction Server," for more information on MTS.

Locking

Locks are a major concern in OLTP applications. With a lot of transactions, you have a lot of locks, so there are potential blocking problems. You should know all the types of locks, their potential blocking problems, and the way to correct them if they occur.

Please note that lock modes, granularity, and ANSI transaction isolation levels are explained in Chapter 3.

Identifying and Correcting Blocking Problems

If you don't know about lock types and modes, and their use with transactions, you might want to revisit Chapter 3 before continuing with this section.

First of all, blocking doesn't mean a deadlock. For example, try running the two queries in Listing 30.23 in two different connections (you can try it using the Query Analyzer).

LISTING 30.23 LOCKING QUERY

Query 1

```
BEGIN TRAN
    UPDATE customer SET city = 'Walnut Creek' WHERE cust_id=12234
```

Query 2

```
BEGIN TRAN
    UPDATE customer SET city = 'Shoshone' WHERE cust_id=12235
COMMIT TRAN
```

If you run Query 1 and then Query 2, Query 2 waits indefinitely for a lock. The problem is that Query 1 has not committed or rolled back its transaction, so an exclusive lock remains on the page. If the rows for customers 12234 and 12235 are on the same page, and a page lock is in place, Query 2 waits for the exclusive lock to be released. There is no timeout on the lock, so Query 2 waits until the administrator kills the connection or the users abort the transaction.

This blocking problem is frequent in OLTP systems, caused by a missing COMMIT or ROLLBACK statement or by bad programming techniques.

TIP

If you want to check whether you have all the associated COMMIT and ROLLBACK statements, use the @@TRANCOUNT global variable. After the last COMMIT or ROLLBACK, the value of this variable should be 0. If it is 1 (or more), you forgot one (or more) COMMIT or ROLLBACK.

30

DATA WAREHOUSING AND OLTP

A common mistake is to separate the BEGIN TRAN and the COMMIT statements and associate them with different buttons on the user's screen. But what happens if that user takes a coffee break or lunch break? The system hangs until he or she clicks the commit button. If you decide to use this somewhat dangerous strategy, always add a timer. If the user is not doing anything after a few minutes, roll back the transaction to release the locks. Nevertheless, I don't think this strategy is a good one for OLTP systems.

If you have a blocking problem, you can track it with SQL Enterprise Manager or with the stored procedures sp_lock2 and sp_who, as shown in Listing 30.24.

LISTING 30.24   sp_who AND PARTIAL RESULTS

```
sp_who
spid   status      loginame      hostname         blk    dbname      cmd
------ ----------  ------------  --------------   -----  ----------  ----------
-----
1      sleeping    sa                             0      master      MIRROR
HANDLER
2      sleeping    sa                             0      master      LAZY WRITER
3      sleeping    sa                             0      master      CHECKPOINT
SLEEP
4      sleeping    sa                             0      master      RA MANAGER
10     sleeping    sa            P133MARC         0      master      AWAITING
COMMAND
...
14     sleeping    sa            P133MARC         0      Receiver    AWAITING
COMMAND
15     sleeping    sa            P133MARC         14     Receiver    UPDATE
16     runnable    sa            P133MARC         0      Receiver    SELECT
```

These results indicate (thanks to the blk columns) that process #15 is blocked by process #14. You can use the procedure sp_lock2 to determine what kind of lock is causing the block. This procedure gives you the the table and database name involved in the block. You can, then, use the DBCC INPUTBUFFER(*spid*) statement to know what statement has been issued by the blocking process (or you can use SQL Trace, if the trace has been activated).

> **NOTE**
>
> DBCC INPUTBUFFER displays the last statement sent from a client to the SQL Server.

> **WARNING**
>
> If the statement has been handled by the SQL Server RPC manager, it won't appear with the DBCC INPUTBUFFER statement. This is particularly true when using dbrpcexec() with DB-Library and SQLPrepare(), SQLBindParameter(), and SQLExecDirect() with ODBC.

Of course, the answer to blocking problems is row locking. Although SQL Server 7.0 implements row locking, it is a good habit to keep the transactions as short as possible.

Insert-Row Locking

Row locking was introduced for insert operations in SQL Server 6.5. In SQL Server 7.0, the default locking level is row locking with the possibility of promoting the locks to the level of page, table, and so on. Row locking can minimize trouble if a lot of inserts occur at the same time. It's common to have many inserts at one time in OLTP applications.

Deadlocks

Deadlock is an infinite blocking problem. SQL Server handles deadlocks automatically, but don't think you don't have to worry about them. They can kill your application performance. It is important for you to make a clear difference between blocking and deadlocking, so let's take a look at the types of deadlocks first, and then discuss the ways to handle or avoid them.

The Two Types of Deadlocks

You can have two types of deadlocks in SQL Server:

- **Cycle deadlock**   Occurs when a transaction owns an exclusive lock and wants to acquire another exclusive lock held by a transaction trying to get the first held lock.
- **Conversion deadlock**   Occurs when a transaction owns a shared lock and needs to acquire an exclusive lock.

These two types of deadlocks, explained in more detail in the following sections, can occur with page, table, or even row locks.

Cycle Deadlocks

A cycle deadlock is the classic, most well-known type of deadlock. Try the two queries in Listing 30.25 in two different connections.

LISTING 30.25 PROVOKING A CYCLE DEADLOCK

Query 1

```
WHILE 1=1
BEGIN TRAN
    UPDATE customer SET city='Walnut Creek' WHERE cust_id=12234
    WAITFOR DELAY '00:00:02'
    UPDATE sales SET amount='100' WHERE sales_id='6789'
COMMIT TRAN
```

Query 2

```
WHILE 1=1
BEGIN TRAN
    UPDATE sales SET amount='100' WHERE sales_id='6789'
    WAITFOR DELAY '00:00:02'
    UPDATE customer SET city='Walnut Creek' WHERE cust_id=12234
COMMIT TRAN
```

> **NOTE**
>
> The WAITFOR statement is here only to speed up the occurrence of the deadlock. Without the WAITFOR, the deadlock will still happen.

One of the two queries is killed, producing the 1205 error, shown in Listing 30.26.

LISTING 30.26 1205 ERROR MESSAGE

```
(Msg 1205, Level 13, State 1)

Your server command (process id #5) was deadlocked with another
process and has been chosen as a deadlock victim. Rerun your command.
```

The other query finishes normally. So when a deadlock is detected, SQL Server kills the query that has closed the circle—that is, the query that has asked for the lock that provoked the deadlock. This is because each one of the two transactions uses the tables in a different order, possibly acquiring locks before the other.

> **NOTE**
>
> In SQL Server 4.x and 6.0, SQL Server killed the query owned by the process that consumed less CPU time. That algorithm has been abandoned in SQL Server 6.5 and 7.0.

Conversion Deadlocks

The other type of deadlock is more subtle. With the conversion deadlock, the deadlock occurs because the two transactions hold a shared lock on the same resource and cannot transform it into exclusive locks for the UPDATE statement because they are both waiting for each other to release the resource.

Avoiding Deadlocks

Experiencing deadlocks is never pleasant, so you should always try to avoid them. Some possible solutions are discussed in the following sections.

> **NOTE**
>
> Many people think that row locking is the solution to deadlocking, but deadlocks occur with row locking. Imagine having row locking on an update operation. If a transaction needs to update two records on the same page, it needs to acquire two row locks. Meanwhile, another transaction needs to acquire the same locks, but in reverse order. The deadlocks could have been avoided with a page lock—so row locking is not the solution to all deadlocks.

Cycle Deadlock Solutions

Cycle deadlocks occur when two transactions access at least two resources in reverse order. The main solution to this kind of deadlock is to always access resources in the same order throughout the transaction.

It is crucial to define the access order of tables at the beginning of the project. If all the procedures access the tables in the same order, you can almost completely eliminate cycle deadlocks.

Conversion Deadlock Solutions

Conversion deadlock occurs with the Serializable or Repeatable read isolation level. In fact, with these levels, the shared locks are held until the end of the transactions. You have two possibilities to avoid that kind of deadlock. The first is to use another isolation level, if possible. The second is to ask for an update lock, as shown in Listing 30.27.

LISTING 30.27 AVOIDING CONVERSION DEADLOCKS

```
SET TRANSACTION ISOLATION LEVEL SERIALIZABLE
WHILE 1=1
```

continues

30

DATA
WAREHOUSING
AND OLTP

LISTING 30.27 CONTINUED

```
BEGIN TRAN
    SELECT * FROM customer (UPDLOCK) WHERE cust_id=12234
    WAITFOR DELAY '00:00:02'
    UPDATE customer SET city='Walnut Creek' WHERE cust_id=12234
COMMIT TRAN
```

The update lock is incompatible with another update lock, so if the same two transactions run at the same time, the first one that acquires the update lock blocks the others (but no deadlock occurs) until the commit, and then the other one runs normally.

> **WARNING**
>
> Always place the lock hint between square brackets; otherwise, SQL Server will think it is a table alias.

Handling Deadlocks

You cannot always avoid deadlocks, so you should prepare your code to handle the 1205 error.

> **WARNING**
>
> You can't test the 1205 error in Transact-SQL because following a deadlock, the process is killed by the system. You need to test it client-side.

You can decide what to do in case of deadlock. Listing 30.28 shows a possible Visual Basic error handler.

LISTING 30.28 DEADLOCK ERROR HANDLER

```
Error_Handler:
    If rdoErrors(0).Number=1205 Then
        intNbErr = intNbErr + 1
        If intNbErr<10 then
            Resume 'Restart the stored procedure call
        Else
            Msgbox "The update fails, please reexecute it later !"
            Exit sub
        End If
    End If
```

In this example, I inserted a retry counter and decided to stop rerunning the procedure if the system got the 1205 error ten times. You can modify this error handler to handle more cases, but remember to always include a 1205 error handler in your OLTP applications.

> **TIP**
>
> If you are writing your application in C/C++, you'll find an error handler already written for you in SQL Server Books Online.

Optimizing SQL Server as an OLTP System

After you have the idea (or the project) to create an OLTP database, you should configure your system as described in the following sections, monitor it, and follow the transaction checklist to see whether you forgot something.

Transaction Checklist

Use the following checklist for all transactions and tables in your system:

1. **Keep your transaction short**. Place variable declarations, loops, and so forth outside the transaction and keep it as short as possible. If it can be shortened, shorten it.

2. **Use a fill factor**. Use a fill factor to leave space for inserts and updates in pages, thus avoiding page splits.

3. **Create only the useful indexes and drop all the others**. Indexes are useful for finding and selecting data, but they slow down updates, so keep only the ones that speed up queries. All the others should be dropped.

4. **Always use the correct isolation level**. If you don't need Repeatable Read or Serializable, don't use them; otherwise, you'll overuse your shared locks. If you need this isolation level, think of update locks.

5. **Define table access order**. Always accessing tables in the same order lowers the possibility of cycle deadlocks dramatically.

6. **Always test deadlocks**. Testing and handling deadlocks allows you to rerun a killed transaction without any message to the end user.

Following all these rules doesn't guarantee you a fast, reliable application, however. You may still need to modify certain configuration options, as shown in the next section.

30

DATA WAREHOUSING AND OLTP

Configuration Options

Although SQL Server can adjust most of the configuration options, some of them can be checked and modified to produce the best response time and throughput.

Fill Factor

The ability of modifying the fill factor value ensures that you will create your indexes with what you think is the correct fill factor after you perform a long analysis. Nevertheless, I prefer asking for a particular fill factor with CREATE INDEX or DBCC DBREINDEX statements, instead of setting the same fill factor for all indexes.

max async IO

My advice is to use excellent I/O subsystems (controller and disks). With Mylex or Compaq controllers, you can set higher values, thus improving the I/O throughput. Values above 20 are typical of such controllers.

Recovery Interval

The recovery interval option indicates the frequency of the cache flushing to disk. If that operation happens too often, the overall performance will suffer because of the amount of physical I/O. The default is 5 minutes. In fact, the 5 minutes are evaluated from the number of transaction log records. The system estimates that each record requires 10 ms to be redone. So a recovery interval of 5 minutes equals 30,000 ($5 \times 60 \times 1000/10$) transaction log records.

On an OLTP system, with an average of 200 transactions per second, the physical checkpoint occurs every 2.5 minutes. If you have 100MB of memory dedicated to SQL Server and a maximum physical throughput of 10Mbit/second (typical practical throughput for SCSI systems), the cache flushing requires 80 seconds. That means that every two and a half minutes, the I/O subsystem hangs for more than a minute.

Unless you want to stick with the self-configuring option for the recovery interval, you need to think about giving a higher value to the recovery interval in heavy transaction systems. Values above 60 are generally good ones, if you have a good backup strategy and an UPS on your server.

Physical Data Repartition

If you need to increase the capacity of your I/O subsystems, I recommend the following hardware:

- Raid 5 for data: Excellent reading performance and protection against one media failure.

- Raid 1 for transaction logs: Excellent writing performance and protection against one media failure. If possible, use disk duplexing instead of simple mirroring.

If you set the correct value for the recovery interval, you won't have a lot of writing on your data; all the updates are done in data cache. However, the transaction log writing is almost continuous (especially in heavy-transaction systems). If the log is on its own disk, the disk heads are not moving away between two log writes, so the I/O subsystem is fully optimized.

Monitoring Performance

Every modification you make to your system should be monitored. You have different tools to monitor your system performance, from DBCC to Windows NT Performance Monitor.

The following sections give you some hints on what to monitor and what to do.

Memory and Procedure Cache

It is important to monitor the cache hit ratio and the procedure cache to get a clear idea of how memory is used. The *cache hit ratio* indicates the possibility of finding data in memory instead of reading it from disk. It should always be above 80. You can monitor it with the Windows NT Performance Monitor (object: SQL Server; counter: cache hit ratio) or by using DBCC SQLPERF(LRUSTATS). If you have an average cache hit ratio that's under 70, try to increase the memory allocated to SQL Server, add more memory, or check that procedure cache is not overallocated.

Input/Output

It is recommended to minimize the use of disk and maximize the use of the physical memory. You monitor the effectiveness of the memory with the cache hit ratio, but you need to check that you don't overuse the disk either.

30

DATA
WAREHOUSING
AND OLTP

First of all, you should know the physical limits of your I/O subsystem. As a rule of thumb, I use the 10Mbits/sec value as an average throughput for SCSI systems. Then you can measure the effective throughput.

You should try to lower the number of batch writes (object: SQL Server, counter I/O – batch writes/s) or use DBCC SQLPERF(LOGSPACE). That value should always be 0 except during cache flushing. Increasing the recovery interval decreases the frequency of cache flushing. During cache flushing, you probably want to increase the overall throughput. Increasing the max async IO (with a good I/O subsystem) can have a positive effect on the throughput.

Transactions Configuration Options

You probably want to know how many transactions per second your system is able to manage. You can monitor this value with Windows NT Performance Monitor (object: SQL Server; counter: I/O – Transaction/s.) or by using DBCC SQLPERF(LOGSPACE). Of course, the higher, the better; there is no perfect value. Remember, this is not really the number of transactions per second, but the number of batches per second.

You can monitor a lot of other counters, but the ones I discussed are the most important ones for OLTP databases.

Summary

Saying that you now know everything you should know about data warehouse and OLTP systems with SQL Server wouldn't be true, but you do know enough to create good applications. Of course, you'll probably discover new things on the road to creating your own applications.

For data warehouses, you have discovered that indexing plays a major role in performance. As far as SQL Server goes, it offers good features for Decision Support Systems, such as remote stored procedures, INSERT...SELECT statements, replication, and the CUBE statement. With CUBE and ROLLUP, you can prepare multidimensional datacubes with only one query.

In an OLTP application, response time and overall throughput play the most important role. With optimizer and lock hints, you can modify the behavior of queries and increase performance dramatically. You have also discovered the tools for avoiding and handling blocking and deadlocking problems.

Appendixes

APPENDIX A

The System Tables of the Master Database

You cannot develop applications on SQL Server 7.0 without a good knowledge of the system tables. This appendix gives you a quick reference for the system tables of the Master database. I chose a logical and nonalphabetical order for the tables, grouping them as login, database, and systemwide tables.

Generally, system tables are not directly queried, but are accessed or modified with a stored procedure. After the description of each table, I give you the main stored procedures used to query or to modify this table, with a quick explanation.

Login Tables

Two tables are in charge of the login into SQL Server: syslogins and sysremotelogins.

syslogins (sysxlogins)

The syslogins table, shown in Table A.1, contains one row for each valid user account. When you first install SQL Server, this table contains:

- sa: The system administrator. The associated password is NULL, so change it if you want a secure system.
- Local NT administrator, and the NT administrators group account of the machine on which the installation is performed.

TABLE A.1   THE syslogins TABLE

Column	Data Type	Description
suid	smallint	Server user ID
sid	varbinary(85)	Security identifier
status	smallint	For internal use only
createdate	datetime	Date login was created
updatedate	datetime	Last date at which the login was modified
accdate	datetime	Reserved
totcpu	int	Reserved
totio	int	Reserved
spacelimit	int	Reserved
timelimit	int	Reserved
resultlimit	int	Reserved
dbname	nVarchar(128)	Name of user's default database when connection is established

Column	Data Type	Description
name	varchar(30)	Login ID of user
password	nVarchar(128)	Password of user (encrypted if not NULL)
language	nVarchar(128)	User's default language (NULL for us_english)
denylogin	int	Value is 1 if the login is an NT user or group and has been denied access
Hasaccess	int	1 if login has access to the server
Inntname	int	1, if login is an NT user or group; 0 if the login is a SQL Server login
Isntgroup	int	1, if login is an NT group
Isntuser	int	1, if login is an NT user
Sysadmin	int	1, if login is a member of the sysadmin server role
Security_admin	int	1, if login is a member of the securityadmin fixed server role
Server_admin	int	1, if login is a member of the serveradmin fixed server role
Setup_admin	int	1, if login is a member of the setupadmin fixed server role
Process_admin	int	1, if login is a member of the processadmin fixed server role
Disk_admin	int	1, if login is a member of the diskadmin fixed server role
Dbcreator	int	1, if login is a member of the dbcreator fixed server role
Loginname	nVarchar(128)	Actual login name

Stored Procedures Used With `syslogins`

- `sp_addalias`: Adds a new alias to the database (mapping from `syslogins` to `sysusers`).
- `sp_addlogin`: Adds a new login.
- `sp_addremotelogin`: Adds a new remote login (mapping between `sysremotelogins` and `syslogins`).
- `sp_adduser`: Adds a new user (mapping between `sysusers` and `syslogins`).

- `sp_changedbowner`: Changes the dbo of the database (mapping from `syslogins` to `sysusers`).

- `sp_defaultdb`: Changes the default database of a login ID.

- `sp_defaultlanguage`: Sets the default langage for a specific login ID.

- `sp_droplogin`: Deletes an existing login ID.

- `sp_helpdb`: General information on the database.

- `sp_helpuser`: General information on a specific user.

- `sp_password`: Changes the password of a specific login ID.

- `xp_trace_setuserfilter`: Specifies the username filter—that is, the names of logins to include or exclude in the events specified.

- `xp_sqlinventory`: Captures configuration and inventory information on the SQL Server in an asynchronous manner and stores it in a database.

- `sp_change_user_login`: Changes the relationship between the SQL Server login and the current user in the database.

sysremotelogins

This table, shown in Table A.2, was kept for backward compatibility with previous versions of SQL Server. `sysremotelogins` contains a row for each user authorized to execute remote stored procedures on this SQL Server. It's used with `sysservers` to define who is authorized to log in the remote server. Note that the remote login has to be defined only on the remote server, but both servers have to be defined as remote for each other.

TABLE A.2   THE `sysremotelogins` TABLE

Column	Data Type	Description
remoteserverid	smallint	Remote server ID
remoteusername	nVarchar(128)	User's login name on the local server
suid	smallint	Remote server user ID
status	smallint	Bitmap of options
sid	varbinary(85)	NT security identifier
changedate	datetime	Date and time the remote user was added

The description I give in the columns is different from the one given in Books Online. For me, the remote server is the one containing the stored procedure to run, so it's also the one on which to declare the remote logins. The local server is the server from which the remote procedure is called.

Stored Procedures Used with `sysremotelogins`

- `sp_addremotelogin`: Adds a new remote login (mapping between `sysremotelogins` and `syslogins`).

- `sp_addsubscriber`: Adds a new subscription server.

- `sp_dropremotelogin`: Deletes an existing `remotelogin`.

- `sp_dropserver`: Deletes the reference of an existing server in `sysserver` (check the remote logins).

- `sp_dropsubscriber`: Deletes a subscription server.

- `sp_remoteoption`: Defines the remote option for a specific remote login.

Database Tables

The database tables are in charge of space management—that is, the location of devices and the location of databases on devices.

sysdevices

This table, shown in Table A.3, was kept for backward compatibility with previous versions of SQL Server. `sysdevices` contains one row for each device. This table stores the reference of dump devices (tape, disk, and so forth) and of database devices. When you first install SQL Server, `sysdevices` contains three database device entries—`Master`, `MDSBData`, and `MSDBLog`—and three dump devices—`diskdump`, `diskettedumpa`, and `diskettedumpb`.

> **WARNING**
>
> Never use the `diskdump` device for your backup. This device is called the "bit bucket." If you dump a database or a log in that device, the dump is lost (in other words, it is *really* dumped).

TABLE A.3   THE sysdevices TABLE

Column	Data Type	Description
low	int	First virtual page number on a database device (not used for dump devices).
high	int	Last virtual page number on a database device (not used for dump devices).
status	smallint	Bitmap indicating the type of device: 1: Default disk 2: Physical disk 4: Logical disk 8: Skip header 16: Dump device 32: Serial writes 64: Device mirrored 128: Reads mirrored (reserved) 256: Half-mirror only (reserved) 512: Mirror enabled 4096: Read Only
cntrltype	smallint	Controller type: 0: Non–CD-ROM database device 2: Disk dump device 3 – 4: Diskette dump device 5: Tape dump device 6: Named pipe device
name	sysname	Logical name of the dump device or database device.
phyname	varchar(127)	Name of the physical device.
size	int	Size of the file in 2KB pages.

You probably noticed that the virtual device number has no associated columns. That's because the vdevno is the last byte of the high or low word value. For example, msdbdata has a low value of 2130706432 (hex 7F 00 00 00), so its vdevno equals 7F (127), and the device starts at the virtual address 0.

Stored Procedures Used with sysdevices

- sp_addsegment: Adds a new segment to the database.
- sp_adddumpdevice: Adds a new dump device.

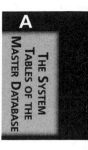

- `sp_coalesce_fragments`: Updates the database fragments.
- `sp_configure`: Displays or sets configuration options.
- `sp_dbinstall`: Installs a removable database on your system.
- `sp_dbremove`: Deletes a database (corrupted or not). Possibility to drop the devices on a single statement.
- `sp_devoption`: Displays or sets device options (useful for removable devices).
- `sp_diskdefault`: Defines the device as part of the default device pool.
- `sp_dropdevice`: Deletes an existing device (if it is empty).
- `sp_dropsegment`: Deletes an existing segment.
- `sp_extendsegment`: Extends an existing segment.
- `sp_helpdb`: General information on the database.
- `sp_helpdevice`: General information on the device.
- `sp_helplog`: Finds the position of the transaction log for a specific database.
- `sp_helpsegment`: General information on segment mappings.
- `sp_logdevice`: Places the log device on a specific device.

sysdatabases

The `sysdatabases` table (see Table A.4) contains one entry for each database created on the system. Initially, when SQL server is installed, it contains entries for `Master`, `Tempdb`, `Model`, `msdb`, and `mssqlweb`.

TABLE A.4   THE `sysdatabases` TABLE

Column	Data Type	Description
name	sysname	Name of the database.
dbid	smallint	Database ID.
sid	varbinary(149)	System ID for database creator.
suid	smallint	Server user ID of database creator.
mode	smallint	Used internally for locking a database while it is being created.

continues

TABLE A.4   CONTINUED

Column	Data Type	Description
status	smallint	Status bits, some of which can be set by the user with the `sp_dboption` system stored procedure (`READ ONLY`, `DBO USE ONLY`, `SIN GLE USER`, and so on):
		2: Database is in transition
		4: `select into/bulkcopy`
		8: `trunc. log on chkpt`
		16: `no chkpt on recovery`
		32: Crashed while the database was being loaded; instructs recovery not to proceed
		64: Database not recovered yet
		128: Database is in recovery
		256: Database is suspect; cannot be opened or used in its present state
		512: Database is offline
		1024: `read only`
		2048: `dbo use only`
		4096: `single user`
		8192: Database being checkpointed
		16384: `ANSI null default`
		32768: Emergency mode
		4194304: Autoshrink
		1073741824: Cleanly shut down; multiple bits can be `ON` at the same time
status2	int	16384: `ANSI NULL DEFAULT`
		65536: `CONCAT` null yields null
		131072: Recursive triggers
		1048576: Default to local cursor
		8388608: `quoted identifier`
		33554432: `cursor close on commit`
		67108864: `ANSI Nulls`
		268435456: `ANSI Warnings`
		536870912: `Full Text` enabled
		Most of these options are set with the stored procedure `sp_dboption`.

Column	Data Type	Description
version	smallint	Internal version number of the SQL Server code with which the database was created.
crdate	datetime	Creation date.
category	int	Used for publication and subscription databases.
reserved	datetime	Reserved for future use.
cmptlevel	tinyint	Compatibility level for the database.
filename	nVarchar(260)	Operating system full path and name for the database primary file.
version	smallint	Internal version number of the SQL Server code with which the database was created.

TIP

Like all the system tables, `sysdatabases` should not be updated manually. But if you have enough experience, and suspect a database should be accessed, you may modify the bit in the `status` field. This operation seems to be without danger.

Stored Procedures Used with `sysdatabases`

- `sp_addlogin`: Adds a new login.
- `sp_addpublication`: Adds a new publication.
- `sp_changearticle`: Modifies an existing article.
- `sp_changedbowner`: Changes the `dbo` of the database.
- `sp_changepublication`: Modifies an existing publication.
- `sp_databases`: Displays the list of table name and size.
- `sp_dboption`: Displays or sets option of the database.
- `sp_defaultdb`: Sets the default database for a specific user.
- `sp_devoption`: Displays or sets device options (useful for removable devices).
- `sp_dropdevice`: Deletes an existing empty device.
- `sp_droplogin`: Deletes an existing login.
- `sp_helpdb`: General information on the database.

- `sp_logdevice`: Places the log device on a specific device.
- `sp_renamedb`: Renames a database (the database should be in single-user mode).
- `sp_spaceused`: Displays information on space used by a database/object.
- `sp_tables`: Displays the list of tables and views of the database.

Systemwide Tables

Systemwide tables are tables in charge of the overall configuration of SQL Server or in charge on what's happening on the server, but not dedicated to a particular user or database.

syscharsets

The `syscharsets` table (see Table A.5) contains one entry for each character set and sort order defined on the server. All the available character sets and sort orders are stored, but only one is referenced in the configuration options of SQL Server to use.

TABLE A.5   THE `syscharsets` TABLE

Column	Data Type	Description
type	smallint	Type of entity this row represents. 1001 is a character set, and 2001 is a sort order.
id	tinyint	Unique ID for the character set or sort order. Note that sort orders and character sets cannot share the same ID number. ID numbers 0 through 200 are reserved.
csid	tinyint	Unused for character set. ID of the character set if the row represents the associated sort order.
status	smallint	Internal system status information bits.
name	varchar(30)	Unique name for the character set or sort order.
description	sysname	Description of the features of the character set or sort order.
description	nVarchar(255)	Description of character set or sort order (optional).
binarydefinition	nvarbinary(255)	Reserved for internal use only.
definition	image	Internal definition of the character set or sort order.

Stored Procedures Used with `syscharsets`

- `sp_helpsort`: Displays the current character set and sort order.
- `xp_sqlinventory`: Captures configuration and inventory information on the SQL Server in an asynchronous manner and stores it in a database.

sysconfigures

The `sysconfigures` table (see Table A.6) contains one entry for each configurable option. This table is loaded at the start of SQL Server with the content of the configuration block.

TABLE A.6 THE `sysconfigures` TABLE

Column	Data Type	Description
config	smallint	Configuration variable number.
value	int	User-modifiable value for the variable.
config	smallint	Configuratrion variable number.
comment	nvarchar(255)	Explanation of the configuration option.
status	smallint	Bitmap indicating the status for the option: 1: Dynamic (the variable takes effect when the RECONFIGURE statement is executed). 2: Advanced (the variable is displayed only when the show advanced option is set).

The content of the table is are written back in the configuration block when the RECONFIGURE statement is run.

Stored Procedure Used with `sysconfigures`

- `sp_configure`: Displays or sets configurable options. Remember to run RECONFIGURE [WITH OVERRIDE] after sp_configure.

syscurconfigs

The `syscurconfigs` table contains one entry for each configuration option, as `sysconfigures` does. This table contains the running values of these options. This table is a pseudo-table because it does not exist on the disk, but is created when a user or process queries it. Its structure is identical to that of `sysconfigures`.

When you update a static option (one that needs restarting of SQL Server), its value is written in `sysconfigures` but does not appear in `syscurconfigs`.

Stored Procedure Used with `syscurconfigs`

- `sp_configure`: Displays or sets configurable options. Remember to run `RECONFIGURE [WITH OVERRIDE]` after `sp_configure`.

`syslanguages`

The `syslanguages` table (see Table A.7) contains one entry for each language installed on SQL Server, except for U.S. English because it is the default language.

TABLE A.7   THE `syslanguages` TABLE

Column	Data Type	Description
langid	smallint	Unique language ID.
dateformat	nChar(3)	Date order (for example, dmy).
datefirst	tinyint	First day of the week. 1 for Monday, 2 for Tuesday, and so on, up to 7 for Sunday.
upgrade	int	Reserved for system use.
name	sysname	Official language name (for example, Français).
alias	sysname	Alternate language name (for example, French).
months	nvarchar(372)	Comma-separated list of full-length month names, in order from January through December (20 characters max).
shortmonths	varchar(132)	Comma-separated list of short-month names, in order from January through December (9 characters max).
days	nvarchar(217)	Comma-separated list of day names, in order from Monday through Sunday (30 characters max)
lcid	int	Windows NT local ID for the language.
mslangid	smallint	SQL Server message group ID.

Stored Procedures Used with `syslanguages`

- `sp_configure`: Displays or sets configurable options. Remember to run `RECONFIGURE [WITH OVERRIDE]` after `sp_configure`.

- `sp_droplanguage`: Deletes an existing language. With the `dropmessages` option, you drop all existing messages in this language.

- `sp_helplanguage`: Displays the defined languages.

- `sp_setlangalias`: Defines an alias for a specific language.

sysmessages

The `sysmessages` table (see Table A.8) contains all the warning, informational, and error messages of SQL Server. Another table has been added to the `msdb` database (`sysservermessages`) for systemwide messages.

TABLE A.8   THE `sysmessages` TABLE

Column	Data Type	Description
error	int	Unique error number.
severity	smallint	Severity level of the error.
dlevel	smallint	Reserved. For internal use only.
description	nvarchar(255)	Explanation of the error with placeholders for parameters.
mslangid	smallint	System message group ID.

Stored Procedures Used with `sysmessages`

- `sp_addmessage`: Adds a new message.

- `sp_droplanguage`: Deletes an existing language and, eventually, all associated messages.

- `sp_dropmessage`: Deletes an existing message.

- `sp_add_alert`: Creates an alert.

- `sp_altermessage`: Allows changing a message.

- `sp_update_alert`: Allows updating an alert.

sysprocesses

The sysprocesses table (see Table A.9) contains one row for each process running or idle on SQL Server.

TABLE A.9   THE sysprocesses TABLE

Column	Data Type	Description
spid	smallint	SQL Server process ID
kpid	smallint	Windows NT thread ID
blocked	smallint	SPID of a blocking process
status	nchar(30)	Process ID status (runnable, sleeping, and so on)
suid	smallint	Server user ID of user who executed command
hostname	char(10)	Name of workstation
program_name	nchar(128)	Name of application program
hostprocess	nchar(8)	Workstation process ID number
cmd	nchar(16)	Command currently being executed
cpu	int	Cumulative CPU time for process
physical_io process	int	Cumulative disk reads and writes for
memusage	int	Number of 2KB pages of the procedure cache that are currently allocated to the process
blocked	smallint	Process ID of blocking process, if any
waittype	binary(2)	Reserved
waittime	int	Current wait time in milliseconds
lastwaittype	nchar(32)	Name of last or current wait type
waitsource	nchar(32)	String representing a lock resource
dbid	smallint	Database ID
uid	smallint	ID of user who executed command
gid	smallint	Group ID of user who executed command
login_time	datetime	The time at which a client process logged into the server, or for system processes, the time at which SQL Server startup occurred

Column	Data Type	Description
last_batch	datetime	The last time a client process executed a remote stored procedure call or an EXECUTE statement, or for system processes, the time at which SQL Server startup occurred
ecid	smallint	Execution context ID; identifies the sub-threads of a single process
open_tran	smallint	Number of open transactions for the process
sid	nbinary(85)	Globally unique identifier for the user
nt_domain	nchar(128)	The Windows NT domain for the client (if using integrated security) or a trusted connection
nt_username	nchar(128)	The Windows NT username for the process (if using integrated security) or a trusted connection
net_address	nchar(12)	The assigned unique identifier for the network interface card on each user's workstation
net_library	nchar(12)	The client's network library name
loginname	nchar(128)	Login name

Stored Procedures Used with sysprocesses

- sp_dboption: Displays or sets the database options.
- sp_who: Displays information on the current processes.
- sp_lock: Reports information about locks.

sysservers

The sysservers table (see Table A.10) contains one entry for each remote server on which remote stored procedures can be executed. Remember that to be able to execute remote stored procedures, you have to declare remote logins on the remote server.

TABLE A.10   THE syslanguages TABLE

Column	Data Type	Description
srvid	smallint	ID number (for local use only) of the remote server
srvstatus	smallint	Bitmap of options
srvname	sysname	Name of the server
srvproduct	nvarchar(128)	Product name of the remote server
providername	nvarchar(128)	OLE DB provider name for access to this server
datasource	nvarchar(4000)	OLE DB data source
location	nvarchar(4000)	OLE DB location
providerstring	nvarchar(4000)	OLE DB provider string
schemadate	datetime	Date of last update of the row of interest
srvnetname	char(30)	NetBIOS name of the server, if it is not compliant with identifier rules
topologyx	int	Used by the SQL Enterprise Manager server topology diagram
topologyy	int	Used by the SQL Enterprise Manager server topology diagram
catalog	sysname	Catalog used to make connection to the OLE DB provider

Stored Procedures Used with sysservers

- sp_addpublisher: Adds a new publisher server.
- sp_addremotelogin: Adds a new remote login.
- sp_addserver: Adds the reference of a new server.
- sp_addsubscriber: Adds a new subscription server.
- sp_addsubscription: Adds a new subscription.
- sp_changesubscriber: Changes subscriber options.
- sp_changesubscription: Changes the subscription information for an existing publication.
- sp_changesubstatus: Change subscription status.
- sp_droppublisher: Drop an existing publishers.
- sp_dropremotelogin: Deletes an existing remote login.
- sp_dropserver: Deletes the reference of an existing server.

- `sp_dropsubscriber`: Deletes a subscription server.
- `sp_dropsubscription`: Deletes an existing subscription.
- `sp_enumfullsubscribers`: Displays the subscribers of a specific publication.
- `sp_helparticle`: General information on an existing article.
- `sp_helpdistributor`: Displays information on the distributor server.
- `sp_helppublication`: General information on publications.
- `sp_helpremotelogin`: General information on remote logins.
- `sp_helpserver`: General information on existing referenced servers.
- `sp_helpsubscriberinfo`: General information on subscribers.
- `sp_helpsubscription`: General information on subscriptions.
- `sp_remoteoption`: Displays or sets remote login ID options.
- `sp_serveroption`: Sets the options (roles) of a server.
- `sp_setnetname`: Sets the real NetBIOS name of the machine if it contains invalid SQL Server character for identifier.
- `sp_subscribe`: Subscribes to an existing publication.
- `sp_unsubscribe`: Unsubscribes to an existing article.

Special Tables

The master tables contain special system tables, not identified as system tables (they have U type in the `sysobjects` table), but used as system tables by specific procedures or by ODBC. These tables are not documented and should not be updated manually:

- `spt_datatype_info_ext`
- `spt_datatype_info`
- `spt_server_info`
- `helpsql`
- `spt_committab`
- `spt_monitor`
- `spt_values`
- `spt_fallback_db`
- `spt_fallback_dev`
- `spt_fallback_usg`

The names are generally self-explanatory. Some of these special tables should become system tables in the next version of SQL Server.

The System Tables of All Databases

APPENDIX B

The 18 system tables of the model database are copied in each new database. In fact, the whole content of the Model database is copied to newly created databases. If you add new objects (tables, views, stored procedures, users) to the Model database, they will be copied into the new databases as well.

These 18 tables represents all the necessary information to self-manage each database. You will find explanations about these 18 tables in this appendix, plus stored procedure used to query or to update them, and special undocumented gifts for some.

Object Tables

The object tables contains all the information needed to manage user and system tables, views, stored procedures, user-defined data types, default, rules, constraints, triggers, and indexes.

syscolumns

The syscolumns table, as shown in Table B.1, contains one row for each table and view column and each stored procedure parameter.

TABLE B.1   THE syscolumns TABLE

Column	Data Type	Description
id	int	ID of the table/view to which this column belongs or of the stored procedure to which the parameter is associated.
number	smallint	Procedure number. Used when some procedures have the same name and are identified by a number (0 for nonprocedure entries).
colid	smallint	Column ID.
status	tinyint	Bitmap used to describe a property of the column or the parameter:
		8: The column allows null values.
		16: ANSI_PADDING was set during creation of a varchar or a varbinary column; trailing blanks are preserved when varchar data is updated or inserted, and trailing zeroes are preserved when varbinary data is updated or inserted.
		32: A varchar or a varbinary column is a fixed-length data type that accepts NULLS; varchar data is padded with blanks to the maximum length, and varbinary data is padded with zeroes.
		64: Output parameter.
		128: Identity column.

Column	Data Type	Description
type	tinyint	Physical storage type (copied from systypes).
length	smallint	Physical length of data (copied from systypes or supplied by the user).
offset	smallint	Offset of this column into the row; if negative, variable-length column.
usertype	smallint	User type ID (copied from systypes).
cdefault	int	ID of the stored procedure that generates the default value for this column.
domain	int	ID of the stored procedure that contains the rule for this column.
name	sysname	Column name (length is 128 characters).
printfmt	varchar(255)	Reserved.
prec	smallint	Level of precision for this column.
scale	int	Scale for this column.
xtype	tinyint	Physical storage type from systypes.
typestat	tinyint	For internal use only.
xusertype	smallint	ID for extended user data type.
xprec	tinyint	For internal use only.
xscale	tinyint	For internal use only.
xoffset	tinyint	For internal use only.
bitpos	tinyint	For internal use only.
reserved	tinyint	For internal use only.
colorder	smallint	For internal use only.
autoval	varbinary(8000)	For internal use only.
iscomputed	int	Indicates if a column is computed (1) and non-computed (0).
isoutparam	int	Indicates whether the stored procedure parameter is an output parameter (1) or not (0).
isnullable	int	Indicates whether the column accepts null values; 1 for accepts, and 0 if not.

B

THE SYSTEM
TABLES OF ALL
DATABASES

Stored Procedures Used with `syscolumns`

- `sp_articlecolumn`: Modifies the existing column of an article.
- `sp_bindefault`: Binds a default to a column/data type.
- `sp_bindrule`: Binds a rule to a column/data type.
- `sp_column_privileges`: Displays current rights for a specific table.
- `sp_columns`: Displays a list of columns of a specific table.
- `sp_droptype`: Deletes a user-defined data type.
- `sp_fkeys`: Displays foreign key information.
- `sp_help`: Displays information about a database object.
- `sp_helparticle`: Displays information about a specific article.
- `sp_helparticlecolumns`: Displays all the columns of the article.
- `sp_helprotect`: Displays rights for a specific user/group/object.
- `sp_pkeys`: Displays primary key information.
- `sp_rename`: Renames a database object.
- `sp_special_columns`: Displays the optimal column names uniquely identifying rows.
- `sp_sproc_columns`: Displays column information for a specific stored procedure.
- `sp_statistics`: Displays index information for a specific table.
- `sp_tables`: Displays a list of object to be queried.
- `sp_unbindefault`: Unbinds a default from a column/data type.
- `sp_unbindrule`: Unbinds a rule from a column/data type.

`syscomments`

The `syscomments` table, shown in Table B.2, contains one or more entries for each stored procedure, trigger, view, rule, CHECK constraint, and DEFAULT constraint. This table contains the source code of each object. The `text` column contains the code and is 255 characters long. So if the code is longer than 255 characters (this is often the case for stored procedure and triggers), the code spans more than one line.

TABLE B.2 THE syscomments TABLE

Column	Data Type	Description
id	int	Object ID of to which the object code belongs.
number	smallint	Number of the procedure, if it is grouped (0 for nonprocedure entries).
colid	smallint	Row sequence number for code longer than 255 characters.
texttype	smallint	1: User-supplied comment—users can add entries describing an object or column.
		2: System-supplied code for views, rules, defaults, triggers, and stored procedures.
		4: Encrypted code for procedures, triggers, and views.
language	smallint	Reserved.
text	nvarchar(4000)	SQL definition code.
status	smallint	For internal use only.
ctext	varbinary(8000)	Actual text of the SQL definition statement.
compressed	bit	Indicates whether the procedure is compressed (1) or not (0).
encrypted	bit	Indicates whether the procedure is encrypted (1) or not (0).

Be careful not to get confused between syscomments and sysprocedures.

Stored Procedures for syscomments

- sp_helpconstraint: Displays information about constraints.
- sp_helpextendedproc: Displays a list of extended stored procedures.
- sp_helptext: Displays the code of a specific object.
- sp_addextendedproc: Adds a new extended stored procedure.
- sp_dropextendedproc: Drops an existing extended stored procedure.

sysconstraints

The sysconstraints table (shown in Table B.3) is only a mapping table and a list of constraints; it does not contain any code or other table references. This table is linked with syscomments for CHECK and DEFAULT constraints code, with sysreferences for FOREIGN KEY constraints, and with sysindexes for PRIMARY KEY and UNIQUE constraints.

TABLE B.3 THE sysconstraints TABLE

Column	Data Type	Description
constid	int	Constraint ID.
id	int	ID of the table that owns the constraint.
colid	smallint	ID of the column on which the constraint is defined (0 if table constraint).
spare1	tinyint	Reserved.
status	int	1: PRIMARY KEY 2: UNIQUE 3: FOREIGN KEY 4: CHECK 5: DEFAULT 16: Column-level constraint 32: Table-level constraint
actions	int	Reserved.
error	int	Reserved.

sysdepends

The sysdepends table, shown in Table B.4, describes functional dependencies between stored procedures, views, and tables. It contains one row for each stored procedure, view, and table referenced by a stored procedure, view, or trigger.

TABLE B.4 THE sysdepends TABLE

Column	Data Type	Description
id	int	Object ID.
number	smallint	Number of the procedure, if it is grouped (0 for nonprocedure entries).
depid	int	Dependent object ID.
depnumber	smallint	Number of the dependent procedure, if it is grouped (0 for nonprocedure entries).
depdbid	smallint	Reserved.
depsiteid	smallint	Reserved.
status	smallint	Internal status information.
selall	bit	On if the object is used in a SELECT * statement.
resultobj	bit	On if the object is being updated.
readobj	bit	On if the object is being read.

Stored Procedures for `sysdepends`

- `sp_depends`: Displays information about object dependencies.

- `sp_rename`: Renames a database object.

`sysindexes`

The `sysindexes` table, shown in Table B.5, contains one row for each index, for each table that does not have a clustered index, and for each table that has `text`, `nText`, and `image` fields. The entry is created by the `CREATE INDEX` statement and by the creation of `PRIMARY KEY` and `UNIQUE` constraints.

B

THE SYSTEM
TABLES OF ALL
DATABASES

TABLE B.5   THE `sysindexes` TABLE

Column	Data Type	Description
name	sysname	Name of table for indid = 0 or 255; otherwise, name of index.
id	int	ID of table to which the index belongs (if indid<>0 and <>255; otherwise, ID of the table).
indid	smallint	ID of index:
		0: Table.
		1: Clustered index.
		>1: Non-clustered index.
		255: Entry for tables that have text, nText, or image data.
dpages	int	If indid=0 or indid=1, then the number of used data pages is equal to dpages. If indid=255, then the number of used data pages is 0. Otherwise, dpages is the number of leaf-level index pages.
reserved	int	For indid=0 or indid=1, it is the number of pages allocated for all indexes on the table and for data pages. For indid=255, it is the number of pages allocated for text or image data. Otherwise, it is the number of pages allocated only for this index.
used	int	For indid=0 or indid=1, it is the number of pages used for all indexes on the table and for data pages. For indid=255, it is the number of pages used for text, ntext, or image data. Otherwise, it is the number of pages used only for this index.

continues

TABLE B.5   CONTINUED

Column	Data Type	Description
rows	int	For indid>=0, it's the data-level row count. For indid=255, it is set to 0.
first	binary(6)	Pointer to first data or leaf page.
root	binary(6)	For indid>=1 and <255, pointer to the root page of the index. For indid=0 or indid=255, pointer to the last page.
distribution	int	Pointer to distribution page (if entry is an index).
origfillfactor	tinyint	The original fillfactor value used to create the index. This value is never updated but used by DBCC REINDEX for re-indexation purposes.
segment	smallint	Number of segments used by this object.
status	int	System-status information:
		1: IGNORE_DUP_KEY
		2: Unique index
		4: IGNORE_DUP_ROW
		16: Clustered index
		64: ALLOW_DUP_ROW
		2048: PRIMARY KEY constraint index
		4096: UNIQUE constraint index
rowpage	smallint	Maximum count of rows per page.
minlen	smallint	Minimum size of a row.
maxlen	smallint	Maximum size of a row.
maxirow	smallint	Maximum size of a nonleaf index row.
keycnt	smallint	Number of keys.
soid	tinyint	Sort order ID that the index was created with. It's 0 if there is no character data in the keys.
csid	tinyint	Character set ID that the index was created with. It's 0 if there is no character data in the keys.
updatestamp	varbinary	This column is used for internal synchronization of changes to row and page counts.
groupid	smallint	ID of file group where the index resides.
rowcnt	binary(8)	Data-level row count. This value is 0 for indid=255.

Column	Data Type	Description
rowmodctr	int	Includes the number of updated, inserted, and deleted rows since the last time statistics were collected.
xmaxlen	smallint	Maximum size of the row.
reserved1	tinyint	Reserved.
reserved2	int	Reserved.
firstiam	binary(6)	Reserved.
impid	smallint	Reserved. Index implementation flag.
lockflags	smallint	Used to constrain the lock level of an index.
pgmodctr	int	Tracks the number of pages that have changed in an index.
keys	varbinary(816)	Column IDs of the columns that make up the index.
statblob	image	Statistics BLOB.

This table is used to store statistics information.

Stored Procedures Used with `sysindexes`

- `sp_dropsegment`: Deletes an existing empty segment.
- `sp_fkeys`: Displays foreign key information.
- `sp_helpconstraint`: Displays information about constraints.
- `sp_helpindex`: Displays information about indexes.
- `sp_helplog`: Displays the name of the device containing the transaction log.
- `sp_helpsegment`: Displays information about existing segments.
- `sp_pkeys`: Displays primary key information.
- `sp_placeobject`: Places future allocation of an object on a specific segment.
- `sp_rename`: Renames a database object.
- `sp_spaceused`: Displays the space used by an object or a database.
- `sp_special_columns`: Displays the optimal column names that uniquely identify rows.
- `sp_statistics`: Displays index information for a specific table.

sysobjects

The sysobjects table, shown in Table B.6, contains one row for each object of the database. These objects are tables, views, defaults, rules, triggers, CHECK constraints, DEFAULT constraints, FOREIGN KEY constraints, and PRIMARY KEY constraints.

TABLE B.6 THE sysobjects TABLE

Column	Data Type	Description
name	sysname	Object name.
id	int	Object ID.
uid	smallint	User ID of the owner.
type	char(2)	Object type: C: CHECK constraint D: Default or DEFAULT constraint F: FOREIGN KEY constraint K: PRIMARY KEY or UNIQUE constraint P: Stored procedure R: Rule RF: Replication stored procedure S: System table TR: Trigger U: User table V: View X: Extended stored procedure
userstat	smallint	Reserved.
sysstat	smallint	Internal-status information.
indexdel	smallint	Index delete count (incremented if an index is deleted).
refdate	datetime	Reserved.
crdate	datetime	Creation date.
version	datetime	Reserved.
deltrig	int	Stored procedure ID of the delete trigger.
instrig	int	Reserved.
updtrig	int	Reserved.
seltrig	int	Reserved.
category	int	Used for publication, constraints, and identity.
cache	smallint	Reserved.
xtype	char(2)	Same as type.

Column	Data Type	Description
info	smallint	Reserved. For internal use.
status	int	Reserved. For internal use. base_schema_verint Version number of the statistics
replinfo	int	Reserved for internal use.
parent_obj	int	The ID of the parent object—for example, the ID of the table if the object is a constraint or a trigger.
ftcatid	smallint	Identifies the full-text catalog for all user tables registered for full text indexing.
schema_ver	int	A number that increments when the schema of a table is changed.
stats_schema_ver	int	Version number of statistics.

Stored Procedures Used with `sysobjects`

- `sp_addarticle`: Creates a new article and adds it to an existing publication.
- `sp_bindefault`: Binds a default to a column/data type.
- `sp_bindrule`: Binds a rule to a column/data type.
- `sp_changearticle`: Modifies an existing article.
- `sp_changesubstatus`: Changes the status of an existing subscriber.
- `sp_column_privileges`: Displays current rights for a specific table.
- `sp_columns`: Displays a list of columns of a specific table.
- `sp_depends`: Displays information about object dependencies.
- `sp_droparticle`: Deletes an existing article.
- `sp_dropgroup`: Deletes an empty existing group.
- `sp_droptype`: Deletes a user-defined data type.
- `sp_dropuser`: Deletes an existing user, if he or she is not the object owner.
- `sp_fkeys`: Displays foreign key information.
- `sp_help`: Displays information about a database object.
- `sp_helparticle`: Displays information about a specific article.
- `sp_helpconstraint`: Displays information about constraints.
- `sp_helpextendedproc`: Displays a list of extended stored procedures.
- `sp_helprotect`: Displays rights for a specific user/group/object.

- `sp_pkeys`: Displays primary key information.
- `sp_placeobject`: Places future allocation of an object on a specific segment.
- `sp_rename`: Renames a database object.
- `sp_replica`: Sets a table as being a replica.
- `sp_spaceused`: Displays the space used by an object or a database.
- `sp_sproc_columns`: Displays column information for a specific stored procedure.
- `sp_statistics`: Displays index information for a specific table.
- `sp_stored_procedures`: Displays a list of stored procedures.
- `sp_table_privileges`: Displays rights for a specific table.
- `sp_tables`: Displays list of object to be queried.
- `sp_unbindefault`: Unbinds a default from a column/data type.
- `sp_unbindrule`: Unbinds a rule from a column/data type.

sysreferences

The syreferences table, shown in Table B.7, contains the referenced columns of a foreign key. This table is used to enforce relational integrity.

TABLE B.7   THE sysreferences TABLE

Column	Data Type	Description
constid	int	Constraint ID.
fkeyid	int	ID of referencing table.
fkeydbid	smallint	Reserved.
rkeyid	int	ID of referenced table.
rkeydbid	smallint	Reserved.
rkeyindid	smallint	Reserved.
keycnt	smallint	Number of columns in key.
forkeys	varbinary(32)	For internal use only.
refkeys	varbinary(32)	For internal use only.
fkey1 to fkey16	tinyint	Column ID of referencing column.
rkey1 to rkey16	tinyint	Column ID of referenced column.

Stored Procedures Used with `sysreferences`

- `sp_fkeys`: Displays foreign key information.
- `sp_helpconstraint`: Displays information about constraints.

systypes

The `systypes` table, shown in Table B.8, contains one row for each system data type and for each user-defined data type.

TABLE B.8   systypes TABLE

Column	Data Type	Description
uid	smallint	User ID of the creator.
usertype	smallint	User type ID.
variable	bit	1: Variable-length data type. 0: Other types.
allownulls	bit	Indicates the nullability of this data type. This nullability is overridden by the one specified in the CREATE TABLE or ALTER TABLE statement.
type	tinyint	Physical storage data type.
length	tinyint	Physical length of data type.
tdefault	int	ID of stored procedure that generates the default value of this data type.
domain	int	ID of stored procedure that contains integrity checks for this data type. The name of this column has nothing to do with NT domains.
name	sysname	Name of the data type.
printfmt	varchar(255)	Reserved.
prec	tinyint	Precision.
scale	tinyint	Scale (function of the precision).
xtype	tinyint	Physical storage type.
status	tinyint	For internal use only.
xusertype	smallint	Extended user type.
xprec	tinyint	Internal precesion as used by the server.
xscale	tinyint	Internal scale used by the server.
reserved	smallint	For internal use only.

B

THE SYSTEM TABLES OF ALL DATABASES

Stored Procedures Used with systypes

- sp_addtype: Creates a new user-defined data type.
- sp_bindefault: Binds a default to a column/data type.
- sp_bindrule: Binds a rule to a column/data type.
- sp_columns: Displays list of columns of a specific table.
- sp_datatype_info: Displays supported data types.
- sp_droptype: Deletes a user-defined data type.
- sp_dropuser: Deletes an existing user, if he or she is not the object owner.
- sp_help: Displays information about a database object.
- sp_rename: Renames a database object.
- sp_special_columns: Displays the optimal column names uniquely identifying rows.
- sp_sproc_columns: Displays column information for a specific stored procedure.
- sp_unbindefault: Unbinds a default from a column/data type.
- sp_unbindrule: Unbinds a rule from a column/data type.

User, Group, and Security Tables

The database security is managed by the database and stored in the three following tables.

sysprotects

The sysprotects table, shown in Table B.9, contains one row for each granted or revoked user right. By default, if a right is not granted for a user, a group, or the public, the user has no rights. This table lists the rights for individual users, groups, and public.

TABLE B.9 THE sysprotects TABLE

Column	Data Type	Description
id	int	ID of object to which this permission applies (taken from sysobjects).
uid	smallint	ID of user or group to which this permission applies (taken from sysusers).

Column	Data Type	Description
action	tinyint	One of the following permissions: 26: REFERENCES 193: SELECT 195: INSERT 196: DELETE 197: UPDATE 198: CREATE TABLE 203: CREATE DATABASE 207: CREATE VIEW 222: CREATE PROCEDURE 224: EXECUTE 228: DUMP DATABASE 233: CREATE DEFAULT 235: DUMP TRANSACTION 236: CREATE RULE
protecttype	tinyint	Type of the protection 204: GRANT WITH GRANT 205: GRANT 206: REVOKE
columns	varbinary(4000)	Bitmap of columns to which this SELECT or UPDATE permission applies. Bit 0: Columns Bit 1: Permission applies to that column NULL means no information.
grantor	smallint	The user ID of the user who issued the GRANT or REVOKE permission.

Stored Procedures Used with sysprotects

- sp_column_privileges: Displays current rights for a specific table.
- sp_dropgroup: Deletes an empty existing group.
- sp_dropuser: Deletes an existing user, if he or she is not the object owner.
- sp_helprotect: Displays rights for a specific user/group/object.
- sp_stored_procedures: Displays a list of stored procedures.
- sp_table_privileges: Displays rights for a specific table.
- sp_tables: Displays a list of object to be queried.

sysusers

The sysusers table, shown in Table B.10, contains one row for each database user or group and for the public.

TABLE B.10   THE sysusers TABLE

Column	Data Type	Description
suid	smallint	Server user ID (copied from syslogins). If it's 1, it's sa; -1, guest; and -2, public. Groups have negative suid; individuals have mapped suid.
uid	smallint	User ID, unique in this database. If it's 1, it's dbo.
gid	smallint	Group ID to which this user belongs. If uid = -gid, this entry is a group; if it's 0, it's public.
name	sysname	Unique username or group name.
environ	varchar(255)	Reserved.
status	smallint	For internal use.
sid	varbinary(85)	Security identifier.
role	varbinary(2048)	For internal use only.
createdate	datetime	Date account was created.
updatedate	datetime	Date of last update done to the account.
altuid	smallint	For internal use only.
password	varbinary(256)	For internal use only.
hasdbaccess	int	Indicates if account has database access (1).
islogin	int	Indicates if the accout is a valid NT user or group, or SQL Server login account (1 if true).
isntname	int	Indicates if account is Windows NT name or group (1 if true).
isntgroup	int	Indicates if the account is an NT group.
isntuser	int	Indicates if the account is an NT user.
issqluser	int	Indicates if the account is SQL Server user.
isaliased	int	Indicates if the account is aliased to a different name.
issqlrole	int	Indicates if the account is a SQL Server role.
isapprole	int	Indicates if the account is an application-defined role.

Stored Procedures Used with `sysusers`

- `sp_addalias`: Creates a new database alias.
- `sp_addgroup`: Adds a new group.
- `sp_adduser`: Creates a new database user.
- `sp_changedbowner`: Changes the database owner.
- `sp_changegroup`: Puts the specified user in a new group.
- `sp_column_privileges`: Displays current rights for a specific table.
- `sp_dboption`: Displays or sets database options.
- `sp_depends`: Displays information about object dependencies.
- `sp_dropgroup`: Deletes an empty existing group.
- `sp_droplogin`: Deletes an existing non-mapped login.
- `sp_droptype`: Deletes a user-defined data type.
- `sp_dropuser`: Deletes an existing user, if he or she is not the object owner.
- `sp_helparticle`: Displays information about a specific article.
- `sp_helpgroup`: Displays information about groups or the specified groups.
- `sp_helpprotect`: Displays right for a specific user/group/object.
- `sp_helpuser`: Displays information about database users.
- `sp_stored_procedures`: Displays a list of stored procedures.
- `sp_table_privileges`: Displays rights for a specific table.
- `sp_tables`: Displays a list of object to be queried.

Replication Tables

Several replication tables exist in the master database. These tables store information about the publisher database and its subscribers. Some of the tables also keep track of the synchronization between the different servers participating in the replication process. These tables are described below.

sysarticles

The `sysarticles` table, shown in Table B.11, contains one row for each published article on the publication server. That table has all the necessary information concerning publishing operations. This table is stored in the published database.

TABLE B.11 THE sysarticles TABLE

Column	Data Type	Description
artid	int	Identity column, unique ID number for the article.
columns	varbinary(32)	Columns published in the table.
creation_script	nVarchar(255)	Schema script of the article.
del_cmd	nVarchar(255)	Command to execute upon delete, or else built from the log entry.
description	nVarchar(255)	Comments for the article.
dest_table	sysname	Name of the destination table.
filter	int	Stored procedure ID, used for horizontal partitioning.
filter_clause	nText	WHERE clause of the article, used for horizontal filtering.
ins_cmd	nVarchar(255)	Command to execute upon insert, or else build from the log entry.
name	sysname	Unique name of the article.
objid	int	Published table object ID.
pubid	int	ID of the publication to which the article belongs.
pre_creation_cmd	tinyint	Command for dropping, deleting, or truncating, to run before the creation of the table: 0: None 1: Drop 2: Delete 3: Truncate
status	tinyint	Bitmap used to describe a property of the column or the parameter: 8: Column allows null values 64: Parameter is an OUTPUT parameter 128: Identity column
sync_objid	int	The ID of the table or view that represents the article definition.

Column	Data Type	Description
type	tinyint	Type of article:
		1: Log-based article
		3: Log-based article with manual filter
		5: Log-based article with manual view
		7: Log-based article with manual filter and manual view
upd_cmd	nVarchar(255)	Command to execute upon update, or else built from the log entry.
schema_option	binary(8)	Indicates what is to be scripted out.
dest_owner	sysname	Owner at the table at the destination database.

B

THE SYSTEM TABLES OF ALL DATABASES

Stored Procedures Used with `sysarticles`

- `sp_addarticle`: Creates a new article and adds it to an existing publication.
- `sp_addsubscription`: Adds a subscription to an article and sets the subscriber's status.
- `sp_articlecolumn`: Displays the columns of an existing article.
- `sp_changearticle`: Modifies an existing article.
- `sp_changesubscription`: Changes the subscription status of an article/publication.
- `sp_changesubstatus`: Changes the status of an existing subscriber.
- `sp_droparticle`: Deletes an existing article.
- `sp_droppublication`: Deletes an existing publication.
- `sp_dropsubscription`: Deletes an existing subscription.
- `sp_enumfullsubscribers`: Displays the list of the subscribers of a specified subscription.
- `sp_helparticle`: Displays information about a specific article.
- `sp_helparticlecolumns`: Displays the columns of the specified article.
- `sp_helppublication`: Displays information about a specific publication.
- `sp_helpsubscription`: Displays information about a specific subscription.
- `sp_subscribe`: Subscribes to a specific publication/article.
- `sp_unsubscribe`: Unsubscribes from a specific publication/article.

syspublications

The syspublications table, shown in Table B.12, contains one row for each declared publication. This table is linked to the sysarticles table to find the articles belonging to a publication.

TABLE B.12 THE syspublications TABLE

Column	Data Type	Description
description	nVarchar(255)	Comments.
name	sysname	Unique name of the publication.
pubid	int	Identity column, publication ID number.
repl_freq	tinyint	Type of replication 0: Transaction based 1: Scheduled table refresh
restricted	bit	Security option for the publication 1: Restricted 0: Unrestricted (default)
status	tinyint	Log-based status 0: Log-based (default) 1: Not log-based
sync_method	tinyint	Type of synchronization method 0: Native bcp 1: Chararacter-based bcp
snapshot_jobid	binary(16)	Scheduled task ID.
independent_agent	bit	Publication attribute.
immediate_sync	bit	Indicates whether the synchronization files are created or re-created each time the agent runs.
enabled_for_internet	bit	Indicates whether synchronization files are exposed to Internet protocols, such as FTP and HTTP.
allow_push	bit	Indicates allowing push subscriptions on the publication.
allow_pull	bit	Indicates allowing pull subscriptions.
allow_anonymous	bit	Indicates allowance of anonymous subscriptions on the publication.
immediate_sync_ready	bit	Indicates whether snapshot agent is completed on time for the immediate update publication.

Column	Data Type	Description
allow_sync_tran	bit	Publication attribute.
autogen_sync_procs	bit	Publication attribute.
retention	int	Retention time in days.

Stored Procedures Used with `syspublications`

- `sp_addarticle`: Creates a new article and adds it to an existing publication.
- `sp_addpublication`: Creates a new publication.
- `sp_addsubscription`: Adds a subscription to an article and sets the subscriber's status.
- `sp_articlecolumn`: Displays the columns of an existing article.
- `sp_changearticle`: Modifies an existing article.
- `sp_changepublication`: Modifies an existing publication.
- `sp_changesubscription`: Changes the subscription status of an article/publication.
- `sp_changesubstatus`: Changes the status of an existing subscriber.
- `sp_dboption`: Displays or sets the database options.
- `sp_droparticle`: Deletes an existing article.
- `sp_droppublication`: Deletes an existing publication.
- `sp_droparticle`: Deletes an existing article.
- `sp_droppublication`: Deletes an existing publication.
- `sp_dropsubscription`: Deletes an existing subscription.
- `sp_enumfullsubscribers`: Displays the list of the subscribers of a specified subscription.
- `sp_helparticle`: Displays information about a specific article.
- `sp_helparticlecolumns`: Displays the columns of the specified article.
- `sp_helppublication`: Displays information about a specific publication.
- `sp_helpsubscription`: Displays information about a specific subscription.
- `sp_subscribe`: Subscribes to a specific publication/article.
- `sp_unsubscribe`: Unsubscribes from a specific publication/article.

B

THE SYSTEM
TABLES OF ALL
DATABASES

syssubscriptions

The syssubscriptions table, shown in Table B.13, contains one row for each subscription on the subscriber.

TABLE B.13 THE syssubscriptions TABLE

Column	Data Type	Description
artid	int	Subscribed article ID.
srvid	smallint	Subscription server ID.
dest_db	sysname	Name of the destination database.
status	tinyint	Status: 0: Inactive 1: Subscribed 2: Active
sync_type	tinyint	Type of synchronization: 0: Manual 1: Automatic 2: None
timestamp	timestamp	Initial time of subscription.
login_name	sysname	Login name used when adding the subscription.
subscription_type	int	0 = Push; 1 = Pull.
distribution_jobid	binary(16)	Job ID for distribution agent.
update_mode	tinyint	0 = read only; 1 = immediate updating.
loopback_detection	bit	Indicates whether transactions originating at the subscriber are sent back to the subscriber (True means they are sent back).

Stored Procedures Used with syssubscriptions

- sp_addsubscription: Adds a subscription to an article and sets the subscriber's status.
- sp_changesubscription: Changes the subscription status of an article/publication.
- sp_changesubstatus: Changes the status of an existing subscriber.
- sp_droparticle: Deletes an existing article.
- sp_droppublication: Deletes an existing publication.
- sp_dropsubscription: Deletes an existing subscription.

- `sp_enumfullsubscribers`: Displays the list of the subscribers of a specified subscription.
- `sp_helparticle`: Displays information about a specific article.
- `sp_helppublication`: Displays information about a specific publication.
- `sp_helpsubscription`: Displays information about a specific subscription.
- `sp_subscribe`: Subscribes to a specific publication/article.
- `sp_unsubscribe`: Unsubscribes from a specific publication/article

Common Error
Messages

This appendix lists the many common error messages you can get, gives the text supplied by SQL Server, and explains what the error really means because the descriptions are not always clear. Error messages show %letter, in which the %letter represents a variable output in an error message. The errors are listed in ascending order according to their numbers.

Error Message #103: Severity Level 15

Text Output: The identifier that starts with %s is too long. Maximum length is %d.

Explanation of Error: If you enclose a character string longer than 128 characters in double quotation marks, the application might get this error. Microsoft SQL Server expects quoted identifiers to be enclosed in double quotation marks (") and data values to be enclosed in single quotation marks (') when the QUOTED_IDENTIFIERS option is set on (SET QUOTED_IDENTIFIERS ON). If character parameters are passed to a stored procedure with this option turned on, SQL Server expects such parameters to be shorter than 128 characters.

Error Message #105: Severity Level 15

Text Output: Unclosed quote before the character string %s.

Explanation of Error: You are missing a quote around a character string, usually above the line with the error message.

Error Message #109: Severity Level 15

Text Output: There are more columns in the INSERT statement than values specified in the VALUES clause. The number of values in the VALUES clause must match the number of columns specified in the INSERT statement.

Explanation of Error: This one is self-explanatory. You receive this error when you try to insert values in a table using fewer values in the VALUES clause than you have specified in the INSERT clause.

> **NOTE**
>
> Do not confuse the SQL Server error 109 with the operating system error 109. The latter means that a connection has been dropped and is no longer available.

Error Message #110: Severity Level 15

Text Output: There are fewer columns in the INSERT statement than values specified in the VALUES clause. The number of values in the VALUES clause must match the number of columns specified in the INSERT statement.

Explanation of Error: You have too many values for the number of columns you have specified when inserting values.

Error Message #113: Severity Level 15

Text Output: Missing end comment mark */.

Explanation of Error: SQL Server cannot find the end of comment marker */. You might have mistyped it or forgotten to add it.

Error Message #137: Severity Level 15

Text Output: Must declare variable @mycount.

Explanation of Error: The variable is not declared, or the variable is local but has been attempted to be accessed globally.

Error Message #156: Severity Level 15

Text Output: Incorrect syntax near the keyword %s.

Explanation of Error: This error is usually a result of an improper format for creating a procedure or a typing error when using one of the SQL Server keywords.

Error Message #170: Severity Level 15

Text Output: Incorrect syntax near %s.

Explanation of Error: This usually means that a field name could be wrong or misspelled or two words have run together. It also appears when you are trying to use functions on a line that uses EXEC.

Error Message #174: Severity Level 15

Text Output: The function %s requires %d arguments.

Explanation of Error: This error means that too few or too many arguments were used with a function. Use the online help or, better yet, use sp_sqlhelp to get the list of parameters required for the function.

Error Message #193: Severity Level 15

Text Output: The object or column name starting with %s is too long. The maximum length is %d characters.

Explanation of Error: Attempting to name a column with more than 128 characters produces this error. It is always a good idea to create short column names so that there is less to type when writing queries!

Error Message #201: Severity Level 16

Text Output: Procedure %s expects parameter %s, which was not supplied.

Explanation of Error: If no default parameters are specified, you get this error when missing one or more parameters of a stored procedure.

Error Message #206: Severity Level 16

Text Output: Operand type clash: %s is incompatible with %s.

Explanation of Error: In this case, attempting to convert function output to string value without using CONVERT, such as using STR(GETDATE()). You receive this error message when trying to perform one set of operations with an operator that is incompatible with a data type.

Error Message #207: Severity Level 16

Text Output: Invalid column name %s.

Explanation of Error: You attempted to select a column and entered a column name incorrectly. Use sp_help *tablename* to get a list of all columns in the table quickly.

Error Message #208: Severity Level 16

Text Output: Invalid object name %s.

Explanation of Error: The object name you are referencing does not exist, or you need to add a reference to the owner name of the object using the dot syntax (for example, dbo.authors).

Error Message #229: Severity Level 14

Text Output: %s permission denied on object %s, database %s, owner %s.

Explanation of Error: You have not been granted privileges to that object, such as trying to access a system stored procedure without the appropriate privileges, such as xp_cmdshell.

Error Message #230: Severity Level 14

Text Output: %s permission denied on column %s of object %s, database %s, owner %s.

Explanation of Error: You could either not have full rights to a table or have only certain rights to certain columns in a table, but the column you selected is not one of them.

Error Message #232: Severity Level 16

Text Output: Arithmetic overflow error for type %s, value = %f.

Explanation of Error: This error always occurs when a value you're trying to insert is too large for the field, such as entering 9121212193833 into an integer field. Always test values before saving. If the field needs to store the number, change the data type. Another common problem is creating a loop that doesn't exit because a new condition occurred that was not taken into account by the programmer; the loop continues a calculation until the overflow error occurs.

Error Message #235: Severity Level 16

Text Output: Cannot convert CHAR value to MONEY. The CHAR value has incorrect syntax.

Explanation of Error: This usually occurs when spaces or symbols in the character string are not allowed to convert to money. Could also occur if you are dynamically creating the character string and the output does not comply with MONEY conversion.

Error Message #241: Severity Level 16

Text Output: Syntax error converting DATETIME from character string.

Explanation of Error: Result of typing error when keying in a date in any of the acceptable date/time formats or trying to assign a string value to a date/time value with an improperly formatted string.

Error Message #243: Severity Level 16

Text Output: Type %s is not a defined system type.

Explanation of Error: Attempting to assign a data type to a variable that does not exist, usually as a result of a typing error.

Error Message #257: Severity Level 16

Text Output: Implicit conversion from data type %s to %s is not allowed. Use the CONVERT function to run this query.

Explanation of Error: This error occurs when attempting to use SQL Server to automatically convert one data type to another datatype, and the conversion is not supported. You can always use CONVERT to fix this problem.

C

COMMON ERROR MESSAGES

Error Message #259: Severity Level 16

Text Output: Ad hoc updates to system catalogs not enabled. System Administrator must reconfigure system to allow this.

Explanation of Error: This error occurs when you try to change system variables without using system stored procedures and the allow updates parameter has not been changed to a value of 1. Do not do this because there is always another method!

Error Message #268: Severity Level 16

Text Output: You can't run SELECT INTO in this database. Please check with the Database Owner.

Explanation of Error: This error occurs when you try to use the SELECT INTO statement to enter records into a table, and the select into/bulkcopy option is disabled. Because this process does not allow logged transactions, you might want to consider using INSERT...SELECT. If you must use SELECT INTO (which does work faster), use the sp_dboption stored procedure to set select into/bulkcopy to TRUE.

> **NOTE**
>
> It's important to note that enabling the SELECT INTO/BULK COPY option allows for nonlogged operations to take place. Just keep this in mind, especially when you develop a plan for backing up your database, knowing that the transaction log will not be backed up.

Error Message #270: Severity Level 16

Text Output: Table %s can't be modified.

Explanation of Error: This error occurs when you attempt to change a table and you do not have the appropriate permissions.

Error Message #284: Severity Level 16

Text Output: Rules may not be bound to TEXT, nTEXT, or IMAGE data types.

Explanation of Error: TEXT, nTEXT, and IMAGE data types do not allow the use of rules. If you are attempting to place a rule on TEXT or nTEXT content, you might consider changing the field value to a string data type and bind the rule on this column.

Error Message #308: Severity Level 16

Text Output: Index %s on table %s (specified in the FROM clause) does not exist.

Explanation of Error: This error can be caused from removing the index from the table or typing the index name incorrectly in the query. Also, verify that the correct table has been specified.

Error Message #511: Severity Level 16

Text Output: Cannot create a row of size %d that is greater than the allowable maximum of %d.

Explanation of Error: You get this error when you try to insert a row that is larger than the maximum defined for that table. The error occurs when what you are attempting to insert into a table is too big to fit into a data page. The maximum allowable size of a table row is 8,060 bytes. Make sure the size of the row you are inserting is less than that number.

C

COMMON ERROR MESSAGES

Error Message #515: Severity Level 16

Text Output: Cannot insert the value NULL into column %.*ls, table %.*ls; column does not allow nulls. %ls fails.

Explanation of Error: This error occurs when a NULL value is being inserted into a column in which NULL values are not allowed. One common oversight is to have a stored procedure that adds data to a table. If the stored procedure accepts input values, and NULL is not tested, and you manipulate data with additional stored procedures, this could cause quite a few problems just with one input parameter.

Error Message #544: Severity Level 16

Text Output: Attempting to insert explicit value for identity column in table %s when IDENTITY_INSERT is set to OFF.

Explanation of Error: Using the IDENTITY property for a field allows us to auto-increment the values stored in that field from a starting seed value. You can force your own values in an IDENTITY column by setting IDENTITY_INSERT to ON. The syntax used to do this is SET IDENTITY_INSERT *tablename* ON.

Error Message #601: Severity Level 12

Text Output: Could not continue scan with NOLOCK due to data movement.

Explanation of Error: When using the NOLOCK locking hint to scan a table or when you have the transaction isolation level set to READ UNCOMMITTED, it is possible for the page at the scan's current position to be deleted, which stops the scanning process. If this happens, either resubmit the query or remove the NOLOCK hint.

Error Message #602: Severity Level 21

Text Output: Could not find row in Sysindexes for dbid %d, object %Id, index %d. Run DBCC CHECKTABLE on Sysindexes.

Explanation of Error: This error is the result of trying to retrieve a row of data from a table that might have been dropped. If the table hasn't been dropped, and it is properly indexed, you could have corrupted indexes. Run several DBCC type checks on the table to locate any errors.

Error Message #605: Severity Level 21

Text Output: Attempt to fetch logical page %ld in database %s belongs to object %s, not to object %s.

Explanation of Error: SQL server generates this message when it detects database corruption. One of the two objects or both objects are corrupted. Use DBCC CHECKDB statement to see which database is corrupted. A possible cause of this error is running SQL server using the FAT operating system. I highly recommend using NTFS, and if this problem does occur, you will most likely have to restore to the last known good backup.

Error Message #624: Severity Level 21

Text Output: Attempt to retrieve row from page via RID failed because the requested RID has a higher number than the last RID on the page. %S_RID.%S_PAGE.

Explanation of Error: This error can be a result of accessing data that points to a ROW ID while other users are updating data at the same time. It can also mean that the table's indexes are corrupt, but this is less often the true cause behind the error. Run DBCC CHECKDB to make sure the database is truly not corrupted.

Error Message #625: Severity Level 21

Text Output: Could not retrieve row from logical page %ld via RID because the entry in the offset table (=%d) for that RID (=%d) is less than or equal to 0.

Explanation of Error: This error is almost always a result of database corruption, possibly even problems with the hardware. Certain SCSI cards with on-board memory and write-back caches could lead to data corruption if not properly flushed. You might need to turn off write caching enabled on the controller. Run DBCC CHECKDB to find out the extent of the corruption in the database.

Error Message #701: Severity Level 19

Text Output: There is insufficient system memory to run this query.

Explanation of Error: This error happens when the procedure cache is too low to execute the query, trigger, function, stored procedure, and so forth. Either increase the memory allocation with sp_configure, or create smaller procedures, queries, and so on. In a multiuser environment, set this value relatively high. In addition, make sure the NT SQL server has plenty of memory (at least 256MB).

Error Message #1023: Severity Level 15

Text Output: Invalid parameter %d specified for 1$.

Explanation of Error: One of the parameters specified is invalid. This problem is usually caused by specifying the parameters in the wrong order or by a typing error.

Error Message #1204: Severity Level 19

Text Output: SQL Server has run out of LOCKS. Rerun your command when there are fewer active users, or ask your System Administrator to reconfigure SQL Server with more LOCKS.

Explanation of Error: The number of available locks is too small for the process to execute. Use sp_configure to increase the number of available locks. Additionally, you could run the process with no users logged into the system (no locks are required) or run smaller increments of a process (such as reducing the range when updating data in a table).

Error Message #1205: Severity Level 13

Text Output: Your server command (process id#%d) was deadlocked with another process and has been chosen as deadlock victim. Rerun your command.

Explanation of Error: This error occurs when two processes attempt to access the same resource. The process with the fastest execution time runs, and the second process needs to be run again. This error does not stop batch processing. Resubmit the query again until it runs when the deadlock is lifted.

Error Message #1505: Severity Level 14

Text Output: CREATE UNIQUE UNDEX aborted on duplicate key. Most significant primary key is %S_KEY.

Explanation of Error: This error occurs if you attempt to create a unique index on a table containing data that would cause the uniqueness to be violated. Fix the duplicate data and then reindex the table.

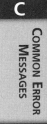

C

COMMON ERROR MESSAGES

Error Message #1508: Severity Level 14

Text Output: CREATE INDEX aborted on duplicate rows. Primary key is %S_KEY.

Explanation of Error: This error happens when you're attempting to create a clustered index, and duplicate data in the table violates the unique settings. You can either change the data in the table or set ALLOW_DUP_ROW to ON to allow for duplicate values.

Error Message #1510: Severity Level 17

Text Output: Sort failed: Out of space or locks in database %.*s.

Explanation of Error: Usually occurs as a result of creating an index and running out of storage space. Can also happen if you're updating or adding an index on a large table, and there are not enough locks available. During a clustered index creation, the space needed is 1.2 times the space occupied by the table. You can increase storage, increase the number of locks with sp_configure, or create the index when no one else is logged into the SQL server.

Error Message #1530: Severity Level 16

Text Output: CREATE INDEX with DROP_EXISTING was aborted because of row out of order. Most significant offending primary key is %S_KEY. Explicitly drop and create the index instead.

Explanation of Error: You're attempting to create a sorted index on a column in a table where data is stored in the column out of sequence. Drop and re-create the index without any additional clauses, or use the SORTED_DATA_REORG clause, which physically reorganizes the data.

Error Message #1702: Severity Level 16

Text Output: CREATE TABLE failed because column %s in table %s exceeds the maximum of 1024 columns.

Explanation of Error: Although it seems rare to create a table with more than 1,024 columns, you could possibly exceed that number of columns when creating a dynamic temporary table. If this occurs, review the normalization and output requirements to see if the data can be broken into two or more tables.

Error Message #1803: Severity Level 17

Text Output: CREATE DATABASE failed. Could not allocate enough disk space for a new database on the disks named in the command. Total space allocated must be at least %d Mbytes (%ld 2048-byte pages) to accommodate copy of Model Database.

Explanation of Error: This error occurs when you run out of storage when creating a table. Free up disk space and try the process again.

Error Message #1814: Severity Level 10

Text Output: Could not create tempdb. If space is low, extend the amount of space and restart.

Explanation of Error: Tempdb is created every time you start SQL Server. The error indicates there's not enough space to create tempdb.

Error Message #1902: Severity Level 16

Text Output: Cannot create more than one clustered index on table %s. Drop the existing clustered index %s before creating another.

Explanation of Error: You can have only one clustered index per table. Either make this index non-clustered, or drop the clustered index and then re-create it.

Error Message #1903: Severity Level 16

Text Output: %d is the maximum allowable size of an index. Composite index specified is %d bytes.

Explanation of Error: This error occurs if the total number of bytes for all columns in the index exceeds 255 bytes.

Error Message #1904: Severity Level 16

Text Output: Cannot specify more than %d column names for index key list. %d specified.

Explanation of Error: This error occurs if the concatenated index has more than 16 columns.

Error Message #2601: Severity Level 14

Text Output: Cannot insert duplicate key row in object %.*ls with unique index %.*ls.

Explanation of Error: You get this error when trying to enter a duplicate record in a table with unique indexes. If the unique key of the row should be duplicated, you need to drop the index and re-create your new unique key after you have reviewed your normalization of the table. For example, in a cash register system that interfaces with SQL Server, the unique key was set to reject the extra purchase if someone bought more than one of the same item.

Error Message #2714: Severity Level 16

Text Output: There is already an object named %s in the database.

Explanation of Error: The table name exists in the current database. Either drop the table and re-create it, or change to a different database.

Error Message #2715: Severity Level 16

Text Output: Column or parameter #1: Can't find type %s.

Explanation of Error: You get this error when assigning a user-defined data type that no longer exists or misspelling the name of a system data type.

Error Message #2729: Severity Level 16

Text Output: Procedure %s group number 1 already exists in the database. Choose another procedure name.

Explanation of Error: A stored procedure already exists with the name you are using. Either change the name or use the DROP PROC statement to remove the old procedure.

Error Message #2750: Severity Level 16

Text Output: Column or parameter #%d: specified column precision %d is greater than the maximum precision of %d.

Explanation of Error: You get this error when attempting to exceed the precision of SQL Server, which goes out to 28 places. Other products, such as Dataease and Visual Basic, carry the precision out much farther. You can round off to 28 places to match SQL Server, or you can specify /p when starting SQL server to increase the precision. However, you will see a performance hit, so it is not generally a recommended solution.

Error Message #2751: Severity Level 16

Text Output: Column or parameter #%d: specified column scale %d is greater than the specified precision of %d.

Explanation of Error: This error occurs when the scale of the column is greater than the precision assigned to the table.

Error Message #2812: Severity Level 16

Text Output: Could not find stored procedure %s.

Explanation of Error: The stored procedure has been deleted, its name was incorrectly typed in the query, or you might need to prefix the procedure with the owner name using the dot notation (such as dbo.sp_myproc).

Error Message #3101: Severity Level 16

Text Output: Database in use. System Administrator must have exclusive use of database to run the restore operation.

Explanation of Error: You get this error when attempting to restore a database when users are logged into it.

Error Message #3604: Severity Level 10

Text Output: Duplicate key was ignored.

Explanation of Error: You get this error when you try to insert a row with an index value that violates the uniqueness property (UNIQUE with IGNORE_DUP_KEY) on an existing index. No action is needed because SQL Server ignores the error and continues execution.

Error Message #5701: Severity Level 10

Text Output: Changed database context to %s.

Explanation of Error: Occurs when the current database context has been changed, which happens whenever a USE Database statement is executed. This is only an informational message and requires no action.

Error Message #5808: Severity Level 16

Text Output: Ad hoc updates to system catalogs not recommended. Use the RECONFIGURE WITH OVERRIDE statement to force this configuration.

Explanation of Error: This error occurs if the sp_configure stored procedure is used with the allow updates option, or when SQL Server thinks you set a configuration value that could interfere with the smoothness of the performance. Make sure you have a valid backup before you perform any system catalog modifications.

Error Message #8101: Severity Level 16

Text Output: An explicit value for the identity column in table %s can only be specified when a column list is used and IDENTITY_INSERT is ON.

Explanation of Error: You get this error when attempting to insert a value into an identity column. If you must add values and bypass the auto-increment (such as to reuse old numbers), make sure IDENTITY_INSERT is set to ON with the SET command.

Error Message #8102: Severity Level 16

Text Output: Cannot update identity column %s.

Explanation of Error: You get this error when you try to update a value in an identity column. If you must update values and bypass the auto-increment (such as to reuse old numbers), you need to copy the data into a temporary table, change the values, and reload the data into the original table.

Error Message #8106: Severity Level 16

Text Output: Table %s does not have the identity property, cannot perform SET operation.

Explanation of Error: You attempted to set the value of an identity column to ON in a table that does not contain an identity column.

Error Message #8146: Severity Level 16

Text Output: Procedure %s has no parameters and arguments were supplied.

Explanation of Error: You provided parameters when none were required.

INDEX

P

X-Y-Z

Get **FREE** books and more...when you register this book online for our Personal Bookshelf Program

http://register.samspublishing.com/

 Register online and you can sign up for our *FREE Personal Bookshelf Program...*unlimited access to the electronic version of more than 200 complete computer books—immediately! That means you'll have 100,000 pages of valuable information onscreen, at your fingertips!

 Plus, you can access product support, including complimentary downloads, technical support files, book-focused links, companion Web sites, author sites, and more!

 And you'll be automatically registered to receive a *FREE subscription to a weekly email newsletter* to help you stay current with news, announcements, sample book chapters, and special events, including sweepstakes, contests, and various product giveaways!

 We value your comments! Best of all, the entire registration process takes only a few minutes to complete, so go online and get the greatest value going—absolutely FREE!

Don't Miss Out On This Great Opportunity!

Sams is a brand of Macmillan Computer Publishing USA.

For more information, please visit *www.mcp.com*

Other Related Titles

Doing Objects in Visual Basic 6
Deborah Kurata
ISBN: 1-56276-577-9
$49.99 USA/$74.95 CAN

MTS Programming with Visual Basic
Scot Hillier
ISBN: 0-672-31425-8
$29.99 USA/$44.95 CAN

Roger Jennings' Database Developer's Guide with Visual Basic 6
Roger Jennings
ISBN: 0-672-31063-5
$59.99 USA/$89.95 CAN

Building Enterprise Solutions with Visual Studio 6
G.A. Sullivan
ISBN: 0-672-31489-4
$49.99 USA/$74.95 CAN

HTML 4 Unleashed, Second Edition
Rick Darnell
ISBN: 0-672-31347-2
$39.99 USA/$59.95 CAN

The Waite Group's Visual Basic 6 Database How-To
Eric Winemiler
ISBN: 1-57169-152-9
$39.99 USA/$59.95 CAN

COBOL Unleashed
Jon Wessler
ISBN: 0-672-31254-9
$49.99 USA/$74.95 CAN

SAMS
www.samspublishing.com

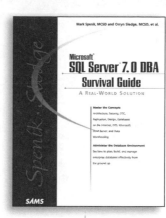

Microsoft SQL Server 7 DBA Survival Guide
Mark Spenik and Orryn Sledge
ISBN: 0-672-31226-3
$49.99 USA/$74.95 CAN

Bob Lewis's IS Survival Guide
Bob Lewis
ISBN: 0-672-31437-1
$24.99 USA/$37.95 CAN

Roger Jennings' Database Workshop: Microsoft Transaction Server 2.0
Stephen Gray and Rick Lievano
ISBN: 0-672-31130-5
$39.99 USA/$59.95 CAN

All prices are subject to change.

<Intranet>   <3developers>
<5 apps>   <5 months>

"With ColdFusion, we turned it on."

– Richard Sebold, Moen Incorporated

COLDFUSION® 4.0
web application server

Ever see a Web development team fly? Richard Sebold has. He's manager of enabling technology at Moen Incorporated. Moen makes the #1 brand of faucet in North America.

In less than 5 months, with 3 Web developers, Sebold launched the *MoenZone* corporate intranet. Complete with applications for workgroup productivity, product design tracking, engineering change management and customer service. All built with ColdFusion.

ColdFusion is the proven Web application server that offers the fastest way to build and deploy scalable Web apps. Easily integrate browser, server and database technologies. From commerce to collaboration, intranets to the Internet, ColdFusion lets you turn on the power. **It's your time.**

Download
www.coldfusion.com/cf4/
CALL 888-939-2545